"Today's political discourse artificially and problematically separates discussion of the dignity of the human person into 'social justice' and 'pro-life' approaches. But in this fantastic book David Gushee articulates how sacred Scripture and tradition offer a coherent and timely defense of the sacredness of life that refuses to accept this simplistic and polarizing binary. A dynamic, readable, and historically aware account of issues like war, abortion/infanticide, racism, biotechnology, and women's rights."

— CHARLES CAMOSY
Fordham University

"This magisterial volume draws upon biblical studies, philosophy, theology, history, and law in order to illustrate the breadth and richness of the concept of the sanctity of human life. Gushee shows us that the ideal of life's sacredness must not be confined to the narrow quarters of the abortion debate."

— M. CATHLEEN KAVENY
University of Notre Dame

"In the face of today's heated debates over ethical issues, Gushee does a fine job of laying out so-called progressive, conservative, and other Christian perspectives. This book is a valuable resource for all those who want to understand and thoughtfully engage perspectives other than their own."

— JOHN F. KILNER
Trinity International University

"I welcome this new study on the sacredness of human life including, but not limited to, those members of the human family still waiting to be born. Drawing on both biblical wisdom and the witness of Christian tradition, David Gushee makes here an impressive case that the whole church needs to hear — and heed."

— TIMOTHY GEORGE
Beeson Divinity School

"This book's subtitle perfectly conveys the way scholarship of classical texts can speak to contemporary culture wars. David Gushee has identified a crucial debate over the relationship between the modern Western value of human dignity and classical Christianity that seems to be driving an ill-considered polemical political wedge between 'liberals' and 'conservatives.' . . . May Gushee's sophisticated contribution enhance the religious axiom of the sacredness of human life."

— NOAM ZION
*Shalom Hartman Institute,
Jerusalem*

The Sacredness of Human Life

*Why an Ancient Biblical Vision
Is Key to the World's Future*

David P. Gushee

WILLIAM B. EERDMANS PUBLISHING COMPANY
GRAND RAPIDS, MICHIGAN / CAMBRIDGE, U.K.

Published 2013 by
Wm. B. Eerdmans Publishing Co.
2140 Oak Industrial Drive N.E., Grand Rapids, Michigan 49505 /
P.O. Box 163, Cambridge CB3 9PU U.K.

Printed in the United States of America

19 18 17 16 15 14 13   7 6 5 4 3 2 1

Library of Congress Cataloging-in-Publication Data

Gushee, David P., 1962-
    The sacredness of human life: why an ancient Biblical vision
    is key to the world's future / David P. Gushee.
        p.   cm.
    Includes bibliographical references.
    ISBN 978-0-8028-4420-0 (cloth: alk. paper)
    1. Theological anthropology — Christianity
    2. Dignity — Religious aspects — Christianity.
    3. Life — Religious aspects — Christianity.
    4. Apologetics.   5. Christianity and culture.   I. Title.

BT701.3.G87   2013
241'.697 — dc23

                                        2012028392

www.eerdmans.com

In honor of my beloved parents,
David and Janice Gushee

Contents

Contents

Contents

Prelude

A moral code for physicians. — The invalid is a parasite on society. In a certain state it is indecent to go on living. To vegetate on in cowardly dependence on physicians and medicaments after the meaning of life, the *right* to life, has been lost ought to entail the profound contempt of society. Physicians . . . ought to be the communicators of this contempt — not prescriptions, but every day a fresh dose of *disgust* with their patients. . . . To create a new responsibility, that of the physician, in all cases in which the highest interest of life, of *ascending* life, demands the most ruthless suppression and sequestration of degenerating life — for example in determining the right to reproduce, the right to be born, the right to live.

Friedrich Nietzsche, 1889

*   *   *

We must be honest, decent, loyal, and comradely to members of our own blood and to nobody else. What happens to a Russian or a Czech does not interest me in the slightest. . . . Whether 10,000 Russian females fall down with exhaustion while digging an anti-tank ditch interests me only in so far as the anti-tank ditch for Germany is finished. . . . Most of you know what it means to see a hundred corpses lying together, five hundred, or a thousand. To have gone through this and yet — apart from a few exceptions, examples of human weakness — to have remained decent fellows, this is what has made us hard. This is a glorious page in our history that has never been written and shall never be written.

Heinrich Himmler, 1943

*   *   *

Close to six-in-ten white evangelicals in the South say that torture can be often (20%) or sometimes (37%) justified in order to gain important information. This compares to roughly half (48%) of the general public who believe that torture can be justified.

Pew Research Center, 2008

*   *   *

Eternal Father,
Source of life and light,
Whose love extends to all people, all creatures, all things:
Grant us that reverence for life which becomes those
      who believe in You:
lest we despise it, degrade it, or callously come to destroy it.
Rather let us save it, serve it, and sanctify it, after the
      example of Your Son,
Jesus Christ our Lord. Amen.

Robert Runcie

Acknowledgments

More than with any other book that I have written, this long and arduous project involved the collaboration and assistance of many kind and wonderful individuals and even institutions. I am happy to name them all here, even while fearing that I will omit someone.

The book was launched through a summer research grant at Union University in 2004. I am grateful to Union for that funding and for so many other ways in which the university supported me during my eleven years of service there.

Mercer University, where I have served since 2007, likewise has been very gracious in providing me with time for writing and funding for research assistants. The completion of this project without any sabbatical leave is a testament to the generosity of Mercer University with my schedule.

Students at both Union and Mercer also served as the first guinea pigs for the book, as I taught two courses related to the material here to undergraduate and seminary students, respectively.

Students in general played a critical role in making this book possible. Let no one underestimate the potential contribution of superior undergraduate and seminary students! My student researchers were Matt Elia, Josh Hays, Jill and Drew Zimmer, my own daughter Holly Love, Shanna Wood, and Andi Sullivan. Andi deserves special praise as the chief researcher on the book during its most intensive stage (2008-2011), as the one who compiled the bibliography, and as the first person to read the entire manuscript in full. I am so deeply grateful to you, Andi, and to all my student assistants.

I am deeply grateful to Jon Pott and Eerdmans Publishing Company for their confidence and their patience through the long development process of this manuscript. I am also grateful to John Kilner, Francis Beckwith, and Dennis Hollinger and to the Center for Bioethics and Human Dignity for early and ongoing substantial support in this project.

I am appreciative of the Center for Theological Inquiry at Princeton for inviting me to participate in a consultation on theology and international law in which I presented a synopsis of the material on the image of Christ. I thank Will Storrar, director of the Center, for his gracious support of my work and especially for his willingness to host a private consultation with leading scholars to review the manuscript.

A wonderfully generous group of scholar-friends read the manuscript in its near-final stage and provided critically important comments. What a gift! Those who read and commented on the whole terribly long manuscript include my Mercer colleagues Tim Floyd, Jack Sammons, and Rick Wilson, former Union colleague Jim Patterson, and Sondra Wheeler, Glen Stassen, Coleman Fannin, Jennifer Crumpton, and Charlie Camosy. Those who read and commented on parts of the book include Mercer colleague Dave Garber, as well as Ron Sider, and Andrea and Kim Strübind. I received helpful comments from several gracious scholars along the lecture circuit I traveled in working out the themes of the book; these are mentioned in footnotes where their particular contributions are noted.

Most of my professional presentations over the last eight years have had something to do with the topic of this book. Audiences subjected to early presentations of this material include the Baptist World Alliance, the Center for Bioethics and Human Dignity, Missouri Baptist University, Lincoln Christian University, the University of Mary Hardin Baylor, Wheaton College, the University of Notre Dame, Fuller Theological Seminary, Princeton University, Wayland Baptist University, the Evangelical Ethics group of the Society of Christian Ethics, the University of Minnesota, Oral Roberts University, All Saints Episcopal Church (Pasadena), People of Faith against the Death Penalty, Rabbis for Human Rights North America, Biola University, and Wingate University.

I gratefully acknowledge prior publications in which draft versions or small overlapping sections of this book have previously appeared:

Life in the Spirit (IVP, 2010)
Keeping God's Earth (IVP, 2010)
Perspectives in Religious Studies
Notre Dame Journal of Law, Ethics and Public Policy
Reflections: Yale Divinity School

Acknowledgments

As always, I stand in awe of the goodness of God for reaching out and finding me in grace so long ago. And of God's gracious gifts, my wife Jeanie, and my children Holly, David, and Marie, are the best of all. I am deeply grateful for their patience, support, and sacrifice during the long development of this manuscript.

Introduction

0.1. Why a Book about the Sacredness of Human Life?

The belief that each and every human life is sacred is a grand moral conviction of ancient origin. This is a book that traces that grand conviction to at least one of its sources — the Christian faith — and explores its surprising, winding, perilous journey into our present moment. Through both conceptual analysis and historical narrative, this book offers forays into understanding what it has meant and what it means today to say that human life is sacred, a conviction that is not only a core belief of the Christian church but also the greatest moral contribution of the Christian tradition to world civilization. This examination is offered with the primary aim of contributing clarity and depth to the moral vision of the church and, perhaps, contributing something constructive to national and global struggles to secure a livable human future.[1]

Both the grandeur and the provenance of the moral conviction that human life is sacred have been obscured over the last forty years, at least in American culture. Most people today encounter the term "sacredness of life" only as a political slogan that surfaces occasionally at events such as candidate debates. The term has been embraced by political-religious con-

---

1. This will be a study in Christian ethics, and will trace the development of the idea that human life is sacred within the Christian tradition. It will be apparent from the very beginning that this conviction in Christian ethics is inextricably rooted in and related to the Jewish tradition and the Hebrew Scriptures; I am not claiming any exclusive Christian provenance. I also recognize that other religious and cultural traditions offer variations on the same theme, but I lack membership and scholarly competence in those other traditions and cannot speak for them.

servatives, its use restricted to expressing opposition to American abortion law, with a quite stunning lack of application to other issues having to do with human well-being. The concept often has been, as a corollary, reflexively rejected by those repulsed by conservative religious politics. The culture war fight over abortion and the deployment of "sacredness" and "life" rhetoric on one side of the debate — always intensified during election years — have put at even greater risk what survives of the ancient moral tradition affirming the sacred worth of each and every human person. One reason I offer this book at this time is to help rescue this tradition before it is completely discredited by the politics of the moment.

0.2. How This Book Came to Be

This project actually began almost a decade ago as an effort to help Christians committed to "human dignity" and "the sacredness of human life" to reach a deeper understanding of these key concepts. The book was recruited for use in a Christian bioethics series and was intended primarily for the kind of audience attracted to such a series. It was related to an aspect of my vocation in which I have sought to broaden and deepen the evangelical Christian social and political agenda.[2]

I hope that my original intended readers will find the result valuable. But creative projects take on a life of their own, developing an inner logic and momentum. As Rowan Williams, the archbishop of Canterbury, has written, creative acts involve "the setting in being of something that is both an embodiment of what is thought or conceived and also a radically independent reality with its own logic and integrity unfolding over time."[3] That has certainly been the case with this project.

I started research on this book in the summer of 2004, and signed a contract for it with Eerdmans on January 26, 2006. Two major things happened to me at almost exactly the time that this contract made its appearance in my filing cabinet — one took place in my personal life, the other in

2. See David P. Gushee, *The Future of Faith in American Politics: The Public Witness of the Evangelical Center* (Waco, Tex.: Baylor University Press, 2008), and *A New Evangelical Manifesto* (St. Louis: Chalice, 2012). For those trying to locate my work via social media, go to http://www.facebook.com/davidpgushee and http://twitter.com/#!/dpgushee.

3. Rowan Williams, *Grace and Necessity: Reflections on Art and Love* (Harrisburg, Pa.: Morehouse Publishing, 2005), p. 160.

my professional life. These events deeply affected the direction of this project — and of my life.

On January 28, 2006, my oldest daughter, Holly, eighteen at the time, was in a very serious car accident. Broadsided in her puny little car by an SUV, she was left unconscious and with a traumatic brain injury along with facial cuts, a broken pelvis, and other injuries. There is nothing quite like seeing your bloodied daughter unconscious in an emergency room to focus your mind on the ineffable sacredness of a single human life. I am beyond grateful to report that after months of medical treatment and loving care, Holly made a full recovery. We saw her graduate college and get married in 2010. Our gratitude and wonder are too profound to be fully described. But suffice it to say that we were all changed by the experience, and it came with me into the book project that has now come to fruition.

The professional development I speak of was my unanticipated immersion in a national fight over the treatment of prisoners held by the United States government after the 9/11 attacks. On February 1, 2006, in the flagship evangelical magazine *Christianity Today*, I published a cover article on "five reasons torture is always wrong"[4] — so it was hitting the newsstands at the same time I was keeping vigil by Holly's bed in the hospital, and around the time I was filing away the contract for this book. Writing, organizing, and speech making related to our nation's counterterrorism policies consumed much of the next three years of my life, and today I serve on a high-level nonpartisan panel investigating the detainee interrogation policies of the United States. This involvement brought many costs, including the delay of this manuscript and attacks from many erstwhile friends in the conservative American evangelical world. It drove me into new communities of moral commitment and taught me much about the politically captive condition of Christianity in America.

And it shed an entirely new light on this project. I became more resolutely convinced that the sacredness of human life is not just about abortion or euthanasia. If any human life is sacred, every human life is sacred. If "the sacredness of human life" is just a political slogan trotted out on convenient occasions but ignored the rest of the time — when lives other than those of embryos, unborn infants, and the elderly are at stake — then the concept has been corrupted beyond repair. With the fight over prisoner abuse I discovered how fragile Christian commitments to respect for life can turn out to be, how deeply and crassly utilitarian we have become in

---

4. "Five Reasons Torture Is Always Wrong," *Christianity Today*, February 2006, pp. 33-37.

what passes for public moral reflection, and therefore how important it is that we have the sturdiest possible understanding of the sacred worth of each and every human being.

Forty years of scalding arguments over abortion have deeply damaged the appeal of "sacredness of life" language among progressives, including Christians. When speaking to politically liberal Christian groups in recent years, I have been struck by how difficult it is for them to even hear the term "sacredness of life" without recoiling. But I want to invite them to reconsider. I want them (you?) to consider the possibility that in overreacting to bad right-wing politics they are unnecessarily abandoning a central Christian conviction that cannot be reduced to those politics — and that actually undergirds progressive Christian commitments to social justice. At the same time, I am challenging my conservative Christian brethren to reconsider the frequent narrowness of their application of life's sanctity and move to a more demanding moral vision that treats *every* life as sacred.

0.3. Joining the Archaeologists

So in this book I go back to the idea of life's sacredness, at its origins. In doing so I have joined a community of scholars from various religious and intellectual traditions who in the last couple of decades have been doing archaeology on some of our culture's most important convictions. I don't think these excavations are just an expression of routine portfolio-building by underemployed professors. No, scholars in our postmodern context are returning for very profound reasons to the deepest sources of the convictions, values, and practices that have helped shape both the church and Western civilization. This trend can be seen in Catholic and Protestant theology, ethics, and liturgics, as well as in numerous works in political and moral thought exploring such core concepts as law, equality, freedom, dignity, justice, liberalism, democracy, and human rights. These excavations, whether on the religious or the secular side, seem to me to result from a nauseating sense of insecurity and decay, both in our institutions and in their foundations.

So I join the intellectual archaeologists of our time, in my case to dig around in the history of the conviction that human life is sacred — a majestic moral tradition that is not only related to other ideas like equality and human rights, but was in fact the ultimate origin of these convictions as they developed in what was once called Christian civilization.

0.4. Plan of the Book

Here is how I will proceed. In chapter 1 I look at the etymology as well as historic and contemporary uses of "sacredness of life" language to see what these words are actually understood to mean, especially in Christianity.

Most Christians who claim that life is sacred say that the Bible is the ultimate source of this belief. Therefore I next excavate both the Hebrew Scriptures and the New Testament to see what texts and themes have been, or could be, important for grounding belief in the sacredness of life, while also offering some attention to biblical materials that pose challenges to human life's sacredness as defined in this book (chapters 2–3). Moving out of the biblical materials, I turn in chapter 4 to early Christianity and explore whether the churches of the first three centuries taught a broad sacredness-of-life ethic, as is often claimed by Christian scholars, and what shape that ethic actually took.

I make a further historical turn in chapters 5 and 6. Chapter 5 explores the fateful transition to Christendom, when the church moved from persecuted minority to empowered majority. Chapter 6 offers three case studies in the history of European Christendom that demonstrate a culture morally divided against itself. A tender Christian ethic elevating the sacred worth of all persons eventually competed with a different kind of ethic more interested in political, religious, and territorial domination. This was Christendom divided, with Christians both honoring and desecrating life in God's name.

These vignettes will also help illuminate some of the impulses that shaped the gradually secularizing modern Western world of the eighteenth and nineteenth centuries. In chapters 7 and 8 I trace the arc of the sanctity-of-life idea in a European cultural context that first rejected official Christian political power, then turned away from Christian theology, and finally abandoned Christian morality. In chapter 7 I explore late medieval natural rights theories, the work of John Locke, and the philosophy of Immanuel Kant to take this story part of the way forward. Then I devote an entire chapter (chapter 8) to the endlessly fascinating and troubling Friedrich Nietzsche, whom I describe as among the first, and the most influential, to explicitly abandon the whole legacy: Christendom, the Christian God, and the Christian sacredness-of-life ethic.

As a climax to the historical explorations of this book, I devote chapter 9 to Adolf Hitler and the Nazi movement. The twentieth century saw repeated bloodbaths, beginning with World War I, which opened the floodgates to total war and multiple instances of genocide. Taking just one especially terrible example, I show that Nazism was not just a tyrannical political ideology but a self-consciously developed worldview that explicitly rejected the idea of each single life's immeasurable worth. But I also show that Hitler himself appeared to believe (or presented himself as believing) that his fanatical racism, anti-Semitism, and commitment to violence on behalf of race and nation actually advanced the purposes of God.

Despite the deaths of hundreds of millions in war and genocide, our battered world survived the twentieth century and staggered forward into the twenty-first. Two chapters explore where we go from here, and what it means to advance the sacredness of life in the face of current challenges. Chapter 10 tackles a half-dozen contemporary moral issues in which life's sacredness is at stake, including nuclear weapons, abortion, and systematic abuses against women. Chapter 11 takes on the question of whether the ancient biblical "sacredness of *human* life" ethic is adequate for an era of global environmental degradation and potential disaster, or whether it must be abandoned in the face of threats that extend to the planet itself and not just its human inhabitants. Here is where I will grapple directly with whether we should hold a "sacredness of human life" ethic or a "sacredness of all creation" ethic. A concluding chapter (chapter 12) offers final words to the church and to its neighbors, reflecting on lessons learned and the way ahead.

In our fallen, bloody world, the sacredness of human life is not just an interesting intellectual concept or a convenient American political slogan. It is not just a principle to be applied to hard cases like abortion and biotechnology, though the effort must be made. Treating life as sacred is a necessity for survival. Human history appears to be a race between forces that motivate us to honor our neighbors and forces that motivate us to desecrate them. Everything that can be done to strengthen the forces for hallowing life must be attempted.

0.5. Notes about My Approach

This is a work for both the general reader and the academic, and so I am attempting to keep both audiences satisfied throughout. There is indeed intellectual heavy lifting to be done to understand the critically important concepts, history, and moral issues we consider here. There are definitions to ponder, fine distinctions to draw, scholarly literature to engage. Probably the general reader will be less interested in some of the methodological or definitional questions that will preoccupy the scholar. For the latter, I can say here that I do think that certain key questions of theological and ethical method surface in this book, and that this study intersects with a number of important debates in contemporary Christian ethics, moral theory, and political philosophy. I hope that this will be a study useful both for normative ethics in the churches and metaethics in the academy, as well as a contribution to public ethics.[5] Let me clarify here my approach to some of the methodological questions at stake in this book, after which we can mainly do the work rather than worry explicitly over methodology.

1. What kind of academic discipline is being practiced here?

This is primarily a work in Christian ethics, the academic discipline rooted in the church and fundamentally aimed at understanding and refining the moral vision and moral practices of Christian people for the sake of our fidelity to Jesus Christ. More specifically, this is a work in *constructive* Christian ethics. I am not just undertaking a history of the belief that human life is sacred, or some kind of comparative or analytical or philosophical study. I am proposing that, rightly understood, a moral norm called the sacredness of life *should be* central to the moral vision and practice of followers of Christ. I am offering a constructive account of that norm. If you are a Christian, I want your assent to the proposition that every life's sacredness is an important moral norm for followers of Christ — and your decision to practice that ethic more fully. If you are not a Christian, I invite you to consider the relevance of this ethic to your own vision and practice of life.

2. Methodologically speaking, how does one do a work in Christian ethics?

There is no consensus on the answer to this question in our field. However, my understanding of Christian ethics is that, at least for a constructive work, one uses whatever intellectual resources are most helpful and significant in order to commend to the churches and Christian disciples the clearest and most compelling statement of Christian moral conviction and obligation. For this study, those intellectual resources have included biblical studies, history, moral philosophy, and contemporary Christian social ethics. This work offers a combination of Christian ethics as conceptual

---

5. "Metaethics" is a term widely used among moral philosophers to discuss that dimension of ethics that seeks to determine the meaning of ethical terms and how one gives good reasons, or warrants, for moral claims.

analysis (telling about the meaning of terms and ideas) and Christian ethics as historical drama (telling about moments, movements, and people that embodied or negated the key convictions under consideration here). This is certainly an interdisciplinary work, like many books in Christian ethics. Most Christian ethicists learn how to be creative borrowers from the work of other kinds of scholars. We reach into the toolbox for whatever tools we need to do our work on behalf of Christian discipleship.

3. Does this book offer an ethic for the church or for society?
My primary goal is to clarify for the church and for Christians what it means to claim, and to practice the claim, that human life is sacred. As I have said, this is a conviction long held by the Christian community. It is extremely important to clarify the meaning of this moral conviction for Christians before it is destroyed through misuse or abandonment. However, the reader will also encounter many references to culture and society in this book. I am very much interested in the way that belief in life's sacredness has affected those cultures that have come into contact with this conviction, as well as the continuing implications of this belief (or its abandonment) for societies today. Therefore, this book simultaneously points in the direction of an *ecclesial ethic* (guiding our way of living as followers of Christ) and a *social ethic* (guiding our Christian moral witness in culture and public life). As a moral norm, the sacredness of life has the intrinsic character of spilling outside of ecclesial bounds to the wider world. It will become clear in this book that this norm has never been understood by Christians merely as a churchly ethic, with society free to desecrate life just as much as it wants.

4. How is the Bible employed in this study?
I work from a Christian theological perspective that treats the Bible as the premier context in which the record of God's divine revelation to humanity can be found, and as one of the primary vehicles by which God's word and will are still communicated and encountered in the world today. This statement must be immediately clarified from a Christian perspective by saying that Jesus Christ is God's ultimate self-communication to humanity, and that therefore the criterion by which all Scripture is to be interpreted is Jesus Christ himself. When I say that the Bible offers a sacredness-of-life ethic, I am claiming that God has communicated to humanity — first to the Jewish people, then in Jesus Christ, then in the church — such an ethic. The communication of this divine demand (and human responses to it) is recorded in the pages of sacred Scripture for the instruction of all who will

listen today. The proper response to this communication by the people of God is to hear and obey God's moral will, now and always. In doing so they can be trailblazers for the whole human family, clearing a path for others to follow.

I also believe that the Bible is a human book, the book (or library of books) that bears witness to God's revelation to the Jewish and Christian peoples in the earliest days of their sojourn with God. It also bears witness to their own successes and failures in hearing and heeding God's word. Any human book bears the traces of humanity, including growth and development, advances and regressions. I therefore do not embrace a "flat Bible" but instead see peaks and valleys in the sacred texts. I will readily acknowledge here that the written pages of the Bible offer moments of extraordinarily profound proclamation of and response to the sacred worth of each person, and other moments in which the written words or narrated events of Scripture fall considerably short of that vision. It might be more politic to fail to mention problematic texts, but honesty compels attention to them, especially where they have contributed to distortions in Christian behavior. I believe the sacredness-of-life norm represents biblical morality at its peak, that it is preeminently embodied and taught by Jesus Christ, and that it is therefore appropriate to test biblical and postbiblical texts and traditions by the criteria established by this ethical norm.

One further note: when I say that the Bible teaches or contributes to a sacredness-of-life ethic at this or that point, I am making a constructive claim, for example, "This text has potential to inform and shape a sacredness ethic," or "This text should be employed in such and such a way in articulating a sanctity-of-life ethic." I am not automatically making the *historical* claim that the Jewish or Christian people always read these texts in the manner described — though they have done so with most of the texts we will consider. I am saying that these texts offer profound resources for a contemporary sacredness-of-life ethic as we articulate it today.

This itself implies that Christian ethics (or any religious ethic) interacts with communal traditions of reading sacred texts as people of faith attempt to shape a faithful way of life over the centuries, and that this conversation between text, tradition, and contemporary faith communities is never finished. I see myself in this project as interacting with a historic Christian sanctity-of-life tradition that has recently drifted off track and is at risk of being abandoned by significant parts of the Christian community and laughed off the field by secular critics. I want to help prevent that from happening.

5. In this book, is the sacredness of life a Jewish ethic, a Christian ethic, a Judeo-Christian ethic, or something else?

This is a delicate question. In this study I begin with the Hebrew Bible, and from that study as well as my familiarity with contemporary Jewish ethics, I am quite confident that a very great percentage of what I say about the sacredness of life as a Christian could be and often is paralleled in Jewish ethics. I *never* want to be heard in this book claiming the sacredness-of-life tradition for Christianity as if Christians own it or gave birth to it. If it weren't for my distaste for the phrase, "Judeo-Christian" would be an accurate description of what I am talking about at many places in this book. However, I do think that the New Testament and then Christian tradition take the sacredness-of-life conviction in some new directions. And I am a Christian ethicist rather than a Jewish ethicist. Therefore the best summary is that this is a Christian treatment of the sacredness of life that stands respectfully and humbly appreciative of the Elder Brother whose privilege it was to first receive this word from the Lord. Because Christians have so desperately and horribly mistreated that Elder Brother, it is extremely important to me to get this right.

6. Was there ever really a Christian concept of the "sacredness of human life" in the Bible and Christian tradition? Or was it cooked up for contemporary debates about abortion, euthanasia, and stem cells?

Finding the answer to this question requires digging in biblical, historical, and theological sources. But this book will clearly show that the idea that human life is sacred was *explicitly articulated* in early Christian writings and became a foundational element of Christian moral tradition. It has roots that extend to the Bible, though no exact cognate of a "sacredness of life" phrase is used there. It is definitely not a modern concoction, though use of the term or its cognates surged in the second half of the twentieth century, during which time it developed into an element of Christian moral dogma in some Christian communities.

7. Is it "sacredness of life," "sanctity of life," or "sacred worth"? What about "human dignity"?

In the next chapter, I will show that the distinctions between the English terms "sacredness" and "sanctity" have faded and that the terms are often used interchangeably. Yet close etymological study will show that for our purposes the term "sacredness of life" is preferable, and this is the term I will most often employ. A greater distinction in meaning is visible in the term "human dignity," as I will also seek to show.

8. What are the faith commitments of the author who is guiding this study?
I am a journeying and wondering human being who was found by Jesus Christ at the age of sixteen and have been personally seeking to follow him since that time. That took me from a lapsed Catholicism to an active practice of a Southern Baptist form of Protestantism. I now describe myself religiously first as one who seeks to be a follower of Jesus Christ, and second as a committed member-servant at First Baptist Church in Decatur, Georgia. In Baptist polity, the primary locus of Christian community, identity, and service is the local congregation, and that is certainly how I would now locate myself. I am nationally affiliated with and known to be an "evangelical" but have had to spend considerable energy defining what part of that community and identity I claim and what part I firmly reject. (I identify most strongly with the sturdy and holistic evangelicalism of people like my mentors Ron Sider and Glen Stassen.) I have been deeply affected by my years at Union Theological Seminary and the social ethical tradition of historic mainline Protestantism embodied by that grand old school and exemplified by figures such as Reinhold Niebuhr. I also have been deeply affected by the Roman Catholicism in which I was raised, and my work is by now heavily influenced by the Catholic social teaching tradition. I hope that the best of all these strands of my identity will be apparent in this work, while anticipating that I will fall short of fulfilling the possibilities of every one of them.

0.6. Two Scenes from Europe

What is this book really about? What drives us into this work? Two scenes tell the tale.

Corrie ten Boom was a devout Dutch Christian who led a rescue operation during the Holocaust that saved hundreds of lives. Here is her account of a conversation with a pastor who had stumbled upon the rescue operation one day when he came into her watch shop. He had come on a routine errand, looking for a part for his broken timepiece; Corrie, on the other hand, was looking for another rescuer.

> Back in the dining room I pulled the coverlet from the baby's face. There was a long silence. The man bent forward, his hand in spite of himself reaching for the tiny fist curled round the blanket. For a moment I saw compassion and fear struggle in his face. Then he straightened. "No. Def-

initely not. We could lose our lives for that Jewish child!" Unseen by either of us, Father had appeared in the doorway. "Give the child to me, Corrie," he said. Father held the baby close, his white beard brushing its cheek, looking into the little face. . . . At last he looked up at the pastor. "You say we could lose our lives for this child. I would consider that the greatest honor that could come to my family."[6]

In the end, Corrie and her father were captured and imprisoned for their rescue efforts. Caspar ten Boom died in a Nazi prison camp in Holland within days. He had indeed lost his life for this child. Corrie's sister and several other family members also paid the ultimate price for hallowing human life. But their rescue operation had saved Jewish babies from what awaited them in Poland:

When the . . . Jews arrived, we used a music camouflage. At the time, the children were burned on big piles of wood. The crematoriums could not work at the time, and therefore, the people [after being gassed to death] were just burned in open fields with those grills, and the children were burned among them. Children were crying helplessly and that is why the camp administration ordered that an orchestra be made of 100 inmates and should play. They played very loud all the time . . . so that even the people in the city of Auschwitz could not hear the screams. Without the orchestra they would have heard the screams of horror. . . .

And then, on one special day they started burning them to death. The gas chambers at the time were out of order . . . and therefore the children were not gassed, but just burned alive. When one of the SS men sort of had pity on the children, he took the child and beat the head against a stone first before putting it on the pile of fire and wood, so that the child lost consciousness. However, the regular way they did it was just by throwing the children onto the pile.

They used to put a sheet of wood, then the whole thing was sprinkled with gasoline, then wood again, and gasoline and wood, and gasoline — and then people were placed on them. Thereafter, the whole pile was lit.[7]

6. Corrie ten Boom, *The Hiding Place* (New York: Bantam Books, 1971), p. 99.

7. Prisoner testimony translated by Irving Greenberg, quoted in Greenberg, *For the Sake of Heaven and Earth: The New Encounter between Judaism and Christianity* (Philadelphia: Jewish Publication Society, 2004), p. 21. That the Nazis on occasion actually burned children alive at Auschwitz has been confirmed by numerous other accounts.

One family risks everything to save a stranger's child . . . one pastor remains a bystander . . . both decisions affecting how many children get shipped to a place in which children are being burned alive. All are stories of human moral choices. All reflect understandings of human worth and what price is worth paying on life's behalf. The unimaginable, unbearable contrast between these two scenes from what had once been Christian Europe lies at the motivational center of this book. It is my hope that by the end of this journey, readers will understand both what happened in the watch shop and what happened at Auschwitz as incidents in the history of the conviction that each and every human life is sacred. And more — that they will be inspired not just to believe in the sacredness of human life, but to act on that belief with all their strength.

0.7. Sacredness as Moral Reality and Moral Task

That last point raises one more critical issue.

I have already introduced the claim that the sacredness of human life is an aspect of divine revelation. It is therefore a *moral reality* that God has declared and demonstrated. I am claiming firmly and foundationally here that one can say "human life is sacred" and be making a truth claim rooted in trustworthy divine revelation. It is not just a human aspiration, ideal, or invention.

And yet, from a historical perspective, it is also a fact that this claimed reality has been cruelly rejected in practice and in thought, often by Christians themselves.

This means that we must speak both about the sacredness of human life as a revealed moral *reality* and about treating human life accordingly as a human moral *task*. One might just as accurately say that the sacredness of human life is a divine *gift*, and treating life as sacred is a divine *command*. We must never collapse this tension between our *conviction* concerning an aspect of divine revelation and our *obligation* to live out its implications; both are required, we can get either or both wrong, and it is easier to affirm a belief than to live it.

Jewish theologian and rabbi Irving Greenberg helps clarify this subtle but critical distinction. His voice — and that of the agonized post-Holocaust Jewish theological tradition — has been significant in shaping the perspective taken in this volume. After decades of deeply personal struggle to relate the Jewish theological tradition to the horrors of the Holocaust, Greenberg concluded that one theological implication of the Holocaust is that God has chosen to elevate human responsibility to bring God's will into realization. God does not do it all for us. One central aspect of God's will is "the creation of a human being with a fulfilled image of God — a creature truly of infinite value, equal, and unique, living in a world that fully sustains these dignities."[8] God invites us to what Greenberg calls a "voluntary covenant" in which we commit to become human beings who will fulfill God's image and who will make decisions that lead to a world that fully sustains and protects God's image in all people. So Greenberg rarely if ever speaks of life's sacredness as a reality — Auschwitz has almost made it obscene to call it a reality — but the concept of human sacredness certainly remains before all of us, as a task. For Greenberg the desperately urgent task facing anyone who would claim to be in covenant with God is to choose, today and each day, to exercise his or her freedom, power, and responsibility so as to respect the sacredness of human life.[9]

Classic Christian theology in the Augustinian tradition, with which I still resonate deeply, teaches an interpretation of the first pages of the Bible in which "in the beginning" all was originally harmonious, beautiful, and holy in human life. One might say that life began with an *original sacredness*. But human beings in their pride and fear turned against God. The entry of sin led swiftly to the desperate *desecration* (a word I will use frequently in these pages) of human life, as wickedness reigned — especially in the form of bloodshed and violence (Gen. 6:5-8). But the text goes on to say that God acted to make covenant with humanity, then Israel, and finally the church. Through such covenants God sought partners who would participate in God's *reconsecration* of the world. Both Jews and Christians wait and live in hope for the time in which the world is finally and fully healed. Christians have been taught to be confident that this time is surely coming, when Jesus returns and at last there is no more killing, no more desecration, no more torture, and "he shall reign forever and ever." Every effort we make now to live into that promised future, to embody it as individuals and in Christian communities, can be seen as an anticipatory participation in a resacralized world — and no such effort is wasted.

8. Greenberg, *Heaven and Earth*, p. 28.

9. In general, I see in Jewish ethics more of an emphasis on sacredness of life as a task, and in Christian ethics more of an emphasis on sacredness of life as a reality. I think Christians need to learn from Jews here.

One might say provisionally that in Christian theological terms all acts that honor life's sacredness participate in this resacralizing of God's beloved world. When that task is accomplished, when every tear is wiped away at last, this will be the reign of God.[10] But, oh, the horrors that still surround us even now! Oh, the difficulty some days of believing in a world made whole and holy still to come!

This book is written by a brokenhearted Christian believer hoping and working for a world in which every human life is treated as precious. I seek not just to clarify an understanding of this beautiful moral tradition and its course through history. I aim to bear witness to one of the most precious aspects of God's revelation to this world. I aim to make some kind of contribution to the dawning of that world. I aim to persuade the reader to believe that practicing the ancient concept of the sacredness of human life is the key to the world's future, and to live accordingly.

10. The kingdom of God has been a central theme of my theological-ethical work and plays a key background role in this volume. See Glen H. Stassen and David P. Gushee, *Kingdom Ethics: Following Jesus in Contemporary Context* (Downers Grove, Ill.: InterVarsity, 2003).

1. *What It Means to Say That Human Life Is Sacred*

> The person is the clearest reflection of the presence of God among us. To lay violent hands on the person is to come as close as we can to laying violent hands on God. To diminish the human person is to come as close as we can to diminishing God. . . . From our recognition of the worth of all people under God flow the responsibilities of a "social" morality.
>
> Cardinal Joseph Bernardin

When people say they believe in "the sacredness of human life,"[1] what exactly are they affirming? Does the term have any clear and specific meaning? What is its history and pattern of usage? Is it an element of historic Christian doctrine? Is it a recognized concept in Christian ethics? Or is it a cipher, a meaningless slogan?

To explore these questions I will first dig around in the etymologies and definitions of the terms "sanctity" and "sacredness" as well as a few closely related words. I will extract from this analysis a **sacredness paradigm**[2] delineating what humans normally mean when they call something sacred, and offer an **analytical definition** of the "sacredness of human life" on the basis of this analysis. Then I will examine whether use of

---

1. Note that for now I am primarily interested in exploring the sacredness, sanctity, dignity, etc., of *human* life, rather than all life — this is the case even when I drop the word "human" as a modifier, for brevity's sake. Later in the book I will focus on the very important question of the sacredness of nonhuman life.

2. The rare terms placed in bold are intended as guides to help the reader label and recall **terms of art** used as key concepts in this book.

the term "sacredness," and especially "sacredness of human life," requires a religious grounding. I will consider the hypothesis that the term as used by Christians today is a recent innovation pretending to be an ancient Christian doctrine. I will then sample standard contemporary Christian definitions of the term "sacredness of human life" and its cognates and describe their commonalities and differences. I will close by settling on a working **Christian definition** of the sacredness of human life for the purposes of this book, while also naming seventeen major **puzzles** that require further reflection and analysis in the course of this study. In all this I will move as briskly as possible, because definitional considerations are rarely thrilling. But it will not do to use a term without knowing what it means. And that occurs too often with this extraordinarily loaded term "sacredness of human life."

1.1. Definitions and Etymologies

In contemporary usage the terms "sanctity of (human) life" and "sacredness of (human) life" are often used interchangeably. It is worth examining whether they have been and should be treated as synonymous. This is one good reason to go back to the etymologies of the words.

The English word "sanctity" is derived from the Latin *sanctitas*. The widely used *Langenscheidt Pocket Latin Dictionary* attributes the following range of meanings to *sanctitas,* in its noun form: "sacredness, sanctity; a) inviolability; b) holiness, purity, virtue, integrity, chastity, piety." The adjectival form of the word *sanctitas* is *sanctus*. This is defined as "sacred, inviolable; a) venerable, august, divine; b) virtuous, holy, pious; innocent, pure; chaste, just."[3] If searching in the other direction, from English to Latin, one seeking the Latin translation for "holy" would use *sanctus* or *divinus;* if looking to translate the word "sacred," one would go with *sacer* or (again) *sanctus.*

Webster's Unabridged Dictionary defines "sanctity" as follows: "1. holiness, saintliness, or godliness. 2. sacred or hallowed character. 3. a sacred thing." It flows directly from the Latin *(sanctitas)* into Middle English *(sauntite)*, and now to our contemporary "sanctity."[4]

---

3. *Langenscheidt's Pocket Latin Dictionary* (Berlin: Langenscheidt, 1955), p. 286.
4. *Webster's New Universal Unabridged Dictionary* (New York: Barnes and Noble, 1989), p. 1265.

By contrast, *Webster's* treatment of "sacred" yields the following:

1. devoted or dedicated to a deity or to some religious purpose; consecrated. 2. entitled to veneration or religious respect by association with divinity or divine things; holy. 3. pertaining to or connected with religion (opposed to *profane* or *secular*). 4. reverently dedicated to some person or object. 5. regarded with reverence. 6. secured against violation, infringement, etc., by reverence, sense of right, etc. 7. properly immune from violence, interference, etc. Synonyms include venerable, divine, holy, consecrated, revered, sacrosanct, inviolable.[5]

Let's press a bit further, both in Latin and in English. A review of the authoritative *Dictionary of Latin and Greek Theological Terms* yields the following definition for *sanctitas:* "sanctity, holiness, inward or intrinsic righteousness."[6] The primary doctrinal use of this term is listed as *sanctitas Dei* (holiness of God). This dictionary, oriented toward classic Reformation theology, lists no use of the term *sanctitas* or cognates in relation to human beings. This is significant.

The world's premier English dictionary, the *Oxford English Dictionary (OED),* offers the following definitions for "sanctity": "(1) holiness of life, saintliness; (2) the quality of being sacred or hallowed; sacredness, claim to (religious) reverence; inviolability."[7]

But the *OED's* more extensive definition of the word "sacred" yields a striking discovery. This English adjective actually emerges from an obsolete verb, *sacre,* which meant to consecrate, sacrifice, worship, hallow, bless, sanctify, or make holy; to dedicate (a person) to a deity, to make a class of things sacred to a deity.[8] Thus the adjective "sacred," derived from this now-obsolete verb *sacre,* carries forward this range of meanings. A sacred thing is an object or being that someone (or Someone) has *sacre-ed,* has *made sacred,* for example, dedicated, consecrated, venerated, or hallowed. The adjective ("sacred") now assumes the action of the lost verb *(sacre),* but because we have lost the verb, it is easy to lose a sense of *agency* — of who (if anyone) bears responsibility for having made something sacred.

"Sacredness" and "sanctity" are today treated as essentially synony-

5. *Webster's,* pp. 1258-59.
6. Richard A. Muller (Grand Rapids: Baker, 1985), p. 270.
7. *Oxford English Dictionary* (hereafter *OED*), 2nd ed. (Oxford: Clarendon, 1989), pp. 441-42.
8. *OED,* pp. 338-39.

mous and often defined with reference to each other. However, this closer examination reveals that "sanctity" carries a particular *moral* connotation — such as purity, holiness, or virtue — linking the term to character qualities *achieved by the person* who has attained sanctity. "Sacredness," by contrast, clearly reflects an *ascribed status*, referring to something or someone having received a special status through consecration by another. This gets us to the heart of our project, because *it is precisely the idea that all human beings have been consecrated to a special status by the agency of God that marks ordinary Christian understandings of the sacredness of human life.* Therefore, precision in terminology dictates that for the most part we use the term "sacredness" rather than "sanctity" in this volume, even though contemporary usage conflates the two terms, as we will often encounter even in this chapter.

We must consider also what is meant by the term "human dignity." Derived from the Latin *dignitas,* "dignity" means worthiness, elevation, nobility, honor, and distinction. While Christians often use "human dignity" as a term equivalent to "sacredness of life," legal philosopher Jeremy Waldron has shown that "dignity" has a developmental history that is definitely not traceable to the Bible or Christianity. It originally emerged from the classical world and carried the connotation of *rank.*[9] In the Greco-Roman world the term originally signaled the proper recognition appropriate to the highest-ranking members of societies in which people were sharply stratified according to class, citizenship, gender, or other characteristics.

The term "dignity" later came to signify (with the Stoics) that, *collectively,* humans "outrank" nonhuman creatures and claim a unique place as a species in the natural order. On this account, *every* human being has a kind of dignity in the sense that every human outranks every other kind of creature. But this unsatisfactory formulation wins human dignity at the expense of the indignity of nonhuman creatures, a move that left a tragic ecological legacy. (This question of whether all claims to the sacredness of human life or human dignity require animal indignity still resonates today. It will stay with us throughout this study and will occupy our full attention in chapter 11.) What is now called "human dignity" eventually became and today remains a very important concept in law, ethics, and religion. In law,

9. Jeremy Waldron, "Dignity and Rank," *Archives Européennes de Sociologie* 48 (2007): 201. See also his work "The Image of God: Rights, Reason and Order" (paper presented at Center for Theological Inquiry, Princeton, September 2009). See also the discussion in R. Kendall Soulen and Linda Woodhead, eds., *God and Human Dignity* (Grand Rapids: Eerdmans, 2006), pp. 3-8.

for example, it functions simultaneously as the *grounding* for concepts of human rights and as the *content* of specific rights.[10] The term is used in public discourse to speak of human life's great worth, most often by secular thinkers but also by Christians who have sacredness/sanctity language available to them and choose not to deploy it. "Human dignity" is a useful crossover term bridging diverse intellectual and religious communities, but it does not fully convey the depth of theological meaning carried by the language of life's *sacredness*. We can incorporate a proper use of "dignity" language into our understanding of sacredness, but it is a subordinate concept related to elevated rank, rather than the central conviction of the Christian tradition when it comes to human worth.

One other often-used term is "respect for (human) life." This term sometimes functions as shorthand for sacredness or human dignity. But it is more precisely understood as one way of describing *the appropriate human response to human life's sacredness*. To respect someone is to recognize that person's worth. It also connotes treating people with due regard. The term "respect" has gained traction and wide use in a secular age less comfortable with terms more clearly associated with religion and the church. For example, some authors (even secular ones) prefer to speak of "reverence" for (human) life. Such a term moves beyond respect into the precincts of *awe or veneration,* carrying its connotations much closer to a religious sensibility.[11] This is probably why "respect" rather than "reverence" is the more commonly used term in our era. I will incorporate both "respect" and "reverence" language into the paradigm I will develop around the language of sacredness of life.

1.2. A Sacredness Paradigm

The dictionaries and etymological studies clearly link both of our key terms — "sanctity" and "sacredness" — to religion. The Latin origins are

10. See also Jeremy Waldron, "Dignity, Rank, and Rights," Tanner Lectures, University of California at Berkeley, April 2009, accessed at http://www.law.nyu.edu/ecm_dlv3/groups/public/@nyu_law_website__news/documents/documents/ecm_pro_061884.pdf, September 30, 2009.

11. Classicist Paul Woodruff has sought to reclaim "reverence" as a virtue for highly irreverent contemporary culture. See Woodruff, *Reverence: Renewing a Forgotten Virtue* (New York and Oxford: Oxford University Press, 2001). He links it to the capacity for awe, leading to proper respect for persons as well as shame when we show damaging moral flaws.

not accidental. As these terms come to us through Latin into English, they bear the unmistakable traces of the Western Christian tradition. Those secular critics who disdain these terms and their generally understood meanings have noticed this, which is one reason why they reject them.

The Latin and Christian origins of our English words "sanctity" and "sacredness" could lead to the conclusion that all ascriptions of sacredness are irreducibly religious, that is, irreducibly linked to the divine. This is certainly the conclusion one would most naturally draw both from looking at the dictionaries and from hearing how these words are almost always used today, especially by Christians.

But further examination of the *Oxford English Dictionary*'s treatment of sacredness yields a clue to a better approach. I went to the *OED* looking for any reference to "sacredness of human life." But the *OED*, which generally can be relied upon to offer examples of every significant historic type of usage of a term in English, has not a single example of any phrase such as "sacredness of human life." It does, however, have listings related to the "sacred" for all kinds of other objects, such as kings, mothers, gods, temples, lovers, knights, and rivers. All are declared sacred by one writer or another, but never does "human life" receive such a designation.

My final work on this chapter was undertaken the weekend of the tenth anniversary of the September 11 terrorist attacks in the United States. It was abundantly clear on that weekend that September 11 has become a permanently set-apart day on the national calendar; it is, in fact, now called Patriot Day, and joins other special national days such as Memorial Day and Veterans Day. Also on that day, the striking new memorial to the victims of the September 11 attacks was dedicated at the World Trade Center site in New York City, as part of a long day of solemn commemoration.

Why this reference to September 11? I propose that in the United States, this particular day has become a national *sacred day*, and will remain so indefinitely. And "Ground Zero," as it is called, that particular spot in New York, now marked by a profound memorial, has become a national *sacred place*. Sacredness is a treasured concept in the United States. The National Archives in Washington house our national *sacred documents*, such as the original text of the Declaration of Independence. I can certainly attest that August 4 (a thoroughly ordinary day for everyone else) is a personal sacred day, because it is the day my wife and I married in 1984. And those roadside crosses one sees next to highways all over the country — they mark *sacred places* for family members to commemorate where loved ones were killed in car accidents.

We can identify a pattern here in human life, which I want to call a **sacredness paradigm**. It is not inextricably tied to belief in God. It goes something like this:

1. One from among a class of ordinary things (we will call it X from among a large group of x's) is lifted up from the midst of its ordinary companions and designated as of elevated rank (dignity), special status, or even sacredness. There are many days, places, and documents in human experience, but X days, X places, and X documents are elevated above the rest and declared to be special, different, set apart, sacred.
2. The consecration, hallowing, blessing, dedicating, or sacralizing of this now-sacred X is undertaken by some agency, whether collective or individual, whose authority to make such a designation is accepted by the community affected.
3. A variety of reasons can exist for why this particular X is declared sacred, but for those making and acknowledging the designation the reasons are compelling.
4. This special/sacred status generally evokes in relation to X an attitude or posture of awe, veneration, honor, or reverence; at least such an attitude toward X is held by the agent that does the designation, and expected from others in the community.
5. This attitudinal posture is accompanied by, or expected to be accompanied by, concrete moral obligations to treat X with due respect and even special care, and in particular to prevent any *desecration* of X by those who refuse to recognize its sacredness.
6. This moral obligation to preserve what is often called the "inviolability" of the sacred X is normally accompanied by negative sanctions for those who do violate the sacred; the more sacred the X, the more severe the sanctions for its violation.

1.3. Sacred Human Beings

Are human beings among those who can be set apart or consecrated as sacred? The *OED*, as already noted, demonstrated English usages in which kings, mothers, lovers, knights, etc., had been designated as sacred. Therefore it is certainly possible for human beings to designate other particular human beings or categories of human beings as sacred. It is something we have often done. The sacredness paradigm identified above can easily apply to such circumstances. A person is elevated from among the ordinary run of people, designated or "dignified" as sacred by some agent for any number of reasons, and granted special status in the community because of this designation; this designation evokes toward that person a posture of honor and respect, accompanied by concrete moral obligations to treat that person with special care and to prevent harm or violation from coming to him or her, with stern sanctions for violating these norms.

But when contemporary Christians use the phrase "sacredness of human life," they are not saying that *some* small number of human beings are sacred, that some human X's from a large class of human x's are set apart and designated as of sacred value. They are instead saying that each and every human life is thus designated. Every human being x is to be set apart as a sacred X.

This move conforms to the sacredness paradigm while departing from it in one crucial way. It conforms because those who make a claim that every human being is sacred intend something like the six steps I have identified in the sacredness paradigm. The only difference is in the first step. No longer is *one* from among a class of ordinary things lifted up above the others and designated as sacred. Now each and every member of the class human being is elevated.[12] The rest of the steps remain the same:

1. The consecration, hallowing, blessing, dedicating, elevating, or sacralizing of each and every human being is undertaken by some authoritative agent.
2. A variety of reasons can exist for why each human being is declared sacred — but for those making and acknowledging the designation the reasons are compelling.
3. This special status evokes in relation to each human being an attitude or posture of awe, veneration, honor, or reverence, or at least such an attitude toward human beings is held by the agent that does the designation and is expected from others in the community.
4. This posture is accompanied by, or expected to be accompanied by, a moral obligation to treat each human being with due respect and special care, and in particular to prevent any desecration of a human being by anyone.

12. However, one way the original paradigm can be viewed as unaltered here is to say that claims that every human being is sacred lift up humanity as a species from among other species; only this species X is elevated in value above all other species. We will have ample opportunity to see if this is what Christians and others are really doing when they make the claim that human life is sacred.

5. This moral obligation to preserve the "inviolability" of the human being is accompanied by negative sanctions and punishments for those
   who do in fact violate a human being.

Let me streamline these categories to offer an **analytical definition** of the
sacredness of human life, based entirely on linguistic analysis and on what
we have observed about how human beings and human communities ascribe sacredness, and without any religious reference at this point:

> *Human life is sacred: this means that each and every human being has been
> set apart for designation as a being of elevated status and dignity. Each hu-
> man being must therefore be viewed with reverence and treated with due
> respect and care, with special attention to preventing any desecration or vi-
> olation of a human being.*

1.4. Does Sacredness Require God?

What would be the origin of such a radical valuing of human beings as
such, of each and every human being? We are forced to return to the question of whether the ascription of sacredness is always and everywhere associated with God or the divine, as the English dictionary definitions and
contemporary usage would lead us to believe, and as contemporary religious believers who hold to the sacredness of human life would certainly
assume.

The sacredness paradigm and the analytical definition outlined above
suggest that certainly some ascriptions of sacredness are not associated
with God, and that it is possible to ascribe sacredness without reference to
God. Something in the human psyche, or in human community and experience, gives us both the capacity and the need to elevate some days, places,
texts, and people as set apart from the ordinary, as sacred. These ascriptions of sacredness appear to be connected to the deepest human experiences of joy and sorrow, of greatness and smallness, of permanence and
transience, of goodness and evil, of love and hate.

But the designation of *each and every human being* as sacred does not
seem quite natural in the same way as these other designations. It seems
perfectly natural for human beings to designate a royal class, or a beloved
mother, or one's fellow citizens, or one's coreligionists, as sacred. But it is
not natural, and certainly not routine in human life, to ascribe sacredness

to each and every other human being. In fact, indifference toward most members of our fellow species, with special hatred for a few and special reverence for a different few, seems the common human experience.

I propose that the conviction that each and every human being is sacred comes to humanity from beyond humanity. It is an aspect of divine revelation, and could only have come to us that way. The only agent (Agent) who could imagine designating all humans as sacred, and who could have the authority to do so, is God. I hope to show through the pages of this book that this breathtaking divine Word to and about humanity is embedded in the biblical canon, that this consecrating Word of God about human worth is most clearly spoken in Jesus Christ, and that this conviction has never entirely disappeared from the church's life — or from cultures where Christian influence has been felt.

Here is where we reconnect to the religiously laden definitions and etymologies of sacredness with which we began. We have imagined the possibility and even seen examples of human ascription of sacred status apart from a role for the divine. But the etymologies associated with our words "sacredness" and "sanctity" echo with the cadence of the religious — and for very good reasons. In most of human history, and certainly in Christian cultures, to ascribe "sacredness" to something or someone usually involved some special kind of connection with God or the things of God. Sacred texts (the Bible), sacred places (cathedrals), sacred leaders (the clergy), sacred days (the feast days), even sacred foods (the bread and wine) became sacred through divine consecration. In each case, the full sacredness paradigm applied. The object of such special hallowing and blessing was elevated from the ordinary by God or God's representatives, was granted special status, evoked reverence or veneration, and required treatment that included respect, special care, and protection from desecration or violation. There are numerous examples: one might think about how a cathedral is consecrated by religious leaders as sacred space during a special worship service, after which that "sanctuary" is to be viewed and treated with reverence and honor, its sacredness respected and protected from any desecration or violation.

To speak in religious terms of the sacredness of each and every human life, then, is basically to claim that all human beings are something like cathedrals that have been consecrated by God and must not be violated. God has *sacre-ed,* has consecrated, the human being, each human being, who is now sacred, and must be treated accordingly.

1.5. Humanity as Sacred: Ancient Christian Doctrine or Recent Innovation?

The *OED* can find no usage of an English phrase "sacredness of human life" (or "sanctity of human life"). But I am claiming it is an aspect of divine revelation from two millennia ago that is embedded in the ancient biblical canon. Today millions of Christians treat this concept as a settled piece of Christian theology or ethics. Yet critics suggest that the language is a recent innovation, and mainly for political use. Is there a way to find out which side is right?

In 2009, I asked my intrepid student researcher Andi Sullivan to employ a JSTOR search to find all English-language articles, editorials, and pamphlets (reviews were omitted) that contained the terms "human dignity," "sanctity of (human) life," or "sacredness of (human) life." JSTOR searches extend as far back as 1869. Here is what she found:

1869-1939: 239 articles used these terms (3-4 per year)
1940-1945: 171 articles (34 per year)
1946-1969: 1,837 articles (79 per year)
1970-2009: 6,467 articles (165 per year)

The earliest reference Andi found was in an 1893 article on the rights of laborers. The terms began to be used in legal, philosophical, and religious journals, and were applied to a wide range of issues in this early stage, including the death penalty, the family, suicide, euthanasia, labor laws and workers' rights, the effects of war, women's rights, self-esteem, the nature of law, and the treatment of animals. A 1918 article on euthanasia by Herbert L. Stewart noted that Western culture's "belief in the sanctity of life" remains, though it "may well be independent of those theological considerations which first gave rise to it, and might even without consequence survive their total abandonment."[13] Linger over that important (1918!) quote for a moment, for it contains three pivotal claims: there is a recognized concept in Western thought called the sanctity of life; it has been sheared from its theological moorings; and that shearing might not be a problem in the long run. Each of these claims will be considered carefully in this book.[14]

---

13. Herbert L. Stewart, "Euthanasia," *International Journal of Ethics* 29, no. 1 (October 1918): 48-62.

14. Oddly enough, in the great 1868 novel *The Moonstone,* by Wilkie Collins (New York:

During and after World War II, use of the language of life's sacredness and dignity intensified. Sometimes this involved reflections on the massive desecrations of life during World War II and in dictatorial regimes such as Nazi Germany and the Soviet Union. Beginning in the 1950s, the language of *human dignity* was widely employed to discuss race, desegregation, and civil rights issues. In the 1960s, the bloody transition to a postcolonial world occasioned numerous discussions of demands for respecting human dignity in Asia, Africa, and Latin America. This period also saw a number of treatments of human rights issues with much reference to international efforts to protect human rights, including declarations like the Universal Declaration of Human Rights, treaties, conventions, the United Nations, and international tribunals.

After 1973 there was indeed a huge increase in the number of references to our three key terms ("dignity," "sanctity," "sacredness"). Much of this increase had to do with abortion and, to a lesser extent, euthanasia. But these terms were also used quite extensively in relation to issues such as race, apartheid, immigration, ethnic conflict, indigenous peoples, torture, contraception, population, human organ transplantation, genetics, and privacy.

In summary: the hypothesis that language ascribing universal dignity, sacredness, or sanctity to human beings is a contemporary innovation is incorrect. Writers employed dignity/sanctity language as far back as our searches will go into the nineteenth-century literature. Most of the time they felt no need to explain their usage of these terms, assuming that their audiences would be familiar with these concepts and would assent to their use in discussions of major contemporary moral issues. Sanctity/sacredness/dignity language was employed most often to offer strong grounding for claims on behalf of the rights or well-being of a wide range of vulnerable or victimized groups. The research indicates that sanctity/sacredness language retained broader appeal for specifically religious audiences, while dignity language tended to prevail in more secular sources, but the terms crossed over quite a bit as well.

It seems most accurate to say that a broad Christian-then-civilizational "sacredness of human life tradition" survived into the twentieth century

---

Signet Classics, [1868] 2009), I found an even earlier reference to the sanctity of life that also demonstrates the assumption that readers would know what the concept meant: "The mastiff and the bloodhound have one great merit — they are not likely to be troubled by your scruples about the sanctity of human life" (p. 97).

and then surged after the desecrations of World War II. It carried forward into the great freedom struggles of the 1950s-1960s and then spiked again in the United States during the fight over abortion. Talk about life's sacredness or dignity has never been restricted to the antiabortion cause. Conservative Christians can certainly be criticized for narrowing the scope of concern for human dignity/sanctity to the beginning (and end) of life after the 1970s, but not for inventing the concept to help win political battles.

So it turns out that the secular philosopher Peter Singer is right when he claims that the "doctrine" or "tradition" of the sanctity of human life is part of the "religious legacy" of our culture. He believes the idea must be rejected in favor of a different vision of life's value, and so he writes books with titles like *Unsanctifying Human Life*. But he does not doubt the ancient religious provenance of the concept.[15] Neither did Sigmund Freud a century earlier, when he wrote of the "character of sanctity and inviolability" given to the prohibition of murder in Western culture through its historic association with (in his view, illusory) divine command.[16]

And yet, what are we to make of bioethicist Daniel Callahan's claim that "the phrase 'the sanctity of life' is not a traditional religious concept. It has no fixed meaning and is not an official part of any church's doctrine. No doubt the western religions now uphold the view that it is 'wrong intentionally to end the life of an innocent human being,' but that position has taken a long time to develop — and is still developing — with many twists and turns along the way."[17]

Callahan, oddly enough, is also (partly) right. One cannot find in the official pre-twentieth-century doctrinal and moral formulations of the Christian churches a well-developed concept called "the sacredness of human life" that takes its place alongside other theological doctrines such as the Trinity, the deity of Christ, or justification by grace. It is not to be found in the classic creeds and confessions of the ancient church. It is not in the codes of canon law. It is not a phrase one finds in Augustine, Aquinas, Luther, Calvin, or Wesley.

But the absence of "the sacredness of life" as a fixed doctrine in Christian tradition does not mean that the idea was cut from whole cloth begin-

---

15. See Peter Singer, *Practical Ethics*, 2nd ed. (Cambridge: Cambridge University Press, 1993), p. 150 and elsewhere, and *Unsanctifying Human Life*, ed. Helga Kuhse (Oxford: Blackwell, 2002).

16. Sigmund Freud, *The Future of an Illusion*, trans. James Strachey (New York: Norton, 1961), p. 41.

17. Daniel Callahan, "Defending the Sanctity of Life," *Society* (July/August 2001): 16.

ning in 1893 or even 1973. The rapid acceleration of language relating to human life's sacredness, especially after World War II, *was a crisis-induced recovery of an older moral tradition rooted in biblical faith but never previously formulated as a matter of dogma.* In Catholic terms, this would fall under the rubric of the "development of doctrine," a concept that describes how even authoritative Christian doctrinal claims believed to be inspired by the Holy Spirit can evolve over time.[18] The sacredness of human life became a way of offering urgent articulation of moral and theological commitments that had gone underground for several centuries due to the pressures of Enlightenment secularization, but in two millennia of Christianity had never disappeared entirely from the Christian tradition or the cultures affected by it. The sacredness of human life did not have to be articulated as an official religious doctrine to have long functioned as a key theological-moral norm in Christianity or in a Western culture rooted in biblical religion. It was only when that norm was massively violated, and perhaps when it seemed clear that merely secular formulations of the norm had proven insufficient, that it became necessary to articulate it afresh and even to raise it to the level of official Christian doctrine.

1.6. Current Christian Definitions of the Sacredness of Life

In this section I want to look at five Christian definitions of the sacredness of human life — two evangelical, one Anglican (in an authoritative Christian ethics sourcebook), and two Catholic. Whatever might be said about the history of "sacredness of human life" as Christian dogma, by now it has arrived and occupies a significant place on the Christian landscape, especially in Roman Catholicism and conservative Protestantism. It is worth our time to see how it is being defined. I will test these representative definitions against the sacredness paradigm I developed earlier in the chapter.

Protestant evangelicals Jay Smith and the late Stanley Grenz offered the following definition for "the sanctity of life" in their *Pocket Dictionary of Ethics:*

> The belief that human life is unique and thus to be treated as sacred. The sanctity of life generally arises out of a theological perspective in which

18. See John T. Noonan Jr., *A Church That Can and Cannot Change* (Notre Dame, Ind.: University of Notre Dame Press, 2005).

each human being is considered to be incalculably precious to God and created for an eternal *telos,* and for this reason ought to be treated with dignity, protected and preserved. The sanctity of life is often invoked as providing the foundation for the existence of a supposed right to life, which forms in turn the basis of all other human rights. The sanctity of life also shapes the responses of many Christians to a variety of social issues, including abortion, homicide, cloning, capital punishment and euthanasia.[19]

A widely used evangelical dictionary of ethics is the *IVP New Dictionary of Christian Ethics and Pastoral Theology.* Here is its entry for "sanctity of human life":

> This phrase is best understood as referring to the particular respect which is owed to human life as the gift of God (Acts 17:25), as created in his image (Gn. 1:26-27) and as subject to the laws of the covenants with Noah and with Moses (Gn. 9:5-6; Ex. 20:13). Everyone has a duty to conserve and respect human life (Gn. 9:5; 4:8-10, 15), and to accept responsibility for the life of their fellow humans (Gn. 4:9, Dt. 21:1-9). Human life is sacred because it is precious to God (Ps. 116:15), and because God took human nature at the incarnation (Jn. 1:1, 14), thus demonstrating the value he places upon it.[20]

The leading mainstream Christian ethics compendium for years has been the *Westminster Dictionary of Christian Ethics.* Its entry for "Life, Sacredness of" is written by Anglican ethicist Thomas Wood:

> Christian belief in the sanctity of human life is derived from the doctrine of God as Creator. Humankind was made in God's image with power to reason and the capacity to choose. Each individual is infinitely precious to God and made for an eternal destiny. Thus the Christian attitude to human life can only be one of reverence — enjoined by the whole of the Decalogue . . . and confirmed by the incarnation — which is to be extended to every individual from the moment of conception to extreme

---

19. Stanley J. Grenz and Jay T. Smith, *Pocket Dictionary of Ethics* (Downers Grove, Ill.: InterVarsity, 2003).

20. David J. Atkinson et al., eds., *IVP New Dictionary of Christian Ethics and Pastoral Theology* (Downers Grove, Ill.: InterVarsity, 1995), pp. 757-58.

old age and death. Our right to life, grounded in our divine origin, is the basis of all other human rights, natural and legal, and the foundation of civilized society. Our worth to God implies the duty of cherishing, protecting, and preserving human life. . . . Since God remains the absolute owner of all our lives, the Christian tradition has held that it is a sin deliberately and directly to kill an innocent person.[21]

The authoritative *Catechism of the Catholic Church* offers the following statement of the church's official stance on the sacredness of life:

Human life is sacred because from its beginning it involves the creative action of God and it remains forever in a special relationship with the Creator, who is its sole end. God alone is the Lord of life from its beginning until its end: no one can under any circumstance claim for himself the right directly to destroy an innocent human being.[22]

A leading American Catholic cleric identified with a sacredness-of-life ethic was Cardinal Bernardin of Chicago. He became known in the 1970s and 1980s for his pioneering work on a "seamless garment" ethic, sometimes called the "consistent ethic of life." This is one way he described this ethic:

The common element that links [our moral] concerns is our conviction about the unique dignity of each human person. The very first chapter of Genesis states unequivocally that humanity represents the summit of the creative process. The Creator places all creation in our hands, giving us the awesome responsibility of stewardship over the earth's resources, including the gift of each human life. . . . God makes each human person in his own image and likeness. . . . The person is the clearest reflection of the presence of God among us. To lay violent hands on the person is to come as close as we can to laying violent hands on God. To diminish the human person is to come as close as we can to diminishing God. . . . From our recognition of the worth of all people under God flow the responsibilities of a "social" morality. . . . Because we esteem human life as

---

21. James F. Childress and John Macquarrie, eds., *The Westminster Dictionary of Christian Ethics* (Philadelphia: Westminster, 1986), p. 353.

22. *Catechism of the Catholic Church*, 2nd ed. (New York: Doubleday, 1997), paragraph 2258, p. 602, italics in original.

sacred, we have a duty to protect and foster it at all stages of development, from conception to death, and in all circumstances.[23]

Let's analyze these five statements via the sacredness paradigm and see what results:

1. Human life is elevated as carrying "sacred" status. It is also declared "unique" and "incalculably precious" (Smith/Grenz), "infinitely precious" (Wood), and of "unique dignity" (Bernardin).
2. This consecration or ascription of unique, precious, sacred status comes from God, Christian theology and doctrine, and various parts of sacred Scripture that attest to it.
3. The specific reasons given for ascribing sacred status to human beings range widely. They include our creation by God, who is humanity's sole end (Catholic catechism); our human origins as the peak of the divine creative process (Bernardin); our status as a "gift of God" (IVP dictionary), made for an eternal telos or destiny (Smith/Grenz, Wood), and fashioned in God's image (Wood, Bernardin); our subjection to the laws of the covenants with Noah and Moses (IVP); our identity as objects of a special relationship with the Creator (catechism), which includes standing under God's ownership/sovereignty (Wood); and our powers as a species, including reason and choice (Wood).
4. The sacredness of human life requires of all our fellow humans an attitude of "particular respect" (IVP), even "reverence" toward and "cherishing" of human life (Wood), along with a duty to "accept responsibility" for human life (IVP), defined more sharply as the responsibility to exercise "stewardship" over the "gift of each human life" (Bernardin).
5. This posture flows into concrete moral obligations to treat human beings with "dignity" (Smith/Grenz), a universal duty to "respect and conserve" (IVP), or to "protect and preserve," human life (Smith/Grenz, Wood, Bernardin), in particular to recognize a right to life (Smith/Grenz, Wood) and a broader panoply of human rights (Smith/Grenz), and to reject any right to "destroy directly an innocent human being" (catechism, Wood). As well, we have a broad obligation to "foster" human life (Bernardin). These obligations extend to all stages of development, from conception through old age to death, and in all circumstances (Wood, catechism, Bernardin).

23. Joseph Cardinal Bernardin, *Consistent Ethic of Life* (Kansas City, Mo.: Sheed and Ward, 1988), pp. 28-29.

1.7. My Christian Definition of Life's Sacredness — and Puzzles That Remain

Earlier I attempted to offer an analytical definition of the sacredness of human life derived from linguistic analysis and observation of common human practices related to ascribing sacredness. That definition went like this:

Human life is sacred: this means that each and every human being has been set apart for designation as a being of elevated status and dignity. Each human being must therefore be viewed with reverence and treated with due respect and care, with special attention to preventing any desecration or violation of a human being.

Now we have the resources to offer at least a working definition of what Christians today mean in claiming that human life is sacred. I propose the following **Christian definition** (henceforth to be distinguished from the earlier **sacredness paradigm** and **analytical definition**) as a synthesis of what we have discovered thus far:

Human life is sacred: this means that God has consecrated each and every human being — without exception and in all circumstances — as a unique, incalculably precious being of elevated status and dignity. Through God's revelation in Scripture and incarnation in Jesus Christ, God has declared and demonstrated the sacred worth of human beings and will hold us accountable for responding appropriately. Such a response begins by adopting a posture of reverence and by accepting responsibility for the sacred gift that is a human life. It includes offering due respect and care to each human being that we encounter. It extends to an obligation to protect human life from wanton destruction, desecration, or the violation of human rights. A full embrace of the sacredness of human life leads to a full-hearted commitment to foster human flourishing.

This rather lovely Christian definition (if I do say so myself!) may seem to conclude our work. But this is a beginning, not an end. This definition, which I am confident will gain very wide assent in the Christian community, opens the way to the deeper explorations needed to offer a lucid and compelling articulation of Christian moral obligation. But a close look at the definition yields questions that demand further examination, puzzles that need to be addressed, if not solved, through the course of this book. I will call these our seventeen **puzzles**, and will refer to them by number throughout the rest of the book. You may want to bookmark these pages, or, for easy reference, consult the last two pages of the book, where these puzzles have also been printed.

(Puzzle #1) Does the elevation of "each and every human being" to special dignity and rank require or imply a denigration of other species, even if the definition as stated says nothing about other species? How does this old-new Christian tradition of human life's sacredness relate to the value of other forms of life? Can it be sustained alongside proper valuing of God's creation and its other species?

(Puzzle #2) Is the focus of "the sacredness of human life" on the human individual, the human community, or the human species? Or is it perhaps even some aspect of the individual, such as the human body, the human spirit, or even the human "personality" or human "potential"? Might there ever be conflicts of interest and vision between those seeking to defend human worth and well-being at these various levels?

(Puzzle #3) What does it mean to say that the sacredness of human life applies "without exception and in all circumstances"? Is it clear from divine revelation that this includes the developing human being in the womb, for example? Or the embryo in the lab? Or the human being lingering in a persistent vegetative state?

(Puzzle #4) What does it mean to say that human beings are "incalculably" precious? Does that mean the same thing as "infinite" or "immeasurable"? Can any kind of "price" be put on a human life? Are some human lives ever "worth" more than others?

(Puzzle #5) What exactly makes human life so precious and sacred? Is it some quality, capacity, or particular set of characteristics that (most) humans have? Is it possible for a human being to lose whatever characteristics or qualities make him or her worthy of the designation "sacred"?

(Puzzle #6) Does human behavior matter at all to this ascription of sacredness? Can a human being behave in such a way as to forfeit his or her sacredness — or at least forfeit the respect and protection that goes with that status,

as defined here? Does the mass murderer or perpetrator of genocide still hold sacred worth?

(Puzzle #7) The definition never uses the words "intrinsic" or "inherent," as in "intrinsic worth" or "inherent dignity." Why not? If human worth is not intrinsic, does this mean it can be forfeited?

(Puzzle #8) The definition also never uses the word "person." Can there ever be a difference between a "human being" and a "person"? What about the distinction that is sometimes drawn between "potential" and "actual" human beings and/or persons?

(Puzzle #9) Is it possible to specify minimum and maximum obligations to human beings? "Respect" sounds minimal in comparison with "reverence." Are some human beings worthy of respect and others of reverence? Could different obligations be related to different relationships, such as the differences between a parent-child relationship and that of two strangers on a subway?

(Puzzle #10) The definition speaks of protecting human life from "wanton destruction" but does not say "killing" or "destruction of an innocent human being." Does belief in the sacredness of human life require rejection of any and all violence and killing? Is this book embracing a "consistent ethic of life" that rejects all violence?

(Puzzle #11) What is meant by "human rights" here? How would one know what these rights are? Does belief in the sacredness of human life require belief in (a particular set of) human rights?

(Puzzle #12) That's a pretty large statement at the end about a "commitment to foster human flourishing." What exactly does that entail? And whose responsibility is it to foster whose flourishing in particular? Is there no limit to this obligation?

(Puzzle #13) Who exactly is the recipient of this purported divinely established set of obligations? To whom did/does God communicate these obligations? Are these obligations for believers only, or for all people? Is this a religious/Christian ethic or a universal human ethic? Who exactly will be held accountable, and by whom?

(Puzzle #14) If one grants the obligations imposed on humanity by these claims to life's sacredness, what are the best ways to move toward their fulfillment? In particular, what are the respective roles of the individual, the faith community, and the state?

(Puzzle #15) These claims are grounded in divine revelation, Scripture, and Christ. But what weight can they carry for those who do not accept such authorities? Could the ethic survive if it were retrofitted back to the analytical definition and stripped of all the religious language and authority? Could secular people embrace at least the spirit of this ethic? As a matter of historical fact, have they done so? Does secularization of this ethic change it in any fundamental way?

(Puzzle #16) Christians have purportedly received this moral obligation through ancient divine revelation. How have they done with it? Have they always recognized and lived by it? What has gone right, and what has gone wrong, in their effort to advance life's sacredness? What can history tell us?

(Puzzle #17) The definition is pretty vague about exactly what elements of the Bible teach this moral obligation to honor human life as sacred. What does the Bible really say that can fill out the details left unexplored here?

These questions in a sense constitute the agenda of the rest of this book. But it is that last question that will especially occupy our attention in the next two chapters. We turn now to explore the Bible and what it has to say about honoring human life as sacred. Close exploration of sacred Scripture will begin to yield some answers to our other puzzles as well.

2. The Old Testament and the Sacredness of Human Life

> When a man or a woman wrongs another, breaking faith with the LORD, that person incurs guilt and shall confess the sin that has been committed.
>
> Numbers 5:6-7a[1]

This obscure text illuminates what may be the most important contribution of the Bible to the conviction that human life is sacred. The text implies (in passing, as if it were obvious) that no human interaction is merely a human interaction. There is always something more than meets the eye when human beings harm and help, love and hate, one another. If it is true that when we wrong another person we "break faith" with God, everything that happens in human life takes on an entirely new cast. Every encounter between human beings is simultaneously an encounter with a God who cares deeply about what happens in those moments. The Jewish and Christian tradition that human life is sacred, and the rich repertoire of moral expectations associated with that tradition, has for centuries hinged on the assumption embedded in Numbers 5:6, echoed throughout the biblical drama, and refined in later theological formulations about God and humanity. Meanwhile, every moral tradition that has abandoned belief in God but still seeks to encourage human beings to serve rather than exploit each other must find a different basis for its exhortations.[2]

---

1. Unless otherwise noted, all quoted Scripture in this book is taken from the New Revised Standard Version of the Bible.

2. We will see in this chapter that grounding moral obligation in the divine will carries

Four primary elements of the witness of the Hebrew Bible/Old Testament[3] were most powerfully important in contributing to the religious-ethical traditions that came to view human life as sacred: (1) its creation theology, specifically the concept of God as Creator and of humans as made in the image of God; (2) its depiction of God's compassionate care for human beings, especially suffering people, and most particularly God's liberation of oppressed Hebrew slaves in Egypt; (3) its covenantal/legal materials, specifically the protections offered to human life in the law codes of the people Israel; and (4) its prophetic vision of a just wholeness *(shalom)* for Israel and all creation in the promised eschatological future. Ultimately, in every genre of Scripture, the conviction that human life is sacred receives its firmest grounding in the Bible's revelation of the character, activity, and decision of God, which lies at the root of all its proclamations related to how human beings should be perceived and treated. In relation to humanity, the Bible declares that God has chosen to be Creator, Sustainer, Liberator, Lawmaker, Judge, and Deliverer. If this is true, the obligations that we humans take in relation to other human beings must be of a form properly responsive to God's actions toward us.

In this chapter, most of my attention will be directed to the biblical materials that prove most constructive for hallowing human life, and which often have been deployed accordingly in the history of Jewish and Christian moral thought. Acknowledgment of materials that point in other directions, however, is also required. Deeply problematic elements that do not cohere with the sacredness-of-life ethic are visible in the Old Testament. Along the way, I will seek to address some of the most important of these countervailing elements with unflinching honesty, precisely because a clear and compelling rendering of the sacredness of life requires straightforward discussion of its violations — even in the canon itself.

---

dangers as well as strengths, and so this is not meant here as any kind of triumphalistic claim about the superiority of a religious ethic.

3. Because I write as a Christian, and because for the Christian tradition the Hebrew Bible becomes the "Old Testament," I primarily use that historic Christian name for the Hebrew Scriptures. I do not intend any offense to the Jewish community, for whom the working term tends to be "Tanakh," "Hebrew Bible," or simply "the Bible."

2.1. Creation, Humanity, and the Image of God

Despite the tendency of Christians to read and cite the New Testament far more frequently, seemingly every recent Christian work related to the sacredness of human life begins with the Old Testament. On few issues do all branches of the church do a better job these days of avoiding the practical Marcionism that so often seems to affect Christians — the tendency to think, preach, and teach almost entirely from the New Testament. In this case, though, Christians usually "begin at the beginning," not just in the Old Testament but almost always in Genesis 1. The effort to articulate a compelling sacredness-of-life ethic may have done more than almost anything else in recent decades to help both grassroots Christians and their teachers recover a theology of creation — long-neglected, especially in Protestant circles dominated by a theology of redemption.[4]

Most Christian declarations about life's sacredness begin with the claim that human life is sacred because it was created by God. Genesis 1–2 tells us that humans do not come from nowhere but are the creative handiwork of God. God is the Creator of humanity, and this claim by itself elevates human worth. Of course, what has just been said about humans as creatures of their Creator also can be said, from the biblical account, about all other creatures on the planet. This is pivotally important for helping human beings to remember that they are part of a *community* of God's earth creatures and that other creatures have divinely ascribed status as well (puzzle #1).[5]

God is *equally* the Creator of *all* humans. All references to humanity in Genesis 1 are references to *all* humanity, and the blessings and tasks given to human beings are given to all. God says, "Let us make humankind in our image." This explicitly includes "male and female" (Gen. 1:26-27), and implicitly includes *every* male and female. There is one God who makes one humanity. This note in Genesis 1 helps explain why my Christian definition of the sacredness of human life applies to "each and every human being." It applies to the species as a whole and to every individual human being, without exception (puzzles #2-3). This is a pivotal element of bibli-

---

4. This is not to say that there are no problems with a theological schema heavily dependent on a theology of creation. We need the full movement of the biblical drama, in all its acts, and very careful consideration of how those acts relate to each other.

5. A phrase taken from the wonderful book by Larry L. Rasmussen, *Earth Community, Earth Ethics* (Maryknoll, N.Y.: Orbis, 1996).

cal creation theology, and it contributes at least an implicit primal human *egalitarianism* and *unity.*

The creation narrative found in Genesis 2, believed by biblical scholars to be the older account, adds another important element. It tells a story in which God begins to create humanity by creating one person first. God creates humankind by creating a first man. The first woman is then formed out of the first man. From these first parents come absolutely everyone else. In this sense we are all kin, all part of one vast human family. Paul put it this way at Mars Hill: "From one he made all nations to inhabit the whole earth" (Acts 17:26). Paul actually offers a wordplay here — from *enos* (one) to *ethnos* (nations/peoples). However different from each other the various *ethnoi* may seem, we all have the same divine Creator and the same earthly forebears. Genesis 1 and 2 teach a *primal human unity and equality* by narrating a story in which all human beings come from one common ancestor. In our origins, we are one race — the human race. There is one universal human family. These claims equalize human status and teach us to value human beings far beyond those most closely connected to us. All are God's creation, all are children of Eve, all are part of our one human family.[6]

Those familiar with the Bible tend to take this element of the creation account for granted or not even to notice it, but every worldview (even purportedly Christian ones) based on an ontologically divided or fundamentally hierarchical view of humanity poses a threat to this theology of creation, which in turn poses a threat to such worldviews. Adolf Hitler, for example, in supporting his noxious anti-Semitism, wrote that "The Jew is the creature of another god, the anti-man. . . . He is a creature outside nature and alien to nature."[7] For Nazi ideology, the higher "Aryan race" shared neither a common origin nor a common humanity with Jews. In fact, Nazi instruction to primary school students emphasized the fundamental and irrevocable division of humanity into separate and hierarchically ordered "races."[8] There was no such thing as "humanity as such," only distinct races and peoples competing with one another for supremacy on the planet. We will explore Nazi ideology more thoroughly later in this vol-

6. I am not here attempting to address the questions raised about this account of human origins on scientific grounds. I am engaging the Jewish and Christian *theological* traditions and the moral claims grounded in this biblical account of human origins.

7. Quoted in Leni Yahil, *The Holocaust* (New York: Oxford University Press, 1990), p. 44.

8. *The Nazi Primer: Official Handbook for Schooling the Hitler Youth,* trans. Harwood Childs (New York: Harper and Brothers, 1938); see especially chapter 1, "The Unlikeness of Men."

ume. Suffice it to say at this point that Hitler was quite clear that the egalitarianism, democratization, and universality of biblical creation theology stood in stark contradiction to his authoritarian political racism.

Genesis 1 makes another quite specific and quite memorable claim about human beings. This one sets them as a species apart from other creatures. The text says they alone are made in the image *(tselem)* of God:

> Then God said, "Let us make humankind in our image *(tselem)*, according to our likeness *(demuth);* and let them have dominion over the fish of the sea, and over the birds of the air, and over the cattle, and over all the wild animals of the earth, and over every creeping thing that creeps upon the earth."
>
> So God created humankind in his image,
>   in the image of God he created them;
>   male and female he created them. (Gen. 1:26-27)

Further references to human beings as made in God's image and/or likeness are extremely rare in the Old Testament, and are worth recounting briefly: Genesis 5:1 begins an antediluvian genealogy with the words "When God created humankind, he made them in the likeness of God." Two verses later, the text reads "When Adam had lived one hundred thirty years, he became the father of a son in his likeness, according to his image, and named him Seth." After the flood, in Genesis 9:6, the image of God is linked to a ban on murder. Many Old Testament references prohibit the crafting of any "image" or "likeness" of God (Exod. 20:4; Deut. 4:16; etc.). This may be linked to the concept of the image of God in humanity: God cannot be represented by any icon of stone or wood. But the human being is an icon, "a kind of representation of God on earth,"[9] and in fact was made by God precisely to be the *only* such representation of God. The *imago Dei* is also discussed in Sirach, an intertestamental book, and surfaces in an interesting way in the New Testament with reference to Jesus and the image of God, a theme we will consider in the next chapter.

---

9. The moral connection seems to be that as the only appropriate "image and likeness" of God visible on the earth, human beings carry special dignity and offer a special glimpse into the character of God, especially when they live as God designed. It is also interesting how often idolatry is linked to moral degradation in the Old Testament, including the mistreatment of human beings. See Walter Harrelson, *The Ten Commandments and Human Rights* (Philadelphia: Fortress, 1980), p. 64.

So then, what exactly is going on when the Old Testament refers to human beings as the image and likeness of God?[10] We will need to linger here for a few moments.

One place to begin is with the claim that the image refers first to some kind of correspondence, similarity, or *resemblance* between humans and God (and/or the *elohim*/heavenly court — see Gen. 1:26a). A clue is found in the Genesis 5 reference to Seth as a son in the likeness and image of his father Adam. This might lead us to view the *imago Dei* as akin to the resemblance between parent and child.[11] Humans are thus described as resembling God, with the terms "image" and "likeness" synonymous, an example of Hebrew poetic parallelism.[12] This claim to resemblance of God is extraordinary, especially in light of the vast gulf so often depicted between God and God's created world throughout the Hebrew Bible. Such a claim certainly elevates human status.[13]

The precise nature of that supposed human-divine resemblance is not spelled out and can only be speculated about — but those speculations matter immensely. One intertestamental interpretation was offered in Sirach, which emphasizes human

> discretion and tongue and eyes,
> ears and a mind for thinking. . . .
> He filled them with knowledge and understanding,
> and showed them good and evil. (Sir. 17:6-7)[14]

---

10. A key question at this point is whether to work *exegetically* — sticking as closely as possible to a narrow reading of the original Hebrew text — or *theologically,* opening up to the expansive, diverse, and often speculative (and even destructive) theological interpretations of the *imago Dei* developed through the centuries. My decision is to stay close to the exegesis even while being mindful of the theological tradition. For an important, classic review of that tradition, see Paul Ramsey, *Basic Christian Ethics* (Louisville: Westminster John Knox, 1950), pp. 249-83.

11. Gerhard von Rad, *Old Testament Theology,* trans. D. M. G. Stalker, vol. 1 (Louisville: Westminster John Knox, [1957] 2001).

12. Later Christian theology sometimes made much of a purported distinction between "image" and "likeness," but these are better viewed as examples of Old Testament poetic parallelism. For discussion, see Anthony A. Hoekema, *Created in God's Image* (Grand Rapids: Eerdmans, 1986), p. 13, though he does see subtle distinctions between the two words. Hoekema's book is a significant study in the theology of the image of God.

13. Harrelson, *Ten Commandments,* p. 64.

14. As a Protestant, I follow our tradition in not accepting Sirach as canonical. Yet I recognize the role of Sirach and the intertestamental literature in shaping Christian thought

Sirach goes on to mention how God

> put the fear of him into their hearts. . . .
> He bestowed knowledge upon them,
>   and allotted to them the law of life. (17:8-11)

One could read this significant text to mean that the image of God includes our human intellectual, spiritual, and moral capacities, in particular our capacity (and obligation) to respond relationally to God with proper fear and respect, to understand the difference between good and evil, and to obey God's law.[15]

The Christian tradition long developed its reflections on the divine image along a "capacities" line (puzzle #5), emphasizing human rationality, spirituality, and moral freedom (and a long list of other proposed attributes) as the uniquely God-resembling capacities granted to us as the *imago Dei* and separating us from other earthly creatures. These greater capacities, it was thought, gave us greater value. But a "capacities" rendering of the divine image proves vulnerable to all kinds of problems, and not just the problem of setting up a persistent humans-over-animals dichotomy. One of these is presented by cases in which human beings have not yet developed (fetuses), never will develop (the severely mentally retarded), or eventually lose (those with severe Alzheimer's) the greater and higher capacities deemed essential to their "image-bearing" status. Do human beings who lack the designated package of image-bearing capacities stop being human beings, or at least stop being image-bearers?

Identifying the image of God with specific *rational, spiritual,* or *moral* capacities also risks a subtle denigration of human physicality and embodiment. If our physicality links us to the beasts, while our rationality/spirituality links us to God or the heavenly host, a trajectory is established that can sever and often has severed God-imaging human capacities, potential, and value from the humble human body and its functions. This has led to a damaging devaluation of the significance of bodily life in Christian tradition. Neuroscience helps us now to see more clearly that it is the body,

---

(and in reflecting intertestamental Jewish thought). We are doing intellectual archaeology here and cannot eschew visiting any relevant site.

15. Von Rad suggests that the resemblance might have been understood to extend even to physical characteristics. *Old Testament Theology,* pp. 145-46. This makes more sense in light of von Rad's interpretation that humans were made in the image of the angels *(elohim,* Septuagint *angeloi).*

and especially the brain, that hosts all "higher" human capacities. More broadly, it is clearer now that all distinctions (and gradations) between the various "parts" of the human self are speculative and debatable.

A shift toward a focus on embodied human *responsiveness* to God, rather than on achieving and maintaining some delineated package of fully human rational-spiritual *capacities,* helps to ameliorate this problem. Old Testament scholar Claus Westermann sees it when he says that the image of God means simply that "mankind is created so that something can happen between God and man."[16] Even this approach, though, focusing on responsiveness to God, risks making a concept of sacred human worth a human *achievement* rather than a divine *ascription,* if it is understood that only the properly responsive human being is truly a bearer of God's image.[17] Human worth or even sacredness as *God's decision about the worth of all humans* can be transformed into human worth as *an earned achievement of some humans,* with lesser-achieving human beings rapidly losing their equal worth before God in the process (puzzle #6). In short, it is not only mistaken but has proven problematic if not disastrous, time and again, to define the image of God in terms of any kind of quality that (some) human beings possess. Westermann rightly concludes that "no particular quality of man is meant, but simply being man," that is, a species created by God for relationship with God.[18]

This leads us into a needed discussion of one of the most difficult of our seventeen puzzles (puzzle #8). Neither here nor elsewhere in this book do I make a distinction between "human beings" and "persons." I use the terms interchangeably. This discussion of the image of God offers the best moment to explain why. I acknowledge that a vast literature in theology, philosophy, and ethics focuses exactly on such a distinction.[19] A key insight lies at its root: biologically alive human beings can differ dramatically in terms of their (capacity for) actualization of those attributes and characteristics that fulfill human potential (puzzle #2) and make a human be-

16. Claus Westermann, *Creation,* trans. John J. Scullion (Philadelphia: SPCK and Fortress, 1974), p. 56.

17. Westermann explicitly disavows this in terms of his own view. "No human being can be excepted." Nothing about the human response changes the human's status before God. *Creation,* p. 60.

18. Westermann, *Creation,* p. 59.

19. I am grateful to Michael Robinson for sharing with me his unpublished essay, "Divine Image, Human Dignity and Human Potentiality," as a guide to the issues considered here.

ing a fully realized individual-in-community. One way to account for these vast variations in human experience, and to make moral/legal judgments in relation to them, is to claim that some human beings do not (currently) possess all the capacities that make a human being a person. Usually this list of "person-making capacities" tracks closely with the kinds of "higher" human *imago Dei* resemblances just discussed: reasoning, loving, relating, choosing, planning, etc. A "person" on this account is a human being who currently has such capacities. It can then be claimed that a "potential person" (like a fetus) is one who will likely someday exercise such capacities, while a "former person" (like someone with total and irreversible dementia) is one who once possessed such capacities but — though still physically alive — no longer has them.

The most common labels employed here name as "essentialists" those who say that "personhood is something that all biological humans have or are intrinsically," and as "developmentalists" those who believe that "some but not necessarily all biological humans possess personhood."[20] Within the latter approach it is also possible to draw distinctions between "potential persons," "actual persons," and even "former persons," such distinctions being tied to those person-making capacities just named.

I contend that all distinctions between human beings and persons are purely speculative, lack grounding in biblical revelation, and have proven hugely dangerous. Such distinctions hinge on somebody's definition of what makes a human being a person. These definitions can and do differ dramatically and have often been skewed by self-interest and degrading ideologies. We will see in this book a number of occasions in which certain groups or classes of human beings were classified right out of the human family and stripped not just of sacred worth but of their freedom and their lives. Certainly the developmentalists are right that human beings grow (and sometimes decline) in their exercise of the full panoply of human capacities. Indeed, if these capacities are taken to include spiritual depth and moral excellence, one might rightly conclude that every human life is a drama of struggle toward or away from moral and spiritual excellence. All this matters greatly to the quality of a human life but not in the slightest to its ascribed status as sacred by divine agency (puzzles #5-6).

The "essentialists," on my view, are closer to the truth in refusing to draw a distinction between biological human life and personhood. They rightly see that there is not and can never be a clear line of demarcation be-

20. Quotations from Robinson, "Divine Image," p. 1.

tween a biological human, a potential person, and an actual person. But along with Westermann and others I reject their claim that there is something *intrinsic* or *inherent* (puzzle #7) about biological humanity that makes it valuable or constitutes it as the image of God. I claim that humanity's sacred worth is an ascribed status willed by God and communicated through God's actions, commands, and declarations, one of them being God's revelation that all human beings are made in the image of God. We can't go looking for something in humanity that *in and of itself* gains us value or worth — the sacredness of human life is God's decision, to which we human beings must accede and by which we must orient our lives.

The link between the image of God in humanity and the command to *exercise dominion* over the creatures deserves careful consideration as well.[21] God makes humankind in the divine image, and follows that immediately by commanding humans not only to be fruitful and multiply (like other creatures) but also to have dominion over the rest of the created order (unlike other creatures). The implication is that (part of) what it means to be made in God's image is to exercise dominion over the world and its creatures, and accordingly to be responsible to God for our collective and individual exercise of rule over creation.[22]

Old Testament scholar Gerhard von Rad argues from the dominion mandate that the meaning of the image of God is our "status as lord in the world."[23] God has dominion over the earth, and delegates or transfers divine sovereignty to us, on the model of a human monarch who delegates royal authority to a chosen emissary (compare Pharaoh's delegation of authority to Joseph in Genesis 41:37-45). The emissary then "images" or represents the monarch wherever he or she is sent. The concept, common in the ancient Near East, that the king was the image of the high god on earth might suggest another theme: if human beings are by definition the image of the Creator God, they are *each and all* in this sense God's designated earthly "kings" or at least royal representatives, a theme reinforced when

21. Christopher J. H. Wright: "The two affirmations are so closely linked in the text that there can be no doubt that they are meant to be related." *Old Testament Ethics for the People of God* (Downers Grove, Ill.: InterVarsity, 2004).

22. The Hebrew word for dominion here (from *radah*) may carry connotations of domination rather than service or care, akin to the power of an ancient Near East tyrant-king. Certainly it carries royal connotations. For a good discussion, see Wright, *Old Testament Ethics*, pp. 120-22.

23. Von Rad, *Old Testament Theology*, p. 146.

we remember that the dominion mandate of Genesis 1:28 extends to the other creatures but not to fellow humans.[24] Old Testament scholar William P. Brown is confident that "such language . . . transfers the tasks and trappings of royalty and cult, the offices of divine representation and habitation, to humanity."[25] If *all* human beings are royalty, this not only fundamentally undercuts the ubiquitous ranking-distinction between royalty and commoner in royalist regimes but also implicitly challenges other human ranking-distinctions.

Psalm 8 picks up the theme of dominion and a suggestion of royalty in its own magnificent reflection on the connection between God's grandeur and human worth:

> When I look at your heavens, the work of your fingers,
>   the moon and the stars that you have established;
> what are human beings that you are mindful of them,
>   mortals that you care for them?
> Yet you have made them a little lower than God [Heb. *elohim*],
>   and crowned them with glory and honor.
> You have given them dominion[26] over the works of your hands;
>   you have put all things under their feet. (Ps. 8:3-6)

Here the psalmist expresses a simultaneous human smallness and greatness. When he looks *up* to the heavens, humans appear dwarfed by the grandeur of creation and *elohim*. When he looks *down* from a God's-eye perspective, humans are in fact all kings, in status just a little lower than *elohim*, exercising a royal dominion over the entirety of creation. This elevation of collective human dignity is a staggering contribution to human culture, especially in light of its contrast with the far less exalted vision of humanity found in contemporaneous ancient Near Eastern texts.[27]

---

24. Claus Westermann: "It is not in accordance with biblical reflection on man as a creature that some groups are born to dominate and other groups are born to serve. The Creation narrative understands dominion as something which belongs to all men and for which all are created." Westermann, *Creation,* p. 54.

25. William P. Brown, *The Ethos of the Cosmos* (Grand Rapids: Eerdmans, 1999), p. 43.

26. Here the Hebrew root is *mashal,* which is linked to royal authority but does not carry the same authoritarian/dominative connotation of *radah*. For Christians, Jesus' treatment of what it truly means to carry kingly authority (cf. Luke 22:24-27) helps clarify the proper interpretation of these texts.

27. John Barton, *Understanding Old Testament Ethics: Approaches and Explorations*

Genesis 9:1-6 may be more significant than any other single text related to the image of God and to the sacredness of human life.[28] Here the image is linked to morality proper for the very first time in Scripture. It is only here that the *imago Dei* concept is used to tell this royal species what it may *not* do. And in canonical context the prescription offered here is for all human beings, not just for the nation Israel, which at this point in the text does not exist (puzzle #13). So what is said here has staggeringly broad implications for humanity.[29]

It is important to read this passage in the context of the new divine-human beginning that takes place after the great and terrible flood (Gen. 6–8). According to the text, humanity's horrendous violence triggered God's angry, heartbroken decision to end human life through a flood (Gen. 6:11-13).[30] But at the last moment Noah's goodness stays God's ultimate judgment. After sparing a remnant through Noah, God promises to bear with human beings, despite their deeply and pervasively evil inclinations (8:21-22). Noah becomes the mediator of God's first covenant relationship with humanity and other species. In this covenant, God first renews the creational commands related to procreation and dominion (9:1-2). Then God offers new moral laws in relation to the animals: human beings are now allowed to kill and eat animal flesh, but with the proviso that they abstain from eating "its life, that is, its blood" (9:3-4). And then come the first laws applying solely to human-to-human relations: the shedding of human blood (that is, the killing of human beings by other human beings) is prohibited, and God will "require a reckoning for human life" (9:5).

(Louisville: Westminster John Knox, 2003), pp. 1-2. This is a great development for making each and every human life sacred, but it does raise the question most acutely of whether this moral advance happens by teaching human beings to think of themselves as dominant rulers of the creation and the rest of its creatures, or as having spiritual and moral capacities that the other creatures do not possess.

28. Christopher Wright simply asserts: "The sanctity of human life is one of the earliest explicit moral values in the Old Testament, based as it is on the creation of human beings in God's image." *Old Testament Ethics*, p. 307.

29. But, of course, it must not be forgotten that this text talking about universal moral law for all people is found in the sacred scriptures of the Jewish people and is an aspect of their particular way of telling the human story and describing human (e.g., Gentile) moral obligation. Even this most "universal" of Old Testament moral claims is embedded in a particularistically Jewish text and tradition.

30. I am not overlooking the massive divine violence-as-judgment that the flood itself represents.

"Whoever sheds the blood of a human,
    by a human shall that person's blood be shed;
for in his own image
    God made humankind." (9:6)

Human violence had triggered God's judgment, and now such violence is expressly forbidden. Because human beings are made in God's image, they must refrain from murdering each other. The text is frustratingly elliptical — it does not tell us *what exactly it is about the image of God* in humanity that makes murder so profoundly wrong. It could be that to murder a human being is to come as close as we humans can to killing the God each of us *resembles* as son or daughter, like Seth resembled Adam (5:1). In this sense, to murder a human being is to strike at God, not unlike the way in which those seeking to wound me could hardly do anything worse *to me* than to kill my son or daughters. Or, thinking along the lines of the Sirach text, murder could be seen as the ultimate abandonment of the exalted human *capacities* of spirituality, rationality, and morality, or the ultimate *lack of responsiveness* to God our Creator, or to the ultimate rejection of the knowledge of God and God's moral law that we have been given. Or murder could be viewed as a terrible abuse of our *dominion responsibilities* over the earth and its creatures, a cruel form of tyranny, a taking of unjust dominion over another human. Or if *humanity is a collective royalty,* to murder a human being is regicide, the ultimate rebellion against the crown of God's creation. Or perhaps murder is wrong fundamentally because it constitutes *rejection of God's sovereignty;* if we are all royal emissaries whose very lives are held under God's rule and commissioned for God's purpose, murder marks a kind of treasonous usurpation in which we become gods over others, decreeing death for them at our whim.

That last point is suggested by another text from Sirach:

The Lord created human beings out of earth,
    and makes them return to it again.
He gave them a fixed number of days,
    but granted them authority over everything on the earth.

(Sir. 17:1-2)

Scripture regularly reflects on the brevity of our lives and the sense of their quick passage (cf. Ps. 90). But the allotted three score and ten are under

God's control rather than our own. One thing that we do *not* have authority over is the decision of when to end the life of another human being — or, for that matter, our own lives. Our delegated dominion authority does not extend that far.

Genesis 9:6, of course, couples the ban on murder with the command (or perhaps the observation) that those who shed blood will have their blood spilled in return. This text has long been pivotal for debates over the morality of the death penalty; in fact, that debate has often distracted Christians (and others) from what is most important about the text — that here the image of God is employed as motivation and grounding for a blanket moral ban on murder that became central in Jewish law and is also reflected in the law codes of most known communities.

The question of what to do to the murderer must be seen as a *second step.* Genesis 9:5 says murderers must face a reckoning, and surely they must. Murderers must be held accountable (and must be prevented from killing again). That reckoning cannot merely be through some kind of financial penalty, such as is imposed for many crimes. This is because it is not fitting to put a cash value on a human life, whose worth is beyond price. In this sense, the sentence of death *for this one crime of murder* has been one way of reinforcing the critically important point that a human life is incalculably precious (puzzle #4). Whether a just reckoning for murder today requires the death penalty is a matter both of biblical interpretation and of analysis concerning the morality and efficacy of capital punishment as instituted and employed in particular contexts (see chapter 10).

However we read Genesis 9:5-6, it does strictly ban the wanton murder of one human being by another, and this is established as the first and most fundamental moral implication of human beings as the image of God. Here we reach the origin of why most biblically informed accounts of the sacredness of human life (mine included) offer clear articulations of a claim that life's sacredness requires that human life not be wantonly destroyed. This is what was meant when several of the Christian definitions of life's sacredness reviewed in the last chapter referred to bans on the killing of "innocent" human beings.[31]

---

31. "Innocent" here does not mean "sinless" or "perfect." It means "having performed no act for which death might be deserved as punishment or in self-defense." Still, I prefer the term "wanton killing/destruction" to "killing of innocent human beings," in part because of problems with the connotation of the word "innocent."

Whether that same sacredness of human life requires (guilty) murderers' lives to be taken in recompense, or to be spared in mercy, deserves debate. But I do believe that Genesis 9:5-6 authorizes us to draw a meaningful distinction between murder and recompense for murder. The same act — ending a life — can have a different moral status depending on whether it is randomly inflicted by a murderer or instead socially inflicted as a way of making reckoning for murder. The same point could be made about imprisonment, for that matter. If I imprison you for twenty years in my basement, that's kidnapping and unlawful imprisonment; if society imprisons me for twenty years as punishment for my kidnapping and unlawful imprisonment of you, that's a proper social reckoning for my wrongdoing. And facing such a reckoning does not mean that my life is no longer being treated as having sacred worth in God's sight. By holding me accountable to act according to the standards appropriate to those made in God's image, it might mean quite the opposite.

All this is to say that Genesis 9:5-6a has shaped a Christian tradition that bans murder, understood as the wanton killing of an innocent human being, while Genesis 9:6b has shaped a Christian tradition that authorizes some kind of proportionate punishment for murderers. A proper Christian understanding of the sacredness of human life cannot, *ipso facto,* be understood to treat both the murder and the social response to murder as morally equivalent acts. I say this even as one who opposes the contemporary use of the death penalty. Where those advocating a "consistent ethic of life" (as raised in puzzle #10) obscure this distinction, they miss something very important morally, and hurt themselves strategically, with those for whom the distinction matters greatly.

Genesis 9:5-6 carries yet one more critically important implication. If God's sovereignty over the lives of our image-bearing neighbors bans murder, it might also set other limits on what we can do to them. This greater-to-lesser argument is even suggested by the literal language of "bloodshed" rather than "murder" in the text. Many forms of bloodshed are not murderous. Perhaps this suggests that lesser offenses, such as assault, rape, or torture, are covered under the ban against murder, and bans on all such acts are rooted in our status as the *imago Dei*. Just as I cannot murder you because you are one made in God's image, so also I cannot assault you, for the very same reason. An assault may violate or even desecrate another human being without taking her life. In fact, hard human experience offers ample reminders that some violations of human beings can actually be as bad as or worse than murder. Sadistic, extended torture, even if it draws no blood, is a very good example of a violation of a human being that can be worse than simply killing the person.[32]

But what else is banned under the same rubric? And can these bans on certain kinds of treatment of human beings ("here is what you cannot do to human beings just because they are made in God's image") be turned around and reframed in positive terms ("here are the *rights* that belong to human beings not to have certain things done to them, just because they are made in God's image")? Once again we confront one of the puzzles mentioned in the last chapter, the question of human rights (puzzle #11).

One way to move forward here is to begin with the *rights of God* rather than the rights of people. God as sovereign Creator has rights in what he has made, including the right to due respect for the sacred worth God has designated to his works in creation. If God has decided to make human beings in the divine image and has demanded that human life be treated as sacred, God has a right as Creator and Lord to see that this status is respected and that sacredness honored. These are *God's rights.*[33] Human rights are not inherent (puzzle #7) in humanity;[34] they are derivative from God, but no less real for being derivative. Genesis 9 begins but does not end the accounting of God's rights. Human beings have the right not to be murdered (and assaulted, raped, and tortured, etc.) by other human beings because God has rights in them. To violate human rights is to violate God's rights. All human rights claims, then, begin as the *rights of God* vis-à-vis humanity, and then become the *rights of human beings* in relation to one another, but always *before God.*

This also further clarifies the answer to our puzzle about whether sacred human worth should be spoken of in the language of the "intrinsic" (puzzle #7). This discussion of rights would suggest that neither rights nor human worth is "intrinsic" or "inherent" to something about the nature of

---

32. This helps to explain why torture is always, everywhere, and without exception banned by international law and the laws of war, but killing of an enemy is not universally banned.

33. This is not familiar language in Christian ethics, at least not today. I first encountered it in Irene Oh, *The Rights of God: Islam, Human Rights, and Comparative Ethics* (Washington, D.C.: Georgetown University Press, 2007). If God has rights in his human creatures, this would be true of God's rights in the other creatures as well. Emphasizing God's rights as Creator and Sovereign over all that God has made decenters humanity and human rights and shifts the focus to God's rights in *all* that God has made.

34. A claim to which Richard Hiers agrees in his helpful discussion of human rights and Old Testament law. See Richard H. Hiers, *Justice and Compassion in Biblical Law* (New York and London: Continuum, 2010), p. 216.

humanity, as if we can somehow just look at a human being and "know" that she is inherently "sacred" and has intrinsic "rights."[35] Both sacredness and rights claims are ultimately theological on the account I am offering based on this reading of Genesis 1–9.[36] Yet it has proven just as easy in Western culture to lose the ultimate Agency that ascribes rights to human beings as to lose the ultimate Agency that ascribes sacredness. Our secular age attempts to preserve both "intrinsic" human sacredness/dignity and human rights without divine agency.[37]

The very idea that the concept of human rights is traceable to the Bible is disputed, including among Christians who are suspicious of "rights talk." Certainly some contemporary approaches to human rights do not fit with the biblical witness. But actual reference to "rights" is explicitly employed in scattered Old Testament texts (Prov. 29:7; 31:9; Job 29:12, 16-17), undergirds the entire structure of Old Testament law, and ultimately follows as an implication of the *imago Dei* as explicated by Genesis 9. The first and most fundamental right is the right not to be murdered; all subsequent rights depend on respect for this first right. The Old Testament assumes that the powerful have the capacity to protect their own rights, and thus Old Testament rights-commands are generally focused on motivating the Jewish community to protect the rights of the physically and socially powerless, such as widows, orphans, aliens, and the poor, to get their basic needs met.[38] I believe that at least the germ of the concept of human rights

---

35. This is obviously a very important claim and is carefully considered. One might attempt an alternative account based on the *imago Dei* material, and claim that, having been made in the image of God, humans now have intrinsic or inherent dignity or rights. This is mainly misleading, however. "Intrinsic" means "belonging to a thing by its very nature," and "inherent" means "existing in something as a permanent and inseparable element or quality." I am claiming that to say that human life is sacred or that human beings have rights is to make claims about God's ascription of status to humanity and God's rights in relation to humanity. If we then want to say that, given God's acts and declarations, human life has a certain intrinsic status or inherent rights, we risk obscuring the divine agency that is the source and ground of any such declaration.

36. Christopher Marshall also argues that contemporary dignity claims as well as claims to human rights make little sense if not grounded in biblical theology, including in this kind of theology of creation. See Marshall, *Crowned with Glory and Honor* (Telford, Pa.: Pandora Press, 2001), especially chapter 3.

37. The reference to philosopher Charles Taylor's magisterial *A Secular Age* (Cambridge: Harvard University Press, Belknap Press, 2007) is intentional. No one has more effectively demonstrated the trajectory of our culture from sacred to secular, with religiously informed moral traditions surviving in sedimented layers.

38. Christopher Wright points out that human need trumps legal rights in Old Testa-

in the Old Testament — and every culture touched by it — is found right here in the *imago Dei* teaching of Genesis 9:5-6.

Looking back on the entire discussion of humanity as the image of God, we easily see the power of this concept in elevating and equalizing the status of human beings, birthing a rights tradition, and even consecrating human life. Still, it does take quite a bit of work to move from here to a full-blown sacredness vision as offered in the Christian definition of the last chapter. Often contemporary theologians and ethicists simply play the *imago Dei* card and assume that this is sufficient for grounding all sacredness-of-life claims they might like to make, including vast, expansive appeals to a holistic commitment to human flourishing. While the *imago Dei* is a pivotal aspect of the biblical witness, it is too narrow a foundation upon which to build an entire ethic for dignifying human life. The thinness of the biblical materials has invited theological extrapolations through the centuries that are sometimes taken for revealed truth but instead often extend far beyond what can reasonably be claimed from the few biblical texts themselves.[39] Still, with the image of God we can legitimately claim to have found the first essential building block in the sacredness-of-human-life ethical tradition.

2.2. God's Compassionate Care and Liberating Deliverance

The Old Testament teaches that God does not just create us in the divine image and declare us "crowned with glory and honor." God also cares for us with deep compassion, for despite our ascribed grandeur we are physically vulnerable creatures, subject to great misery and suffering. The Bible records that God's universal care for humanity took a more focused form in God's compassionate response to the suffering of God's people Israel when they were enslaved and threatened with the mass murder of their children in Egypt. It is a universal element of human experience that we care for those

---

ment law, especially where the legal right is held by the more powerful party. *Old Testament Ethics,* pp. 312-14.

39. German ethicist Christiane Tietz claims that "the concept itself is not that clear"; she has found "many different explications in Jewish and Christian thinking" and says it "is not even a central biblical concept." See Tietz, "Particular Justifications for Universal Claims — Exemplified through the Protestant Concept of Imago Dei as Foundation for Human Rights" (unpublished paper for Center for Theological Inquiry Consultation, September 2009, in possession of the author).

we value, and that the suffering of those we love evokes our deepest compassion and most focused acts of care. The numerous examples of God's care for needy and suffering human beings have impressed themselves deeply on the consciousness of those peoples and cultures most affected by the biblical witness, and especially those whose suffering has been the gravest.

God's care begins in Genesis itself. God offers initial care in setting the man and woman in a garden in which their physical and aesthetic needs are met without great labor. And of course, God gives the man and the woman to each other, that they might not be lonely and without help or partnership (Gen. 2:18-25).

They distrust and therefore disobey God, which brings shame to the first couple and evokes God's sorrowful wrath. And yet immediately after the curses are pronounced in Genesis 3, the text offers this striking little note: "And the LORD God made garments of skins for the man and for his wife, and clothed them" (Gen. 3:21). Naked people need to be clothed (cf. Matt. 25), not just for physical protection but because human beings are ashamed of their nakedness. God becomes the first clothier, and in so doing introduces animal killing for human well-being for the very first time. Even a human race under judgment receives divine protection and care.

Biblical narratives abound with the same theme. In Genesis 4 Cain slays his brother Abel. It is an atrocious crime, introducing murder (fratricide!) into the human experience. Abel's blood cries out from the ground (Gen. 4:10), and Cain is afraid he will be hunted down and murdered in return. God spares him this, placing his "mark" on Cain as a signifier of divine mercy (4:15). From this we might learn that even one who has murdered evokes the compassionate mercy of God.

In Genesis 8–9, God makes a covenant with Noah, and through him to all flesh, and in that covenant promises to care for humanity and the world through sustaining a creation in which life can endure and physical needs can be met (8:22). Jesus later uses God's universal provision of such care as an example for his disciples to love people, friend and foe alike: "Love your enemies and pray for those who persecute you, so that you may be children of your Father in heaven; for he makes his sun rise on the evil and on the good, and sends rain on the righteous and on the unrighteous" (Matt. 5:44-45). This unexpected link between rain showers, good harvests, and enemy love surprises us. It helps reinforce the universality of who counts as sacred and explicitly draws enemies (both God's and ours) into the circle of those who must be included.

The Old Testament, of course, makes a turn beginning in Genesis 12, moving from universal/primeval history to the particular history of that people who came to be called the Jewish people. God chooses one people from among the rest to be his partners in covenant and agents of divine reconciliation with the world. From this point in the Old Testament forward, really all the way through the rest of the Bible, a tension emerges between God's general love for all and God's particular love for his chosen. Does God care about one people, his "treasured possession" (Heb. *segullah*), or are all people treasured by God?[40] (This tension is worth noting here and keeping in mind throughout because it highlights the immense challenge of valuing the sacredness of *each and every human life,* when our natural tendency is to place great value on a small number of particular people and relationships.) More than a few times in Scripture the particular seems to crowd out the general entirely. God seems to love *this* people — his chosen, the apple of God's eye, the elect — to the *exclusion* of other peoples, by gaining victories (often violent) over other peoples,[41] raising the question whether the Bible really can be taken to teach the sacredness of *all* human life.[42] And yet the texts themselves sometimes contain striking reminders that God relates in a redemptive way to all people and nations, not just Israel. This is quite striking in a text from Amos:

> Are you not like the Ethiopians to me,
>   O people of Israel? says the LORD.
> Did I not bring Israel up from the land of Egypt,
>   and the Philistines from Caphtor and the Arameans from Kir?
>
> (Amos 9:7)

Still, it is the particular story of God's deliverance of the Hebrew people from slavery and infanticide in Egypt that we are told in Scripture and that so profoundly shaped the Jewish people. You will recall the story: the Hebrew community, apparently a peaceable alien minority amidst the Egyptian population, was forced into backbreaking slavery. "The Egyptians became ruthless in imposing tasks on the Israelites, and made their lives bitter with hard service" (Exod. 1:13-14). The situation took a decisive

---

40. I thank Walt Zorn for pointing out the significance of this Hebrew term.

41. Some of these enemies become permanent ones, and Israel is at times explicitly instructed not to care about their well-being. Speaking of Ammonites and Moabites, Deut. 23:6 reads: "You shall never promote their welfare or their prosperity as long as you live."

42. Bruce C. Birch, *Let Justice Roll Down: The Old Testament, Ethics, and Christian Life* (Louisville: Westminster John Knox, 1991), p. 252.

turn for the worse when Pharaoh moved from enslavement to a policy that can only be described as genocidal: "Every boy that is born to the Hebrews you shall throw into the Nile" (Exod. 1:22).

"The Israelites groaned under their slavery, and cried out. Out of the slavery their cry for help rose up to God. God heard their groaning, and God remembered his covenant with Abraham, Isaac, and Jacob. God looked upon the Israelites, and God took notice of them" (Exod. 2:23-25).[43] Cornel West has highlighted this crucial moment in the biblical narrative: "God hears their cries and is moved by their tears because God is first and foremost a lover of justice. . . . Divine compassion undergirds the divine love of justice."[44]

God selects Moses as the means by which the Israelites will be delivered. We know the rest of the story — after Moses' initial resistance, under God's direction he embarks on an escalating confrontation with the Egyptian king that finally leads to their miraculous escape out of Egypt, through the waters of the sea, with their pursuers "dead on the seashore" (Exod. 14:30) when the waters come crashing down. Liberation has come, as God's gift. The texts celebrate the death of Israel's pursuers, the tragic though apparently necessary cost (given Pharaoh's intransigence) of Israel's liberation.[45]

It is hard to overstate the significance of the exodus narrative for the consciousness of the many cultures that have been affected by it. Beginning at the most particular level, for the Jewish people this founding narrative of God's compassionate deliverance has been fundamental to their life and thought for three thousand years or more. "The hour of the Exodus was the birth of a people, the people chosen and called to a destiny. Israel's consciousness of being a people was first awakened at the Exodus; the event was the *fons et origo* of her life."[46] Its echoes resound through

---

43. One might say that deliverance begins even earlier, when the midwives Shiphrah and Puah refuse to participate in this murder of the Hebrew boys (Exod. 1:15-22). Even more interesting is the possibility that they were Egyptian rather than Hebrew.

44. Cornel West, *Democracy Matters* (New York: Penguin, 2004), p. 214.

45. This is a reminder that where compassion and justice bring liberation, and therefore life's sacred value is affirmed, such gains almost always require confrontation with victimizers. In a world gone so terribly wrong, life's sacredness is often defended through the defeat and punishment of those who violate it. The suffering of those on the "wrong side" of divine judgment is then often overlooked. I am grateful to Sondra Wheeler for this insight.

46. James Muilenberg, *The Way of Israel: Biblical Faith and Ethics* (New York: Harper and Row, 1961), p. 50.

later Old Testament writings and in every generation of Jewish life. "Remember that you were a slave in the land of Egypt and the LORD your God redeemed you" (Deut. 15:15). This memory instructs Israel as to the character of her God: one who keeps his covenant promises to the chosen people, one who looks with compassionate love on Israel, and one who delivers Israel when it appears that all is lost. God is a God of justice who fights for Israel's liberation when she is victimized. In the words of Moses' song (Exod. 15:13):

> "In your steadfast love you led the people whom you redeemed;
>   you guided them by your strength to your holy abode."

This foundational understanding of God's character also demands of Israel that her way of life as a people reflect a responsive covenant fidelity, compassionate love, and justice, a central theme in both the Law and the Prophets.[47]

This exodus-shaped vision has been embraced by many suffering peoples in human history. Michael Walzer has shown the endless fecundity of the exodus texts for inspiring social revolutions in the name of justice.[48]

This motif, for example, surfaced quite powerfully during the turn toward liberation theology in the Third World. Latin American, Asian, and African Christians toiling under conditions of colonialism and oppression turned to the God who hears the cries of the oppressed for dignity and a decent life. Catholic theologian Gustavo Gutiérrez helped set the tone when he argued that the exodus account is paradigmatic of a God who acts to liberate the oppressed from their political subjugation and delivers them to a life of freedom in community. God's action in history is fundamentally concerned with such liberation of the oppressed, and the exodus-Sinai narrative reveals that "to love Yahweh is to do justice to the poor and oppressed."[49]

Catholic authorities resisted elements of liberation theology, notably its flirtations with Marxist ideology, but did weave into the teaching tradition of the church the idea of God's "preferential option for the poor." God chooses to side with the poor precisely because he is a God of compassion

---

47. How easy it is for Israel or any people to focus on God's care for us instead of the moral obligations toward others that flow from God's care.

48. Michael Walzer, *Exodus and Revolution* (New York: Basic Books, 1985).

49. Gustavo Gutiérrez, *A Theology of Liberation* (Maryknoll, N.Y.: Orbis, 1973), p. 194.

and justice, and because failure to side with the poor means siding with their oppressors by default. God demands that all who would be his people must do the same — especially those who hold social power:

> Give justice to the weak and the orphan;
>   maintain the right of the lowly and the destitute.
> Rescue the weak and the needy;
>   deliver them from the hand of the wicked. (Ps. 82:3-4)

Perhaps the paradigmatic case of an exodus motif surfacing in the North American context is in African American life. No biblical narrative proved more important for the slave communities in the Americas, or for the development of the black church tradition, and the exodus remained influential all the way through the civil rights movement. As slaves toiled in seemingly endless servitude under their supposedly Christian masters, the subversive power of this narrative offered sustenance and revolutionary hope and undercut the false version of Christianity that blessed slavery as God's will.[50]

In the days of Jim Crow, when slavery had given way to legalized segregation and second-class status, black Americans again found great strength in the exodus narrative of a delivering God. As black theologian James Cone has written, "In the Exodus-Sinai tradition Yahweh is disclosed as the God of history, whose revelation is identical with his power to liberate the oppressed. There is no knowledge of Yahweh except through his political activity on behalf of the weak and helpless." The biblical God is a "God of the oppressed," which means that "God discloses that he is the God of history whose will is identical with the liberation of the oppressed from social and political bondage."[51] This sets the terms for black theology and, according

---

50. I just called the slaveholder version of Christianity "false." I believe that. But note that in situations of conflict participants view reality differently. The more intractable the conflict, especially where both sides have the capacity to hurt each other, the more difficult it is to determine who is "victim" and who is "oppressor." Think about how nothing is quite as predictable and fruitless as hearing estranged spouses blame each other for being abusive or oppressive. Liberation theology dealt with this perceptual gulf in conflicted situations by speaking of the "epistemological privilege of the poor/oppressed." This meant: the view of the truth of a conflictual situation is clearer from the underside than from the position of power. But this assumes that we know who is on the underside and who holds the power. I am not saying that the exodus-liberation-deliverance motif is invalidated; I am saying that few situations present themselves to us in such clarity as Exod. 1–2 enslavement and infanticide do.

51. James H. Cone, *God of the Oppressed* (New York: HarperCollins, 1975), p. 65.

to Cone, applies to all legitimate Christian theology, which is not just private but public, not just personal but political, and not just impartial in situations of social injustice but instead sides with the oppressed.

Consider again the Christian definition of the sacredness of life that I offered in the first chapter. Test that definition against the exodus narrative. A paradox emerges. There is a kind of stringent impartiality and universality in that definition. The exodus narrative pushes us toward a kind of partiality amidst that impartiality, a particularity amidst that universality. God demonstrates special concern not just for each and every person, but for the Jewish people in particular, as we have already discussed. But also, and this is the point here, God demonstrates special concern not just for each and every person but *especially for the enslaved, the suffering, the victimized, those whose groans too deep for words rise up to a just God who compassionately delivers them.* This may help us with puzzle #2, which asks which aspects of the human experience or the human person should be seen as the focus of a conviction concerning the sacredness of human life. The exodus narrative teaches us to focus on *suffering, victimized human beings, whether individuals or groups.*

The concept of a God who demonstrates impartial love for all people may seem to contradict the idea of a God whose ear inclines especially to the oppressed and especially a God who confronts those who do such oppression. This tension has kept many from accepting a divine "preferential option" for the subjugated and victimized, and it is often articulated as a main reason to reject liberation theology. But in a sinful and unjust world, in which many people are not perceived with reverence, are not treated with respect and care, and do not enjoy protection from destruction or desecration, justice requires special divine (and human) help for those who cannot help themselves. Some must be lifted up from the dust — even at the price of confrontation — to join the ranks of others who are already blessed with the privilege of standing up straight.

The exodus narrative of God's deliverance of the suffering Hebrew people deepens our understanding of what it might mean to treat every human life as sacred as well as what it might cost to do so. It challenges any purely noncoercive or even nonviolent understanding of the *means that might have to be employed* to protect human life from desecration (puzzle #10). And it links together a sacredness-of-life theological ethic (more popular with conservatives) with a liberative ethic of social justice (more popular with liberals). They belong together, and rightly understood, they essentially converge.

2.3. Biblical Law and Life's Sacredness

The Old Testament narrative moves from exodus to Sinai, from God's miraculous deliverance of the covenant people to God's articulation of the laws that shall govern Israel. Let us now explore the manner and extent to which biblical law stands in continuity with the vision of the sacredness of each and every human life so richly suggested by the creation, care, and deliverance motifs in the Old Testament. I cannot here offer an expansive treatment of the entirety of Old Testament law, and so will focus on the significance of (moral) law itself for a sacredness ethic, and then give specific attention to the Ten Commandments.

The first foundational resource for a sacredness ethic is that *God is depicted as the ultimate source of law in Israel, and God holds his people accountable for obedience.* From Exodus through Deuteronomy the text depicts God as literally dictating (primarily through Moses) the laws that shall govern Israel — beginning memorably with an awe-inspiring, indeed terrifying, divine appearance at Sinai.[52] A profound role is given in the Old Testament to teaching a proper fear of God as lawgiver, who holds Israel accountable for compliance with his laws.[53] This motif of God as awesome lawgiver is of course quite unbelievable to many who live on this side of the Enlightenment. Figuring out how these texts came to exist has occupied many fine minds since that time. But our task here is to consider the impact of the texts as they stand within the canonical narrative, especially as this impact has been felt in history in those cultures most affected by the Bible. If God is the source of law — cultic, civil, criminal, social welfare, moral, all of which flow together here — then the full weight of God's sovereign majesty and power falls upon the laws thus offered. One might say, as Freud suggested so many centuries later, that God's own sacredness transfers to the law (for Freud, this was a mythical God with mythical sacredness). The law therefore carries a holiness and authority. God commands, humans must obey — beginning with Israel, God's chosen people. And there are severe consequences for disobedience.

The very idea that there is a divinely given moral law that governs Israel

---

52. Patrick Miller, "Divine Command and Beyond: The Ethics of the Commandments," in *The Ten Commandments: The Reciprocity of Faithfulness,* ed. William P. Brown (Louisville: Westminster John Knox, 2004), p. 15.

53. Texts like this one abound: "God has . . . put the fear of him upon you so that you do not sin" (Exod. 20:20). There is a reason people used to be called "God-fearing," and a reason they are no longer often called that.

— and perhaps governs more than Israel — is itself a major contribution to a sacredness-of-life ethic. It means that God sets the terms for how human beings must relate to both the divine Person and human persons. Human moral obligation is ultimately rooted in God's will, especially as recorded in sacred Scriptures.[54] "The foundation for all morality . . . is the character and will of God [who] is supreme and without any competitors . . . there will be no higher standard of obligation."[55] Such an ethic is thus starkly differentiated from any ethic based on personal preference, social power, unaided human reason, or communal tradition. God's revealed will establishes a transcendent reference point by which all life is to be governed and by which all human laws and actions can be evaluated and critiqued.

Certainly a variety of complexities can be identified related to an ethics rooted in God's will, most especially how to adjudicate differences in interpretation of that will, as well as the applicability of a particularistic understanding of God's will in a pluralistic society and world. But for now the point is to suggest that such a formulation of ethics at its best causes the human being to consider the divine source of moral obligation and therefore the great and sometimes even terrifying responsibility before God to meet that obligation. This tradition is still felt whenever anyone pauses before a dubious course of action and considers whether that action conforms to God's moral will or might evoke God's judgment.

Second, *this elevation of a transcendent legal/moral standard over human life creates or reinforces momentum toward human equality before the law.* In many cultures, especially in the ancient world, the ruler defined the law and was above the law. No one in ancient Egypt could hold Pharaoh accountable. But the kings of Israel found that they were indeed accountable to the same divinely given moral law that governed everyone else. David Pleins has written, "We . . . see in these formulations of the Ten Commandments the makings of a subtle critique of monarchy and an attempt to limit its powers. . . . Unlike elsewhere in the ancient Near East, where law was a royal prerogative, [here] each and every member of the community has a religious, moral and social duty toward the nation's deity."[56] Con-

---

54. See Richard J. Mouw, *The God Who Commands* (South Bend, Ind.: University of Notre Dame Press, 1991); cf. Rémi Brague, *The Law of God: The Philosophical History of an Idea,* trans. Lydia G. Cochrane (Chicago: University of Chicago Press, 2007).

55. Walter J. Kaiser Jr., *Toward Old Testament Ethics* (Grand Rapids: Zondervan, 1983), p. 85.

56. J. David Pleins, *The Social Visions of the Hebrew Bible* (Louisville: Westminster John Knox, 2001), p. 48.

sider how the mighty King David was called to account by Nathan for his crimes/sins of adultery and arranged murder in the Bathsheba affair (2 Sam. 11–12), even though he was spared the death penalty. The many kings who were tempted to forget that their will was not absolute in Israel often ended up paying a serious price for their pride and disobedience. But the only context in which that could happen was in a society that believed in divinely given moral law and the accountability of all to God's law, with a socially acknowledged role for prophets who could demand compliance in God's name. This is a good place to remind ourselves that we are dealing with the particular religious and moral traditions of Israel, which powerfully affected later cultures influenced by these texts (puzzle #13).

The power of law (especially if understood to be divinely given) to level the playing field in human life has the effect of weakening the strong and strengthening the weak. The standard is clear: all stand equal before the law and before those human courts charged with enforcing it. If any member of a particular political community is understood to have moral and legal rights, all have such rights.[57] One way that we come to know that all human beings, of all classes and races, are to be perceived as sacred and treated with respect is because we see it happen in the administration of the law — if the law is functioning properly. In Israel, where law was seen as divinely given, a failure to administer justice in this way was treated as a direct affront to the God who authored the law. This is one reason why so much attention is given in biblical law to the functioning of the justice system itself, beginning with the command in the Decalogue against bearing "false witness" (Exod. 20:16), which clearly has a primary reference to the necessity of truthful testimony in the administration of justice (cf. Exod. 23:6-8).

Third, *the grounding of all moral obligation in God's law had a deep impact on the understanding of human law.* A just society lives not by royal fiat but under the rule of law, and law itself must be anchored in the will of God or it can become cruel and arbitrary. A long tradition of Jewish and Christian thinking about law developed that came to argue that no human law

---

57. The question then becomes who counts as a member of a political-legal community. The first step is to say "every member of this political community stands equal before the law." The second step is to include more and more people in the agreed political community. Women, children, slaves, foreigners, indigenous peoples, homosexuals, religious dissidents, etc., are among those who have not been counted as members of the political community to whom all laws apply equally. Thanks to Sondra Wheeler for reminding me of this critically important point.

carries authority if it stands in fundamental contradiction to divine law. This issue carries forward into legal theory to this day, though it is not the preferred position of most Western legal theorists. One legacy of the biblical tradition is the rejection of the theory of legal positivism, that law is to be understood as an amoral expression of human will in human communities, with a validity that can only be evaluated based on procedural fairness in the legislative process. Instead, this older tradition argues that the legitimacy of law is connected to whether the actual content of legislation reflects and responds to a preexisting moral order (established by God and knowable by all human beings) that precedes the lawmaking process. On this view, laws that violate the moral order are morally illegitimate and without binding force, requiring a response of disobedience and resistance.

Here I am backing us into an initial discussion of the natural law tradition, quite relevant to our puzzle related to the recipient of the obligation to treat life as sacred (puzzle #13). To very briskly summarize a massive tradition such as this one hardly does justice to it, and it will receive more extensive treatment in chapter 7. But for our purposes, let's understand the natural law tradition as emerging from a synthesis of biblical and classical strands of thought as these coalesced in historic Christianity. Biblically, its sources include the Noahide covenant, the Decalogue, the biblical wisdom tradition, and the apostle Paul's claims in Romans 1 and 2 about the knowledge of God's moral law available to all through creation and conscience.[58]

The development of a natural law tradition allowed Christian thinkers to claim that God revealed moral law through both Scripture (for Israel and the church) and a complementary natural law (for everyone), which among other things helped to reduce the potential arbitrariness of a pure divine command ethic based solely on scriptural texts (or somebody's report of what God told them in the night). The tradition provided grounds for conversation with non-Christians about the proper structure and provisions of human law. And when a spirit skeptical of biblical and ecclesial authority came upon Western culture, the natural law tradition for a time became the main way that earlier Christian understandings of the nature of moral and legal obligation made their way forward into the modern

---

58. An important recent Catholic treatment of natural law is found in Eberhard Schockenhoff, *Natural Law and Human Dignity: Universal Ethics in an Historical World,* trans. Brian McNeil (Washington, D.C.: Catholic University of America Press, 2003); on the Protestant side, J. Budzeszewski has been especially prolific on this tradition. See his *Written on the Heart: The Case for Natural Law* (Downers Grove, Ill.: InterVarsity, 1997), and *What We Can't Not Know: A Guide* (Dallas: Spence Publishing, 2003).

world — until that tradition itself was rejected. Morally, it survived primarily in the Catholic rather than the Protestant tradition, the latter being dubious about the capacity of sinful humans to apprehend God's will using fallen reason. Legally, it survived with sufficient strength that most scholars of Western law, especially the origins of international law, recognize the formative role of the natural law tradition even as they now reject its continuing validity.[59]

Even long after its general rejection in mainstream philosophy and legal theory, natural-law reasoning still continues to surface in surprising ways, for example, in the civil rights movement of the 1950s and 1960s. Schooled in the tradition of Western Christian thought, Martin Luther King argued for civil disobedience to segregationist laws on a natural law basis during the struggle for African American equality in the United States.[60] As King put it, "an unjust law is no law at all." Respect for the sacredness of human life has often been well served by the continuing survival of this principle, as laws that violate human dignity and well-being (such as those permitting slavery, segregation, torture, forced euthanasia, mistreatment of immigrants, and racial discrimination) have been tested against the transcendent standard of natural law, recognized as flawed, and resisted until they have been rewritten. When God's will and/or the natural law are understood as the ultimate foundation of legitimate human law, it creates an understanding of law that goes far beyond a mere social contract. Of course, two key problems are determining what exactly the natural law consists of and who is capable of knowing it.

Today, natural law claims appear to be most popular with conservative Catholics and evangelicals, who often work in coalition to resist cultural trends they believe to be in obvious violation of the natural law. But those tempted to dismiss natural law arguments need to think twice before entirely abandoning one of the major legacies of the Christian inheritance on Western culture, now visible via globalization throughout much of the world.

Fourth, *the leveling and inclusive nature of Old Testament law are re-*

59. Natural law as the basis of international law is discussed but essentially dismissed in the classic textbook on international law: Louis Henkin et al., *International Law: Cases and Materials,* 2d ed. (St. Paul: West Publishing Co., 1987), pp. 12, 36. The issue has received important recent attention by Mary Ellen O'Connell of Notre Dame Law School. See her book, *The Power and Purpose of International Law* (New York: Oxford University Press, 2008).

60. Martin Luther King Jr., "Letter from Birmingham City Jail," in *A Testament of Hope,* ed. James Melvin Washington (San Francisco: Harper and Row, 1986), p. 293.

inforced by the narrative framework in which they are offered — and that narrative itself comes down through the ages into our culture. Law begins in Israel with these words: "I am the LORD your God, who brought you out of the land of Egypt, out of the house of slavery" (Exod. 20:2). Every subsequent word of command carries an implicit "therefore." The entire narrative of merciful deliverance that we have already discussed serves as the framework and wellspring of Israelite law.[61] The God of compassion, kindness, and justice has delivered his covenant people Israel from destruction and established them in a great and fruitful land.[62] This means that God the Deliverer is God the Lawgiver, and so God's law (and all Israelite law written in response to it) is characterized by a commitment to love, mercy, and justice, understood again as focused especially on behalf of vulnerable and victimized people. It means that God's law itself is an expression of grace and further evidence of God's care, which also has implications for the writing and administration of human law. Simple gratitude on Israel's part will require that love, mercy, and justice must characterize Israel's life as a people and must be felt in her legal system. To treat the rich better than the poor, the powerful better than the powerless, the native better than the alien, not only violates the rights of the weak but also is a slap in the face of a gracious God who did the reverse *on Israel's behalf.* The motivational wellspring for Israel's obedience to a legal code especially designed to protect the weak will be her constantly reinforced memory of her own hour of desperate weakness and God's mercy on Israel's behalf at that critical hour.

2.4. The Decalogue

The great and central expression of Old Testament law is the Ten Commandments (Exod. 20:1-17). This grand summary of the law that shall govern Israel begins with duties toward God and moves seamlessly into duties toward neighbor. Both are vitally important for a sacredness-of-life ethic, for reasons suggested above. It is precisely because "I am the LORD your

---

61. Cf. Kaiser, *Toward Old Testament Ethics*, p. 83.

62. Of course, this establishment in the land, according to the text of Joshua, comes at the expense of the destruction of many Canaanite peoples. Slavery-exodus-Sinai is one way to say it; Slavery-exodus-Sinai-*genocide* is quite another. More on this critically important issue will be offered below.

God, who brought you out of the land of Egypt" that "you shall have no other gods before me" (20:2-3). Israel must stay entirely free of confusion as to the name, identity, and character of her God; she must refrain from crafting images that might tempt her to reduce God to one among many nature-divinities; and having been informed of the holy name of the one God, Israel must never misuse that name (20:4-7). The majesty, power, uniqueness, transcendence, and holiness of God join with God's demonstrated compassion, kindness, and justice to anchor moral law for Israel. The *sanctitas Dei* undergirds the sacredness of human life and the sacredness of the civil/moral law that protects that life. This drives us back to puzzle #15 from the end of chapter 1: *Can the sacredness of human life survive the loss of this transcendent reference point?* In the Decalogue, duties to humans flow from duties to God, and obedience to God is motivated by a rich, textured understanding (and worship) of the awesome and transcendent God who commands. When that disappears, as it has in part or in full in large parts of Western culture, the fate of moral law and of the lives it protects becomes an open question.

The Decalogue pivots in the command to "remember the Sabbath day, and keep it holy." In the Exodus version of the Ten Commandments, this requirement is rooted in God's creation of the world in six days; we imitate God by resting on the seventh day. But suggested here and made more explicit in the Deuteronomic version of the Decalogue is the broader dimension of Sabbath observance: "But the seventh day is a Sabbath to the LORD your God; you shall not do any work — you, or your son or your daughter, or your male or female slave, or your ox or your donkey, or any of your livestock, or the resident alien in your towns. . . . Remember that you were a slave in the land of Egypt" (Deut. 5:14-15a). The Sabbath simultaneously honors God and protects the neighbor, even the slave neighbor, even the resident-alien neighbor, even, yes, the livestock neighbor.[63] Due to the divine command, one might quite fairly say that all creatures have *a divinely mandated right to rest* on the seventh day, in memory of that time of oppression when no Israelite ever had the right to rest at all. Sabbath observance is among the most egalitarian provisions of biblical law, working toward the preservation, protection, and flourishing of the lives of all flesh in Israel.

The command to "honor your father and your mother" (Exod. 20:12)

---

63. This is very important, and is not the only example in OT law of divinely commanded concern for animals.

once again takes us to particularity rather than universality in moral obligation. Just as the Old Testament teaches that God has a special relationship with Israel while loving all humanity, so this command teaches that children have a special obligation to care for aging and increasingly vulnerable parents (as elsewhere we see that parents have a special obligation to young and totally vulnerable children) even while having general obligations to all human beings.

This issue — often called "the problem of special relations" — is not a simple one, and raises interesting concerns related to the sacredness of human life.[64] Most moral obligations, as we saw in relation to the Sabbath and will see in relation to the other commands of the Decalogue, are universal. "You shall not murder" (anyone). "You shall not steal" (from anyone). But the obligation to "honor your father and mother" has to do with *your* father and mother, not the parents of someone else. The command is universal in the sense that every person addressed is commanded to honor his or her father and mother; but I am to honor *my* father and mother, not yours.[65] Our Christian definition of the sacredness of life stresses universality; this command to honor father and mother stresses particularity. It does lead us to wonder whether it is best to say that everyone deserves respect, but only particular people deserve reverence; or, in turn, whether I have minimal obligations to everyone, but maximal obligations only in a handful of particular relationships (puzzle #9).

One solution is to remember that in everyday human experience most of us do better in sensing the obligations we have to our nearest and dearest than to those distant from us. Most of us naturally understand that among those who fall within what Holocaust scholar Helen Fein called the "sanctified universe of obligation" are our families.[66] The moral challenge, most often, is to learn to *broaden the boundaries* of that universe so that they extend to include not just my parents and children and fellow tribesmen but also strangers and aliens and even enemies. The sacredness of life is served, then, not as we *diminish* our sense of obligation to parents or

---

64. Gene Outka, *Agape: An Ethical Analysis* (New Haven: Yale University Press, 1972), and subsequent discussion, such as Stephen J. Pope, "'Equal Regard' vs. 'Special Relations': Reaffirming the Inclusiveness of Agape," *Journal of Religion* 77, no. 3 (July 1979): 353-79.

65. Walter Harrelson points out, however, that the implications of this command extend to the overall attitude of a community toward aged ones who no longer can work or "contribute" anything to the society. Harrelson, *Ten Commandments*, p. 95.

66. Helen Fein, *Accounting for Genocide: National Responses and Jewish Victimization during the Holocaust* (Chicago: University of Chicago Press, 1984), p. 4.

other kinfolk, but as we *extend* as much of that sense of kinship as possible to broader and broader circles of people. As we come to see every elder in a sense as "my father or mother," and every child in a sense as "my son or daughter," and every peer in a sense as "my brother or sister," then we move into the precincts of the sacredness of life as we ought to understand it. The entire human race becomes "my family," and my obligations extend as far as humanity itself — even as I still recognize the specific and heightened obligations that come to me because this particular human being is in fact my father or mother, sister or brother, son or daughter.[67]

The Decalogue famously forbids adultery (Exod. 20:14), the violation of the sexual exclusivity appropriate to the covenant relation of marriage.[68] Here once again we see a command directed at special relations rather than our obligations to all humanity. I am commanded to remain sexually faithful to my spouse, not your spouse. The command reflects the particular vulnerability of married persons to the harm that only one other person — their one spouse — can do to them. While it was especially directed to the protection of men's interests in patriarchal Israel, the egalitarian implications of the command were intrinsic to its very formulation and eventually came to dominate both Jewish and Christian interpretation of this command.

One reason for the command against adultery was to protect children. Adultery damages marriage, and marriage most of the time is a relationship that brings forth children; thus adultery damages and in some cases destroys the lives of children. This occurs because uncertainty about a child's parentage can destroy parental love for that child and even threaten his or her survival — and more broadly because children are deeply dependent upon the stability and quality of the marital bond of their parents. Children — such small, dependent, and powerless creatures among us —

67. The idea of a universal "fatherhood of God" and "brotherhood of man" became very important in late-nineteenth- and early-twentieth-century liberal theology and ethics, and continues to be discussed today, though almost always in more gender-inclusive terms. A good example was the work of Adolf von Harnack (1851-1930) in Germany. The concept has powerful meaning even if theological liberalism used it to thin out Jesus' identity and message inappropriately.

68. Here a desire to make Old Testament law look more like contemporary Christian understandings must be resisted. We now say that adultery is extramarital sex on the part of either a husband or a wife. In the Old Testament, adultery was any extramarital sex on the part of a married woman, or sex between a man and another man's wife. A married man could have sex with a single woman or a prostitute, and married men did at times take more than one wife.

ought to be viewed as falling into that category of vulnerable human beings discussed earlier who deserve special attention because they are so likely to be oppressed and unable to protect themselves. Jesus certainly attended to children in this way, behaved with particular tenderness toward children, and sternly warned adults not to harm children. It is no coincidence that both Matthew and Mark place Jesus' teaching about divorce right next to sayings about children's well-being (cf. Mark 9:33–10:16; Matt. 19:1-15). In this way the command against adultery serves the sacredness of children's lives.[69]

The command also protects what some call the *sacredness of marriage,* as the prior command protects what some call the *sacredness of the family.* If we grant the concept, then the moral meaning of "sacredness" takes on a new dimension: covenant relationships, even social institutions like marriage and family, can be viewed as having a divinely given sacredness. Notice that our Christian definition of the sacredness of life focuses on "each and every human being," not on relationships or institutions. It moves from the particular (each human being) to the universal (every human being) without resting anywhere in between. This command against adultery, together with the command to honor father and mother, suggests that it is not inappropriate to ascribe sacredness to marriage and family life as God intended it. One might say that marriage and family are the God-given contexts in which the sacred lives of the individuals cocooned within can be preserved, protected, and nurtured toward flourishing. A society that successfully nurtures marriage and family as social institutions, then, contributes cumulatively to the well-being of its millions of people.

This argument could be pushed even further to say that one way to honor the sacredness of every human life is to recognize and enhance those particular social institutions and relationships in which human beings move from being just-one-of-the-crowd to valued-as-part-of-our-particular-group. There are dangers here, but also possibilities. Family is the first and foremost of these collectivities, which have been called "mediating institutions" in recent literature.[70] Schools, social clubs, sports teams,

69. I explore these themes further in my *Getting Marriage Right* (Grand Rapids: Baker, 2004), chapter 3.

70. A concept originally suggested by Alexis de Tocqueville in his brilliant early analysis of American democracy, *Democracy in America* (Washington, D.C.: Library of America, [1835] 2004). See Pierre Manent, *Tocqueville and the Nature of Democracy* (New York: Rowman and Littlefield, 1995).

artistic ensembles, youth groups, and other human institutions also nurture the individual-in-community. It is no coincidence that these are the places in which *human flourishing* in one dimension of life or another is most often the central object. We learn from this that to care comprehensively about the sacredness of human life requires us to attend to the institutions of human culture that aim for full human flourishing (puzzle #12). We are not just *against* killing; we are *for* family, education, sports, and the arts, and for the flourishing of human potential that these make possible. Perhaps law is best positioned to protect individuals from wanton destruction or desecration, while mediating institutions are better situated to advance human flourishing. This speaks to puzzle #14, about which particular obligations to respect the sacredness of life belong to which particular sectors or groups.

All human flourishing goals do indeed require the preservation of human lives from harm. We cannot pursue musical training or learn how to hit a baseball if we have been shot dead in the streets. Therefore, "You shall not murder" (Exod. 20:13). Everything depends on general obedience to this command, which is one reason why it is often treated in Christian ethics as *the single most foundational biblical mandate in relation to the sacredness of human life,* "the basis of all life together in society," according to John Paul II.[71] Already visible in the creation materials, as we have seen (Gen. 9:5-6), the command against murder (or narrative depiction of its tragic violation) shows up in various forms in all genres of Scripture and in both the Old Testament and the New Testament.

As suggested earlier, the Old Testament does not teach a ban on all forms of killing, nor does it treat every taking of a human life as morally equivalent.[72] It mandates the communal (not private) imposition of the death penalty for various crimes while also authorizing war in various circumstances facing Israel. The implications of these teachings in light of the

---

71. John Paul II, *The Gospel of Life* (New York: Random House, 1995), p. 95.

72. Brevard Childs helpfully points out nuances within the Old Testament in understanding the precise meaning of the verb here, *rashah.* He concludes that it "first had an objective meaning describing a type of illegal slaying which called forth blood vengeance." Eventually it designated "acts of violence against persons which arose from personal feelings of hatred and malice." These are the acts that are rejected. Childs also points out that case law is plentiful in the Old Testament that deals with various situations, motivations, intentions related to killing and its consequences. Childs, *Old Testament Theology in a Canonical Context* (Philadelphia: Fortress, 1985), pp. 75-76. Provisions for cities of refuge are rooted in distinctions related to purposeful and accidental killing.

New Testament are debated, and will be discussed later in this book.[73] But for now the place to begin is by recognizing that what is clearly banned in Old Testament law is the intentional killing of one person by another apart from certain specific circumstances: reasonable personal/household self-defense (Exod. 22:2-3), communally sanctioned acts of proportionate justice (21:23-25), and divinely authorized warfare (23:23-33). Murder is distinguished in biblical law from unintentional killing (21:13-14), or death through acts of negligence (21:28), though gross negligence is sometimes treated as a capital crime (21:29). Life's sacredness is further affirmed as those guilty of accidental homicide or whose cases need further examination are protected through the establishment of cities of refuge (cf. Num. 35, reinforced in Joshua's tribal land distributions).

This body of legal/moral instruction is sometimes summarized, as in Catholic social teaching, as a ban on *direct, intentional killing of the innocent, that is, murder.*[74] The full weight of divinely sanctioned biblical law stands against such killing. God holds murderers accountable through community-sanctioned punishments, while the Old Testament also repeatedly suggests that those murderers who evade such punishments in this life will still somehow be recompensed by the transcendent God of justice (cf. Ps. 37). This vision of a God who both prohibits murder and judges those who violate that command comes down through the centuries as one of the most significant and sometimes quite compelling moral legacies of biblical religion.

Old Testament exceptions for permitted killing still leave room for a terrible amount of killing, however. God kills in judgment, soldiers kill in war, and the community kills in capital punishment. Many of the most grotesque instances of the violation of life's sacredness that we have witnessed in human history (and many of the most troubling parts of the Bible itself) fall within these exception categories.[75] God killing in the name

---

73. Lutheran scholar Gary Simpson argues flatly that "'Thou shalt not kill' is the first commandment of the 'just war tradition.'" He argues strongly against abandoning the distinction between defensive violence in legitimate wars and aggressive attacks on the innocent in war. Issues related to violence will continually occupy us in this volume as they do throughout Christian moral tradition. See Simpson, "The Sixth Commandment," in Brown, *The Ten Commandments,* chapter 19.

74. See, for example, *Catechism of the Catholic Church,* 2nd ed. (New York: Doubleday, 1997), 2258-69, pp. 602-6.

75. Tremper Longman III and Daniel G. Reid, *God Is a Warrior* (Grand Rapids: Zondervan, 1995), chapter 2.

of God, people killing in the name of the community, people killing in the name of God, or most potent of all, an entire community/nation and its people killing another people in the name of God — space is opened for all these possibilities in the Old Testament itself.

In my view, the single most dangerous dimension of this material is found in those instances in which God's very holiness, or Israel's sanctity as a community, is linked *directly* to killing. It happens in Numbers 16 within the Israelite community when a Levite rebellion ("the sons of Korah") is snuffed out at the cost of the lives not only of the rebels but also of their families. The very metal censers the rebels were holding when they were killed are hammered into plates for the sacred altar: "for the censers of these sinners *have become holy at the cost of their lives*" (Num. 16:38, italics added). God's holiness is linked to killing again when the zealous Phinehas spears an Israelite who has taken a presumably idolatrous Midianite wife, and he is commended and blessed for his actions (Num. 25:6-13). And it certainly happens in texts like Joshua 6, where to "devote to the LORD for destruction" means to set a city apart *for God* as a kind of holy sacrifice by killing everything that breathes (Josh. 6:21). Here we are not talking about death as sad but necessary penalty for murder, or death as an unfortunate by-product of communal self-defense; this is sacred death, or sacred killing, where *precisely because God is sacred,* people must be killed. The most basic restraints on what we can do to other people are overridden because loyalty to God trumps such ethical limits. Indeed, God is the one perceived as commanding that overriding.

Jewish scholar Donniel Hartman has suggested that a paradox is built into monotheistic religious traditions, including his own. He argues that "The mere presence of God creates a problem for the ethical."[76] The same God who demands ethical treatment of others also can be viewed as requiring and motivating actions that undercut those ethical demands.[77] God calls on believers to honor the ethical, but believers are tempted to discount the ethical as they act so passionately to please and honor God. Hartman says: "We will go to extreme lengths to do the wrong thing to others in the name of God." The biblical tradition is itself aware of this problem. Hartman points out how in the Hebrew Bible the prophets criti-

76. Donniel Hartman, "'I Am the Lord Your God': God as Advocate — God as Foe of the Ethical" (unpublished paper, dated February 8, 2011).

77. Danish philosopher Søren Kierkegaard explored these themes brilliantly in his exploration of the Abraham narrative. See Kierkegaard, *Fear and Trembling,* trans. Howard V. Hong and Edna H. Hong (Princeton: Princeton University Press, 1983).

cize Israel's misbehaviors, many of which were undertaken to please God — such as the slip into prioritizing religious ritual over basic ethical obligation (cf. Amos 5:21-26). Then the Talmud and later Jewish writers comment on the same pattern in later Jewish life and tradition. Hartman concludes that *our religious tradition itself, beginning in the sacred text itself, must constantly heal itself.* Or perhaps better: God must intervene in our religious tradition to prevent its turn toward the desecration of the human in the name of God.

This mix of ethically constructive and destructive texts goes beyond the issue of sacred killing. I will focus on two other issues: problems in relation to the status of women, and the acceptance of a debt slavery system. We cannot address these issues in detail here, but they do need at least brief discussion.[78]

The Old Testament does indeed reflect the power relationships and anthropological assumptions of a patriarchal society, in which women were not perceived as persons of equal legal status and often were not treated as having an inviolable dignity. Scholarly discussion of biblical patriarchalism is well established, and does not need to be rehashed here. The basic problems are clear. At a microlevel, women were not treated as free and full persons in society and before the law but instead as falling under the authority and jurisdiction of their fathers or husbands. They were most often the *acted upon* rather than the *actors* in their own lives, often leading to the experience of profound oppression, suffering, terror, and even death.[79] To some extent they occupied a netherworld between property and person, a moral status that advocates of the sacredness of life now understand is inappropriate for any human being. The most deeply critical feminist analysts have concluded that women's marginalization was rooted in a patriarchalized understanding of God.[80] A male God (it was understood) had established a male-dominated religious and cultural system in which men held power in every sector of life: male tribal heads, male clan leaders, male prophets, male priests, male kings, male everything.

---

78. Probably the best biblical/ethical exploration of these themes is found in Willard Swartley, *Slavery, Sabbath, War, and Women* (Scottdale, Pa.: Herald, 1982), especially the way Swartley reflects on the way in which Christians have used and abused these texts for more recent debates.

79. The classic treatment is Phyllis Trible, *Texts of Terror: Literary-Feminist Readings of Biblical Narratives* (Philadelphia: Fortress, 1984).

80. Mary Daly, *Beyond God the Father: Toward a Philosophy of Women's Liberation* (Boston: Beacon Press, 1993).

It helps to remember that the Old Testament's treatment of women marks a considerable advance over other cultures in the ancient Near East, even while falling far short of contemporary standards or the norms entailed by the concept of the sacredness of life.[81] The Old Testament itself offers counternarratives that feature at least somewhat empowered women (e.g., Miriam, Deborah), and the New Testament arguably offers dramatic advances in the recognition of women's worth and dignity. The ambiguity of even the New Testament evidence is such, however, that it has been employed to reinforce patriarchal religion by most branches of the Christian church over most of the last two millennia. It is my view that a commitment to the sacredness of life requires a commitment to the empowerment of women, and that therefore movements that have won dramatic social gains for women in the last two hundred years are in fact part of the struggle for the sacredness of life.

The long fight for full agency for women over these millennia teaches us that advance in recognitions of the sacred worth of all people requires the power to speak for oneself, to make free and self-directed decisions, and to enjoy full political, economic, and legal rights, including full participation in decisions that affect one's own destiny.[82] Until that happens, a person, class, gender, or group depends on the mercy, compassion, and justice of others for the recognition of its sacred worth or even basic human rights, and such dependence rarely works out well, because, as Reinhold Niebuhr so frequently reminded us, self-interestedness usually trumps moral pressures to act on behalf of others.[83] A sacredness ethic requires those who have power to offer mercy, compassion, and justice to those who need it. But it also pushes us into the structural work of using our power to eliminate situations in which entire groups of people must depend on the right actions of others for the basic provision of their fundamental rights. This means that efforts to advance the enfranchisement and empowerment of marginalized groups are also part of a sacredness-of-life ethic, rightly understood. It also draws our attention to the relationship between social power and the sacredness of life.

A similar dynamic can be noted in relation to debt slavery. On the face of it, the very existence of any form of slavery in ancient Israel constitutes a

81. Barton, *Understanding Old Testament Ethics*, p. 2.
82. I acknowledge that both law and custom do not grant full agency to small children, and that this is proper in most circumstances.
83. Reinhold Niebuhr, *Moral Man and Immoral Society* (New York: Scribner's, 1933).

gross violation of at least the spirit of the Hebrew liberation narrative. It makes little sense that a God who brought Israel out of the "house of slavery" (Exod. 20:2) should then institute slavery in the land of promise, both with Israelites and with foreigners. It softens the contradiction just a bit to view debt slavery as a common practice in the ancient world and in fact a common practice in agricultural societies even into the modern period (sometimes even today). It was one of the only ways in which people who had desperately few tradable commodities could settle debts incurred due to mismanagement or to lean years on the farm. Old Testament law itself tries to set both moral and legal limits on usurious lending practices and on the practice of debt slavery. Provisions to protect at least the limited human rights of slaves are found in the Covenant Code (Exod. 20–23), including punishments for excessive violence against them (21:20), recognition of their marital status prior to and during enslavement (21:3), some protections for female slaves vis-à-vis their sexual and marital rights (21:7-11), and means of liberation and return to one's land and family rather than permanent servitude (21:2). All these ancient provisions offered more protections for slaves than existed three millennia later in slaveholding America. Still, the very fact that texts were available in the Bible (both Old Testament and New Testament) that could easily be quoted to justify slavery ("the slave is the owner's property" — 21:21) proved deeply problematic and undoubtedly delayed the abolition of slavery in "Christian" Europe and America.[84]

It should be abundantly clear that I am not attempting to argue that the Bible offered perfect and unexceptionable resources for the development of a sacredness-of-life ethic. It was quite possible to whip up a stew of hatred and dehumanization out of elements found in the sacred texts. Indeed, those possibilities remain with us today, as so many terrible "Christian" examples can attest. (Consider Qur'an burners and Westboro Baptist Church.) But ingredients for a tender life-affirming ethic could be found there, and they were found. Through the Scripture-sifting process that occurs in every faith community built on fixed sacred texts, the peoples of God found profound resources for an emergent ethic in which every human being was viewed as having incalculable worth. Believers gradually found ways to reread or to diminish the impact of texts and strands that were less constructive, though the perennial presence of these problematic texts requires the perennial success of this Scripture-sifting, tradition-

---

84. Stephen Haynes, *Noah's Curse: The Biblical Justification for American Slavery* (New York: Oxford University Press, 2002).

healing project in the Jewish and Christian communities. Bruce C. Birch describes this as a process of "reclaim[ing] the biblical text from elements that distort or limit its moral witness."[85]

Who dares to attempt such a reclaiming/sifting project? There is no alternative: the work is done by communities of committed believers, well led and well formed, reading together, praying together, listening to God's Spirit together, trying to be God's faithful people together. And this process is happening all the time, whether or not a faith community's theology permits acknowledgment of it.

2.5. The Prophetic Demand and Yearning for Shalom

Finally, one of the Old Testament's key resources for a sacredness ethic is found in the demand, and the yearning, for a transformed world of justice and peace. *The concept of shalom names that state of affairs in which human beings flourish in community and the sacredness of each and every human life is finally honored.* Often defined simply as well-being or as a "just wholeness," shalom, as Walter Brueggemann so memorably put it, is "the dream of God" for a redeemed world and an end to our "division, hostility, fear, drivenness, and misery."[86] The prophets (our key source for the shalom vision) both demand shalom *now* and yearn for it *then,* when the time comes when God finally prevails. In this final section I want to demonstrate the links between shalom and the sacredness of human life.

Ethicist Karen Lebacqz has argued that an ethic of justice is often developed most profoundly amidst the experience of a particular injustice.[87] Likewise, the Old Testament yearning for shalom begins with the particular, especially Israel's experiences of wrenching violence and injustice. Prophets speak about shalom for Israel, from within the cataclysm of war (cf. Jer. 33). From exile, they speak of the land and people of Israel coming back from the dead (Ezek. 36–37), in a kind of "new exodus," as Waldemar Janzen has put it.[88] They yearn for a new Jerusalem, from within the expe-

---

85. Birch, *Let Justice Roll Down*, p. 43.

86. Walter Brueggemann, *Living toward a Vision: Biblical Reflections on Shalom,* 2nd ed. (New York: United Church Press, 1982), p. 16.

87. Karen Lebacqz, *Six Theories of Justice: Perspectives from Philosophical and Theological Ethics* (Minneapolis: Augsburg Fortress, 1987).

88. Waldemar Janzen, *Old Testament Ethics* (Louisville: Westminster John Knox, 1994), p. 170.

rience of Jerusalem's destruction (cf. Isa. 65). Earlier prophets, prophesying in times when all appeared secure, warned that the violations of shalom within the Jewish community would someday bring upon Israel judgments that she could hardly imagine. Thus the prophetic writings leave a legacy both of particularity and of universality — they speak to specific events, injustices, and dreams of the Jewish people while also evoking powerful demands and yearnings on the part of millions of people for the kind of world they envision.

The narrowest translation for the Hebrew word *shalom* is "peace," as in the opposite of war, and peace as commonly understood is certainly an ingredient of it. The prophets *demand* peace from the covenant people Israel when they decry Israel's violence and murder (Mic. 7:2-3), and her turn to military alliances and military might, especially the royal development of the military killing apparatus symbolized by horses and chariots (cf. Isa. 31:1; Hos. 1:7; Mic. 5:10).[89] They *yearn* for peace as an end to war when they envision a time when "there shall be endless peace" (Isa. 9:7) and

> they shall beat their swords into plowshares,
>   and their spears into pruning hooks. (Mic. 4:3; cf. Zech. 9:9-10)

Shalom means peace, as in straightforward security from physical threats to bodies, homes, and communities. God promises just such a "covenant of peace" in which threats even from animals no longer exist (Ezek. 34:25; Isa. 65:25; cf. Num. 25:12). Shalom happens when the sixth commandment is obeyed, and people stop murdering each other; but it extends to a time when even "legitimate" killing is no longer undertaken in human life.

> Violence shall no more be heard in your land,
>   devastation and destruction within your borders. (Isa. 60:18)

Security is so complete that

> your gates shall always be open;
>   day and night they shall not be shut (Isa. 60:11),

for there are no more security threats at last (cf. Jer. 33:6, 15; Mic. 5:4-5). Eventually, shalom in this sense is so complete that God

---

89. Walter Brueggemann, *A Social Reading of the Old Testament: Prophetic Approaches to Israel's Communal Life* (Minneapolis: Fortress, 1994), chapter 15.

will destroy on this mountain
    the shroud that is cast over all peoples, . . .
    he will swallow up death forever. (Isa. 25:7-8)

Shalom, as Irving Greenberg has put it, means "the triumph of life" and "the overcoming of death," which he describes as the mission of both Judaism and Christianity.[90]

Taking shalom seriously points us strongly toward what it really means for human beings to flourish. For example, the shalom vision includes the *(re)building of community.* The prophets speak most often in a particularistic voice, but they leave a legacy relevant to all of us. The prophets of the exile, for example, speak of the liberation and return of the dispersed Jewish people (cf. Isa. 60–61; Jer. 16:14-15; Ezek. 34:11-13; Amos 9:14-15), scattered to the four winds by war and the deliberate policies of exile, imprisonment, and enslavement of imperial powers such as Assyria and Babylon. The slaves, prisoners, and exiles shall be set free at last (cf. Isa. 61:1). The prophets dream of the rebuilding of a glorious Jerusalem and the return of a growing (Ezek. 36:10) and vibrant community to Israel's most important city (Isa. 61:4; Jer. 30:18-22). The people will come back, they will rebuild their homes and public buildings, and they will live securely there, in a newfound unity. As a community and as individuals and families, they will not only survive but also flourish, and thus experience the honoring of life's sacredness.

Shalom means not just rebuilt community but inclusive community. The egalitarianism and universality that we saw when discussing the image of God surface in powerful new ways here. Shalom overcomes ethnic divisions as even the "foreigner" who lives in covenant faithfulness before God becomes a full and honored member of the Jewish community. The eunuch, previously considered inferior and unclean, is also welcomed as a full member of the community (Isa. 56:3-6). All are welcomed on the same basis; all "who choose the things that please me / and hold fast my covenant" (56:4) will be welcomed into the house of the Lord and gain there a "monument and a name / better than sons and daughters" (56:5). The temple will become "a house of prayer / for all peoples" (56:7), as all nations will come to worship God in Jerusalem.[91] Shalom restores the original

---

90. Irving Greenberg, *For the Sake of Heaven and Earth: The New Encounter between Judaism and Christianity* (Philadelphia: Jewish Publication Society, 2004), pp. 18, 39.

91. *Mercer Commentary on the Old Testament,* gen. eds. Watson E. Mills and Richard F. Wilson (Macon, Ga.: Mercer University Press, 2003), p. 613.

unity of humankind, at last. All made in the image of God finally come to-gether in one peaceable human community.

Shalom means that everyone has enough to eat and drink, in a world (and land) so often full of desperately hungry and thirsty people. We are reminded of human neediness and bodiliness, and that there can be no vi-brant human community for long if some have enough to eat while others starve to death. Honoring the sacredness of life means meeting these basic physical needs of all. Shalom means, then, abundant material well-being and prosperity (Isa. 60:5-7; 66:12; Jer. 31:12; Ezek. 34:14-15, 29; Joel 2:23-24; Amos 9:13-14; Zech. 9:17) fairly distributed to all, in a flourishing land of ecological health and well-being (Isa. 32:15-20; 45:8) that also symbolizes spiritual renewal in Israel.[92] It means that those who work on the land will not have their produce stolen from them, but will instead "eat it and praise the Lord" (Isa. 62:9; cf. Isa. 65:21-22; Jer. 31:5). Shalom means economic justice — everyone has the means necessary to work successfully to meet material needs, and no one is permitted to take away from anyone either the means of production (mainly land) or the goods it produces. The pro-phetic vision of a restoration of economic justice (Ezek. 34:16) and an end to economic oppression finds rich complement in the Levitical Holiness Code, which unexpectedly includes commands, such as the Jubilee Year provision (Lev. 25), intended to give every Israelite family a chance to re-gain access to its land every fifty years.

Shalom means the healing of broken bodies and spirits. This healing is both individual and collective:

> Then the eyes of the blind shall be opened,
>   and the ears of the deaf unstopped;
> then the lame shall leap like a deer,
>   and the tongue of the speechless sing for joy. (Isa. 35:5-6a)

> I have seen their ways, but I will heal them;
>   I will lead them and repay them with comfort. (Isa. 57:18)

"Your days of mourning shall be ended," as God promises to "bind up the brokenhearted" and "comfort all who mourn" (Isa. 60:20; 61:1-2). Ezekiel has God saying, "I will seek the lost, and I will bring back the strayed, and I will bind up the injured, and I will strengthen the weak" (Ezek. 34:16). In Zephaniah, God declares,

---

92. Brown, *Ethos of the Cosmos*, pp. 254-56.

I will save the lame
    and gather the outcast,
and I will change their shame into praise
    and renown in all the earth. (Zeph. 3:19)

The sick will be set free to move toward their full human flourishing and their full inclusion in community.

Shalom means both human and divine delight. It means joyful smiles and deep satisfaction, for

as a young man marries a young woman,
    so shall your builder marry you,
and as the bridegroom rejoices over the bride,
    so shall your God rejoice over you. (Isa. 62:5)

Shalom means that after endless suffering, humans will receive

a garland instead of ashes,
the oil of gladness instead of mourning,
    the mantle of praise instead of a faint spirit. (Isa. 61:3)

Shalom is like a party:

Out of [the city] shall come thanksgiving,
    and the sound of merrymakers. (Jer. 30:19)

Their children shall see it and rejoice,
    their hearts shall exult in the LORD. (Zech. 10:7)

Finally, shalom means obedience to God, and is therefore linked to the covenantal themes considered earlier. For the prophets, disobedience is the source of Israel's suffering, and obedience will therefore be central to Israel's healing — and the healing of the world. The problem had been that

justice is turned back,
    and righteousness stands at a distance;
for truth stumbles in the public square,
    and uprightness cannot enter. (Isa. 59:14)

Peace, justice, inclusive community, restored human unity, food for all, joy and delight — all come as God's gracious response to people who "maintain justice, and do what is right" (Isa. 56:1).[93] The nations will stream to Jerusalem (Mic. 4:1) to worship and serve the one Lord of all —

> these I will bring to my holy mountain,
> and make them joyful in my house of prayer.
> (Isa. 56:7; cf. Zeph. 3:9)

God promises that in the time of restoration, "I will put my spirit within you, and make you follow my statutes and be careful to observe my ordinances. Then you shall live in the land that I gave to your ancestors, and you shall be my people, and I will be your God" (Ezek. 36:27-28; cf. Zeph. 3:11-13).

It is possible to select a central organizing motif of the Old Testament, and then run all other materials through the grid created by this motif. I have named several candidates for that role in this chapter: creation, *imago Dei,* human rights, liberation, justice, covenant, law, and of course, the sacredness of life. This foray into the shalom theme in the later prophetic writings names a vision of how things ought to be in Israel, of how things *will be* in Israel when God fulfills his promises. Shalom in this sense draws up numerous motifs already named in the chapter; it suggests others that could have been named, such as "salvation," for the glorious picture here of redeemed Israel is essentially synonymous with "saved" Israel.[94] *Shalom is what happens when God saves Israel.* And the texts themselves suggest that *shalom is what happens when God saves the world.* For the prophets often suggest that Israel's salvation lies at the center of and is inseparable from the final salvation of the world.

All is not sweetness and light in the prophetic vision of the coming shalom. Interspersed with many of the glorious promises identified here are words of woe and judgment upon those who stand in the way of the fulfillment of this vision. Often these are woes upon other nations, especially enslaving imperial powers like Assyria and Babylon. What survives from some prophets is little other than these words of woe to specific powers (cf.

---

93. On the other hand, God's abundant blessings can be seen as coming first, leading to obedient response, leading to further blessing. "I have seen their ways, but I will heal them" (Isa. 57:18a).

94. James Muilenburg, *The Way of Israel: Biblical Faith and Ethics* (New York: Harper and Row, 1961), p. 136.

Nahum) or even notes of celebration of a coming global apocalypse of divine judgment on the "day of the Lord" (cf. Zephaniah, Zechariah).[95] And careful reading reveals that many of the promises in the prophetic texts of a coming human unity and peace are premised on the victory of God over Israel's enemies and their subjection before Israel at last. Isaiah 60–61 offer great examples of this: the marvelous "year of the Lord's favor" for Israel is also "the day of vengeance of our God," and "the nation and kingdom that will not serve you shall perish" (Isa. 60:12).

2.6. Toward Jesus Christ

This is our Christian definition of what it means to say that life is sacred:

> *Human life is sacred: this means that God has consecrated each and every human being — without exception and in all circumstances — as a unique, incalculably precious being of elevated status and dignity. Through God's revelation in Scripture and incarnation in Jesus Christ, God has declared and demonstrated the sacred worth of human beings and will hold us accountable for responding appropriately. Such a response begins by adopting a posture of reverence and by accepting responsibility for the sacred gift that is a human life. It includes offering due respect and care to each human being that we encounter. It extends to an obligation to protect human life from wanton destruction, desecration, or the violation of human rights. A full embrace of the sacredness of human life leads to a full-hearted commitment to foster human flourishing.*

This chapter has shown the significant building blocks toward this conviction that are embedded in the Hebrew Bible. Through exploration of the themes of God's creation of humanity in the image of God, God's liberation of the oppressed, God's covenant making with Israel, and God's revelation of the coming glories of a transformed world, we have seen numerous ways in which, by divine decision and command, human worth was elevated, extended in the direction of universal and equal applicability, and treated as the ground not just for a posture of basic respect but also for specific moral obligations to protect innocent human life and seek its holistic, joyful flourishing. These are not just literary themes or abstract

---

95. Longman and Reid, *God Is a Warrior,* chapter 4.

theological and moral beliefs but are the particular convictions and perceived responsibilities of that specific community, Israel. The sacred texts reflect the theological beliefs and moral convictions of that community, as they responded to God's self-revelation.

The New Testament bears witness to God's continued self-revelation. God continues to speak this transcendent Word about humanity's sacred value in God's sight. That divine Word takes flesh in Jesus Christ, and dwells among us (John 1:14). The ministry, message, and career of Jesus give birth to a new global community convinced that in Jesus they have seen God's ultimate expression of love for humanity, and have learned what such love requires in human life.

3. Jesus Christ, the New Testament, and the Sacredness of Human Life

> In Christ's incarnation all of humanity regains the dignity of bearing the image of God. Whoever from now on attacks the least of the people attacks Christ, who took on human form and who in himself has restored the image of God for all who bear a human countenance.
>
> Dietrich Bonhoeffer

The New Testament contributes profoundly to the conviction that human life is sacred. In the ministry of Jesus Christ, in the church's theological reflection on the meaning of the incarnation, and in the character and ministry of the early church, the incalculable value of human life gains powerful, even overwhelming, affirmation. Plumbing the depths of that affirmation over the centuries, Christian theologians and moralists have found ever-new ways to say that in Christ, God offered the ultimate demonstration of the extraordinary value he places on humanity. While there are countermotifs in the New Testament, as with the Old Testament, these are finally overridden by the broader implications of God's redemptive Yes to humanity in Jesus Christ. The witness of the New Testament helped shape a Christian church in which for two thousand years some believers could always be found demonstrating their conviction that every human life has sacred value.

3.1. The Ministry of Jesus Christ

The strands of text and tradition cited in the last chapter flow forward into this one because Jesus was a faithful son of Israel and a creative expositor of

85

Israel's best traditions. Whatever else one may say about his identity, or about the intent and strategy of his earthly ministry, Jesus carried forward in profound ways all four themes noted in the last chapter. He articulated a *creation theology* affirming God as Creator and God's sustaining care for human beings, while employing his power over creation to manifest that care in healing people, rescuing people, and raising people from the dead. He taught and exemplified the *compassionate deliverance* for suffering people that God had exhibited to Israel, though he offered deliverance through suffering love rather than violence. He offered a rendering of *Jewish legal and ethical norms* that affirmed and heightened the protections offered there to human life. And he both articulated and embodied the *prophetic vision of an eschatological shalom* in God's coming future.

I could cite an abundance of examples from his ministry to demonstrate the numerous ways in which Jesus taught and embodied a transformed world in which each and every life is hallowed as God wills. Different readers of the Gospels will undoubtedly be impressed with different teachings, incidents, patterns, or themes. My goal here is to consider the primary ways in which the ministry of Jesus and the teachings of the New Testament contribute to shaping an emerging sacredness-of-life tradition in Christianity. I find the themes set forth below to be some of the most germane patterns in the ministry of Jesus, as these are recorded in the Gospels.

Jesus' Consistent Opposition to Violence and Teaching of the Way of Peace

A central commitment in the sacredness-of-life tradition is to the protection of human life from wanton destruction. A central sign of the terrible brokenness of our world is the depth and pervasiveness of aggressive violence, often followed by defensive or retributive violence in the name of the dead, often followed by more violence, in humanity's ultimate vicious cycle. Jesus rejected this cycle of human violence, despite the abundant provocation to violence that existed for all Jews under Roman occupation.[1] This point is disputed by few careful readers of the New Testament.

---

1. One of the first and still most persuasive expositions of the explosive context of oppression and the hunger for retaliation in the first-century Palestinian Jewish context was offered by Howard Thurman. His *Jesus and the Disinherited* (Richmond, Ind.: Friends United Press, [1949] 1981) remains deeply influential for me, and helps shape this account.

Our problem is not really in understanding that Jesus rejected violence and refused to employ it when he had opportunity, but in deciding whether to imitate him at this critical point, in all circumstances and without exception (puzzle #10). This issue will surface repeatedly in this book, and it is obviously critical for a constructive rendering of what it means to honor the sacredness of human life.

Jesus rejected violence as a way to deal with personal affronts, conflicts, or assaults, and as a response to the humiliations of Roman subjugation (cf. Matt. 5:38-48). He rejected violence when it was proposed by James and John as a response to Samaritans who rejected his ministry (Luke 9:54-55). He rejected it yet again when swords were flashed at the time of his arrest, saying that "all who take the sword will perish by the sword" (Matt. 26:51-52). He rejected it when he could have called legions of angels as he headed to the cross (Matt. 26:53). In his several comments on Jerusalem (cf. Luke 13:34-35; 19:41-44; 21:5-6; 23:27-31), Jesus seems to reject both the everyday violence of Jewish and Roman rulers and the guerrilla violence of rebels, and foresees the coming terrible destruction of the city, which was eventually destroyed in the catastrophic Jewish-Roman War of 66-70. Jesus' earliest disciples saw that violence had no part in the way he had lived and died and thus could not be a part of their own way of life as his followers. This is quite striking, not just because of their context of oppression, but also because of the elements of the Hebrew Bible that permit violence for liberation and against oppression. The early church, originally an entirely Jewish movement, became convinced that such violence did not fit a community seeking to imitate and obey Jesus.

But Jesus didn't just say no to violence. He taught his followers how to find creative alternatives that could bring deliverance from violence. He taught what Glen Stassen has called "transforming initiatives," such as going the second mile with the Roman soldier's pack, turning the other cheek as an unexpected response to being struck, and taking the first step to make peace by finding one's adversary and beginning the conversation (Matt. 5:23-24, 39, 41).[2] He taught that forgiveness should be extended repeatedly to those who wound us (Matt. 18:22), and embodied such forgiveness throughout his ministry, perhaps most notably when he prayed for his persecutors even from the cross (Luke 23:34). He characterized God his heavenly Father as offering such gracious forgiveness in the same way, call-

---

2. On "transforming initiatives," see Glen H. Stassen, ed., *Just Peacemaking: The New Paradigm for the Ethics of Peace and War* (Cleveland: Pilgrim Press, 2008).

ing his listeners to the imitation of God and warning them against with-holding forgiveness (Matt. 6:14-15; Luke 17:3-4).[3] He described God the Father as showering love rather than violence on God's enemies (Matt. 5:43-48), as one who seeks those who walk away from him (cf. Luke 15).[4] Jesus' harshest words of judgment are reserved for those who turn religion itself into an instrument of violence, judgmentalism, and exclusion (cf. Matt. 23), words that Christians today would do well to consider more seriously.

We face a paradox here that cannot be sidestepped. In the Old Testament teaching that we reviewed, divine and human violence has a place in upholding life's sacredness. Through laws banning and punishing murder, and through the liberating divine violence that rescued Israel from Egyptian slavery, death (or the threat of death) protects and liberates human beings from those who would harm or subjugate them. Yet Jesus and his earliest followers take a different path. Even today the debate rages, including among Christians, as to which approach to violence best protects human well-being in our broken world. For now let us simply register the sharp turn toward nonviolence that was taken by Jesus and the movement he created, and watch how that plays itself out over the succeeding centuries.

Jesus' Inclusive Ministry

A key element both of the kingdom of God and of the sacredness of life is its expansive inclusiveness, its hospitable universality. Every individual is called, claimed, and welcomed; no groups are diminished vis-à-vis other

3. For a very thoughtful Christian theological reflection on forgiveness, see L. Gregory Jones, *Embodying Forgiveness: A Theological Analysis* (Grand Rapids: Eerdmans, 1995).

4. On Jesus as peacemaker, and the peacemaking theme in the New Testament, see Joseph A. Grassi, *Jesus Is Shalom: A Vision of Peace from the Gospels* (New York: Paulist, 2006); Perry B. Yoder and Willard M. Swartley, eds., *The Meaning of Peace: Biblical Studies* (Louisville: Westminster John Knox, 1992); Willard M. Swartley, ed., *The Love of Enemy and Nonretaliation in the New Testament* (Louisville: Westminster John Knox, 1992); Willard M. Swartley, *Covenant of Peace: The Missing Piece in New Testament Theology and Ethics* (Grand Rapids: Eerdmans, 2006); Ulrich Mauser, *The Gospel of Peace: A Scriptural Message for Today's World* (Louisville: Westminster John Knox, 1992); Lisa Sowle Cahill, *Love Your Enemies: Discipleship, Pacifism, and Just War Theory* (Minneapolis: Augsburg Fortress, 1994); Daniel L. Smith-Christopher, *Jonah, Jesus, and Other Good Coyotes: Speaking Peace to Power in the Bible* (Nashville: Abingdon, 2007); J. Massyngbaerde Ford, *My Enemy Is My Guest: Jesus and Violence in Luke* (Maryknoll, N.Y.: Orbis, 1984).

groups; no categories of people are the privileged recipients of God's love. Everyone matters. Jesus embodied that inclusiveness throughout his ministry. His example pushed Christians toward the development of love for "each and every" human being, without exception, as a fundamental element of a Christ-following way of life.

In a religious culture in which women were consistently shunted into second-class status, Jesus spoke with women, traveled with women, touched and healed women, and taught and ministered to women (cf. Matt. 15:21-28; John 4; 20:15).[5] In so doing he laid the foundations for an elevated role for women within the church and within cultures later affected by Christianity. It is to our shame as Christians that we often have dishonored women and thus disobeyed Jesus in the life of the church.

In a religious culture in which, apparently, major religious leaders had developed a reading of Jewish law that tended to elevate religious separatism in the interest of ritual purity (cf. Matt. 12:1-14; 15:1-20; Mark 7:1-23; Luke 13:10-17), Jesus consistently acted to welcome and care for the "impure" and the "unclean," thus demonstrating a reading of religious obligation that elevated the worth of all people. In a retrieval of the prophetic strand of the Jewish tradition, holiness for Jesus meant justice, mercy, and welcome for the excluded. This is what a holy God demands — "I desire mercy, not sacrifice" (Matt. 9:13a; 12:7) — not an exclusionary practice protecting purity by rigid separation.[6]

In a religious culture in which obvious "sinners" were often treated as beyond the reach of God's love, Jesus purposefully welcomed such people at his dinner table (cf. Matt. 9:10-13; Luke 5:29-32). He ate with tax collectors and prostitutes! And he taught many times about God's welcoming and forgiving love toward those who had been on the wrong path but repented (cf. Luke 15:11-32; 19:2-9). His "open table" hospitality embodied

---

5. See Richard Bauckham, *Gospel Women: Studies of the Named Women in the Gospels* (Grand Rapids: Eerdmans, 2002); Mary Ann Getty-Sullivan, *Women in the New Testament* (Collegeville, Minn.: Liturgical Press, 2001); Elisabeth Schüssler Fiorenza, *In Memory of Her* (New York: Crossroad, 1987); Ben Witherington, *Women in the Ministry of Jesus: A Study of Jesus' Attitude toward Women and Their Roles as Reflected in His Earthly Life* (Cambridge: Cambridge University Press, 1987); and numerous other works.

6. On the contested meanings of purity and holiness, see Stephen C. Barton, ed., *Holiness: Past and Present* (London and New York: T. & T. Clark, 2003). See also Marcus J. Borg, *Conflict, Holiness, and Politics in the Teachings of Jesus* (Harrisburg, Pa.: Trinity, 1984). It is, however, important to avoid disastrous anti-Pharisee and anti-Jewish stereotypes in interpreting these difficult texts. See Amy-Jill Levine, *The Misunderstood Jew: The Church and the Scandal of the Jewish Jesus* (New York: HarperOne, 2006).

God's redemptive love, rather than angry rejection, of those who strayed. This "prodigal" (prodigious!) divine love strains every effort to include rather than exclude, to convert rather than destroy.[7]

In a culture in which children were held of little account, Jesus welcomed and honored children, touched and held and cared for them (cf. Matt. 18:1-9; 19:13-14; Mark 9:33-40).[8] He taught his reluctant disciples to welcome rather than reject children, and said that "whoever welcomes one such child in my name welcomes me, and whoever welcomes me welcomes . . . the one who sent me" (Mark 9:37). This saying, which in a powerful way echoes Matthew 25:31-46, teaches disciples to see in the face of each child the face of Jesus, and to receive each child as if receiving God the Father. It is hard to imagine a more profound way to communicate the sacred worth of a child.

In a religious context in which the sick and disabled were often cast out from community or blamed as sinfully responsible for their own maladies, Jesus spoke with, touched, and healed thousands of sick ones, attending not only to their physical well-being but also to their spiritual needs and their restoration into community (Matt. 4:23-24; 8:16-17; etc.). His example set the church on a historical trajectory of intensive commitment to health-care ministries and to the disabled all around the world, and inspired millions of caregivers from Florence Nightingale to Mother Teresa.[9] Christians care about human health and do not abandon the sick and dying. Jesus blazed the trail.

In a political context in which the occupying Romans were hated, Jesus ministered to and spoke with Roman soldiers, and on one occasion honored a Roman centurion for his great faith (Matt. 8:5-13; Luke 7:1-10). He was somehow able to see in the Roman soldier more than an enemy, and was able to respond to soldiers as individuals loved by God rather than

7. Marcus J. Borg and John Dominic Crossan have clarified the significance of Jesus' own table fellowship as central to his ministry. See Borg, *Jesus: A New Vision; Spirit, Culture, and the Life of Discipleship* (San Francisco: Harper and Row, 1987), and Crossan, *The Historical Jesus: The Life of a Mediterranean Jewish Peasant* (New York: HarperSanFrancisco, 1991), chapter 13. Compare N. T. Wright, *Jesus and the Victory of God* (Minneapolis: Fortress, 1996), chapter 7.

8. Judith M. Gundry-Volf, "The Least and the Greatest: Children in the New Testament," in *The Child in Christian Thought*, ed. Marcia J. Bunge (Grand Rapids: Eerdmans, 2001), chapter 1.

9. Stevan L. Davies, *Jesus the Healer* (London: SCM, 1995); cf. John P. Meier, *A Marginal Jew: Rethinking the Historical Jesus*, vol. 2, *Mentor, Message, and Miracles* (New York: Doubleday, 1994), chapter 21.

merely as national enemies hated by his people.[10] His example has been continually imitated as oppressed believers in various settings have sought to rise above their all-too-natural hatred and thirst for vengeance against their persecutors.

Against a historic backdrop of tensions between Jews and Samaritans, Jesus spoke with and ministered to a Samaritan woman and through her to her community (John 4). He also elevated a compassionate Samaritan to a memorably praiseworthy role in perhaps his most widely quoted parable (Luke 10:25-37). In so doing Jesus worked to overcome one of the most powerful tensions of his context, setting an example always available to his followers whenever they have been prepared to listen and to follow.[11] As Dietrich Bonhoeffer points out, the parable of the Good Samaritan forever recasts the question of who counts as my neighbor, as one worthy of my concern and care. "Being a neighbor is not a qualification of someone else; it is their claim on me, nothing else. At every moment, in every situation I am the one required to act, to be obedient. There is literally no time left to ask about someone else's qualification. . . . I must be a neighbor to the other person."[12] Jews considered Samaritans to be practicing a heretical form of Judaism, so in treating Samaritans with kindness, both in person and in parable, Jesus teaches his followers to honor the worth even of those with whom they might have the most acute religious differences. Even today Christians (and others) often feel entitled to denigrate people of other faiths in ways they would never countenance on grounds of race or any other criteria. Consider the Muslim-bashing quite popular among many Christians today.[13]

In an economic context in which a woman alone in the world faced desperate financial challenges, Jesus compassionately raised a widow's son from the dead and restored him to his mother, thus restoring her to economic and social well-being (Luke 7:11-17). The profound compassion of this particular story leaves an indelible impression. Here is one who grieves with and responds to bereft widows. Jesus' response to the widow who gave her very last penny (Luke 21:1-4) strikes the same chord. His anger at a religious system that would demand that last penny of her (Luke 20:46-47) is also important — to value vulnerable ones means to confront those who exploit them.

10. An early, quite sensitive discussion of how Jesus related to Roman soldiers is found in Thurman, *Jesus and the Disinherited*.

11. See Wright, *Jesus*, pp. 305-7.

12. Dietrich Bonhoeffer, *Discipleship*, vol. 6 of *Dietrich Bonhoeffer Works* (Minneapolis: Fortress, 2003), p. 76.

13. I am grateful to Sondra Wheeler for this acute observation.

In a political context in which social-economic divisions were acute, Jesus preached "good news to the poor" (Luke 4:18), welcoming the desperate in his band of followers (cf. Matt. 5:1-12). He taught the rich to share with the poor and live in simplicity rather than to be greedy, to hoard, or to ignore the poor (cf. Matt. 6:19-24; 19:16-24; Luke 12:13-21; 16:19-31). He ministered to extortionate and collaborationist tax collectors in such a way that some were moved to divest, make restitution, and follow him (Matt. 9:9-13). He also told a memorable parable about self-righteousness in which a penitent tax gatherer is described as justified before God (Luke 18:9-14). Jesus treats the poor with dignity, proposes a way of life in which everyone has enough and no one has too much, calls the rich and especially the unjust rich to repentance, and creates an egalitarian community of economic sharing and justice. The powerful impact of Christ's treatment of the poor and his vision of a just and dignified economic community has been felt down through the centuries until today, continuing to motivate personal and social efforts among Christians toward economic justice.[14]

In sum: Jesus did much to overturn the religious, cultural, economic, and political barriers of his context and demonstrated love, respect, and inclusion toward people of all descriptions, in doing so often shocking and scandalizing those around him. He treated all human beings as persons of sacred worth. He sought to meet them at the point of their need and to act to advance their flourishing in whatever dimension was most needed. And he taught those who would be his followers to be "neighbors" to each and every person.

Jesus' Teaching about God's Love for Human Beings

In a variety of different ways, Jesus taught the very "good news" that God loves human beings with an immeasurable love. The theme resonates

---

14. Two fairly recent celebrations and applications of the economics of Jesus can be found in Obery Hendricks Jr., *The Politics of Jesus* (New York: Doubleday, 2006), and Shane Claiborne and Chris Haw, *Jesus for President* (Grand Rapids: Zondervan, 2008). Drawing on much recent biblical scholarship, these contemporary Christian leaders suggest that Jesus offered a social-economic justice program (Hendricks) that can and must be embodied in communities of Christian discipleship today (Claiborne). All contemporary work on the economics of Jesus is indebted to John Howard Yoder, *The Politics of Jesus* (Grand Rapids: Eerdmans, [1972] 1994).

through the pages of the Gospels in a way that has left a profound imprint on the church.

I have already suggested that ultimately the concept of the sacredness of human life is grounded theologically in God's free decision to consecrate human life by divine declaration, command, and action. God speaks, and creation comes into existence; just so God speaks, God commands, God acts, and in so doing designates human beings as immensely precious. Christians believe in the sacredness of human life not fundamentally because of some potential, capacity, or inherent function, characteristic, or quality of human nature (puzzle #5), but because God has decided that human life has such a value. God is love, and God loves what God values. Human beings must respond to God's claim on human life as God commands.[15]

Jesus declared that divine decision to love us when, for example, he announced the coming reign of God (Matt. 4:17; Mark 1:14-15), which is nothing other than God's loving decision to save humanity and the world rather than leave us to our own destructive devices. This gracious divine decision was, in a sense, first announced in Genesis 8–9, when God made covenant with Noah and all creatures after the flood, declaring that he would bear with them despite their sinfulness (Gen. 8:21-22). Jesus declared that God continues to love humanity, and not just those who return that love, but those who reject it (Matt. 5:43-48).

Jesus said that God pays attention even to the life of a sparrow, and all the more attends to providing for our material needs — therefore freeing us to trust him and serve others (Matt. 6:26). He describes God as like a loving Father who can be counted on to "give good gifts to [his] children," which authorizes and encourages us to ask for what we need and trust that it will be given to us (Matt. 7:7-11; Luke 11:13; 18:1-8). He said that each child has an angel in heaven who intercedes for him or her before the Father (Matt. 18:10), and that God is like a shepherd who goes after the one lost sheep even if he has the ninety-nine at hand (Luke 15:3-7).

Jesus frequently offered reminders of God's special care for those who especially needed it — the children, the poor, the abandoned, the sick, the hungry. These reminders were often accompanied by teachings requiring all who would be his followers to imitate this preferential love or face judg-

---

15. As we saw earlier, a critically important benefit of this view is that it prevents the devaluing of a human life that somehow lacks, loses, or fails to develop the supposedly central quality, such as rationality, that God values or that is viewed as making human life truly human.

ment for failing to do so (cf. Matt. 25:31-46). Love attends especially to those who need love the most, and God will hold us accountable for doing so. These Old Testament themes are carried through powerfully in the life and teachings of Jesus, and we cannot allow accountability before God for the lives of the most vulnerable to drop out of our understanding of the sacredness of human life.

John's Gospel has either Jesus or the narrator sum up this theme in words memorized by many thousands of Christians: "For God so loved the world that he gave his only Son, so that everyone who believes in him may not perish but may have eternal life" (John 3:16). The bottom line of the New Testament is this divine saving love for the world, for humans, for each and every human. This is the ultimate foundation of Christian belief in the sacredness of human life. Any claim here about "life's sacredness" should be heard as the theological claim that *for God's sake, and in obedience to God, we must prize and protect the life of human beings.*

3.2. The Incarnation of Jesus Christ

We saw in chapter 1 that Christian discussions of the sacredness of human life often make reference to the very fact of the incarnation as somehow elevating human worth. This deserves further reflection. I want to reflect on implications of the major movements of Christ's earthly journey, which (having already considered briefly the nature of his earthly ministry) I will summarize here as his birth, crucifixion, resurrection, and ascension.

God Became Human

"The Word became flesh and lived among us" (John 1:14). The Word, which in the beginning was "with God," and "was God" (John 1:1), became human in Jesus the Christ. The eternal gulf between divinity and humanity was bridged in the God-man Jesus. The New Testament writers consistently marvel at the divine condescension, in which God stooped low to take on our frail, humble flesh, carry our nature, suffer humiliation and death at our hands, and bear our sins as God's suffering servant (cf. Phil. 2:1-11). The paradox of the incarnation is that when divinity stooped low and took on humanity, humanity revealed its desperate debasement — and yet was elevated through God's mercy. And it was elevated forever, for this moment in

God's history marked an irreversible change in God's relation to humanity and the world. After the incarnation, God is the One who became a human to save us in Jesus Christ. Karl Barth says that "Jesus Christ is *the* man, and the measure, the determination and limitation of all human being." He is "the decision as to what God's purpose . . . is, not just for Him but for every man."[16] If this is so, our understanding of humanity itself must be fundamentally transfigured and permanently elevated through its association with the God-man Jesus Christ.

Old Testament resources taught us to see the depth of God's loving and valuing of human beings. The incarnation sees this loving and valuing incarnated in the person of Jesus Christ. When God became human, when divine nature and human nature joined in Jesus Christ, when God our Father became Christ "our brother,"[17] God's sacredness touched humanity in an unprecedented way. We are no longer "just" made in God's image, cared for in creation, delivered from our distress, protected by God's laws, and promised eschatological shalom; now God becomes one of us. In Christ, God literally embodies care, deliverance, protection, and shalom in, with, and to humanity.

Christian theologians have often been moved to proclaim that if God became human, the status of the human changes. No human can be seen as worthless. No human life can be treated cruelly or destroyed capriciously. Human dignity can never again be rejected, or confined to only a few groups or individuals of supposedly higher rank. God's incarnation in Jesus Christ elevates the worth not only of the one human, Jesus of Nazareth; not only of the woman who carried him, Mary; and not only of the followers who believe in him, the church. The incarnation elevates the status of every human being everywhere on the planet at every time in human history. It elevates the worth of every human being at every stage of life, because the arc of Jesus' own life included every stage of existence, from conception to death and even resurrection, which is our own destiny in Christ. The incarnation is highly relevant to whether we understand human life's sacredness to extend to the hidden beginnings of life, in the womb, and to the sometimes bitter end of life, at death — leading me and many other Christians to extend sacred status to every stage of life that Jesus experienced (puzzle #3).

There is a paradox here in Christian thought that must not be evaded.

---

16. Karl Barth, *Dogmatics in Outline* (New York: Harper and Row, 1959), p. 89.
17. On Christ as our "brother" in the incarnation, see Bonhoeffer, *Discipleship*, p. 123.

Many voices in the Christian tradition find in the incarnation confirmation of desperate human *unworthiness* rather than worthiness. As Barth also said, "We may realize the utter depth of our human sin and need in the fact that this immeasurable thing had to happen and did happen."[18] Pessimism about human sin and "the total depravity of humanity" runs deep in Christian thought. That would be a problem for the thesis being pursued in this volume — if that thesis depended upon some intrinsic goodness in humanity (puzzle #7). But the depth of human sin, as Barth says, only highlights the even greater depth of God's love for humanity: "The Church and all Christendom looks in its message at this immeasurable and unfathomable fact, that God has given Himself for us."[19] Christian thought proclaims the immeasurable, incalculable value of the human person not because of any intrinsic goodness on our part, but because God has acted in so many ways to communicate his own immeasurably, incalculably great love for human beings (puzzle #4). In this sense, the deeper and more realistic our understanding of the fallenness of the human condition, the more we find confirmation of the immeasurable (God-given) sacredness of human life.

Speaking in the past tense about what he feared was a fading Christian belief in the simultaneously exalted and debased human condition, G. K. Chesterton wrote:

> In one way Man was to be haughtier than he had ever been before; in another way he was to be humbler than he had ever been before. In so far as I am Man I am the chief of creatures. In so far as I am *a* man I am the chief of sinners. . . . Christianity thus held a thought of the dignity of man that could only be expressed in crowns rayed like the sun and fans of peacock plumage. Yet at the same time it could hold a thought about the abject smallness of man that could only be expressed by fasting and fantastic submission. . . . Let him say anything against himself short of blaspheming the original aim of his being; let him call himself a fool . . . but he must not say that fools are not worth saving. He must not say that a man, *qua* man, can be valueless. . . . One can hardly think too little of oneself. One can hardly think too much of one's soul.[20]

---

18. Barth, *Dogmatics in Outline*, p. 86.
19. Barth, *Dogmatics in Outline*, p. 86.
20. G. K. Chesterton, *Orthodoxy: The Romance of Faith* (New York: Doubleday, [1908] 1990), pp. 94-95.

One particular teaching of Jesus has proven particularly influential in linking the incarnation to human life's sacredness. It is the eschatological judgment parable from Matthew 25. The scene is familiar to Christian readers: the Son of Man/king (presumably Jesus himself) sits on his throne, with all nations (peoples — *ethnoi*) gathered before him for the final judgment. He separates "sheep" from "goats," approved from disapproved, on the basis that "I was hungry and you gave me food, I was thirsty and you gave me something to drink, I was a stranger and you welcomed me, I was naked and you gave me clothing, I was sick and you took care of me, I was in prison and you visited me." The "sheep" have no memory of having cared for the Son of Man/king in this way, and so they are told, "Just as you did it to the least of these who are members of my family, you did it to me."[21]

In a profoundly important twist on the theme of incarnation, Jesus here suggests that God enters humanity not just in one human, but in all people, especially the most needy. Jesus teaches us to see in the face of every person his own face. This judgment parable (if it is a parable!) particularly instructs us to see Jesus Christ in and through the face of every *suffering person*, everyone who counts as among "the least of these," enumerated here as the hungry, the thirsty, strangers, the naked, the sick, and the imprisoned.[22]

Mother Teresa of Calcutta saw this with perhaps more clarity than any known Christian leader. She was driven by this Matthew 25 vision into a ministry with the lepers and dying of Calcutta. There she was sure she encountered Jesus Christ himself: "Jesus comes to meet us. To welcome him, let us go to meet him. He comes to us in the hungry, the naked, the lonely, the alcoholic, the drug addict, the prostitute, the street beggars. He may come to you or me in a father who is alone, in a mother, in a brother, or in a sister. If we reject them, if we do not go out to meet them, we reject Jesus himself."[23] Mother Teresa's ministry embodied this insight offered by

21. A more narrow reading of the text in its original context confines the "least of these" in this passage to persecuted believers, and therefore the king's blessing is for those who cared for persecuted Christian believers. Even if this is the better reading, the text has often invited and provoked the broader, richer interpretation I am presenting here.

22. Vladimir Lossky has written: "Only the eyes of faith recognize the form of God beneath the form of the slave and, deciphering beneath the human face the presence of a divine person, learn to unveil in each face the mystery of the person created in the image of God." Lossky, *Orthodox Theology: An Introduction* (Crestwood, N.Y.: St. Vladimir's Seminary Press, 1978), p. 102.

23. Mother Teresa and José Luis González-Balado, *Mother Teresa: In My Own Words* (New York: Gramercy Books, 1996), p. 29.

Barth: "There is a general connection of all men with Christ, and every man is his brother. . . . It is the most important basis, and the only one which touches everything, for what we call humanity. He who has once realized the fact that God was made man cannot speak and act inhumanly."[24] Why? Because in every human being we encounter the person of Jesus Christ; behind every human face we glimpse the face of God incarnate.

Barth offers another way to link the incarnation to action on behalf of other people in reminding us that Jesus is "not man for nothing, nor for Himself," but is "for God's own glory" by being the "man for men, for other men." The incarnate God exists to be for others. If we grant this, and also grant that Jesus is the model and measure of what it means truly to be human, then we must conclude with Barth that "A man without his fellows, or radically neutral or opposed to his fellows, or under the impression that the co-existence of his fellows has only secondary significance, is a being which *ipso facto* is fundamentally alien to the man Jesus and cannot have Him as Deliverer and Saviour."[25] The incarnation therefore reveals that what it means to be human is to act on behalf of the well-being of others, as God-in-Christ acted on our behalf.

Jesus came as a human being, and thus he came in a body, which (as Matthew 25 reminds us) was fully capable of hunger, thirst, loneliness, and suffering, and experienced all these to the uttermost. Because most religious traditions, including Judaism and Christianity, identify God as a spirit (cf. John 4:24), it has been all too easy for adherents to denigrate the significance of human bodily existence. Christians have often struggled to accept the full bodily humanity of Jesus (and of ourselves), perhaps out of an enduring human embarrassment at such humble functions as eating, drinking, lovemaking, excreting, aging, and dying.

But the incarnation forever elevates human bodiliness, an important correction to any tendency to diminish the significance of the body (puzzle #2). What happens to human bodies (not just minds and spirits and souls) matters to God and must matter to us. One way we know this is because Jesus Christ came in a body; he was embodied, as a baby, a child, a teenager, and a man. He enjoyed the proper functioning of his body. He

24. Barth, *Dogmatics in Outline*, p. 138, spelling Americanized.

25. I am grateful to Christopher Chenault Roberts, *Creation and Covenant: The Significance of Sexual Difference in the Moral Theology of Marriage* (London: T. & T. Clark, 2007), for this particularly apposite discovery in Barth. For the original, see Karl Barth, *Church Dogmatics III/2: The Doctrine of Creation*, trans. H. Knight et al. (Edinburgh: T. & T. Clark, 1960), p. 132.

also suffered grievously in his body. What happens to people's bodies must matter to us because God came in a body in Jesus Christ. This reality is a powerfully important contributor to Christian sacredness-of-life commitments as these relate to the protecting and flourishing of human life, which is always bodily life.

In teaching about sexual morality (1 Cor. 6:12-20), the apostle Paul links bodiliness to sacredness in an especially complex and provocative way. Arguing against moral indifference to embodied behavior in the Corinthian Christian community, Paul says that "the body is meant not for fornication but for the Lord, and the Lord for the body" (1 Cor. 6:13). The believer's body was created for God, called to God's service, and destined for resurrection (6:14). Paul then employs the central ecclesiological image of the church as Christ's body to warn Christians against using their own bodily members for sexual sin (6:15-16), thus violating the integrity of the church as corporate body of Christ, which is a kind of theft from Christ and the church.[26] He declares that our bodies are temples of the Holy Spirit, who comes to believers as a gift from God (6:18-19). The holy God dwells in human bodies — at least the bodies of believers — through the Holy Spirit. The collective body of the church, and all its constituent individual bodies, has become the new sacred temple! Our bodies are the site of sacredness. Paul finally alludes to Christ's bodily suffering on the cross in saying that "you were bought with a price; therefore glorify God in your body" (6:20). Bodies matter. What happens to and in and through our bodies matters to God. The incarnation of Jesus Christ helps ground these important convictions.

The Cross

The sacred body of Jesus Christ was nailed to a cross. On that cruel Roman cross Jesus suffered and died. There is no more central image in the iconography, piety, and theology of Christian faith than the suffering Christ on the cross.

The implications of the cross for the sacredness of life are abundant. One place to begin is with Christian grief over Christ's grief, Christian anguish over Christ's anguish. This grief and anguish are central to Christian

26. Anthony C. Thiselton, *The First Epistle to the Corinthians* (Grand Rapids: Eerdmans, 2000), pp. 464-66.

piety in many traditions and tend to overflow during the annual Lenten season:

> O sacred head, now wounded, With grief and shame weighed down.
> Now scornfully surrounded, With Thorns thine only crown;
> How pale thou art with anguish, With sore abuse and scorn!
> How does that visage languish Which once was bright as morn![27]

It is right that Christians should grieve Christ's grief and anguish over Christ's anguish — especially if that grief and anguish come to extend to all who suffer bodily humiliation, suffering, and death. The cross serves as a resource for honoring life's sacredness when it functions to ground and motivate compassionate concern and intervention on behalf of all those who suffer in their bodies.

That concern can be sharpened and extended in appropriate ways if we focus more closely on the details of Christ's suffering and death and look around our world for parallels. This could lead us to special concern for those whose victimization occurs at the hands of the state; those who are victims of unjust legal processes; those who suffer humiliation, abuse, and torture; and perhaps especially those who have done nothing worthy of such cruelty, punishment, or death. In other words, Christ's suffering and death lead to concern about the violation of life's sacredness by those who hold political power and use it to oppress and abuse the innocent or defenseless. This is a major field of struggle in defense of life's sacredness, though obviously not the only one.

It seems appropriate to draw the connections between the cross and the disastrous turn toward prisoner abuse by the United States after 9/11. That many American Christians would endorse not just abuse and cruelty but outright torture in the interests of "national security" has marked a fundamental repudiation of the ethical meaning of the cross. Certainly the link between the torture-death of Jesus Christ and the torture of others, including other Christians around the world, has not been lost on those who have experienced torture and have protested it. As a Christian antitorture activist in Chile has written, "If to some extent we share the sufferings of the tortured, He who was tortured by Roman justice and

27. "O Sacred Head, Now Wounded," words by Paul Gerhardt, 1656, Hymn 105, *Baptist Hymnal* (Nashville: Convention Press, 1975).

nailed on the Cross accompanies us and we for our part accompany Him, because He identifies Himself with the tortured."[28] The cruel torture and death of Jesus Christ should sensitize us, rather than inure us, to similar cruelties inflicted on others. During the torture debate, some American Christians intuited the connection between torture and the cross, but most were unable or unwilling to see the link.

Jesus' death is always portrayed as an evil. It is *not good* that he was abused and killed. This is a reminder that it is not good that anyone is ever abused or killed. And yet, of course, the New Testament teaches that this particular death somehow brought the salvation of the world. "With his stripes we are healed" (Isa. 53:5 KJV). The precise theological formulation of the salvific meaning of Christ's death varies in the New Testament and has varied throughout Christian history. We need not settle on one single interpretation in the church, and certainly not here. But what all such interpretations have in common is the basic claim that *Jesus died for us.* "God so loved the world that he gave his only Son" (John 3:16) — and that giving culminated at the cross.[29]

God not only took flesh in Jesus Christ, God sacrificed that flesh at Golgotha, for our salvation. This staggering New Testament claim only deepens belief in the extent of God's love and care for humanity. God stopped at nothing to reach out to us. God-in-Christ suffered and bled and died for us. What more can anyone — what more could the divine One — do to demonstrate love for the world? The intensity of this conviction is deepened when, especially as in evangelical traditions, Christians emphasize that Christ died for *each and every one* of us, friend and foe, good and evil. It is a commonplace saying in some Christian communities that "even if you were the only person on the planet, Christ would have died for you." Belief in the sacredness of life is deepened considerably by reflection on the ultimate nature of the price God paid at the cross to demonstrate how valuable each and every human life actually is to him (puzzle #2). The in-

---

28. José Aldunate, "La Acción que Habla a las Conciencias," in *La No Violencia Activa: presencia y desafíos,* ed. José Aldunate, S.J., et al. (Santiago: ILADES, 1988), p. 5, translated by William T. Cavanaugh and quoted in his "Torture and Eucharist: A Regretful Update," in *Torture Is a Moral Issue,* ed. George Hunsinger (Grand Rapids: Eerdmans, 2008), p. 111.

29. It is worth pointing out that Christians who love their lives often have been willing to lay them down if that is what fidelity to Christ requires. Christian martyrs such as these help clarify that what matters ultimately in Christian perspective is faithfulness to Christ. This does involve a proper valuing of our own and others' embodied lives. But it may involve a willingness to sacrifice our own life, as Jesus did.

calculably terrible suffering and death of Jesus Christ, and what it says about how very much God values each and every human being, has contributed profoundly to a Christian moral tradition that exalts the immeasurable worth of the human being.

New Testament teaching and later Christian thought include some related beliefs that are also highly significant for a consideration of life's sacredness. One is that "all have sinned and fall short of the glory of God" (Rom. 3:23). This communicates a primal human equality before God in our shared, desperate need for divine rescue at the cross. A key part of our Christian definition of life's sacredness is its *equalizing force* — all human life is sacred, in the most significant sense all stand equal in value, and all must be viewed and treated that way (Gal. 3:26-28). This equality is grounded in the Old Testament in many ways, beginning with the claim that all are made by God in God's image. Now again, if "all have sinned," this means that in this very significant fact about humanity there is another dimension of irreducible equality. Everyone stands equal "at the foot of the cross." All need the sacrificial rescue that Jesus offered there. Christian piety has often reinforced this theme.

The New Testament also teaches that Jesus died for "the world," that is, everyone, people in all states, conditions, nations, ethnic groups, races, and orientations toward God and neighbor. Paul reminds us that Christ laid down his life not just for his friends but also for his enemies (Rom. 5:10). The trajectory of the New Testament chronicles the ever-unfolding universality of those sought and reached by the good news of God's love in Christ. A movement that began as a Jewish splinter group spread geographically, linguistically, culturally, and ethnically, so that John's Apocalypse could celebrate that "by your blood you ransomed for God / saints from *every tribe and language and people and nation*" (Rev. 5:9, italics added).

In the global reach of Christ's saving death, the universality of life's sacredness is affirmed. Christ died for everyone, and people have come to his new family from every part of the world. Paul's formulation becomes highly influential here: Who am I to harm one "for whom Christ died" (Rom. 14:15/1 Cor. 8:11)? If the population of those "for whom Christ died" includes every human being in the entire world, beginning with those who believe but extending outward in every direction to those who have not (yet) believed, the moral implications are clear. Everyone must matter to us, because everyone matters to God, who sent Christ, who died for all. Certainly there are moments in the New Testament, and strands of Christian thought, in which this universality of moral concern seems to narrow to the church; this seems especially problematic in the Johannine literature, apparently emerging from an embattled community in a defensive crouch.[30] The same tendency had appeared in strands of the Old Testament, as noted earlier. Perhaps it is an inevitable tendency in religious movements — and in human life generally — to focus on those within rather than outside the community, especially when that community is under threat. But in the canon the universalizing impulses simply cannot be denied: all have sinned; all need salvation; Christ suffered and died for all.[31]

The Resurrection

And then Christ rose again. Entire theologies have been built on the significance of Christ's resurrection. There is no need to recapitulate them here. But a few comments germane to our present exploration should be made.

First, it is significant that Christ rose in a body. It was a new, different kind of body. But it was still a body. This was a body that could be seen and touched. In this body Jesus ate and drank. Paul concludes from Christ's bodily resurrection that we too shall have bodies at our own resurrection (1 Cor. 15:42-49). Human life never ceases to be bodily, even at the resurrection. Once again, human bodiliness gains powerful affirmation. Christians never escape embodiment and its implications.

The resurrection of Christ also signifies the victory of God over evil, including the evil that took Jesus to the cross. In the resurrection, God triumphs, and God signals that in the end he will triumph over Satan and all forces that bring suffering and death; even death itself is destroyed (1 Cor. 15:26).[32] The sacredness of life, when fully realized, will be part of this ultimate victory of God over the evil that has harmed and destroyed so many human lives.

The resurrection marks the triumph of life. The Gospel of John de-

30. Richard B. Hays, *The Moral Vision of the New Testament: Community, Cross, New Creation* (New York: HarperOne, 1996), p. 146.

31. There are many reasons to critique the hyper-Calvinist claim that Christ died only for the elect; one of them is precisely here, that it undercuts a key theological rationale for universal moral concern and the universal equality and sacredness of human life.

32. I first encountered this formulation in J. Christiaan Beker, *Paul the Apostle: The Triumph of God in Life and Thought* (Philadelphia: Fortress, 1980). Since then it has become a familiar concept, linked to the kingdom of God.

clares that "all things came into being through him [the Word], and without him not one thing came into being. What has come into being in him was life" (John 1:3-4a). In the incarnation, the one through whom all things were made, the one who sustains and holds together the creation itself, became flesh, took on human life. At the cross this human being suffered and lost his life. But in the resurrection, Jesus lives again; God wins; and therefore life wins. God is for life.[33] All that wars against life is enemy to God, and God has defeated it proleptically at the cross. This demands that God's people participate in combating and, with God's help, defeating all that wars against life until Christ comes again.

The Ascension

The historic confession of the church is not just that Jesus rose from the dead, but that he ascended to heaven, where he now sits at the right hand of the Father, and from which he shall come to judge the living and the dead. Remembering that the Jesus who rose from the dead was fully God and fully human, this means, as Barth puts it: "The real mystery of Easter is not that God is glorified in it, but that man is exalted, raised to the right hand of God and permitted to triumph over sin, death and the devil."[34] In a sermon for Ascension Sunday, Leo the Great put it this way: "With all due solemnity we are commemorating that day on which our poor human nature was carried up in Christ above all the hosts of heaven, above all the ranks of angels, beyond those heavenly powers to the very throne of God the Father."[35]

God stoops low so that humanity can be exalted even to the right hand of God. Human beings must be viewed and treated as those whose divinely intended destiny is to dwell eternally along with Jesus the Son in the presence of God the Father. Humanity was made for an eternal destiny; this theme is often sounded in Christian declarations on the sacredness of human life. The theme can be strengthened if we link it to the ascension. Those who belong to Jesus Christ will follow him to the throne of God. We come from God and are returning to God. Jesus blazed the trail.

33. This theme has perhaps never been expressed more profoundly than by Pope John Paul II, in *The Gospel of Life* (New York: Random House, 1995), chapter II.

34. Barth, *Dogmatics in Outline*, p. 115.

35. Quoted in Thomas C. Oden and Christopher A. Hall, eds., *Ancient Christian Commentary on Scripture: Mark* (Downers Grove, Ill.: InterVarsity, 1995), p. 254.

3.3. The Image of Jesus Christ

As the early Christians formed churches and began Christianity's long historical journey, they sought to proclaim and embody the kingdom ministry of their Lord Jesus Christ. And their earliest literature reflects ongoing development of their understanding of the impact of Jesus Christ on their own lives and on the human condition and its value.

A profound strand running through the New Testament concerns the relationship between Jesus Christ and the image of God.[36] The image of God plays a critically important role in almost all contemporary treatments of the sacredness of life. But some Christians raise theological questions about the meaning or even the survival of the *imago Dei* after the entry of sin into the world, and in seven places in the New Testament, five of them in the (probable) writings of Paul, the *imago Dei* is reinterpreted in light of Jesus Christ. Let us consider implications of what has been called an "image Christology."[37]

One place to begin is in 1 Corinthians 15. In verses 42-49, Paul moves toward the culmination of his argument that not only is the resurrection of Jesus Christ central to all Christian thought, but also the Christian hope of eternal life must be a hope for bodily resurrection rather than some kind of disembodied immortality. He acknowledges that what is "sown" in our deaths (a physical body) is different from what is "raised" (a spiritual body). Nonetheless, this is a bodily resurrection (further evidence of the significance of human bodily existence). To help his readers understand the difference, Paul contrasts the first man, Adam, who was a "living being," with the "last Adam," Christ, who was a "life-giving spirit" (v. 45). This first man was a "man of dust," the second man is the "man of heaven." Those human beings who are not in Christ are still "of the dust" (v. 48) and will return to the dust like the first man, whereas those who are associated with Christ the man of heaven are "of heaven" and will share in his bodily resurrection. The argument climaxes: "Just as we have borne the image of the man of dust, we will [variant: let us] also bear the image of the man of heaven" (v. 49).

---

36. The theme is today largely neglected outside of Reformed theological circles. One exception is found in John Howard Yoder, *The War of the Lamb*, ed. Glen Stassen et al. (Grand Rapids: Brazos, 2009), chapter 14.

37. Besides the texts we will consider from Paul below, the development of this image in Christology is most attributable to Irenaeus. For a discussion of his contribution to this line of thought, see Kurt Anders Richardson, "Imago Dei: Anthropological and Christological Modes of Divine Self-Imagining," *Journal of Scriptural Reasoning* 4, no. 2 (October 2004).

This difficult argument seems to work like this: Genesis 1 says human beings were made in the image of God. We were creatures (created ones), yet made to be like the God who created us in a way that differentiated humans from other creatures. But under temptation Adam tragically and disobediently grasped for the godlike status that was already his as God's gift, and so humanity fell, with a great and terrible crash. Ever since the Fall, human beings have become estranged from what God made us to be, and from the God who made us.[38]

Christian traditions and theologians disagree among themselves concerning whether (or what components of) the image of God in humanity survived the Fall. Given the great significance attributed to the *imago Dei* in most discussions of the sacredness of life, this is no small matter. If the *imago Dei* was lost with the Fall, then to make contemporary moral claims based on the *imago Dei* is entirely illegitimate, at least from a Christian perspective.

A review of the creeds and confessions of the church reminds us that the focus of Christian theology is properly and has always been the saving activity of God in Christ, not fine details concerning human nature. However, the general pattern in relation to our question appears to be that Catholic tradition affirms a weakened but still present *imago Dei* even in fallen humanity and uses it today to ground its human rights and human dignity claims;[39] Eastern Orthodox theology draws a distinction between "image" and "likeness" to claim that humans always retain God's image but can lose God's likeness by choosing evil;[40] and Reformed Protestant theology (especially Lutheran thought) tends toward a stance in which the image of God was entirely destroyed with the Fall, so it is dubious about grounding moral claims on the *imago Dei*.[41] Dietrich Bonhoeffer, for example, says that the image of God was totally "lost" when Adam fell: "Hu-

38. I acknowledge that the very notion of a "fall" is a particular theological construction of Gen. 1–3, and that it cannot be taken for granted. However, it is central to the Christian theological traditions we are considering here.

39. "Created in the image of the one God and equally endowed with rational souls, all men have the same nature and the same origin." *Catechism of the Catholic Church* (New York: Doubleday, 1995), article 1934, p. 522.

40. Timothy Ware, *The Orthodox Church* (London: Penguin, 1993), p. 219, and Lossky, *Orthodox Theology*, pp. 128-29.

41. Martin Luther, *Luther's Works*, vol. 1, ed. Jaroslav Pelikan, trans. George V. Schink (St. Louis: Concordia, 1958), pp. 63-64. For this summary I acknowledge with gratitude Rev. Angus Stewart, "The Image of God in Man: A Reformed Reassessment," accessed online at http://www.cprf.co.uk/articles/imageofgod.htm, July 8, 2009.

man beings have lost their own, God-like essence, which they had from God. They now live without their essential purpose, that of being the image of God. Human beings live without being truly human."[42] He therefore does not make moral arguments based on the *imago Dei.*

My reading of Scripture is that even after sin enters the picture, the *imago Dei* is affirmed in passing in Genesis 5:1-2 and affirmed *theologically* in Genesis 9:5-6. Human beings are still described as *imago Dei* creatures in the same primeval history in which the story of human sin is introduced, and the image of God still grounds claims about human life's God-given value.

Our main interest here is how Paul seems to be reworking the theme in an important way. Ever since Adam sinned, whatever one may say about the image of God in humanity, human beings have existed in the *image of Adam,* the first man. Then God sent Jesus Christ into the world. He was truly human. But he was also the "man from heaven." Those who belong to Christ now receive the benefit of the *imago Christi.* One aspect of that image is his spiritual body; for example, spiritual-bodily resurrection. If the majority reading of 1 Corinthians 15:49 is accepted, the text stands in the indicative: "we will also bear the image of the man of heaven." If the variant reading is accepted, the meaning shifts to the imperative: "let us bear the image of the man of heaven." The former seems more appropriate to the context of Paul's argument in 1 Corinthians. The latter is certainly plausible; those who belong to Christ *should* bear the *imago Christi* in their pattern of living. As we are transformed, we (are to) become more and more like Jesus Christ, the "man of heaven," and less and less like Adam, the "man of dust" (1 Cor. 15:48).

But what is the content of this *imago Christi?* The author of Colossians, possibly Paul, states straightforwardly that Jesus Christ "is the image of the invisible God, the firstborn of all creation" (Col. 1:15). Colossians goes on to enumerate aspects of Christ's nature and work including his role in shaping and sustaining creation, his headship of the church, his reconciling death on the cross, and his trailblazing resurrection from the dead (vv. 16-20). If Jesus is now the *eikon tou theou,* what has happened to the Genesis declaration that human beings were made in that image of God? Perhaps this: if considered sequentially in salvation history, Jesus Christ *repairs and restores* the image of God in fallen humanity. Human beings can at last be what they were made to be because Jesus has made it possible. Je-

42. Bonhoeffer, *Discipleship,* p. 282.

sus assumed the image of humanity, indeed, the humblest form of humanity (Rom. 8:3/Phil. 2:1-11). While doing so he perfectly embodied the image of God in humanity, and restored humanity to its divinely intended nature. And Jesus has gathered to himself and around himself and in himself a community that shares in the capacity to do the same through the Spirit's power at work in them.

If viewed in terms of the mystery of the preexistent Christ and the triune God, the Son of God always was and always will be "the image of the invisible God." He has always defined what it means both to be God and to be human. He is where perfect divinity and perfect humanity meet and are exhibited. On this reading, when human beings were made in the image of God, *it always was the image of Christ in which and for which they were made.* He has always defined what humanity is to be. But only in "the last days" has he walked the earth and dwelt among us, publicly displaying in his life, death, and resurrection what it means to be truly human.

Bonhoeffer emphasizes that the work of Christ is a fact, a reality that has its effect whether particular people respond or do not. Christ's incarnation has restored the image of God in all humanity, regardless of whether people believe in Christ or not. And for Bonhoeffer, this has profound moral implications: "In Christ's incarnation all of humanity regains the dignity of bearing the image of God. Whoever from now on attacks the least of the people attacks Christ, who took on human form and who in himself has restored the image of God for all who bear a human countenance."[43]

So Christians are not the only beneficiaries of this restorative work of Christ. But we Christians are that community that gazes "with unveiled faces" at Jesus Christ (2 Cor. 3:18). When we look directly at the divine through the face of Jesus, we do not perish, unlike in the days of Moses. Our gaze at Jesus Christ transforms rather than destroys us. We "are being transformed into the same image from one degree of glory to another," and the image we see of ourselves "as though reflected in a mirror" is the image of Jesus Christ (2 Cor. 3:18). The more we look at him, the more like him we become, the more the form of our life takes the form of his life. The "light of the gospel of the glory of Christ, who is the image of God" (2 Cor. 4:4), changes us. We become who we were meant to be, and are "conformed to the image of his Son" (Rom. 8:29), who is the firstborn of "a large family" filled with people who share the image of the One who is the image of God. This is how God is reconstructing the world — by gathering

---

43. Bonhoeffer, *Discipleship*, p. 285.

a family of people who conform to the image of the Son, who conforms to the image of his Father.

The author of Hebrews continues the Pauline theme in saying that Jesus is "the reflection of God's glory and the exact imprint of God's very being" (Heb. 1:3). Jesus is the image of God. Human beings were made in the image of God. Jesus incarnates that image. In so doing he has demonstrated the possibilities available to every human as God intended — we were made to reflect God's glory and bear God's imprint. Since sin entered the world, we have borne its shattering consequences. But in Christ, the image of God has been restored, and now human beings are invited into their own personal instantiation of Christ's image. In the church, at least a part of the human race, according to the New Testament, is even now being restored to its original majesty. One New Testament term given to this is "sanctification" — a process of becoming more holy, more like God, and more like God intended human life to be from the beginning.[44]

The New Testament discussion of the image of Christ clarifies and confirms the distinction between *sacredness* and *sanctity*, offered in chapter 1 (puzzle #6). All human beings are *ascribed sacredness* by God, and gain the divinely given status and protections that go with it. The image of God exists in people no matter what they do with their lives. One justification for that claim is Old Testament teaching about the image of God in Genesis 9, which is used to ground the ban on the murder of any person. Human beings, however, are also invited to *achieve sanctity*, which means reaching the full moral potential God intended in creating humanity. Jesus Christ is the only human who has reached that potential, but the church exists as a community seeking to conform to the image of Christ. The apostolic indicative voice proclaims that this conformation to the image of Christ is a fact. The apostolic imperative calls for followers of Christ to cooperate with a Christ-shaped transformative process, always remembering that the agent of this transformation is Christ, who seeks to take shape and form in us.[45]

The church is not different in status before God, as if only those who are in the church and are actually making progress in conforming to the

---

44. For one excellent discussion of sanctification, see Richard F. Lovelace, *Dynamics of Spiritual Life* (Downers Grove, Ill.: InterVarsity, 1979), pp. 102-19.

45. For the language of Christ taking form in us, see Bonhoeffer, *Discipleship*, p. 285. For a careful analysis of the entire process of growth in Christian maturity, see James George Samra, *Being Conformed to Christ in Community: A Study of Maturity, Maturation, and the Local Church in the Undisputed Pauline Epistles* (London: T. & T. Clark, 2006).

image of Christ are viewed as persons of worth. The church is instead that community that goes ahead of the rest of humanity in *seeing realities that others do not yet see, and behaving accordingly.* So the church, the body of Christ, is a pioneering community determined to treat all human beings with a dignity proper to the redemptive work that God has done on humanity's behalf in Jesus Christ, even where others have not said yes to God. Again, we listen to Bonhoeffer: "Inasmuch as we participate in Christ, the incarnate one, we also have a part in all of humanity, which is borne by him. . . . Our new humanity now also consists in bearing the troubles and the sins of all others. The incarnate one transforms his disciples into brothers and sisters of all human beings. The 'philanthropy' (Titus 3:4) of God that became evident in the incarnation of Christ is the reason for Christians to love every human being on earth as a brother or sister."[46]

3.4. The Expansive Reach of the Body of Christ

We have been considering certain rather subtle implications of New Testament teachings concerning transformed human existence in Christ. Now let us briefly sketch ways in which early Christian communities embodied (or were instructed to embody) an expansive vision of the sacredness of human life. The primary evidence we have for the extent to which the early church moved in this direction can be found in the New Testament itself.

The book of Acts depicts a rapidly growing church led by the Holy Spirit toward an ever-more inclusive and hospitable community ethos. The initial community of approximately 120, gathered around the bereft eleven apostles (Acts 1:15), quickly expands into the thousands after the coming of the Holy Spirit at Pentecost (2:1-13). The Spirit-instilled ability to tell the story of Jesus in multiple languages leads to the conversion of "devout Jews from every nation under heaven" (2:5). What had initially been a "Hebrew" Jewish community of Christ-followers rapidly expands to include large numbers of "Hellenists," that is, Greek-speaking Jewish Christians (6:1). The tensions involved in integrating and meeting the needs of this newly diverse community are portrayed honestly in Acts 6. The gospel next spreads through the ministry of Philip to neighboring Samaria, whose inhabitants were despised, as we have seen, by most Jews

---

46. Bonhoeffer, *Discipleship*, p. 285.

(Acts 8). The Jew/non-Jew barrier has been breached to include the anomalous Samaritans; soon enough it is shattered as the gospel is taken to Gentiles, beginning with the conversion of the Roman centurion Cornelius (Acts 10–11). The transition is accomplished via Peter's agonizing struggle to reconcile the divine voice demanding an end to categorizing not just Gentile food but Gentile people as "profane or unclean" (10:28) with biblical laws that had seemed to demand precisely that kind of categorization.[47] When law and divine voice collide, the latter prevails, and the church is opened to the Gentiles.

The rest of Acts and much of the rest of the New Testament tell the story of the progressive spread of Christian faith to both Jews and Gentiles throughout the ancient world. Opening the church to Gentiles, and not requiring them to live according to the strictures of Jewish law, was clearly the most contested decision of the early church era. Traces of that contest are clearly visible throughout the writings of the New Testament, especially in Paul, the most aggressive exponent of this vision.[48]

Paul also offers the most expansive theological effort to defend this revolutionary transformation of relationships between Jews and Gentiles. His oft-quoted words in Galatians 3 are nothing short of breathtaking in their context: "There is no longer Jew or Greek, there is no longer slave or free, there is no longer male and female; for all of you are one in Christ Jesus" (Gal. 3:28). Paul has worked out a new theological anthropology, or perhaps better, a theological ecclesiology, in which all humanly significant distinctions are transfigured and overcome by and in and through Jesus Christ. Clearly the root distinction to be overcome for this once-most-passionate Jewish leader is that barrier that divides Jew and Gentile. Now Christ "has made both groups into one and has broken down the dividing

---

47. This line is very important: "God has shown me that I should not call anyone profane or unclean" (Acts 10:28). Peter's amazed declaration concerning what God is teaching him marks a major breakthrough in the early Christian movement. It is not a long step from his statement to its correlated positive formulation: "God has taught us to call all human beings sacred."

48. The New Testament gives evidence of the early church wrestling toward creating a new kind of community that includes both Jews and Gentiles who believe in Jesus Christ. This was quite an accomplishment. But honesty compels that I name our first New Testament countermotif right here: the New Testament is not always quite so sanguine about Jews who do not believe in Jesus. The problem seems especially acute in the Gospel of John, but there are problematic texts elsewhere as well. Certainly Christianity later developed a disastrous tradition of anti-Judaism (contempt for Jewish faith) and anti-Semitism (contempt for Jewish people). I will offer a detailed examination of this issue in chapter 6.

wall . . . the hostility between us" (Eph. 2:14).[49] This revolutionary sacrificial peacemaking (Eph. 2:16-17) on Christ's part then lays the groundwork for all other distinction-shattering. If even Jews and Gentiles can now be "one new humanity" (Eph. 2:15), other distinctions can and must also fall — between male and female,[50] slave and free,[51] and so on. In Christ, we are one new humanity, and this is what ultimately matters. God has begun to reclaim this divided world and to bring peace to its warring members through the peace and unity now available in Jesus Christ.

The early church's ecstatic experience of the Holy Spirit, poured out upon both sons and daughters, young and old, slave and free (Acts 2:17-18), combined with its Spirit-led decision to shatter the Jew-Gentile boundary line, combined also perhaps with the special appeal of its message to those most hurting and vulnerable, created powerful momentum toward radically inclusive and egalitarian community. This would be a multiethnic, multilinguistic, multiracial, gender-inclusive, class-inclusive community, and a community that would not accept the dehumanization and

49. New Testament scholars continue to argue about Pauline authorship of Ephesians, but do see deep Pauline influence in this epistle.

50. Second countermotif: the literary witness of the early church shows that it did not fully eliminate the second-class status of women as found in Judaism and the Greco-Roman world, but it did make real progress in that direction. Women's dramatic inclusion in communities of early Christians did not eliminate questions about, and differences regarding, leadership roles in the life of the church (cf. 1 Cor. 11:3-10; 14:33-34; 1 Tim. 2:11-15), nor did it create a fully or universally egalitarian understanding of male and female roles in marriage (Eph. 5:21-33; Col. 3:18-19), though it did soften the hard edges of patriarchalism. The literature on this issue is vast. One especially valuable work is Craig S. Keener, *Paul, Women, and Wives* (Peabody, Mass.: Hendrickson, 1992). My view of what the New Testament says is found in Glen H. Stassen and David P. Gushee, *Kingdom Ethics: Following Jesus in Contemporary Context* (Downers Grove, Ill.: InterVarsity, 2003), chapter 15.

51. Third countermotif: New Testament teachings enjoin slaves to obey their masters (Eph. 6:5; Col. 3:22; 1 Tim. 6:1; Titus 2:9; 1 Pet. 2:18). These teachings were (of course) deployed by Christian slaveholders in North America and elsewhere to compel submission to their often cruel rule. These slaveholders often failed to acknowledge that the same New Testament texts urged masters to be kind and just and to remember that "you also have a Master in heaven" (Col. 4:1), undercutting cruel absolutism and tyranny. Paul's letter to Philemon is a fascinating example of this undercutting process at work. The literature on this issue is vast as well, but seems to me to yield the conclusion that Christian leaders whose writings made it into the canon urged a softening of the cruelties of slavery while offering a logic of God's sovereignty and every person's worth that undercut the logic of slavery altogether. See William J. Webb, *Slaves, Women, and Homosexuals* (Downers Grove, Ill.: InterVarsity, 2001), for one fine treatment, as well as Willard Swartley, *Slavery, Sabbath, War, and Women* (Scottdale, Pa.: Herald, 1982).

degradation of any category of people, as occurred all around it in the Greco-Roman world. It would also be a community committed to pressing toward enemy-love, in obedience to Christ. What mattered was not how enemies treat Christians, but how Jesus responded when he was mistreated (1 Pet. 2:21-25). When reviled and abused, we must not return evil for evil but should instead walk "in his steps" (1 Pet. 2:21) in patient endurance and forgiving love.[52] Reminded that "while we were enemies, we were reconciled to God through the death of his Son" (Rom. 5:10), as Christians we are both grateful for that reconciliation and called to our own "ministry of reconciliation" (2 Cor. 5:18). This is why "we regard no one from a human point of view" (2 Cor. 5:16). All the old divisions have passed away, and there is "a new creation . . . everything has become new!" (2 Cor. 5:17).

What ultimately emerged were congregations that believed that in their own experience of transformed human relations lay the beginnings of the redemption of the world. Their leaders addressed them with such seriousness on these points because so very much was at stake. Christ came, died, and rose again. The world at large remains in the grip of dark forces, of principalities and powers, and evidences evil at every turn; and yet in Christian churches new seedlings of eschatological community can be found — and must be protected. Here rich and poor, young and old, male and female, Jew and Greek, slave and free, celebrated God's transforming love in Jesus Christ. And before this love all stood equally needy, equally blessed, and equally overwhelmed with gratitude. Until Christ returned, these communities would seek to live in love toward one another and to all. Instructed to avoid all forms of malice and ill-will to anyone, Christians would instead seek and contribute only good to their neighbors — beginning with their near neighbors in Christian community but extending far beyond "the household of faith." They would do so until Christ returned, the hope of which was often invoked as ground and motive for their way of life.

---

52. Final possible countermotif: the book of Revelation does not seem to exude the patient love described here. This is clearly the work of a church under persecution, enduring extreme suffering, hurt and angry at the cruelties and martyrdoms it was experiencing. And yet the apocalyptic holy war imagined in Revelation involves Christ's death ("the lamb who was slain") and the church's continued faithfulness to his way, and certainly offers no authorization for Christians to take up arms. It was a word of encouragement, comfort, and promise to a martyred church, as well as a stark condemnation of imperial Rome and its cruelties. See Richard Bauckham, *The Climax of Prophecy* (Edinburgh: T. & T. Clark, 1993).

3.5. The New Testament and the Sacredness of Life: A Dialogue with Richard Hays

Near the end of his magisterial *Moral Vision of the New Testament*, Duke University scholar Richard Hays, whom I respect highly, says that "the 'sacredness of life' is a sacred cow that has no basis in the New Testament."[53] He makes this claim near the end of his brief chapter on abortion, in a section in which he lists certain "argumentative strategies [that] cannot be accommodated within the symbolic world rendered by the New Testament."[54] To buttress this claim, Hays draws on a quote from his colleague Stanley Hauerwas to the effect that Christians must oppose the taking of life not because of its inherent value but because God is sovereign over all life and thus human life is not ours to take.

I hope that during the course of these two chapters it has become clear that belief in the sacredness of human life — rightly understood — is no mere "sacred cow." These two chapters have filled out the often sketchy claims of adherents to a sacredness-of-life ethic related to the biblical basis of their beliefs (puzzle #17). I have sought to show that in multiple strands of Scripture and above all in Jesus Christ, God has indeed declared and demonstrated the sacred worth of human beings in his sight. This worth is entirely a divine ascription, not tied to our purported capacities, not tied to anything "inherent" or achieved by human beings, but rooted in God's relationship to humanity, his decisions, declarations, and commands toward us. At least, I believe that is the best reading of the scriptural evidence we have reviewed, as well as the dangers we must avoid.

This aspect of divine revelation gave birth to a moral tradition that has powerfully shaped the church and all civilizations affected by the church. That tradition taught Christians to adopt a posture of reverence toward all human beings; to accept responsibility to care for all, and especially the most marginal among humanity; and to stand against the wanton destruction and degradation of human life. It also led to a commitment to human flourishing. These convictions motivated a permanent Christian interest in life-sustaining ministries such as feeding the poor, life-saving ministries such as health care, and life-enriching ministries such as education and the arts.

Writing in 1996, undoubtedly weary of the Christian Right, Hays ap-

---

53. Hays, *Moral Vision*, p. 454.
54. Hays, *Moral Vision*, p. 454.

pears to have been responding to the shallow and politicized version of language about life's sacredness that I also have strongly critiqued. He may also be picking up a strand of Christian thought that dismisses all rights-claims and any other public ethical claims that sound as if they are related to Enlightenment liberalism rather than a theocentric Christian ethic. We will see in the next three chapters the complex historical trajectory that has contributed to such confusions. I will try to show in chapters 4 through 6 that the moral conviction that each and every human life is of equal and incalculable value is embedded in the Christian faith and goes with Christianity wherever it goes — even when Christian people fail to live up to its implications, as is so often the case.

Chapter 7, in turn, will show how epic Christian failures contributed to the secularization of belief in the sacredness of life so that its theological roots became even more deeply buried, underground and beyond inspection. Eventually, the idea that God has demonstrated and declared the sacred worth of the human person gives way to talk about more abstract moral and legal norms. The biblical roots of these norms became so deeply invisible (or contemptible) to those who advocated for them from the Enlightenment period forward that the norms themselves eventually became viewed as secular or Enlightenment products — eventually evoking a theological backlash on the part of some Christians. The backlash against such norms took far more disastrous shape in some of the intellectual and political movements of the nineteenth and twentieth centuries, as will be discussed in chapters 8 and 9.[55] This is a caution for those who still participate in that backlash. But that is to get ahead of our story.

---

55. Every Christian should read Fritz Stern's *Politics of Cultural Despair: A Study in the Rise of the Germanic Ideology* (Berkeley and Los Angeles: University of California Press, 1961), if tempted toward a solely reactionary position in relation to culture.

4. The Sacredness of Life in Early Christianity

For think not that stones, and stocks, and birds, and serpents are sacred things, and men are not; but, on the contrary, regard men as truly sacred, and take beasts and stones for what they are.

Clement of Alexandria

4.1. The Christendom Question

An acute paradox has become visible in contemporary Christian writings about the history of the church. It is a paradox extraordinarily relevant to our study of the sacredness of life as a central moral norm in Christian thought.

It seems most of the highly regarded thinkers in progressive Christianity attack the history of the church, at least after the conversion of Constantine, as at best a detour from the church's originally peaceable and liberating vision, and at worst a grotesque moral capitulation to violence and imperialism. Often this is coupled with an implicit or explicit contemporary critique of the United States as an imperialist *faux* Christian superpower, and American Christianity as far too long infected by a Constantinian-style Christianity that has underwritten that imperialism. I think here of the work of Christian ethicists such as John Howard Yoder and Stanley Hauerwas; biblical scholars such as John Dominic Crossan, Richard Horsley, and Neil Elliott; pastors such as Gregory Boyd; and younger evangelical Christian activists such as Shane Claiborne.[1] Despite

1. See John Howard Yoder, *The War of the Lamb*, ed. Glen Stassen et al. (Grand Rapids:

116

various differences in background and perspective, all seem to agree that when Christianity became Christendom, or "Christian civilization," the church (despite exceptions) fell into a desperate moral confusion that essentially destroyed its moral witness. Such criticisms are all the more intense when offered by leading feminist theologians such as Rosemary Radford Ruether, African American thinkers such as Howard Thurman, liberationist theologians such as Gustavo Gutiérrez and other Latinos/ Latinas, and numerous Native American theologians and postcolonial thinkers,[2] all of whom link Christendom with the historic experiences of subjugation and abuse endured by so many women, African slaves, indigenous peoples, and colonized lands.

On the other hand, one finds a number of culturally more conservative Christian thinkers whose writings generally celebrate the achievements of Christendom, its positive legacy to Western civilization, and (at times) the general superiority of Christian/Western civilization over other alternatives. Baylor University sociologist Rodney Stark comes to mind, with his publication of books with titles like *The Victory of Reason: How Christianity Led to Freedom, Capitalism, and Western Success.*[3] Catholic contributions to Western culture have been celebrated by Thomas Woods in *How the Catholic Church Built Western Civilization,*[4] and recent Catholic leaders such as the current Pope Benedict often have sought to highlight the con-

---

Brazos, 2009), and numerous other works; Stanley Hauerwas, *After Christendom?* (Nashville: Abingdon, 1991), among other works; John Dominic Crossan, *God and Empire: Jesus against Rome, Then and Now* (New York: HarperCollins, 2007); Richard A. Horsley, ed., *In the Shadow of Empire: Reclaiming the Bible as a History of Faithful Resistance* (Louisville and London: Westminster John Knox, 2008); Neil Elliott, *The Arrogance of Nations: Reading Romans in the Shadow of Empire* (Minneapolis: Fortress, 2008); Gregory A. Boyd, *The Myth of a Christian Nation: How the Quest for Political Power Is Destroying the Church* (Grand Rapids: Zondervan, 2005); and Shane Claiborne and Chris Haw, *Jesus for President* (Grand Rapids: Zondervan, 2008).

2. See, for example, Rosemary Radford Ruether, *America, Amerikkka: Elect Nation and Imperial Violence* (London: Equinox Publishing, 2007); Howard Thurman, *Jesus and the Disinherited* (Richmond, Ind.: Friends United Press, [1949] 1981); Gustavo Gutiérrez, *A Theology of Liberation* (Maryknoll, N.Y.: Orbis, 1973); Vine Deloria et al., *God Is Red: A Native View of Religion,* 30th anniversary ed. (Golden, Colo.: Fulcrum Publishing, 2003); and Catherine Keller, Michael Nausner, and Rivera Mayra, *Postcolonial Theologies: Divinity and Empire* (St. Louis: Chalice, 2004).

3. Rodney Stark, *The Victory of Reason: How Christianity Led to Freedom, Capitalism, and Western Success* (New York: Random House, 2005).

4. Thomas E. Woods Jr., *How the Catholic Church Built Western Civilization* (Washington, D.C.: Regnery, 2005).

structive and even indispensable contributions of Christianity to European culture.[5] One finds books like Robert Royal's *The God That Did Not Fail* and Jonathan Hill's *What Has Christianity Ever Done for Us?*, with the answer being quite a lot, really, including the arts, education, philosophy, morality, and politics.[6] Popular American conservative activist-authors such as the late Chuck Colson and Richard John Neuhaus have tended to focus on the constructive public contributions of Christianity to the United States and other Western nations and to lament Christianity's declining influence.[7] Anti-imperialist and postcolonial critiques of Great Britain and now the United States have evoked responses from those, like Britain's Niall Ferguson, who have sought to identify and defend the positive legacies of their nations in the many lands they touched during the colonial ascendancy, while also acknowledging the wrongs done.[8] Defending Christianity, always a popular cottage industry within certain sectors of contemporary evangelicalism, has come to be understood in many culturally and politically conservative Christian quarters as defending the legacy of Christian/Western civilization and of historically Christian lands against our cultured despisers, angry atheists, or Islamist religious enemies, all of whom, if successful, would eventually eliminate the positive cultural legacy of Christianity.[9]

It might be easy to dismiss such defenders of Christendom as retrograde reactionaries. But one is brought up short by discovering similar themes in the work of a theological giant like Dietrich Bonhoeffer. In the

5. Sometimes this case is made in ways starkly counter to the received secular wisdom about the role of the church in history. For example, Pope Benedict has argued that Christianity played an indispensable role in creating and sustaining the concept of freedom of conscience in Western culture. For a discussion, see Fr. Vincent Twomey, S.V.D., "Pope Benedict XVI on Conscience," accessed at http://www.catholicculture.org/culture/library/view .cfm?recnum=8598, February 17, 2010.

6. Robert Royal, *The God That Did Not Fail: How Religion Built and Sustains the West* (New York: Encounter Books, 2006); Jonathan Hill, *What Has Christianity Ever Done for Us?* (Downers Grove, Ill.: InterVarsity, 2005).

7. Charles Colson, with Ellen Santilli Vaughn, *God and Government* (Grand Rapids: Zondervan, 2005); Richard John Neuhaus, *The Naked Public Square* (Grand Rapids: Eerdmans, 1984).

8. Niall Ferguson, *Empire: How Britain Made the Modern World* (London: Penguin Books, 2003).

9. An influential contribution to the idea of starkly different world civilizations rooted in culture and religion was made by Samuel P. Huntington in his controversial book, *The Clash of Civilizations and the Remaking of World Order* (New York: Simon and Schuster, 1996).

striking "Heritage and Decay" essay in his *Ethics*,[10] Bonhoeffer reflects back on a cultural legacy he still understands as "western history," rooting that history in the centuries-long legacy of Jesus Christ. By this Bonhoeffer means to include the "Israelite-Jewish people" from whom Jesus Christ emerged, the classical Greco-Roman world that first rejected and eventually embraced Christ, and the history that flowed forward in Western cultures via this Jewish-Christian-Greek-Roman synthesis. And he means to correct anti-Semitic and Nazi mythology that excluded the crucial Hebraic contributions to Western culture, as part of the overall project of pushing the Jewish people entirely out of Germany and Europe — the project that culminated in their mass murder.

Bonhoeffer apparently finalized this essay sometime in late 1941, in a Nazi Germany that had begun to make the horrifying transition to total extermination of the Jewish people, beginning on the eastern front.[11] Reading his culture with crystalline clarity, Bonhoeffer contrasts the cultural heritage built on Jesus Christ with the disastrous ideology that had overtaken his nation. In the shadow of Nazism, Bonhoeffer sees in Western history, by contrast, cultural patterns that once reflected a deeply embedded belief in God-in-Christ and contained constructive moral resources based on that belief. These patterns, according to Bonhoeffer (speaking in a sad past tense), had marked off Western culture in important ways from other cultures. For example, he claims that

> Western war has always distinguished between what is permitted and prohibited, between just and criminal means of warfare. The renunciation of perhaps effective but criminal means — killing of innocents, torture, extortion, and so on — was possible on the basis of faith in a just divine rule of the world. War was always something like an appeal to divine judgment to which both sides were willing to bow. Only when Christian faith in God is lost do people feel compelled to make use of

10. Dietrich Bonhoeffer, *Ethics*, vol. 4 of *Dietrich Bonhoeffer Works* (Minneapolis: Fortress, 2005). The "Heritage and Decay" essay is found on pp. 103-33 and will be cited in-text.

11. This analysis is derived from careful study of the footnotes in the recent English edition of *Ethics*. See notes 9, 24-28. See also the editors' "Afterword," pp. 422-23, which suggests that Bonhoeffer began "Heritage and Decay" in the autumn of 1940 and edited it in the autumn of 1941. The first draft was thus written after the invasion of Poland with its vast atrocities; the second after the invasion of the Soviet Union with its even greater and more systematic mass killings, as well as the first public deportations of Berlin Jews to the east. For more, see chapter 9.

all means — even criminal — to force the victory of their cause. (pp. 109-10)

Bonhoeffer is probably talking here in a thinly veiled way about Hitler's war of annihilation on the eastern front with the Soviet Union, which began when Germany invaded on June 22, 1941. He may also have known about the systematic mass shootings of Jews already under way there. Bonhoeffer is here proposing that these atrocities stand in radical discontinuity with the history of the Christian West. Bonhoeffer does not offer an uncritical celebration of Western Christian history; nor does he reject every intellectual development since that time. But he is able to articulate in a way that few could the conviction that then-current "Western godlessness" (p. 122) is a nihilistic force that threatens to consume everything in its wake: "Uncontrolled powers clash with each other. Everything that exists is threatened with annihilation. This is not just one crisis among others, but a conflict of ultimate seriousness" (p. 127). He believes that Nazism represents a total negation of a four-thousand-year-old cultural legacy related inextricably to Jesus Christ.[12] He sees that such ideologies threaten to destroy that cultural legacy and an immense number of human beings as well. Four years later, the total body count of World War II was approximately 55,000,000. Bonhoeffer sensed the opening of that abyss.

I want to explore in the next three chapters whether God's revealed will that every human life be treated as sacred survived the emergence of a religion called Christianity (puzzle #16). In this chapter I will consider the witness of the church prior to Constantine's embrace of Christianity. In the next two chapters I will explore what happened in post-Constantinian Christendom. By **Christendom** I refer to *lands that adopted orthodox Christianity as their official religion, beginning with the late Roman Empire, then its successor European states, and finally the lands colonized by Europeans beginning in the fifteenth century.* I will be speaking of those lands in which most of the people would have understood the term "Christian kingdom," "Christian nation," or "Christian civilization" as an accurate or desirable description of who they were or sought to be. Such a concept survived in Europe until World War II, and even in the officially separationist United States the concept survives to some extent to this day.

I have already signaled the thesis-antithesis-synthesis paradigm that

---

12. We will complicate Bonhoeffer's account when, in chapter 9, we review evidence that Hitler actually believed that he was doing God's will and representing the true spirit of Jesus.

strikes me as the most accurate approach. Stated starkly for clarity, the thesis is that in Christendom, the constant employment of violence in the name of God marked a negation of the ethic taught and lived by Jesus Christ, including the sacredness of each and every human life. The antithesis is that in Christendom, Christ's ethic valuing human life was largely affirmed and advanced, in ways that positively mark Western culture to this day. *My synthesis-hypothesis is that in Christendom, the sacredness ethic was both negated and advanced; everywhere that Christian civilization traveled, so did the elevating and the desecrating of human life.*

*   *   *

I suggested in the last chapter a number of powerful factors that led to the emergence of a church that treated all human life with reverence. These included the nature of Christ's ministry, the church's theological reflection on the deepest meaning of the incarnation, and the Spirit's direction of the church into a posture of expansive, inclusive, and hospitable community. These factors are both reflected in the descriptive dimension of New Testament texts and required in the hortative teachings. The earliest followers of Jesus were, and were called to be, communities that learned how to value human life in a way that often set them radically apart from their neighbors. They were not perfect, but they were visibly different from their cultural peers in valuing life's sacredness. They invited others to consider and to embrace their way of life and the Lord to whom they were devoted, but they continued in their steadfast way even as others rejected it. This was a countercultural ethic lived by a small religious minority (puzzle #13).

As our gaze extends beyond the New Testament, the literary evidence for a peculiarly reverential treatment of human life by the early Christians remains quite strong. Those Christian leaders who sought to instruct Christians on the nature of their way of life, or who sought to defend Christian morality against the cultured despisers of their own time, left numerous traces of this vision. In what follows, I will offer a large number of representative quotations from a diverse array of the early church's leaders, serving all over the Greco-Roman world.[13] These will give us a significant glimpse into the moral vision church leaders sought to imprint on the faithful.

---

13. When possible, primary sources are cited in the text from the *Ante-Nicene Fathers* collection, edited by Alexander Roberts and James Donaldson (Buffalo: Christian Literature Publishing Co., 1885), hereafter *ANF*, followed by volume and page number. Other primary texts are footnoted. Archaic formulations ("thee," "thou shouldst," etc.) are updated.

4.2. The Church against War

The earliest Christians are instructed repeatedly by numerous key leaders that killing is forbidden to followers of Christ, and these instructions had their effect. Christian nonparticipation in the Roman military and resistance to the evils of war were one result. Philip Wogaman reflects what remains the majority view when he claims that "no Christian is known to have served in the imperial armies until about AD 170,"[14] though after that the situation was more mixed, as were the pastoral responses.[15] We know that at least a small number of Christians participated tenuously in branches of the Roman military by the late second and then in the third century; we know this mainly because some began to be martyred in persecutions during and after that time.[16] Still, the early church leaders from whom we have surviving writings did not rest easy with Christian involvement in government (with its use of violence), military service, and especially warfare, and for most of early church history all three were forbidden to Christians by their pastors. Consider the exhortations offered by some of the early church's most revered leaders, from all over the Christian world:

We who were filled with war, and mutual slaughter, and every wickedness, have each through the whole earth changed our warlike weapons

14. J. Philip Wogaman, *Christian Ethics: A Historical Introduction* (Louisville: Westminster John Knox, 1993), p. 32. The question becomes more complex later, as gradually some Christians did serve in the Roman military, even before the conversion of Constantine. There were, for example, military martyrs in the church in the early fourth century. For competing perspectives on the evidence, see Frances M. Young, "The Early Church: Military Service, War and Peace," *Theology* 92, no. 750 (November 1, 1989): 491, and Alan Kreider, "Rediscovering Our Heritage: The Pacifism of the Early Church," in *Waging Peace*, ed. Jim Wallis (San Francisco: Harper and Row, 1982), p. 122. These sources and others offer considerable discussion not just about whether, how, and why Christians served in the Roman military but also about the various factors that affected their decision making about this critical issue, including the corrupting religious effects of military service in a pagan empire.

15. Summarizing recent research, Kirk MacGregor argues that it is "relatively noncontroversial" to now assert that "no Christians served in the military or assumed government offices" from the close of the New Testament era until 174 C.E., and that after 174, "the ancient church treated those Christians who played such roles, including previous officeholders who converted, with great suspicion." Kirk R. MacGregor, "Nonviolence in the Ancient Church and Christian Obedience," *Themelios* 33, no. 1 (2008): 16-17.

16. Roland Bainton, *Christian Attitudes toward War and Peace* (Nashville: Abingdon, 1960), p. 68. Some of the instructions in this section are clearly directed to Christians attempting to serve in the Roman military without violating their faith and its commitments.

— our swords into ploughshares, and our spears into implements of tillage — and we cultivate piety, righteousness, philanthropy, faith, and hope.

Justin Martyr (100-165), *Dialogue with Trypho,* ANF 1:254[17]

For it is not in war, but in peace, that we are trained. War needs great preparation, and luxury craves profusion; but peace and love, simple and quiet sisters, require no arms nor excessive preparation.

Clement of Alexandria (150-211), *The Instructor,* ANF 2:234-35

Now inquiry is made about this point, whether a believer may turn himself unto military service, and whether the military may be admitted unto the faith, even the rank and file, or each inferior grade, to whom there is no necessity for taking part in sacrifices or capital punishment. There is no agreement between the divine and the human sacrament, the standard of Christ and the standard of the devil, the camp of light and the camp of darkness. One soul cannot be due two masters — God and Caesar. . . . How will a Christian man war, nay, how will he serve even in peace, without a sword, which the Lord has taken away? . . . The Lord . . . in disarming Peter, unbelted every soldier.

Tertullian (160-225), *On Idolatry,* ANF 3:73[18]

A soldier, being inferior in rank to God, must not kill anyone. If ordered to, he must not carry out the order, nor may he take an oath to do so. If he does not accept this, let him be dismissed from the church. . . . Any catechumen or believer who wishes to become a soldier must be dismissed from the church because they have despised God.

Hippolytus (170-236), *The Apostolic Tradition* 16.17-19[19]

---

17. MacGregor points out that Justin Martyr is probably referencing a large number of conversions from paganism to Christianity that had occurred among Roman soldiers. These soldiers had risked everything to leave the army and join the church. MacGregor, "Nonviolence," p. 18.

18. "Sacrament" is a translation of the Latin *sacramentum,* probably meaning here a military oath. Significantly, Tertullian is saying that the military oath/sacrament and the Christian oath/sacrament are incompatible.

19. Translation by MacGregor, "Nonviolence," p. 22.

For we must delightfully come to the counsels of Jesus by cutting down our hostile and impudent swords into plowshares and transforming into pruning-hooks the spears formerly employed in war. So we no longer take up the sword against nations, nor do we learn war anymore, since we have become children of peace, for the sake of Jesus, who is our leader.

Origen (185-254), *Against Celsus,* ANF 4:558[20]

For since we . . . have learned from His teaching and His laws that evil ought not to be requited with evil, that it is better to suffer wrong than to inflict it, that we should rather shed our own blood than stain our hands and our conscience with that of another, an ungrateful world is now for a long period enjoying a benefit from Christ, inasmuch as by His means the rage of savage ferocity has been softened, and has begun to withhold hostile hands from the blood of a fellow-creature.

Arnobius (ca. 300), *Against the Heathen,* ANF 6:415

These representative selections of early Christian moral teaching focus not so much on what Rome is doing as on what kind of community the church of Jesus Christ is called to be. The church includes some who have previously fought and killed, but they laid aside their weapons of war once they were called into the service of Christ. Christ is the one and only Lord whom Christians may obey, and Christ has made his will clear on the matter of war through both his example and his teaching. He now trains a peaceful army of love and service to others, a community willing to bear violence for his name but not to inflict violence on others. Arnobius is among the Christian writers who point to positive social consequences of a growing faith-community that by means of Christ has tamed the "savage ferocity" and violence within its midst, though he expects little gratitude for this very real social benefit — and that is not the reason for the church's opposition to war.

4.3. The Church against Abortion and Infanticide

This absolute loyalty to Jesus requires abstaining not only from war but also from *abortion, abandonment of infants ("exposure"), and direct infanti-*

20. Translation by MacGregor, "Nonviolence," p. 24.

cide.[21] These were quite common practices in the Greco-Roman world, and had especially devastating effects on women and female children.[22] Under Roman law, the father was granted extensive power over the members of his household. This could include the power to kill, abandon, or sell his child or to order any female in his household to abort, which involved primitive methods that often ended women's lives or ruined their health.[23] But for Christians, the child's life too was sacred, even in the womb and in infancy, as was the life of the woman carrying the child. For both Jews and Christians, abortion and infanticide were absolutely banned, a fact that remains highly important for those Christians today who oppose abortion as a violation of life's sacredness (puzzle #3).[24] Here are a few of the many surviving Christian texts:

Practice no magic, sorcery, abortion, or infanticide.

The Didache[25]

You shall love your neighbor more than your own soul. You shall not slay the child by procuring abortion; nor again, shall you destroy it after it is born.

Epistle of Barnabas (ca. 100), *ANF* 1:148

21. Robin Lane Fox has written, "Like the Jews, Christians opposed much in the accepted practice of the pagan world. They vigorously attacked infanticide and the exposure of children." Robin Lane Fox, *Pagans and Christians* (San Francisco: Harper and Row, 1986), p. 351. See also Michael J. Gorman, *Abortion and the Early Church: Christian, Jewish, and Pagan Attitudes in the Greco-Roman World* (Eugene, Oreg.: Wipf and Stock, 1998).

22. Rodney Stark, *The Rise of Christianity* (New York: HarperCollins, 1996), p. 97.

23. Stark, *The Rise of Christianity*, p. 120. A substantial literature about infanticide has been developed among classicists, with special debate as to how often it was practiced in Roman culture, and for what reasons. The evidence appears to be clear that deformed or disabled infants were sometimes "exposed," along with those conceived by rape or incest or in cases of poverty. The principle of *patria potestas* did allow a father to kill his own children. Christianity rejected this principle and any moral legitimacy for infanticide, first in its own communities and then in society when Christianity had power to affect laws in the Roman state. See J. R. Sallares, "Infanticide," in *The Oxford Classical Dictionary*, ed. Simon Hornblower and Antony Spawforth, 3rd ed. (Oxford and New York: Oxford University Press, 1996), p. 757. I am grateful to Brian Messner for his help in clarifying this issue.

24. Josephus, quoted in Stark, *The Rise of Christianity*, p. 124.

25. Probably dated to the late first century. See Maxwell Staniforth and Andrew Louth, trans. and eds., *Early Christian Writings: The Apostolic Fathers* (London: Penguin Books, 1987), p. 191.

But as for us, we have been taught that to expose newly-born children is the part of wicked men; and this we have been taught lest we should do any one an injury; and lest we should sin against God.

Justin Martyr (110-165), *First Apology*, ANF 1:172

We say that those women who use drugs to bring on an abortion commit murder, and will have to give an account to God for the abortion . . . [for we] regard the very fetus in the womb as a created being, and therefore an object of God's care . . . and [we do not] expose an infant, because those who expose them are chargeable with child-murder.

Athenagoras (ca. 177), *A Plea for the Christians*, ANF 2:147

In our case, murder being once for all forbidden, we may not destroy even the fetus in the womb. . . . To hinder a birth is merely a speedier man-killing; nor does it matter whether you take away a life that is born, or destroy one that is coming to the birth.

Tertullian (160-225), *Apology*, ANF 3:25

Without pressing these quotes too far, it is striking that these early Christian proscriptions of abortion do not draw a meaningful distinction between a "fetus" and a "child," and certainly not between a "human being" and a "person" (puzzle #8). The developing child is a "neighbor" like any other neighbor and must be spared killing accordingly. Killing of the fetal/child neighbor is described as "murder" unequivocally, which is quite striking and certainly less restrained than the language most often used in our own time, even by many who oppose abortion. Abortion, infanticide, and exposure are treated as equivalent sins against God and neighbor.

4.4. The Church against Judicial Torment and Killing

This opposition to bloodshed extended to *all forms of killing*, even capital punishment, which was one reason for opposition to service in the military and in the government, both of which employed the death penalty:

We cannot endure even to see a man put to death, though justly.

Athenagoras, *A Plea for the Christians*, ANF 2:147

Note the mention of other horrendous features of the criminal "justice" system in this statement by Tertullian:

> Shall it be held lawful to make an occupation of the sword, when the Lord proclaims that he who uses the sword shall perish by the sword? And shall the son of peace take part in the battle when it does not become him even to sue at law? And shall he apply the chain, and the prison, and the torture, and the punishment, who is not an avenger even of his own wrongs?
>
> Tertullian (160-225), *The Chaplet, ANF* 3:99

Athenagoras seems to recognize a distinction between just and unjust exercise of the death penalty, presumably tied to the actual guilt or innocence of the condemned. But he describes an alternative community unable or unwilling to "endure" the sight of anyone's life being ended. Tertullian's comment is extremely relevant not just to the death penalty, but also to the broader dehumanization and mistreatment of prisoners, including torture. Tertullian also speaks of a particular, distinct community, which cannot countenance or participate in routine social practices of its culture due to fidelity to its Lord. The church, for both of these writers, is simply *not the kind of people* that can witness or participate in the horrors of what passed for a criminal justice system.

4.5. The Church against the Mayhem of the Arenas

Early Christian writings also took aim at the bloody spectacle of the gladiator games, and at eating the meat of slaughtered animals. These comments speak acutely to our culture's attraction to violent, bloody entertainment spectacles, contrasting sharply with an alternative Christian way of life. These are words of social criticism, which carry the integrity and power of leaders speaking for communities that refuse to participate in such practices.

> Do such exhibitions as these redound to your credit? He who is chief among you collects a legion of blood-stained murderers, engaging to maintain them; and these ruffians are sent forth by him, and you assemble at the spectacle to be judges . . . and he who misses the murderous exhibition is grieved, because he was not doomed to be a spectator

of wicked and impious and abominable deeds. You slaughter animals for the purpose of eating their flesh, and you purchase men to supply a cannibal banquet for the soul, nourishing it by the most impious bloodshedding.

Tatian (110-172), *To the Greeks, ANF* 2:75

Blush for your vile ways before the Christians, who have not even the blood of animals at their meals of simple and natural food.

Tertullian (160-225), *Apology, ANF* 3:25

The chaos and misery of humanity's constant bloodshed are often decried by early Christian leaders:

The whole world is wet with mutual blood; and murder, which in the case of an individual is admitted to be a crime, is called a virtue when it is committed wholesale.

Cyprian of Carthage (ca. 250), *Epistle, ANF* 5:277

4.6. "Regard People as Truly Sacred"

Christians take a different path, because of the value they place on human life, a value itself derived from God's high valuing of all people. Consider the following two very important texts, which explicitly use the language of sacredness. These are among the most important statements to be found anywhere in Christian history on the issue we are considering in this book. The first is from Lactantius (240-317). The late date is significant, for a rise in the number and power of Christians had not affected his view:

Thus it will be neither lawful for a just man to engage in warfare . . . nor to accuse any one of a capital charge, because it makes no difference whether you put a man to death by word, or rather by the sword, since it is the act of putting to death itself which is prohibited. Therefore, with regard to this precept of God, there ought to be no exception at all; but that it is always unlawful to put to death a man, whom God willed to be a *sacred animal.*

Lactantius, *Institutes* 6.20, *ANF* 7:187, italics added

For think not that stones, and stocks, and birds, and serpents are sacred things, and men are not; but, on the contrary, *regard men as truly sacred, and take beasts and stones for what they are.*

> Clement of Alexandria (150-211),
> *Exhortation to the Heathen, ANF* 2:201, italics added

4.7. An Army of Peace and Piety

Martial imagery is often transfigured in Christian moral rhetoric to suggest that the Christian posture is different because Christians follow a different commander, serve in a different army, and pursue a different mission. Apologists often claim that this alternative Lord, community, and mission actually serve the broader community — but they do so in the face of fierce criticisms to the contrary:

> The loud trumpet, when sounded, collects the soldiers and proclaims war. And shall not Christ, breathing a strain of peace to the ends of the earth, gather together His own soldiers, the soldiers of peace? Well, by His blood, and by the word, He has gathered the bloodless host of peace, and assigned to them the kingdom of heaven. The trumpet of Christ is His Gospel. He hath blown it and we have heard. "Let us array ourselves in the armor of peace."

> Clement of Alexandria (150-211), *Exhortation to the Heathen* 2:204

> And as we by our prayers vanquish all demons who stir up war . . . we in this way are much more helpful to the kings than those who go into the field to fight for them. . . . And none fight better for the king than we do. We do not indeed fight under him, although he require it; but we fight on his behalf, forming a special army — an army of piety — by offering our prayers to God.

> Origen (185-254), *Against Celsus, ANF* 4:668

4.8. Love without Partiality

Christian leaders instruct their followers not only to refrain from killing, but also in humility[26] to *love all without partiality, as God is without partiality,* and as Jesus was recognized even by his critics to be one who showed "deference to no one; for you do not regard people with partiality" (Matt. 22:16; cf. Acts 10:34-35).[27] In a society torn by social status distinctions, here was the germ of a Christian social revolution that elevated the status of the poor, enemies, women, children, the sick, the disabled, those considered physically ugly, the enslaved, and all who stood at the bottom of the social hierarchy. Robin Lane Fox considers this Christian conviction a key reason for the spread of Christianity in a Greco-Roman world increasingly resentful of status hierarchies.[28] It was not so much that Christians had such an attractive theological message as that they were, by their striking communal way of life, such enormously attractive messengers.[29] Even if at the time Christians did not (and could not) destroy such entrenched social structures as slavery and patriarchy, primal Christian norms such as the demand to treat all without partiality, and the experience of congregations in which women and men, highborn and lowborn, slave and free, worshiped and served one another side by side, were at least a "first step"[30] toward undercutting these structures at their foundations. This first step has been described as an "inner revolution . . . which must necessarily produce in time a corresponding change in all external social and economic relationships."[31] Consider, then, the following typical exhortations that subtly initiated this great social revolution:

---

26. Robin Lane Fox points out the revolutionary nature of the early Christian emphasis on voluntary humility in a pagan culture that heretofore had never considered humility a virtue, but instead an aspect of being ignoble, low, or unworthy. See Fox, *Pagans and Christians,* p. 324.

27. Note the link between humility and being "no respecters of persons." Christians were to view neither themselves nor anyone else as "higher" or "lower" than others. See Robert Bruce Mullin, *A Short World History of Christianity* (Louisville: Westminster John Knox, 2008), p. 39. Compare Paul Hanly Furfey, "Social Action in the Early Church, 30-180 A.D.," *Theological Studies* 2, no. 2 (1941): 90.

28. Fox, *Pagans and Christians,* pp. 334-35.

29. I am grateful to church historian Andrea Strübind for this insight.

30. Wogaman, *Christian Ethics,* p. 29.

31. Christopher Dawson, *The Formation of Christendom* (San Francisco: Ignatius, [1965] 2008), p. 128.

See then, dear friends, what a great and wondrous thing love is. Its perfection is beyond all words. Who is fit to be called its possessor, but those whom God deems worthy? Let us beg and implore of his mercy that we may be purged of all earthly preferences for this man or that, and be found faultless in love.

Clement of Rome (30-100), *First Epistle to the Corinthians*[32]

You shall not issue orders with bitterness to your maidservant or your manservant, who trust in the same God, lest you should not reverence the God who is above both; for he came to call men not according to their outward appearance, but according as the Spirit had prepared them.

Epistle of Barnabas (ca. 100), ANF 1:148

It is not by ruling over his neighbors, or by seeking to hold the supremacy over those that are weaker, or by being rich, and showing violence towards those that are inferior, that happiness is found; nor can anyone by these things become an imitator of God. . . . On the contrary he who takes upon himself the burden of his neighbor; he who, in whatever respect he may be superior, is ready to benefit another who is deficient; he who, whatsoever things he has received from God, by distributing these to the needy becomes a god to those who receive; he is an imitator of God.

Epistle to Diognetus (ca. 130), ANF 1:29

Thus we admit all who desire to hear, even old women and striplings; and in short, persons of every age are treated by us with respect. . . . We do not test them by their looks, nor do we judge of those who come to us by their outward appearance.

Tatian (110-172), *To the Greeks,* ANF 2:78

That [Christian] faith is the one universal salvation of humanity; and . . . there is the same equality before the righteous and loving God, and the same fellowship between Him and all.

Clement of Alexandria (150-211), *The Instructor,* ANF 2:217

32. In Staniforth and Louth, *Early Christian Writings,* p. 43.

We never do good with respect of persons; for in our own interest we conduct ourselves as those who take no payment either of praise or premium from man, but from God, who both requires and remunerates an impartial benevolence. We are the same to emperors as to our ordinary neighbors. For we are equally forbidden to wish ill, to do ill, to speak ill, to think ill of all men.

Tertullian (160-225), *Apology, ANF* 3:44-45

4.9. Sojourners of Christ

Defending the overall Christian way of life, one writer described followers of Christ with these famous words:

They dwell in their own countries, but simply as sojourners. As citizens, they share in all things with others, and yet endure all things as if foreigners. . . . They marry, as do all; they beget children; but they do not destroy their offspring. They have a common table, but not a common bed. They are in the flesh, but they do not live after the flesh. . . . They obey the prescribed laws, and at the same time surpass the laws by their lives. They love all men, and are persecuted by all . . . they are put to death, and restored to life. They are poor, yet make many rich.

Epistle to Diognetus (ca. 130), *ANF* 1:26-27

Others summarized it this way:

We who valued above all things the acquisition of wealth and possessions, now bring what we have into a common stock, and communicate to everyone in need; we who hated and destroyed one another, on account of their different manners would not live with men of a different tribe, now . . . live familiarly with them, and pray for our enemies, and endeavor to persuade those who hate us unjustly to live in conformity to the good precepts of Christ, to the end that they may become partakers with us of the same joyful hope of a reward from God the ruler of all.

Justin Martyr (100-165), *First Apology, ANF* 1:167

For [our funds] are not taken thence and spent on feasts, and drinking bouts, and eating houses, but to support and bury poor people, to supply the wants of boys and girls destitute of means and parents, and of old persons confined to the house; such too as have suffered shipwreck; and if there happen to be any in the mines, or banished to the islands, or shut up in the prisons for nothing but their fidelity to the cause of God's Church, they become nurslings of their confession.

Tertullian (160-225), *Apology, ANF* 3:46

This care extended beyond the boundaries of the Christian community:

There is nothing remarkable in cherishing merely our own people with the due attentions of love, but that one might become perfect who should do something more than heathen men or publicans, one who, overcoming evil with good, and practicing a merciful kindness like that of God, should love his enemies as well. . . . Thus the good was done to all men, not merely to the household of faith.

Cyprian (200-258), *Epistle to the Carthaginians*[33]

These literary traces depict communities of Christians who consecrate life. These Christians view everyone they encounter with reverence, even as "sacred," in the words of Lactantius and Athenagoras quoted above. This is a community that holds loosely to national or ethnic identities as subordinate to their primary identity as followers of Jesus Christ. They humbly welcome and serve the poor, the sick, the enslaved, and the imprisoned.[34] They treat people without partiality because God also views and treats people that way. They are committed to the preservation of human life and do not participate in its destruction in any form or at any stage. They are unafraid to die for Christ or in service to others but are never willing to kill, and they understand that Christ was likewise willing to die for the world's salvation but never to kill.

Rodney Stark offers an apt summary of the picture available from these Christian documents. "Perhaps above all else, Christianity brought a new conception of humanity to a world saturated with capricious cruelty and

---

33. Quoted in Stark, *The Rise of Christianity,* p. 212.

34. Mullin, *Short World History,* p. 40, suggests that Christian care for the sick was a major contributor to the spread of Christianity, and stood in marked contrast with the pagan abandonment of the sick during epidemics and plagues.

the vicarious love of death. . . . Christians effectively promulgated a moral vision utterly incompatible with the casual cruelty of pagan custom. . . . [W]hat Christianity gave to its converts was nothing less than their humanity."[35]

4.10. Christians as the Romans Saw Them

Is this a truthful picture of how the earliest Christians scattered around the Greco-Roman world actually lived? Historical sources from the Christian side are mainly available precisely in the form of the exhortations just encountered as well as in apologetic documents. Yet there is evidence from the Greco-Roman side as well, beginning early in the second century.[36] Especially in the earliest days of Christianity, Christians were viewed as a Jewish sect indistinguishable from other expressions of Judaism, and some of the charges brought against Christians paralleled older charges against Jews — who had been negotiating the pressures of first Greek and then Roman culture for three hundred years.[37] These included accusations of "atheism," *amixia* (failure to mingle, or participate), and *misanthropia* ("hatred of humankind"),[38] as well as criticisms for refusing to serve in the Roman military. Jews and Christians shared an unwillingness to participate in the very many Roman social activities that were tainted by pagan worship practices, which were pervasive. But both also shared a deeper unwillingness to compromise their loyalty to God.

Roman authorities and cultural leaders were deeply concerned that this steadfast refusal to acknowledge the traditional Roman gods undermined cultural unity and perhaps even risked divine retaliation, including the catastrophic collapse of the Roman world order.[39] Where they had reluctantly granted Jews a special exemption from most religio-social expectations due

35. Stark, *The Rise of Christianity,* pp. 214-15.

36. Robert L. Wilken, *The Christians as the Romans Saw Them* (New Haven and London: Yale University Press, 1984), p. 31.

37. See Luke Timothy Johnson, *Among the Gentiles: Greco-Roman Religion and Christianity* (New Haven and London: Yale University Press, 2009), chapter 8.

38. Tacitus, *Annals* 15.44, quoted in Justo L. González, *The Story of Christianity,* vol. 1 (New York: HarperCollins, 1984), p. 35.

39. Howard Clark Kee et al., eds., *Christianity: A Social and Cultural History* (Upper Saddle River, N.J.: Prentice-Hall, 1998), p. 67. Compare W. H. C. Frend, *The Early Church* (Philadelphia: Fortress, 1982), p. 9.

to their antiquity as a distinct people who had once also been a nation with a land, Roman leaders did not want to grant the same exemption to the newer, transnational Christian movement. Robert Wilken names the broader issue well when he suggests that the most perceptive Roman observers discerned that Christianity was a subversive new kind of religion in how it was genuinely severed from the way of life of any particular nation, tribe, or people. Christians were a weird new "third race" distinct from pagans and Jews and scattered around the known world.[40] Here was a religion that by its very self-definition and structure sat loosely with national loyalties of all types, which made it inherently destabilizing to the established social order of the Greco-Roman world.[41]

Even those critiquing the Christian movement occasionally reported or revealed at least a grudging respect for the internal life of Christian communities. Pliny, a provincial governor, in 110 noted the strict moral code, weekly shared meals, and high internal cohesion of the Christians even as he worried over what to do about them.[42] The second-century Roman satirist Lucian was struck by the internal solidarity among Christians, their economic sharing, fearlessness in the face of death, and intense commitment to Jesus and his way of life, even while lampooning what he considered their strange beliefs.[43] The Christian leader Tertullian wrote that the pagan crowds would shout "See how they love one another" of Christians brought to die in the arenas, evidence of a kind of awe at the manner of life of the Christians dying before their eyes.[44] The revanchist late-fourth-century pagan emperor Julian complained that Christianity was growing because of its adherents' "benevolence toward strangers and care for the graves of the dead," and he fumed that "the impious Galileans support not only their poor, but ours as well."[45]

On the other hand, the most vicious rumors about Christian behavior also circulated, treating the misunderstood rites and practices of these close-knit Christian communities in their private gatherings as occasions for orgies, incest, infanticide, cannibalism, and more.[46] These charges were easy to refute, and those written refutations provide some of the docu-

---

40. Fox, *Pagans and Christians*, quoting Tertullian, p. 325.
41. Wilken, *The Christians*, p. 124. Celsus is credited with this key insight.
42. Kee, *Christianity*, p. 23.
43. Kee, *Christianity*, p. 64.
44. Cited by Fox, *Pagans and Christians*, p. 324.
45. Quoted by Stark, *The Rise of Christianity*, p. 84.
46. Fox, *Pagans and Christians*, p. 427.

ments we have already seen related to the actual Christian way of life, helping to reinforce our confidence that Christians most of the time actually
lived in a way that aligned with the exhortations and descriptions of these
early Christian texts.

Rodney Stark sums up the nature of the Christian way of life and the
difference Christianity made in the chaotic and miserable cities of the Roman Empire:

> Christianity revitalized life in Greco-Roman cities by providing new
> norms and new kinds of social relationships able to cope with many ur-
> gent urban problems. To cities filled with the homeless and impover-
> ished, Christianity offered charity as well as hope. To cities filled with
> newcomers and strangers, Christianity offered an immediate basis for at-
> tachments. To cities filled with orphans and widows, Christianity pro-
> vided a new and expanded sense of family. To cities torn by violent eth-
> nic strife, Christianity offered a new basis for social solidarity. And to
> cities faced with epidemics, fires, and earthquakes, Christianity offered
> effective nursing services. . . . No wonder the early Christian missionaries
> were so warmly received. . . . For what they brought was not simply an
> urban movement, but a *new culture* capable of making life in Greco-
> Roman cities more tolerable.[47]

4.11. How the Early Church Retained Its Moral Vision

The attractiveness of this way of life against the backdrop of the available
alternatives contributed to the rapid expansion of Christianity in the late
third century and finally to its fateful adoption by the emperor Constantine. We will consider the implications of that transition in Christianity's
status in the next chapter. Our task in the remainder of this one is to consider whether there were factors "wired in" to early Christianity that enabled it to retain this distinctive character. I propose the following five factors that seem most significant.

*a. Their interpretation of reality within the Jewish-Christian narrative
framework of the reign of God, and their attempt to embody that reality in
the churches*

47. Stark, *The Rise of Christianity,* pp. 162-63, italics in original.

Justo González rightly emphasizes that the earliest Christians did not see themselves as founding a new religion but as celebrating God's fulfillment of his long-awaited promise to redeem Israel.[48] Primitive Christianity began as a species of Jewish apocalyptic, and emerged on a kind of parallel track to other forms of Jewish apocalyptic religion swirling about during this dramatic period in Jewish and world history.[49] Christians believed themselves to be living through the joyful fulfillment of Israel's covenant with God, most crucially the promise of a God-sent Messiah who would help

> "his servant Israel,
>   in remembrance of his mercy,
> according to the promise he made to our ancestors,
>   to Abraham and to his descendants forever." (Luke 1:54-55)

In Christ the reign of God has broken in, and not just Israel but the whole world is now being redeemed.

This kingly reign of God proclaimed and inaugurated by Jesus was at least initially understood to be a concrete reality in which the world actually begins to be characterized by justice, peace, and the deliverance of the oppressed rather than its oppressive daily injustice, violence, and bondage.[50] It is striking that over 120 years later Justin Martyr articulated that same kingdom vision when defending Christianity against charges of sedition in a letter to the emperor Antoninus Pius. Christians were not seditious; instead, as Kirk MacGregor summarizes his message, Christians "lived as citizens . . . of an already inaugurated divine kingdom, presently ruled by Christ from the heavenly realm and soon to be physically implemented when Christ returns."[51]

The fact that the life, death, and resurrection of Jesus the Christ by no means brought an end to the world's evils led to a focus not just on the return of Christ but also on the quality of Christian moral living. I would argue that a robust countercultural, or even counterworldly, ecclesiological practice became theologically necessary, or else the kingdom claims of Jesus and his earliest followers could not be sustained. As historian Christo-

---

48. González, *The Story of Christianity*, p. 31.

49. This is now widely recognized — a nice, fairly early statement of the issue is in Dawson, *The Formation of Christendom*, pp. 93-110.

50. Frend, *The Early Church*, p. 47, says the Bar Kokhba revolt killed Jewish apocalyptic and affected Christian apocalyptic as well.

51. Summarized in MacGregor, "Nonviolence," p. 17.

pher Dawson put it, "The Church which was constituted by the outpouring of the Holy Spirit at Pentecost . . . was the organ of the kingdom in a special sense, since it was the body of Christ and it was in and through the Church that Jesus established his kingdom on earth."[52] This expectation for the role of the church both required and created the theological space for the evolution of churches into alternative communities that in their life embodied the evidence of God's reign.

In short: *the kingdom was the Christian story; living into its reality was the purpose of Christian existence; and the church was the embodied platform for this apocalyptic experiment in human community, until Christ returned.* The earliest Christians remained tethered to this founding Jewish-Christian narrative of the in-breaking reign of God and to their exalted role in the churches as embodying that reign until the Lord returned for his final victory.[53]

With the passing of time the role of this kingdom narrative inevitably faded, and new converts from the Greco-Roman world had little feel for Jewish apocalyptic.[54] Eschatological expectations shifted to a focus on the church's vindication at the Great Judgment and the believer's entry into the blessedness of eternal life. The understanding of the relationship between the church and the kingdom also tended to shift, with a general trend toward a heightened focus on the church *as* the kingdom of God on earth rather than as the *agent* of the kingdom of God. Still, the founding apocalyptic-messianic kingdom narrative left its mark on emerging orthodox Christianity. Christians would tell a story about Christ as King and about his already/not yet kingdom, and would live as "the society of the world to come" amidst the "debris of a wrecked world"[55] even while they awaited the full transition to the new aeon.[56] This was their story, and for a

52. Dawson, *The Formation of Christendom*, p. 96.

53. If Rodney Stark is correct about the likely strong ties and even blurred identities between Jews and Christians throughout the period under consideration here, this would increase the plausibility of my claim that Jesus' version of Jewish apocalyptic messianism would still hold meaningful resonances long after and far beyond his time and place. Stark, *The Rise of Christianity*, chapter 3.

54. Fox, *Pagans and Christians*, pp. 333-34.

55. Dawson, *The Formation of Christendom*, p. 101.

56. Contrary to Stark's hypothesis, most scholars have held that the pressure of the Jewish-Christian schism increased the temptation for Christians to slip free of the Jewishness of their founding narrative very early. Marcion is the most extreme embodiment. See Mullin, *Short World History*, p. 29. The authoritative decision to keep the Old Testament helped stave off the utter loss of Christianity's Jewish roots and kingdom narrative, at least for a while.

very long time they would reject any other "master narrative" relating a competing interpretation of reality.

b. The looming centrality of their beloved Jesus, his teachings and example
The New Testament and later writings of the early church are suffused by the impact of Jesus Christ. Almost all the earliest Christian teaching documents contain numerous allusions to the teachings and examples of Jesus. Some teaching texts are little more than collected sayings of Jesus. The Sermon on the Mount is especially central in early Christian teaching, with allusions to these teachings both in the New Testament and in countless postcanonical teaching documents. It is not accidental that communities steeped in Jesus' teachings would become committed to advancing the vision announced there: the steadfast rejection of violence; the tender care for children; the welcoming inclusion of "sinners," the weak, the ill, women, Gentiles, and servants; the resolute impartiality and fearlessness in the face of hierarchies of power; and above all, the command to love God and neighbor with every fiber of one's being (cf. Matt. 22:34-40).[57]

Everything that Jesus taught he also exemplified. The powerful congruence between Jesus' life and his teachings intensified the impact of both. The teachings could be read in light of the life and the life in light of the teachings, and both blazed the trail for the believers to follow. Jesus had incarnated his teachings and thus demonstrated the possibility and path of that embodiment for others. Early Christians were called to imitate Jesus, not just obey him.[58]

And this was a Jesus who was *loved,* not just imitated. To allude to Jewish philosopher Martin Buber, we can say that for the earliest Christians Jesus was the ultimate *Thou.*[59] He was a Savior to be loved, not just a teacher of truths, founder of a religion, or center of a faith. He was adored, worshiped, cherished, and clung to; he was alive, more real than any other reality. The power of this personal attachment to a beloved and living Jesus must not be underestimated.

---

57. Mullin, *Short World History*, p. 39, says it is *love* that truly sets Christian teaching about both God and ethics apart from paganism. Wogaman, *Christian Ethics*, p. 35, and Bainton, *Christian Attitudes*, p. 77, concur.

58. This is the central theme of the recent text in New Testament ethics by Richard A. Burridge, *Imitating Jesus: An Inclusive Approach to New Testament Ethics* (Grand Rapids: Eerdmans, 2007).

59. Martin Buber, *I and Thou* (New York: Simon and Schuster, 1970).

c. Their carefully maintained distance from Greco-Roman culture and its practices and concurrent protection of Christian identity

Greco-Roman writers excoriated both Jews and Christians for their social distancing strategies, which both groups found necessary to develop to protect their distinctive identity amidst Greek and later Roman cultural hegemony.[60] For Christians, in great continuity with Jews, this social distancing was pivotal in enabling the formation of communities that remembered their primary loyalty to Jesus Christ and primary narrative of the kingdom of God. It was not just that the Christians sought to avoid participation in the pervasive Greco-Roman religious associations, public rituals, and worship practices; they sought to avoid acculturation to the broader Greco-Roman way of life insofar as it contradicted Christian identity.[61] As Kenneth Scott Latourette has said of the early church: "They would not compromise with paganism, but held themselves apart from it, and in so doing withdrew from much of current society."[62] This distancing began when Christianity was primarily a Jewish movement and reflected the views and strategies long held by diaspora Judaism. But it continued when the transition to a primarily Gentile Christianity occurred.[63] This is how Christopher Dawson summarizes the matter: "The early Church could not but be conscious that she was separated by an infinite gulf from this great material order [of Rome], and that she could have no part in its prosperity or in its injustice. She was in this world as the seed of a new order."[64]

Navigating the currents of Greco-Roman society through such social distancing required structures of community discipline to define and preserve Christian identity. One aspect of this discipline was the extraordinarily careful and lengthy preparation process for catechumens before entry into the Christian community. This two- to three-year preparation process "became . . . one of the faith's particular appeals. People felt that

---

60. Great discussion of these religious identity challenges first in Judaism and beginning with the Greeks can be found in Kee, *Christianity,* chapter 1.

61. Luke Timothy Johnson points out how very difficult it was to participate in any way in the life of Greco-Roman society without encountering the religious symbols, practices, and institutions of "the deeply enmeshed religious associations" of that society. Johnson, *Among the Gentiles,* p. 23.

62. Kenneth Scott Latourette, *A History of Christianity,* vol. 1 (New York: Harper and Row, 1975), p. 81.

63. Differences over how much distancing to maintain were of course endemic, as they are today. Consider the struggles discussed in 1 Corinthians as a signal example.

64. Dawson, *The Formation of Christendom,* p. 126.

they were exploring a deep mystery, step by step. They were advancing with a group of fellow explorers along a route which required a high moral effort."[65] Having been initiated into the community through such a disciplined process, believers were held there through not only personal loyalty but also ongoing structures of discipline and accountability.[66] It is not coincidental that early church writings, beginning with the New Testament, describe and commend internal processes for the correction of believers seen as straying from Christ's Way (Matt. 18:12-15; 1 Cor. 5; Gal. 6:1; James 5:20). Exhortations to correct the straying continue in the early post–New Testament period (cf. *Didache* 2.7; Ignatius, *To Polycarp* 2.1). Protection of doctrinal and moral purity preoccupies church leaders throughout the period we are considering. The pattern surfaces powerfully in relation to violence. Church leaders either refused to readmit to full communion in the church believers guilty of shedding blood or required a rigorous process of repentance and rehabilitation.[67] Church discipline of such rigor became central to the emerging ecclesiastical structures and their leaders as early as the late first century.[68] Such rigorism has its downside. But it helped to ensure the integrity of the distinctive Christian way of life attested here.

d. Their searing experience of persecution at Roman hands

Evidence from early Christian writings reveals a measure of respect for the general benefits of Roman rule, such as the maintenance of order and suppression of crime and piracy. This kind of general appreciation of divinely given and evangelistically providential Roman order may lie behind texts like Romans 13 and 1 Peter 2:13-17, which strongly counsel submission to government authority. That strand of thought remains visible in the Christian teaching offered in the period we are considering.[69] These kinds

65. Fox, *Pagans and Christians*, p. 317.

66. Johnson points out that both Greek and Jewish religious and philosophical movements offer examples of similar structures involving extensive probation periods, rigorous discipline, and excommunication. So we must not posit an airtight sealing off of Christianity from other religious traditions in the way they went about initiating, training, and retaining adherents, and even, at times, in the content of moral instruction. Johnson, *Among the Gentiles*, pp. 25-31.

67. MacGregor documents this. See "Nonviolence," pp. 22-23.

68. Mullin, *Short World History*, pp. 26-27, 41-42. He writes (p. 41): "The Christian community was constructed as a tightly knit fellowship, with strong and fixed boundaries between inside and outside."

69. Bainton, *Christian Attitudes*, p. 74.

of texts apparently were most often written during periods in which the Roman state was not harassing the church.

On the other hand, and entirely to be expected, the sporadic experience of imperial, provincial, local, and mob violence against Christians evoked a theological-political-ethical strand of contempt for the violence of Roman government and Greco-Roman culture.[70] One might say that the book of Revelation strand, with Rome as bloody anti-Christ, could not disappear from Christianity as long as such hostility and persecutions endured, with an appeal directly related to the viciousness of those persecutions at any given time.[71]

Thus Christopher Dawson is correct in saying that "from the beginning the pressure of external hostility and persecution [on the Church] was so great that it provided a natural barrier that separated the Christians from the rest of the Roman world."[72] Understanding the resoluteness of Christian rejection of participation in Roman social practices and governmental violence is aided immeasurably by considering briefly the persecution Christians experienced in that world from time to time. Beginning with Nero (reigned 54-68 C.E.), who slaughtered Christians for their supposed responsibility for the burning of Rome, believers sporadically but memorably endured such tortures and murders as the following, reported by the Roman historian Tacitus: "Before killing the Christians, Nero used them to amuse the people. Some were dressed in furs, to be killed by dogs. Others were crucified. Still others were set on fire early in the night, so that they might illumine it. Nero opened his own gardens for these shows, and in the circus he himself became a spectacle, for he mingled with the people dressed as a charioteer, or he rode around in his chariot."[73] This vicious round of persecutions probably took the lives of both Peter and Paul. A later first-century persecution of Christians for resisting Domitian's (81-96 C.E.) version of the emperor cult took many more martyrs. The persecution of Christians in Asia Minor during this period apparently drove the apostle John into exile and helped create the ethos for the book of Revelation.

---

70. Fox argues that most persecutions of Christians were local until at least the 250s, and that imperial authority was sometimes employed to protect Christians rather than attack them. *Pagans and Christians*, pp. 422-23.

71. A very helpful discussion of Revelation as shaping Christian ethos and practice can be seen in Wayne A. Meeks, *The Moral World of the First Christians* (Philadelphia: Westminster, 1986), pp. 143-47.

72. Dawson, *The Formation of Christendom*, p. 105.

73. *Annals* 15.44, quoted in González, *The Story of Christianity*, p. 35.

Persecutions of individual Christians resurfaced periodically but brutally across the empire, even before the emperor Decius began a centralized, concerted attack against Christianity as a religion from 250 to 251.[74] The last round of persecutions, under Diocletian (284-305) and Galerius in the early fourth century, was especially grotesque and climaxed the era of imperial terror against the church. It was the last such persecution before the age of Constantine.

As with earlier Jewish martyrs to pagan tyranny, Christian theology, identity, and community loyalty in these early centuries were deeply affected by the experience of martyrdom.[75] Among other effects, persecution required Christians to count the cost of affiliation and thus helped screen the casual out of the church. It helped believers identify even more closely with Jesus the persecuted. It seemed to confirm the truth of the biblically recorded warnings that his true followers would suffer for their faithfulness (cf. Matt. 5:10-12). It elevated martyr-heroes of courage and steadfastness whom later believers could emulate along with Jesus. Persecution forged a Christian memory of the dead that deepened identification with and loyalty to the church for all who persevered. Most germane to our purposes, it stiffened the spine of the church against any temptation to assimilate to Greco-Roman culture. And it might well have helped the church to remain crystal clear about its commitment to affirm and protect life in the teeth of such brutality, torture, and killing. That is, it did so at least until the era when Christians themselves found uses for state power and violence.[76]

e. Their relative marginality and social powerlessness

The earliest Christians were a splinter Jewish sect in the vast Roman Empire. They were initially a minority of a minority amidst the greatest power the world had ever seen. The formative childhood of the early Christian community occurred in a context of marginality. According to Rodney

74. Fox, *Pagans and Christians*, pp. 450-62.

75. Fox, *Pagans and Christians*, pp. 436-37, points out the precedent of Jewish martyrdom, especially in the Maccabean period, and some similarities in the role of martyrdom in both traditions.

76. In my *Righteous Gentiles of the Holocaust: Genocide and Moral Obligation*, 2nd ed. (Minneapolis: Paragon House, 2003), I argue that the remembered experience of religious persecution served some Christian communities during the Nazi era quite powerfully both to encourage resistance to the Holocaust and to discourage any seductions from Nazism or its collaborators.

Stark's estimate, there were only 40,000 Christians, constituting 0.07 percent of the population of the Roman Empire, as late as 150 C.E.[77] This does not mean that every Christian, or every Christian community, was utterly marginal or powerless. The situation varied in different communities and across time, and especially the social class position of the early Christians remains debated.[78] It is indisputable that Christianity was mocked by pagan critics precisely for its disproportionate appeal to those perceived as being on the margins, especially women and those of humble birth.[79]

What cannot be argued is that for its first two centuries the Christian community learned to conduct its affairs as a tiny minority without the benefit of economic and political power, and often in the teeth of such power. This apparent disadvantage, as Justo González points out, actually helped Christians avoid "spiritualiz[ing] Christian hope" or losing the powerful, mournful yearning of history's nobodies for God's coming reign.[80] I am suggesting that their relative social marginality enabled them to retain the other four essential elements of Christian distinctiveness we have been discussing — and thus their moral integrity, including their lived commitment to the sacred worth of all persons.

So this is my thesis concerning the primary elements that contributed to the uniquely powerful moral existence and witness of pre-Christendom Christians: their inhabiting of a vivid, life-shaping Jewish-Christian reign-of-God narrative; the centrality for them of their beloved Jesus and of his concrete teachings and example; their careful distance from Roman culture and immersion in a carefully guarded community identity; the searing experience of sporadic but vicious Roman persecution; and the experience of social marginality. These factors all combined to create communities that honored human life rather than destroying it, that "preached and at their best . . . practiced, love in a world of widespread brutality."[81]

In the next chapter we will consider the changes that political power brought into this moral heart of Christianity. I will suggest that the fateful Constantinian transition affected every one of these five primary elements: the central kingdom narrative changed; Jesus remained central but in ways that de-emphasized his teaching and example; and the social distance be-

---

77. Stark, *The Rise of Christianity,* p. 7.

78. González, *The Story of Christianity,* p. 91. Cf. Latourette, *A History of Christianity,* p. 80; Stark, *The Rise of Christianity,* chapter 2; Fox, *Pagans and Christians,* pp. 299-301.

79. Stark, *The Rise of Christianity,* chapter 5.

80. González, *The Story of Christianity,* p. 92.

81. Fox, *Pagans and Christians,* p. 335.

tween church and culture collapsed along with the transition from marginality to social power for the church. The era of persecution and martyrdom for the church transitioned all too quickly to the use of persecution by the state on behalf of the church. And yet the moral vision of life's sacredness so beautifully expressed and embodied in the life of the early church survived — often expressing itself in struggles against Christendom's own worst abuses.

5. The Fateful Transition to Christendom

> We command that those persons who follow this rule shall embrace the name Catholic Christians. The rest, however, whom we adjudge demented and insane, shall sustain the infamy of heretical dogmas ... and they shall be smitten first by divine vengeance and secondly by the retribution of our own initiative, which we shall assume in accordance with the divine judgment.
>
> Emperor Theodosius

From 100 to 300 C.E., according to Rodney Stark's well-known estimate, the Christian movement grew from 7,500 souls to 6.3 million, at an average growth rate of 40 percent per decade. Christians had gone from a tiny flyspeck on Rome's periphery to 10 percent of the entire population of the empire. By 300, Christians could be found almost everywhere in the empire, from Britain to India, from northern Europe to Sudan. By 350, nearly forty years after the emperor Constantine's conversion to Christianity, the number of Christians had grown to 33 million and represented over half of the empire's population.[1]

By any customary measure, Christian faith had succeeded. A small, marginal, often persecuted church had become the dominant religious community of the vast Roman Empire, and in fact spread far beyond the empire. And its numerical dominance was soon enough matched by a political rise to power that took the church from outlaw group to tolerated minority to established state religion in a mere seventy years.

1. Rodney Stark, *The Rise of Christianity* (New York: HarperCollins, 1996), p. 7. Stark's estimates are disputed and cannot be taken as conclusive.

Great success — and yet, as we saw in the last chapter, many Christian scholars have argued that this burst of numerical and political success was one of the worst things that ever happened to the Christian movement. These scholars essentially claim that the church gained the whole world but lost its soul. Another band of scholars strongly dissents from this judgment.

This chapter will clarify what exactly happened in the "Constantinian transition" and the birth of what became known as Christendom. I will try to move beyond oversimplification and stereotype to get the key facts on the table. Our ultimate purpose in entering this old debate is to advance our excavation of the history and practice of the conviction that human life was held sacred during the years of Christian cultural ascendancy.

The next chapter will offer three case studies of *Christendom divided against itself.* Having made the fateful political transition to Christendom in the Roman Empire and its successor realms, the church collectively and Christians as individuals exercised real worldly power for the first time, with significant consequences for the treatment of large numbers of human beings. In each case study, we will see disastrous "Christian" desecrations of life's sacredness; we will also see Christians who resisted these violations, embodying a life-revering vision that has left a lasting legacy. We will see Christendom desperately divided against itself, making moral errors so grave that they have stained the church's reputation to this day. But we will also see that the vision of the holy sacredness of every human life simply could not be eradicated, even in a church whose moral integrity was badly damaged by its exercise of worldly power within Christendom.

5.1. The Constantinian Transition

Though every detail of their significance is disputed, the key events in what is often called "the Constantinian transition" are well known.

Constantine came to power in the western part of the increasingly fractured Roman Empire after "the most severe persecution which Christianity had yet experienced,"[2] under Emperor Diocletian and his son-in-law Galerius, beginning in 303. Prodded by Galerius, a spate of anti-Christian decrees were offered by Diocletian. These ordered the destruction of church

---

2. Kenneth Scott Latourette, *A History of Christianity,* vol. 1 (New York: Harper and Row, 1975), p. 90.

buildings, confiscation and burning of Christian sacred texts, demoting of Christians from places of honor, loss of legal rights, reversion to enslavement for Christians who had been freed, and enslavement of Christian household servants who would not renounce their faith. A later decree ordered the imprisonment of Christian clergy; the most radical decree demanded sacrifice to the Roman gods throughout the empire on pain of imprisonment or death.[3] Thousands of Christians were executed and murdered during this reign of terror, while others died under astonishingly cruel tortures. Kenneth Scott Latourette reports that "on occasion there was wholesale slaughter," such as the time a Christian town in Asia Minor was burned to the ground together with all its inhabitants.[4] Despite being unevenly enforced, the persecution claimed lives all across the empire. It also evoked varying responses from Christians. These ranged from courageous and sometimes eager martyrdom to understandable but lamentable recantations under threat of torture, leaving the church with unforgettable heroes and major losses — as well as the task of figuring out how to respond to those members who did not bear up well under persecution.

The man we know as the emperor Constantine was the son of Constantius Chlorus, who as Caesar of the West was governing Britain, Gaul, and Spain when the persecutions were ordered by Diocletian. He seems to have largely refused to enforce the decrees, and this was the policy of his son as well when he took over upon his father's death in 306. At least in Constantine's zone of influence there would be no slaughter or torture of Christians, despite the decrees from Rome. It is not exactly clear why.

The late empire was torn by succession struggles, and that is how Constantine first enters the stage of history. Every student of church history knows the famous story of Constantine's purported embrace of Christianity as the result of his interpretation of signs received in 310 and in 312, the latter just before a critical battle in his fight to consolidate control as western emperor.[5] These signs, confirmed in Constantine's mind by his victory against the larger and stronger army of his pagan rival Maxentius at the Milvian Bridge, contributed to his personal identification with Christianity and a lifetime commitment to support and advance the church.

3. Details of the persecution summarized in Peter J. Leithart, *Defending Constantine* (Downers Grove, Ill.: InterVarsity, 2010), p. 21.

4. Latourette, *A History of Christianity*, p. 91.

5. One finds a very rich discussion of the pagan background to this experience and a creative interpretation of what it all meant to him in Robin Lane Fox, *Pagans and Christians* (San Francisco: Harper and Row, 1986), pp. 613ff.

Having consolidated power, Constantine moved quickly on the religious front. In 313, together with his eastern imperial rival Licinius, Constantine confirmed a policy of religious toleration that granted freedom of worship to Christians and others. This new policy also reversed some of the effects of the former persecution by requiring the return of confiscated goods and property to Christians throughout the empire.[6] For the first time, the Roman imperium had formally ordered the toleration of Christianity in all parts of the realm, and also required religious freedom for people of other faiths. And yet, as W. H. C. Frend has written, "the scales tipped insensibly toward Christianity."[7]

Constantine had not been baptized, but his policies advanced Christian interests. His rhetoric and public iconography were part of this advance; they leaned toward Christian imagery and belief, as he increasingly filled public spaces and public ritual with Christian architecture and imagery. Constantine also used his imperial power to decree the empire-wide abandonment of a number of the practices that Christians had most abhorred. He ended the practice of crucifixion and condemned the exposure of children. He banned the bloody gladiator shows, as well as the branding of the faces of criminals, explicitly in the name of the image of God.[8] He offered funding for the church to expand dramatically its benevolence ministries to the poor and sick. The church could not help but be overjoyed to see an end to its heartbreaking persecution, while these imperial bans on barbaric Roman practices that Christians had long criticized led Christians to rejoice that the Christian vision of respect for every human life seemed to be advancing rapidly.[9]

---

6. Historically called the Edict of Milan, the full text can be found in http://gbgm-umc .org/UMW/Bible/milan.stm, accessed March 26, 2010. This historic document is actually a letter, just two lengthy paragraphs, which requires freedom of religious worship for Christians and others, and grounds this decision in a desire to please "any Divinity whatsoever" who may reside in the heavens, to preserve good order and peace, and to uphold the dignity of subjects of various religious convictions. It followed an earlier edict of toleration by the exhausted former persecutor Galerius (in 311) that was not quite as far-reaching.

7. W. H. C. Frend, *The Early Church* (Philadelphia: Fortress, 1982), p. 124.

8. Robert Bruce Mullin, *A Short World History of Christianity* (Louisville: Westminster John Knox, 2008), p. 55. Chris Wickham, however, shows that the games continued into the early fifth century. *The Inheritance of Rome* (New York: Viking Penguin, 2009), p. 21.

9. On the other hand, Constantine remained ruthless in employing death to maintain power; for example, he had his own son Crispus killed for a supposed conspiracy against him. Justo L. González, *The Story of Christianity*, vol. 1 (New York: HarperCollins, 1984), p. 118.

If this is where Constantine's relationship with Christianity had stopped, there would be little controversy about him, and skeptics would not be talking ruefully about the Constantinian transition. But Constantine went further. His religious policy moved beyond evenhanded religious liberty and increasingly favored Christianity with imperial support. These moves included endowing and building large Christian churches,[10] financing the production of new copies of the Bible to replace those earlier destroyed, and giving the bishop of Rome a former imperial palace. Constantine revised marriage laws in a way that enshrined Christian convictions, exempted clergy and church lands from the heavy taxation and civic duties of that era (a nice inducement to join the clergy), mandated Sunday as a day of rest,[11] ordered the civic recognition of holy days on the Christian calendar, and offered bishops extensive judicial authority, including the authority to release slaves.[12] Constantine also sent his mother Helena — a longtime Christian — to Jerusalem to restore it as a Christian city. With his support, she built two great churches there, in Bethlehem and on the Mount of Olives.

In 324, after defeating the non-Christian Licinius in another imperial battle heavily marked by religious overtones, Constantine moved the capital of the empire to Byzantium, refounding it as a Christian city and "the symbol of the new Christian Roman Empire."[13] The city, soon known as Constantinople, was filled with Christian churches and other Christian symbols and spaces. Constantinople became an ornate Christian imperial city, symbolizing the dramatic transition for the church from persecution to tolerance to imperial favor.[14]

Constantine's entanglement with the church also led to his controversial intervention in internal church matters. This happened very early in his reign, when he intervened (at the repeated request of church officials)

10. Fox, *Pagans and Christians*, p. 623. "This deluge of publicity exceeded any other programme in precious stone which was realized by a ruler in antiquity."

11. However, this may have been in homage to the sun-god he (once?) worshiped more than to the Christian God. Frend, *The Early Church*, pp. 137-38.

12. Mullin, *Short World History*, pp. 54-55; Latourette, *A History of Christianity*, pp. 92-93. Christian impulses motivated the widespread release of slaves, according to Christopher Dawson, *The Formation of Christendom* (San Francisco: Ignatius, [1965] 2008), p. 138.

13. Mullin, *Short World History*, p. 55.

14. Leithart, generally a fan of Constantine, acknowledges that Constantine not only favored Christianity but also suppressed the religious practices of pagans and intensified legal limits on Jewish proselytism. He "destroyed some [pagan] temples, plundered more, [and] decreed that sacrifice should end." *Defending Constantine*, p. 302.

in the Donatist controversy in 314. This involved the question of the legitimacy of church leaders believed to have betrayed their commitment to Christ under the Diocletian persecutions. Constantine could have stayed out of this fight but, probably motivated by a desire to prevent the church from falling prey to disastrous divisions,[15] instead responded to a doomed appeal for his intervention by the Donatist party. Constantine called a meeting of the bishops at Arles, in 314. Over the next few years he and this council not only resolved the question of who would be the proper bishop from North Africa — Caecilian, against the Donatists — but in 316 Constantine also ordered the confiscation of the property of the followers of Donatus.[16] This enforcement of doctrinal decision through state sanction marked a fateful turn. Constantine here seems to have violated his own edict of religious toleration by imposing on Christian schismatics a type of punishment that not long before had fallen on Christians as a whole. In this he set an unfortunate precedent.

Less than ten years later Constantine responded to several other doctrinal disputes by calling a general council of bishops at Nicaea in 325. The main issue had to do with how to understand the divinity and humanity of Christ. For our purposes the central significance of this first ecumenical council was the very fact that it was called by Constantine and yielded results enforced by Constantine. Also, Constantine added to the church's decision to depose the Arians his own decisions to banish them from their cities and to confiscate their meeting places.[17] This was yet another major step in using the power of the state to enforce the official doctrine of the church.[18]

The fact that this first general council of bishops was attended almost exclusively by leaders from within the Roman Empire helped to solidify the identification of the Roman Empire with Christianity.[19] And the creed that

15. Leithart argues that these divisions mattered to Constantine not just politically but theologically; God might take vengeance on church, empire, and emperor for such divisions. Thus he rejects the argument, below, that Constantine was attempting to secure Roman imperial unity by deploying Christianity as a tool. *Defending Constantine,* p. 84.

16. Howard Clark Kee et al., eds., *Christianity: A Social and Cultural History* (Upper Saddle River, N.J.: Prentice-Hall, 1998), p. 106.

17. Fox, *Pagans and Christians,* p. 656.

18. Eventually Constantine reconsidered, calling for Arius's recall from exile and for the bishop of Constantinople to restore him to communion. Arius died before the bishop had to make a decision. Constantine was eventually baptized by a loyal Arian bishop, Eusebius of Nicomedia. González, *The Story of Christianity,* p. 166.

19. Kee, *Christianity,* p. 118. Bauer: From the Persian perspective, "Christianity was less a

emerged from this council helped to set a precedent in which official talk about Jesus Christ focused almost exclusively on theological details rather than on his kingdom ministry or the specific demands of his teachings.

Constantine's intervention in such doctrinal matters may provide a clue that helps us understand his embrace of Christianity. It is not that Christianity was numerically dominant in his realm — when he took power, perhaps one in ten people in the empire was a Christian, and Christians were politically quite disengaged. But Constantine may have seen in Christianity a force for unification of an empire so dangerously fragmented that its very survival was threatened. Susan Wise Bauer puts it this way: "A Christian could be a Greek or a Latin, a slave or a free man, a Jew or a Gentile. Christianity had begun as a religion with no political homeland to claim as its own, which meant that it could be adopted with ease by an Empire that swallowed up homelands as a matter of course. By transforming the Roman Empire into a Christian Empire, Constantine could unify the splintering Empire in the name of Christ, a name that might succeed where the names of Caesar and Augustus had failed."[20]

Whatever may have motivated Constantine, a unified Christianity could plausibly serve as a way to solve the worsening problem of Roman imperial and cultural disintegration.[21] Success, of course, would require a reasonably unified Christianity. But anyone very familiar with Christianity has to smile a bit ruefully at the idea that its fractious faith could be a source of unity for such a vast and diverse population. What Constantine and later rulers discovered was that if Christianity was going to function as a source of unity, emperors would have to use their coercive power to deal with Christianity's own internal tendency toward doctrinal disunity. As Christopher Dawson observes, "This concern of the emperors with the cause of religious unity led them to interfere in every theological controversy by imposing an.official solution which they then proceeded to enforce by bureaucratic action."[22] This pattern also proved fateful.

---

religion than a symbol of loyalty to the Romans." Susan Wise Bauer, *The History of the Medieval World* (New York: Norton, 2010), p. 85.

20. Bauer, *History,* p. 7.

21. Fox instead argues for the centrality of Constantine's Christian convictions and that his efforts to achieve Christian unity were motivated by "simple fears for God's anger at heresy" — that is, he fought hard for Christian unity because he saw it as his responsibility before God. Fox says that Constantine was clearly a "sincere and convinced adherent of the faith." *Pagans and Christians,* p. 658.

22. Dawson, *The Formation of Christendom,* p. 140.

Constantine died in 337. He was honored by the church as a saint in the city renamed Constantinople in his honor.[23] His patronage of the church probably assured not only its survival but also its growth into one of the world's largest religious communities. His legislation offered the church the opportunity to replace routine pagan barbarisms with its more exalted understanding of human life. It is an unfortunate telescoping of history to pin all that went wrong later in Christendom onto Constantine himself. He *was* the first ruler to kill under the banner of Christ, and he certainly had plenty of blood on his hands throughout his reign. He *was* the first to establish an imperial entanglement with the church. But Constantine did not manifest most of the worst desecrations later undertaken in the name of a Christian state.

The centuries-long struggle between Christianity and the pre-Christian pagan gods flared again during the brief reign of the emperor Julian ("the Apostate," to Christian history), who in 362-363 sought to return the Roman Empire to classic Roman paganism. He did not embark on a persecution of the church, but he did strip it of many of its privileges and sought to revive both the spirit and the practices of the old Roman religion.[24] He failed, dying in battle in 363, but the pre-Christian religions of the ancient Greco-Roman world continued to have adherents well into the fifth century. Augustine (354-430) felt it necessary to devote considerable attention in his writings to defending Christian faith against its still-vocal pagan critics. This helps us understand that the Constantinian transition did not lead directly or ineradicably to the establishment of a securely Christian Roman Empire.

5.2. Theodosius Mandates Orthodox Christianity

It was really the ardently orthodox Christian emperor Theodosius (379-395) who took the steps that we now think of as constituting the full "Christianization" of the Roman Empire. It was Theodosius, not Constantine, who first used the power of the state to ban entirely both unorthodox Christian beliefs and the old Roman religion. He was the first to declare

---

23. And the Roman Senate declared him a pagan god — a nice indicator of the complexity and confusion around Constantine's faith and legacy, then and now. González, *The Story of Christianity*, p. 123.

24. See the thoughtful discussion in Robert L. Wilken, *The Christians as the Romans Saw Them* (New Haven and London: Yale University Press, 1984), chapter 7.

(Nicene) Christianity the official state religion of the empire, and he also outlawed Arianism, the heterodox Christian movement that continued to have many adherents, including numerous priests and their entire congregations. His decree in this regard (in 380) threatened both divine and human punishments for continued unorthodox practice:

> It is our will that all the peoples who are ruled by . . . Our Clemency shall practice that religion which the divine Peter the Apostle transmitted to the Romans. . . . We command that those persons who follow this rule shall embrace the name Catholic Christians. The rest, however, whom we adjudge demented and insane, shall sustain the infamy of heretical dogmas . . . and they shall be smitten first by divine vengeance and secondly by the retribution of our own initiative, which we shall assume in accordance with the divine judgment.[25]

In 381 Theodosius followed the example of Constantine and called an ecumenical council, the second, at Constantinople. This new council further clarified Christian doctrine, including reaffirming that Arianism was a heresy. Theodosius followed up with Arianism's total disestablishment and with the confiscation of its church properties.

Theodosius also went beyond Constantine when he banned the sacrifices and religious rituals of the old Roman religions and closed their ancient temples and monuments. By 388 he had sent an emissary through large parts of his empire with the aim of not just closing but also destroying the pagan temples. His assault on the old gods inspired mob violence, which in some cases was undertaken in tandem with the church: "The archbishop of Alexandria rounded up a posse of monks to demolish the great Serapeum, shrine of the Egyptian god Serapis and one of the wonders of the ancient world. Theodosius congratulated the perpetrators."[26] Ruined temples were often quickly rebuilt as churches with the emperor's blessing. Eventually Theodosius declared that "any act of worship of the old Roman gods would be an act of treachery against the emperor himself."[27]

There was yet one last gasp of the old pagan world. In 394, a revolt centered in the old families of the Roman senatorial class publicly revived Rome's ancient pagan rites in an obvious slap at the Christian emperor.

25. Quoted in Mullin, *Short World History,* p. 56.
26. Kee, *Christianity,* p. 119.
27. Bauer, *History,* p. 70.

"Once again, Rome saw processions for Magna Mater and Isis, along with sacrifices to Jupiter and Saturn, Mithras and the Unconquered Sun, and Ceres and Proserpina. . . . Then the Roman senatorial pagans rode out under pagan standards to defend their antiquarianism, patriotism, and the old ways."[28] Theodosius won, and Christian writers interpreted the circumstances of his victory as further evidence of God's favor on a Christian warrior-emperor. Once again the Christian God had won.[29]

It is fair to say, along with Susan Wise Bauer, that "the interweaving of the two traditions [Roman imperial and Christian] continued to change both of them in ways that would prove impossible to undo."[30] The decision of Constantine and most of his successors to embrace Christianity produced numerous worldly benefits for Christianity. It had legally empowered and privileged the church, established its symbols and calendar as central to the state, motivated a huge numerical increase in adherents, and dramatically heightened the power of church officials. This latter was demonstrated when Bishop Ambrose of Rome overpowered Theodosius through excommunication in 390.[31] The church had proven itself, at least for a time, even more powerful than the officials that had empowered it. In turn the Roman imperial state had gained a temporary resource for unity. It had been purged of many of its worst practices. And it had gained a powerful new religious interpretation of its meaning and purpose. Church leaders were now at times describing the Roman Empire as "the kingdom of God on earth,"[32] a way of interpreting political realities that long outlived the Roman Empire itself.

Fifteen years after the death of Theodosius, in 410, the ancient city of Rome was sacked by Visigoths — the first time in 800 years that Rome had been unable to successfully defend itself from outside invasion. The last vestige of the western Roman Empire officially fell with the young puppet emperor Romulus Augustulus in 476, though in reality the empire had collapsed well before then. The Roman Empire fell into tribal fragmentation. Any semblance of order and unity in the various realms was provided by the surviving Catholic Church, which thenceforth carried forward both Roman and Christian cultural values and traditions.[33] The eastern empire survived

28. Kee, *Christianity*, p. 124.
29. Kee, *Christianity*, p. 124.
30. Bauer, *History*, p. 57.
31. Bauer, *History*, p. 70.
32. Bauer, *History*, p. 49.
33. Bauer, *History*, p. 173. *Unity:* Consider the example of Clovis, first king of all the

another 1,000 years, anchored in Constantinople and deeply rooted in the understanding of Christendom pioneered by Constantine, deepened by Theodosius, and finally intensified by Justinian (527-565), whose autocratic rule as "representative of Christ on earth" took the marriage of church and state to a new level.[34] That state-dominated model of Christendom[35] remained prevalent throughout the later Eastern Orthodox world until overturned by revolutionary political developments in the nineteenth and twentieth centuries.

5.3. Moral Damage at the Foundations

The earliest Christian moral vision sustained foundational damage in the years we have been considering — damage whose full consequences became visible only later.

Let's return to the five key factors offered in the last chapter for why the earliest Christians were able to retain their sharply differentiated life-honoring moral vision. Events during the transition from roughly 312 to 395, from Constantine to Theodosius, weakened these factors at their very foundations. Recall these factors as articulated in the last chapter:

a. The earliest Christians' interpretation of reality within the Jewish-Christian narrative framework of the reign of God, and their attempt to embody that reality in the churches;

b. The looming centrality of their beloved Jesus, his teachings and example;

c. Their carefully maintained distance from Greco-Roman culture and its practices and concurrent protection of Christian identity;

d. Their searing experience of persecution at Roman hands; and

e. Their relative marginality and social powerlessness.

Franks, who converted to Christianity in 496, which would thenceforth "serve as the new glue of the Frankish nation." Thus Catholic France was born. *Order:* Pope Gregory (Gregory the Great, 590-604) organized food distribution in Rome, repaired the aqueducts, supervised the rebuilding of the military, and even negotiated for peace with the Lombards. González, *The Story of Christianity,* p. 246.

34. Bauer, *History,* pp. 200-201.

35. González, *The Story of Christianity,* p. 251. See also Jeffrey Burton Russell, *A History of Medieval Christianity* (Arlington Heights, Ill.: Harlan Davidson, 1968), p. 35.

Every one of these five factors that had safeguarded the identity and vision of early Christianity was damaged during the transition from Constantine to Theodosius. Without going into deep detail, I claim the following:

a. The Christian narrative framework changed.

The earliest Christians inhabited an apocalyptic Jewish narrative in which the coming of Jesus the Messiah initiated the eschatological events leading to the ultimate consummation of God's reign, beginning with Israel and extending to the whole world. That divine reign, in turn, was an already/not yet reality with specific characteristics such as deliverance, justice, peace, inclusive community, healing, and the joyful experience of God's presence, all embodied by Jesus himself. While awaiting Christ's return, the church sought (and was called) to embody God's reign through a way of life committed to treating every human being as sacred, and the truthfulness of the Christian message required evidence in the church's own moral practices.

As Jaroslav Pelikan has pointed out, the indefinite delay of Christ's return meant that "it could no longer serve as the premise for the affirmations of Christian doctrine, which had to be transposed into another key."[36] This problem presented itself to Christian thought long before the period we have been considering in this chapter. Literary evidence available in Christian writings shows a variety of exegetical and theological strategies deployed to address the issue. These ranged from a millenarian teaching that Christians should expect Christ to return and to initiate a thousand-year reign on earth (Papias, Irenaeus), to spiritualizations of the millennium as having to do not with the body but with the soul (Origen), to the "decisive shift from the categories of cosmic drama to those of being" that were articulated in the creeds of the fourth century.[37]

Perhaps the latter development would have occurred in any case. But it is at least interesting that the codification of Christian doctrine that began in Constantine's era and was carried forward by later emperors cemented a shift in the focus of Christian thought toward a Platonic ontology of being rather than a Hebraic historical drama. One result was to strip the kingdom of God of its original dynamic framework rooted in Jewish eschatology. Now the "kingdom of God" could denote almost anything other than

---

36. Jaroslav Pelikan, *The Christian Tradition: A History of the Development of Doctrine,* vol. 1 (Chicago: University of Chicago Press, 1971), p. 123.

37. Pelikan, *The Christian Tradition,* pp. 123-32.

its original Hebraic meaning. It could be identified with the earthly reign of Roman emperors who claimed belief in Christ or who favored the church. The thousand-year reign of Revelation 20 could be identified with the church triumphant in its new political symbiosis with the state, or with the (Christian) state itself. The triumph of God in human life, which had included a final end to violence, could be viewed as no longer partial and awaiting God's decisive final intervention, but as fulfilled through God's intervention on behalf of violent earthly Christian rulers such as Constantine, Theodosius, and Justinian — and their successors. It could be seen as confirmed whenever a Christian ruler gained a victory in battle or bestowed a favor on the church. When violence moved from being a mark of the *need for* God's kingdom to a mark *of* God's kingdom, there indeed was a dramatic negation of Christianity's original moral vision.

The church's top thinkers got into the act. Eusebius (260-339), the early church's most influential historian, declared Constantine to be God's "commander in chief," put forward "as a lesson in the pattern of godliness to the human race," his victories clearly the product of divine providence, his triumph the triumph of God, his enemies the enemies of God.[38] With the present political order in good hands, Christians could transfer their remaining eschatological hopes to their own personal resurrection, a pressing concern in a world where illness and death loomed as such constant threats.[39] In short, Jesus' apocalyptic Hebraic eschatology originally involving the inaugurated-but-not-consummated transformation of the world was subsumed into a fulfilled eschatology around a Christian state/established church (especially one expanding in power) and a heightened theology of personal salvation. These patterns of thought lived on, and remain with us to this day in many Christian communities.

Identifying God's reign with the reign of Rome (and later Byzantium) damaged the spread of God's actual reign to any realm not politically allied with Rome or its successor states. Rome was not in fact universal, and so to identify God's reign with Rome's realm was both theologically mistaken and politically dangerous. One example of this problem is seen in the precarious status of Christianity in the Persian Empire in the third through fifth centuries. Christians who had once been tolerated were often persecuted when Persian leaders came to identify Christianity with Rome. A precedent was

---

38. Quoted in Mullin, *Short World History,* p. 62. See Eusebius, *The History of the Church,* trans. G. A. Williamson (London: Penguin, 1965), book 10, especially pp. 328-33.

39. González, *The Story of Christianity,* p. 134.

set: Roman and Byzantine Christians tangled violently with Persian Zoroastrians on the eastern edge of the Roman Empire; European Christians tangled violently with Arab Muslims through much of Europe, Africa, and the Middle East; and indigenous Arabs or other Christians outside the "Christian West" remain hugely vulnerable.[40] If "Christianity" meant "Roman Empire" or "European Christian states," it was easy to treat the Christian faith as a political entity that was an enemy to every other tribe or kingdom in the world. The aftereffects of this problem remain with us to this day.

b. The role played by Jesus changed, from teacher/exemplar to object of religious dogma and its enforcement.
The earliest Christian writings reveal an extraordinarily sharp focus on the life and teachings of Jesus Christ. Christians were repeatedly taught to imitate his life and obey his teachings. The Sermon on the Mount played an especially visible role in early Christian moral exhortations. Early Christian commitment to nonviolence in such a desperately violent world offers the best example of a faith community transfixed by the example of its source and head, its Savior and Lord. To say "Jesus Christ is Lord" meant not just or even primarily that Jesus Christ reigned in the heavens but also that Jesus Christ set the pattern by which his followers were committed to live. This example was powerful enough to lead the church to resist both the holy violence of large swaths of the Old Testament and the imperial violence of the Pax Romana. The church was a different kind of community following a different way of living.

Perhaps it was inevitable that three centuries after the end of Christ's earthly ministry his followers would be fixated on determining questions such as how to understand the exact nature of his divinity or how his human and divine natures were transmitted and related to each other. Such questions were not entirely new. The intellectual credibility of Christianity eventually required their resolution. The Roman emperors did not create such disputes, but they intervened and used their earthly power in attempts to resolve them once and for all. And a day spent arguing about fine points of dogma related to the person of Christ was a day *not* spent focusing on how to live out the moral teachings of the Jesus whose words are recorded in the New Testament, which enabled their primacy to slip further from view. A pattern was established that continues today — followers of Christ could grotesquely violate the moral teachings of Christ in the name

40. Bauer, *History,* chapter 12.

of defining and enforcing the tiniest points of doctrine about Christ. The actual teachings and example of Jesus could be evaded without anyone really noticing it, because they had ceased to be central to standard understandings of Christianity.

The use of state power — including the power to intimidate, shame, disadvantage, confiscate, imprison, torture, and kill — to enforce religious dogma against Roman "pagan" religionists, unorthodox Christians, and sometimes Jews represented a great moral collapse for Christianity and a fruitless effort on the part of the state. It also set a terrible precedent for later violence in the name of Jesus Christ. A faith that began in tender adoration and imitation of the executed Jesus of Nazareth became the cooperating partner in state abuses against the tender faith of others — including variant versions of Christian faith. In its cooperation with state religious persecution, the church left behind the Jesus of the New Testament and the moral vision that had for so long anchored its life.

c. Christians lost their social distance from Roman culture and conveniently became the majority, thus losing their distinctive identity.
Again using Rodney Stark's rough estimates, when Constantine came to power roughly 10 percent of the population of the empire was Christian; by 350 that number had soared to 56 percent.[41] Most historians, even Christian ones, acknowledge that this massive growth rate cannot be attributed solely to the intrinsic appeal of the Christian message or even to natural growth. Robert Mullin sums up the issue concisely:

> The support of the emperors assured that the church would grow. . . . To be a Christian was no longer a detriment in the Empire, but rather an advantage. To profess Christianity opened doors to a career in the administration of the Empire, and such positions could be quite lucrative. Enterprising towns could win better charters by proclaiming that they had become Christian. To profess Christianity now became for some not simply a path for doing good, but for doing well. The inevitable result of this shift in fortune was that insincere conversions began to be reported.[42]

Early Christian communities had constituted a tiny minority of the population, an often persecuted sect. The only reason people joined these

41. Stark, *The Rise of Christianity,* p. 7.
42. Mullin, *Short World History,* p. 59.

communities was because they believed their message and wanted to share in their way of life. With Constantine, Christianity became the privileged religion of the empire; with Theodosius, Nicene Christianity became the official and only sanctioned religion of the empire. The empire half-converted to Christianity; but it also half-converted Christianity. Certain egregious practices, like gladiator games and infanticide, were abandoned along with the worship of the old gods; but the violence and injustices true of any empire remained constitutive of this one. This is easy to miss if one is focusing on doctrinal and institutional developments, in which Christianity as doctrine and church was indeed triumphing over the Vestal Virgins and the old Roman gods. But if one attends to Christianity as adherence to the moral vision of Jesus, it is easy to see how much of this kind of religion was being lost in the accommodation to late Roman imperial politics and culture.

d. Christians forgot the bitter taste of their own persecution and accepted the persecution of others.

It is hard not to grieve very deeply the transition of Christianity from a persecuted to a persecuting religion in the period from Constantine to Theodosius.

Christians who once had their sacred books confiscated and destroyed now participated in confiscating and destroying the sacred books of others, including fellow Christians. A group whose leaders had been arrested and killed now supported the arrests and eventually supported the killing of the leaders of other groups. Christians whose churches and properties had been invaded and confiscated and destroyed now supported the invasion and confiscation and destruction of the temples and churches of others. Christians who had borne the full brunt of Roman imperial power employed to suppress their conscientiously held beliefs now supported the employment of Roman imperial power to suppress the conscientiously held beliefs of others. Christians who had once been martyred for rejecting the identification of the imperial will with the will of God now blessed that identification when the imperial will was avowedly Christian.

The Bible records numerous terrible persecutions of first Jews and later Christians. Sometimes the texts consciously demand that the reader remember these persecutions, as if they had happened to the reader's later generation (Deut. 5:14-16; 24:17-19; etc.). And of course, we Christians, at the very heart of our faith, remember the abuse and murder of Jesus himself at the hands of Pontius Pilate. Sometimes exhortations to remember the persecutions and suffering of our religious ancestors function to generate resistance to the victimization of others. Sometimes they motivate Christians, Jews, and others to become fierce opponents of any form of religious persecution by the state. But in this particular historical transition in the fourth century, the church appears to have suffered a tragic loss of historical memory. All that elaborate martyrology, all that sanctification of the memory of the murdered believers, did not prevent the church from supporting the persecution of others. The church was not long content to enjoy its newfound "peace" from imperial persecution before it acquiesced in violating the peace of others.

e. The church lost its marginality and became immensely powerful.
Whether for reasons of conviction or convenience, Roman emperors beginning with Constantine made a decision to favor the church with privileges and power, in order to try to hold together a fractured Roman Empire. Certainly the bloodied and exhausted church was going to rejoice at the dawning of a new era of peace and security and was very likely to attribute this newfound peace to God's providential care. But peace became privilege and eventually power and then persecution. Susan Wise Bauer, a Christian historian, is a bit too gracious when she says that "Christians in turn, would have had to be more than human to resist what Constantine was offering: the imprint of imperial power."[43] Looking back, one wonders if the Holy Spirit, who sustained the church's moral vision for three centuries, was whispering to church leaders at this pivotal moment that while peace for the church was a good gift, the "imprint of imperial power" was an offer that must be refused.[44] By the end of the fourth century the bishop of Rome was able to drive the emperor of Rome to his knees. By the end of the fifth century, in the west there was no emperor of Rome, and western Catholicism had inherited his fragments. In the east, the marriage of throne and altar had settled in for a good long run. Christendom had been born.

Luke Timothy Johnson summarizes aptly the developments we have been reviewing thus far in this chapter:

Christians moved from a place of hiding to a posture of display, from a condition in which their property could be dispossessed to a condition

43. Bauer, *History,* p. 11.
44. That was what most of the monastics concluded in any case. González, *The Story of Christianity,* chapter 15.

in which property was bestowed on them, from a marginal to a central social status, from a status of mockery to one of privilege, from a situation in which the cross of Christ was the signal for danger to themselves to a situation in which the cross of Christ was emblazoned on the banners of imperial troops carried into battle. History has known few such profound reversals of fortune and it is not in the least surprising that the majority of Christians should gladly embrace their new status as the Empire's favored religion.[45]

5.4. Advances and Regressions for the Sacredness of Life

During the fateful transition to Christendom, reverence for the sacred worth of every human life expanded in some important respects and receded in others. A world without authorized gladiator contests, crucifixion, and infanticide was a better world, in large part due to Christian influence translated into imperial law. But the church now far too often blessed the mistreatment of those classified as heretics, schismatics, and enemies of the emperor and the empire. Its marriage with state power compromised its original resistance to violence, which became not just permissible but, all too often, holy.

Christianity's life-revering vision was badly damaged. The question we now face is whether it even survived the transition to worldly power. I believe that three case studies — in war, colonialism, and anti-Judaism — will help us see both the damage to the church's original moral vision of every life's sacred value and the survival of that vision as embodied by several of the church's most memorable dissenters and movements.

45. Luke Timothy Johnson, *Among the Gentiles: Greco-Roman Religion and Christianity* (New Haven and London: Yale University Press, 2009), p. 258.

6. *Christendom Divided against Itself: Three Case Studies*

It is not my purpose to offer the three case studies in this chapter as a replacement for the history of the era of Christendom. Nor do I pretend that they are any kind of comprehensive study of the events considered. Think of them as extended vignettes. They are intended to sketch the corruption of Christian behavior within Christendom, as well as the Christian faithfulness of individuals and communities that resisted it. These vignettes succeed in their purpose if they bring into vivid relief the consecration and the desecration of life within Christendom. They will also build a bridge to the rest of the book, helping us understand why leading voices in Western culture eventually sought to end Christendom both intellectually and politically. This is Christian ethics as historical drama, rather than conceptual analysis. But it is precisely amidst these historical dramas that important truths about what it means to honor life's sacredness can be most clearly discerned.

6.1. The Crusades, Francis, and the Sacred Lives of Enemies

> The Christian glories in the death of the pagan, because Christ is glorified.
>
> Bernard of Clairvaux

We have grappled with the issue of violence in every chapter of this book, because the tradition we are considering has never failed to grapple with violence — and because human history is awash with bloodshed. This first vignette will especially give us opportunity to think more deeply about how violence relates to the sacredness of life. Consider it an extended meditation on puzzle #10 — whether believing in the sacredness of life requires the rejection of all violence.

It is commonplace in (Christianity-friendly, generally nonpacifist) presentations of historic Christian ethics to treat the development of Christian tradition on war as beginning under conditions of powerlessness with a primitive pacifism; transitioning under the leadership of Ambrose and Augustine to responsible and constrained support for justifiable wars with just-war theory; straying to an aberrant "crusade" ethos during two unfortunate medieval centuries; and then returning once again to a civilized and restrained just-war theory as the predominant Christian view to this very day.[1] Sometimes the positive historic achievement of Christian just-war theory is contrasted with Islamic jihadism, which is paralleled with the abandoned Christian crusade mentality, both treated as examples of "holy war" thinking.[2] We have already seen that Dietrich Bonhoeffer sharply contrasted the historic Christian constraints on war with the unrestrained slaughter he was hearing about on the eastern front during World War II. He certainly believed that Christian tradition had to some extent modified the practice of war in human life, and that the savagery of this new war marked the abandonment of those restraints.

Following this basic paradigm, the arguments within Christian circles about the morality of war rarely stray from certain well-defined tropes that the experienced ethicist could recite while asleep. Pacifists argue that faithfulness in following Christ requires abstention from war or any support for war. (They differ on the details of exactly what that abstention requires.) Just-war people argue that in a fallen world violence is, tragically, sometimes required as a necessary evil. Christian fidelity comes into play in determining when a war is morally justified and then in constraining the application of force once the war has begun — but it does not require pacifism. Both sides agree, at least in principle, that the crusade was and is a very bad and aberrant idea that has no standing as a Christian moral norm or practice. Both generally agree that Christians must not accept any and every war — and any and every use of force within war — as acceptable simply because a government demands it.

1. David L. Clough and Brian Stiltner, *Faith and Force: A Christian Debate about War* (Washington, D.C.: Georgetown University Press, 2007), is an excellent recent book that offers a fairly typical presentation of this type; see pp. 6-10.
2. J. Daryl Charles, *Between Pacifism and Jihad: Just War and Christian Tradition* (Downers Grove, Ill.: InterVarsity, 2005), p. 125.

One can hear both Christian pacifists and just warriors make sacredness-of-life claims, at least if pressed. Pacifists regularly claim that human life is so sacred that it must never be taken, including in war. Just warriors claim that life's sacredness can, at times, only be upheld by forcefully constraining the hand of those who would unjustly take it, as when an invading force crosses national borders and attacks an innocent land and its people. They are usually careful to draw a distinction between what can be done to *noncombatants* and what must be done to deter and defeat *aggressors*. And they emphasize that war can never be celebrated but only mourned.

Let us grant that no simple appeal to life's sacredness can resolve the question of whether Christians can support or participate in war. But let us not be under any illusions concerning the extent to which the Christian tradition or historic Christendom actually restrained "the dogs of war" under the guise of just-war theory. Nor can we be sanguine about the extent to which the Crusades, or the crusade mentality, proved aberrational in Christian history. To the contrary, in large stretches of Christian history, *"just wars" that were supposed to be fought with Augustinian mournfulness and careful limits became crusades fought with zealous piety and without restraint.* Just-war theory has been pristine only in theory, not where the bodies pile up. Clues for such a view can be seen not just in the constant violations of just-war theory in both word and deed in every period in which Christians have attempted to employ it.[3] But in the very period we are considering, the Crusades were themselves justified explicitly in the terms of just-war theory.[4] Indeed, just-war theory took shape precisely during the period of the Crusades, in which its terms as we now understand them were so systematically violated.[5]

Here we benefit from entering into a particularly striking story from Christendom. I want us to attend with some care to the way in which one of the most serious Christian disciples of his own or any era — Francis of Assisi — understood and responded to the Christian warring of his day.

---

3. See John Howard Yoder, *The War of the Lamb*, ed. Glen Stassen et al. (Grand Rapids: Brazos, 2009), pp. 87-89, 95-96, 101, 113, 119.

4. Roland Bainton, *Christian Attitudes toward War and Peace* (Nashville: Abingdon, 1960), p. 114. See also Lisa Sowle Cahill, *Love Your Enemies: Discipleship, Pacifism, and Just War Theory* (Minneapolis: Augsburg Fortress, 1994), pp. 123-25.

5. Thomas Aquinas (1225-1274) and Stanislaw of Skarbimierz (1360-1431) both played key roles in solidifying the terms of just-war theory and wrote in crusading contexts. A considerable literature can be found debating the continuities and discontinuities between "just war" and "crusade" thinking in figures such as Augustine and Aquinas.

His story makes an excellent example of a Christendom morally divided against itself. He experienced the blood-drenched, always (purportedly) "just" wars of his day and place, and eventually found the contrast between these wars and true fidelity to Christ simply unbearable. He took a very different path. Let us enter into his story.

As a young man, Francis di Bernardone, the son of a rich merchant, participated in a typically stupid battle between his town of Assisi and neighboring Perugia. The background of the fight has to do with conflicts between the merchants of Assisi and the wealthy noblemen who ruled that town as representatives of the Germanic "Holy Roman Empire." In this series of events that culminated in 1202, when young Francis was just twenty years old and aspiring to become a knight, the first bloodshed was internecine, in the narrow streets of Assisi. Then, fleeing Assisi, noblemen were sheltered by the Perugians, who allied with these nobles in a planned attack on Assisi. It became a matter of honor for Assisi to go to war preemptively to defeat Perugia.[6] Though not all historians agree, Francis may well have participated in this bloody battle, in which the Assisians were routed, with most of their young soldiers massacred: "The battlefield was covered with severed limbs, entrails, and mutilated heads."[7] Paul Moses, in *The Saint and the Sultan,* makes a case for the likelihood that Francis himself killed enemies on the battlefield that day.[8] Assisi had been fighting for "God and commune" in a battle his townsmen believed to be morally and religiously obligatory. But it was led by an excommunicated mayor, who headed a temporarily excommunicated city, against a foe closely allied with the papacy, in a fight about civic honor. In this dubious cause the Assisians shed much of their own blood and that of their enemies in a fruitless battle that ended numerous young lives. And it was just one of many stupid, forgettable battles in "Christian" Europe, one that would have been forgotten long ago if it had not likely played a role in radicalizing one of its participants.

We have grown accustomed to justifying, excusing, and taking for granted the sheer carnage of war. A moment before, there had been a living human being, body, soul, and spirit, with uncut skin and brains safely nestled inside the skull and memories and hopes and loves. A moment

---

6. For a more thorough telling of the background to this key event, see Adrian House, *Francis of Assisi: A Revolutionary Life* (Mahwah, N.J.: HiddenSpring, 2000), chapter 5.

7. Paul Moses, *The Saint and the Sultan* (New York: Doubleday, 2009), p. 22.

8. Moses, *Saint and the Sultan,* pp. 22-24.

later, there lies a shredded corpse, its body torn apart and its memories and hopes and loves gone with it. There is nothing normal, natural, or routine about either being shredded or shredding another human being. Given that today's soldiers, heavily armed, often killing from a distance, still often end up psychologically destroyed by the battles they have to fight, imagine how much worse it must have been to participate in the close hand-to-hand combat of medieval warfare in which young men like Francis participated.

By the time of Francis, the church founded by Jesus had been blessing war for almost nine hundred years. The fact that this blessing was rationalized and supposedly constrained by the categories of just-war theory, with limits as to participants and times imposed by the church, and with penitential disciplines imposed on warriors tainted by blood, would have made little difference in the battlefield experience of Francis and his (now mainly dead) friends that day.[9] Then, as now, any war that honor or self-interest or anger or pride or territorial defense compels my side to fight is by definition a just war, until perhaps history sees it in its true light when the passions later cool. And the restraints imposed by the Catholic Church look a little less impressive when we recall that by the time of Francis it was often the church itself calling its sons to war. The message became, in effect: war is tainted by sin, but go, kill, and die, when we tell you to go.

Francis was clearly a sensitive soul, like many of the very young people who still today go off to fight and kill and die in our own wars. His year as a hostage in a Perugian prison provided ample time to reflect on what he had seen and done — the fact that he became quite ill in his fetid dungeon[10] and the possibility that he was "tortured and humiliated" help us understand the changes soon to emerge in him.[11] During his recovery he experienced healing and finally a conversion not primarily in belief but in way of life. Through dreams he was literally turned around when he was preparing once more to fight in "chivalric" battle. He went back home, sold his warhorse and weapons of war, gave away the money gained from the sale, and eventually embarked on a new journey of radical discipleship that earned him the bitter rejection of his father and nearly everyone in his community. Though not an overnight conversion, his became a classic ex-

9. All nicely discussed by Bainton, *Christian Attitudes,* chapter 7.

10. Carol Kelly-Gangi, *Saint Francis of Assisi: His Essential Wisdom* (New York: Fall River Press, 2010), p. 8, suggests the possibility of either tuberculosis or malaria.

11. Moses, *Saint and the Sultan,* p. 26.

perience of repentance, a total turning around and away, and an embrace of a new way of life.

Francis the saint is best known for his radical commitment to poverty and his loving relationship with the nonhuman creatures of God's world. These important aspects of his understanding of Christian discipleship must be linked to his broader commitment to peace after the shattering experiences of his earlier days. Francis himself explicitly linked his abandonment of earthly possessions with his commitment to nonviolence: "If we had any possessions we should also be forced to have arms to protect them, since possessions are a cause of disputes and strife, and in many ways we should be hindered from loving God and our neighbor."[12] This comment also reveals his understanding that much war-fighting actually is motivated not by selfless defense of human lives but instead by selfish defense (or acquisition) of property, which sheds light on the doubtfulness of many justifications for war.

Francis's love and compassion for the animals represented the extension of his commitment to Christ's peace even into the animal kingdom. It was as if his awareness of the majestic sacredness of human life before God could not be contained at the boundaries of the human. I will return to this theme at the end of the book. There we will see that only recently have a large number of Christian and other thinkers begun to (re)sacralize the nonhuman creatures and the created order itself. Francis was ahead of his time in seeing that nonviolent love is a total way of life that sweeps everything up into its wake, and his witness remains an important inspiration for care of creation today.

Francis also understood that the way of life that requires the routine resort to war could only be countered by the creation of an alternative community bound by a different way of life. Thus he did not merely preach peace to a violence-drenched culture, though this he did do, and sometimes to great effect; he also created a new community bound by commitment to a *rule* that got at the problem of war from its roots. This rule was the covenant for what became Franciscan communities, which attempt to carry forward Francis's vision to this day. It required economic simplicity and thus no need to defend possessions, the practice of reconciliation within the community and thus a pattern of peacemaking in daily life, a ban on bearing arms and thus an inability to fight, and a rejection of making oaths like those that bound young men to their lords and to the wars

---

12. *The Legend of the Three Companions*, quoted in Moses, *Saint and the Sultan*, p. 38.

undertaken by their lords. Those living obediently under the terms of Francis's order simply could not be drawn into the social system that created the perpetual wars of his era. They were bound to a different community that operated by different rules. They were fighting a different set of battles than their fellow countrymen. The story we tell of Francis in this chapter must not be abstracted from the Christian community in which his life was embedded.

It was inevitable that Francis and his peaceable countercommunity would be forced to encounter the version of Christian moral practice that we now know as the Crusades, which gripped Christendom for two centuries. I want to define the Crusades here not just as the effort by western European Christians to retake the Holy Land between 1095 and 1291 after Muslim conquest, but also as *a moral practice primarily motivated and organized by the Roman Catholic Church that employed military force aggressively, in the name of Jesus Christ and as an expression of Christian piety, to accomplish a number of the church's political/religious aims.* These aims began with reclaiming from Muslims the land where Jesus walked, but they extended to include broader efforts to roll back, (re)claim territory from, or destroy Islam; programs to contain or destroy splinter/heretical groups like the Cathars and Hussites and eventually to combat individual heretics; and attempts to destroy the political and religious enemies of various popes or of Christendom. These official aims of the Crusades, most highly questionable in themselves, were often corrupted or diverted so that Crusaders also became deeply involved in wars for material gain, in massive pogroms against Jews, in attacks on Eastern Orthodox Christians, and in merely political or territorial conflicts within Europe. At a religious level the Crusades were in part motivated by the church's aim of inspiring a deepening of pious devotion to Christ among Europe's drifting Christian population, and many rank-and-file Christians indeed experienced the Crusades as an act of Christian devotion.

Francis never opposed the Crusades openly. Perhaps he knew that his movement could not gain and keep the support of the church hierarchy if he directly opposed its principal project. But it is hard to imagine that a man and a movement so devoted to peacemaking and so averse to violence could have supported them. We know that he and members of his order became well known for passionate peacemaking efforts in Italy from early in their history as a movement.[13] Their preaching inspired enemies who

---

13. Bainton, *Christian Attitudes*, p. 119.

hated each other to drop their weapons and make peace. Perhaps these successes help to explain Francis's decision to try to reach out to Muslim leaders personally. This is especially striking in light of the dehumanizing rhetoric so often directed by church leaders against Muslims. For example, the first crusading pope, Urban II, rallied his troops by describing the Muslims as "an accursed race, a race utterly alienated from God," and proclaiming a Christian duty to "exterminate this vile race from our lands."[14] This kind of "othering" rhetoric routinely precedes and accompanies desecrations of human life, and Francis would have none of it.

Francis made three attempts to encounter directly Muslim leaders during this period in which Christians and Muslims were slaughtering each other in dreadful numbers as cosmic enemies. In 1211, he boarded a ship with the intent of going to the Holy Land; it was blown off course and he had to return home. In 1213 or 1214, after a bloody battle in Spain that cost 100,000 Muslim lives, he attempted to travel by land to the court of Sultan Muhammad an-Nasir in Morocco. His journey across France and Spain became significant for the worldwide development of Francis's order, but he never reached Morocco. Finally, Francis made it to Egypt when he accompanied the Fifth Crusade.

Francis landed in Egypt in late July 1219 and walked into a military stalemate. He entered a scene of vicious if periodic fighting, and stayed in a Crusader camp of 40,000 soldiers and thousands of hangers-on, plagued by growing conflict and disease. Crusaders had been besieging for more than a year the northern Egyptian city of Damietta, a fortified walled city that was home to 80,000 (only 3,000 of whom survived the conflict). Various attacks and counterattacks, along with war's evil cousins, hunger and disease, had already left tens of thousands of soldiers and civilians on both sides dead by the time Francis arrived.

Francis believed war participated in the demonic, and he had plenty of occasions to witness its demonic excesses in Damietta. In one memorable engagement large numbers of Muslim soldiers were slaughtered, many beheaded: "So many Muslims were decapitated that the Christians set to hurling their heads into Damietta with their siege engines."[15] These Christian head-hurlers, incidentally, were led by the universally loathed and feared Cardinal Pelagius Galvani, who had seized power from the actual military

---

14. There are various versions of Urban II's call to the crusade at Clermont. This one is found in Karen Armstrong, *Holy War* (New York: Anchor Books, 1992), p. 3.

15. Moses, *Saint and the Sultan,* p. 88.

leaders on hand. He had rallied the troops around a sacred relic (a purported sliver of the true cross), and in a typical moment prayed that God would help the Christians win "so that we may be able to convert the perfidious and worthless people, so that they ought duly to believe with us in the Holy Trinity and in Your Nativity and in Your Passion and death and resurrection."[16]

Cardinal Pelagius decided that it was time for a major attack, and planned it for August 29, 1219. He was opposed by most of the military leaders on the Christian side, including John of Brienne, who wanted to take up a peace offer from the sultan that would have given the Crusaders control of Jerusalem, along with several other generous provisions. (Note that just-war theory says that war must be a last resort; the rejection of this peace offer that *would have fulfilled the entire original purpose of this conflict* clearly violates that provision.) On the morning of this first major battle after his arrival, Francis "rushed to the Christians crying out warnings to save them, forbidding war and threatening disaster." Francis was understood to mean that this particular battle was not God's will, a kind of inspired prophetic warning. Paul Moses suggests that this was the only way Francis had of implicitly saying that the whole *war* was not God's will. This would have been a far more radical stance, of course, because it would have put Francis in direct conflict with the pope and his representative in Damietta.[17] In any case, his warning for the day's battle was ignored. He stayed behind in the camp while both warriors and the clergy blessing them headed off. The Crusaders were crushed in battle, losing thousands.

Even after this battle the Egyptian sultan renewed his peace offer. It was rejected, again, not by the military men but by Cardinal Pelagius and the clergy. Francis, hearing of this development, decided that it was time to undertake a direct peacemaking effort with the sultan. Crossing enemy lines and stinking, body-littered battlefields, totally unarmed and without any letter or document that might provide protection, Francis and his friend Illuminato set out to meet the sultan or their deaths, or both.

Many different accounts of this famous meeting survive from the thirteenth century. They do not agree in details, and the various layers of accounts have propaganda interests. Here is the version that seems most plausible to me.[18] Francis and Illuminato were clearly risking their own lives on what seemed a suicide mission. They were grabbed by an enemy

16. Moses, *Saint and the Sultan*, p. 89.
17. Moses, *Saint and the Sultan*, pp. 114-15.
18. I am largely following House, *Francis of Assisi*, pp. 210-13.

patrol, beaten, chained, and taken to a guard post. They could easily have been killed on sight. Their obviously nonmilitary bearing and dress, and the folly of their mission in any military sense, must have convinced the guards to spare their lives and grant their request to be taken to the sultan. The sultan asked Francis if they were messengers or had come seeking to convert and join the Muslim side (the latter did happen occasionally). Francis proceeded to say that, to the contrary, they had come as messengers of Christ to talk with the sultan about the Christian faith and indeed to convert him. Rather than lopping off their heads, Sultan al-Kamil immediately sent for his leading scholars, saying he could not participate in such a conversation without them. Once the theologians arrived several days later, the dialogue commenced.

Clearly this was an evangelistic effort, but if we follow the contemporaneous account of Bishop Jacques of Vitry, who was on the scene, rather than Bonaventure's later embellishment, it was a largely peaceable encounter. The wait for the scholars and then the conversation went on for several days; all the while Francis and Illuminato were offered Middle Eastern hospitality within the sultan's camp. During this time Francis would have witnessed the daily religious practices of the Muslims who hosted him, and he seems to have been especially impressed by the periodic daily call to prayer. The Muslims in turn allowed him to discuss his faith with them, though at least some reports suggest that ultimately al-Kamil's religious advisers recommended the execution of the monks. The sultan, to his credit, refused to do this. In this pivotal personal encounter neither side gave in to religious dehumanization.

The way the visit ended is most interesting. Francis refused the lavish monetary gifts offered by the sultan. However, he did accept a horn to call people to prayer, and an offer to visit Jerusalem under the sultan's protection; and he did tell the sultan that he would take a meal before parting. Perhaps he and the sultan actually ate this meal together; we do not know. Finally the sultan sent Francis and Illuminato back to the Christian camp under his royal protection.

Francis had reached out to the sultan in peace. He seems to have hoped that peace could be found between warring communities through shared faith in (the one, true) God, the God in whom Francis believed. As G. K. Chesterton famously wrote: "It was, of course, simply the idea that it was better to create Christians than to destroy Moslems."[19] One thinks of the

---

19. G. K. Chesterton, *Saint Francis of Assisi* (New York: Image Books, [1924] 1957), p. 114.

Old Testament theme considered earlier: that shalom will happen when the nations stream to Jerusalem (Mic. 4:1) to worship and serve the one Lord of all —

> these I will bring to my holy mountain,
>   and make them joyful in my house of prayer.
>
>   (Isa. 56:7; cf. Zeph. 3:9)

Peace with the Muslims through dialogue leading to voluntary conversion was Francis's goal. This was far better than doomed efforts to achieve peace through conquest and killing, which was being undertaken by the church and its Crusaders and certainly at times by Muslims and their warriors. While it did not lead either to the sultan's conversion or to the end of the war, this was an extraordinarily rare, deeply human encounter at a time of relentless dehumanization and the carnage of war. And it apparently ended with mutual respect despite unresolved religious disagreements. It could only have occurred if Francis (and Sultan Malik al-Kamil) had already cultivated the capacity to see a kind of sacred fellow-humanity across the lines of religion — or even, to be a bit more provocative, some mysterious core of shared piety underneath the differences of religious tradition and conviction. Chesterton summarizes this theme quite nicely in the following reflection on Francis:

> To him a man was always a man and did not disappear in a dense crowd any more than in a desert. He honored all men; that is, he not only loved but respected them all. What gave him his extraordinary personal power was this; that from the Pope to the beggar, from the sultan of Syria in his pavilion to the ragged robbers crawling out of the wood, there was never a man who looked into those brown burning eyes without being certain that Francis Bernardone was really interested in him; in his own inner individual life from the cradle to the grave.[20]

The sacredness of the lives of our religious "enemies," especially when those enemies profess Islam, has become one of the most important issues in American life since the 9/11 attacks, just as the sacredness of Christian lives is an issue in certain sectors of Islam. We know that a radical version of Islamic holy war thinking motivated the terrorists of 9/11. But we also

---

20. Chesterton, *Saint Francis of Assisi*, p. 88.

know that our invasions of Afghanistan and Iraq since then have sometimes been accompanied by our own crusader language — and that is how our actions have been interpreted by many in the overwhelmingly Muslim nations we invaded and occupied.[21] While former President Bush was careful to avoid verbal attacks on Islam as a religion, or any equating of U.S. military action with historic clashes between Christians and Muslims, others were not always so careful in the heat of the moment.

The spiking of Christian-Muslim tensions around the world and in the United States has led to what once would have been an unthinkable development in the ethics of war. Earlier I outlined the standard exposition of Christian thinking about war and how the "crusade" or "holy war" is routinely ruled out as aberrant. But today one begins to hear the open embrace of an interpretation of current U.S. wars as a defense of Christian/Western civilization or Christian America from Muslim enemies. And the once universally discredited Crusades are now being described by some as an earlier episode in the same struggle, which should be viewed positively rather than rejected as an aberration.[22] In other words, the Crusades are being rehabilitated by some ideologies, with Christian America now at the forefront of the new (defensive, just, even holy) wars of religion against Islam. An equally dangerous interpretation within Islam also continues to circulate, with similar claims and justifications of holy killing, only from the other side.[23] In fact, they evoke and justify each other, in the classic vicious spiral of religiously sanctioned contempt and violence against the dangerous infidel other.

This is disastrous. Perhaps it helps to illustrate my core claim in this section. A majority of us Christians like to tell ourselves that we moved from the primitive pacifism of the powerless early church to a realistic and responsible just-war theory with an aberrant Crusade exception. But the crusade mentality remains a far more powerful and vibrant element of our

21. Moses, *Saint and the Sultan,* p. 230.

22. Samuel P. Huntington, *The Clash of Civilizations and the Remaking of World Order* (New York: Simon and Schuster, 1996); Rodney Stark, *God's Battalions: The Case for the Crusades* (New York: HarperOne, 2009).

23. The development and current status of crusade-type thinking in the Muslim world are very carefully discussed by Jonathan Phillips, *Holy Warriors: A Modern History of the Crusades* (New York: Random House, 2009), pp. 344ff. Phillips shows that while jihad is intrinsic to Islam, jihad as crusade-type holy war against the West has not been a consistent theme in Muslim thought. It has, though, been deployed more frequently since nineteenth-century colonialism brought ever more frequent incursions by Western nations into Arab lands — especially when those Westerners have employed crusading language or imagery themselves.

moral imagination than we are willing to admit.[24] This is indeed a moral degradation of the original Christian vision, a turn far away from honoring each and every human life. It is ultimately traceable to forces unleashed in the Constantinian transition. But the moral witness of a Francis of Assisi is traceable to forces unleashed by the example and teaching of Jesus himself, and this witness also survives. The story told here of Francis's careful but clear subversion of the Fifth Crusade through application of Jesus' peacemaking teaching[25] that we are to go and talk with our enemies (Matt. 5:21-26) reveals that all the powers of Christendom and its just-war/holy crusade against the Saracen infidels were not capable of destroying the simple but clear moral witness of Jesus. That witness survived, and was embodied at a particularly important moment by Francis of Assisi, a moment in attempted conflict transformation that is warmly remembered today by many Christians *and Muslims.*

One final footnote seems appropriate. Perhaps this episode teaches us that a truly realistic Christian debate about war ought not to be treated as pacifism versus just-war theory. Perhaps realism about human nature suggests that our choice most often is between *two kinds of crusades* — one for holy peace and the other for holy war.[26] It's just a suggestion, but perhaps the God-given human awareness that something ultimate is at stake whenever we shred a human being on the battlefield (or risk being shredded) makes it psychologically and spiritually necessary to treat every war as a crusade — for nation, security, territory, Christ, God, justice, democracy, etc. R. H. Tawney caught this insight about the ultimacy of war when he wrote, "War is either a crime or a crusade."[27] The midcentury Christian historian Roland Bainton, a deep skeptic of war, essentially agreed when he said: "[War] ought to be so overwhelmingly right as to be manifestly the will of God or else not right at all."[28]

---

24. Therefore it must be considered seriously in ongoing Christian thinking and writing about war. No presentation of the Christian history and ethics of war is complete without such discussion. For two good recent examples, see Mark J. Allman, *Who Would Jesus Kill? War, Peace, and the Christian Tradition* (Winona, Minn.: St. Mary's Press, 2003), chapter 3, and Cahill, *Love Your Enemies,* chapter 7.

25. Glen H. Stassen, *Just Peacemaking: Transforming Initiatives for Justice and Peace* (Louisville: Westminster John Knox, 1992), pp. 102-3.

26. Bainton, *Christian Attitudes,* p. 120, makes a similar claim: "The religious sect is almost bound to be either pacifist or crusading."

27. Quoted in Bainton, *Christian Attitudes,* p. 242.

28. Bainton, *Christian Attitudes,* p. 242.

I submit that it would be very difficult to find *any* American war that has not been treated by at least some visible advocates as a holy crusade, beginning with the wars against the peoples that the settlers found when they got here, up to the Revolution, through the Civil War, including the early imperialist episodes in Cuba and the Philippines, and extending through World Wars I and II and the Cold War. Similarly, British historian Jonathan Phillips offers abundant, even devastating evidence of the regular evocation of the Crusades or the crusade motif in relation to wars fought by Italy, France, Britain, Spain, and Germany.[29] As Phillips, among others, has shown, World War I certainly was described as a holy crusade throughout the world (on opposing sides), as is evidenced by this statement from the bishop of London: "I look upon it as a war for purity; I look upon everyone who dies in it as a martyr."[30] This sentiment was far from unusual in Britain or the United States at the time, and not much different in spirit than these words of the crusading preacher par excellence, Bernard of Clairvaux, writing in the twelfth century: "The Christian glories in the death of the pagan, because Christ is glorified."[31] Holy war, indeed: Christ is glorified either through killing the infidel enemy or in dying a martyr's death in the effort to kill that enemy. This may help explain why the Tomb of the Unknown Soldier in Westminster Abbey (built in 1920) is adorned with a medieval sword, and why a group called the Order of Crusaders honored the Unknown Soldier in 1923 as "Principal Knight and Supreme Head" of their order.[32] The Crusades appear to be the gift that keeps on giving.

The staggering thought arises that perhaps just-war theory was little more than an illusory pagan and then Christian effort, valiant but doomed, to desacralize war. Many Christians have treated it as a profound Christian contribution to the ethics of war, and this is not entirely without merit. Its principles are rational and its limits have spared many lives from wanton destruction and violation. But on balance it has not proven capable of desacralizing war and setting limits on the passions war evokes. Perhaps the only way that war really can be desacralized is through the resacralizing of human life and of the peacemaking that saves human life. Perhaps holy crusades of violence against subhuman infidels cannot be defeated by cool

29. Phillips, *Holy Warriors*, chapter 12.

30. Bishop A. F. Winnington-Ingram, *The Potter and the Clay* (London, 1917), pp. 41-42, quoted in Bainton, *Christian Attitudes*, p. 207.

31. Quoted in Michael Walsh, *Warriors of the Lord: The Military Orders of Christendom* (Grand Rapids: Eerdmans, 2003), p. 82.

32. Phillips, *Holy Warriors*, p. 327.

principles like just-war theory, but only by even more holy crusades of *deliverance from violence* in the way of Jesus Christ. This may be the ultimate lesson taught by our brother Francis of Assisi.

6.2. Colonialism, Las Casas, and the Sacred Lives of Indians

> With what right and with what justice do you keep these poor Indians in such cruel and horrible servitude? By what authority have you made such detestable wars against these people who lived peacefully and gently on their own lands? Are these not men? Do they not have rational souls? Are you not obliged to love them as yourselves?
>
> Fr. Antonio Montesino

Christopher Columbus offers an unexpected link between the discussion we have just completed and the one we now undertake. So also does that momentous year, 1492. On the second day of 1492 the last Muslim stronghold on the Iberian Peninsula capitulated to an international array of Christian forces led by the Spanish Crown. Granada was wrested from Muslim hands after 780 years. This culmination of the *Reconquista* was experienced as a glorious victory not just for Spain but also for Christendom. It might reasonably be named the end of the Crusades, or far past the end. But in that same year 1492, and in that same frenzied atmosphere of Christian triumphalism and pious fervor, the Spanish Crown authorized Christopher Columbus's first great expedition. Columbus's diary entry from December 26, 1492, records his desire to find gold and spices to pay for an expedition — strikingly enough — "to conquer the Holy Sepulchre, for thus I urged Your Highnesses to spend all the profits of this, my enterprise, on the conquest of Jerusalem."[33] Columbus was at least partly motivated by a kind of apocalyptic crusading fervor, and by his 1501-1502 voyages he clearly saw himself as an agent of God's will. Jonathan Phillips argues that Columbus "hoped to create the conditions for the Second Coming of Christ by the conversion of all peoples to Christianity and the recapture of the holy city."[34] Phillips says that Columbus garnered this vision from the writings of contemporary Franciscans — another, quite terribly ironic,

---

33. Phillips, *Holy Warriors*, p. 305.
34. Phillips, *Holy Warriors*, p. 306.

connection to the story just narrated. Once again, the Crusades show up as the gift that keeps on giving.

Of course, all of history knows that, instead of reaching India in the east, Columbus landed in what became known as the Americas, in the west. And instead of a peaceful mission for trade and evangelism, the Spanish colonial presence quickly became characterized by brutality, enslavement, and the decimation of the indigenous population. The story of the encounter between the purportedly Christian Spanish and the native populations is of titanic historical and moral significance. One particular figure from that history is the subject of this vignette.

Portugal, Spain, and Christian Imperialism

Our story actually begins with Portugal. The late fifteenth century marked the ascendancy of that Iberian nation to the heights of its greatest power. Portuguese advances in seafaring took that nation to Africa, where the Portuguese became the first European colonizers since the days of Rome — and, as they saw it, the defenders of Christendom in taking the Christian fight to the Muslims. The Spaniards were quickly to follow in these first forays in modern European imperial colonialism. Competing Portuguese and Spanish claims to various newly discovered territories threatened to disrupt their relationship with one another and to slow colonial progress.

This situation garnered a series of interventions by the Roman Catholic Church, which inserted itself into diplomacy between the Iberian kingdoms as well as offering papal statements, or "bulls," on the matter. These interventions, including the Treaty of Alcáçovas (1479); the papal bulls *Aeterni regis* (1481), *Inter caetera,* and *Dudum siquiedum* (1493); and the Treaty of Tordesillas (1494), were important not just because they managed temporarily to calm the tensions between Spain and Portugal. Of deeper significance was the way they did so — by dividing the newly colonized territories into demarcated spheres of influence, on the basis of a supposed papal authority over the peoples to be ruled in these colonized regions of the world. The theological-legal theory at work was "papal donation" — the papacy was sovereign over these new lands and peoples, but was delegating, donating, or transferring its sovereignty to Portugal and Spain.[35] (Of

35. Whether the papacy intended something more like a feudal investiture, in which it retained sovereignty but entrusted temporary control to these kings as vassals, was never en-

course, the papacy's authority to claim such sovereignty and make such "donations" was not accepted by other European powers and has been eternally resented by the peoples to whom it applied and who were never consulted.) This divine authorization of the Spanish or Portuguese to take over native civilizations and populations was for the explicit purpose of spreading Christian faith and Christian morality to "barbarous nations," in the words of the bull *Inter caetera,* and this provided its justification.

Beginning in 1492, everywhere Spanish adventurers, soldiers, settlers, traders, and churchmen went in the New World they staked their claim to territory in the name of Christ and with the sign of the cross. This was often done, quite literally, with large wooden crosses staked in visible places on the ground.[36] The cross became a sign both of Christianity and of Spain, a symbol both of Christian rule and of the Christianization expected or demanded of the indigenous peoples. As early as his second voyage Columbus carried priests with him to advance the evangelization project, while *every* new landing in the New World carried warriors ready for conquest and settlers ready to claim land — or exploit people and raw materials. The indigenous peoples could easily be forgiven for assuming that Christianity was interchangeable with ruthless Spanish conquest, for that was their experience, even though on the Spanish side the mix of motives was both complex and contested. Warriors, politicians, and churchmen who cared nothing for native souls and employed the language and symbols of Christianity with cruelty or indifference competed with other Spaniards, notably members of the monastic orders, most of whom were interested in genuine evangelization.[37]

Robert Mullin claims that the kind of Spanish Catholicism in operation during this period was especially rigid and full of the crusader spirit. Fresh off of the *Reconquista,* Spain at this time represented the apotheosis

---

tirely clear. This question came to matter because who exactly held sovereignty over these subjugated territories was far more than theoretically important. Of course, it was a dispute within the thought-world of imperialism. Neither the pope nor Spain held morally legitimate sovereignty in the New World.

36. Howard Clark Kee et al., eds., *Christianity: A Social and Cultural History* (Upper Saddle River, N.J.: Prentice-Hall, 1998), p. 526.

37. This raises the question of the moral legitimacy of evangelization, an issue that comes up in works especially by native American and postcolonial thinkers. See, for example, George Tinker, *Missionary Conquest: The Gospel and Native American Cultural Genocide* (Minneapolis: Fortress, 1993), and Luis N. Rivera, *A Violent Evangelism: The Political and Religious Conquest of the Americas* (Louisville: Westminster John Knox, 1992).

of church/state unity in the West and the attempt to establish a thoroughly and aggressively homogeneous Christian society. This was the Spain of the Inquisition, a Spain that moved quickly from *Reconquista* to the suppression, forced conversion, and expulsion of Jews and Muslims, a Spain attempting to cleanse itself of all religious diversity. The year Columbus first sailed was the same year the Jews of Spain were forced into exile, and Spain had little interest in religious toleration toward its ancient Muslim population. Mullin says it was this authoritarian and violent version of Christianity that came with Spain into the New World.[38] And yet a different strand of Christianity, one much closer to the spirit of Jesus, also made its way across the Atlantic. Our story is located in the clash between these two Christianities, a clash with echoes down to our own day, and not only in Latin America.

Hypocrisies, Delusions, and Bad Conscience

The papacy had made a deal with Europe's first colonizing powers. One might in retrospect call it a devil's bargain. The deal came to involve a great deal of delusional self-deception on the part of the Catholic Church and the Spanish monarchy. Each had to tell a sanitized story to itself about what it had authorized and (soon enough) about what the results of its authorization were turning out to be. These delusions could not easily be sustained in the face of the evidence on the ground, leaving the church and the Spanish monarchy with, as Anthony Pagden has written, "a deep moral unease."[39] Leaders who believed they were "the champions of Christendom . . . lived in constant fear of finding themselves out of favour with their God."[40] Some wanted to know the truth as it emerged from the New World. But most wanted their delusions reinforced. Local authorities benefiting from their exploitation of native land and peoples were only too happy to oblige the latter wish.

In the New World, the church first had claimed an illusory sovereignty over the peoples and vast territories of all the lands soon to be conquered. This entailed believing it was God's will that European Christian nations,

38. Robert Bruce Mullin, *A Short World History of Christianity* (Louisville: Westminster John Knox, 2008), p. 157.

39. Anthony Pagden, introduction to *A Short Account of the Destruction of the Indies*, by Bartolomé de Las Casas, trans. Nigel Griffin (London: Penguin Books, 1992), p. xxiv.

40. Pagden, "Introduction," p. xxiv.

with authority delegated by the church, could simply take control of the Americas and its various peoples without the consent of the peoples themselves. The church and the Spanish Crown soon tried to convince themselves that the violence that erupted in the New World upon this conquest was the fault of the divinely subjected peoples, who had no right to "rebel" against the leaders established by God and brought to them for their salvation and improvement. Thus the "pacification" (Columbus) of such rebels was an expression of just(ifiable) war, a tragic necessity but ultimately an expression of Christian love.[41] To ensure (again, delusionally) that all good order was being maintained in the waging of legal and just wars, in 1513 the Crown instituted the tragically laughable *Requerimento*. This was an actual prepared statement that was to be read, in Spanish, to villagers. It narrated the historical and theological grounds of Spanish sovereignty and gave the natives a chance to surrender to their rightful sovereign or face the stern consequences of their rebellion. Every conquistador carried a copy of it in his pocket. It was often read out of earshot of the native villages, or in a whisper at night while the people spent their last hours of peace asleep in their beds.[42]

The new hegemons of Latin America also repeatedly tried to convince themselves that they had not authorized slavery in the New World and had reined in the rampant wildcat enslavement that occurred during the first decade of Spanish rule. The supposed solution was the establishment of the *encomienda* system.[43] If, as La Rochefoucauld said, "hypocrisy is the tribute that vice pays to virtue," *encomienda* may be hypocrisy's ultimate poster child. This new policy involved what was described as a kind of benevolent trusteeship. A certain number of natives were "entrusted" *(encomienda,* from *encommender)* to Spanish colonists who were given control (though not "ownership") of parcels of territory and also parcels of indigenous people to share the work of that territory. The Indians were not permitted to refrain from accepting their assignment in the *encomienda* system. They were instead to offer their work to the Spanish, and in return

41. Justo L. González, *The Story of Christianity,* vol. 1 (New York: HarperCollins, 1984), p. 383.

42. Pagden, "Introduction," pp. xxiv-xxv; Bartolomé de Las Casas, *A Short Account of the Destruction of the Indies,* trans. Nigel Griffin (London: Penguin Books, 1992), pp. 33, 56.

43. Justo González argues that the Spanish Crown enacted a number of laws to protect the natives, but these were regularly disregarded by the settlers. A structural conflict of interest existed between the local settlers and the far-off monarchy. Neither was fundamentally motivated by the good of the indigenous. *Story of Christianity,* p. 381.

would graciously be offered religious instruction (their greatest need, after all), the protection of the Spanish Crown, and, according to at least one source, a small regular wage.[44] So the Spanish Crown could tell itself that the Spanish did not enslave their subject populations but instead exercised a benevolent and evangelistic trusteeship over indigenous populations that had been generously incorporated into its political community. In actual fact, it looked more like this: "*Encomienda* became a system of brutal slavery. Distributed like cattle to greedy fortune hunters, put to work in gold mines without adequate food, subject to European diseases, unable to escape and losing their will to live, the Indians of the Caribbean began to die off."[45]

Introducing Las Casas

One of the men who landed early in the conquest of the New World was a young Spaniard named Bartolomé de Las Casas, a figure little known in most North American Christian circles but of legendary and disputed status both in Spain and in Latin America. Though he was by no means alone in his moral vision, and though some of his words and actions can be criticized on various grounds, perhaps more than any other European Christian in the Americas he resisted the dehumanization and desecration of the indigenous population that were the actual reality of Spanish colonization. He fought back against the brutalities of Christendom precisely in the name of Christ. In so doing he bore witness to the enduring power of a Christian vision of the sacredness of every life.

Bartolomé de Las Casas was a prolific writer but left little evidence of his life prior to joining Nicholas de Ovando's large expedition to the New World in 1502, when Las Casas was twenty-eight. According to his own account, Las Casas landed on April 15, 1502, in Santo Domingo, on the island known to the natives as Guanahaní and renamed Hispaniola by Columbus. Today the Dominican Republic and Haiti share that island. By 1503 Las Casas was a reasonably prosperous Spanish colonizer and a master of a number of Indian slaves under *encomienda*.

Las Casas became a priest in 1510 — likely the first Spaniard ordained

---

44. Pagden, "Introduction," p. xx, says there was a small wage; I find that in no other account.

45. Kee, *Christianity*, p. 530.

in the New World — but this did not prevent him from initially being a full participant in the new economy of enslavement that the Spanish were establishing. Yet a change began stirring in him. Various milestones can be identified in his movement toward conscientious objection to the system in which an entire hemisphere was rapidly being engulfed. He claims that a sermon preached in Santo Domingo at Christmas 1511 by the Dominican friar Antonio Montesino began a serious process of reconsideration. In that sermon, on December 4, 1511, the newly arrived friar Montesino shocked his audience by decrying what was happening all over colonial Latin America: "With what right and with what justice do you keep these poor Indians in such cruel and horrible servitude? By what authority have you made such detestable wars against these people who lived peacefully and gently on their own lands? Are these not men? Do they not have rational souls? Are you not obliged to love them as yourselves?"[46]

Pay attention to the form and vocabulary of these critically important questions. Eventually it was Las Casas himself who became the leader of those who persistently asked them. At the time, predictably, the population of the colony was outraged at this impudent sermon and demanded that Montesino recant and be sent back to Spain. Montesino was immovable, and the local leadership of the Dominicans stood with Montesino — who heightened his criticism the next week, announcing that the Dominicans would no longer hear the confessions of slaveholding colonists. (Notice again the role of a resistant *community*, not just an individual.) Las Casas records that though he himself remained silent, he did not share his townsmen's indignation against Montesino. Later in 1511 Las Casas traveled with the conquistador Diego Velázquez to Cuba, and there he saw blood-curdling massacres. He reports that he protested against the especially vicious actions of one Pánfilo de Narváez, but apparently not aggressively enough to lose his good standing with Velázquez. Any resistance stirring in him was not yet visible enough to cost him anything.

It was not until 1514 that Las Casas experienced his conversion to a full defense of the indigenous population. He reports that in working on his Easter sermon, Ecclesiasticus (Sirach) 34:25-27 struck him with extraordinary force. That text reads (NRSV):

> The bread of the needy is the life of the poor;
> whoever deprives them of it is a murderer.

---

46. Quoted by Pagden, "Introduction," p. xxi.

> To take away a neighbor's living is to commit murder;
> to deprive an employee of wages is to shed blood.

If we take Las Casas at his word, this text catalyzed a rethinking of the colonial enslavement and brutalizing of the natives, which he now saw as little more than organized theft and murder. He reports that he spent days reflecting on the matter until concluding that "everything which had been done to the Indians in the Indies was unjust and tyrannical."[47] Las Casas became a changed man. He renounced his possession of Indians as servants, and within a year left Cuba with Friar Montesino to report to King Ferdinand about the evils they had witnessed in the New World — and to beg for his intervention. Las Casas had begun a fifty-year, largely unsuccessful career (he died in 1566) as gadfly, goad, and conscientious objector to the brutalities of Spanish imperialism.

Eyewitness and Legal Protest

Bartolomé de Las Casas was, at least for a time, willing to accept large portions of the fantastical story that the Catholic Church and the Spanish Crown told themselves. He believed that Columbus (whose diaries Las Casas is responsible for copying and summarizing) had been chosen by God to bring the gospel to the New World, and that he came with an originally peaceful mission of trade and evangelism that was ruined by later settlers.[48] He did not dispute the legitimacy of the Spanish presence in the New World or the papal grant of power over the peoples there. He agreed that the indigenous population was subject to Spanish authority. In all these ways, he shared the presuppositions of most faithful Catholic Spaniards, presuppositions that almost every reader of this volume would reject out of hand. As Anthony Pagden shrewdly observes: "Like many radicals, he was, in all respects but one, the staunchest of conservatives."[49] For the extent to which he shared imperialist presuppositions, he has been rightly criticized.

But Las Casas had seen with his own eyes and had heard from others about such a pattern of atrocities that he came to conclude that his fellow

47. Pagden, "Introduction," p. xxii.
48. Pagden, "Introduction," p. xv.
49. Pagden, "Introduction," p. xix.

Spaniards were perpetrating a wicked continent-wide crime against the indigenous population. First as a priest, then as a Dominican friar (beginning in 1523), finally as bishop of Chiapas (1544), and always as an activist, reformer, and extraordinarily prolific writer, he devoted the rest of his life to protesting the evils he had witnessed, proposing new laws, and trying to persuade the Spanish Crown to end the worst abuses of Spanish colonial rule.

Las Casas's first strategy was to offer eyewitness accounts of what he had seen. He offered these eyewitness accounts orally before ruling authorities both in the New World and, following repeated return journeys, in Spain, as well as in a massive series of writings — many of which remain in print today. His first major book, begun in 1527, was his massive *Apologetic History of the Indies*. He abbreviated this work in 1542 when he wrote his *Short Account of the Destruction of the Indies* (published 1552). He also wrote a kind of ethnography describing the practices of the native populations, a very important project in light of the significance of degrading Spanish depictions of the purportedly low intelligence and depraved lifestyle of indigenous peoples. In these books, Las Casas presents himself as an eyewitness both to the dignity of remote but fully humane and in their way quite civilized societies and to Spanish atrocities too grotesque to fully comprehend if one had not been present. As he writes in *A Short Account,* he seeks to break "the conspiracy of silence about what has really been happening."[50] He writes to bear witness to evil in order to prevent its continuation — a reminder of literary projects from the twentieth century that sought to do exactly the same thing amidst the atrocities of that era. One might call him the first holocaust memoirist.

I use the term "holocaust" intentionally and with care. I had intended to give here just a few examples of the vicious inhumanity Las Casas summarizes in his *Short Account of the Destruction of the Indies* — a book that every Christian, indeed every human being, should read. But such an effort seems now deeply inappropriate, something like offering a brief précis of Raul Hilberg's three-volume *Destruction of the European Jews*. For that is what Las Casas saw — a holocaust. And that is where his account begins — with a survey of the desolate landscape of the New World, once teeming with Amerindians, but by the time he published his book, largely bereft of them. Why? Because so many native Americans were dead, their commu-

---

50. Las Casas, *Short Account*, p. 127. Page references to this work have been placed in the text for the next few paragraphs.

nities holocausts ("burnt offerings") to Spanish imperialism: "This whole region, once teeming with human beings, is now deserted over a distance of more than two thousand leagues: a distance, that is, greater than the journey from Seville to Jerusalem and back again . . . the despotic and diabolical behavior of the Christians has, over the last forty years, led to the unjust and totally unwarranted deaths of more than twelve million souls, women and children among them" (p. 12).

Las Casas describes how this happened in vivid and bloodcurdling accounts of events that took place from island to island, kingdom to kingdom — most of which, he repeatedly says, he witnessed with his own eyes. Vainly attempting to summarize the "two main ways in which those pretending to be Christians" have created such devastation, Las Casas breaks down the evils he has witnessed into "unjust, cruel, bloody, and tyrannical war," and the murders of "anyone and everyone who has shown the slightest sign of resistance" (p. 12). But that schema falls short of even beginning to capture the wanton and sadistic cruelty he narrates.

Take just one example. In his four-page summary of events in Hispaniola, at the very beginning of the conquest, Las Casas names the following: the mass slaughter of men, women, and children; mass enslavement; torture; rape; verbal mockery of the suffering of those dying; gamesmanship and wagers among the conquerors related to their skills in torture and murder; smashing babies against rocks; the slow roasting of men and women in groups as a form of torture-execution; the use of dogs to track those trying to escape and to kill them; and the execution of 100 natives for every one European killed in self-defense (pp. 14-17).

I came to this study as one most familiar with mass inhumanity through research on the Holocaust. With that more recent evil as a reference point, from reading Las Casas's *Short Account* I identified the following resemblances between what was done to the indigenous populations of the Americas and what was done to the Jews from 1939 to 1945:

- Mass murder, sometimes of entire communities and often of large parts of communities
- Mass "reprisals" for various "offenses"
- Use of deception to trick unsuspecting communities before destroying them
- Slavery for extracting work (e.g., in the mines)
- Slavery for the purpose of slow torture-murder
- Forced relocation of communities

- Systematic rape and sexual slavery
- Pillage of land, food, and property
- Torture for various reasons, including as "interrogation"
- Systematic starvation
- Bartering of people as hostages for goods and property
- Use of dogs to frighten, torture, and kill
- Branding with marks of domination and servitude
- Executions of the innocent for terror purposes
- Hunting down those trying to flee and killing them mercilessly
- Special efforts to identify, torment, and kill community leaders
- Mockery of the grief and suffering of the victims
- Escalating patterns of cruelty and sadism
- Destruction of millions, a significant majority of the region's population

A close reading of *A Short Account* reveals that Las Casas was no mere reporter of atrocities. He was, after all, a student of the Bible, and by the time of this writing had been a cleric, friar, and Christian leader for decades. As such, Las Casas offers what I would describe as a twofold biblical diagnostic for interpreting what he had witnessed, together with its ultimate moral sources. First: five times, by my count, Las Casas names "greed" and "ambition" or a direct variant as the ultimate source of the evils being inflicted on the natives (pp. 3, 7, 53, 105, 129). He uses these categories at the very beginning and very end of the book, and several times in between. This scheme cannot be accidental.

These conquerors, says Las Casas with great bitterness, "have taken no more trouble to preach the Christian faith to these peoples than if they had been dealing with dogs" (p. 126). (So much for the papal donation for the purposes of evangelization.) These men want, above all, *gold*. They want whatever else they can extract from or terrorize out of the natives. They will steal the food right out of their mouths. And they want *position*. They are ambitious to be the rulers of all they survey. They want power, and they know there is no greater or purer symbol of power than the ability to kill and enslave with impunity. Out-of-control greed and ambition have morally degraded the conquerors and led directly to mass murder — to the utter desecration of human life.

The second diagnostic move Las Casas repeatedly makes is found in his employment of Romans 1. Though he never cites chapter and verse, he often repeats variations on a theme that is critically important in that biblical text (Rom. 1:26ff.): "Having abandoned all Christian sense of right and wrong [they have] been totally given over to a reprobate mind" (p. 69). Or, in a somewhat more fulsome statement, he declares: "The longer they spent in the region the more ingenious were the torments, each crueler than the last, that they inflicted on their victims, as God finally abandoned them and left them to plummet headlong into a life of full-time crime and wickedness" (p. 80). Las Casas has personally witnessed the God-given gifts of human imagination and creativity descend to ever more ingenious forms of cruelty and sadism among the Spanish conquerors. They have gotten better and better at being more and more evil. (I have spared the reader a narration of almost all these cruelties, just as Las Casas says he has narrated only a fraction of what he saw.) Las Casas adopts Paul's interpretation in Romans 1. The God-given restraints on wickedness provided by conscience and other forms of divine restraint have been removed. All that remains is the abyss of spiraling evil. They have been left to their own devices and are spiraling toward eternal punishment as the richly deserved reward for their wickedness.

Las Casas repeatedly demonstrates the ability to enter with sympathy into the sufferings he has witnessed. He wrote in a culture in which, as Pagden notes, ancient texts and traditions had primary authority, not contemporary eyewitness accounts. The Bible, the church fathers, and a handful of classical authors, authoritatively interpreted by the church, communicated all the truth needed for life.[51] But Las Casas brought a new kind of authority to bear — the authority of personal experience — in particular, the personal experience of the victimization of others.

Honoring life as a practice hinges on *a way of perceiving* other people, leading to a posture of reverence toward them and then a consequent sense of responsibility for them.[52] Human beings have demonstrated an extraordinary capacity to *fail to see* the fellow-humanity of (certain categories of) others; indeed, to train ourselves via our ideologies, greed, ambition, and xenophobia *not to see* that fellow humanity. During my research on those Christians who rescued Jews during the Holocaust, I discovered that it was precisely the experience of becoming an eyewitness to the suffering of Jews that, for some at least, pierced the veil of a trained *not noticing* and *not caring* and *not recognizing* the Jew as a fellow human being. It was only seeing

---

51. Pagden, "Introduction," p. xxxiv.

52. I refer readers to Glen H. Stassen and David P. Gushee, *Kingdom Ethics: Following Jesus in Contemporary Context* (Downers Grove, Ill.: InterVarsity, 2003), chapter 3.

a Jew shot in the streets, or thrown crudely onto a truck, or weeping at the door, that made the difference.[53]

Nearly everyone who has wept has the capacity to recognize the significance of the tears of another — and nearly everyone who has grieved a dead loved one can find some common ground with another who has done the same. Something in the human suffering that Las Casas witnessed overrode his training-in-dehumanization and helped him to perceive the victimized native as a fellow human being. Every rhetorical strategy he later employed was secondary; the perception of fellow-humanity through suffering was primary. His grief over the victimization of fellow humans is palpable throughout his *Short Account.* Speaking of the conquest of Guatemala by Pedro de Alvarado, Las Casas ends his description with these stirring words:

> Oh, if one were to catalogue all those orphaned by him, all those whose children he stole, all those whose wives he took, all the women he widowed, and all the adultery, violence and rape that could be laid at his door, as well as all those he deprived of liberty, and all the torment and calamity countless people suffered because of him! If one could calculate how many tears were shed and how many sighs and anguished groans were caused by his actions, how much grief he occasioned in this life, and how many souls he consigned to eternal damnation in the life hereafter. . . .[54]

Las Casas was able to grieve with those who grieved, to see the natives as his fellow human beings. His narratives convey something of both their grief and his. But readers of Las Casas easily discover that besides atrocity narration he indeed makes appeals to various kinds of textual authorities. Sometimes he turns to the kinds of biblical motifs we discussed in earlier chapters, for example, when he critiques the mistreatment of natives "created in God's image" (p. 74). Several times in *A Short Account* he appeals to the significance of the cross, calling for better treatment of "these poor wretches for whom our Lord died" (p. 72). He speaks with sarcasm of "How closely they [the conquerors, fail to] obey that commandment to love one's neighbor that underpins the Law and the books of the Prophets" (p. 93).

---

53. David P. Gushee, *Righteous Gentiles of the Holocaust: Genocide and Moral Obligation,* 2nd ed. (Minneapolis: Paragon House, 2003), chapter 5.

54. Las Casas, *Short Account,* p. 64. Page references to this work have been placed in the text for the next few paragraphs.

But occasionally in his *Short Account,* and far more in nearly everything else he wrote, Las Casas turns to legal discourse. He argues that the mistreatment of the Indians violates "natural, canon, and civil law" (p. 6), or "natural, divine, and Roman law" (p. 70), or "justice" and "rights" (p. 69), and he pleads in legal terms for better treatment. His ceaseless advocacy for legal change did in fact help bring some results, such as the "New Laws" of 1542 — though the Crown's decrees were largely ignored, if not openly resisted. Anthony Pagden draws a connection between these two approaches in Las Casas when he says that during his era "the only science which provided any guidelines as to how to [transmute experience into text] was the law."[55] Pagden apparently sees experience as primary and legal/forensic argumentation as secondary for Las Casas, who was simply employing the main literary tool available to him.

But this is probably not correct. Las Casas was a Catholic cleric/monastic who would have been deeply familiar with the theological-legal tradition of Catholicism as it had developed over the centuries. He wrote in the wake of the systematizing of Catholic thought by Thomas Aquinas (1225-1274) and those who followed in his wake. Las Casas argued and apparently thought like one steeped in this particularly law-oriented version of Christian theological ethics. Like a good Thomist, he structured numerous arguments based on the kinds of law recognized in Catholic theology and culture at the time. He argued that the law of God (divine law/natural law), the laws of the church (canon law), the laws of Spain (civil law), and the laws of war (codified in canon law, civil law, and incipient international law) were being violated by the Spanish settlers and that this had to change, not least because such lawbreaking courted the fierce wrath of God.[56]

We dare not overlook both the contemporary and the long-term significance of the recourse by Las Casas to legal argument, and of the specific kinds of legal arguments he made. In our discussion of Old Testament law, it became clear that law in Israel was viewed as coming from God and as one of the primary means by which the sacred lives of the most vulnerable were protected (puzzle #14). Everyone in principle needs the protection of law because everyone is vulnerable to victimization. The powerless, though, need the protection of law not just in principle but, moreover, in the midst of the abuses they experience in everyday life. That is because

55. Pagden, "Introduction," p. xxxvi.
56. Pagden, "Introduction," p. xxxviii.

they lack the power to protect their own interests. A well-constructed, fairly enforced body of laws that treats everyone as a person, and every person as equal before the law, is one of the most important ways that cultures honor the sacredness of human life. This is equally true in ancient Israel, sixteenth-century Hispaniola, twentieth-century Germany, or twenty-first-century Sudan. Human beings who do not fall under the protection of law are the most vulnerable on the planet. Law, fairly written and rigorously enforced, consecrates life! Las Casas seems to have understood this. A massive amount of his work was devoted to legal argumentation on behalf of the rights of native Americans.

Status under the three primary categories of law is accorded only to human beings.[57] Incredibly — or not so incredibly, depending on the depth of one's knowledge of human nature and history — *whether the native Americans were really to be viewed as fellow humans* therefore became a fundamental point of debate between Las Casas and his adversaries. Indeed, the (human?) nature and moral status of the natives had been a matter of fierce discussion since the beginning of the Spanish Conquest.[58] If opponents could argue that the natives were not quite, not really, not fully human beings, the arguments of activists like Las Casas could be blunted. Anthony Pagden says Las Casas himself had been fighting various versions of this fight since 1513.[59] But it culminated in his famous 1550-1551 debates with Juan Ginés de Sepúlveda, a Spanish theologian who became the most articulate defender of the idea that the native populations were not quite human beings, or at least not human beings of the same type and rank as the Spaniards. Ordered by the Spanish king — who suspended all conquests until the debates were concluded — the Las Casas–Sepúlveda debates ultimately hinged on the moral status of the colonized. The results echo through history.

Sepúlveda's arguments, which were certainly not unique to him, went essentially as follows.[60] The natives, or "Indians," are barbarians, of very limited rational capacity and incapable of any learning beyond technical

---

57. Of course, today we rightly recognize categories of animal rights and ecosystem rights as well.

58. Lewis Hanke, *All Mankind Is One: A Study of the Disputation between Bartolomé de Las Casas and Juan Ginés de Sepúlveda on the Religious and Intellectual Capacity of the American Indians* (De Kalb: Northern Illinois University Press, 1974), pp. 7-9.

59. Pagden, "Introduction," p. xxviii.

60. Bartolomé de Las Casas, *In Defense of the Indians*, trans. Stafford Poole (De Kalb: Northern Illinois University Press, 1992), pp. 12-16.

skills. They are immoral, cruel, and unable to govern themselves. Therefore, following an argument made by Aristotle, they are natural slaves who
by natural law are obligated to submit to the control of their moral and intellectual superiors. If they do not willingly submit to their superiors, they
legitimately can be forced to do so by war. Therefore Spanish wars against
the natives of the New World are just according to natural law, and in the
end the subjugation of the natives to the Spaniards amounts to their liberation in their own best interests.

Sepúlveda also argues from Scripture for a parallel between the conquest of the native peoples in the Promised Land and the conquest of the
natives of the New World. The parallel hinges on the shared practice of human sacrifice among both groups of natives. Scripture shows that it is just
to wage war against peoples that practice both idolatry and the heinous
crime of human sacrifice. Indeed, it is obligatory to stop them from continuing such practices as an act of protection of the innocent from harm,
another feature of natural law reasoning as it relates to just war.

Sepúlveda also argues that once the Indians have been subdued, the
door will be open to their evangelization, by force if necessary. He supports this argument with reference to Augustine, Constantine, and others.
He buttresses his overall argument with an appeal to the authority of the
pope, who declared the use of arms against the natives to be just and authorized the Spanish king to conquer them.

Las Casas attacked Sepúlveda in a massive book-length series of arguments bringing together his observations of indigenous cultures, legal analysis, historical argument, biblical interpretation, and theological reasoning.

We take up the latter arguments first. Las Casas rejects the legitimacy
of any form of coercive evangelization. The Christian faith can only be
advanced, among those who have never encountered it, by persuasion,
preaching, and good example. Las Casas says that he and others have been
personally involved in the successful spread of Christian faith among the
peoples of the New World in this way.[61] He argues from Scripture and tradition to make the dubious claims that force may be legitimately employed to deal with relapses of Christians into heresy or for recovering
formerly Christian provinces from the Muslims. But he then says that
there is *no* legitimate use of force to coerce the "conversion" of peoples
who have never been exposed to the Christian message.[62] He bitterly re-

61. Las Casas, *In Defense*, chapters 39–40.
62. Las Casas, *In Defense*, chapters 7–12; 26–28.

jects the claim that war against the natives prepares them for a later peaceful evangelization, instead arguing that it is far more likely to turn them against the Christian faith: "Now if Christians unsettle everything by wars, burnings, fury, rashness, fierceness, sedition, plunder, and insurrection . . . where are the holy deeds that should move the hearts of pagans to glorify God?"[63]

In a move that was astonishing in its own time and not much less astonishing in ours, Las Casas suggests that the use of human sacrifice in some indigenous religions (he rejects the claim that the natives routinely and broadly practiced human sacrifice) does not constitute grounds for their conquest. He counters Sepúlveda's use of Scripture by claiming that the war stories from Joshua and Deuteronomy must not be read as standing divine commands to kill all idolaters.[64] More daringly, Las Casas also suggests that such sacrifices, where they occur, have a kind of internal logic related to the sincerely held religious beliefs of the peoples who practice them, and are therefore not always evil.[65] In other words, Las Casas was able to respect the internally consistent religious reasoning and the desire to serve God motivating the practices of people whom he believed religiously misguided and with whom he profoundly disagreed.[66] He also argues on a just-war basis that, in any case, killing natives to prevent human sacrifice fails the test of proportionality. (Notice the constructive use of just-war theory here.) Making massive wars that kill millions to prevent human sacrifices that kill far fewer fails just-war reasoning.[67] Las Casas also argues on the basis of a jurisdictional logic that it is not legitimate for the Spaniards or the church to punish violations of natural law or Christian belief on the part of the indigenous populations.[68]

But what is finally most significant for our purposes, and echoes most strongly through the ages, is the way Las Casas dismantles the idea that the indigenous are somehow not quite fully human. He does this by working with the thinking of Aristotle and Aquinas related to four different catego-

---

63. Quoted in Hanke, *All Mankind Is One*, p. 97. See Las Casas, *In Defense*, chapters 42–48.

64. Las Casas, *In Defense*, chapter 13.

65. Las Casas, *In Defense*, chapters 33–37.

66. Willie James Jennings describes Las Casas's move here as a kind of breakthrough in "theological generosity." See his *The Christian Imagination: Theology and the Origins of Race* (New Haven and London: Yale University Press, 2010), pp. 100-101.

67. Las Casas, *In Defense*, chapter 28.

68. Las Casas, *In Defense*, chapters 6–10; Hanke, *All Mankind Is One*, pp. 87-95.

ries of "barbarians."[69] These include (1) those who are barbarians because of their wicked and savage behavior, (2) those who are barbarians because they have no written language, (3) those who are by definition barbarians because they are non-Christians, and (4) those who are barbarians because they are "freaks of nature" who lack rational capacity, laws, or any other evidence of a way of life appropriate to human beings. Regarding these four categories, Las Casas argues (1) that the natives are not generally characterized by wicked, merciless, and savage behavior; indeed, the Spaniards have far better fitted that definition; (2) that not having a written language makes a people "barbaric" only in a very restricted sense; other Spanish missionaries who had learned native tongues emphasized that the natives had beautiful and intricate languages with detectable grammatical structures, and had demonstrated the capacity to learn and speak Spanish and Latin; (3) that it is incorrect to classify all non-Christians as barbarians in any sense that would justify their domination or subjugation; and, most importantly, (4) that the natives are not "freaks of nature" who lack rational capacity or other evidences of human function but instead have visible and impressive structures of intellectual life, politics, law, and morality. Even in making these kinds of arguments Las Casas was bending dangerously in the direction of tying human worth to the achievement of certain human-making characteristics (puzzle #5).

Undoubtedly Las Casas had encountered and heard about native tribes with very different levels of "civilization" as a Westerner would evaluate it. But he seems to reject at a theological level the idea that there could be large groups of human beings who are not quite human, or that there could be "greater and lesser" human beings.[70] This would, says Las Casas, frustrate God's "love of mankind" and his great "will to save all men."[71] Las Casas appears to be theologically committed to the idea that there could not be any subhumans or lesser ranks of human beings or peoples on the planet. He seeks to buttress his case with empirical claims related to the behaviors that he observes among the indigenous, behaviors evidencing their rationality and immortal souls, categories for human worth so important in the thought-world of his era. He seeks further support in the structures of natural, canon, and civil law. But the ultimate foundation for his resistance to the desecration of indigenous life is the theological lens with which he

69. Las Casas, *In Defense*, chapters 1–5.
70. Las Casas, *In Defense*, chapter 4.
71. Hanke, *All Mankind Is One*, pp. 83-84.

views the world. Las Casas, and the many that followed in his footsteps, were committed to "the essential unity of mankind," as Lewis Hanke has put it. Las Casas writes in his *Defense:* "The nature of men is the same and all are called by Christ in the same way."[72] Or, as Las Casas sympathizer Tomás López wrote, "All the world is one."[73] People committed to the sacredness of each and every human life under the sovereignty of God are trained to see this common humanity. Their perceptions follow their convictions. Those committed to other convictions, or driven by interests or ambitions or hatreds, train themselves to see the differences among individuals and groups, and immediately to classify the differences hierarchically and in their own selfish interests. One can accurately say that the argument between Las Casas and Sepúlveda was not merely an argument between them alone — it resounded through the Americas until the end of the era of Spanish rule, if not to this day.[74] And it resounds everywhere some are classified as less than fully human, with desecrations immediately to follow.

Bartolomé de Las Casas was far from perfect, and his legacy is not unmixed. Critics said he enjoyed the spotlight far too much and had more than a touch of pride and narcissism. Some, mainly aggrieved Spaniards, still suggest that he exaggerated both Spanish excesses and native innocence. He has been charged with being ineffective in his activism, of accomplishing little for the American natives, and of having little direct relationship with them. He was a paternalist who worked for rather than with the Amerindians. He has been bitterly indicted for proposing, even though quickly reversing, the idea that Africans rather than native Americans should be employed as slaves. He has been charged with being a useful stooge of the Spanish Crown in its efforts to pacify and dominate the New World and gain the upper hand against the settler population. His evangelistic fervor has been treated as in itself an aspect of the "peaceful conquest" (e.g., cultural genocide) foisted on the Amerindians, even while he resisted their physical annihilation.[75] Some contemporary thinkers, such as Daniel Castro, indict him as representing simply a kinder, gentler ecclesiastical imperialism that helped the Spanish feel better about their inherently oppressive enterprise.[76]

72. Quoted in Hanke, *All Mankind Is One*, p. 96.
73. Hanke, *All Mankind Is One*, p. 130.
74. Hanke, *All Mankind Is One*, pp. 122ff.
75. See Tinker, *Missionary Conquest*, p. 7. The quote is from a 1539 statement about Las Casas by the governor of Guatemala.
76. Daniel Castro, *Another Face of Empire: Bartolomé de Las Casas, Indigenous Rights, and Ecclesiastical Imperialism* (Durham, N.C., and London: Duke University Press, 2007).

There is reason for sympathy for some of these accusations, but I believe that in the context of his era such criticisms are largely overdrawn. Overall, Las Casas stands the test of time as an exemplar of a life-revering Christianity that stood against the vast power of a desecrating Christendom. And the way he made his arguments echoes with claims made through the rest of this book. He spoke on behalf of those who had little voice or power; eventually, as is completely fitting, the indigenous and oppressed would speak and act for themselves, and articulate their own indigenous theologies and ethics of justice and liberation.[77] He spoke and wrote of human suffering and a God who responds to the cries of the victimized, anticipating what later came to be known as liberation theology. He made legal arguments that contributed to the very early human rights tradition of the modern West as well as to the foundations of international law (puzzle #11). And he found his way to bold arguments on behalf of not just religious *liberty* but also religious *respect* for those whose religions were profoundly different from our own.[78] He demonstrates, as Francis did, the indispensable connection between respect for people of other religions, their religious liberty, their right not to be killed by us over religious differences, and respect for the sacredness of life. Las Casas helps us see, dimly but clearly, the religious origins of modern rights and liberties traditions that are too often called "secular" and "individualistic." But we see here that such efforts were deeply Christian and other-centered, focused on the needs of vulnerable strangers. We will see something similar in the arguments of the early Baptists for the right to religious liberty not just for themselves but for everyone — including Jews, Christianity's ultimate other, and the recipient of some of Christendom's worst abuses.

6.3. Anti-Semitism, Overton, and the Sacred Lives of Jews

> Then the people as a whole answered, "His blood be on us and on our children!"
>
> Matthew 27:25

---

77. It is simultaneously possible to affirm that oppressed people's own voices must be heard and that it is morally good to stand in solidarity with the oppressed and speak up on their behalf when no one will listen to the victimized themselves.

78. Gustavo Gutiérrez, *Las Casas: In Search of the Poor of Jesus Christ* (Maryknoll, N.Y.: Orbis, 1993), praises Las Casas much as I have done in this chapter and treats him as a trailblazer, well ahead of his time, in such areas as liberation theology, religious freedom, and respect for non-Christian religions.

In my argument so far, I have sought to keep two claims in tension that often are collapsed in favor of one or the other: (a) that a powerfully life-honoring ethic flows out of the biblical tradition and predominates in the life of the early church, and (b) that a disastrous subversion of that ethic develops after the transition to Christendom.

I think both claims are generally true, otherwise I would not make them. But I am painfully aware of a group whose treatment by the early Christians raises acute questions to this thesis: Jews. We need to ask whether the two-part thesis holds for Christian treatment of the Jewish people. We will find that it does not hold, which is both tragic and also a helpful corrective for anyone tempted to posit a sinless church prior to Constantine. The bit of good news to be found here is that finally, beginning in the seventeenth century, some Christian dissenters began to speak up for Jews. We will catch a glimpse of their story.

The Origins of Anti-Semitism

If we define anti-Semitism as hatred of the Jewish people,[79] its origins go back deeply into the history of the Jewish people themselves.

Anti-Semitism in antiquity was related to a too-standard human contempt for difference. But it was also uniquely tied to certain distinctive features of the identity and experience of the Jewish people. The Jewish people believed in a God worshiped nowhere else in the ancient world. They believed this God had specially chosen Israel from all the peoples of the earth to be his servant-people. They believed that they stood in a covenant relationship with God that required of them a comprehensive, distinctive religio-cultural-ethical way of life. And, for several hundred years, they had control of a slice of land in which to live out this way of life.[80]

---

79. The term is deeply problematic. It was invented in the 1870s by the German Jew-hater Wilhelm Marr to refer specifically to "non-confessional" hatred of Jews; in particular, opposition to Jewish emancipation and social equality in European societies, on the basis of supposedly objective racial, scientific, or political considerations. Like many terms, it eventually grew beyond its origins to become the catchall term for hatred of Jews. See Robert Wistrich, *Antisemitism: The Longest Hatred* (New York: Pantheon Books, 1991), pp. xv-xvii. A distinction is often drawn between anti-Semitism, now defined broadly as *hatred of Jews or the Jewish people,* and anti-Judaism, defined as *hatred of Judaism as a religion.* The terms obviously cannot be entirely distinguished, and certainly not for any exculpatory reasons; for example, to claim that Christians did not hate Jews, only Jewish religion.

80. Richard L. Rubenstein and John K. Roth appear to argue that anti-Semitism is trace-

The series of conquests that we remember in two primary movements — the Assyrian destruction of the northern kingdom of Israel in 722/721 B.C.E., and the Babylonian conquest of the southern kingdom of Judah in 587/586 B.C.E. — decimated but did not destroy the Jewish people. The conquests weakened their numerical presence in their historic homeland, cost them political control over that homeland, and furthered their dispersion across the ancient world. It would have seemed inevitable that the assimilating pressures of living as minority communities in other lands over hundreds of years would have cost the Jewish people their distinctive identity. But while some Jews did fully assimilate to the cultures of Babylonia, Persia, Greece, Rome, Egypt, and elsewhere, the Jewish people as a whole did not assimilate, and Jewish peoplehood survived.

The formative expressions of anti-Semitism in the pre-Christian world were directed at these minority Jewish religious communities attempting to live faithfully Jewish lives while situated in lands dominated by others.[81] One primary strategy for retaining Jewish identity was careful social separation, including, in some cases, voluntary ghettoization in separate Jewish quarters of major cities.[82] Sometimes this carefully protected Jewish differentness was treated with respect by outside observers, and even drew imitators and converts. More often it was treated with incomprehension and contempt, and drew mockery, hatred, threats, and even expulsions and violence. Pressures to assimilate by forced worship of national gods, and threats of violence for failing to do so — or even just for being Jewish — echo through the awe-inspiring biblical books of Esther and Daniel, and the realities that lay behind the stories told in these books are well attested beyond the Scriptures. Certainly conditions for Jews varied. But it is not too much to say that anti-Semitism directed at diaspora Jews was widespread, especially after the conquests of Alexander the Great and the birth of an aggressive Hellenism.[83] The suppression and seething unhappiness

---

able ultimately to the distinctive Jewish religious identity birthed in the time of Moses. See their *Approaches to Auschwitz: The Holocaust and Its Legacy,* rev. ed. (Louisville: Westminster John Knox, 2003), pp. 26-29.

81. Here I follow Fr. Edward Flannery in tracing the origins of "anti-Semitism" proper to events that occurred amidst the Jewish experience of diaspora. Flannery is concerned not to trace anti-Semitism to the very origins of the Jewish people, as if it is somehow an inevitable "eternal" concomitant of Jewish existence. Flannery, *The Anguish of the Jews* (New York: Macmillan, 1965), pp. 3, 22-23.

82. Flannery, *Anguish of the Jews,* p. 6.

83. Flannery, *Anguish of the Jews,* p. 6.

of the Jewish people in their subjugated historic homeland were also a perennial reality.[84] After the successful Maccabean revolt of 166 B.C.E., Jewish confidence soared and Jewish influence spread in noticeable and resented ways in the world of the Mediterranean basin. Verbal and physical attacks on Jews heightened. Many of the anti-Semitic canards that appeared later were birthed during this period, including such atrocious charges as Jewish ritual murder of Gentile babies.[85] And, again, all this long predates the emergence of Christianity.

The Emergence of Christianity and the Great Jewish-Christian Schism

The emergence of a great world religion centered on the crucified Galilean Jew permanently linked what became the Jewish and Christian peoples in an often uneasy and sometimes disastrous embrace. We are and always have been religiously related, as siblings, or perhaps better, as mother and daughter,[86] but for the great majority of our shared tenure on this planet our filial ties have been hostile. Sometimes they have been deadly. The birth of Christianity introduced an entirely new dimension into anti-Semitism.

The Jesus movement was initially a Jewish eschatological sect constituted by those who believed that Jesus was the Messiah (the "Anointed One" from God) long promised to Israel, that he had inaugurated the messianic age even though he had unexpectedly suffered crucifixion, and that by God's redemptive power he had risen from the dead and was still present among his followers. They believed that in his Son Jesus, God had initiated the climax of the redemption of Israel and of the world.

---

84. This is perhaps most profoundly symbolized by the brutal overreaching of Seleucid ruler Antiochus IV Epiphanes in his desecration of the Jewish temple, and the Maccabean revolt that followed and brought a fragile Jewish independence for seventy-five years.

85. Flannery, *Anguish of the Jews,* pp. 13-14.

86. Christianity and Judaism are often metaphorically described as sibling religions, with Judaism as the elder brother. I think it more honest to join with Jules Isaac and others in describing Christianity as a daughter religion to Judaism. See his *Jesus and Israel,* trans. Sally Gran (New York: Holt, Rinehart and Winston, [1959] 1971). Isaac, a leading French historian of Jewish descent, lost his wife and daughter to the Nazis. His incredibly poignant writings about the origins of the hatred that shattered his family were precedent-setting in causing a reconsideration of Jews and Judaism, especially in Catholic thought.

The first followers of Jesus were Jews. The Jesus sect began life as a tiny messianic movement within the sprawling and squabbling religious landscape of first-century Palestinian Judaism, a context deeply marked by the strains of Roman domination and the consequent pressures on Jewish survival, self-definition, and community cohesion.[87] Most of the world's Jews were not in Palestine during Jesus' ministry but were scattered in dispersion throughout the world, a point often overlooked by later Christians. As Jules Isaac notes, "the Jewish people 'as a whole'" never encountered the historical Jesus.[88] Or as John Howard Yoder puts it, "The Jews did not reject Christianity."[89] Those Jews who became believers in Jesus Christ shared with those Jews who did not believe in Jesus a millennia-old religious heritage, including the Hebrew Bible, numerous liturgical and ethical traditions, and an entire thought-world. They also shared a common context of imperial oppression that threatened Jewish survival, bitterly divided the subjugated people, and served as a hothouse of desperate religious creativity.

Scholarly theories abound as to both where the most intensely felt religious differences were perceived to lie and also about the timing of the hostility that developed between what gradually became two separate groups named "Jews" and "Christians." But for the sake of simplicity, let me suggest three main developments.

In the period after the death of Jesus (ca. 30 C.E.) and before the Roman War (66-70 C.E.), it seems likely that the most intense point of conflict that emerged between the messianic Jesus movement and the predominant leadership of the Jewish religious community concerned the Christian reinterpretation of the demands of Torah observance.[90] In Paul's letters, conflicts both within the Christian community and with external Jewish critics over the abandonment or weakening of Torah observance

---

87. The first century was a time of great ferment and transition in Jewish religiosity. James Carroll, following Alan Segal and others, suggests that both "Christianity" and rabbinic Judaism emerged during this time of ferment. There were multiple competing Judaisms in Jesus' day, not one thing that can be called "Judaism." Carroll, *Constantine's Sword* (New York: Houghton Mifflin, 2001), pp. 75-76, emphasizes the centrality of Roman subjugation and its pressures on Jews and Judaism in Palestine.

88. Isaac, *Jesus and Israel*, p. 94.

89. John Howard Yoder, *The Jewish-Christian Schism Revisited*, ed. Michael G. Cartwright and Peter Ochs (Grand Rapids: Eerdmans, 2003), p. 51.

90. John C. Meagher, "As the Twig Was Bent: Antisemitism in Greco-Roman and Earliest Christian Times," in *AntiSemitism and the Foundations of Christianity*, ed. Alan T. Davies (New York: Paulist, 1979), p. 20. "They were persecuted for abusing Torah."

are very clear. The decision to propel the Jesus message forward to the Gentiles by creating a new option for how they might affiliate with Judaism both disrupted the status quo in Jewish life and made the Christian Way far more appealing to Gentiles (cf. Gal. 2; Acts 10; 15:5-11; 21:21; etc.).[91] This struggle over Torah became the major internal challenge facing the earliest Christian communities and also a source of considerable conflict beyond the churches.

It has been argued that a significant fissure between Palestinian Jewish Christians and non-Christian Palestinian Jews emerged after the Roman War.[92] Palestinian Jewish Christians refused to participate in the fighting, fleeing to Pella, provoking the anger of some of their fellow Jews and perhaps deepening the emerging schism between the Jesus followers and others.[93] After the devastation it became common for Christians to interpret the brutal destruction of Jerusalem, the desecration and destruction of its temple, and the massive slaughter of Jews as evidence of divine judgment on "Jerusalem" for rejecting Jesus, a theme signaled in several New Testament texts (Matt. 21:33-46; 22:1-14, 24, and parallels; cf. especially Luke 19:41-44).[94] It was not a small matter when one of the Jewish people's three greatest historic disasters was interpreted as a sign of God's judgment on Jews for rejecting Christ.

Then there is the New Testament itself. Much of the New Testament — including at least three of the four Gospels (Matthew, Luke, and John) — was written after this catastrophic war.[95] The writing of these Gospel accounts was itself a historical event that clearly reflected the state of relations in each author's specific context between those Jews who believed in Jesus

91. The best and most accessible description of what happened has been offered by Amy-Jill Levine in *The Misunderstood Jew: The Church and the Scandal of the Jewish Jesus* (New York: HarperOne, 2006), pp. 68-71.

92. The second great cataclysm for Palestinian Jewry, during 135, in which many hundreds of thousands more Jews were killed at Roman hands, should also be noted here.

93. But not everyone fought the Romans; indeed, the Palestinian Jewish community as a whole was desperately split during this rebellion. Those who did not fight included key leaders among the Pharisees — which is one of the reasons why the Pharisees and the Jesus movement were the only two major surviving movements within Palestinian Jewish life after that war.

94. Flannery, *Anguish of the Jews*, p. 28.

95. And even Mark was probably written *during* that war. Each of the Gospel accounts therefore must be understood as having been affected by this epoch-shaping war. See Elaine Pagels, *The Origin of Satan: How Christians Demonized Jews, Pagans, and Heretics* (New York: Vintage Books, 1995), p. 8.

and those Jews who did not. Honesty requires Christians to face acute questions concerning retrospective interjection of later conflicts into earlier narratives about Jesus. In a time when Israel as a people was under threat, intense conflicts over the identity of the "true Israel" lay behind the texts both of the New Testament and of early rabbinic Judaism.[96] The increasingly bitter conflicts became inscribed in the sacred texts themselves, with fateful consequences through the ages.

The Gospel narratives and other New Testament texts routinely depict (disbelieving) Jews as antagonists to Jesus and his followers. There are nuances, and nuances matter; each Gospel handles the "Jewish problem" differently. But collectively, the texts contain powerfully negative images, words, and themes about the "Jewish" response to the Jew Jesus. It has been all too easy to read the New Testament as telling a story in which God graciously sent his Son Jesus to his own chosen people Israel, and they, incomprehensibly and wickedly, rejected him, sought to block his miraculous and redemptive ministry, and conspired to get him killed. Their leaders, notably the Pharisees but often others as well, are routinely depicted as the worst offenders of all. Amy-Jill Levine lifts up 1 Thessalonians 2:14-16 ("The Jews, who killed" the Lord Jesus and "oppose everyone"), Matthew 27:25 ("His blood be on us and on our children!"), and John 8:44 ("You are from your father the devil") as the three most significantly damaging texts, but a number of others have been named.[97] Alan Culpepper points out incisively that the writers who produced these texts were the most Jewish of all New Testament authors. They were not anti-Semitic; they were debating fiercely with their fellow Jews.[98] But they have too often been interpreted by later Gentiles in an anti-Semitic way, especially once a significant Jewish presence had disappeared from the church.

Looked at in panoramic historical context, Christianity brought the God of Israel far more deeply into the wider world as the messianic Jewish sect was embraced by increasing numbers of non-Jews. Christianity's adaptations of the Jewish religious tradition meant that the beauty of Judaism could become a blessing to billions, down to this very day, including this writer and every Gentile Christian.[99]

96. See Carroll, *Constantine's Sword*, chapter 9.

97. Levine, *The Misunderstood Jew*, chapter 3.

98. With reference to the Gospel of John on this issue, see R. Alan Culpepper, "The Gospel of John and the Jews," *Review and Expositor* 84 (1987): 282.

99. Irving Greenberg goes so far as to say that this is in fact evidence of God's activity — Christianity became the vehicle by which the God of the Jews was introduced deep into the

But Christianity developed a tragic ambivalence toward its own Jewish origins and toward the Jewish people. We Christians kept the "Old Testament," which kept us connected to our Jewish origins in a way, but often as a footnote to the superior "New Testament." We claimed key Old Testament figures such as Abraham but eventually claimed them exclusively for (Gentile) Christianity.[100] Insofar as we continued to read the "Old Testament," we employed Jewish text and tradition, but we cut ourselves off from ongoing Jewish interpretations, often succumbing to foolish hermeneutical errors in the process. We believed it our right to define the meaning of Jewish religion, casually denigrating those elements in "Judaism" that we abandoned or rejected, while ignoring or rejecting actual Jews who practiced an actual living religion. We developed a primordial tendency of bewilderment and even contempt toward these mysteriously blinded Jews who did not believe in Jesus. We assumed a supersessionist narrative that the legitimate Jewish religious journey ended with the birth of Christianity.[101]

Eventually the breach between Christianity and its Jewish mother became irrevocable. It was indeed gradual, taking as long as three centuries, with major milestones of alienation at points along the way. As Yoder points out, the Jewish-Christian schism "did not have to be."[102] But it happened. Gradually, Christianity became a Gentile religion severed from its Jewish origins. Mutual anathemas between Judaism and Christianity eventually came to abound. For Christians, vestiges of the Jewish narrative framework survived; the more strongly that narrative survived, the healthier Christianity tended to be. But especially after the Bar Kokhba revolt of 135 led to Roman exile of the surviving Jewish population of Jerusalem, both Jews and Christians became entirely dispersed minority faiths jostling for survival in an often hostile pagan culture. Both drew on the same

---

marrow of non-Jewish cultures. *For the Sake of Heaven and Earth: The New Encounter between Judaism and Christianity* (Philadelphia: Jewish Publication Society, 2004), especially pp. 41-42.

100. A story told in Jeffrey Siker, *Disinheriting the Jews: Abraham in Early Christian Controversy* (Louisville: Westminster John Knox, 1991).

101. A point strongly emphasized by pioneering, recently deceased Christian theologian Franklin Littell, who long argued that supersessionism — the belief that Christianity has superseded Judaism, and Christians have displaced Jews as God's chosen people — is the fatal flaw at the heart of Christianity. Littell, *The Crucifixion of the Jews: The Failure of Christians to Understand the Jewish Experience* (Macon, Ga.: Mercer University Press, [1975] 1986), p. 2.

102. This is the title of Yoder's primary essay in *Jewish-Christian Schism Revisited*.

religious heritage, texts, and symbols, and both made exclusive claims to the validity of their interpretation of that heritage. Eventually Christians got the upper hand in this disastrous filial rivalry.

A Systematic Theology of Contempt

Tensions between the schismatic religions were probably inevitable. But this does not reduce the shamefulness of the full-blown theology of contempt that Christians eventually developed. The theology was sufficiently systematic that it has its own name — the *adversus Judaeos* tradition — the "against the Jews" tradition. Not a good name — not a good tradition. It built the systematic dehumanization of one particular group of people into the very marrow of Christianity.

The most fundamental and damaging charge leveled by Christians was that the Jews as a people had killed the Messiah, Jesus. This was regicide (killing their own king) or even deicide (killing their own god).[103] No other people had committed so grave an offense. And it was not a onetime problem. Reading back from the death of Jesus, the church's leaders often suggested that Jewish history was a *trail of crimes.* The rejection and murder of Jesus was the most important act in a long history of Jewish rejections of the will of God, the law of God, and the prophets sent by God. Every act of sinfulness ever portrayed in the Old Testament is attributed to the Jews as a people, as representative of their collective character. They are and always have been, in this account, idol worshipers, prophet killers, rebels against God, blasphemers and haters of all righteousness.[104] The self-critical writings of the Hebrew prophets became, in the hands of the church, cudgels with which to bash a morally reprobate Jewish people — while all words of hope and affirmation of God's people in the Old Testament were interpreted as applying to the later church.[105]

In response God has utterly rejected the Jews. Their covenant relation-

---

103. Ruether points out that the regicide and deicide charges tended to emerge rather late, after the Constantinian transition. See Ruether, *Faith and Fratricide* (New York: Seabury Press, 1974), pp. 129-30.

104. Gregory of Nyssa summary from Moshe Lazar, "The Lamb and the Scapegoat: The Dehumanization of the Jews in Medieval Propaganda Imagery," in *Anti-Semitism in Times of Crisis,* ed. Sander L. Gilman and Steven T. Katz (New York: New York University Press, 1991), p. 47.

105. Ruether, *Faith and Fratricide,* p. 131.

ship with God has been ended. And yet as a people they still exist. This is a puzzle. The dominant interpretation that emerged was that though God has irrevocably rejected the Jews, it serves his divine purposes to allow them to continue to survive as a pariah people. Their very rejection of Christ, and the suffering it brings to them (conveniently, at the hands of Christian church and state), forces them to bear ironic witness to Christian faith. The deeper the Jewish suffering, the more triumphant the Christian church, the more obviously homeless and exiled the Jewish people (the "wandering Jew" motif),[106] the more clearly God's salvation-historical plan becomes publicly visible. This is sometimes called the "witness people myth," a theme in Augustine's writings and an important component in centuries of Christian theologizing about Jews and Judaism.[107]

The *adversus Judaeos* tradition never counseled the murder of Jews, though at times it came perilously close, and if we include Martin Luther's "we are at fault in not slaying them"[108] in the tradition, that judgment may need to be revised. But even short of Luther's hateful late polemics, the tradition desanctified the meaningfulness of Judaism as a religion. It awaited the day when God would finally either convert or damn the Jews so that there could be no more questions as to whose interpretation of the biblical tradition was correct. In the hands of "golden-mouthed" leaders like John Chrysostom — who called the Jews dogs, goats, pigs, and fat and lazy drunkards, their synagogues the haunts of demons — it certainly proved capable of inciting corporate Christian contempt, hatred, and violence against Jews, even when this was not sanctioned by the church or by law.[109]

This systematic theology of contempt developed over time, and different leaders specialized in different themes. But the worst of it cannot be

---

106. Ruether, *Faith and Fratricide*, p. 134.

107. Augustine's teaching about the Jews can be, and has been, read more positively. Paula Fredriksen has offered a book-length treatment of Augustine's developed theology of Judaism and the Jewish people and mainly credits him for advancing beyond many of the anti-Jewish tropes discussed in this section. She claims that Augustine's innovation of the Jews as a witness people actually saved many Jewish lives because it provided powerful theological legitimation for their continued existence as a people bearing witness to God. See Fredriksen, *Augustine and the Jews: A Christian Defense of Jews and Judaism* (New York: Doubleday, 2008).

108. Martin Luther, "On the Jews and Their Lies," in *Luther's Works*, vol. 47, ed. Franklin Sherman (Philadelphia: Fortress, 1971), p. 267.

109. See Chrysostom's fateful Antioch sermons in Paul W. Harkins, trans., *The Fathers of the Church*, vol. 32 (Washington, D.C.: CUA Press, 1979).

confined to some mythically bad post-Constantinian transition.[110] Many of the thinkers that I cited so approvingly in chapter 4 — Justin Martyr, Tertullian, Cyprian, Origen, et al. — contributed to it. Theologically anti-Jewish themes can be seen quite early, in the *Didache,* the epistles of Ignatius, the *Epistle of Barnabas,* and the *Epistle to Diognetus,* even though it took another hundred years for the full development of the themes mentioned above.[111] The negative reading of Judaism and the Jewish people goes back deep into the marrow of Christianity, and this to our eternal shame. It is in every layer and stage of the patristic tradition.[112] There is no time of primal innocence for the church on this one.

When Contempt Became Action

But there is one thing worth noticing in that fateful Constantinian transition. Prior to Constantine, Christian theological teaching *adversus Judaeos* was not coupled with the power to do anything about it.

After Constantine, however, it did not take long at all for church and state together to turn contempt for Jews into public policy and social custom. Jews were rapidly demoted to an inferior legal status as Christianity ascended to become the official religion. Raul Hilberg was among the first Holocaust scholars to notice the parallels between 1933-1941 Nazi anti-Jewish laws and anti-Jewish measures in Christendom. Most often, according to Hilberg, church synods first arrived at anti-Jewish provisions in canon law; these were then codified in state policies. "[F]or more than a thousand years, the will of the Church was also enforced by the state. . . . Every medieval state copied the canonical law and elaborated upon it."[113] Among the church/state provisions Hilberg discovered that paralleled later Nazi laws and actions were the following:

- Prohibition of intermarriage and sexual intercourse between Jews and Christians (306 C.E.)
- Jews and Christians not permitted to eat together (306)

110. Here I dissent from Yoder, who works hard to minimize the significance of the anti-Jewish themes in Christian writings prior to Constantine.

111. I am persuaded on this point by Littell, *Crucifixion of the Jews,* pp. 26-28.

112. Carroll, *Constantine's Sword,* pp. 92-93.

113. Raul Hilberg, *The Destruction of the European Jews,* rev. ed. (New York: Holmes and Meier, 1985), p. 11.

- Jews not allowed to hold public office (535)
- Jews not allowed to employ Christian servants (538)
- The Talmud and other Jewish books burned (681)
- Jews obliged to pay taxes to support the church (1078)
- Jews not permitted to be plaintiffs or witnesses against Christians (1179)
- Jewish clothes marked with special badges (1215)
- Construction of new synagogues prohibited (1222)
- Compulsory ghettos mandated (1267)
- Adoption of Judaism by a Christian banned (1310)
- Jews not permitted to obtain academic degrees (1434)

What changed with Christendom, then, was the ability of the church to establish its theological interpretation of Jews and Judaism as public policy. Church authorities were able to force social conditions upon the Jews that caused a deepening of their social and political marginalization and suffering, which itself represented a fulfillment of their theological interpretation of all things Jewish. The trend over the centuries was generally one of ever worsening status during the years prior to the Enlightenment, with progressive loss of rights and progressive intensification of restrictions.[114]

At times it all led to violence. Sometimes it was because "Christian" mobs simply came after them. This is where we get that word "pogrom." We have already seen that the zealous Crusaders more than once inflicted pogroms upon the Jews in their path, and that the Spaniards not only harassed but finally expelled their Jews in 1492, the same year Columbus sailed. Craziness accelerated in the high Middle Ages with charges of ritual murder, well poisoning, and host desecration, and the libeling of Jews as demonic, insidious, disease-like contagions dangerously infecting/afflicting Christian civilizations. Ghettoization, pogroms, forced conversions (and mistrust of those conversions), and expulsions were a direct result of this systematic theology of contempt — after centuries of social inculturation and legal implementation. Anti-Semitism, Christianity's original sin, had reaped the whirlwind.

---

114. Ruether, *Faith and Fratricide*, p. 186.

But the Early Baptists Said No

There is no contemporaneous Francis of Assisi, no figure like Las Casas, to celebrate when it comes to resisting Christian contempt for and subjugation of Jews. The Christian community did not begin the long, slow process of resacralizing Jewish lives in any broad and thoroughgoing way until after the mass annihilation of the Jews in the twentieth century. Only then did any significant number of Christian scholars and church leaders begin to come to terms with the poisonous tradition that we have been reviewing here. It took decades for many to see the organic relationship between Nazi anti-Semitism and the Christian Jew-hatred of earlier centuries.

But I do think there is one relevant set of voices. They emerged on the fringes of the Reformation and the cusp of the modern era. It will not do to overstate their contribution to honoring Jewish lives, but the Christian dissenters who first made the case for religious liberty in the English-speaking world in the very early seventeenth century must at least receive some attention here. These were men and women of devout Christian faith who found themselves and their communities on the receiving end of state persecution for holding religious convictions different from the majority. Some of these persecuted Christians came to understand that the religious liberty they so earnestly sought for themselves could not, in principle, be denied to people of other faiths, even non-Christian faiths or no faith at all. This articulation of an increasingly comprehensive principle of religious liberty and freedom of conscience for all people in a political community had revolutionary consequences.

Roger Williams and Richard Overton were among these early Baptists. They were contemporaries and allies even though their theological perspectives were not identical. As the story of the mercurial Roger Williams is much more familiar to most readers,[115] I will focus here on Richard Overton, whose story was retrieved from the shadows of history by Baptist ethicist Glen Stassen.[116] Stassen shows that Overton, who first surfaces in

---

115. For a compelling recent account, see James Calvin Davis, *The Moral Theology of Roger Williams: Christian Conviction and Public Ethics* (Louisville: Westminster John Knox, 2004). See also William Lee Miller, *The First Liberty: America's Foundation in Religious Freedom* (Washington, D.C.: Georgetown University Press, 2003), part 3.

116. Glen H. Stassen, *Just Peacemaking: Transforming Initiatives for Justice and Peace* (Louisville: Westminster John Knox, 1992), chapter 6. One could just as easily focus on Thomas Helwys's groundbreaking book, *Mystery of Iniquity,* probably written as early as 1611. I am grateful to Jim Patterson for this insight.

documents in 1607, was a member of a group of separatist English Puritans who fled to Holland because of fierce persecution at the hands of the Anglican state establishment in England. Overton became a member of the very first Baptist church, led by John Smyth and Thomas Helwys. This was a General Baptist church with strong Anabaptist leanings. In 1612, these Baptists offered a confession of faith that affirmed freedom of conscience and separation of church and state, and linked these protections to the maintenance of civil peace, as persecution for religion did nothing other than harden opposition and evoke fruitless bloodshed and religious war. In 1615, in his own written declaration of faith, Overton drew on themes we have seen throughout this book, emphasizing that all human beings are created in the image of God, and that Christ died for all (not just for the Christian elect, as in Calvinism). Overton also strongly emphasized that Christ alone is Lord of the church.

Overton reappears in 1642, as a pamphleteer, fighting against the social and ecclesiastical hierarchy with its combination of power, violence, and greed. In his 1645 work *The Arraignment of Mr. Persecution,* Overton offered the first of several declarations attacking all forms of state persecution of religious dissenters. Imaginatively framing his work as a trial of "Mr. Persecution," Overton charged "him" with violating Christ's Lordship and commands, causing division in families and nations, creating war and eating up wealth in the conduct of war, torturing dissenters with many instruments of torture he specifically names, and depriving fellow citizens and fellow Christians of their just liberty.[117]

Overton was especially appalled at how the state, aided and abetted by the church, actually tortured and killed dissenters and unbelievers in the name of Christ. In a statement that sounds remarkably similar to Las Casas, Overton writes in 1645 that this religious killing completely violates the will of Christ, "who came not to destroy, but to save men's lives; and therefore would have all *taught* in the nations, that all might be *persuaded* to the obedience of the truth, that all might be saved — therefore to kill the unbeliever, as Turk, Pagan, Jew etc. is to slay such as Christ would have to live to repent."[118] Jesus prescribed preaching and persuasion and never coercion and compulsion to reach people for faith in Christ. *Fifty years before John Locke's argument for civil toleration,* Richard Overton demanded full religious liberty, primarily on New Testament grounds, for every religious

---

117. Stassen, *Just Peacemaking,* p. 145.
118. Stassen, *Just Peacemaking,* p. 146.

group in the state. He became one of the first thinkers to describe religious liberty as a human right that, as Stassen puts it, "belong[s] to all persons as persons, not only to Englishmen or persons of one particular faith."[119] These are rights that precede government, must be recognized in law by government, and cannot be overridden by government.

In a series of pamphlets that followed, Overton developed his arguments further and marshaled various kinds of claims to support them. With state violations of religious liberty rights at the heart of his arguments, Overton began to articulate ever more wide-ranging claims. He says that people have a right not to be taxed to support the established church; that all people should be treated as having equal liberties; that state power actually comes from the people; and that the state is answerable to the people for the fulfillment of its limited responsibilities to secure peace and protect natural and just liberty. He argues for freedom of the press and regular elections, for the right not to be imprisoned without cause, for the right not to be tortured, for the rights of the poor and hungry, and for the right not to be subject to the draft for war. He says that justice is "my inheritance by lineal descent from the loins of Adam," and that this is of course applicable "to all the sons of men as their proper right without respect of persons."[120] Eventually the full body of Overton's works combined claims from Scripture, reason, and hard personal and group experience to argue for wide-ranging human rights and liberties for all persons and an incipient democratic egalitarianism. He argues for limited government that never attempts to legislate belief or religion, and for a church that never makes use of the weapons of force to coerce belief. His final major declaration includes a remarkably comprehensive list of human rights, including what would now be called "negative rights" (not to be harmed) and "positive rights" (to receive a certain limited roster of goods); in another classification scheme, Overton clearly combines civil, economic, and political rights in his statement. These include freedoms of religion among a wide range of civil liberties related to the right not to be mistreated by government, basic economic rights such as a right to a free education, and the rights of all to participate in self-government.[121]

When it came to Judaism as a religion, thinkers like Richard Overton were convinced that Jews were doctrinally erroneous. As men of convinced

119. Stassen, *Just Peacemaking*, p. 148.
120. Stassen, *Just Peacemaking*, p. 151.
121. Stassen, *Just Peacemaking*, pp. 154-55.

Christian faith, they did not consider these doctrinal errors insignificant. Overton makes clear in the quote above that he believes that Jews fall among those groups who need to hear the gospel, repent, and believe. These early Baptists were not making any *theological* challenge to historic Christian rejection of Judaism. But what they did accomplish was the inclusion of Jews (and Muslims) among those who, because of their God-given worth and status before God, and because of their basic rights and liberties as persons, must never be coerced into belief — or even into supporting by taxation the majority belief. These beliefs ultimately blossomed into the religious liberty protections that became a part of the United States First Amendment and eventually spread around large parts of the world. Thus began the unwinding of fifteen hundred years of persecution of Jews in Christendom. In its very beginning, it was Christians themselves, beginning with those who had tasted the bitter lash of religious persecution, who led the way, and for explicitly Christian reasons.

6.4. A Tragically Mixed Legacy

In this chapter we have considered three cases of Christendom divided against itself — or, perhaps better, of faithful Christian witness within a corrupted Christendom. We have watched Francis attempt peacemaking with the Muslim sultan amidst the carnage of the Crusades. We have witnessed the Spanish conquerors killing the indigenous Americans in the name of Christ, and being resisted in the name of Christ by Christian leaders like Bartolomé de Las Casas. And we have watched Christian theologians and then Christian states persecuting the Jewish people, and finally being resisted by early Baptists like Richard Overton — the beginnings of religious liberty. These vignettes provide at least a glimpse of the extent to which some Christians, embedded in and strengthened by countercultural Christian communities,[122] obeyed the life-honoring ethic given to them in Scripture, tradition, and Jesus Christ in opposition to a morally corrupted Christendom (puzzle #16).

As this chapter closes we are right on the brink of "liberal modernity," but not yet in the era in which claims based mainly on Scripture or Chris-

---

122. Rarely is resistance a matter of individual dissent, but instead it is most often nurtured in a countercultural alternative or subcommunity, even within a culture putatively sharing the same faith.

tian tradition have given way to claims based mainly on reason and science. We can see clear acknowledgment of human dignity and human rights, beginning with respect for religious liberty and freedom of conscience, that long precede the Enlightenment or any move to sever belief in human dignity from belief in God as the author of human dignity. This is important evidence for a claim that will be made forcefully in the next chapter: critically important convictions about respect for persons, human rights, universal human dignity, and individual liberties cannot be traced to modern secular Enlightenment liberalism. The late Scottish ethicist Duncan Forrester is closer to the mark when he claims that the germ of the idea of an ineffable sacred human worth flows from the biblical-Jewish-Christian traditions through the bloodstream of Western civilization.[123] It went everywhere Jews and Christians went and simply could not be destroyed — even by Christians. Where Christians went most badly astray, other Christians arose to protest. We have seen notable exemplars of resistance in our brief profiles of Francis, Las Casas, and Overton.

But in truth, it was a tragically mixed legacy that Christendom bequeathed to the modern world. In the next chapter, we will explore some of the key ways in which what were once explicitly theological commitments to the sacredness of every human life before God gradually became philosophical and political commitments to respect for the dignity of persons. These commitments were often stripped of any explicitly theological grounding and, indeed, sometimes treated as opposed to theological commitments of any type. Through its mingling of Christian faith and unjust domination over many centuries, Christendom managed to poison its own moral well so profoundly that the Christian faith's best legacy to the modern world would eventually be understood as incompatible with Christianity — rather than as an expression of its highest moral norms. Western civilization soon embarked on an attempt to retain the best insights of Christianity's ethic while shearing it from its theological foundation (puzzle #15). In the next three chapters, we will explore what happened.

---

123. Duncan Forrester, *On Human Worth* (London: SCM, 2001), p. 56 and throughout.

7. Enlightenment Transitions: Natural Rights, Rule of Law, and Human Dignity

> Act in such a way that you always treat humanity, whether in your own person or the person of any other, never simply as a means but always at the same time as an end.
>
> Immanuel Kant

7.1. Enlightenment Transitions and the Sacredness of Human Life

The discussion we take up in this chapter is exceedingly complex; we enter into debates that have exercised scholars intensively in recent decades. Many historians, theologians, political philosophers, and Christian ethicists have been attempting to understand the significance for Christianity and for Western culture of the gradual transition from the religiously drenched medieval world to the dominant rationalism and secularism of "liberal modernity" and "the Enlightenment." Pretty much everything about this transition has been up for reconsideration in recent scholarship. This includes what to call this period (if it was a "period"), when it started and ended, how much continuity and discontinuity can be identified with what came before, and whether from a Christian perspective it marked a laudable expression or a lamentable rejection of Christian thought and values.[1]

---

1. For three pivotal recent treatments, see Michael Allen Gillespie, *The Theological Origins of Modernity* (Chicago and London: University of Chicago Press, 2009); Charles Taylor, *A Secular Age* (Cambridge: Harvard University Press, Belknap Press, 2007); Mark Lilla, *The Stillborn God* (New York: Knopf, 2007). These works reveal, among other things, how much we are *not* attempting to do in this chapter. This is not a history of political theology or secularism or the Enlightenment. Our project is more limited, and therefore more conceivable.

Our inquiry will certainly intersect with these kinds of questions. But our fundamental purpose is narrower. This book tells the story of the greatest moral conviction of the Christian tradition — that each and every human being is sacred, of unique, incalculable worth and elevated status, to be viewed with reverence and treated accordingly. So far I have attempted to trace the biblical origins of this conviction and key moments in the history of its presentation, embodiment, and negation on the part of Christian people themselves. From Constantine on, this historical presentation, embodiment, and negation of the sacredness of life occurred in political and cultural contexts that explicitly claimed Christian identity and allegiance. Beginning with this next period, those Christian allegiances begin to weaken and in some cases to be abandoned. In this chapter, then, I am interested in exploring how the sacredness-of-life conviction fared amidst what eventually became a much more weakly Christian political and cultural context. Was the notion entirely abandoned? Was it preserved in something like its classic Christian form? Or did it take on new forms?

I will focus here on Enlightenment transitions. My claim will be that during the Enlightenment the idea that human life has great worth was not abandoned but did take on new forms and was grounded in new ways. Gradually during this period, leading political and moral philosophers shifted away from religious language in describing the content of the moral norm we have heretofore called "sacredness of human life," in naming the foundations for belief in it, and in prescribing the best ways it could be actualized. These shifts ultimately had dramatic consequences, many of them problematic. But ironically, during this period much of the *substance* of the sacredness norm survived, such as a posture of respect for persons and bans against wanton violence. Moreover, political innovations in the direction of democratic egalitarianism and the recognition of human rights meant that in some ways the practice of the norm actually improved over what had taken place in high medieval Christendom. Yet these steps forward occurred simultaneously with a slow, gradual shearing of the norm from its original theological foundation.

In this chapter I will follow three interwoven strands of this complex story, knowing that were there space I could explore many more such strands.[2] I will start where this period starts, with frequent and widespread

---

2. In particular, I am coming to believe that the Christian humanism of the earlier Renaissance period is extremely important as it relates to our study. For an authoritative treatment, see Charles Trinkaus, *In Our Image and Likeness* (Notre Dame, Ind.: University

appeals to a concept initially called "natural rights," and explore the background to that concept in medieval natural law theories. I will next consider the thought of John Locke, with special attention to the new political philosophy he developed emphasizing liberty, the social contract, and the rule of law. I will finally look at the moral philosophy of Immanuel Kant, with its thunderous proclamation of human moral dignity against a backdrop of epistemological skepticism. This is heavy philosophical sledding, but it must be undertaken. I hope you will hang in there with me for this surprisingly important part of the story.

7.2. Natural Right/s: Bridge Concepts between the Medieval and Modern Worlds

Recall that Bartolomé de Las Casas and Richard Overton, in very different contexts one hundred years apart (1540s and 1640s), both made arguments on behalf of desperately mistreated people in protest against the state powers that were mistreating them. Both arguments were explicitly, deeply, and thoroughly Christian; both reflected a passionate concern for what I have been calling the sacredness of human life. And both made those arguments using, among other tools, the language of *natural rights,* which became the predecessor for the *human rights* tradition so dominant in global religion, ethics, and law today, so important in contemporary defenses of life's sacredness, and so disputed in contemporary political and moral philosophy.[3]

The concept of natural rights upon which these men drew has been

---

of Notre Dame Press, 1995). The Christian humanists sought an elevated understanding of "the dignity of man" (Pico della Mirandola) and our extraordinary powers and potential, all of which come to us as gifts from God. Gillespie suggests that "modernity" has roots in the medieval period and includes both these Renaissance developments and the Reformation, but the Enlightenment, strictly speaking, is a later development. We will focus on the latter.

3. The term "natural rights" preceded by centuries the widespread use of the term "human rights." Both terms mean "the rights that people have, not by virtue of any particular role or status in society, but by virtue of their very humanity." Brian Tierney, *The Idea of Natural Rights* (Grand Rapids: Eerdmans, 1997), p. 2 n. 4. But, as we will see below, the term "natural rights" is derived from Latin use and is an aspect of ancient Christian tradition that crossed over into the modern world. Its theological and philosophical presuppositions lost their consensus, however. The concept of "human rights" survived, shorn of its basis in "nature." We will say more about human rights in chapter 10.

traced to the medieval period in learned studies by the intellectual historians Richard Tuck, Brian Tierney, Eberhard Schockenhoff, and others.[4] The once influential belief that rights claims are a (fictive and lamentable) product of early liberal modernity with its turn against God has been decisively repudiated by numerous historians, though this view unfortunately retains its hold in some circles. With the aid of medieval intellectual historians, we can now see that the language of rights finds its origins in that era. Indeed, given the influence of Greco-Roman thought and law on medieval Christian civilization, the story can actually be traced back to the classical origins of Western civilization.

Needing one primary guide through this dense thicket, I have turned to medieval historian Brian Tierney to structure this discussion. Tierney argues that both a *natural right* and a *natural rights* strand are visible in the medieval Catholic writers. He is quite aware that the seemingly arcane difference between these two strands of thought is actually a subject of intensive contemporary debate, and that those involved in this debate generally believe that much of contemporary significance is at stake — basically the moral health of civilization and the well-being of its inhabitants. (Oh, that's all.) So it is worth paying attention to the difference between natural right and natural rights.

Tierney argues that the medieval Catholic natural *right* tradition followed strands of ancient Greek and Roman thought in the belief that there exists "an objectively right state of affairs," a natural right, or *right order,* in the universe itself. This natural right/right order is real; it is external to humans (sometimes called "extramental," existing beyond the human mind);[5] and it is discoverable by humans using the faculty of reason. In the words of one medieval Catholic thinker, it is "what nature teaches all living beings."[6] For Aristotle, the metaphysical basis of this natural order of things was the *logos,* the principle of "order and harmony and purpose" visible in

---

4. Besides Tierney, see Richard Tuck, *Natural Rights Theories: Their Origin and Development* (Cambridge: Cambridge University Press, 1979); Eberhard Schockenhoff, *Natural Law and Human Dignity: Universal Ethics in an Historical World,* trans. Brian McNeil (Washington, D.C.: Catholic University of America Press, 2003). For an effort to argue for the continuing value of natural law today, see John Finnis, *Natural Law and Natural Rights* (Oxford: Clarendon, 1980).

5. Gillespie, *Theological Origins of Modernity,* p. 30.

6. Rufinus, "Summa Decretorum," in *From Irenaeus to Grotius: A Sourcebook in Christian Political Thought,* ed. Oliver O'Donovan and Joan Lockwood O'Donovan (Grand Rapids: Eerdmans, 1999), p. 300.

the universe.[7] For the Stoics, this same principle was described as divine reason pervading the universe and embedded in all life, including human life. For Catholic thinkers like the great classical-biblical synthesizer Thomas Aquinas (1225-1274), this right order was the God-given moral design of the universe, including the human. The link to *nature* in terms of an objective cosmic moral order in the nature of things, beyond the human self but binding on every rightly ordered human self, lay at the heart of the metaphysic undergirding the classical and Thomistic understanding of natural right.

The term "nature" or "natural" in this tradition includes a belief in a God-given and relatively stable *human nature*. One can discern an objective right order and in-built structure in human nature. This includes a visible right order in terms of the ultimate *telos* (goal or end) of human life, identified by Aristotle as the quest for the good and by Aquinas as beatitude with God. There are visible subsidiary natural ends such as (right) sexuality, (right) procreation, (right) begetting and parenting, and so on.[8] If humans pursue such natural *teloi* in a disciplined manner through the development of virtuous habits of thought and action, they can flourish; otherwise they will fall short of their intended end. On this account, if one's interest is in the well-being and especially the flourishing (puzzle #12) of human lives sacred in God's sight, the path forward is the pursuit of God-given right order in human life.

Human nature is also relevant, and stable, in terms of human *needs*, which we do not create but which we experience and to which we must respond. These needs include, among other things, both the physical need for sustenance and the social need for community. In Christian thought, human needs are understood to have been affected by the disordering consequences of sin. This, as Eberhard Schockenhoff points out, introduces an element of great complexity into the heart of reflection about what is "natural" for humans. All natural right or natural law theories must decide whether to speak of *created* or "ideal rational nature" as humans were designed, or *fallen* nature as humans actually have it in the current human condition.[9] This is but one of many perplexing puzzles associated with efforts to ground what is right in what is "natural."

---

7. Tierney, *Idea of Natural Rights*, p. 22.

8. This list is drawn from the helpful summary of the natural law tradition in O'Donovan and O'Donovan, *From Irenaeus to Grotius*, p. 238.

9. Schockenhoff, *Natural Law*, p. 13.

Schockenhoff offers a very helpful summation of this entire pattern of natural right and natural law thought: "The deepest concern of all theories of natural law [is] the yearning to learn how to understand the essence of the human person and to use this insight to formulate prescriptive statements about the goals in life that are appropriate to his essence and about the political-societal conditions that mark the parameters of a truly human existence."[10] And further: "This kind of ethic bases its normative affirmations on an objective foundation in 'the ethics of Being' that exists antecedently in the nature of the human person and in those existential ends that are in accordance with his essence."[11]

At least for the Catholic tradition as developed by Thomas Aquinas, the central thinker of medieval Catholicism, it is through a superstructure of law that God has inscribed both the objective foundations of the good and the means to discern the good. This is how *natural right* links to *natural law*. In his magisterial *Summa Theologiae*, Aquinas describes this superstructure under the terms "eternal law," "natural law," "divine law," and "human law" (along with the negative category he calls "the law of sin"). *Eternal law* is essentially how God operates in relation to creation and humanity; it is exemplary for humans, but only barely accessible to the human mind. Rémi Brague points out the significance of this idea of eternal law, even though it plays little substantive role in prescribing moral norms. That "there is a law common to God and his creatures, and that God, in a certain manner, submits himself to a law," links God to humanity in a community under law and means that human life is never merely subject to arbitrary divine or human will.[12]

Natural law is "an inner apprehension of right, an inborn habit of judgment and persistent impulse to specific conduct" in keeping with our design as biological, social, and rational creatures.[13] So natural law in this more narrow sense refers to our human moral capacity to understand and perform natural right. *Divine law* is Thomas's term for the scriptural revelation (further broken down into the Old Law and the New Law) that directs human conduct beginning with Israel and the church; its precepts extend beyond the knowledge available in natural law while supplementing and confirming them. *Human law*, finally, is "constructed [by humans]

10. Schockenhoff, *Natural Law*, p. 6.
11. Schockenhoff, *Natural Law*, p. 10.
12. Rémi Brague, *The Law of God: The Philosophical History of an Idea*, trans. Lydia G. Cochrane (Chicago: University of Chicago Press, 2007), p. 221.
13. O'Donovan and O'Donovan, *From Irenaeus to Grotius*, p. 324.

from natural law by reasoned deliberation under particular historical conditions."[14] This is sometimes also called *positive law,* and can be broken down further into such categories as civil law *(ius civile),* moral custom *(ius consuetudinus),* and the law of nations *(ius gentium).*[15] For Thomas, as we saw briefly in chapter 2, all just human laws derive from the natural law, which ultimately derives from God's eternal law; therefore human laws have legitimacy precisely because and insofar as they advance natural right. This has the pivotal implication that it is not human law that *makes* something right (or obligatory, or permitted, or forbidden); human law simply *recognizes* what is already right, obligatory, permitted, or forbidden.[16] More broadly, Thomas envisions an entire society turned toward the quest for a "common good" that, as Joan Lockwood O'Donovan and Oliver O'Donovan put it, "embraces the mesh of communal ends — religious, moral, legal, political, and economic."[17] This vision of an entire society holistically oriented around the quest for a God-given right order, with all people and institutions understanding themselves to be under the authority of God, and nature as God has designed it,[18] remains powerfully compelling for many traditionalist Christian thinkers today. Yet it has been left behind in the main channels of Western politics and culture, as we shall see.

Tierney illustrates natural right or right order with a familiar example from ancient culture and the natural law tradition — family relations. Nature (it is argued) reveals to the observation of reason that human children "need a long period of nurture and education; whence one can conclude that stable marriage between parents is a naturally right relationship."[19] Correspondingly, reason easily discovers that the objectively right relationship between parents and children consists of a long period of childhood nurture at home. A rightly ordered family is to be characterized by a pattern of respect and honor toward parents by children (and presumably, a

14. O'Donovan and O'Donovan, *From Irenaeus to Grotius,* p. 324.

15. Here is one font of the concept of international law, which will receive more attention in chapter 10 as one significant way human beings have attempted to protect and sanctify human life.

16. The same would apply if we were speaking of natural rights. See Nicholas Wolterstorff, *Justice: Rights and Wrongs* (Princeton and Oxford: Princeton University Press, 2008), p. 316.

17. O'Donovan and O'Donovan, *From Irenaeus to Grotius,* p. 323.

18. O'Donovan and O'Donovan, *From Irenaeus to Grotius,* p. 325.

19. Tierney, *Idea of Natural Rights,* p. 22.

host of responsibilities of parents toward children as well, which Tierney does not discuss). This right order in filial relations is properly encouraged or even demanded by moral norms that take the form of natural law, divine law, and even civil law. These right relationships can also be framed in terms of the duties of each party: children have a duty to honor their parents, parents to raise their children properly.

Tierney says that it could just as easily be said that parents have a *natural right* to the respect of their children, as a corollary to the *duty* that children have to offer that respect. It is only here that we catch a glimpse of the more controversial concept of natural rights, or "subjective natural rights," that is, "rights inhering in the individual person as such,"[20] and requiring toward that individual, or perhaps toward all individuals, certain behavioral duties from one or more neighbors. To continue our example in the language of natural rights, a parent might say: "As your parent, I have a *right* to be treated by you, my child, with respect." More commonly, subjective natural rights claims are broader, as in: "All people, just because they are human, have the right to be treated with respect."

But such claims are decidedly *not* the focus of the right order tradition. Some scholars claim, in fact, that they have no place whatsoever in the right order tradition. The right ordering of human community demands of each of us conformity with nature's God-given design for the human in community, through adherence to the obligations of natural law and performance of our proper natural moral duties.

Tierney claims, however, that natural right, or right order, was not the only perspective handed down to the modern world from the Catholicism of the medieval period. Nor was a shift away from a tight focus on natural right a late corruption after Aquinas.[21] Tierney considers eleventh- and especially twelfth-century voices among the medieval commentators and canon lawyers and shows that many of their writings already included at least preliminary presentations of *natural rights,* not just natural right.

Tierney notes that the twelfth century was a time of considerable ferment and intellectual creativity. Political and ecclesial clashes between various actors, especially between the papacy and the empire, led to numerous civil and canonical legal rulings clarifying various disputed claims,

---

20. Tierney, *Idea of Natural Rights,* pp. 32-33; see p. 20 for his definition of subjective rights.

21. Every treatment of shifts in natural law wrestles with the role of William of Ockham and the move toward theological voluntarism. To explore this issue would take us too far afield. Cf. Gillespie, *Theological Origins of Modernity,* chapter 1.

duties, freedoms, protections, immunities, and rights.[22] Oliver O'Donovan and Joan Lockwood O'Donovan write of a "rivalry of imperial projects" between the church and the empire that lasted not just one but three centuries.[23] John Milbank suggests that the inability of the various parties to resolve their disputes within the parameters of natural right forced rights-claims regularly to the surface, from which (unfortunately, he claims) they never fully receded.[24]

Meanwhile, in a separate but important strand, an early flowering of Christian personalism and humanism, deeply marked by the piety and ethics of Francis of Assisi, with its especially profound version of Christian belief in "the supreme value of the individual soul,"[25] led to a heightened emphasis on the unique character, intentions, choices, and, yes, *rights* of the individual. Here we are catching a glimpse of the theological resources that eventually helped fuel a kind of Christian individualism, or Christian humanism, focused not on personal self-aggrandizement or soulless autonomy (as so often today) but on the individual human being's irreducibly personal relationship with and accountability toward God.[26] This also helped fuel the natural rights tradition.

The canon lawyer Rufinus (1160), for example, argued that *ius naturale* (the same term we have been translating "natural right") is "a certain force instilled in every human creature by nature to do good and avoid the opposite."[27] By this Rufinus and other commentators claimed that what is natural to humans is a certain capacity, power, or faculty of moral discernment. The later Thomistic account also stressed that the objective moral

---

22. Tierney, *Idea of Natural Rights*, pp. 35-36. See also John Witte, *God's Joust, God's Justice: Law and Religion in the Western Tradition* (Grand Rapids: Eerdmans, 2006), p. 36.

23. O'Donovan and O'Donovan, *From Irenaeus to Grotius*, p. 231.

24. John Milbank, *Theology and Social Theory: Beyond Secular Reason* (Oxford: Blackwell, 1990), p. 15.

25. This is acknowledged by Michel Villey, but as a source of the deformation of law when transferred to that realm. Tierney, *Idea of Natural Rights*, p. 27. Gillespie also points to the role of the Franciscans in embodying and articulating a challenge to the "order of nature" as taught by the papal hierarchy and in emphasizing a kind of radical individuality of the disciple in relation to Christ and his revealed will. Gillespie, *Theological Origins of Modernity*, pp. 25-27.

26. This "responsibility individualism" must be distinguished from an "isolated individualism," the latter rightly worthy of criticism and concern. The terms are drawn from Jesse Couenhoven, "Christianity, the Enlightenment, and Political Life: A Transformed Landscape?" (paper presented at the Society of Christian Ethics, New Orleans, January 2011).

27. Quoted in Tierney, *Idea of Natural Rights*, p. 62.

order is discernible by reason. But in Rufinus the focus shifts away subtly from the objective moral order to the faculties of the human who discerns it. The emphasis is on the profound, God-given rationality and free will of humans, and on the implications of humans having such capacities. Here we see some of the earliest seeds of the elevation of the dignity of the human that came to characterize first Renaissance humanism and then, in a more secular vein, the Enlightenment.[28]

Rufinus and others in his line especially attended to the exercise of these moral discernment faculties with regard to those limited but important arenas of life in which "nature does not command or forbid." This refers to those areas in which both nature and Scripture show that the person is genuinely free to choose — for example, whether and whom to marry — and in which any of several outcomes of such choices would fall within right order (cf. 1 Cor. 7). This recognition opens the door a crack to a focus on the *proper freedom* belonging to human beings when they choose among legitimate options in those areas that are not otherwise prescribed or proscribed by the natural law. Here it is — a first broaching of the theme of freedom that later became so central in Western thought. This understanding of freedom could be framed under natural law in terms of "permissive law," as Tierney points out.[29] Further: "Once a subjective definition of *ius naturale* came to be widely accepted — and associated with ideas of reason and free will — the language could readily be used to define the natural rights that humans could exercise in acting freely or claiming something due."[30]

Some medieval thinkers also reached back to a strand of ancient Roman law to link liberty and rights with *power*. Natural rights came to be understood as the individual's "rightful power" to act unhindered by others on certain matters.[31] This was no modern claim of unfettered personal

---

28. See Gillespie, *Theological Origins of Modernity,* chapters 2–3.

29. See Tierney, "Natural Law and Natural Rights," in *Christianity and Law: An Introduction,* ed. John Witte Jr. and Frank S. Alexander (Cambridge: Cambridge University Press, 2008), p. 93.

30. Tierney, "Natural Law," p. 94.

31. Tierney, *Idea of Natural Rights,* p. 67. The use of the word "power" here is intentional and grounded in this same tradition and these writers. A subjective natural right became linked to the individual's "licit power," or in more contemporary terms, "rightful power," to exercise this right. Tierney, p. 41. Others have a duty to protect my exercise of this licit power, as I have the duty to protect theirs. The state eventually becomes the guarantor of these powers; indeed, for Locke and many successors this becomes the primary rationale for the existence of the state. And of course, various checks against the state's own violation of my

autonomy or will to power in all things, nor was it severed from the idea of an objective right order. The zone of free choice and licit power was not unlimited; far from it. But it did introduce the pivotally important concept that natural subjective rights include the right to claim, and the power to protect, one's liberty, in that small but important zone in which liberty properly belongs to the individual. Together, this emphasis on the rights, liberties, faculties, powers, and dignity of each person represented an egalitarian leveling of the more hierarchical natural law tradition inherited from Aristotle and accepted in hierarchical form by Aquinas. Duncan Forrester describes it as a kind of triumph of biblical and Stoic themes over Aristotelian-Greek hierarchicalism.[32]

This deep concern about natural rights such as liberty was in part motivated by those numerous occasions in medieval Christendom in which that zone of liberty was indeed violated. As we saw with Richard Overton, people most forcefully demand rights when they believe their basic humanity and dignity are being trampled upon. And this is essentially what Schockenhoff believes happened with the natural law tradition. The majority *right order* strand, exemplified by Aquinas, ultimately was displaced by the minority *natural rights* strand, largely ignored (or suppressed)[33] by Aquinas, and instead exemplified by a chain of lesser-known thinkers such as Jean Gerson, William of Ockham, and Marsilius of Padua, and in later days such thinkers as Vitoria, Suárez, Grotius, and Pufendorf.[34] Schockenhoff speaks of this latter strand of tradition as "the subterranean contrary current of another natural law, whose waves of protest continually broke the surface and joined battle under the banner of liberty and equality, autonomy and human dignity against the misuse of the doctrine of natural law by theocratic systems of government and absolutistic theories of the state. Ultimately, the idea of natural law itself became obsolete, thanks to the use made of it by such worldviews."[35] So, even in late medieval/pre-

---

licit power to exercise my natural rights and liberties must be built into state structures and procedures as well.

32. Duncan Forrester, *On Human Worth* (London: SCM, 2001), pp. 49-50.

33. John Headley suggests that Aquinas must have deliberately excluded subjective natural rights from his presentation of natural law. This is one claim in his very thoughtful book, *The Europeanization of the World: On the Origins of Human Rights and Democracy* (Princeton: Princeton University Press, 2008), p. 105.

34. For a sophisticated account of key thinkers and moments in this strand, see Milbank, *Theology and Social Theory,* chapter 1.

35. Schockenhoff, *Natural Law,* p. 8.

Enlightenment Europe, natural law as natural right began giving way to natural law as natural rights, in part because of the excesses and errors of Christendom itself as supposed guardian of natural right.

Critics of the transition from natural right to natural rights often deeply lament all that was lost. But they usually fail to account for the flaws within Christendom's own practices that led to the gradual abandonment and finally the total rejection of the natural law as right order tradition. John Milbank, among those who have most trenchantly lamented the secularization of formerly Christian Europe and the loss of the natural right tradition, also lays the blame squarely at the church's feet: "It was the increasing failure of the Church to be the Church . . . which created a moral vacuum," and ultimately the conditions for a secularized understanding of politics and privatized understanding of religion.[36]

Once we enter the seventeenth century, it is not hard to spot two fundamental reasons for the decisive and final shift from natural right to natural rights and the abandonment of the natural law tradition. The first was an irreducible religious pluralism in seventeenth- and eighteenth-century England and America, which meant that multiple and competing accounts were in circulation at all times about what exactly right order and natural right looked like. (These remain with us today, even in seriously Christian circles; as we have seen, they had bedeviled even the medieval natural right tradition. Knowledge of these differing accounts is one major reason why it is today implausible to go back to Aquinas's cathedral-like vision of an ordered hierarchy of natural law with whole civilizations bending their efforts toward that vision.) The second reason was simple exhaustion with governmental strife, violence, and tyranny, especially in matters of religion. Too many kings had imprisoned and killed too many dissenters over too many fine points of religious doctrine. As Mark Lilla has said, "They [modern political philosophies] were also developed for local reasons, to help Europe escape the grip of Christian political theology, which the early moderns blamed for centuries of political and religious violence."[37] Early modern religious and intellectual pioneers believed that the effort to ground politics on religion was destroying Europe, and that a new approach was desperately needed.[38] Thus their focus shifted to rationally de-

36. Milbank, *Theology and Social Theory*, p. 16; cf. p. 6.
37. Lilla, *The Stillborn God*, p. 32.
38. The argument has been made on the other side that the "wars of religion" actually had more to do with the consolidation of state power than with religion.

rived natural rights rather than a no-longer-agreed, theologically derived, right order.

A number of influential scholars appear to be nostalgic for the lost world of right-order Christian civilization. Some want to see a return to Christian states pursuing a shared vision. (Others, more ecclesially focused, see the consequences of social fragmentation but emphasize the pivotal role of churches in forming small alternative communities of disciples committed to a shared vision of life.)[39] They believe we lost a shared vision of the good, of God's will for the community as a whole, of moral virtue, or of any kind of social unity. What we got in return was an increasing plurality of incoherent subjective rights-claims.[40] They worry that one consequence has been the degradation of the moral quality of Western civilization. (It is easy to conclude the malignancy of the path we took after, say, watching one episode of MTV's *Real World*.) More deeply, they worry that there can be no sustainable human civilization without a shared account of the good, and that abandoning natural law leaves the field wide open to every kind of tyrant and every kind of desecration. This was the leaning of thinkers such as Isaiah Berlin and Leo Strauss after World War II and its horrible degradations. But for now, back in the seventeenth century, we must consider what was gained, as well as what was lost, in this transition; what was intended, as opposed to what finally developed. And we must understand the roots of both approaches in the Christian tradition itself.

7.3. John Locke: Equality, Rule of Law, and Resistance to Tyranny

"The Enlightenment" is a term that generally denotes the birth of liberal modernity with its skeptical rationalism and empiricism, shucking off of Christian beliefs and church authority, and abandonment of the right order tradition. There is certainly truth to this general understanding of intellectual developments in the period we are considering, but if we want to speak with precision about John Locke (1632-1704), and about the hugely influential statement he offered in his *Two Treatises on Government*, it is hard to consider Locke as some kind of unequivocal exemplar of Enlightenment

---

39. I am grateful to Coleman Fannin for this insight.

40. Oliver O'Donovan, *The Desire of the Nations: Rediscovering the Roots of Political Theology* (Cambridge: Cambridge University Press, 1996), p. 247.

thinking. He is instead a complex transitional figure. Much of his writing is suffused with biblical and theological argumentation; and yet it can be argued that the implications of his thought are profoundly secularizing.[41]

Locke's written legacy marks him as one who carried forward the ancient Christian commitment to the value of human life while altering that tradition in important ways. He drew on the natural rights strand of the Christian tradition, and then went beyond it to develop an elaborate political philosophy designed to protect those natural rights against governmental tyranny. After centuries of Christian governments and their abuses in the name of God, Locke was among the first to see that *one of the most critically important ways to protect human life is to construct political systems that sharply limit state power,* with its perennial tendency toward a claim to what he called "Sovaraign Arbitrary Authority over the Persons of Men" (*1st T:* 40).[42] Locke knew all too well that such claims were often made by states purporting to possess such authority in the name of God and, yes, in the name of right order. So Locke's articulation of a new kind of natural rights theology, ethic, and political order was an effort to protect human beings from the abuses of those in Christendom so tempted to violate human rights in God's name. In this way, Locke offered an answer to our fourteenth puzzle: the best way to move toward fulfillment of life's sacred worth is to establish political structures that prevent government from abusing individual rights.

Locke is famous for his so-called social contract theory, which is both badly described by that term[43] and arguably the place where Locke *ends* rather than *begins* his political philosophy. At least if we take Locke's *First Treatise* on government as significant in itself and not just a preliminary to the more famous *Second Treatise*, the starting point of Locke's political theory is his theological account of God's relationship to human beings as

41. The most important essays for our purposes are his first and second treatises on government, which will be referred to below as *1st T* and *2nd T,* followed by paragraph number(s). John Locke, *Two Treatises of Government* (New York: New American Library, 1963). Locke's famous *Letter concerning Toleration, Essay concerning Human Understanding,* and *The Reasonableness of Christianity* are also relevant but will be secondary to our discussion here.

42. The theme of ending the use of arbitrary power, especially the power to take life and property, and restricting all exercises of power to those authorized by law is central for Locke. Cf. *2nd T:* 35. Good discussion in Peter Laslett, introduction to *Two Treatises of Government,* by John Locke (New York: New American Library, 1963), p. 125.

43. Far more often Locke speaks of a "compact" or "agreement" rather than a "contract." The former language has a more covenantal feel and implies a greater degree of trust.

well as his related account of human nature. In Locke's *First Treatise*, these accounts are grounded primarily in a reading of the book of Genesis and other scriptural texts. Locke affirms there that all members of the human species are created by the omnipotent God, are made in the image of God, and dwell under the sovereignty of God. Humans belong absolutely to God their Maker, not to their fellow humans, and not even to themselves in any absolute sense. Locke describes human beings as duty-bound before God to subordinate themselves to their omnipotent Sovereign and to obey God's moral law, the knowledge of which is accessible to them through reason. Jeremy Waldron argues that these theological claims, redolent with elements of the natural right tradition, were not an optional or detachable part of Locke's political philosophy but were instead fundamental to its coherence.[44]

Like much of the Christian tradition before and after him, Locke identified the image of God, so central to his theological anthropology, primarily with the human rational capacity. (We considered, in chapter 2, the inadequacies and dangers of this approach.) More precisely, Locke viewed human beings as characterized by *corporeal rationality*.[45] We are *corporeal*, or embodied, which distinguishes us (presumably) from nonembodied rational creatures such as angels, and also gives us physical needs, desires, and interests that sometimes lead us astray morally. But other creatures, such as the birds, cattle, and fish, are also corporeal. So Locke emphasizes that we are *rational*, which distinguishes us from all embodied but nonrational creatures, such as the animals. In his *Essay concerning Human Understanding*,[46] Locke the relentless empiricist-rationalist-philosopher does wrestle with evidences for a blurry distinction between human rational capacity and that of the higher animals and is willing to admit that the distinctions we delineate between species do not correspond with some kind of ultimate reality (*E*: III:vi).[47] This actually has some potential to

---

44. This is the central claim of Jeremy Waldron's entire analysis in Waldron, *God, Locke, and Equality: Christian Foundations in Locke's Political Thought* (Cambridge: Cambridge University Press, 2002). Much depends on whether one follows secularist scholarly tradition in dismissing the real significance of Locke's *First Treatise*, with its abundant biblical argumentation.

45. Waldron, *God, Locke, and Equality*, p. 71.

46. John Locke, *An Essay concerning Human Understanding*, in *Great Books of the Western World*, vol. 35, ed. Robert Maynard Hutchins (New York: Encyclopaedia Britannica, 1952). Hereafter cited in the text as *E*, followed by book:chapter:paragraph.

47. Discussed in Waldron, *God, Locke, and Equality*, chapter 3.

contribute to a contemporary ethic for animal rights (puzzle #1). But Locke the political philosopher requires a clear distinction between human and nonhuman creatures of God, and finally appears to claim that what makes humans distinct from rabbits and birds is reason. Humans possess the capacity for sufficiently abstract rational thought to be able to arrive at knowledge of God, to live a life pleasing to God, and to be held accountable by God when they face divine judgment after death.[48] This rational-spiritual-moral capacity is what makes a particular kind of creature a member of the human species, one made in God's image.[49] And since *all* humans "share in the same common Nature, Faculties, and Powers," therefore they "are in Nature equal" (*1st T:* 67).

Locke's way of grounding the nature of human equality is certainly not beyond disputing. But Locke's approach did the constructive work of drawing the boundaries of human species membership, and thus moral and political equality, as *broadly* as possible. Locke played a pivotal role in the gradual recognition of what should have been clear in Christendom from the Bible alone — that each and every human being is a person of equal and immeasurable worth; no one is excluded from a place in divine-human community; there are no ontological tiers or ranks of human beings; and we are duty-bound to create what Jeremy Waldron calls a "single-status political community."[50] Locke "[held] constant an element of respect" based on "the sheer fact of [the] underlying humanity" of every person.[51]

There is a sober dignity to Locke's vision of the human. We are creatures of special dignity and worth, all of us. Made in God's image, we are (echoing von Rad) "all of us lords, all of us kings."[52] This must have been a profoundly ennobling word to "commoners" everywhere, after centuries of deeply entrenched human rank and hierarchy. But Locke also says that before God (only God) we are all subordinates. While we no longer bow before human "betters," we *each* must bow before God in humble submis-

48. Waldron, *God, Locke, and Equality*, pp. 78-79; Charles Taylor, *Sources of the Self: The Making of Modern Identity* (Cambridge: Harvard University Press, 1989), p. 171.

49. It is legitimate to ask, as many now do, whether Locke's delineation of the great theological, ethical, and political significance of the distinction between humans and "lesser" species — which was undertaken to prevent any such distinctions being drawn between human beings — has had negative implications for Western understandings of the nonhuman creation. I think it has. This is, again, our puzzle #1. See chapter 11.

50. Waldron, *God, Locke, and Equality*, p. 108.

51. Waldron, *God, Locke, and Equality*, p. 10.

52. This is Waldron's language; Waldron, *God, Locke, and Equality*, p. 6.

sion and obedience. And because each of us is equally lordly and equally subordinate in this theological sense, before one another we are and must be equals. Each of us, says Locke, is "equal to the greatest, and subject to no body" (*2nd T:* 123). Locke deserves credit for being among the first in modern times to retrieve the radical egalitarianism to be drawn upon in Scripture. That to retrieve these basic claims of revelation and reason he had to reject the "Currant Divinity of the Times" taught by "The Pulpit" (*1st T:* preface) of his day, may help us to understand his general tendency toward suspicion of church authorities and their claims. Indeed, this is a major clue to understanding the often antiecclesial and anticlerical spirit of this entire era.

For Locke, equality is not just an aspiration or a principle but a divinely given fact that must be honored in human relations. This lays the foundation for a core move in his political philosophy, that any subordination of one person to the political power of another must be done by consent, and there are natural law limits even to what we are permitted to consent to (e.g., the natural law bans our choosing to be enslaved; *2nd T:* 23).[53] Notice the continuity with the medievalists as Locke sets limits on our legitimate liberties. This is no absolutizing of autonomy. *No one* is above the law of nature, which Locke defines in one pivotal passage as the very will of God (*2nd T:* 135). And therefore no one is above (or beneath!) the rule of human law, when (in another medieval-sounding move) it properly corresponds with the law of nature. Societies must be governed by law, first the natural law and then the agreed human law. For "wherever Law ends Tyranny begins" (*2nd T:* 202). How very often that claim has proven true in human history.[54]

Locke's understanding of the theological roots of comprehensive human equality also shaped his frequently progressive and sometimes radical attitudes toward other time-honored social and political distinctions between people in his society, such as those related to lineage, age, gender, educational attainment, and social class.[55] None of these distinctions was fundamental — however long society may have treated them as such —

---

53. Waldron, *God, Locke, and Equality,* p. 142.

54. Waldron, *God, Locke, and Equality,* p. 141. Locke regularly contrasts the rule of arbitrary will with the rule of natural law or civil law that applies equally to all members of the body politic. The former invites the worst tyrannies; the latter is far preferable. I strongly concur, and will return to this issue again in discussing the life-desecrating tyrannical regimes of the twentieth century, notably the Nazis.

55. Waldron, *God, Locke, and Equality,* chapters 4 and 5.

and none overrode shared species membership, rationality, and equality before God.

In his important study of Locke's political thought, Jeremy Waldron carefully surveys what Locke writes about some of these specific relationships and structures, against the backdrop of a society characterized not just by unequal moral status but also by the belief (often supported by church authorities) that this unequal moral status was part of a hierarchical right order itself. For example, as Waldron points out, in his treatment of the relations between husbands and wives, or more broadly, between men and women, Locke attempts to refute contemporary readings of the Adam and Eve narratives in Genesis 1–3 insofar as these purported a comprehensive God-given or natural law subordination of women to men. Responding to the arguments offered by Robert Filmer, Locke claims that the divine grant of dominion over the earth was given jointly to Adam and Eve (not just Adam), that *both* of them were made in the image of God without distinction or hierarchy between them, that both were endowed with reason, that the Fall was their *joint* responsibility, and that God enjoins children to honor both father *and mother* (*1st T*: 29-30; cf. 44-49, 61-63).[56] (Three hundred years later I experienced Southern Baptists tearing themselves apart arguing over some of these very issues.) Waldron concludes that Locke's writings as a whole at least laid the foundation for full social and political equality for women, even if one can still see vestiges of patriarchalism in his thoughts about marriage.[57] Waldron also notes that for Locke, not even the authority of parents over children can be considered lordly or absolute, for God is the Maker and Sovereign over children as well (*1st T*: 52-53).[58] No human dare claim to be the maker or owner of a child. Parents hold children in trust from God until children reach their majority.

56. Waldron wrestles with statements in Locke that suggest that when it comes down to a conflict of wills between a husband and a wife over a decision, the husband should decide because he is, quoting Locke, "abler and stronger." But I think Waldron is correct in seeing that here Locke contradicts the logic of his own deeper principle, probably reflecting his "not altogether successful" effort to free himself from existing cultural assumptions. Waldron, *God, Locke, and Equality*, chapter 3, especially p. 40.

57. A much debated point in Locke literature. A key text is *1st T*: 48. It seems to me that Locke accepts as customary and perhaps "natural" that wives are subjected to their husbands in domestic affairs, but does not argue for a general subjection of women to men or subjects to rulers. See Waldron, *God, Locke, and Equality*, pp. 122-23.

58. And Locke is careful to reject Filmer's ideas, not just of the sovereignty of the father over his children, but his ignoring of the equal status and role of the mother as parent. See *1st T*: 55.

Locke's emphasis on the significance of the capacity of each adult person to make spiritual and moral choices freely and in good conscience had other implications. It helped reinforce the need for a political order that protected freedom of conscience and inquiry. This became important for his thinking about religious toleration that, though not nearly as absolute or as satisfactory as that found in Overton or Williams, overlaps with their thinking and is still far ahead of his time.[59] For Locke, in an area as pivotal to our human nature and eternal destiny as the task of discerning what God our Maker requires of us, each of us must remain free and uncoerced in conscience. It is our freely developed beliefs for which each of us will answer to God (*LCT*, p. 10).

The natural *right to life*, so important in Locke's politics and in every political theory affected by Locke, and so central to any concept of the sacredness of life, is also theologically derived. Because each of us belongs to God and not to ourselves, "Every one . . . is bound to preserve himself, and not to quit his station willfully; so by the like reason when his own Preservation comes not in competition, ought he, as much as he can, to preserve the rest of mankind" (*2nd T:* 6). In another famous line, he writes that we are "made to last during his [God's], not one another's Pleasure" (*2nd T:* 6). In other words: I have a *right* to act to protect my own human life and those liberties and faculties most essential to it, not because I am selfish or individualistic, but because my life ultimately belongs to God and must be protected for the sake of God's ownership rights in it. (This provides important grounding for a theologically rooted right to self-defense.) One could just as easily say I have a *duty* before "God the Maker of Heaven and Earth, who is sole Proprietor of the whole World" (*1st T:* 39) to preserve my life as well and as long as possible for continued service to God. Indeed, this kind of duty had long been understood in Christian thought, for example, in moral prohibitions of suicide. But Locke says I have a similar duty not to take others' lives or even harm them, and indeed an obligation to come to their aid if I can, because God is *their* Maker and Sovereign too,

---

59. Cf. John Locke, *A Letter concerning Toleration*, in *Great Books of the Western World*, vol. 35, edited by Robert Maynard Hutchins (New York: Encyclopaedia Britannica, 1952), pp. 17-21 (hereafter cited in text and notes as *LCT*). Groups not to be tolerated for Locke: those teaching opinions "contrary to human society" and basic moral order; religious zealots who would seize political power and depose kings who do not believe the doctrines that they do (presumably Catholics); those whose religion is actually service to another prince (he mentions "Mahometans," but then later extends toleration to them); those who "deny the being of a God." For discussion, see Waldron, *God, Locke, and Equality*, pp. 225-28.

and it is by natural right that they be preserved for their own service to God. Locke can write quite eloquently of this fundamental theological, moral, and political obligation to protect and preserve human life: "Doth God forbid us under the severest Penalty, that of Death, to take away the Life of any man . . . and does he permit us to destroy those he has given us the Charge and Care of, and by the Dictates of Nature and Reason, as well as his Reveal'd Command, requires us to preserve?" (*1st T:* 56).[60] Or consider this categorical statement: "Unless it be to do Justice to an Offender," we "may not . . . take away or impair the life, or what tends to the Preservation of the Life, Liberty, Health, Limb, or Goods of another" (*2nd T:* 6).[61]

Locke is often criticized for his innovative developments of the theory of private property, which proved so important in the regime we now think of as liberal democratic capitalism. Locke's complex treatment of property is easily misunderstood, in part because of semantic peculiarities related to the use of the term "property." The term, rooted in the Latin *proprius,* had a very long and complex heritage in classical and Christian thought and is very important in the natural law tradition. By the time of Locke, it was understood to extend to all things belonging to a person, and thus to go far beyond material possessions. Property, then, includes everything that is one's own, including one's physical existence and liberties. The idea seems to be that, *always under God's sovereignty,* I first possess myself, my life (*2nd T:* 27). This is where "property," or "propriety," begins. This pivotal idea, at least for Locke, does not offer grounds for my "license," or my doing just anything, as Locke himself points out. Instead my freedom is a natural liberty constrained by natural law. As one who possesses himself or herself under God, my proper interest in my physical well-being, personal liberties, and legitimate needs must not be encroached upon by others.

As is typical for Locke, this treatment of property is rooted in a reason-inflected reading of the Genesis account. In continuity with much of Christian tradition, and joining a very long argument in that tradition, he interprets these texts as providing "a Confirmation of the Original Community of all things amongst the Sons of Men" (*1st T:* 40). In other words,

---

60. Notice also the way Locke assembles his authority claims here: nature, reason, and revelation.

61. Note that in this and other statements Locke clearly grants the legitimacy of the death penalty, at least for those who take the lives of others. See *2nd T:* 11. This does not settle the contemporary question of whether we should now understand the death penalty as a violation of the sacredness of human life. More on that issue later.

property was originally given by God to humans to share in common. But if this was so, then the existence of private property is a great puzzle, maybe even a great sin. Locke's solution is that every person's preservation of his or her life requires the *personal* appropriation and use of at least a subsistence level of private property. Since it is not God's will that "so curious and wonderful a piece of Workmanship" (*1st T:* 86) as the human should die of starvation, God has given to each person a right to work with God's provisions to provide all that is needed for subsistence. This includes making use of the other creatures given to us humans by God in the Garden, which is why it is appropriate for us to own animals and mix our labor with theirs for our survival, as well as to kill and eat them (*2nd T:* 27). It is labor that turns the commonly shared God-given gifts of nature into private property (*1st T:* 86). While Locke's doctrine of property can be criticized as "lacking the humanity and the sense of social co-operation to be found in the [medieval] canonists,"[62] it is not entirely individualistic. Developing property is also a kind of social duty, a duty to the community, to posterity, and to God; all people have a duty to work hard to make the most of the resources God has placed in their hands and on the planet for the flourishing of a multitude of people on the earth (*2nd T:* 42).[63] When we work hard, for example, in finding new ways to feed more people, we make it possible for humans collectively to obey the divine mandate to "be fruitful and multiply" (Gen. 1:28). This approach puts significant responsibility for human flourishing in the hands of each individual as a creative laborer (puzzle #14).

And property rights are not absolute. Locke is often misread here. No one has a right, for example, to own slaves or to establish any slave system, a state that Locke described as "vile and miserable" and that cannot be supported by the principles of his political philosophy (*1st T:* 1).[64] No one

---

62. Laslett, "Introduction," p. 120.

63. Noted by Waldron, *God, Locke, and Equality*, p. 164.

64. Locke begins his *First Treatise on Government* with an attack on slavery, though in context he seems to mean the slavery of those subjected to a monarch with absolute power. But his entire political philosophy undercuts the legitimacy of any political order in which some human beings exercise absolute power over others. From time to time he explicitly mentions slavery as a violation of the natural right to freedom (*2nd T:* 17; cf. 22-24). Yet I do not find evidence that he ever launched an explicit attack on the slavery system as practiced in Great Britain and the colonies. He also may have been personally implicated in that system in terms of his economic interests and role in drafting the constitution of South Carolina. For a discussion of this matter, see Waldron, *God, Locke, and Equality*, pp. 197-206.

has a right to take more of a perishable product like food than she can use, and thus to waste it and deny it to others who could have used it (the principle of "spoilage" — *2nd T:* 31). No one has a right to take a parcel of land unless the next person has access to at least "as much and as good" a tract of land — the so-called sufficiency proviso (*2nd T:* 33). And no one (of means) has a right to turn his back on the needs of the poor, who, says Locke, "have a Title to so much out of another's Plenty, as will keep him from extreme want, where he has no means to subsist otherwise" (*1st T:* 42). So Locke's cherished/criticized emphasis on property rights, in its original form, was hedged about with qualifications deeply rooted in the Christian tradition, with both the primary theory and the qualifications intended to contribute to human preservation and flourishing. I do believe Locke can be criticized for a tendency to reduce the function of government to the securing of "estate" or "property" (cf. *2nd T:* 94 and numerous other texts), a problem worsened by the semantic difficulty mentioned above. But I wonder if he would have turned out to be as rigid as today's libertarians who claim his legacy in limiting government's function entirely to this role, and who so readily deny the responsibility of government to establish any social safety net for the poor.[65]

Rejecting a much darker view found in Thomas Hobbes's influential 1588 *Leviathan,* Locke describes the original human condition, or "the state of nature," as one in which humanity, or "natural man," is perfectly free, equal, and independent, living peacefully in sociable community (not as a lone individual) with no one subject to anyone else and no one in fear of anyone else (cf. *2nd T:* 4). These original humans are able to live in this way because they are equipped by God with reason to obey the natural law, which is readily accessible to rational discovery. Locke seems influenced here by a reading of the original Edenic state of humanity as presented in Genesis, and seems to be rejecting Hobbes's dystopian vision in his *Leviathan* of a primal "State of War" of all against all as the natural human condition.[66] This latter view has proved itself again and again to be potentially

65. Waldron, *God, Locke, and Equality,* pp. 177-87, seems to see more generosity in Locke on property than does Laslett, "Introduction," p. 120. An interesting question concerns whether Locke draws a distinction between what "Justice" requires and what "Charity" requires, and perhaps therefore, what responsibilities belong to government as a demand of justice and to individuals or associations as a call for charity. I don't think Locke is altogether clear on this issue.

66. John Milbank considers Lockean liberalism little different from Hobbesian absolutism in its founding narrative of an original "ontological violence" and its implications, in-

dangerous, tending toward support for absolutist rule. For Locke, a kind of loosely anarchic peace among equals is the starting point (cf. *2nd T:* 19).

But Locke does understand that we do not live in the Garden, and that there was such a thing as a fall of humankind. We are no longer immortal, apart from God's redemptive grace; and we are also no longer fully rational in how we think or how we treat others. We are not free from selfishness or misunderstanding of the natural law (cf. *2nd T:* 13, 124-125). We are tempted to abuse one another's vulnerability, and we do need protection from one another. It is within the natural law to protect one's life, liberty, and property and to refrain from harming others. We should always honor this natural law. But we do not always do so, especially in relation to others. This means that our peace and security in the state of nature are uncertain, with everyone uneasy about his neighbor and dependent on himself for self-protection (cf. *2nd T:* 123).

So we agree to give up some of our natural liberties — which in the state of nature included the liberty to do whatever we chose for self-preservation and for punishment of those who violated the law of nature.[67] We "join in society with others, who are already united, or have a mind to unite, for the mutual preservation of their lives, liberties and estates" (*2nd T:* 123).[68] From this agreement to form a civil society comes the origin of government, to which is delegated the responsibility to do the work that each individual once had to try to do in the state of nature. The legislative power writes and the executive power impartially enforces statutes within the body politic that conform to the natural law, beginning with the prevention and punishment of unjust violence (cf. *2nd T:* 124-131).[69]

---

cluding the centralization of violence in the state. See Milbank, *Theology and Social Theory,* p. 13. I do think there is a difference, but grant that both Hobbes and Locke assume the need for a state prepared to do violence to preserve security. For other connections and divergences, see the brilliant discussion in Lilla, *The Stillborn God,* pp. 75ff.

67. Laslett, "Introduction," p. 120.

68. The main problem here is the implication that in the imagined state of nature we are solitary individuals rather than humans in community. But in reality we are always social creatures, from the moment we are conceived until the day we die. Locke's state of nature can easily be read to reinforce radical individualism, with government's role being to protect the individual from obligations to other people. I am grateful to Glen Stassen for this insight.

69. Notice that in this theology/philosophy of the origins and purposes of law Locke clearly reflects great continuity with the medieval natural law tradition. See *2nd T:* 12-13; 168. Locke was not a legal positivist; he believed human law should reflect the natural law, or "a Law antecedent and paramount to all positive Laws of Men." See the discussion in Waldron, *God, Locke, and Equality,* p. 131.

By treating violence as an aberration rather than the natural state of things, and by emphasizing the use of reason to establish civil society, with political processes that forestall the need for violence and set strict limits on state violence, *Locke embeds in liberal political philosophy that respect for human life that came forward from the Christian tradition.*[70] The entire system is built upon full and equal human worth before God and the need to protect each and every human life from harm. Government's fundamental delegated responsibility is of "preserving him [every person] from the Violence or Injury of others" (*1st T:* 92). And government itself must be prevented from doing unjust harm to those it is responsible precisely to protect from such harm. "For wherever violence is used, and injury done, though by hands appointed to administer Justice, it is still violence and injury, however colour'd with the Name, Pretences or Forms of Law" (*2nd T:* 20).

Therefore, though we trade some portion of our liberty to create a government that will protect our "Fundamental, Sacred, and unalterable" (*2nd T:* 149) right to life, we always have a duty and a right to challenge or even depose governments that violate the rights they were created to protect. The *rule of law* is supreme, not the persons or individual will of legislators or executives. These men and women forfeit their claim to obedience as soon as they violate the rule of law. In a striking section, Locke says that the ruler "has no Will, no Power, but that of the Law" (*2nd T:* 151), and that any oath of fealty taken to a prince or other ruler must be understood as an oath extending only insofar as that ruler is a faithful executor of the law. The oath is not to the person but to the law. (One thinks of Sir Thomas More.) This is indeed a sacredness of human life ethic, in a shrewd new incarnation, and again brings to mind history's numerous tyrants who so often have demanded unconditional oaths of personal allegiance during their reigns of terror.

Locke scholar John Dunn has said that Locke's *Two Treatises on Government* are simply "saturated with Christian assumptions."[71] Alasdair MacIntyre has quipped mordantly that Locke's political philosophy is so rooted in Christian thought that it could not today be taught in American public schools.[72] Jeremy Waldron is so impressed by the Christian founda-

---

70. I do not share the belief that Locke's ratification of a place for state violence to protect people from aggressors marks a fatal flaw in his theory. I do agree that the Christian community is called to be a people marked by peacemaking as an ecclesial practice and public witness.

71. Quoted in Waldron, *God, Locke, and Equality*, p. 12.

72. In Waldron, *God, Locke, and Equality*, p. 44.

tions of Locke's thought that he appears to suggest not only that Locke's thinking about equality is incomprehensible apart from them, but also that contemporary secular efforts to defend equality apart from any religious basis represent a "squander[ing] of our ethical inheritance" and a very risky venture indeed.[73]

As we consider Locke's legacy to us, on the plus side Locke can be credited with carrying forward both a principled commitment to the equal God-given worth of each human being and a rule-of-law political philosophy that has the potential to protect human beings from one another and from government tyranny. The laudable conviction that every person is equal, is free, and has a right to life, and that government exists to secure these rights, stands at the foundation of political thought in the United States and in every society affected by Locke. Even a cursory reading of the documents associated with the founding of the United States reveals the profound impact of Locke's thought. Locke says in his treatise that "in the beginning, all the world was America" (*2nd T:* 49). He is speaking of what he takes to be the state of nature as it pertains to property. We could just as easily say that all Americans are Lockeans, at least all who appreciate the political system that the Founders created on Lockean premises even as they eventually extended and improved upon Locke in key regards.[74]

Of course, criticisms of Locke are appropriate as well. Jeremy Waldron, whose writing reveals a great respect for Locke, admits that Locke "flinched at a number of points" from the implications of his own radical egalitarianism.[75] He specifically mentions things Locke says about the power of husbands over wives as well as some of his statements about criminals. We have already discussed problems with Locke's treatment of property, and of the created order, and scholars have noted at least potential problems in his beliefs and practices in relation to slavery as well as aboriginal rights in America. It is sadly interesting that the American Founders and the American experience have replicated these same problems even as Americans have often embraced the best of Locke. It has taken the entire course of American history for the "equality-radicalism"[76] of Locke and of the Declaration of Independence to fight its way through the irrational, immoral, and ungodly structural discriminations already visible in the seventeenth and eighteenth

73. Waldron, *God, Locke, and Equality,* pp. 242-43.

74. For example, the U.S. Constitution includes an independent judiciary, a stronger set of checks and balances, and fuller religious liberty and freedom of conscience.

75. Waldron, *God, Locke, and Equality,* p. 6.

76. Waldron, *God, Locke, and Equality,* p. 5.

centuries. And now, in the days after chattel slavery, women's disenfranchisement, and racism *de jure,* many would agree that Locke remains problematically with us, because American democracy may be more threatened by the unfettered capitalism grounded in his robust theory of property rights than by any other single force.[77]

I already indicated that many who lament the loss of "right order" thinking in Western culture blame the "natural rights" crowd, which by any account would have John Locke near the front of the line. But I hope it is now clear that Locke himself was still functioning as a kind of natural law thinker, with a version of natural right still present in his thought. He believed in a God-given moral order, and believed that human law must conform to God's will, which equals the law of nature, which equals natural right. So Locke himself cannot be blamed for the deterioration of the natural right tradition into the "anything goes" rights ethic that we so often find in Western culture today. Locke decidedly did not believe that there are no God-given boundaries set for human choices, or that anything anyone wants to do is her right.

The seeds of danger are already visible in Locke, however. Perhaps they are traceable to his idea that each of us possesses ourselves first of all, and that we are "perfectly free" individuals. My exposition of Locke has shown that he *meant* that we possess ourselves as a subsidiary to God's possession of us, and that we are perfectly free *only insofar* as we do not violate the natural law. But these not-so-small provisos have gradually weakened almost to the point of invisibility, not only in our cultures but also in most of our churches.

Critics such as the right-order thinkers are justified in being worried about people sliding into moral chaos. But right-order thinkers seem less worried about what the thinkers of the early modern era were worried about — the hubris and tyranny so frequently exercised by the state (often in tandem with the church), in pursuing *their vision, at that moment, of right order,* which inevitably conflicted with the pluralistic visions of right order already present in the society, thus triggering civil conflict and great bloodshed. Think of Great Britain's constant conflicts over religion during and after the reign of Henry VIII. The United States and those nations that followed its political example took a different path. They

---

77. One recent work related to this issue is H. W. Brands, *American Colossus: The Triumph of Capitalism, 1865-1900* (New York: Doubleday, 2010). Brand claims that democracy and corporate power have been fighting for preeminence since very early in American history.

moved toward a *political* order based in natural/human rights with a limited government hedged about by all kinds of checks and balances to prevent tyranny; and they hoped for a *social* order in which the morally indispensable pursuit of virtue and right order was cultivated by individuals, religious institutions, voluntary associations, educational structures, and civil society.[78] Government itself would no longer pursue a broader vision of right order, of forming virtuous lives that conform to the will of God. *But that did not mean that no one would or should do so.* This division of social-ethical responsibilities was carefully considered, a product of hard experience and hard decisions. Perhaps, as of 2012, we can conclude that it has at last failed, at least in cultivating any kind of shared moral vision and the virtues that go with it. But this remains a matter of legitimate debate.

It is the underlying narrative and the implications of a Lockean vision that most disturb Christian moral philosophers and theologians like John Milbank and Oliver and Joan Lockwood O'Donovan — and ought to disturb all of us. Locke tells a mythological story of origins — the "state of nature" — in which "the detached, pre-social individual"[79] warily gives up his primal freedom and contracts his way into a society of strictly limited engagement and then a state, all the while intent on the self-interested protection of his rights. Locke's core narrative, on this view, is a narrative from below (the state of nature) rather than above (God's eternal law); it sees the individual rather than the community (or God) as the fundamental actor in history; it envisions no shared social good/right but only the aggregation of individual rights in "property" and other interests; it does not see the social order as a gift from God but instead as a human creation preserved by contract, law, and force. As John Headley puts it, natural law begins to lose any real transcendent power in this account. The same term is used — "natural law" — but it primarily describes a universal human condition and its remedy rather than a transcendent, objective, divinely inscribed moral order from which all rights are derived. And the idea of a limited state pursuing a very limited security-based menu frees (or robs, depending on one's perspective) the state of any transcendent religious or

---

78. A point made in a somewhat different way by Gertrude Himmelfarb, *The Roads to Modernity: The British, French, and American Enlightenments* (New York: Knopf, 2004), pp. 198-203. She also points out that at least at the beginning, the Constitution was understood to leave moral and religious formation in the hands of state governments if they should choose to pursue it. It was the federal government that was banned from establishing religion.

79. O'Donovan, *Desire of the Nations*, p. 276.

moral reference. The state secularizes; religion and morality are gradually reduced to the private sphere where they can be safely cordoned off from politics and public life.[80] Critics wonder if this religiously denuded social order leaves people hungry for a shared sense of transcendence and meaning, so that a formerly Christian vision subject to tyrannical pretensions is simply traded out for a society with religious toleration but with potential secular, nationalist, commercial, or racist visions at least as tyrannical as the earlier religious regimes.[81]

The philosophers among us might say the real issue with Locke is his epistemology. In his *Essay concerning Human Understanding,* an extraordinarily searching document about how we know what we know, Locke does conclude that it is possible to be certain of some things. And he concludes that these occasional certainties, and more frequent probabilities, are gained through our (God-given) natural faculties of "sensation" and "reflection" (*E:* IV.xviii.2), the two key components of rationality. It is possible to have "faith," which Locke defines as "a firm assent of the mind," but there must be "good reason" for that assent, and much of what passes for good reason Locke dismantles during the course of the *Essay.* Locke thus became an early addition to a train of Western philosophers who were in the process of becoming less and less sure about more and more things — in terms of both *what* we thought we knew and *how* we thought we knew. So the John Locke of the *Treatises* quotes the Bible extensively, while the John Locke of the *Essay* is extremely careful about accepting any claims from "traditional revelation," and finally says that "Reason must be our last Judge in everything" (*E:* IV.xix.14). Claims from direct divine revelation are ruled out (cf. *E:* IV.xix); claims from traditional revelation (Scripture, apparently) are supplemental, are less reliable than deductions from reason, and can communicate no new ideas (*E:* IV.xviii.2-4). Nor does Locke accept the concept of innate moral principles imprinted on the human mind.[82] As Nicholas Jolley has observed, "We know that Locke was a theist and a Christian (if a rather unorthodox one) who seems to have believed that the Bible contains divinely revealed truths. But his most sus-

---

80. Headley, *Europeanization of the World,* pp. 114-19.

81. The argument that religious toleration simply prepared the way for profit-driven and nationalist secularism is made by A. J. Conyers in his *The Long Truce: How Toleration Made the World Safe for Power and Profit* (Dallas: Spence Publishing, 2001).

82. Himmelfarb makes this point, noting that even in his own day "Locke was admired more for his politics than for his metaphysics." See Himmelfarb, *The Roads to Modernity,* pp. 26-29, for her complete discussion.

tained discussion of the philosophy of religion [the *Essay*] is highly corrosive; whatever he intended, it gives aid and comfort to the enemies of revealed religion."[83] Mark Lilla is so impressed with this that he goes so far as to suggest the possibility that Locke may not have believed his own theological arguments.[84] The key Enlightenment philosophers after Locke resembled and followed his path — both in attempting to offer substantive moral claims about how human life should be protected and human dignity respected, and in offering epistemologies subtly undercutting the reasons for believing any such thing at all.

7.4. Immanuel Kant: Dignity, Autonomy, and the Moral Law

A remarkable figure now moves to the center of our reflections. All scholars of Western intellectual history recognize the pivotal significance of Immanuel Kant (1724-1804), the German philosopher whose thinking perhaps more than any other single person's brought an end to the confident Enlightenment era and initiated the transition into the deep uncertainty about the grounds of knowledge that remains with us today.[85]

Our focus in this brief discussion will be, as just suggested, on both the epistemological skepticism of Kant's philosophy and his memorable defense of an ethic of human dignity. The best example of the former is found in Kant's still-staggering *Critique of Pure Reason* (1781, rev. 1787), the latter in his *Groundwork of the Metaphysic of Morals* (1785).[86] These works will receive most of our attention.

It is hard to know how much to emphasize the personal background and biography of scholars whose work lives on primarily because of its rich intellectual content. I said little about the Puritan background, revolutionary English context, and life-threatening political maneuverings that surely had an impact on the thought of John Locke. Perhaps it is therefore

83. Nicholas Jolley, "Locke on Faith and Reason," in *The Cambridge Companion to Locke's "Essay concerning Human Understanding,"* ed. Lex Newman (Cambridge: Cambridge University Press, 2007), p. 455.

84. Lilla, *The Stillborn God,* p. 100.

85. Allen W. Wood, *Kant* (Malden, Mass.: Blackwell, 2005), p. 1.

86. Immanuel Kant, "The Critique of Pure Reason," in *Great Books of the Western World,* vol. 42, ed. Robert Maynard Hutchins (New York: Encyclopaedia Britannica, 1952), hereafter abbreviated in text as *C1*; *Groundwork of the Metaphysic of Morals,* translated and analyzed by H. J. Paton (New York: Harper and Row, 1948), hereafter abbreviated in text as *G.*

unfair to claim here the very likely impact of Immanuel Kant's immersion in, and general rejection of, the German Pietism of his childhood and youth. But it seems that both the immersion into and the rejection of this form of sectarian Protestantism played a pivotal role in forming Kant's mature philosophy, and his personal journey stands as such a symbol of his era.

Allen W. Wood, a leading scholar of Kant, draws these biographical connections in his authoritative survey of Kant's life and thought. Those readers who, like me, have experienced populist religion at an impressionable age might recognize something of our experience when we read Wood's claim that Kant "found the atmosphere of religious zealotry, especially the intellectual tyranny of the catechism, insufferably stifling to both mind and spirit." Or this: "[Kant] typically identifies pietism either with a spirit of narrow sectarianism in religion or with a self-despising moral lethargy." Or this: "[Kant defined] a pietist as someone who 'tastelessly makes the idea of religion dominant in all conversation and discourse.'"[87] Wood discloses that the adult Kant on principle refused to set foot in church even when it was expected of him as a faculty member at the University of Königsberg.

To note these facts is not to reduce Kant's thinking to their influence. But it may help us understand the deeper wellsprings of the relentless skepticism of the Kant we see in *Critique of Pure Reason,* his first memorable work. Amidst that extraordinarily rigorous probing of how human beings know anything they purport to know, Kant regularly returns to attacks on "dogmatism" and on fanciful metaphysical and religious claims that extend far beyond the reach of human experience and rationality. He seems especially committed to destroying the claims, so frequently found in Christianity, to *know* things about the supernatural realm on the basis either of biblical revelation or of some kind of philosophical or rational proof. His efforts certainly left their mark. Such claims never quite recovered.

All the Christian thinkers we have encountered so far in this book did indeed believe that they *knew* certain truths about metaphysical or supernatural realities. But Kant utterly breaks with this tradition as he claims that there can be no sure knowledge of any objects that cannot be experienced through the senses. Of course, he further claims that even those sense experiences we have of objects are not unmediated, but instead are processed through categories that our mind imposes upon them. In his

87. Wood, *Kant,* p. 4.

words, "the object conforms to the nature of our faculty of intuition . . . we only cognize in things *a priori* that which we ourselves place in them" (*C1*, p. 1). This is a way of saying that we do not encounter things in themselves, but only a mediated experience of things as filtered through our categories of thought and experience. As Richard Tarnas puts it, "In the act of human cognition, the mind does not conform to things; rather, things conform to the mind."[88]

If this is true even of objects that we can encounter with our senses, it is perhaps not surprising that Kant would go on to say that we can have *no knowledge* of any idea or (purported) object that is not accessible to the senses. Therefore, when he finally discusses the traditional objects of metaphysics, that is, ideas such as God, human freedom (and thus real moral choice), a beginning of the universe through creation, or the immortal soul, he says we literally cannot know such things.[89] Therefore we can neither affirm nor deny real knowledge of such matters. The fact that we can think an idea of God does not mean that our thoughts correspond to anything beyond our thoughts. Here is a typical statement of his position: "The notion of a Supreme Being is in many respects a highly useful idea; but for the very reason that it is an idea, it is incapable of enlarging our cognition with regard to the existence of things" (*C1*, p. 182).

The truth of such theological claims, for Kant, simply cannot be settled through any means that humans have of reliably knowing anything. The same is true of claims related to the content of morality. In a very important statement, Kant says: "The real morality of actions — their merit or demerit, and even [the morality] of our own conduct, is completely unknown to us" (p. 169). Kant says of any claim to metaphysical knowledge: "It stretches its wings in vain, to soar beyond the world of sense by the mere might of speculative thought" (p. 179). From a Christian perspective, it is slight comfort that Kant just as readily dismisses supposedly sure knowledge that there is *no* God or *no* real morality. Dogmatic claims both for and against such knowledge overreach their bounds. Indeed, Kant seems to suggest that overwrought positive claims to such supernatural knowledge (from Christians and others) have produced the climate for overwrought negative claims from aggressive atheists (p. 10). This state-

88. Richard Tarnas, *The Passion of the Western Mind* (New York: Ballantine Books, 1991), p. 343.

89. Kant eventually argued that we can (must) affirm belief in God and immortality because morality needs such grounding, but that is far different from claiming we have sure knowledge of the existence of God and the reality of immortality.

ment and the situation that lies behind it sound remarkably contemporary. The best posture, for Kant, is to accept that we simply cannot know things that are unknowable, and metaphysical claims are unknowable.

And yet, Kant opens a window where he has closed a door. He draws a distinction between *theoretical knowledge* and *practical knowledge,* which appears to parallel his distinction between *pure reason* and *practical reason.* Pure reason produces theoretical knowledge pertaining to what *is,* says Kant, while practical reason produces practical knowledge pertaining to what *ought to be.* While human beings can have no theoretical knowledge about the actual existence of a Supreme Being who created the world, or who created morally free rational creatures, they find it highly practical to believe in the existence of such a God and such moral freedom (p. 190). In fact, he says it more strongly: "The practical interests of morality require" these assumptions (p. 10). This then becomes the basis for an eventual Kantian proposal for a "rational moral faith" that includes belief in God and the practice of a purified version of Christianity.[90]

Before we consider further the kind of practical morality that Kant proposed, let's review what we have just witnessed. Kant has claimed that it is not possible to know whether there is a God, or whether humans are really free to make meaningful moral decisions. Further, he has denied the entire heritage of the natural law tradition insofar as it claimed to perceive an objective moral order in nature, outside the self and discovered by the self. Kant's epistemology requires the conclusion that such a "moral order" does not exist *out there* but is instead a construction of our speculative reason. More broadly, he rejects the idea of any "thing in itself" outside the self; at least, we cannot know what that thing in itself would be, because we access such "things" indirectly. We carry around the concepts and categories in our minds that we need to make sense of objects that our senses perceive as existing outside ourselves. And if that is true of objects that we can see and touch, like tables, it is certainly true of ideas, like an invisible objective moral order.

After Kant, philosophy at least, and much theology, would give up on the project of attempting to describe realities such as God, or a "pre-given good"[91] as in natural law, or moral rights and wrongs as they are in themselves, independently of us; instead, after Kant, all we can undertake is, as Wood says, "second-order study of the way human inquiry itself makes

90. Lilla, *The Stillborn God,* p. 142.
91. Wood, *Kant,* p. 1.

possible its access to whatever subject matter it studies."[92] In a famous statement in the introduction to the *Critique of Pure Reason,* Kant writes, "I must therefore abolish *knowledge,* to make room for *belief*" (*C1,* p. 10, italics in original). Henceforth, mainstream philosophy would focus primarily on the limitations or the groundlessness of our knowledge claims. Ethics, such as it was, often became nothing more than analysis of the meanings of our humanly invented ethical systems and languages (analytic philosophy),[93] along with "paralysis" in terms of any normative proposals for what might actually be moral and immoral, right and wrong.[94] Theology tore in two, with the "liberal" and sometimes pietistic side increasingly focused on the dynamics of human belief and religious feeling in the absence of knowledge in the Kantian sense, and the other (fundamentalist, orthodox, or neo-orthodox) side clinging resolutely to the older belief that Christian claims to *know* certain things about God, the self, morality, etc., are based on the sure foundation of Scripture and/or tradition and/or church authority and/or reason and/or natural law. This theological schism remains very much with us to this day.[95]

In the next chapter we will consider one brilliant and deeply disturbing philosophical response to these developments in the work of Friedrich Nietzsche. As for Kant, he still had a substantive moral philosophy to propose. Kant himself does *not* appear sanguine about the shaking of the foundations of morality that his "critical philosophy" requires of him. He says even in the first *Critique* that the skeptical mode of inquiry is not the only one we need. And the survival of a meaningful morality to govern the behavior of men and women is never far from his mind. He writes, "There are certain practical laws — those of morality — which are absolutely neces-

92. Wood, *Kant,* p. 1. Mark Lilla claims that, long before Kant, Hobbes was the first and most significant modern thinker to argue in this vein. See *The Stillborn God,* pp. 77-78.

93. See J. L. Mackie, *Ethics: Inventing Right and Wrong* (New York: Penguin, 1977). For a discussion of analytic moral philosophy, see Richard Norman, *The Moral Philosophers: An Introduction to Ethics* (Oxford: Oxford University Press, 1998), chapter 10.

94. MacIntyre concurs, lamenting that this left academic philosophy without the confidence to offer either religious or rational justifications for morality; they still carried on their academic debates, but "in much greater isolation from [the] public than previously." Alasdair MacIntyre, *After Virtue,* 2nd ed. (Notre Dame, Ind.: University of Notre Dame Press, 1984), p. 50. For "paralysis," see Robert M. Veatch, *The Foundations of Justice: Why the Retarded and the Rest of Us Have Claims to Equality* (New York and Oxford: Oxford University Press, 1986), p. 78.

95. See Nancey Murphy, *Beyond Liberalism and Fundamentalism* (Valley Forge, Pa.: Trinity, 1996).

sary" (*C1*, p. 190). He returns again and again to this theme. Human civilization cannot do without a sure belief in a universally applicable morality, and indeed, the rigorous practice of this morality as if it were absolutely binding. Individuals must act, and often do act, as if such a morality exists: "But if [a person] were called to action, the play of the merely speculative reason would disappear like the shapes of a dream, and practical interest would dictate his choice of principles" (p. 149). But the previous supports for belief in morality no longer hold. Therefore, Kant's primary project in the arena of "practical reason" came to be the construction of a moral theory that could ground obligation for all rational creatures. And, interestingly enough, he discovered that this moral theory actually "demand[s] or postulate[s]" the "existence of a Supreme Being" (p. 190). He found a kind of back door to God, though not one that most Christian theologians have found terribly inviting.[96]

*   *   *

Four years after the first edition of his *Critique of Pure Reason* appeared, Immanuel Kant began to fulfill the promises he made there to present the "practical laws of morality." In Kant's own conception, the relatively brief book he produced in 1785 toward this end — the *Groundwork of the Metaphysic of Morals* — was only a starting point in this project. But it remains the work most cited in Kant's corpus, certainly in ethics. Our primary goal in revisiting this work is to see whether he carried forward the ancient Christian ethic of the sacred worth of each and every human life, and if so how he did it.

Kant begins by cordoning off the work of moral philosophy proper from the task of identifying "laws for the will of man" pertaining to what "ought to happen" (*G*, p. 55). At first he sounds as if he is committed merely for technical reasons to abstracting the search for these moral laws for the human will away from any consideration of actual human experi-

---

96. In *Groundwork of the Metaphysic of Morals*, p. 76, Kant argues that we derive the idea of God as the morally perfect being from the idea of moral perfection as we reason our way to it. We don't need the idea of God to see that this vision of moral duty is binding and obligatory. God is entirely supplemental. No information or sanction comes from God or Scripture that is not accessible to reason. Kant eventually goes a bit further toward an ethically based practical justification for belief in God. See Karl Ameriks, "Immanuel Kant," in *The Columbia History of Western Philosophy*, ed. Richard Popkin (New York: Columbia University Press, 1999), p. 500.

ence. But quickly he also makes clear at a *substantive* level that proper understanding of moral obligation *requires* bracketing off human experience, as well as human inclinations, goals, feelings, self-interest, happiness, and the consequences of human actions.[97] Kant liked to speak of the "pure" in philosophy, and here his pivotal methodological move is to identify the pure in ethics with a pure moral law based in "pure reason" and motivated purely by duty (*G*, pp. 57-58). We must train ourselves away from any other consideration if we want to understand morality.

That moral law, which actually culminates the first chapter of the *Groundwork*, is Kant's famous categorical imperative in its first formulation: "I ought never to act except in such a way that I can also will that my maxim should become a universal law" (p. 70); or, stated positively, "Act only on that maxim through which you can at the same time will that it become a universal law" (p. 88). He contrasts this ethical principle with any approach — such as in utilitarianism — that identifies right action with an action yielding a desired result, the satisfaction of inclinations, or the increase of happiness. Kant is totally convinced that mixing the pursuit of such ends into the motives for one's actions poisons moral decision making. For example, he contrasts a prudent consequences-maximizer who might knowingly make a false promise to attain a desired goal with a person who knows that he cannot will the making of false promises as a universal law (pp. 70-71). Only the latter person will never compromise the moral obligation to make truthful promises and to keep them. And we need every bulwark to keep us from sliding into such moral compromises.

In his run-up to this first formulation of the categorical imperative, Kant makes several moves that are important for our purposes. First, he proposes and then defends the proposition that the only thing "which can be taken as good without qualification, [is] a *good will*" (p. 61). In perhaps the clearest statement of what he means by this, he says the good will is "the straining of every means as far as they are in our control" (p. 62) to allow reason rather than inclination, desire, or self-interest to function as governor of our actions. A will thus governed by reason acts on the basis of the moral duties reason dictates, even when (and especially when) these

---

97. Kant was an enemy of any form of utilitarianism, which he pokes repeatedly in these pages. He knew it in the form offered by Jeremy Bentham; John Stuart Mill's more refined utilitarianism came later, but the two schools of thought became permanent antagonists. More broadly, as Franklin I. Gamwell has written, "Kant stands radically opposed to all teleological theories of ethics." Gamwell, *The Divine Good: Modern Moral Theory and the Necessity of God* (New York: HarperCollins, 1990), p. 38.

duties contrast sharply with that course of action that might produce the greatest personal happiness for ourselves. A "holy will" (p. 81), in turn, is a will so aligned with duty's demands that they are no longer experienced as demands at all. He offers several cases in which a person's will is directed by (a) self-interest, (b) a mix of self-interest and duty, or (c) duty alone. Kant is convinced that only the latter has "genuine moral worth" (p. 66). Any action motivated by a mix of factors that include anything other than reason-dictated duty is not an action worthy of significant moral esteem. He uses a rare example (in his writings) from the New Testament to buttress his point here, saying that Scripture's command that we love our enemies clearly distinguishes love of friends — driven as that is by inclination or preference — from love of enemies, which is the only kind of love one could actually be *commanded* to undertake (p. 67).

In this first chapter Kant famously introduces the language of "reverence," which is often taken as a synonym for sacredness, as in "reverence for life." But what he actually proposes is not reverence for persons but reverence for the (moral) law: "Only bare law for its own sake . . . can be an object of reverence and therewith a command" (p. 68). Kant rather eloquently communicates a sense of "awe"[98] here, even a sense of sacredness, but it is connected to the moral law itself, "a value which demolishes my self-love" (*G*, p. 69). In a footnote he defines this reverence as "consciousness of the subordination of my will" to a law that commands my adherence apart from either my inclinations or my fears. Kant hastens to add that this moral law is one that we "impose on ourselves," but it is also "necessary in itself" (p. 69). In sum: we do not reverence persons in themselves, but we do reverence the moral law. We are right to reverence people whose dutiful actions give us an exemplary embodiment of reverence for the moral law — if we recognize that it is really the moral law that we are honoring, not the persons themselves.

At the end of the first chapter, Kant reaffirms his belief that what he has presented is nothing other than an elucidation of "ordinary human reason" (p. 71) or, as the title of his chapter suggests, "ordinary rational knowledge." But is it? Would it seem so today? In a key aside, Kant himself admits that he is drawing from "the common Idea of duty and from the laws of morality" (p. 57). One does not have to be much of a practitioner of the "hermeneutics of suspicion" to see that what Kant understands as "the common Idea of duty" was certainly much more common in his own culture than in ours,

98. Taylor, *Sources of the Self*, p. 83.

and the same could easily be said of "the laws of morality." I am not the first to propose that Kant appears to be drawing on a particular version of the moral heritage of Christendom, mixed with some Platonic idealism, in grounding morality in a more-or-less ascetic sense of absolutely binding moral duty, oblivious to personal wants and inclinations — and therefore, at least implicitly, demanding of each person a willingness to sacrifice personal desires for the sake of doing what is right.[99] And the framing of such moral duties in terms of universal law, which the self experiences reverentially as totally obligatory and binding, as commanding my actions and demolishing my self-love, certainly rings with the cadences of the Bible's treatment of the law of God. Read that footnote on reverence for the moral law again (*G*, p. 69), and you will see it. The references to this reverenced law being "self-produced by a rational concept" and "a law which we impose on ourselves" feel forced in this context. Kant very much is committed to saying that reason alone is "the authoress of her own laws" and "not . . . the mouthpiece of laws whispered to her by some implanted sense or by who knows what tutelary nature" (p. 93). But I am suggesting that Kant himself has heard some whispers. He is taking what is indeed a pure and exalted understanding of binding moral-legal obligation that he inherited from the best of his Christian tradition and only half-translating it here into rational terms. This moral law and its supposed *a priori rationality* have origins beyond what Kant is willing to admit.

Now we turn to the heart of the matter, Kant's three formulations and extensive discussion of the "categorical imperative." The first of these, discussed above, is the one most frequently repeated throughout the rest of this short book. But in an early restatement of the categorical imperative in the pivotal second chapter, he makes a slight amendment: *"Act as if the maxim of your action were to become through your will a universal law of nature"* (G, p. 89, italics in original). Kant has now retrieved and imported a version of, or some language of, the natural law tradition that he earlier seemed so resolutely to reject. We know enough already to assume that Kant cannot mean "law of nature" the way Aquinas or even Locke meant it. If we can get some idea of what he does mean by it, it will help us understand his overall perspective much more clearly.

---

99. Richard Tarnas is among those who tie his ethic to his pietist background. Tarnas, *Passion of the Western Mind*, p. 350. Alasdair MacIntyre reaches the same conclusion: "Kant never doubted for a moment that the maxims which he had learnt from his own virtuous parents were those which had to be vindicated by a rational test." MacIntyre, *After Virtue*, p. 44.

I propose that two primary things are going on with Kant's use of this ancient term. First, when Kant says "nature" has a "law" or "laws," he appears in the first instance to be talking about laws such as cause and effect — "Everything in nature works in accordance with laws" (p. 80). He also claims that there is a "universal interconnexion of existent things in accordance with universal laws" (p. 104). He is not making an argument from divine design; he always rejected such arguments. But in his empirical mode he recognizes certain physical "laws" of nature, and the way all existent things are interconnected under the power of these laws. So one meaning of "law/s of nature" for Kant pertains to physical laws of nature such as gravity or cause and effect.

Secondly, Kant seems to accept a teleological view of nature, in which "nature" has a purpose for each of its entities and creatures. As for nature's special purpose for humanity, it goes like this: "there are in humanity capacities for greater perfection" (pp. 97-98), in the life of each human person and perhaps also in the species as a whole. In context, this incredibly striking statement is suggesting that nature's special purpose for us human beings is the full development and exercise of our unique rational capacity, so that we might learn to legislate moral duty for ourselves in accordance with pure reason. So in this sense the "law of nature" for humanity is that humans might become fully rational and autonomous moral agents who disinterestedly do their duty for the sake of duty itself. Kant says that "only a rational being [such as a human] has the power to act *in accordance with his idea of laws* . . . and only so has he a will" (p. 80). What distinguishes the fulfillment of the law of nature on the part of rational beings (with human beings the only group of such rational beings that we have heretofore encountered) is their free decision to direct their will toward the autonomous discovery and implementation of their moral obligations.[100]

Spending a moment with what might seem to be an abstruse dimension of Kant's moral theory proves important to making sense of his other two formulations of the categorical imperative. Here is the famous second formulation: "Act in such a way that you always treat humanity, whether in

100. In their systematic and thoughtful treatment of the foundations for belief in human equality, John E. Coons and Patrick M. Brennan land precisely here. They argue that it is the capacity for moral self-perfection that is the property possessed by all rational creatures and is thus the best ground for human equality. This is clearly a Kantian move. See their *By Nature Equal: The Anatomy of a Western Insight* (Princeton: Princeton University Press, 1999).

your own person or the person of any other, never simply as a means but always at the same time as an end" (*G*, p. 96).

Kant appears convinced that this is just another way of stating the first version of his categorical imperative. But this has not been quite so obvious to everyone else. The connection appears to be this: of all entities in nature, only humans can rationally discover the categorical imperative and choose to direct their will accordingly. This sets human beings apart from all other creatures on the planet; the other creatures are nonrational and operate by instinct rather than will. Our rational capacity, and the freedom to direct our will in accordance with this capacity, means that "man exists as an end in himself, not merely as a means for arbitrary use by this or that will; he must in all his actions . . . always be viewed at the same time as an end" (p. 95). Human rationality — especially humans' unique ability to make free moral choices — "marks [humans] out as ends in themselves" (p. 96). Rémi Brague puts it this way: "For Kant, the presence of the moral law within us is precisely what proves our freedom from the natural laws."[101] We transcend mere cause-and-effect physical laws only and precisely as we legislate morality for ourselves. Kant even says that this capacity is what makes us "persons," with an absolute rather than relative value, and that this capacity of our nature is a proper "object of reverence" (*G*, p. 96).[102]

The normative payoffs for this staggeringly important principle are stated concisely here but have echoed through history. Because "man is not a thing — not something to be used merely as a means" (p. 97), we humans are never free to undertake the "maiming, spoiling, or killing" of another human being, or ourselves (p. 97). We are never free to take away other people's freedom or property arbitrarily. We are never free to treat another human being merely as a means, for any high purpose or interest whatsoever. This is the "supreme limiting condition of every man's freedom of action" (p. 98). We cannot transgress this boundary.

Kant is eloquent in his various efforts to delineate the difference between *objects* upon which a price can be placed and *subjects*, or "ends," that is, human beings, which are "exalted above all price" (p. 102; cf. puzzle #4, about humans as "incalculably precious"). Here is where his highly influential use of "dignity" language enters his theory: "If [an object] has a

---

101. Brague, *The Law of God*, p. 236.
102. I acknowledge that it is exceedingly difficult to interpret the way Kant is using the term "object of reverence" in that sentence.

price, something else can be put in its place as an *equivalent;* if it is exalted above all price and so admits of no equivalent, then it has a dignity." And just below: "That which constitutes the whole condition under which anything can be an end in itself has not merely a relative value — that is, a price — but has an intrinsic value — that is, *dignity*" (p. 102). (For Kant an object that has a price has no "intrinsic" value, and an object that has intrinsic value can have no price. This is his resolution to our puzzles #4 and #7.) And: "Morality, and humanity so far as it is capable of morality, is the only thing which has dignity. . . . fidelity to promises and kindness based on principle (not on instinct) have an intrinsic worth. . . . they exhibit the will which performs them as an object of immediate reverence" (pp. 102-3). This particular *way of being human* is of incomparable value. It is the highest expression of human rationality, and it has a "sanctity" that must be acknowledged and never profaned (p. 103). This is the only use of the term "sanctity" in the book, and it is pivotal.

Kant's murkier third formulation of the categorical imperative is open to a kind of eschatological reading. He tries several versions. Here is the clearest: "So act as if you were by your maxims in every case a legislating member of the universal kingdom of ends" (p. 101). The focus of this formulation at first appears to be the envisioning and even perhaps the creating of a kind of moral community in which each person treats each other person in accordance with the maxim that all are ends in themselves, and never merely means. In other words, it's a *categorical imperative community* such as has never existed but ought to exist. This represents a rich but underdeveloped dimension of the *Groundwork,* a turn from individual self-legislation toward the proper shape of a human "kingdom" or community. Kant developed these themes more broadly in later publications, in some of which he interpreted a role for a purified church in becoming and advancing such a moral vision. In its original form here in the *Groundwork,* Kant's "kingdom of ends" proposal has been foundational for such later projects in moral philosophy as John Rawls's *Theory of Justice.*[103]

Kant concludes the book with a ringing affirmation of the centrality of moral autonomy. This does not mean just doing what one wants; fatefully, that is often what the term is now taken to mean. What it means for Kant is that all externally imposed moral pressures are to be rejected as distracting and spurious to true morality. Any "heteronomous" moral theory that

---

103. John Rawls, *A Theory of Justice* (Cambridge: Harvard University Press, Belknap Press, 1971).

adds human happiness or moral feeling or divine revelation or divine approval/judgment as a factor motivating action is fatally flawed. An absolutely good will, driven by self-legislated action in accordance with the categorical imperative, is the proper form of all human morality. The idea seems to be that human dignity is most clearly exhibited by persons so rational and "disinterested" in their understanding and application of moral obligation that they arrive without any inducement, and therefore autonomously, at fair and rigorous moral principles, that they live according to those principles, and that others would agree to the justice of these principles if they were required to live under them. Everyone, in a sense, becomes a philosopher-legislator in this dreamy universal kingdom of ends.

As for God: sifting through all of Kant's works, we are left again with the idea that it is reasonable and necessary to believe in God as the ultimate author of that precious freedom of will that is the condition of rational moral self-legislation. Belief in God brings hope to the difficult moral enterprise of developing a Kantian "holy will." But God's existence cannot be proved; there is no irrefutable evidence for God, except perhaps as logically necessary for belief in morality. Further, it is risky, in the sense that introducing God into the equation either as Lawgiver or as Eternal Judge tends to undercut the proper dignity of the human being by possibly introducing heteronomous factors into moral deliberation.

So here is the legacy of Kant: in his "theoretical reason" voice he claims that "the real morality of actions . . . is completely unknown to us" (*C1*, p. 169), and in his "practical reason" voice he asserts categorically that "man exists as an end in himself, not merely as a means for arbitrary use by this or that will" (*G*, p. 95). *Those of his readers and interpreters who listen primarily to Kant's first voice have never quite recovered the confidence required to take seriously the claims of Kant's second voice* — while those numerous scholars and professionals who have found that second voice compelling tend to ignore the damaging implications of his first voice.[104] Kantians and neo-Kantians remain with us today, arguing for binding moral obligations and constraints in how human beings are to be treated. The language of reverence for persons, moral worth, and intrinsic dignity echoes through scholarship and activism even today. And at one level that is a very good thing. Numerous medical professionals, for example, have

---

104. "More recently, Kant's moral theory has become very popular because of its normative content, while its metaphysical foundation has been ignored." Ameriks, "Immanuel Kant," p. 501.

now been trained in generations of ethics textbooks to view and treat their patients with dignity, to respect their moral autonomy, and never to use them merely as means to other ends. It is not too much to say that in mainstream Western philosophy and professional practice Kant's rigorous code of moral obligation for persons is the primary way in which older biblical and traditional commitments to the sacredness of human life have been carried forward to us. They suit us, in part, because they appear to require no shared religious foundation. We are a long way from Aquinas.

The nuances are, of course, often lost. It is not usually noticed that Kant mainly identified human dignity with the capacity to make, and with success in making, disinterested moral choices. In the *Groundwork,* at least, he does not really speak of the intrinsic dignity of the human species as such, but of the dignity of autonomous moral choice, and of humanity only insofar as it exercises (or is capable of exercising) such choice in order to impose binding moral constraints on itself. There is certainly a kind of species-based egalitarianism here, which has often been drawn upon by those in Kant's line, and admittedly became central in the later development of Kant's social and political ethics.[105] But there is also an overlooked Kantian inegalitarianism, as Kant at least implies the existence of a kind of moral aristocracy distinguishable from the crowd through the rigor of its moral reflection and practice. These moral exemplars are the only humans truly worthy of "reverence."[106]

The biggest paradox of all, of course, is the way in which Kant rejects any normative role either for religion or for God in vouchsafing morality, while importing from "the common Idea of duty and from the laws of morality" (*G,* p. 57) an ethical norm that looks suspiciously like a Christian

---

105. From philosopher John Ladd: "The key to Kant's moral and political philosophy is his conception of the dignity of the individual. This dignity gives the individual person an intrinsic worth, a value *sui generis* that is 'above all price and admits of no equivalent.' It is the source of one's innate right to freedom, and from the right to freedom follow all one's other rights, specifically one's legal and political rights. Inasmuch as every individual possesses this dignity and right, all persons are equal. Thus, Kant may be regarded as the philosophical defender *par excellence* of the rights of persons and their equality, and of a republican form of government." See John Ladd, translator's introduction to *Metaphysical Elements of Justice,* by Immanuel Kant, trans. John Ladd, 2nd ed. (Indianapolis: Hackett, 1999), p. xv.

106. Nicholas Wolterstorff explores this nuance/paradox in Kant's thought, concluding that Kant's writing is internally contradictory on this point. See Wolterstorff, *Justice,* pp. 325-33. His conclusion is that Kant bases human worth on capacities, in this case the capacity for rational agency, and that because some human beings do not possess or exercise this capacity, it cannot serve as an adequate grounding for justice or human rights.

sanctity-of-life ethic. Allen Wood sees it: "Pietism had already taught him to believe in the equality of all human beings as children of God, and in the church universal, encompassing the priesthood of all believers, to be pursued as a moral ideal."[107] Kant takes the norm, strips it of any grounding in God, church, Scripture, or revelation, and makes it a dictate of practical reason accessible to anyone with a mind to think things through. Nicholas Wolterstorff describes this as "living on inherited capital" and claims that modern-day secularists attempting to defend human rights on a nonreligious basis are still attempting to do the same thing.[108] We will see in the next chapter what happened in the late nineteenth century when, at least for some thinkers, that inherited capital had all been spent.

7.5. Trial Balance: The Journey So Far

We are about to take a significant turn in our narrative. Before we do, it seems timely to sum up our major discoveries thus far.

1. The idea that each and every human life is sacred is an oft-repeated and oft-disputed claim in contemporary theology, politics, and ethics. This book has been tracing its meaning, origins, history, and implications.

2. Both the Hebrew Bible (Christian Old Testament) and the New Testament offer multiple strands of tradition and teaching that planted the seeds for belief in the ineffable value of each and every human life into Judaism and Christianity, and into every culture affected by these sibling religious traditions. I suggested that ultimately this conviction must be viewed as a matter of divine revelation, even as this revelation gave birth to a tradition of thought and action that can be humanly defined, described, and revised.

3. The earliest Christians both taught and demonstrated a way of life that comprehensively sought to honor the God-given sacredness of each human being, and were notable for the countercultural quality of their congregational life.

4. After the Constantinian turn, a divided Christendom often experienced moments in which domination and violence authorized by a church-state establishment (often in the name of God) were protested by resistant Christians in the spirit of the sacredness-of-life tradition. The resistance of

107. Wood, *Kant*, p. 7.
108. Wolterstorff, *Justice*, p. 391.

Francis to the Fifth Crusade and the counteraction of Las Casas to the Spanish cruelties in the Americas are two signal examples of this resistance.

5. Christian contempt for Jews is an exception to this overall narrative because it is traceable far more closely to the origins of Christianity. Christian hatred of Jews, and repeated abuses of Jews, deeply damaged Christianity morally and in its public witness. By the seventeenth century a small number of Christian leaders like Richard Overton began demanding an abandonment of church-state partnerships and an end to religiously driven state discrimination of minority faiths and their adherents, with Jews to be included among those whose religion would no longer be harassed. This was a necessary but not sufficient beginning of the journey to reverse Christian anti-Semitism.

6. Some of these seventeenth-century demands for religious liberty were framed in terms of "natural rights" or "human rights." We can now see that a minority strand of the Christian natural law tradition as far back as the medieval period was the origin of such natural rights claims, with their early development of a concept of subjective natural rights, the dignity of human moral and spiritual capacities, and a zone of personal liberty.

7. Motivated especially by plentiful evidence of state tyranny, especially in the name of religion, John Locke later developed a biblical-rationalist account of human equality, limited government, the rule of law, and the human rights to life, liberty, and property. These were, on the whole, life-protecting innovations, though some Christians then and now have rejected them as anti-Christian innovations with dangerous implications. The American Founders developed the first political system intended to embody these insights, even while compromising them in numerous fateful ways. The liberal democratic and American political regimes are inconceivable apart from the Christian contributions to Locke's theory.

8. Immanuel Kant retained an attractively rigorous ethic affirming the absolute dignity and worth of (rational-moral) persons and our obligation to honor that dignity without compromise. But he grounded this ethic in "practical reason" rather than revelation and rejected any meaningful connection to the older natural law tradition. His God is remote, and the gap between the substantive claims of his ethic and the skepticism of his epistemology made the ethic profoundly vulnerable to later challenge. He is perhaps our best symbol of the gradual de-Christianizing of what were once Christian convictions, retaining a biblically inflected ethic of duty and sacrifice while rejecting its theological foundations.

Contemporary discussions in moral philosophy and Christian ethics continue to wrestle with many of these issues. The social abandonment of a right order tradition, and the fading or ignoring of a richly Christian understanding of human worth and human rights in community (as in Catholic natural rights thought and in early Baptists like Overton), leaves most Western societies dangerously normless. The early canonists' insistence on a small zone of liberty within the limits of natural law laid the foundation for a more robust human rights tradition acknowledging (1) freedoms of religion and civil liberty and freedoms from arbitrary treatment by the law; (2) rights to basic needs of life including economic rights; and (3) rights of participation in choosing one's government and petitioning it. This had it exactly right. But today, rights claims sometimes have expanded to look more like license claims to do anything I want to do, bounded by the merest social restraints necessary — together with a near-total loss of the language of duty and obligation. The church hasn't helped the cause when it has perpetrated its own human rights abuses and when, today, it succumbs to the temptation to abandon rights claims out of reaction to contemporary excesses.

Locke's theory of property rights eventually became absolutized and corporatized. When this occurred his approach was stripped of the influences of an earlier Catholic natural law tradition of a common distribution and universal destination of goods, and of everyone's obligation to care for the poor. It has left many of the poorest among us cruelly neglected. The barbarities of predatory industrial capitalism in the nineteenth century ended up so degrading to human life that Marxism was born in response. Its particular version of morally driven atheistic utopianism eventually contributed, in twentieth-century Communist regimes, to mass killing on a breathtaking scale. Where Marxism did not prevail, as in the United States, the uphill battle to exert some reasonable level of social control or social regulation over the excesses of unfettered capitalism has never abated — nor has resistance to such social regulation, nor has social suffering among capitalism's losers.

A certain type of Christian scholar/apologist likes to claim all the best of the Christian heritage and all the positive impact of Christianity on the world while deriding the modern West for its rebellion against God. But this amounts to nothing more than special pleading when we do not acknowledge the worst of our heritage and the negative impact especially of warring, often oppressive Christendom-type Christianity on the world — and when we do not acknowledge that it was often the church and clergy rather than God that were the object of Enlightenment scorn. Especially when the church stood most defiantly in reaction against movements for social equality, religious liberty, and human rights, using state power to enforce its vision, it created the conditions for its own rejection.

We end this chapter around, say, 1850, with belief in the great dignity, worth, and rights of human beings largely intact in Western thought, and with greater legal measures beginning to be advocated and advanced to protect such dignity, worth, and rights for more and more people. Circa 1850, many still believed in life's sacred worth for religious reasons; others, especially among the intellectuals, had adopted a rationalist rendering of intrinsic human dignity. Despite ongoing political gains for greater justice and broader recognition of human rights (as in the moves to abolish slavery and recognize women's rights), there was serious damage at the intellectual foundations. Alasdair MacIntyre is right when he suggests that "the Enlightenment project" was living off "inherited, but already incoherent, fragments left behind" from earlier moral traditions that actually believed in a "teleological view of human nature" prescribing substantive moral norms.[109] The consequences of that damage were intellectually visible in the writings of Friedrich Nietzsche, and politically visible in the great mass slaughters of the twentieth century. These are the subjects of our next two chapters.

109. MacIntyre, *After Virtue*, pp. 54, 59.

8. Nietzsche Rejects the Christian God and Christian Morality

> When one gives up Christian belief one thereby deprives oneself of the *right* to Christian morality. For the latter is absolutely *not* self-evident. . . . Christianity is a system, a consistently thought out and *complete* view of things. If one breaks out of it a fundamental idea, the belief in God, one thereby breaks the whole thing to pieces.
>
> Friedrich Nietzsche

8.1. New Challenges to Belief in the Sacredness of Human Life

In the late nineteenth and early twentieth centuries, belief in the inherited religion of Christian Europe faded profoundly. The doubts expressed by cutting-edge philosophers of an earlier day spread extensively throughout the European populations, especially among the elites. We saw in the last chapter that this was beginning to occur well before the late nineteenth century. But we also saw that to a very profound extent the core moral commitments of Christianity came forward even while the theology was gradually being discarded. Both parts of the last sentence clearly apply to Immanuel Kant and arguably to John Locke. One of these core moral commitments was belief in the worth and dignity of each individual life. Indeed, the conviction that all people, without exception, should be viewed as equal and treated with dignity actually spread during this early modern and Enlightenment period. It was easy, at the time, to view the era from Locke to Kant as a period of great human progress, with the husks of religious dogma and church power thrown off even while the kernel of great moral truth in Christianity was preserved and improved for a new era.

Many forces began to challenge this scenario by the end of the nineteenth century. My top-six list would include:

1. The discoveries and theories of Charles Darwin, insofar as they undercut the belief in God as the creator of a human species that is unique, distinct from, and superior to other species; we can now see that this purportedly unique and superior human status vis-à-vis other species had always been an important feature in Christian accounts of human worth, and in secularized form survived through the Enlightenment period (puzzle #1).

2. The discoveries and theories of Darwin, insofar as they proposed a new "survival of the fittest" narrative about planetary history that challenged the long-accepted Western story of origins, including the biblically rooted belief in a gracious, superintending, providential God who does not let a sparrow fall apart from his will (Matt. 10:29-31).

3. The emergence of a crude "social Darwinism" that projected Darwin's primal narrative onto the human stage both retrospectively and prospectively, opening the door to a moral vision in which mass violence, killing, and loss of life (especially of the weakest individuals and species) were simply to be expected and might even need to be encouraged as part of the historical process.[1]

4. The development of a reductionistic scientific or philosophical materialism that rejected the reality of a "real" metaphysical, spiritual, or moral realm, viewing these instead simply as products of the physiology, psychology, and history of humanity.

5. The birth and spread of Marxism, which affirmed the worth of all in fighting for the suffering working classes in industrializing Europe, but shifted the focus of moral attention from individual moral restraint (in obedience to God) to structural economic conflicts between groups, with the claim that revolutionary violence would inevitably be required to bring about economic justice.

---

1. The relationship between the work of Darwin and the thought of Nietzsche is complex. One major Nietzsche scholar, R. J. Hollingdale, suggests that Nietzsche would have accepted the truthfulness and significance of point 1 above, would have rejected point 2, and would have qualified point 3 to say that the weak prevail over the strong more often than the reverse. See Friedrich Nietzsche, *Twilight of the Idols,* ed. and trans. R. J. Hollingdale (New York: Penguin Books, 1968), p. 201. Henceforth abbreviated in text as *TI*.

6. The first full and unconstrained public articulation of atheistic perspectives that totally rejected the theological commitments of both Judaism and Christianity; and the concurrent rejection, among some, of the morality inherited from Judaism and Christianity through centuries of influence in European culture.

The most influential philosopher whose work reflected the impact of these developments was Friedrich Nietzsche (1844-1900). This chapter will examine this brilliant but troubling philosopher, an "utterly lonely man" with a "weird, paradoxical personality,"[2] who became, and remains today, perhaps the ultimate symbol of explicit intellectual rejection of the inherited morality and religion of western European culture.

8.2. Reading Nietzsche

I do not undertake this chapter-length exploration of the work of Friedrich Nietzsche in order to add my small contribution to the Christian scorn heaped upon our long-dead ex-Christian friend. We do not need any more works simply castigating Nietzsche — or, for that matter, simply praising him. It is far better to try to understand him. He so much wanted to be understood, and was little understood or appreciated during his own active career, leading him to conclude that he was an "untimely" or even a "posthumous man" (*TI*, p. 24). Nor was his memory necessarily benefited by the cult of adulation that grew up around him at the time of his death, much of it fanned into flame by his sister Elisabeth, who served as his literary executor for a long and pivotal period. She bears considerable responsibility for turning Nietzsche into the presumed philosopher of Nazism. We will explore to what extent the Nazi appropriation of his language and themes had to do with what Nietzsche actually said.

Nietzsche's primary editor and biographer for a very long time was Walter Kaufmann, an anti-Nazi German refugee and, like Nietzsche, a fierce critic of Christianity, who taught philosophy at Princeton from 1947 to 1980. Kaufmann's opinionated defenses of Nietzsche are not to be taken as gospel truth, but one of his claims makes much sense when one has read

---

2. These are the words of Walter Kaufmann, perhaps Nietzsche's most devoted translator, editor, and interpreter, in the translator's preface to *Thus Spoke Zarathustra* (New York: Penguin, 1966), pp. xiii, xv. Henceforth abbreviated in text as *Z*.

Nietzsche. Kaufmann argues that far more than most thinkers, Nietzsche's writings are not "independent creations." Instead they are all part of one grand single work and share an "existential unity."[3] Other interpreters emphasize the developments in Nietzsche's thought from work to work, but do recognize the significance of reading his works in sequence and tracking the growth and development of his ideas.

You will be quite glad to know that you will not be led on a guided tour of the entire body of Nietzsche's works. My strategy will be to present relevant and important themes in Nietzsche roughly in the sequence in which they emerged in his writings. I think it is possible to see sedimental deposits or *layers* over Nietzsche's meteoric sixteen-year literary career, and I want to identify the most important of those layers for our project. This strategy involves devoting more attention to early works than is often customary in studies of Nietzsche. I will therefore begin with his first book, the 1872 *Birth of Tragedy*. We will always keep our eyes on the prize as it pertains to this volume: how Nietzsche interacted with the ancient theological and moral vision of the sacredness of human life: the conviction that because of God's decisions, actions, and declarations toward humanity, all human beings are to be perceived with reverence, as beings of sacred worth who must be respected, cared for, and protected from wanton destruction and violation.

8.3. Biographical Basics

Friedrich Nietzsche was born in 1844 just outside Leipzig. He was the grandson and son of Lutheran clergymen; his pastor father, unfortunately for Nietzsche, died at thirty-six when the young lad was just five years old. Nietzsche also had a younger brother who died at two, just after their father's death. Henceforth Nietzsche's childhood was spent entirely around women — his mother, sister, grandmother, and two maiden aunts. Numerous disdainful comments Nietzsche makes about women throughout his works are often linked to the peculiar circumstances of this upbringing. Nietzsche spent six years at an elite boarding school, the Pforta School, where he excelled. There was no question of his intellectual brilliance or breadth of learning. He entered the University of Bonn as a theology stu-

---

3. Walter Kaufmann, ed. and trans., *The Portable Nietzsche* (New York: Penguin, 1954), p. 4.

dent, but this plan was abandoned after he lost his faith during his first year there. Eventually he completed work at the University of Leipzig in classical philology. At this stage, his major professor described him as a prodigy, a peerless talent.[4] This helped him, at twenty-four, extraordinarily young and without having completed a dissertation, to be appointed to the chair in classical philology at the University of Basel in Switzerland. Nietzsche appeared to be poised for a major career as an academic classicist.

Most casual readers of Nietzsche are unaware of two terms of military service in these early years. In 1867, prior to completing his studies and being appointed at Basel, he signed up for a year in military service. However, this military stint ended prematurely when Nietzsche injured his chest in a fall from a horse, which exacerbated what were apparently already chronic health problems. Nietzsche also served briefly as an orderly during the 1870-1871 Franco-Prussian War, and according to Rick Anthony Furtak, he witnessed numerous "hideous injuries" while serving there.[5] It also appears to have "shattered" his health — he contracted diphtheria and dysentery, and perhaps syphilis, though this latter is disputed, as is its impact on his later health.[6] Nietzsche wrote *The Birth of Tragedy* during his service in the Franco-Prussian War. He speaks in the original foreword to that book of writing amidst "the horrors and sublimities of the war which had just then broken out" (*BT*, p. xxvii). We know that the extremities of war have impacted the writing and vision of many writers. We don't usually think of Nietzsche as one of those wartime writers. It is worth keeping in mind.

Nietzsche's academic career proved a profound disappointment to him and to Basel. He worked hard as a teacher-scholar for seven years (1869-1876), then took a leave of absence as his health worsened. Three years later, in 1879, he took early retirement from Basel, again due to debilitating health problems, including intense stomach ailments, migraines, and chronic insomnia. But Kaufmann suggests that Nietzsche was ready to leave the narrow confines of academia with its demands for specialized publishing in classical philology.[7] Neither university authorities nor reviewers were appreciating his version of what exploring the classics might

4. Kaufmann, *The Portable Nietzsche*, p. 7.

5. Rick Anthony Furtak, introduction to *The Birth of Tragedy*, by Friedrich Nietzsche, trans. William A. Hausmann (New York: Barnes and Noble, 2006), p. viii. Henceforth abbreviated in the text as *BT*.

6. Kaufmann, *The Portable Nietzsche*, p. 9.

7. Kaufmann, *The Portable Nietzsche*, p. 11.

look like (e.g., the brilliant but idiosyncratic and negatively reviewed *Birth of Tragedy*). He was not writing the guild's kind of book and was not intending to do so. His later writings reveal considerable contempt for the scholarly guild and its ways (*Z*, p. 124). Eventually he adopted the work of an independent philosopher, unemployed and eventually unemployable in official higher education.

Nietzsche's writing career lasted just ten more years after his departure from Basel. But what a decade! From 1879 to 1888, living an austere and desperately lonely life (his journey included a failed romance in 1882, as well as numerous broken friendships), moving from place to place in Europe in search of relief from his physical ailments, he churned out over a dozen works that one can still find in bookstores across the world today. These works ranged from sober and fairly "normal" works in philosophy to hyperkinetic and exaggerated polemics, poems, songs, thought fragments, quasi-apocalyptic works, and self-referential musings. Finally, early in January 1889, after an extraordinary burst of creativity that included finishing five manuscripts in one year, he "collapsed in the street, weeping uncontrollably."[8] He spent the rest of his life as an invalid, primarily under the care of his family, and died in 1900. By the time of his death Nietzsche had begun to be a literary celebrity, though his lack of control over his own body of works has led to a century of conflict over what Nietzsche really intended to say.

As we begin to encounter Nietzsche, I think it is important to understand four things. First, by the time he began writing, Nietzsche had already rejected Christianity — but he had not rejected the quest for understanding and even meaning, which was always a matter of urgent concern for him. Second, his training in the ancient classics was extensive and profound, and he turned to the classics in that quest and in much of his writing. One might say that whereas the Renaissance and Enlightenment thinkers sought to retrieve the classics most often as a *supplement* to or purification of Christianity, Nietzsche's retrieval was far more thoroughgoing. He wanted to go back beyond and before Christianity to reclaim what he believed to be an ancient and far more profound vision of life. Third, precisely because he was a (multilingual) philologist, Nietzsche cared about words. He was one of the first thinkers to focus extensively on language itself as a phenomenon; he was also among the first to play with language, to tinker with received terms and their meanings as part of his

---

8. Furtak, "Introduction," p. viii.

philosophical project. This anticipates our era in quite a profound way, and also makes translation disputes rather acute. Finally, Nietzsche was widely read, and was deeply affected by the entire intellectual milieu of his day. His work must not be read as if it emerged *ex nihilo*, entirely disconnected from the world of ideas around him. Nietzsche scholars emphasize his relation to a wide range of figures, perhaps most notably the pessimistic philosopher Arthur Schopenhauer, the materialist Friedrich Lange, and the musician Richard Wagner (whom he once idolized and finally rejected). This rootedness in the intellectual milieu of his time also helps justify so much focus on his work. He represents something beyond himself. He represents an era, or a way of being in the world.

8.4. Tragic Pessimism: *The Birth of Tragedy* (1872)

As we meet Nietzsche's first book, *The Birth of Tragedy*, we are watching the twenty-seven-year-old academic making a literary debut. With the background already offered, it becomes possible to read this book at two levels — as his first and essentially only attempt to make a credible contribution in German-speaking academia, and as the beginning of a far more personal exploration. It failed utterly as an academic work. But it is significantly illuminating as a personal one, and as the beginning of what became an extraordinary career as a philosopher.

The Birth of Tragedy is framed as an exploration of pre-Socratic Greek art, including drama, poetry, and music, with an emphasis on ancient Greek tragedy. Here we have what appears to be a standard academic work in the classics — for a few pages. Nietzsche begins by claiming that the great achievement of pre-Socratic Greek culture was to sustain a dynamic tension between two competing principles or modes that surface first in life and then in art. In *Apollonian* mode (named for Apollo) the individual is especially aware of himself as an individual and of his effort to bring order to what he imagines, dreams, creates, and experiences. The Apollonian mode is characterized by "reasoned limitation . . . freedom from the wilder emotions . . . [and] philosophical calmness" (*BT*, p. 3). The *Dionysian* mode (named for Dionysius) is a primordial, euphoric, exuberant state characterized by "blissful ecstasy" and drunken revelry, joyful song and dance. The Dionysian is filled with primordial energy and with a sense of unity with other human beings and even with nature itself. The Apollonian is the human individual dreaming, reasoning, shaping, and reflecting; the Dionysian is the human collectivity carousing, reveling, singing, and having sex.[9]

The birth of Greek tragedy, for Nietzsche, is found in the creative synthesis of the Apollonian and the Dionysian. But there is a far darker dimension to these two modes than we see at first glance. Greek tragedy in an Apollonian inflection values individual existence and grants that it has meaning, but this meaning is disclosed precisely in the terrible sufferings of the individual, the tragic hero who finds personal meaning but usually at the cost of great suffering. Greek tragedy in a Dionysian inflection altogether denies the significance of individual existence. In this mode we don't face the tragedy of individual suffering. Yet the discovery that our individual life is an illusion, without personal meaning, is its own kind of tragedy.[10]

It looks like Nietzsche is telling us about ancient Greek culture, art, and tragedy. He is purporting to try to get behind what he calls "Apollonian culture" (Apollo mixed with Dionysius, Apollo disciplining Dionysius) to understand what motivates it. The Greeks created Apollo and other gods, says Nietzsche, to deal with "the terrors and horrors of existence" (*BT*, p. 9). But here Nietzsche shows his hand. He is really telling us about how *he* views the world and perhaps how he himself copes with it. He speaks of the world as "eternal primordial pain" (p. 12), of "the most delicate and severe suffering," of "the terribly destructive processes" of history, and of "the cruelty of nature" (p. 26). He speaks of our effort to transcend the "loathing" that seizes us in life, the "nauseating reflections on the awfulness or absurdity of existence" (p. 27). Nietzsche is not here describing a form of Greek literature; he is describing life as he sees it.

Why is life so nauseating and absurd? Because we have "true knowledge" into the "appalling truth" (p. 27) that human beings are simply offerings-up of a blind cosmic will that continues to churn out "innumerable forms of existence which throng and push one another into life" (p. 69). Nietzsche personalizes this will (Will?) at one point as "the Being who, as the sole author and spectator of this comedy of art, prepares a perpetual entertainment for himself" (p. 19). We are "pictures and artistic projections" of this Being, "works of art" for him (p. 19) who is witness to all our "willing, longing, moaning, and rejoicing" (p. 22). But we are only a

---

9. The sexual and even orgiastic dimension of what Nietzsche means by the Dionysian is made quite clear in *TI*, pp. 108-10. It is not quite so explicit in *BT*.

10. Furtak, "Introduction," p. xi.

"phenomenon" of the "eternal life of the will," which is not at all concerned about or affected by our "annihilation" (p. 68). This "god" is only a kind of primal life force that spits out life after life without personal regard or care for the lives produced.

So here is the first layer of Nietzsche's thought: *we human beings are the pointless products of a godless universe that cares nothing for us. But we are intelligent enough to seek some kind of intrinsic meaning, value, and purpose to life. Yet these simply are not available to be found, at least not "out there" in the universe.* Still, here we are, life after life, generation after generation, tragically doomed to seek such meaning.

Nietzsche suggests that the "torment" (p. 13) and terror of such a realization are simply unbearable for us, and so we continuously develop "redeeming vision[s]" in order to make existence tolerable. But all redeeming visions are illusions. The Greeks responded by developing their renowned pantheon of gods: "To be able to live, the Greeks had, from direst necessity, to create these gods" (p. 10). The gods and their narratives — especially the narratives around Apollo, and thus Nietzsche's Apollonian strand — enabled humans to look at life as something to be desired, the continuation of life as something to be sought, despite and in the midst of the terror of existence. (This desire for life, suggests Nietzsche, is itself a product of a cunning Nature/Cosmic Will that fosters such illusions to "compass her ends" — presumably, that humans will want to stay alive rather than kill themselves [pp. 11, 74].) Nietzsche continually contrasts the Dionysian and the Apollonian, and speaks of their creative synthesis in Greek tragedy, but it seems clear that for him the more primal human experience is the dark side of the Dionysian — life is miserable, terrifying, and horrifying; we experience ourselves as victims of chance and misfortune; our efforts to attribute meaning to our lives are illusory (as is belief even in our individual identities); and our most primal response to all this is to wish we had never been born or could soon die (p. 9). The Greeks fully understood this. But Apollo, and Apollonian existence, offered a creative way to ease the "terrible depth of world-contemplation" (p. 10), which was an extraordinary artistic and cultural achievement. Of course, it was an illusion, but a sublimely useful one, and a profound approach to the human condition.

So here is the second Nietzschean layer: *human beings continually create redemptive illusions in order to make life bearable.* This theme never leaves Nietzsche's thought.

Even while in a sense celebrating the cultural achievement of classical Greece's Apollonian illusions, through most of the book Nietzsche appears more personally attracted to a Dionysian life without illusion.[11] He speaks warmly of the great meaning to be found in giving in to the real "terms of individual existence":

> We are really for brief moments Primordial Being itself, and feel its in-domitable desire for being and joy in existence; the struggle, the pain, the destruction of phenomena, now appear to us as something necessary, considering the surplus of innumerable forms of existence . . . consider-ing the exuberant fertility of the universal will. We are pierced by the madding sting of these pains at the very moment when we have become . . . one with the immeasurable primordial joy in existence, and when we anticipate, in Dionysian ecstasy, the indestructibility and eternity of this joy. In spite of fear and pity, we are the happy living beings, not as indi-viduals, but as the one living being, with whose procreative joy we are blended. (*BT*, p. 69)

But still, the Apollonian achievement of ancient Greece, the religious-mythical taming and yet recognition of the terrors of existence, is a re-demptive illusion that contrasts favorably for Nietzsche with the efforts of "another religion," a religion of "asceticism, spirituality, and duty," a reli-gion that looks for "moral elevation, even for sanctity, for incorporeal spiritualization, for sympathetic looks of love" (p. 8). Need we wonder what this religion might be? Earlier he contrasted the exuberant joy of Di-onysian revels with those moderns who would sniff at them as primitive, "with a smile of contempt or pity prompted by the consciousness of their own health: of course, the poor wretches do not divine what a cadaverous-looking and ghastly aspect this 'health' of theirs presents when the glowing life of the Dionysian revellers rushes past them" (p. 4). He also contrasts the "Aryan" tale of Prometheus, which speaks of "the necessity of crime imposed on the titanically striving individual will," against the "Semitic" story of the seduced fall of humanity in the Garden. He prefers the Pro-methean tale, while appreciating the Hebraic as at least a meaningful myth, albeit a "feminine" one (pp. 37-38). He speaks of "our pale and ex-hausted religions, which even in their foundations have degenerated into

---

11. Walter Kaufmann points out that later in his work Nietzsche dropped all talk of the Apollonian and drew his contrast between the Dionysian and Christianity. See Friedrich Nietzsche, *The Gay Science*, ed. and trans. Walter Kaufmann (New York: Vintage Books, 1974), p. 331 n. 126. Henceforth abbreviated in text as *GS*.

scholastic religions" (p. 76). He notes how often founding myths of great vitality get historicized, systematized, dogmatized, and ruined, draining all the power right out of them (p. 41). He appears to be convinced that the founding "myth" of Western culture has entirely lost its energy, and this is a problem because "without myth, every culture loses its healthy creative power" (p. 99).

Here, then, is Nietzsche's first published critique of Christianity. Nietzsche treats Christianity as an exhausted religion, whose once-powerful mythic energies have long become enervated. Christianity survives in the form of a desiccated moralism and scholasticism that satisfies no one, leaving disillusionment and a naked, mythless public square. Nietzsche is suggesting the inferiority of Christianity's otherworldliness, asceticism, and moralism, in contrast with the far more majestic, dynamic, and ennobling achievements of ancient Greek Olympian religion, culture, and art. He is suggesting that a pre-Christian world left behind, a long lost epic Greek world, understood human existence better and provided a better vision for how life is to be lived than the milquetoast Christianity of European culture.

So here is our third layer: *Christianity, the prevailing myth of Western culture since the fourth century, was always inferior to pre-Christian Greek myth as a redemptive illusion for humanity, and in any case stands enervated and exhausted in contemporary "Christian" European culture.*

But in *The Birth of Tragedy,* the true villain of the piece is not yet Christianity. Surprisingly enough, it is Socrates. Nietzsche paints Socrates as the man primarily responsible for the death of Greek tragedy, not just as an art form but as a worldview. The historical figure Socrates is not really guilty of all the sins Nietzsche charges to his account, and indeed, according to Walter Kaufmann, most references to Socrates later in Nietzsche's writings are positive.[12] But what the young Nietzsche does with this attack on Socrates is to offer a trenchant assault on the entire rationalist-empiricist era we discussed in the last chapter.

Nietzsche claims in *The Birth of Tragedy* that Socrates was the antithesis to the Dionysian spirit, because he sought to make an incomprehensible universe intelligible, a purposeless universe purposeful. He seemed to believe that with enough knowledge and insight the world could be understood and, indeed, corrected. Socrates ("that despotic logician" — *BT,*

---

12. Kaufmann, in *GS,* p. 272 n. 70. On the other hand, even in *TI,* pp. 29-34 (1888), Nietzsche levels many of the same charges against Socrates that he did in *The Birth of Tragedy.*

p. 59) was unwilling to accept the tragic nature of existence and, says Nietzsche, sought to tame it through knowledge and moral virtue. This introduced a "profound illusion" into the world that remains with us still: "The imperturbable belief that, by means of the clue of causality, thinking reaches to the deepest abysses of being, and that thinking is able not only to perceive being but even to *correct* it" (p. 61). Nietzsche suspects that the ultimate purpose of this quest is "to make existence appear to be comprehensible, and therefore to be justified" (p. 61).

Nietzsche worries that the Socratic quest is dangerous not only because it is based on a "metaphysical illusion" that is sure to disappoint. He also thinks that the constant effort to "penetrate into the depths of the nature of things" has turned "the mechanism of concepts, judgments, and inferences" into "the highest activity and the most admirable gift of nature" (p. 62). "Socratic" civilization has lost touch with critically important aspects of what it means to be human, such as human instincts and passions, the arts and music, and the tragic sense of life. Nietzsche is also aware that the endless quest for rational and scientific knowledge continually hits its limits, because eventually even the most ingenious scientist bumps up against the frontiers of the inexplicable (p. 63). One might summarize Nietzsche here by saying that while both the Apollonian and the Socratic are illusions, the Apollonian is an illusion that remains in creative tension with tragic Dionysian reality while the Socratic illusion seeks to dismiss Dionysius altogether. For the Socratic society, then, life is not essentially tragic. It has real and not illusory meaning. That meaning can be penetrated through critical rationality and the scientific method. The leaders of Socratic civilization are its scientists and rationalists. Knowledge is the ultimate panacea that can perfect the world. Myth is displaced altogether as the "theoretic" replaces the "tragic" view of the world (p. 71).

Though Nietzsche was never as skeptical of the scientific and rationalist enterprise in any later work, I think it is possible to identify an enduring Nietzschean layer here, our fourth: *no human project of any kind can fully penetrate, master, or correct the world.* Just when we think we have understood, gained control, and found ways to ameliorate the human condition, we are always brought up short. We see this sense of reality's obstinacy and its irresolvable paradoxes throughout Nietzsche's work.

In a brief moment of indirect but revealing political commentary, Nietzsche says that Socratic optimism is dangerous partly because it unleashes "not just a *belief* in the earthly happiness of all but also a *demand* for it" (p. 76). In what seems to be a reference to the Marxism that by 1872 was spreading widely, Nietzsche suggests that the ultimate origin of this "aroused and angry and vengeful" class of workers demanding respect for "the dignity of man" and "the dignity of labour" (p. 76) is the too-widespread belief that earthly happiness for all is a legitimate human expectation. If one had the ancient Greek tragic sense of life, one would know that such an aspiration does not correspond with any metaphysical reality. Neither nature nor the gods nor reason nor science offers anyone earthly happiness. But the Socratic spirit did suggest that such happiness would come, through its relentless quest for the improvement of the human condition via critical rationality. Today's human being is unwilling "to have anything entire, with all the natural cruelty of things, so thoroughly has he been spoiled by his optimistic contemplation" (p. 78). And so the workers march in the streets asking for a justice that cannot be expected in this earthly human existence. We will return to what Nietzsche says about socialism and Marxism, but it strikes me that Nietzsche's consistent pessimism about the burgeoning Marxist movement begins with this existential pessimism about the basic correctability of the world.

Nietzsche concludes by calling for a return of *myth,* which he defines crisply as "the concentrated picture of the world, which, as abbreviature of phenomena, cannot dispense with wonder" (p. 98). He says that cultures need founding myths, and that states "know no more powerful unwritten law than the mythical foundation which vouches for its connection with religion and its growth from mythical ideas" (p. 99). But societies dominated by scientific rationality, such as Nietzsche's own, have suffered "the annihilation of myth," which he describes as a "defect at the heart of this culture" (p. 101). Nietzsche appears to seek a recovery of Greek myth for Germany. (He speaks much of Germany at the end of this book, just at the time that Germany had become a newly united nation. But in general his writing is fiercely antistatist, antinationalistic, and sometimes quite anti-German, which is important to know when considering continuities and discontinuities with later Nazi ideology.) All other centers of meaning have been exhausted. There is no going back to Christianity or rationalism or empiricism; to forestall nihilism, we must return to the ancient myths of Greece.

Is there a fifth layer here? Eventually Nietzsche speaks somewhat less of Greece; he spends far less energy looking backward to borrow Greece's mythic visions and more energy looking forward to the construction of a new human future. One might even say that at the height of his career, especially in the quasi-apocalyptic/messianic *Thus Spoke Zarathustra,* he attempts to construct a new mythology related to the human condition and a new redemptive vision/illusion of a humanity set free from its ancient shackles in (Christian) religion and morality. So perhaps we can dare to conclude that Nietzsche unwittingly ends up illustrating his own fifth layer: *human beings cannot live without myths; if they do away with the old ones, they will create new ones.* Here is the 1872 Nietzsche waxing eloquent as only a young philosopher can:

> Let us imagine a rising generation with this undauntedness of vision, with this heroic desire for the prodigious, let us imagine the bold step of these dragon-slayers, the proud and daring spirit with which they turn their backs on all the effeminate [!] doctrines of optimism in order "to live resolutely" in the Whole and in the Full: would it not be necessary for the tragic man of this culture, with his self-discipline to earnestness and terror, to desire a new art, the art of metaphysical comfort — namely, tragedy? (*BT*, p. 77)

So this is our first encounter with Friedrich Nietzsche. By 1872, he has rejected the Christian story of human origins, purpose, and salvation. But he has not replaced it with either reason or science. At this stage he seems to believe that these are dead ends for humanity as well. Instead he wants a recovery of classic Greek myth. He calls for a kind of moral heroism in facing the nauseating abyss that is human existence, a courageous willingness to live without illusions and cheap optimism.

What does any of this have to do with the sacredness of human life? In 1872 the clergyman's son has already made it plain that he is quite sure there is no Deity who cares about the value of each and every individual human life. At one point he says that our "highest *dignity* is in our significance as works of art" of Cosmic Will (p. 19), but this is no particular comfort, for this Will cares nothing for us and in fact does not recognize us as individuals at all. The very idea of an individual is an illusion. The implications of this belief for any concept of individual human dignity and worth are devastating. Nietzsche does seem to think there is a kind of tragic human dignity to be found in facing the truth about reality, and that this life-without-illusion is more dignified and elevated than the various kinds of illusions we deploy to pacify ourselves. But this is as far as his understanding of human dignity goes.

As we have seen, in his one brief foray into political commentary, where he is talking about how "the barbaric slave class" of our time is currently demanding earthly happiness based on the (Marxist) illusion that it is owed to them, Nietzsche makes clear his disdain for this class and for their world-perfecting political project. It is clear that, for Nietzsche, Kantian, Lockean, and biblical egalitarianism have been entirely rejected. There is no God of justice who cares about human equality to whom these aggrieved workers can apply; there is no confidence here, as in a Martin Luther King Jr., that "the arc of the universe bends toward justice." Nietzsche was consistently anti-Marxist in his writings. Here it is mainly because he believes we ought to be able to intuit the hopelessness of any and all world-correcting dreams. Better to face this unflinchingly. But that is scant comfort for a starving, abused worker in 1870 Berlin.

We are a long way from any Christian understanding of the sacredness of life. But twenty-seven-year-old Nietzsche, in analytical mode, has said some powerfully relevant things already. He is prescient in seeing the desperate limits and perils of a civilization built on scientific rationality. Nietzsche could be prophetic at times, in that he saw the coming implications of current developments. Here he seems to sense that some very serious problems are on their way when Western civilization bumps up finally against the ultimate limits of what we now call technical rationality. One thinks of I. G. Farben's gas chambers. Nietzsche worries over what happens to societies that have abandoned compelling founding myths, suggesting well before Richard John Neuhaus that a secularized public square naked of any metaphysical significance does not satisfy human nature.[13] One hears the Nazi storm troopers singing the "Horst Wessel" song in those heady days when they filled Germany's own naked public square with a terrible, robust millennial myth. The thousand-year Reich. . . .

8.5. The Pathos and Delusion of the Great Quest for "Truth" (1872-1873)

In 1872-1873 Nietzsche wrote two relatively brief essays on the subject of truth. These are not book-length works but are significant in their own right.

Already in *The Birth of Tragedy*, Nietzsche attacked Socrates and the entire tradition of rational and empirical investigation, insofar as these are

---

13. Richard John Neuhaus, *The Naked Public Square* (Grand Rapids: Eerdmans, 1984).

treated as somehow the highest aspirations of human life. He even says that such efforts are based on a "metaphysical illusion." In a brief essay also published in 1872, under the name "On the Pathos of Truth" (hereafter abbreviated "PT"), Nietzsche goes further.[14]

At one level, this little essay is a celebration of the great persons (men, actually; he always speaks of great *men,* and he really seems to mean *males*) of history who have made some great discovery and are certain that it must be made known to posterity. These people — he uses the Greek philosopher Heraclitus as his example in this essay — are certain that they have discovered truth, and such important truth that they, and their truth, will and must always be remembered. Such great ones are much to be celebrated, especially in contrast with the ordinary run of people who scrape around desperately in the pitiful quest merely to extend or improve their "bit of existence" ("PT," p. 7) on the earth. The great ones, caught up in their more exalted quest for truth, can only consider their mediocre neighbors as "dross, rot, vanity, brutishness, or pleonasm, leaving them to perish" (p. 4). These great ones, the boldest of whom are the philosophers (p. 7), must constantly transcend the "hindering, choking, suffocating, deadening, smothering, dimming, deluding" forces of the "customary, the small, [and] the common, [that] fills every nook and cranny of the world" (p. 5). Their achievements form the "mountain peaks" of culture that "unite mankind across the millennia" (p. 5). They appear to achieve immortality, and do so against the backdrop of the general human experience, which looks like this: "pitiful, short-lived creatures who, given over to their cramped needs, rise again and again to the same afflictions and, with great effort, manage to fend off ruin for a short time" (p. 6).

This contrasting of the greatness of the rare great human beings with the mediocrity of the masses — the "herd," "the mob," and "the rabble" — became such a consistent theme for Nietzsche that it must be named our sixth Nietzschean layer. We see a variety of permutations of it over the course of his career, and the late Nietzsche offers a number of morally catastrophic formulations of it. I think it is one of the most fundamental issues in Nietzsche's work related to the sacredness of human life.

But then — and who but Nietzsche could extinguish hope so effectively? — comes this challenge even to the so-called great ones:

---

14. Friedrich Nietzsche, *On Truth and Untruth,* trans. and ed. Taylor Carman (New York: HarperPerennial, 2010).

Truth! Rapturous delusion of a god! What does truth matter to human beings!

And what was the Heraclitean "truth"!

And where has it gone? A vanished dream, wiped from the faces of men, along with other dreams! — It was not the first! (p. 12)

This is the "pathos of truth," indeed! This quest of the greatest of humans, this quest for truth, a quest that sets the greats far above the mass of mortals, is itself delusional. We cannot stop looking for truth: "All that is proper to man . . . is faith in the attainable truth" (p. 13). But it is delusional, for "truth [is] eternally damned to be untruth" (p. 14). And where does the quest culminate? "Knowledge attains its ultimate end only — annihilation" (p. 15). Nietzsche here extends and expands upon what we have called our second layer; redemptive illusions are not just found in religious myths. Any quest for truth, and for meaning through the discovery and publication of truth, is one of those redemptive illusions. And yet human beings — especially the best and most ingenious — are doomed to pursue such quests.

Nietzsche concludes "On the Pathos of Truth" and begins "On Truth and Lie in a Nonmoral Sense" (1873; hereafter abbreviated "TL") with the same three sentences: "In some remote corner of the sprawling universe, twinkling among the countless solar systems, there was once a star on which some clever animals invented *knowledge*. It was the most arrogant, most mendacious minute in world history, but it was only a minute. After nature caught its breath a little, the star froze, and the clever animals had to die" ("PT," p. 13; "TL," p. 17). Fateful words in the history of Western philosophy and culture, embodying a hugely important turn in Nietzsche's thought.

Notice the impact of the scientific picture of the world in this account. This is no longer an Earth-centered cosmos; Earth is a little star in an out-of-the-way corner of the universe. This is an ancient Earth, for our star has a long, long history. Very recently in planetary history some particularly "clever animals" evolved into existence. In cosmic terms, human beings are not significant. Here is how Nietzsche put it in 1888, near the end of his writing career: "Man a little, eccentric species of animal, which — fortunately — has its day; all on earth a mere moment, an incident, an exception without consequences, something of no importance to the general character of the earth; the earth itself, like every star, a hiatus between two nothingnesses, an event without plan, reason, will, self-consciousness, the worst kind of necessity, *stupid* necessity."[15]

And yet the brains of this particular species developed the capacity to invent concepts, including ideas of "knowledge" and "truth." These animals and their concepts were arrogant and deceitful. For that brief moment — which in their arrogance these animals assumed had lasted forever and would last forever — this species came to believe itself to be the center of the universe and to know for certain a number of things about it. But — and here the science kicks in again, the dismal cosmic eschatology of a frozen planetary future — the clever animals were soon dead, along with their grandiose ideas about what they "knew." With this cosmic narrative Nietzsche begins his radical deconstruction of all human notions of "truth."

Here is our seventh Nietzschean layer, and it is a crucial one: *human beings are merely clever animals whose evolved brains deceived them into thinking that they were the central fact of the cosmos, that they were fundamentally different from other creatures, and that they had access to the truth about themselves and their world.* Much of the rest of Nietzsche's philosophical project will be the furious effort to destroy all these human illusions.

Nietzsche continues in narrative vein with a dramatic linguistic recasting and expansion of a Hobbesian account of the state of nature. The clever animals have extensive cognitive skills — not nearly as extensive as they think, but still, extensive. In the state of nature, before the social contract, they use these skills primarily to deceive predators and enemies (human and otherwise) and thus to live another day ("TL," p. 20). The most primal use of the intellect, then, is "dissimulation," constant "deception, flattery, lying and cheating," toward others and themselves (p. 20). This claim adds another dimension to Nietzsche's second layer: our tendency toward delusion and illusion, toward deception and self-deception, is rooted in our primal animality. We learned to deceive in order to survive. We still deceive in order to survive.

The clever animals warily leave the state of nature to enter community. They do so out of "both necessity and boredom" (p. 22). Now the human

15. Friedrich Nietzsche, *The Will to Power*, trans. Walter Kaufmann and R. J. Hollingdale, ed. Walter Kaufmann (New York: Vintage Books, 1968), p. 169. Henceforth abbreviated in text as *WP*. There are serious problems with counting this among Nietzsche's books, as he never published it in his lifetime. However, if Nietzsche titans Kaufmann and Hollingdale were willing to translate, edit, and release this volume as a work of Nietzsche, I am willing to offer a few quotations from it.

task becomes a social one. These animals must learn to create some kind of tolerable community. To do so they must communicate with each other. They must establish all kinds of understandings that will govern their shared life. They use their cognitive and linguistic skills to do this. They create "linguistic conventions" (p. 24). These include a vast array of metaphors, terms, concepts, categories, and designations that are accepted for use within each particular community. "What is henceforth to count as 'truth' is now fixed . . . a uniformly valid and binding designation of things is invented, and the legislation of language likewise yields the first laws of truth" (p. 23). These designations exist, again, for the creation and maintenance of as pleasant and peaceful an experience of community as can be developed. Henceforth what is "true" is what the community has designated as true, and the community has made such designations in correspondence with what it understands the interests of the community to be. "Liars" are those who use the community's agreed-upon words in ways that violate the community's designations as to how those words are to be used. "Liars" are sanctioned when their misuse of linguistic conventions harms the community (p. 23).

Truth, then, is "a mobile army of metaphors, metonymies, anthropomorphisms — a sum of human relations that have been poetically and rhetorically intensified, translated, and embellished, and that after long use strike people as fixed, canonical, and binding: truths are illusions of which one has forgotten that they are illusions" (pp. 29-30). The obligation to be "truthful," in turn, is one "which society imposes in order to exist . . . the obligation to use the customary metaphors, hence . . . the obligation to lie in accordance with a fixed convention, to live in droves in a style binding for all" (p. 31).

Here, then, is Nietzsche's eighth layer: *for the sake of community survival and well-being, human beings construct linguistic conventions to govern their life together. "Truth" is whatever a community conventionally defines as true.* This holds true for every dimension of life, including religious and moral "truths." The community-preserving nature of all truth claims, including moral claims, is the origin of Nietzsche's (in)famous use of the term "herd instinct" (*GS*, p. 174), or "herd morality." "Truth" is what the herd defines it to be, for the sake of its own survival. Nietzsche spent his life striding resolutely away from all such herds.

Nietzsche is impressed with the capacity of human beings "to erect an infinitely complicated cathedral of concepts on shifting foundations and flowing water" ("TL," p. 33). He sees human beings as demonstrating "great architectural genius" in creating their linguistic conventions and building their intellectual towers to the sky. But he indicts humanity for constantly suppressing the recognition that "the original metaphors of intuition were metaphors" and instead thinking that they are "the things themselves" (p. 35). There are no things-in-themselves. On the other hand, Nietzsche suggests that this constant human suppression of the fact that we ourselves are the artists and creators of our entire intellectual superstructure is necessary for us to live with "some degree of peace, security, and consistency" (p. 37). Just as we deceived and dissimulated to misdirect beasts of prey in the state of nature, so we deceive ourselves to misdirect our minds away from the nauseating realities of our existence. Our lies appear to be as necessary now as they ever were, this time for our own *psychic* survival.

Is there any way out of this imprisonment in our own conceptual iron cage? In this essay Nietzsche looks once again to myth and art, contrasting intuitive/artistic people with rationalists. The rational person employs conventional understandings of "truth" and builds his intellectual superstructure primarily to enable human beings to meet their most pressing needs and thus free mortals from some degree of life's immense misery. Here is the bureaucrat, the technocrat, the thoughtful rational engineer of human society, or perhaps the clerk working for a $20 a week raise and a better apartment. But the artist responds to her intuitions, not her concepts — "not seeing" (p. 47) the endless array of human needs but instead catching glimpses of beauty and illumination and joy amidst misery. This appears to be Nietzsche's understanding of himself and his own role as this essay ends. He is not the technocratic engineer of a smidgen of human betterment but the artist in search of glimpses of beauty and illumination. This relates closely to Nietzsche's sixth layer — the contrast between the great minority and the mediocre majority.

What do these 1872-1873 essays mean for the "concept" of the sacredness of life? We should not rush past what we have noticed more than once, and will see throughout his work — Nietzsche's continued tendency to demean the human struggle to eke out a little bit better life for human beings. He mocks in various ways human efforts to "see[k] out the greatest possible freedom from misery" ("TL," p. 48), to extend and prolong life and to improve its quality. He appears to do so both because he considers such projects futile in light of the overall nature of the human condition, and because he does not consider such work to be as great, noble, or exalted as what is undertaken by the genius philosophers or artists. He has lost any sense of a God-given value to the average, humble, ordinary life — the quest of the human being for a little bit more food or a little bit more health or a little bit better treatment at the hands of the powerful. He is so impressed by what a flourishing life looks like for the greatest and most creative geniuses that he cannot appreciate the significance of just a bit of humble improvement in the lives of everyone else.

It is more difficult to reject the epistemological skepticism, or the broad scientific framework within which Nietzsche frames that skepticism, without throwing out impressive achievements over 150 years in the natural and social sciences. His description of how communities form, developing shared language to name important objects and concepts and relations, rewarding those who adhere to the shared linguistic and conceptual apparatus and disciplining those who do not, rings true. Every encounter with people from other cultures, or people who speak different languages, or people whose conceptual apparatus is fundamentally alien to our own, or even people within our own (sub)culture who disagree with us over concepts and language and truth, reminds us of the realities Nietzsche is describing.

But does this mean that "the sacredness of life" is nothing more than a "concept," of which there can be no "knowledge" and about which no one can make claims to "truth" or "falsehood"? Have we reached a dead end in our discussion of this "concept," if all concepts are delusional products of the "miserable, shadowy, fleeting, aimless, arbitrary" ("TL," p. 18) human intellect, which is "simply an expedient supplied to the unluckiest, the most delicate, the most transitory creatures in order to detain them for a minute in existence" (p. 19)?

Perhaps we have reached such a dead end, with all further discussion futile. Perhaps it is best to recede into silence until our illusory individual life ends or the planet freezes or burns. But no one can live that way. Nietzsche himself did not recede into silence. I do believe that to the extent that one takes Nietzsche's epistemological skepticism seriously, we are driven in the direction of a revelational (rather than a "natural") theology, in which a God of love and mercy chooses to speak and act in grace toward his creatures — after which we apply our architectural genius to the difficult but necessary task of giving categories and concepts to God's Word to humanity. One of those concepts is the sacredness of human life. So let us continue.

8.6. Acknowledging That We Are Human, All Too Human (1878)

Nietzsche's next book, *Human, All Too Human* (1878),[16] receives little attention in most renderings of his work. But this book introduces key themes that resonated in the rest of Nietzsche's work.

The book begins with an expansion and sharpening of evolutionary themes introduced in the essays on truth. Now Nietzsche locates the origins of human nature, if we must call it that, in "primeval times, long before those four thousand years with which we are more or less familiar" (*HA*, p. 14). He says that "everything *essential* in human development" (p. 14, italics in original throughout this chapter) occurred during that misty prehistorical period. He is offering a kind of philosophical anthropology based on his reconstruction of what was going on during that period and what it meant and still means for humanity.

These early human beings were not especially delicate or refined. They focused inevitably on their own survival, and leadership went to the "brutal, powerful man" who intimidated others into subordination to his will (p. 69). We human beings, like all other organic beings, perforce learned to focus on our own self-preservation, which was (and remains) the ultimate basis of our actions, even when we deceive ourselves about this (p. 68). Closely related to the instinct for self-preservation was our inclination to seek pleasure and avoid pain or displeasure (p. 68). By now, we do not often have to face the mere daily struggle for survival. Therefore we have learned to pursue more refined tasks, at least during times of peace and order. And yet we can never entirely free ourselves from our primeval past, and its instincts and passions often surface. We are indeed "human, all too human." Every so often we encounter glimpses of the beast in ourselves (p. 45), and sometimes we learn of other human beings who appear to be a kind of throwback to primeval days. But we must not judge such primal throwbacks too harshly, for "we must think of men who are cruel today as stages of *earlier cultures,* which have been left over. . . . they are backward men whose brains, because of various possible accidents of heredity, have not yet developed much delicacy or versatility. They show us what we *all* were, and frighten us" (p. 46).

Here is our ninth Nietzschean layer: *humans are organic beings who,*

---

16. Friedrich Nietzsche, *Human, All Too Human: A Book for Free Spirits,* trans. Marion Faber, with Stephen Lehmann (Lincoln: University of Nebraska Press, 1984). Henceforth abbreviated in text as *HA.*

like all other organic beings, are predetermined to seek self-preservation and pleasure and to avoid pain. These remain the ultimate bases for our actions, whatever lies we may tell ourselves about our motivations.

Nietzsche offers a more famous account of the development of morality in the later *Genealogy of Morals* (1887).[17] That is where he develops his concepts of master and slave morality, and distinguishes between Jewish, Christian, and Greco-Roman moral beliefs. Precisely because of the familiarity of that account, it may be more interesting to focus on this earlier rendering. Offering a "history of moral feelings," Nietzsche argues that everything that humans call right and wrong, good and evil has its ultimate origin in the legitimate and primal organic interest in self-preservation. The first and most basic stage of "moral feeling" is when we assess particular acts as good or evil on the basis of their good or bad consequences for our well-being or survival as communities. This at least has some basis in "reality," for Nietzsche, in the sense that certain acts are indeed generally good or bad for human self-preservation.

But the lies and illusions begin when "we imagine that the quality 'good' or 'evil' is inherent in the actions themselves" (*HA*, p. 43). Nietzsche doesn't say here, but could, that one basic problem with this move is that it involves going beyond a particular act to create a class of acts called, say, "murder," and then ascribing the metaphysical status "evil" to that class of acts. Nietzsche had already made clear in "On Truth and Lie in a Nonmoral Sense" that such moves from particular to universal, or from act to essence, are invalid, a classic error in philosophy. There is for him no moral status that clings to a particular (human-invented and designated) class of acts that makes it intrinsically good or evil. "Between good and evil actions there is no difference in type; at most . . . a difference in degree" (*HA*, p. 75).

But this first error is then compounded with another. Human moral feeling goes on to attribute good or evil not just to the *acts* but also to the *motives* that lie behind the acts (p. 43). When we speak of motives, we are attempting to look inside the minds/hearts/souls of the persons who do acts and to pin a moral label onto the "motives" that led to those acts. Further, says Nietzsche, we then predicate good or evil not just to the *motives* but also to the *persons*. This person, not just his motives, and not just this kind of act, is good or evil. He is an evil, murderous murderer. Then we may step back one more time and attribute good or evil to the forces that shaped this particular person, or

---

17. Friedrich Nietzsche, *On the Genealogy of Morals,* trans. Walter Kaufmann and R. J. Hollingdale (New York: Vintage Books, 1967). Henceforth abbreviated in text as *GM.*

to the forces that shape all people, or to "human nature" itself as a whole (p. 43). So the history of morality involves much building of cathedrals of reflection around such categories as human nature, character, motives, and acts, with much attribution of good and evil to any, all, or none of the above. And often these cathedrals of reflection assume universality and eternity. That is, the moralists of one generation in one culture assume that the claims they are making about good or evil human nature, character, motives, and acts apply to all places, times, and cultures.

But for Nietzsche *everything about all of this is wrong*. It is wrong to believe that acts can be classified as intrinsically anything. *"There are no moral facts whatever"* (*TI*, p. 55). Communities create categories of good or evil, right or wrong, and ascribe them to certain acts, but history clearly shows that these categories and ascriptions change dramatically across time and culture (*HA*, p. 45; *Z*, p. 39; etc.). It is equally wrong to believe that motives or people or humans as a whole can be classified as intrinsically anything. And it is wrong to believe that people are free to choose the acts they will perform, or are responsible for those acts, their motives, or their character. There is no moral freedom, duty, or responsibility, and it was a historic error (as in Kant) to tie human dignity to such illusions (*HA*, p. 74; a theme developed extensively in Nietzsche's neglected *Daybreak*).[18] "No one is responsible for his deeds, no one for his nature; to judge is to be unjust" (*HA*, p. 44). No one is free in her *actions or motives*, because all organic beings are driven by self-preservation and its kinfolk, pleasure-seeking and pain-avoidance. If we are not free, we are by definition not responsible. And no one is really free in *character*, because the forces that shape the person are inexorable. Speaking of cruel persons, but with applicability to his entire approach, Nietzsche says, "They themselves are as little responsible as a piece of granite for being granite" (p. 46). So what is all this talk of morality, of freedom, of responsibility, of eternal and transcendent moral truths? An illusion: "Morality is a white lie, to keep [the beast in us] from tearing us apart." It is a lie we tell ourselves to comfort ourselves with the idea that we are not mere organic beings or beasts: "[Man] has taken himself to be something higher and has imposed stricter laws on himself. He therefore has a hatred for those stages of man that remain closer to the animal state" (p. 45).

So there are no things-in-themselves out there in the world called "sin,"

---

18. Friedrich Nietzsche, *Daybreak: Thoughts on the Prejudices of Morality*, ed. Maudemarie Clark and Brian Leiter, trans. R. J. Hollingdale (Cambridge: Cambridge University Press, 1997).

"guilt," "evil," "goodness," or "virtue." These are labels we stick on the *world*, to make it seem more just and orderly than it actually is, and labels we stick on *acts and people*, to encourage those behaviors that preserve the community and discourage those that harm it (p. 66). We sacralize these communal moral traditions by bathing them in religious myth, to deepen cultural loyalty to them and thus maintain our communities, but this sacralization too is delusional. (Think of Moses coming down the mountain with the two divinely inscribed tablets of stone, an image Nietzsche enjoyed subverting [*Z*, p. 198].) And the particular morality to which we attribute these delusional categories "is in a continual state of fluctuation. . . . There are higher and deeper concepts of good and evil, moral and immoral" (*HA*, p. 53). Also there are lower and shallower concepts; all fluctuate, all are contested. We honor the "moral" person and shame the "immoral," without recognizing that all we are doing is rewarding those who accept age-old traditions in our particular cultures and punishing those who do not (p. 66).

This account prepares Nietzsche to be clearer and more direct in his rendering of the origins of religion and his rejection of all metaphysical beliefs. In *Human, All Too Human,* he extends and deepens his third layer, the rejection of Christianity, by doing more than before to situate the birth of metaphysical beliefs historically, in the primeval human past. Religion is a part of the misty folk history of the human race, still surviving vestigially in advanced modern culture. He proposes a genealogy of worship: it was the vain effort of primitive humans who, in the absence of any accurate understanding of causality, tried to appease and control the awesome and terrible forces of nature (p. 82). He says that while "one can hardly dispute the absolute possibility" (p. 17) of a metaphysical world (with a god, etc.), "we cannot begin to do anything with it, let alone allow our happiness, salvation, and life to depend on the spider web of such a possibility" (p. 18). All knowledge claims made by advocates of metaphysical or theological beliefs, says Nietzsche, are based on "passion, error, and self-deception . . . and [t]he very worst methods of knowledge" (p. 17). This includes such ludicrous ideas, for Nietzsche, as "belief in inspiration and a seemingly miraculous communication of truths" (p. 15). "When one has disclosed these methods [of religious knowledge] to be the foundation of all existing religious and metaphysical systems, one has refuted them" (p. 17).

But moderns now understand that it is time to "get beyond superstitions and religious concepts and fears" (p. 27). We can leave behind belief in "a God [who] is guiding the destinies of the world as a whole" (p. 30) along with correlated beliefs in a heavenly court of angels, virgin births, atoning deaths, miracles, some kind of supernatural salvation, or even "sin" and "evil." After all, "What thinking person still needs the hypothesis of a god?" (p. 33). It is Christianity, and not just religion, that has now come fully into view; Nietzsche is here explicitly rejecting the most central Christian doctrinal convictions as well as the viability of the traditional sources of any Christian claims to theological knowledge. Eventually Nietzsche became the first to make the staggering declaration "God is dead" (*GS*, p. 167) — "God is dead. God remains dead. And we have killed him. . . . What after all are these churches now if they are not the tombs and sepulchers of God?" (*GS*, pp. 181-82). And in *Zarathustra:* "This old god lives no more: he is thoroughly dead" (*Z*, p. 263).[19]

Having abandoned "the hypothesis of a god," those equipped with "a very high level of education" (*HA*, p. 27) can also unlearn, "weake[n]," and "roo[t] out" religiously laden worries over human depravity and how one might obtain salvation (p. 32). It is time to become "free spirits" (*HA*, subtitle and throughout), unbound by these enslaving ancient traditions. Here we first meet Nietzsche's most intense and enduring critique of religion, especially Christianity. This will be our tenth Nietzschean layer: *his claim that both Christian theology and Christian morality have badly damaged human beings, and human well-being therefore requires the total rejection of Christianity.*

In this first foray into the theme, Nietzsche claims that Christianity and its priests made themselves indispensable by first crushing the human spirit and then prescribing a remedy for what they had crushed. "It is a trick of Christianity to teach the utter worthlessness, sinfulness, and despicableness of man" (p. 86). Christianity, and Judaism before it, took certain natural human dissatisfactions with life and self and blew them up into a full-blown myth of human sinfulness, guilt, and depravity before God (pp. 90-93). Humans were taught to picture themselves standing before a perfect God who stands ready to judge them brutally and forever for all their wrongdoings. Into this entirely imaginary human crisis Christianity offered the medicine of sweet redemption through the atoning death of Jesus Christ. "Christianity . . . crushed and shattered man completely, and

---

19. Sometimes Nietzsche sounds gleeful at having made the kinds of intellectual discoveries that lead him, among others, to this conclusion about the "death of God," which should be taken not only as belief in the nonexistence of God but also as an observation about fading belief in God in Western culture. Other times, including in *GS*, pp. 180-82, he sounds somewhat staggered by the epochal nature of this change as well as his role in advancing it. It is a momentous thing being one of the murderers of a culture's god.

submerged him as if in a deep mire. Then, all at once, into his feeling of complete confusion, it offered the light of divine compassion to shine, so that the surprised man, stunned by mercy, let out a cry of rapture. . . . All psychological inventions of Christianity work toward this sick excess of feeling, toward the deep corruption of head and heart necessary for it. Christianity wants to destroy, shatter, stun, intoxicate" (p. 85).

Christianity accompanied this theology of redemption with an "ascetic" moral ideal of self-denial and incessant mortification of all natural desires. "They did not know how to love their god but by crucifying man" (*Z*, p. 92). Both the diagnosis and the prescription had been terribly wrong all along, and had taught people to hate themselves, to cauterize their instincts, and to suppress all natural and life-giving drives — actually, everything great and powerful in humanity. We were taught to become cruel against ourselves, with all that talk of sin, the cross, and penitence (*Z*, p. 218). "All naturalism in morality, that is all *healthy* morality, is dominated by an instinct of life. . . . *Anti-natural* morality, that is virtually every morality that has been taught, reverenced, and preached, turns on the contrary precisely *against* the instincts of life — it is now a secret, now loud and impudent *condemnation* of these instincts. . . . Life is at an end where the 'kingdom of God' begins" (*TI*, p. 45).

Christianity stands profoundly guilty for teaching human beings to repress the irrepressible, to go against every natural drive inherited from our primeval past and essential for our flourishing and even our survival. The offense seems greatest, to Nietzsche, where it crippled the most noble and robust of previous generations — the warriors, the "blond beasts" of every great culture (*TI*, p. 56), which Christianity turned into simpering monastics. More generally, Christian morality has made every person and culture affected by this religion quite sick. "The Christian resolve to find the world ugly and bad has made it ugly and bad" (*GS*, p. 185). This weakening of humanity through spurious guilt and equally spurious punishment or redemption is the worst offense of Christianity against the world — so devastating that by the end of his life Nietzsche describes it as *"the greatest crime against humanity,"*[20] and a "vampirism of pale subterranean bloodsuckers!" (*AC*, p. 165). His ultimate verdict: "I call Christianity the one great curse, the one great intrinsic depravity . . . the one immortal blemish of mankind" (*AC*, pp. 186-87).

---

20. Friedrich Nietzsche, *The Anti-Christ*, trans. and ed. R. J. Hollingdale (New York: Penguin, 1968), p. 165. Henceforth abbreviated in text as *AC*.

Fortunately, all this delusional religion is being left behind. Religion, "that antiquity jutting out from a far-distant olden time," still oddly evoked by the sound of "the old bells ringing out on a Sunday morning" (*HA*, p. 84), is fading. Nietzsche does briefly acknowledge that there are problems associated with the death of religion. "The individual looks his own short life span too squarely in the eye and feels no strong incentives to build on enduring institutions, designed for the ages" (p. 28). Previously he had been motivated by the apparent stability and eternity of such institutions as churches and monasteries, as well as by the sure hope of eternal blessedness as reward for his service and generosity on their behalf (pp. 28-29). Now he is not sure where to invest such hopes and energies. One possibility is in scientific projects, Nietzsche suggests; when built up over time, these will have their own kind of stability and eternity (p. 29), and will evoke a sense of the worthiness and value of their goals.

But for much of *Human, All Too Human,* and in most of his other books (*Daybreak, Zarathustra, Beyond Good and Evil, Genealogy of Morals*),[21] Nietzsche turns instead to his own titanic project of reworking human moral sensibility in light of this new "knowledge" about the delusional nature of Christianity and the damage caused to Western culture by Christian morality. So, based on a new anthropology in scientific materialism and evolutionary biology, and a rejection of any compliance with the extant "herd morality," Nietzsche begins his "immoralist" project of undertaking a "revaluation of all values."

> We need a *critique* of moral values, *the value of these moral values themselves must first be called into question.* . . . One has taken the *value* of these "values" as given, as factual, as beyond all question; one has hitherto never doubted or hesitated in the slightest degree in supposing "the good man" to be of higher value than "the evil man," of greater value in the sense of furthering the advancement and prosperity of man in general (the future of man included). But what if the reverse were true? What if a symptom of regression were inherent in the "good," likewise a danger, a seduction, a poison, a narcotic, through which the present was possibly living *at the expense of the future?* Perhaps more comfortably, less dangerously, but at the same time in a meaner style, more basely? —

---

21. Friedrich Nietzsche, *Beyond Good and Evil: Prelude to a Philosophy of the Future,* trans. and ed. Walter Kaufmann (New York: Vintage Books, 1966). Henceforth abbreviated in text as *BGE*.

So that precisely morality would be to blame if the *highest power and splendor* actually possible to the type man was never in fact attained? So that precisely morality was the danger of dangers? (*GM*, p. 20)

An eleventh Nietzschean layer can be distilled from these critically important, albeit elliptical, musings: *the pivotal human project of our era is the reversal of the antinatural Christian morality of two millennia and the building of a new morality that genuinely serves human flourishing, at least the flourishing of the great ones of our species.* (Note here how a vision of human flourishing — puzzle #12 — is juxtaposed directly against a vision of the sacredness of each individual life.) And Friedrich Nietzsche gradually comes to see that he will be the one leading this epochal project, in the face of great rejection, misunderstanding, and hatred. He will be the "lawbreaker" of his culture's old "tables of values," the "immoralist," the "creator" of a new morality for a new and better future for the earth (*Z*, p. 23). "Man [as currently constituted] is something that shall be overcome." The "overman" *(Übermensch)* is on his way, a breakthrough in species history as great as the leap from beast to man so long ago (*Z*, p. 14). With a malady this severe, a prescription this radical, and a task this huge, and perhaps also with an overly developed sense of his own importance and intense suffering and fear related to his miserable health, Nietzsche's writings from the mid-1880s forward sometimes begin to sound apocalyptic and even messianic. He is a prophet to the human race, a Zarathustra with revelation for humanity,[22] if humanity will but listen. Had Nietzsche — in an echo of our second layer — discovered a redemptive illusion to make his life bearable? Or, in an echo of the fifth layer: Had he invested in a new myth to replace the dead myths of the past?

This new Nietzschean morality will restore humanity to a more natural state and rescue it from the enervating effects of Christian morality: "I mean the morbid softening and moralization through which the animal 'man' finally learns to be ashamed of all his instincts. On his way to becoming an 'angel' . . . man has evolved that queasy stomach and coated tongue through which not only the joy and innocence of the animal but life itself has become repugnant to him" (*GM*, p. 67).

This revaluing will require us to look shrewdly at what behaviors actually benefit the long-term survival of the species — these alone must we

22. Everyone should read *Thus Spoke Zarathustra*. It is impossible to describe, other than to point to it as a kind of naturalist/secularist/messianic/apocalyptic/eschatological book of Revelation.

value. As creators of new tablets of morality, we must "become hard" (*Z,* p. 214) and not flinch at the new morality we must propose: "Even the most harmful man may really be the most useful when it comes to the preservation of the species; for he nurtures . . . instincts without which humanity would long have become feeble or rotten. Hatred, the mischievous delight in the misfortunes of others, the lust to rob and dominate, and whatever else is called evil belongs to the most amazing economy of the preservation of the species" (*GS,* p. 73). The new morality will mean declaring war on the church's old ascetic morality. There can be no compromise with it. "The Church combats passion with excision in every sense of the word; its practice, its 'cure' is *castration.* It never asks, 'How can one spiritualize, beautify, deify a desire?' — it has at all times laid the emphasis of its discipline on extirpation (of sensuality, of pride, of lust for power, of avarice, of revengefulness). — But to attack the passions at their roots means to attack life at its roots; the practice of the Church is *hostile to life*" (*TI,* p. 42). Therefore anyone who would be a friend of life must eradicate the church and its life-destroying morality.[23]

In the remainder of this chapter, I will cull through the rest of Nietzsche's works and identify six major moral reversals that he proposes. Were there space I would name more, for his project is a comprehensive one. His particular proposals evolve, moving in a number of different directions and varying in intensity and radicality. I will seek to identify the moves he makes that I believe are most contrary to an ethic of the sacredness of human life.

8.7. No Justice, No Rights, No Equality

One place to begin is with Nietzsche's deconstruction of any kind of transcendent concept of justice. If we believe that justice involves redressing past social and economic wrongs; or if we believe that justice involves reducing hierarchy in order to treat everyone essentially as on the same level

23. Though it is beyond the purpose of this book to explore this question further, this line from one of Nietzsche's last works must be quoted: "In reality there has been only one Christian, and he died on the Cross" (*AC,* p. 151). Nietzsche's fierce attack on Christianity distinguishes between Jesus and the movement that surrounded him, which "was already the opposite of what *he* had lived" from its very beginnings. He certainly hated Paul. And he hated the New Testament: "One does well to put gloves on when reading the New Testament. The proximity of so much uncleanliness almost forces one to do so. One would no more choose to associate with 'first Christians' than one would with Polish Jews. . . . Neither of them smell very pleasant" (*AC,* p. 161). This is hateful and dangerous talk.

and as having the same worth; or especially if we believe that there is a God who works in history toward justice, we are delusional, and our delusions must be utterly rejected.

Nietzsche's first account of justice begins in the ancient world, with examples from Greece. He claims that initially justice originates "among approximately *equal powers*" (*HA*, p. 64), each seeking self-preservation and advancing its self-interest. I exchange my X for your Y, on positions of equal strength, because both of us believe it to be in our self-interest and because we believe ours was an exchange of value for value. Justice here is barter. But in situations of unequal power between two parties, the weaker party will and must yield to the powerful party precisely in proportion to their relative power. Therefore "justice" is inextricably tied to power; what is "just" is the exchange appropriate between two parties relative to their power relations. Any concept of justice beyond this is a polite fiction.

This same paradigm would hold true for any concept of rights as well: "Each has as much right as his power is worth" (p. 65). There is no such thing as equal rights between persons just because they are persons. There is no transcendent reference point or Being to arbitrate disputes among persons on the basis of an eternal fixed standard of justice or human rights. Notice the complete reversal of the understanding of justice that we found in Old Testament law.

And the very idea of equality is wrongheaded: "'Equality,' a certain actual rendering similar of which the theory of 'equal rights' is only the expression, belongs essentially to decline: the chasm between man and man, class and class; the multiplicity of types; the will to be oneself, to stand out — that which I call *pathos of distance* — characterizes every *strong* age" (*TI*, p. 91). All talk of equality is a sign of social decay. "I do not wish to be mixed up and confused with those preachers of equality. For, to *me* justice speaks thus: 'Men are not equal.' Nor shall they become equal!" (*Z*, p. 101). Here is a rather crisp Nietzschean statement on the matter of equality: "The doctrine of equality! . . . There exists no more poisonous poison" (*TI*, p. 102). The implications of such beliefs about justice, rights, and equality are disastrous for the sacredness of human life.

8.8. No Pity

Nietzsche is known for his attacks on the Christian virtue of pity. These begin in *Human, All Too Human* and extend through much of his work.

In fairness, Nietzsche does not reject the significance of all kindness and love. Indeed, he describes these as "the most curative herbs and agents in human intercourse" (*HA*, p. 48), though he sees them as all too rare. But he holds no brief for pity. Nietzsche rejects pity, at one level, as useless. It doesn't do anything to ease anyone's pain. Further, he doubts the capacity of anyone to enter deeply into the pain of another, and mocks the superficiality of most efforts to "help" (*GS*, p. 269). He believes that pain and suffering are a "personal necessity" for growth and that pity mistakenly attempts to make us all far too comfortable (p. 269). He suggests that if we stopped to help every time we encountered anyone who suffered, we could never pursue any goal or project of our own (pp. 270-71). He condemns pity on the demand side, one might say, speaking of the efforts of whiny sufferers and unfortunates to evoke pity. If I am sick, ill, or depressed, and I can make you feel pity for me, I have gained happiness at the expense of your suffering on my behalf. Weak persons feel consoled that "they still *have* at least one *power:* the power to hurt" (*HA*, p. 50). So efforts to evoke pity are a sly, subterranean expression of the desire to hurt.

Nietzsche ends up grouping pity together with self-denial and self-sacrifice as part of that cluster of life-denying and life-negating ascetic virtues that had so predominated in (Christian = Western) morality. Eventually Nietzsche concludes that pity is more vice than virtue. Writing in *Genealogy of Morals*, he says:

> What was especially at stake was the value of the "unegoistic," the instincts of pity, self-abnegation, self-sacrifice. . . . But it was against precisely *these* instincts that there spoke from me an ever more fundamental mistrust, an ever more corrosive skepticism! It was precisely here that I saw the *great* danger to mankind, its sublimest enticement and seduction . . . the will turning *against* life, the tender and sorrowful signs of the ultimate illness: I understood the ever spreading morality of pity . . . as the most sinister symptom of a European culture that had itself become sinister. . . . For this overestimation of and predilection for pity on the part of modern philosophers is something new: hitherto philosophers have been at one as to the *worthlessness* of pity. (*GM*, p. 19)

Pity, self-denial, and self-sacrifice are hidden paths to self-destruction for human beings and for humanity itself. The natural human being seeks to meet his own needs, to care for himself, to act in the interests of his own survival and flourishing; such desires are rooted in primal human experience, and they are how humanity survives to this day. The same is true of strong cultures: "Strong ages, *noble* cultures, see in pity, in 'love of one's neighbor,' in a lack of self and self-reliance, something contemptible" (*TI*, p. 91).

Nietzsche's suspicion here is that the Western/Christian embrace of the negation of such values is a hidden embrace of death, not just for the person but also for culture and even the species. Eventually he grounds his rejection of all pity in "nature" itself — interestingly enough, given how many times we saw such resorts to claims from nature in the last chapter — but this is a nature red in tooth and claw, and ruthless toward the weak. "'Life always lives at the expense of other life' — he who does not grasp this has not taken even the first step toward honesty with himself" (*WP*, p. 199). Our belief must be that "the species is everything, *one* is always none" (*GS*, p. 74; note relevance to puzzle #2). Pity toward the weak goes against nature, and against the well-being of the species: "Pity on the whole thwarts the law of evolution, which is the law of *selection*. It preserves what is ripe for destruction" (*AC*, p. 118). We see here a direct assault both on the concept of *every* life's sacredness and on the compassion that the suffering of precious human beings ought to evoke in us.

8.9. Cruelty Not Necessarily Evil

So Nietzsche rejects the received moral tradition that pity is morally good; conversely, he is unwilling to accept the received moral tradition that cruelty (or the infliction of suffering on others) is morally evil. His first foray on this issue is in *Human, All Too Human,* when he suggests that different perspectives are inevitable in moral situations and that we have to see things from both sides. Using examples such as a prince taking a plebeian's beloved sweetheart, or a king wantonly killing a subject's beloved son, or the crimes of an unjust judge or a dishonest journalist, Nietzsche argues that power differences, gaps in experience, and the inability of each of us to truly enter into the reality of others mean that the perpetrator and the sufferer inevitably misunderstand each other. "No cruel man is cruel to the extent that the mistreated man believes. The idea of pain is not the same as the suffering of it" (*HA*, p. 61).

Later in this same chapter Nietzsche argues from the widely accepted legitimacy of injuring others intentionally in cases of self-defense to the legitimacy of cruelty, or doing harm out of "so-called malice" (*HA*, p. 73), even when not in self-defense. To make this leap he says first that we don't know and can't really know how much pain our action might be causing another, because of limits to our capacity for experiencing the pain of others. Meanwhile, we *can* feel pleasure in such actions; we know this, because we experience that pleasure. Therefore, "the action [of harming another for pleasure] takes place to preserve the well-being of the individual and thus falls within a point of view similar to that of self-defense or a white lie" (p. 73). Nietzsche is saying that any action that brings me pleasure is related to the quest for self-preservation, which is, for Nietzsche, not exactly "justifiable" (because he doesn't offer moral justifications) but so *primal* as to be beyond the category of justifiability: "No life without pleasure; the struggle for pleasure is the struggle for life" (p. 73). His argument appears to be that if it pleases me to hurt you, then I am acting in the interests of my own self-preservation, just as when a plant reaches toward the sun or an aardvark chews on leaves.

Nietzsche later develops a theory to explain what he describes as a primal human attachment to cruelty, which Christianity had attempted to extinguish in its ethics. Note the harshness of his language here:

> It seems to me that the delicacy and even more the tartuffery of tame domestic animals (which is to say modern men, which is to say us) resists a really vivid comprehension of the degree to which *cruelty* constituted the great festival pleasure of more primitive men and was indeed an ingredient of almost every one of their pleasures. . . . To see others suffer does one good, to make others suffer even more so: this is a hard saying but an ancient, mighty, human, all-too-human principle to which even the apes might subscribe; for it has been said that in devising bizarre cruelties they anticipate man and are, as it were, his "prelude." Without cruelty there is no festival: thus the longest and most ancient part of human history teaches — and in punishment there is so much that is *festive!* (*GM*, pp. 66-67)

Of course, in the Christian moral tradition, unleashing such sadistic and cruel human impulses is a really bad idea.

8.10. The Right and Dignity of Suicide

Nietzsche also regularly comes out in favor of the legitimacy of suicide, and rejects ancient Christian proscriptions against self-killing in favor of a classical (Greek and Roman) honoring of those who choose to end life on their own timetable. His words presaged the collapse of prohibitions on (physician-assisted) suicide that were based on the moral scruples long prevailing in predominantly Christian cultures. "Why, aside from the demands of religion, [is it] more praiseworthy for a man grown old, who feels his powers decrease, to await his slow exhaustion and disintegration, rather than to put a term to his life with complete consciousness? In this case, suicide is quite natural, obvious, and should by rights awaken respect for the triumph of reason. . . . Religions provide abundant excuses to escape the need to kill oneself: this is how they insinuate themselves with those who are in love with life" (*HA*, p. 60).

He put the matter far more strongly in *Twilight of the Idols:*

> To die proudly when it is no longer possible to live proudly. Death of one's own free choice, death at the proper time, with a clear head and with joyfulness, consummated in the midst of children and witnesses: so that an actual leave-taking is possible while he who is leaving is *still there,* likewise an actual evaluation of what has been desired and achieved in life, an *adding-up* of life — all of this in contrast to the pitiable and horrible comedy Christianity has made of the hour of death. One should never forget of Christianity that it has abused the weakness of the dying to commit conscience-rape and even the mode of death to formulate value judgments on men and the past! (*TI*, p. 88)

Instead, we should seek "death at the right time," in the words of Nietzsche's prophet Zarathustra: "Many die too late, and a few die too early. The doctrine still sounds strange: 'Die at the right time!' . . . My death I praise to you, the free death which comes to me because *I* want it. And when shall I want it? He who has a goal and an heir will want death at the right time for his goal and heir. And from reverence for his goal and heir he will hang no more dry wreaths in the sanctuary of life" (*Z*, pp. 71-72).

8.11. Social Contempt and Suppression of "Degenerating" Lives

I have sought to be fair to Nietzsche, and never to caricature his views or link him to later catastrophes unjustly. Many thoughtful contemporaries have made similar arguments related to the right and dignity of death/suicide on one's own timetable. But the next disturbing words must be faced for what they are — morally disastrous, and fateful, especially in light of what happened in Germany merely fifty years later:

> *A moral code for physicians.* — The invalid is a parasite on society. In a certain state it is indecent to go on living. To vegetate on in cowardly dependence on physicians and medicaments after the meaning of life, the *right* to life, has been lost ought to entail the profound contempt of society. Physicians . . . ought to be the communicators of this contempt — not prescriptions, but every day a fresh dose of *disgust* with their patients. . . . To create a new responsibility, that of the physician, in all cases in which the highest interest of life, of *ascending* life, demands the most ruthless suppression and sequestration of degenerating life — for example in determining the right to reproduce, the right to be born, the right to live. (*TI*, p. 88)

So here we have a mandate for physicians to suppress the lives of "parasites" and to show contempt for all such patients. This concept is based on a ranking[24] of human beings in two categories: "ascending" life and "degenerating" (sometimes "descending") life. Nietzsche is abandoning the old Christian ranking system in which the human *qua* human stands higher in rank than the animal, and all humans stand equal to each other; for example, the sacredness of each and every human life. Now only certain humans stand higher in rank — these are the "ascending" lives. Such lives must be protected. One way to protect them is by denying the right of "degenerating life" to be born or to be sustained in illness, because the resources used up by the degenerates should have been used by the ascenders.

Who exactly makes up these two categories? The distinction between the great and the mediocre that we identified in Nietzsche's sixth layer seems to apply here as well. For the sake of the long-term human future, the great must be taken care of: "If [individuals] represent the ascending line, their value is in fact extraordinary — and for the sake of life as a whole, which with them takes a step *forward,* one may take extreme care to obtain and preserve the optimum conditions for them."

However, the reverse also applies: "If he represents the descending development, decay, chronic degeneration, sickening (— sickness is, broadly speaking, already a phenomenon consequent upon decay, *not* the cause of

---

24. Nietzsche actually speaks of "orders of rank" in humanity. See *GS*, p. 334, and elsewhere.

it),[25] then he can be accorded little value, and elementary fairness demands that he *take away* as little as possible from the well-constituted. He is no better than a parasite on them" (*TI*, p. 86).

Nietzsche did not hesitate to speak with utmost harshness about the valueless lives of the mediocre majority: "All-too-many live, and all-too-long they hang on their branches. Would that a storm came to shake all this worm-eaten rot from the tree" (*Z*, pp. 72-73). Nietzsche wants the "overman" to live (p. 79). He cares little if others do.

In the case of "descending lives," forced sterilization is perfectly appropriate, even obligatory, to prevent the expansion of their number:

> *Also a commandment of the love of man.* — There are cases in which a child would be a crime: in the case of chronic invalids and neurasthenics of the third degree. What should one do in such cases? — One might at least try encouraging them to chastity. . . . After all, society has a *duty* here: few more pressing and fundamental demands can be made upon it. Society, as the great trustee of life, is responsible to life itself for every miscarried life — it also has to pay for such lives: consequently it ought to prevent them. In numerous cases, society ought to prevent procreation: to this end, it may hold in readiness, without regard to descent, rank, or spirit, the most rigorous means of constraint, deprivation of freedom, in certain circumstances castration. . . . Life itself recognizes no solidarity, no "equal rights," between the healthy and the degenerate parts of an organism: one must excise the latter — or the whole will perish. — Sympathy for decadents, equal rights for the ill-constituted — that would be the profoundest immorality, that would be antinature itself as morality. (*WP*, p. 389)

The dangerous implications of such a sharp distinction between ascending and descending, worthy and unworthy, human life have been noticed by many who study Nietzsche. Walter Kaufmann is worth quoting at length here:

> Even in the context of Nietzsche's early philosophy it was pointed out that this doctrine was dynamite insofar as it insisted that the gulf be-

25. The significance of this statement should not be missed. Nietzsche seems to be suggesting that physical illness/degeneration reflects a more basic existential degeneration. You are sick because you are degenerate. If degenerates as a type are parasitic on the strong, then there is nothing to do but eliminate or suppress them.

tween some men and others is more significant than that between man and animal. At the same time, however, it was perfectly clear that Nietzsche looked to art, religion, and philosophy — and not to race — to elevate man above the beasts, and some men above the mass of mankind. . . . If the value of a human being . . . were a function of race or indeed of anything purely biological, the consequences would be momentous: the chasm between the "powerful" elite and those others who are doomed to mediocrity would be fixed and permanent, even hereditary — and large masses of people, possibly whole nations, might be reliably determined to be inferior and possibly worthless. . . . On the other hand, if power — and the value of the human being — are construed not in terms of race, nor at all biologically, but in terms of artistic or philosophic creativity, the situation would be very different: the "powerful" and valuable specimens would be widely scattered over the centuries and continents and, as likely as not, unrecognized by their own contemporaries — this last qualification being fulfilled admirably by Nietzsche himself; no man could presume to know with any certainty who among his fellow men might be chosen and who damned; and all men might have to be treated with respect as potentially "truly human beings." It is one of Nietzsche's most serious shortcomings — and has contributed seriously to his "influence" — that he failed to give any emphasis to this common human potentiality and did not consider the possibility that this potentiality might be quite sufficient to re-establish that "cardinal distinction between man and animal" which Darwin seemed to Nietzsche to have denied.[26]

8.12. The Benefits of War

While Nietzsche, unlike the later German ultranationalists who appropriated his language, is relentlessly critical of states and of nationalism (*Z*, p. 49), he generally speaks positively about the wars that peoples must sometimes wage, and that have been so important in human experience. While acknowledging that war "makes the victor stupid and the vanquished malicious" (*HA*, p. 213), it also has positive effects. War "barbarizes through both these effects and therefore makes man more natural"

26. Walter Kaufmann, *Nietzsche: Philosopher, Psychologist, Antichrist,* 3rd ed. (Princeton: Princeton University Press, 1968), pp. 285-86.

(p. 213). Here is more revaluation of values — being "barbarized," and thus more "natural," as opposed to civilized and less natural, is treated as a good thing, as progress for humanity, in this new table of values. Nietzsche goes much further in a memorable statement later in the book:

> It is vain rhapsodizing and sentimentality to continue to expect much . . . from mankind, once it has learned not to wage war. For the time being, we know of no other means to imbue exhausted peoples, as strongly and surely as every war does, with that raw energy of the battleground, that deep impersonal hatred, that murderous cold-bloodedness with a good conscience, that communal, organized ardor in destroying the enemy, that proud indifference to great losses, to one's own existence and that of one's friends, that muted, earthquakelike convulsion of the soul. . . . Europe . . . needs not only wars but the greatest and most terrible wars (that is, occasional relapses into barbarism) in order not to forfeit to the means of culture its culture and its very existence. (*HA*, pp. 230-31)[27]

Certainly Nietzsche's successors were granted his wish, and saw, in fact, two great and terrible wars with more than occasional relapses into barbarism.

He also warns against being deceived by the appeal of peace and good will:

> Refraining mutually from injury, violence, and exploitation and placing one's will on a par with that of someone else — this may become, in a certain rough sense, good manners among individuals if the appropriate conditions are present. . . . But as soon as this principle is extended, and possibly even accepted as the *fundamental principle of society,* it would immediately prove to be what it really is — a will to the *denial* of life, a principle of disintegration and decay. Here we must beware of superficiality and get to the bottom of the matter, resisting all sentimental weakness: life itself is *essentially* appropriation, injury, overpowering of what is alien and weaker; suppression, hardness . . . and at least, at its mildest, exploitation. (*BGE*, p. 203)

Perhaps readers will be able to think of certain regimes and movements after Nietzsche that found quite appealing this vision of life as injury,

---

27. It should be noted that when Nietzsche speaks of "war," he is not always talking about armed conflict between states; sometimes he is speaking metaphorically.

violence, and exploitation; appropriation, overpowering, and suppression; and "hardness" rather than "sentimental weakness" as the order of the day.

8.13. Nietzsche and the Sacredness of Human Life

We could sum up one key dimension of Nietzsche's moral philosophy with his own words: "There is no 'ought' anymore. Morality to the extent that it was an 'ought' has been destroyed by our way of reflection, every bit as much as religion" (*HA*, p. 36). Many contemporary scholars of Nietzsche remember him primarily for this work of deconstruction of the old epistemologies and the assumed moral universals that accompanied them. There are significant reasons for all who wrestle with issues in epistemology and philosophy to take his claims seriously on this level.

But Nietzsche could not leave it there. He was unwilling simply to deconstruct the old morality, religion, and epistemology. He also began a reconstruction, a revaluation of values. Drawing especially on strands of classical thought and on what he believed to be the implications of scientific materialism and evolutionary history, Nietzsche sought to displace the ethics of pity, other-regard, and sacrifice and recover a primal, natural, ethical egoism, for the sake of human flourishing and the human future. "To make a whole *person* of oneself and keep in mind that person's *greatest good* in everything one does — this takes us further than any pitying impulses and actions for the sake of others" (*HA*, p. 66).

This also means the end of guilty consciences: "The advent of the Christian God, as the maximum god attained so far, was therefore accompanied by the maximum feeling of guilty indebtedness on earth. Presuming we have gradually entered upon the *reverse* course, there is no small probability that with the irresistible decline of faith in the Christian God there is now also a considerable decline in mankind's feeling of guilt" (*GM*, pp. 90-91).

Such liberated free spirits were now free to join Nietzsche's reconstruction of social ethics. Sometimes his prescriptions seem harmless, as in his thousands of clever aphorisms. But other times they are chilling, and sometimes disastrous. In what may be the most disturbing section of *Human, All Too Human* (though it pales in comparison with the later works), Nietzsche argues that our loss of belief in a God who is providentially guiding humanity to "somewhere glorious" means that humans "must set themselves ecumenical goals, embracing the whole earth" (*HA*, p. 30). We are on our own, to do collectively what must be done for the good of humanity. This "ecumenical" project cannot necessarily be constrained by the "older morality," the "nice, naïve" (p. 31) ideas of men such as Immanuel Kant, that would require that each of us act in such a way that we could endorse that all act in like manner. Instead, we may discover that "[p]erhaps a future survey of the needs of mankind will reveal [that] . . . in the interest of ecumenical goals, for whole stretches of human time special tasks, perhaps in some circumstances even evil tasks, would have to be set" (p. 31). It was not clear what "special tasks" Nietzsche had in mind when he wrote these words. But is it inappropriate to read this statement in light of his later claims about the worthlessness of the weak, the ill, the rabble, the herd, the all-too-many, and the "degenerate"?

We have been asking about the implications of Nietzsche for the sacredness of human life. He considered this issue quite directly. In one long paragraph of *Human, All Too Human*, Nietzsche asks whether humans should continue to believe in "the value and worth of life" (*HA*, p. 35). He quickly says that any such general belief is "based on impure thinking." He suggests that some of us accept claims to the value and worth of human life because we focus on the exceptional people, the "great talents and pure souls" whose very brilliance tempt us to believe that such great souls are "the goal of all world evolution" (pp. 35-36). But this approach, to which Nietzsche himself is clearly tempted, is "impure" thinking, because it involves overlooking the great mass of others who are not exceptional. Nietzsche says that the average person finds great value in life because he is so inordinately focused on himself. If such a person were actually able to exit his focus on his own affairs and enter into the lives of others, "[he] would have to despair about the value of life; if he were able to grasp and feel mankind's overall consciousness in himself, he would collapse with a curse against existence" (p. 36). This is not because, as might be said in a Christian account, he would in such a moment experience the great sorrows and sufferings of others. Instead his despair would result from being forced to encounter "the ultimate aimlessness of men" (p. 36) and the "squandering" of mankind that is the general human experience. In short: the only possible thing about humanity that gives worth to the species as a whole is the greatness of a few, and even that is overwhelmed by the mediocrity and pointlessness of the many. Human life, in and of itself, cannot be said to have particular worth and value.

Over and over again later in his writings, he says it directly: "In every age the wisest have passed the identical judgment on life: *it is worthless*" (*TI*, p. 29). Or this somewhat more exploratory reflection: "*What is life?* — Life — that is: continually shedding something that wants to die. Life — that is: being cruel and inexorable against everything about us that is growing old and weak — and not only about *us*. Life — that is, then: being without reverence for those who are dying, who are wretched, who are ancient? Constantly being a murderer? — And yet old Moses said: 'Thou shalt not kill'" (*GS*, p. 100).

We cannot make any claims to the worth of human life because our existence is an accident of a godless universe:

> What alone can *our* teaching be? — That no one *gives* a human being his quality, not God, not society, not his parents, not *he himself*. . . . *No one* is accountable for existing at all, or for being constituted as he is, or for living in the circumstances and surroundings in which he lives. The fatality of his nature cannot be disentangled from the fatality of all that which has been and will be. He is *not* the result of a special design, a will, a purpose; he is *not* the subject of an attempt to attain to an "ideal of man," or an "ideal of happiness," or an "ideal of morality" — it is absurd to want to *hand over* his nature to some purpose or other. *We* invented the concept "purpose": in reality, purpose is *lacking*. . . . The concept "God" has hitherto been the greatest *objection* to existence. . . . We deny God, in denying God, we deny accountability: only by doing *that* do we redeem the world. (*TI*, p. 54)

Quite insightfully, Nietzsche will simply have none of this Enlightenment project of preserving the kernel of Christian morality while abandoning the husk of Christian theology:

> When one gives up Christian belief one thereby deprives oneself of the *right* to Christian morality. For the latter is absolutely *not* self-evident. . . . Christianity is a system, a consistently thought out and *complete* view of things. If one breaks out of it a fundamental idea, the belief in God, one thereby breaks the whole thing to pieces: one has nothing of any consequence left in one's hands. . . . Christian morality is a command: its origin is transcendental; it is beyond all criticism, all right to criticize; it possesses truth only if God is truth — it stands or falls with the belief in God. (*TI*, pp. 69-70)

This is why it is critically important to destroy any remaining remnants of belief in the Christian god: "After Buddha was dead his shadow was still shown for centuries in a cave — a tremendous, gruesome shadow. God is dead; but given the way of men, there may still be caves for thousands of years in which his shadow will be shown. — And we — we still have to vanquish his shadow, too" (*GS*, p. 167).

In an oddly comprehensive and accurate way Nietzsche fully recognizes the surviving Christian concept of the sacredness of life that we have been working with throughout this book:

> When Christian prejudice was a power . . . meaning lay in the salvation of the individual soul. . . . For each soul, the gravitational center of valuation was placed within itself: salvation or damnation! . . . Extremest form of personalization — For every soul there was only one perfecting; only one ideal; only one way to redemption — Extremest form of equality of rights, tied to an optical magnification of one's own importance to the point of insanity — Nothing but insanely important souls, revolving about themselves with frightful fear. (*WP*, p. 185)

And this: "'You higher men' — thus blinks the mob — 'there are no higher men, we are all equal, man is man, before God we are all equal.' Before God! But now this god has died. You higher men, this god was your greatest danger. It is only since he lies in his tomb that you have been resurrected" (*Z*, p. 286; cf. *AC*, p. 141). With God dead, and Christian theology thrown aside, its ethics can be abandoned as well: "There is nothing to life that has value, except the degree of power — assuming that life itself is the will to power. Morality guarded the underprivileged against nihilism by assigning to each an infinite value, a metaphysical value, and by placing each in an order that did not agree with the worldly order of rank and power: it taught resignation, meekness, etc. Supposing that the faith in this morality would perish, then the underprivileged would no longer have their comfort — and they would perish" (*WP*, p. 37).

Nietzsche is concerned that despite everything, people still speak of the value of man, equality, and rights. "No man believes now in this absurd [Christian] self-inflation: and we have sifted our wisdom through a sieve of contempt. Nevertheless, the optical habit of seeking the value of man in his approach to an ideal man remains undisturbed: fundamentally, one upholds the perspective of personalization as well as equality of rights before the ideal" (*WP*, p. 185).

302

That meant there was still more work to be done to accomplish the annihilation of the Christian God, and the rejection of Christian morality, in the name of "ecumenical goals" such as remaking the nation, the world, and humanity itself.

The twentieth century saw considerable efforts to that effect.

9. Desecrations: Twentieth-Century Nazi Assaults on Human Life

> Should the Jew, with the aid of his Marxist creed, triumph over the people of this world, his Crown will be the funeral wreath of mankind, and this planet will once again follow its orbit through ether, without any human life on its surface, as it did millions of years ago. And so I believe today that my conduct is in accordance with the will of the Almighty Creator. In standing guard against the Jew I am defending the handiwork of the Lord.
>
> Adolf Hitler

The twentieth century was a bloody mess. History truly became a slaughterhouse. Surely it had been a slaughterhouse before, but the scale and magnitude of the mass killings of the twentieth century stagger the imagination. In a book about the unique, incalculable sacredness of each and every human life, honesty compels us to engage the worst negations, violations, and desecrations of that historic conviction. The twentieth century gives us plenty of material.

My initial plan for this book involved chapters on the murderous regime of the Soviet Union under Joseph Stalin as well as the genocide in Rwanda. To attempt such discussions would make this book too long, so it makes more sense to focus closely on one regime, especially on the one that is most familiar to me. But before focusing on the Nazis, the following sad list of the top fourteen twentieth-century genocides seems worth entering into the record of a book on the sacred worth of the human being.[1] The list includes only civilian noncombatant casualties.

1. This list is drawn from http://www.scaruffi.com/politics/dictat.html, accessed April

1. Mao Ze-Dong. China and Tibet. 1949-1969. 49-78 million
2. Joseph Stalin. USSR. 1932-1939. 23 million
3. Adolf Hitler. Nazi Germany. 1939-1945. 12 million
4. Leopold II. Belgian Congo. 1886-1908. 8 million
5. Hideki Tojo. Japan. 1941-1944. 5 million
6. Ismail Enver. Turkey. 1915-1920. 2.5 million
7. Pol Pot. Cambodia. 1975-1979. 1.7 million
8. Kim Il Sung. North Korea. 1948-1994. 1.6 million
9. Mengistu. Ethiopia. 1975-1978. 1.5 million
10. Leonid Brezhnev. Afghanistan. 1979-1982. 800,000
11. Jean Kambanda. Rwanda. 1994. 800,000
12. Suharto. East Timor/West Papua. 1966-1998. 800,000
13. Saddam Hussein. Iraq, Iran, and Kurds. 1980-1990. 600,000
14. Tito. Yugoslavia. 1945-1987. 570,000

Using the lower of the estimates from China, and only numbers from this top-fourteen list, we count twentieth-century civilian deaths at over 107 million. And again, this does not include military casualties in World War I, World War II, or any of that century's smaller wars. We should tremble before such unimaginable human suffering, such vast desecration of lives made in the image of God.

At least one of these episodes of human evil deserves a closer look. I have chosen to focus my attention in this chapter on the period from 1933 to 1945, on the regime of Nazi Germany, and on the man Adolf Hitler. I will first consider the full range of crimes against life's sacredness inflicted by Hitler and his regime. Then I will turn to the beliefs that were most significant in shaping his regime's murderous actions. At all times the subject of this book will discipline our explorations. We are laying the deeds and beliefs of Hitler next to the conviction that human life is sacred, and trying to figure out how this man and his regime could have gone so badly wrong. We take this sad journey into another of history's most extraordinary dramas to deepen our understanding of what it really means to say that human life is sacred and to protect sacred lives from desecration. We face the mystery of iniquity here. I cannot hope or pretend to fully penetrate it. But I do believe it is necessary to make the attempt, and I think we have sufficient distance now from these events in

---

30, 2011. There are counting challenges and a wide range of other lists, but this is sufficient for our purposes here.

the first half of the twentieth century to take a fresh look at them. Indeed, I believe we must do so.

9.1. Hitler and His Crimes

Adolf Hitler was the forty-three-year-old leader of the extreme rightist National Socialist German Workers' Party when he was named chancellor of Germany on January 30, 1933. His résumé was thin. After a mediocre education and obscurity as a failed artist in his twenties, the onset of the First World War on August 2, 1914, found Hitler enthusiastic to join. Having been found unfit for service earlier in the year by the Austrian military, he slipped across the border to Germany and successfully volunteered his way into a Bavarian regiment. He served for the entirety of that bloody war. Serving as a runner to the front lines, he rose to the rank of lance corporal, was twice decorated with an Iron Cross for bravery, was wounded twice, and was temporarily blinded once by a mustard gas attack. He survived some of the war's worst battles: at Ypres, the Somme, and Passchendaele. He reacted bitterly to the news of Germany's surrender on November 11, 1918. For a heretofore unremarkable young man, these were years of great glory and became the touchstone for his life.

Briefly employed by army intelligence to investigate right-wing German movements in the wake of Germany's defeat in World War I, Hitler ended up finding his purpose as the leader of one of these obscure rightist parties — the National Socialist German Workers' Party (NSDAP = Nazi). He spent the 1920s pressing the rightist agenda along with other like-minded activists while attempting to build his party. A failed 1923 coup that he led against the state government in Bavaria landed him in jail just long enough to write *Mein Kampf (My Struggle)*, an influential political memoir and manifesto to which we will return. Ten years later, amidst the Great Depression and extraordinary suffering and political instability in Germany, the Nazi Party had become a force to be reckoned with — so strong after the November 1932 parliamentary elections (the Nazis received 12 million votes, or 27 percent of those cast)[2] that the aged president Paul von Hindenburg concluded that a new German government had to include Hitler, who represented a party with 196 seats in the

2. This was actually down from July 1932, when the party won 37 percent of the vote in the Reichstag, their highest vote total in a fully free election in Germany.

Reichstag.[3] Everyone hoped Hitler could be useful — and could be tamed if brought into the government. Using democratic means, Adolf Hitler became the legitimately appointed head of the German government.

Hitler entered government as one party's representative in a multiparty parliamentary democracy. He had less than one-third of the legislators with him, though he did have the strongest single party. He did not have control of foreign policy; this rested with Hindenburg. He had not appointed the judiciary. He had inherited the government bureaucracy, over which he had little immediate control. He was a figure of no great pedigree. All these facts make what happened next even more astonishing.

Despite the obstacles Hitler faced, he did now have partial command of a nation in crisis, hungry and poor, divided and aggrieved and looking for strong leadership. He certainly provided "strong" leadership, after a fashion. From 1933 until his "twilight of the idols" suicide in his bunker on April 30, 1945, Hitler created a regime that in the name of what had once been Christian Germany systematically and intentionally violated the ancient Christian understanding of the sacredness of human life. In what follows I will name his regime's major crimes against life's sanctity as if I were laying out the terms of an indictment, though I will take them roughly in the order of their occurrence rather than the level of their magnitude. I think it fair to assume that few readers will be familiar with the full and astonishing range of Hitler's crimes. Let's begin with the period from his ascension to power on January 30, 1933, to August 31, 1939, the eve of World War II.

First, Hitler rapidly destroyed the already weakened parliamentary democracy of Germany, moving quickly beyond authoritarianism into a dictatorship in which he gained absolute power.[4] Within months of taking office his government was able to harass and finally outlaw other political parties (beginning with the Communists on February 27, 1933, extending to all other parties in July), ban trade unions, build concentration camps,

---

3. The next closest was the Communist Party, with 100 seats. Doris L. Bergen, *War and Genocide: A Concise History of the Holocaust* (Lanham, Md.: Rowman and Littlefield, 2002), p. 50. These numbers also help explain why Hitler's first political target was the Communists.

4. A key event was the February 27, 1933, Reichstag fire. Hitler seized on the mood of panic to attack the Communists by law and in the streets and thus consolidate his power on the German right. This was quickly followed by legislation (the Enabling Law of March 23, 1933), which "allowed Hitler to put through any measure without approval from the Reichstag. . . . In effect the Reichstag was now defunct; its own members had voted it out of existence." Bergen, *War and Genocide*, p. 55.

establish the Gestapo (secret police), torture and sometimes kill political dissidents, restrict democratic liberties such as freedom of the press and freedom of assembly, corrupt the criminal justice system and destroy an independent judiciary, and rule by decree. One might say that his initial destruction of democracy and the rule of law was not a violation of life's sacredness in itself but was one of the essential preconditions for other violations. We have seen this theme before.

Hitler brought with him to power a massive nongovernmental street army (the SA [*Sturm Abteilung*], founded in 1921 and with 2.5 million men by 1934)[5] that had terrorized Jews, Communists, and other enemies of the Nazis during the 1920s and early 1930s and continued to do so with Hitler's support when he came to power in 1933. This established the precedent that street violence against anyone deemed a threat or enemy would go unpunished; indeed, it eventually would become official governmental activity as the SA was folded into the Nazi state. Because Hitler did not have full control over this street army, differed with its leader Ernst Röhm on some policy matters, and found Röhm a threat to his absolute power, he eventually ordered Röhm and others killed off in a lawless, bloody purge in mid-1934.[6] In place of the SA he expanded his private militia, the SS *(Schutzstaffel),* into an even more deadly paramilitary force, which replaced thuggish "street violence" with a far more coldly calculating approach and eventually became the elite strike force of his government.

Hitler built upon and inflamed (though he did not create) attitudes of contempt for social outsiders. The premier target was the Jews, but social outsiders included other marginalized or disdained groups such as political dissidents, petty criminals, social nonconformists, religious sects like the Jehovah's Witnesses, Sinti and Roma (Gypsies), naturalized citizens and immigrants from other lands, people of mixed race backgrounds such as Afro-Germans, the handicapped and mentally ill, sexual outsiders such as homosexuals, and juvenile delinquents.[7] His regime's propaganda, together with his own sneering contempt as expressed in his powerful and

5. Bergen, *War and Genocide,* p. 70.

6. "The Night of the Long Knives" killed hundreds or even thousands, including some by mistake. It was actually applauded as a step toward law and order by Hindenburg and others. The significance of this step itself should not be underestimated.

7. For this list and a helpful discussion, see Robert Gellately, *Backing Hitler: Consent and Coercion in Nazi Germany* (Oxford and New York: Oxford University Press, 2001), and Bergen, *War and Genocide,* pp. 56ff. Bergen estimates that there were 20,000 Jehovah's Witnesses, 35,000 Gypsies, 385 Afro-Germans, and 500,000 Jews when Hitler's reign of terror began.

passionate speeches, created a dehumanizing, hateful, and inflammatory insider/outsider social climate in Germany and everywhere this spirit penetrated around the world.[8] (Political hate speech is itself a sacredness-of-life issue.)[9] Each of these groups was eventually targeted for harassment, persecution, exclusion, expulsion, and worse during the Hitler years. Hitler moved cautiously at first, targeting the most hated, feared, and stigmatized groups initially and then, when he encountered little social resistance, moving to other groups and more radical forms of persecution. According to Doris Bergen, the very first group targeted for social ostracism as well as legal and street harassment after January 30, 1933, was Germany's homosexual community, a vulnerable and easily ostracized target, and not just in 1933 Germany.[10]

Hitler created a state where participation, citizenship, and rights were based primarily on race, and secondarily on political conformity. The primary but not exclusive objective of the race-based classification system the Nazis created was to exclude Germany's 500,000 "Jews" and other "non-Aryans"[11] from membership in society — to move them from citizens to

8. One especially acute contemporary observer of this phenomenon was Elisabeth Schmitz, a thoughtful Christian scholar/teacher whose profound written appeals for Germany's evangelical leaders to speak out more forcefully have surfaced in recent years. Schmitz wrote to church leaders in September 1935: "For more than two years, in the name of blood and race, the atmosphere in Germany has been incessantly poisoned by hatred, lies, slander, and defamations of the lowest kind in speeches, appeals, magazines and the daily press, all in order to mold citizens into willing tools of the persecution." Elisabeth Schmitz, "On the Predicament of the Non-Aryans," September 1935, unpublished document provided to me by Steven Martin, producer of "Elisabeth of Berlin" (Vital Visuals, 2008). Consider, for example, the impact of the following kind of speech from the nation's chief press officer. Speaking of the Jews in 1937, Joseph Goebbels proclaimed before a national audience: "Look, this is the enemy of the world, the destroyer of cultures, the parasite among the nations, the son of chaos, the incarnation of evil, the ferment of decomposition, the visible demon on the decay of humanity." Quoted in Peter Fritzsche, *Life and Death in the Third Reich* (Cambridge: Harvard University Press, Belknap Press, 2008), p. 131.

9. I think of how dehumanizing rhetoric so often precedes violence, whether on a small scale as in the U.S. culture wars or on a massive scale as in the genocide in Rwanda.

10. Bergen, *War and Genocide*, p. 57.

11. There were many different types of "non-Aryans." Consider, for example, the memoir of Hans J. Massaquoi, who grew up black (he was the son of an African diplomat and a white German nurse) in Nazi Germany and experienced a parallel process of social marginalization in a society that became obsessed by race. Others of black skin in Germany at the time primarily were found in the Rhineland; these were the children of Belgian and French colonial occupation troops from World War I and thereafter. Some of these Afro-Germans were murdered in Nazi death camps. See Hans J. Massaquoi, *Destined to Witness:*

aliens and finally from aliens to elimination. It was a project of systematic social exclusion that extended to every dimension of life — including excluding non-Aryans from voluntary associations and from public or military service, and denying them participation in the professions and the economy, citizenship status and its associated rights, and eventually any right to live in Germany. That project of exclusion after January 1933 became a society-wide endeavor, with leadership and innovation often coming from below rather than above, as leaders of every type of social and professional group in Germany raced to be the first and most creative to reject Jews and other outsiders.[12] Let us declare a principle here that extends far beyond Nazi Germany: once it is "open season" on any outcast social group in a society, the preferred groups collectively, and many individuals, will quickly join in on the fun and take advantage of their neighbors' powerlessness.[13]

In terms of citizenship, from 1933 forward the Nazi state shifted the basis of German citizenship to an imagined ethnic one, while also simply disenfranchising those deemed politically disloyal. In September 1935 the Jews of Germany and other "non-Aryans"[14] were deprived officially of their citizenship under the Nuremberg Laws, becoming stateless resident aliens in a land they had once fully called home.[15] This was an essential prelude for later persecutions.

Hitler and his party also pursued a eugenicist vision — again he radicalized earlier versions, including some that had been pursued in the United States, to our shame — that ultimately corrupted the practice of medicine in Germany, drawing the helping and healing professions into crimes against human dignity and humanity itself. The goals of this eugenicist vi-

---

Growing Up Black in Nazi Germany (New York: Morrow, 1999). Note that the very term "non-Aryan" is ridiculous, reflecting a vicious and discredited racial theory. One almost needs to put quotation marks around nearly every phrase the Nazis used.

12. For one account of this process, see Konrad H. Jarausch, "The Conundrum of Complicity: German Professionals and the Final Solution" (United States Holocaust Memorial Museum, 2002).

13. Cf. Bergen, *War and Genocide,* p. 60, for the phrase "open season."

14. The Gypsies, for example, were defined by later implementing regulations after the Nuremberg Laws as "alien to the Aryan species" and persecuted/prosecuted accordingly. The language of *species* there is quite significant for a study of the sacredness of each and every human life. Bergen, *War and Genocide,* p. 75.

15. See Diemut Majer, *"Non-Germans" under the Third Reich: The Nazi Judicial and Administrative System in Germany and Occupied Eastern Europe, with Special Regard to Occupied Poland, 1939-1945* (Baltimore: Johns Hopkins University Press, 2003).

sion included enhancing the number of "racially desirable" German citizens, suppressing "race mixing," and discouraging reproduction among those deemed genetically undesirable. This project was undertaken through a variety of means, beginning with a July 1933 law prescribing involuntary sterilization of a large number of groups deemed biologically impure or harmful to the building of the Aryan master race. The targeted groups included those with significant mental illness, retardation, physical deformity, blindness and deafness, epilepsy, and even alcoholism. Targets also included "asocial" persons, which meant by definition those arrested for all kinds of crimes and therefore proclaimed likely to pass on to their offspring "serious hereditary defects of a physical or mental nature."[16] This law provided the eventual basis for a systematic effort to sterilize members of the Sinti and Roma because they were believed to be "asocial" as a people. The tiny Afro-German population was also targeted for sterilization; many were involuntarily sterilized in 1937.[17] A little-known 1935 law "required any pregnant woman who should have been sterilized under the 1933 law but had not been to have an abortion."[18] So this eugenicist program included not only forced sterilization but also forced abortion. Eventually some 250,000 Germans were involuntarily sterilized in a campaign that lasted as long as the Nazi regime and undoubtedly would have continued and expanded long into a Nazi future.[19] As of 1935, Nazi law also banned any sexual relations between Aryans and members of other, "inferior" races, while Nazi-influenced social norms led Germans to shame and stigmatize anyone even suspected of such relations.[20] This eugenicist vision also included efforts to encourage, assist, reward, and honor the "biologically fit" who chose to have large families.[21]

16. Quoted in J. Noakes and G. Pridham, eds., *Nazism: A History in Documents and Eyewitness Accounts*, vol. 1 (New York: Schocken, 1983), pp. 457-58.

17. Bergen, *War and Genocide*, p. 58.

18. Bergen, *War and Genocide*, p. 75. Bergen notes the chilling implications of this law in terms of the overall impact on health care for anyone deemed racially undesirable. Why should doctors treat patients whom the society has declared racially undesirable?

19. Bergen, *War and Genocide*, p. 63. This 250,000 amounted to 0.5 percent of the German population. Interior Minister Wilhelm Frick suggested the proper proportion should be about 20 percent. There was plenty of work still to do to implement the insane Nazi vision. Understanding this regime requires getting a sense of how vast and radical their vision was and how much more they still believed they had to do.

20. See Fritzsche, *Life and Death*, chapter 2.

21. Fellow Holocaust scholar Timothy Crawford of University of Mary Hardin Baylor has shown me his vintage collection of medals awarded to (racially desirable) German

On November 9-10, 1938, Nazi forces attacked the Jewish communities of Germany and Austria in "response" to the shooting of a German diplomat by an aggrieved Jewish teenager in Paris. On *Kristallnacht*, the "Night of Broken Glass," Nazis crossed a major threshold in their assaults on the Jewish people in Germany, Austria, and elsewhere by unleashing quasi-official mobs that desecrated and burned down over 1,000 Jewish synagogues and burned down 7,500 businesses, broke into Jewish homes to pillage and destroy Jewish property, killed 100 Jews, and imprisoned well over 20,000 Jewish men in concentration camps.[22] This desecration of Jewish life and property, followed by the cruelly ridiculous "fining" (e.g., expropriation and plundering) of the German Jewish community to pay for the damages, was a major milestone in the path to the Holocaust, and marked another key moment in the spreading moral degradation of German society. The inhumanity and cruelty of this event can hardly be imagined. It is helpful to focus on little-noticed facts that give a real glimpse into what that night was like: the Nazis assembled the Jewish communities to tell them why they must suffer for their crimes, and then forced them to watch their synagogues burn to the ground; at one synagogue in Germany, which I visited, the Nazis tied a pig to the chandelier and then shot it, so that it bled all over the floor of the synagogue and desecrated it.

One must not forget the wide complicity of the German public in this event, which can stand as a reminder that Hitler's crimes were poisonously seductive and were usually not his alone. Christian laywoman Elisabeth Schmitz, a careful observer, penned an indignant letter to her pastor Helmut Gollwitzer less than one week after *Kristallnacht*. She wrote:

> People of all ages and at all levels of society took part in the looting. Yesterday a friend of mine overheard a general conversation on a streetcar about the fact that people were saying they couldn't get the proper shoe sizes. Young girls were being asked where they had suddenly come by their fur coats. . . . A young man was standing at a shop window offering stockings according to size. Near another window a Hitler Youth was

---

mothers for their output of good Nazi racial stock. Highest honors went to those women having eight or more children. The *Lebensborn* program in the SS was one expression of this impulse.

22. Richard L. Rubenstein and John K. Roth, *Approaches to Auschwitz: The Holocaust and Its Legacy*, rev. ed. (Louisville: Westminster John Knox, 2003), p. 132. Doris Bergen puts the number at 26,000. Bergen, *War and Genocide*, p. 88.

handing out gold watches. . . . British newspapers write that this is the biggest pogrom in the history of the world.[23]

On September 1, 1939, Nazi Germany rolled into Poland on a faux provocation and initiated World War II. After the launch of the war, Nazi crimes against humanity and life's sacredness expanded exponentially. I will try to name the most important ones.

Hitler's forces waged a war of aggression throughout the continent of Europe, as well as in Africa and the Middle East. The war was fought with somewhat fewer atrocities in western Europe than in the east, though in the west bombing attacks on civilian population centers were plentiful. (The Allied forces later also bombed German population centers; there were huge civilian casualties on both sides.) Other German crimes in the west beginning in 1940 included summary executions in occupied lands, constant economic exploitation, theft, destruction, collective reprisals for suspected partisan or resistance activity, and the dragooning of millions for a massive program of forced labor in the German Reich that eventually took 7.5 million unwilling slaves.

Hitler's assault on Poland in 1939 was accompanied by even greater crimes. This invasion included an intentional effort to decapitate Polish society through mass executions of political, religious, and intellectual leaders as well as the installation of a regime of terror, mass rape, mass imprisonment, forced labor, and utter domination of the entire Polish population. This was based partly on belief in the intrinsic inferiority of the Poles and partly on the desire to destroy the Polish nation (and national identity) and expand German territory to the east for more *Lebensraum* (living space) for the German people, which had always been a key foreign policy goal for Hitler. An estimated 3 million Polish civilians were murdered during the war.[24] The country was utterly brutalized — by the Germans from the west and also by the Soviets from the east, the latter given carte blanche to take half of Poland by the secret Hitler-Stalin Pact of August 1939. Following the invasion, numerous atrocities against western Poland's massive Jewish community were also committed, though (through mid-1941 at least) this was undertaken on an "open season" paradigm rather than on a more coldly systematic basis.

23. Schmitz to Gollwitzer, November 15, 1938, unpublished letter provided to me by Steven Martin.

24. Bergen, *War and Genocide*, p. 119, reminds us that the 3 million civilian deaths include casualties at Soviet hands, and not just Nazi hands.

Having gained Soviet compliance and complicity, Hitler also attempted to redraw the map of the region according to a mad vision that can only be described as imperialist-nationalist-racist-colonialist. In Poland, this involved simply incorporating large parts of the occupied land into the Greater German Reich, which had previously swelled to include Austria and much of what was once Czechoslovakia. This new addition of Polish territory comprised 10 million people, 80 percent of whom were ethnic Poles.[25] The area was then to be relentlessly "Germanized." This program included confiscation and use of Polish industry and much of the property of Poles and Jews; deportation of able-bodied Polish workers from their homes and families and into Germany in order to suppress Polish population growth; assimilation/Germanization of those remaining locals deemed to be moldable into loyal National Socialists; the resettlement of thousands of Germans into the incorporated areas, essentially as colonizers; and the deportation of hundreds of thousands of Jews and Poles, in view of their envisioned later demise, to the unincorporated area known as the General Government.[26] This massive colonization/"ethnic cleansing" campaign brought chaos, misery, dislocation, and death to millions. The General Government became a vast temporary dumping ground for unwanted peoples, with no provision made for accommodating such a massive population influx and constant, random enslavement, brutality, and killing there.

The provisional solution for the Jews in particular was ghettoization. The ghettos were sections of major cities in the General Government such as Warsaw and Lodz into which millions of Jews were crowded. Some 500,000 Jews died from 1939 to 1941 in these ghettos and associated labor camps, mainly from forced labor and disease but also from daily murders.[27] Later these ghettos became staging areas from which survivors were shipped to Nazi death camps. The Nazis actually sent German tourists to look upon the misery of some of these ghettos "so that members of the supposed master race could see the degeneracy of their alleged inferiors."[28]

The ultimate plan in the east, if the Nazis had won the war, would have

---

25. Bergen, *War and Genocide*, p. 101.

26. "Nazi Conspiracy and Aggression, Volume 1, Chapter XIII — Germanization and Spoliation," *The Avalon Project: Documents in Law, History, and Diplomacy,* Yale Law School Lillian Goldman Law Library; http://avalon.law.yale.edu/imt/chap_13.asp, accessed April 30, 2011.

27. Bergen, *War and Genocide*, p. 111.

28. Bergen, *War and Genocide*, p. 112.

been a Nazi New Order expanding exponentially on this initial start. In what was called General Plan East, the Nazis comfortably imagined the decimation and enslavement of millions of Slavic peoples and an eastward expansion and colonization as far as the Ural Mountains in a vast Aryan Empire. One aspect of this plan, which was in fact begun, was a program in which Aryan-looking or "Aryanizable" children would be kidnapped from their racially inferior parents to be transformed into Germans as part of an expanded, territory-grabbing German Reich.[29] This was another Nazi project that would have taken decades if not centuries to accomplish.

The Nazi regime also murdered as many as 275,000 handicapped or disabled people, beginning with well over 100,000 of its own citizens,[30] in a half-secret "euthanasia" campaign envisioned by Hitler early in his regime and initiated with children and then adults even before World War II began. This program, a similar version of which was actually proposed in print by distinguished German jurist Karl Binding and leading psychiatrist Alfred Hoche in 1920, targeted the mentally ill, those institutionalized with various disabilities and handicaps, and others who were considered "lives unworthy of living," "useless eaters," and "human ballast."[31] These were actual phrases used by Nazis. To carry out this plan once the war began, the Nazi regime secretly developed a medical review process in which physicians and nurses used a form (not even a personal visit to the patient/victim) to evaluate the continued value of these lives over against the supposed interests of the state.[32] It was in this medicalized killing campaign (which also sometimes involved medical experimentation) that the Nazis first developed the procedures and techniques later used on the eastern front, including "selection" by physicians for life or death, and then death by starvation or gassing.[33]

Scholars are now clear that the biomedical vision that informed this program, as well as the techniques, the facilities, and many of the key personnel, was sent to the eastern front and became central to the annihilationist program against the Jews and other targeted groups. This included

29. Bergen, *War and Genocide*, pp. 163-64.

30. Bergen, *War and Genocide*, p. 129. This program did create considerable backlash in Germany, including on grounds of the sanctity of human life. Christian leaders like Catholic Cardinal August Count von Galen offered vocal protests.

31. The book was entitled, chillingly: *Permission for the Destruction of Worthless Life, Its Extent and Form.*

32. Bergen, *War and Genocide*, p. 99.

33. Bergen, *War and Genocide*, p. 127.

handicapped and institutionalized people there, most of which were simply gunned down in cold blood when the German soldiers arrived in town.[34] The logic went like this: if Germany's own handicapped are "useless eaters" whom we are euthanizing to prevent them from consuming scarce resources better reserved for others, surely this must be all the more true of the ultimate useless eaters, such as the Jews and Gypsies. It is not a stretch to say that what *we* now call the Holocaust, the Nazis considered a vast public health campaign under the supervision of doctors. Robert Jay Lifton put it this way: "At the heart of the Nazi enterprise . . . is the destruction of the boundary between healing and killing."[35]

The wartime domestic front also saw intensified targeting of other "outsider" populations. A steady stream of political prisoners, nonconformists, and those believed to be asocial deviants continued to flow into Gestapo prisons and SS concentration camps throughout the war, almost all of whom were mistreated and many murdered. Religious dissidents such as Jehovah's Witnesses, student protesters such as members of the White Rose "conspiracy" of 1943, homosexuals, Protestant and Catholic clergy raising religious or ethical questions about regime behavior, and anyone else who offered a challenge or threat to Nazi policies were at risk of imprisonment, torture, and death. Over the course of the war the Nazi state began to chew up a larger and larger part of its own population, as the miseries the Nazi regime had perpetrated on other peoples began to be inflicted on their own citizenry with greater frequency. Eventually, "all lives [became] cheap, including those of the German people."[36]

On June 22, 1941, in Operation Barbarossa (notably, named for a medieval German Crusader), Hitler broke his cynical nonaggression pact with the USSR and declared war against that nation. Planning documents surviving from that period demonstrate the regime's explicit instructions

34. Henry Friedlander, *The Origins of Nazi Genocide: From Euthanasia to the Final Solution* (Chapel Hill: University of North Carolina Press, 1997). Friedlander is a leader in tracing the ideological and practical connections between the Nazi euthanasia program and the later mass murder campaigns on the eastern front. On the practical side, similar selection and killing techniques involving the perversion of the medical profession were employed. On the ideological side, both the killings of the handicapped and of Jews and Gypsies were based on belief in the absolute worthlessness of the groups killed and thus the cleansing benefits of these killings to Germany and the world.

35. Robert Jay Lifton, *The Nazi Doctors: Medical Killing and the Psychology of Genocide* (New York: Basic Books, 1986), p. 14.

36. Bergen, *War and Genocide*, p. 217. The war eventually took the lives of 4.3 million Germans.

to ignore all restraints imposed on warfare in custom and law and to wage a ruthless and untrammeled attack against the Soviet Union — not just its soldiers, but also its society. This was the attack against whose backdrop Dietrich Bonhoeffer wrote his "Heritage and Decay" essay in the *Ethics* (chapter 4). Though there is much competition for this prize, documents associated with Barbarossa may offer the most explicit negation of human dignity anywhere among the surviving Nazi policy texts.[37] Hitler explicitly described this conflict as a war to the death between Germany and the USSR (and between National Socialism and Communism). He commanded his military and associated special killing squads and police units to kill ruthlessly and without restraint, and ordered the deaths not just of enemy soldiers but also of enemy political leaders ("commissars"), saboteurs, Jews (e.g., "Jewish subhumans"),[38] and anyone who might pose a threat to the Nazi conduct of the war. Especially given that Communism was defined as a Jewish invention, and thus to kill Jews was (absurdly) also to attack Communism, the attack on the USSR was pivotally important as a path to the Holocaust.

Hitler's overall crimes against Soviet civilians were numerous and grotesque. Doris Bergen estimates that 27 million Soviet citizens were killed — including 3.3 million Soviet POWs, out of 5.7 million captured by the Germans.[39] One must also consider the horrible volume of casualties in military engagements like the Battle of Stalingrad, which numbered 1.1 million on the Soviet side and 1.5 million on the German side.[40] It is hard to overstate the traumatizing impact of this bloodshed and carnage on the Soviet Union and its people.

But the Soviet Union was not the only brutalized nation. Events in what was once known as Yugoslavia rank near the top of the list of Nazi crimes. Nazi Germany invaded Yugoslavia in April 1941, dismembering that ethnic/religious tinderbox into an annexed territory to be added to Greater Germany, a Croatian puppet state under a brutal fascist leader, and a military government in occupied Serbia. Germans and Croatian fascists (the

---

37. André Mineau, *Operation Barbarossa: Ideology and Ethics against Human Dignity* (Amsterdam: Rodopi, 2004). As the title indicates, this book specifically connects the war against the USSR with the Nazi rejection of human dignity, and is therefore central to our project in this volume.

38. Bergen, *War and Genocide*, p. 153, quoting Field Marshal Walter von Reichenau.

39. Bergen, *War and Genocide*, pp. 145, 157.

40. Chris Bellamy, *Absolute War: Soviet Russia in the Second World War* (New York: Vintage Books, 2007), p. 550.

Ustashe) together committed every kind of brutality, especially against Serbs, who died in the hundreds of thousands, but also against Jews, Gypsies, and every other familiar enemy. Though after the war Yugoslavia was stitched back together under its own murderous dictator Tito, the brutalities of the war years remained fresh and unresolved for decades. This helps explain the background to the genocidal crimes committed by Serbian nationalist leader Slobodan Milošević and his henchmen against Croats, Bosnians, and others, as well as the (re)dissolving of Yugoslavia once again in the 1990s, with at least 100,000 civilian victims.[41]

Hitler's regime decided, apparently in the fall of 1941, though the exact date is disputed, to launch a campaign of total annihilation against the Jews of Europe. The dating is somewhat difficult because from the beginning of the war, Nazi forces had killed Jews regularly, and we just saw that after the invasion of the USSR, Nazi killing squads were established specifically to "combat Bolshevism and prevent guerrilla warfare," which meant, among other things, killing Jews.[42] On the eastern front, first Jewish men only were killed, then eventually the floodgates opened as soldiers, mobile killing squads, Order Police units, and others began killing everyone they could find in the numerous Jewish villages, settlements, and ghettos in eastern Poland, Ukraine, Belarussia, the Baltics, and western Russia. These mass shootings killed at least 1.3 million Jews and 250,000 Gypsies after the June 1941 invasion.[43]

The basic outlines of the broader continent-wide plan to kill Europe's Jews (e.g., "The Final Solution to the Jewish Question") are apparent in the breathtaking, even though sanitized, minutes of the Wannsee Conference. This was a top-secret gathering of fifteen senior German leaders held outside Berlin on January 20, 1942. After reviewing the successes and failures of measures taken to resolve the Jewish question to that point, these minutes describe a new plan: to "comb through" Europe from west to east for Jews, then to "evacuate" them to the east. On arrival, the "able-bodied" would be used for "appropriate labor . . . in the course of which action

---

41. See Peter Maass, *Love Thy Neighbor: A Story of War* (New York: Knopf, 1996). I traveled in Croatia, Bosnia, and Serbia early in the decade 2000-2009 and witnessed the personal and physical damage of this conflict.

42. Bergen, *War and Genocide,* p. 149.

43. The numbers are from Bergen, *War and Genocide,* p. 152. One of the most illuminating accounts of these eastern front shootings is offered by Christopher R. Browning, *Ordinary Men: Reserve Police Battalion 101 and the Final Solution in Poland* (New York: HarperCollins, 1992).

doubtless a large portion will be eliminated by natural causes." The "possible final remnant" somehow surviving this "appropriate labor" would have to be dealt with "accordingly," for after all, "it is the product of natural selection and would, if released, act as the seed of a new Jewish revival."[44] There is no mention of the non-able-bodied. We know what happened to them — they were never given the chance to work, but were killed upon arrival. So that was the plan: immediate death for those judged unable to work; forced labor for the rest, leading to mass death by attrition; and then finally the murder of what few hardy survivors might remain.

According to the testimony of Adolf Eichmann at his trial in Israel in 1961-1962, the leaders at the meeting — guided by the ruthless SS figure Reinhard Heydrich, top subordinate to SS Reich Marshal Heinrich Himmler — actually talked openly about how to undertake this total annihilation of the Jewish people in the most efficient manner possible. Men were present at the meeting who already had participated in the mass shootings in the east. The details of their accounts and the new plans were not included in the minutes. But this was the meeting that confirmed that it was preferable to adopt a strategy of taking the victims to the killers to die by labor and gas, rather than taking the killers to the victims for mass shootings.[45] The "Final Solution to the Jewish Question" would now involve the arrest and transit of every remaining European Jew by rail line to a reconfigured camp system, necessitating the construction of six specially equipped killing facilities using industrial-scale gas chambers and crematoria to dispose of the bodies. From early 1942 until the war turned against them, the Nazis dramatically expanded their concentration camp system into a death-camp-plus-concentration-camp system. Jews were indeed rounded up from all over Europe and shipped east to death camps, the most infamous of which was Auschwitz, outside Cracow. This new strategy ended up successfully murdering approximately 3 million Jews.

And so, by the time of the Nazi defeat in May 1945, a total of nearly 6 million Jews from dozens of countries had been starved, worked, tortured, shot, burned, or gassed to death, including over 1 million children. This was approximately two-thirds of all the Jews in Europe in 1939, one-

---

44. "In the course of the practical execution of the final solution, Europe will be combed through from west to east. Germany proper, including the Protectorate of Bohemia and Moravia, will have to be handled first due to the housing problem and additional social and political necessities." Direct quotation of Wannsee minutes, accessed at http://www.historyplace.com/worldwar2/holocaust/h-wannsee.htm, April 28, 2011.

45. Bergen, *War and Genocide*, p. 159.

third of all the Jews in the world. European Jewish civilization has never recovered. It survives mainly as a museum and a graveyard, with flickers of life at best. The trauma inflicted on the Jewish people continues to affect both Jews and the world on a daily basis.

The Nazis also decided to exterminate the Sinti and Roma peoples. This attempted genocide is far less well-known, but similar strategies were deployed for a similar annihilationist goal involving some of the same German personnel, including the infamous Adolf Eichmann, who testified to his role at his trial; and it is certainly known that Gypsies perished in large numbers at the death camp Auschwitz and elsewhere. My best estimate is that 500,000 Gypsies were killed, approximately two-thirds of the prewar Sinti and Roma population of Europe — the same percentage as with Jewish losses.[46] It is fair to say that both Jews and Gypsies, and only Jews and Gypsies, were targeted for *total* extermination, as if in an attempt to kill every single cockroach in a house — for that is how they were viewed by the Nazis.

The vast Nazi camp system, considered in its entirety, constituted an anticivilization through which as many as 18 million human souls eventually passed, 11 million of whom died.[47] This camp world became a demonic universe of forced labor, starvation, physical and mental torture, cruel medical experiments, sexual humiliation, rape, assault, sadism, and mass killing. Whether imprisoned for racial, political, or other reasons, Nazi victims were systematically denied the most basic humane treatment; indeed, the camps became laboratories of cruelty against vast powerless populations. After stealing the property of their victims, the Nazis then dehumanized, desecrated, branded, starved, froze, tortured, and killed their bodies, burned them in crematoria, and dumped them in pits as nameless ashes and bone fragments. Despite the written accounts of thousands of survivors and a number of perpetrators, the sheer evil represented by these camps remains incomprehensible, like the world's worst nightmare — and it was real, all too real.[48]

46. See David P. Gushee and Sheri B. Lovett, "The *Porraimos:* Toward the Reclamation of the Gypsy Experience of the Holocaust" (paper presented at 1999 Scholars' Conference on the Holocaust). Note that within the Sinti and Roma communities the events of World War II have their own name and associated scholarship.

47. Bergen, *War and Genocide,* p. 186.

48. Among the accounts that all educated people should read: Elie Wiesel, *Night,* rev. ed. (New York: Hill and Wang, 2006); Primo Levi, *Survival in Auschwitz* (New York: Collier, 1961).

The total death toll for which Adolf Hitler and his regime are responsible — if we count everyone who died because of the war that the Nazis started — was approximately 55 million. But something else died during those years. Humanity died. For many, God died. Certainly the sacredness of life died, or nearly died. Historian Doris Bergen, writing of the murder of the German handicapped but with implications far beyond that particular crime, put it this way: "Nazi planners measured the value of a human life by its contribution to the national community, not by some inherent worth."[49] There is good reason why the Nazi regime, which collapsed in fire and ashes in May 1945, will live in infamy throughout human history as one of the world's most murderous tyrannies, and one of the ultimate collective negations of the sacred value of human life.

9.2. How They Got There: The Nazi Party Platform of 1920

I said at the beginning of this chapter that we needed to understand both what Hitler did and why he did it. Again, I am using "Hitler" here also to stand in for the party he came to lead and the policies his regime imagined and his people implemented.[50] For this reason, it seems appropriate to look at examples of both party documents and personal writings and declarations when trying to reach into the critical question of how he ended up doing what he did.

For Hitler and the Nazis, we have a very convenient starting point in the still-extant 1920 Nazi Party Platform.[51] This twenty-five-point document from the very earliest days of the then-tiny Nazi Party tells us a great deal about what these men believed and dreamed of doing. Unlike most party platforms, though there is considerable boilerplate language, it appears that the Nazis genuinely intended to keep their promises.[52] In Elie

---

49. Bergen, *War and Genocide*, p. 126.

50. While I do not accept the thesis that Germans as a whole were "Hitler's willing executioners," as in the thesis offered by Daniel Jonah Goldhagen, it is important even in a study focused on Hitler and his party to recall that his policies required many implementers and many more complicit bystanders. See Daniel Jonah Goldhagen, *Hitler's Willing Executioners: Ordinary Germans and the Holocaust* (New York: Knopf, 1996).

51. http://users.stlcc.edu/rkalfus/PDFs/026.pdf, accessed April 17, 2011.

52. German church historian Andrea Strübind suggested to me that party platforms in that era often contained similar formulations stated in a particular order. Thus, for example, though we will see that the Nazi platform leads with nationalism, Strübind argues that Hit-

Wiesel's classic memoir of the Holocaust, an exhausted Jewish concentration camp inmate is quoted as saying bitterly: "I have more faith in Hitler than anyone else. He alone has kept his promises, all his promises, to the Jewish people."[53] I suggest that the 1920 Nazi Party Platform text is the first document in which he and his party made some of those promises. I will use it as my organizing framework for understanding the twisted vision that led to the catastrophic outcomes we have just surveyed. We will look at several of the key articles and their implications, both for Hitler's violations of life's sacredness and as lessons for those of us committed to the sacredness of each and every life today.

9.3. Aggrieved Nationalism

> Article 1. We demand the uniting of all Germans within one Greater Germany, on the basis of the right to self-determination of nations.

> Article 2. We demand equal rights for the German people (*Volk*) with respect to other nations, and the annulment of the Peace Treaty of Versailles and St. Germain.

Nazism was above all an ideology of extreme *nationalism*. It was a kind of ultrapatriotism in which love of fatherland was taken to its most logical and terrifying extreme. Patriots, people who love their countries, are not unusual, nor are they to be condemned. People who love their countries so radically that they come to dismiss the interests, rights, or needs of people of other nations are a different kind of thing altogether. Nazism was this kind of nationalism; it was murderous, genocidal nationalism.

Notice that Article 1 from the outset defines the moral basis of the party's agenda to be *national self-determination*. This, of course, was not a Nazi idea but was the prevailing vision of Woodrow Wilson and others and became the basis of the world order envisioned after World War I.[54] It remains an essential part of international law. The principle of self-determination is that peoples, or ethnic-national communities, have a right to live together in a

---

ler's ideology led with racism, anti-Semitism, and social Darwinism. I am grateful to Dr. Strübind for her input on this chapter.

53. Wiesel, *Night*, p. 81.
54. http://www.mtholyoke.edu/acad/intrel/freeman.htm, accessed April 30, 2011.

nation-state and determine their own future together, rather than having their future determined by subjugating powers. This national "right" to self-determination became especially problematic in post–World War I Europe because history's forces had scattered the various ethnic-linguistic-national groups across much of the continent, and state boundaries had shifted after various wars. The postwar settlement appeared to grant self-determination for some peoples at the expense of others. The Nazis here essentially attempted to claim national self-determination as their own agenda and to suggest that Germany's self-determination had been violated by the terms of the Versailles Treaty.

Article 1 also helps us understand that the Nazis were not just looking for German self-determination. Their agenda extended to a kind of nationalist *pan-Germanism,* an idea whose roots can also be traced to the nineteenth century. The belief was not just that German-speaking people or those who identify as ethnic "Germans" should be able to have a homeland, but that all Germans should be able to live together in a territorially expanded "Greater Germany." This clearly signaled Nazi dissatisfaction with the territorial settlement after World War I, and their intent to press for a larger Germany that could encompass sizable German-speaking populations throughout Europe. This was precisely the program undertaken by the Nazis when they reclaimed western Germany from the French, annexed Austria, intimidated the world into surrendering the Czech Sudetenland, and annexed parts of Poland after conquering it by force. Slobodan Milošević operated on a similar pan-Serbian vision during his reign of terror in the 1990s, and that itself bears at least a genetic resemblance to an earlier pan-Slavism. Rulers interested in reopening border questions and expanding their territories in the name of pan-ethnic ideologies are very dangerous.

Article 2 clearly reveals that this was not just pan-German nationalism but an *aggrieved nationalism.* The document clearly reveals the bruised feelings of many Germans, and not just Nazis, in the wake of World War I and the terms imposed by the Versailles Treaty. Whether Germans were in fact mistreated by that treaty remains a matter of fierce debate. That they believed themselves to be mistreated is not up for debate. Doris Bergen argues that Germany "cultivated a politics of resentment that promoted a bitter sense of humiliation and poisoned the chances for the new German democracy formed in 1918."[55] Fritz Stern wrote famously of the toxic poli-

---

55. Bergen, *War and Genocide,* p. 27.

tics of cultural despair, and his book is a stern warning against ideologies built on reaction and resentment. They can overwhelm crucial checks and balances that are needed for maintaining justice and can lead to authoritarian takeover and violent mistreatment of minorities.[56] Once in power, the Nazis expressed this despairing, aggrieved national rage not just by claiming "equal rights" but by rushing past the correction of whatever wrongs were perceived and waging aggressive war against nations and peoples all across Europe and the world.

In terms of the sacredness of life, Nazism reminds us of the great dangers associated with nationalism, and even with patriotism — especially when combined with resentment over perceived injustice, dishonor, or loss. Human communities are easily tempted to override the moral restraints imposed by belief in human rights or the sacredness of every life when wounded and angry national pride is on the march. On a far smaller scale, one is reminded of excesses in U.S. detainee policies after 9/11, and the continued threat of anti-Muslim xenophobia in our land. Some observers, including some Christian thinkers, believe that the only proper response to such realities is to abandon not only every kind of nationalism but also any kind of patriotism, any distinctive love of homeland and people. I believe that a critical patriotism, in which love of country includes love of God and love of people as sacred in God's sight, and includes disciplines of justice and shared responsibilities for the human rights of all people, better reflects the nature of human beings and better serves the well-being of human communities in the world we actually live in. But any such critical patriotism must have among its first characteristics an unflinching willingness to resist loudly and clearly any time one's beloved nation edges toward violating the sanctity of human life, especially in moments of national anger, grief, and fear.

9.4. Imperialism and Colonialism

> Article 3. We demand land and soil (Colonies) to feed our People and settle our excess population.

It has often been noted that Germany entered the *imperialism* and *colonialism* game relatively late, in part because Germany as a modern state

---

56. Fritz Stern, *The Politics of Cultural Despair: A Study in the Rise of the Germanic Ideology* (Berkeley and Los Angeles: University of California Press, 1961).

was not even born until 1871.[57] We have already explored some early, and also morally disastrous, expressions of European imperialism and colonialism with the fifteenth- and sixteenth-century conquests by the Portuguese and Spaniards. Germany was late to this game, but still, under Bismarck, Prussia did extend an empire across large parts of northern, central, and eastern Europe, claiming territory in which significant numbers of Poles, French, Danes, Lithuanians, Dutch, and others lived. The modern state of Germany was born in part from these imperial advances, but Germany was stripped of much of this territory as well as its overseas colonies after World War I. The Nazis harkened back to the glories of these days in much of their ideology and propaganda.

Article 3 helps us interpret Articles 1 and 2 as implicitly imperialistic. A Greater Germany would once again be territorially extensive and would include other peoples along with the ethnic Germans named in the first article. Having "equal rights" with other European powers implicitly means having the same access to empire that they did. Article 3, then, goes beyond a desire for imperial power to include an explicit colonial project of settling Germans in subjugated lands. The brief statement here signals that this would be both a "settler colonialism," in which "excess" Germans would move to the subjugated territories (not named in the actual article), and an "exploitation colonialism," in which resources would be taken to feed the German people. Neither was a new idea. But here the Nazis "demand" them as part of their basic program.

Adolf Hitler's *Mein Kampf* made clear as early as 1925 that his version of German colonialism was looking primarily to eastern Europe for colonial possibilities.[58] The Nazis never accepted the legitimacy of Poland, which was reconstituted after World War I in part due to the theory of national self-determination. Hitler treated Poland and other small eastern European peoples as vassals to Russia. The real fight was with Russia. So we can already see in this platform, and certainly in *Mein Kampf*, the seeds of what eventually happened — a Nazi colonialist war in the east that extended all the way to Russia, a fight to the finish. Those colonialist ambitions extended as far east as the Urals by the 1940s, and the envisioned sub-

57. These two terms are closely related but can be distinguished. I define "colonialism" here as the establishment of colonies by one people in the territory of another people for settlement and/or economic exploitation. "Imperialism" is the building of an empire through the military, political, economic, or cultural domination of subordinated states or peoples by another state or people.

58. Adolf Hitler, *Mein Kampf* (Boston: Houghton Mifflin, [1925] 1971), chapter 14.

jugated territories included large chunks of the Soviet Union. This was the dream the Nazis were following, and it is apparent in germinal form even in 1920.

After World War II, the moral legitimacy of imperialism and colonialism finally collapsed, in part because of the disastrous impact of both great wars of the century, and in part because of liberation movements in the global south. Peoples do not have any moral or legal right to conquer, subjugate, colonize, and exploit other peoples for their own purposes. Much of the history of the period after World War II involved the international delegitimizing and unwinding of colonialism around the world. This was most apparent in the collapse of British and French hegemony over numerous colonies. But imperial dreams never completely disappear, and empires can be economic ones when direct political rule is deemed inappropriate. Those concerned with the sacredness of life today need to attend to all forms of imperialism, colonialism, and neocolonialism, including that exercised by the United States.

9.5. Racism and Anti-Semitism

> Article 4. Only Nationals *(Volksgenossen)* can be Citizens of the State. Only persons of German blood can be Nationals, regardless of religious affiliation. No Jew can therefore be a German National.

From the beginning the intent was clear: for Nazis, the real Germany was constituted ethnically, according to race or "blood." Citizenship must be confined to those who belonged to the German people *(Volksgenossen)*, and the German people must be defined according to their "blood." This illusory *blood-racism* became the basis for an elaborate racial classification system to define who was fully, partly, or not at all "German." During the Nazi years many hundreds of bureaucrats penned many thousands of regulations in an effort to firm up such definitions, and it was a matter of serious governmental infighting. First employment, and eventually life or death, hinged on the results of the current interpretation of such questions as, for example, whether one was a *Mischling* (half-breed) of first or second degree.[59] How many drops of "Jewish" blood must one have to no longer

---

59. The Nuremberg Laws of 1935 defined a "full Jew" as anyone with three Jewish grandparents who had been enrolled in a Jewish religious community. A person with one or two

be a part of the German national community? Lengthy discussion of the matter actually appears in the minutes of the Wannsee Conference, the same meeting in which it was clarified that Germany would send properly defined Jews to the gas chambers from all over Europe.

"No Jew can therefore be a German National." Eventually Nazi policies and regulations turned against all kinds of people, including Gypsies and Afro-Germans, and the same logic eventually excluded them from national membership and subjected them to persecution. But the initial target, and the one explicitly named, was the Jews. Here a national political party platform targeted one particular group to deny them any share in German identity. From the beginning the Nazis rejected the ancient Christian paradigm of welcoming Jews into the family if they believe in Christ, and "only" casting their opprobrium on Jews who do not believe in Jesus. For the Nazis, blood was thicker than profession of faith, and whether a person in 1935 was a Jewish Christian mattered not at all. (Of course, by defining blood in terms of the religious affiliation of a Jew's grandparents, the definition was, let us say, stretched quite a bit.) Still, the language of Nazi propaganda was a language of blood and race. When we say that the Nazis targeted the "Jews" for annihilation, we are already speaking in Nazi terms unless we quickly speak of "those the Nazis defined as Jews."

A Jew could have dwelt as a productive citizen within the territorial borders of Germany for decades (his family could have dwelt there for generations) but not have been a "German," once defined as being outside German "peoplehood" according to racial classifications. Others could have dwelt outside the territorial borders of Germany their entire lives and still have been a "German National" because of their race/blood — which became national policy as Germany began its conquests and resettlements.

Racism was not new to humanity, and it did not arrive with the Nazis. But, as with so many other issues, the Nazis built upon and inflamed existing racism, and the crimes they performed in the name of race ought to have forever discredited any form of racism in the postwar world. Yet South Africa attempted to maintain a racist apartheid state into the 1990s, and our own country had "white" and "colored" bathrooms and water fountains

---

Jewish grandparents was also classified as Jewish if certain tests were met, such as being enrolled in a Jewish congregation. A person with two Jewish grandparents who did not meet the contemporary tests was a *Mischling* of the first degree. A person with one Jewish grandparent who did not meet the other tests was a *Mischling* of the second degree. One of the evil absurdities of this system was that religious observance was fundamental to the definition, even though the Nazis defined Jewishness as "racial" rather than "religious."

and officially segregated schools into the 1960s, while unofficially segregated schools, churches, and communities remain with us today. Segregationist racism once characterized Christian churches and schools, and (unofficially) sometimes still characterizes such institutions, whose supposed purpose is to glorify Christ and train young people in Christ's way. Anyone who would claim a commitment to the sacredness of human life must reject racism in all its forms. The Nazis are among our best teachers that life's sacredness is fundamentally incompatible with any form of racism.

9.6. Disenfranchisement — Exclusion from Political Community

> Article 5. Any person who is not a Citizen will be able to live in Germany only as a guest and must be subject to legislation for Aliens.
>
> Article 6. Only a Citizen is entitled to decide the leadership and laws of the State. We therefore demand that only Citizens may hold public office, regardless of whether it is a national, state, or local office.

The Nazis quickly kept the "promises" embedded in these articles as well. Let's retrace the logic for a moment: nationalism means that we must do that which, and only that which, advances the interests of the nation. We have now defined who is a part of the nation. It turns out that some among us are not part of the nation — Jews, for example. They are therefore not citizens. They are actually *aliens,* visitors to our land. What does one do with aliens? One begins by making sure that everyone is clear about who is an alien, and who is a citizen. And then, one does not permit those who are merely guests to hold elected office, because this is not really their country to serve. One does not permit them to serve in the military, because they are not loyal to this country. (Jews were quickly banned from serving in the military in Nazi Germany.) One bans them from service in any governmental role. That would have to include all civil service positions, such as posts in the police force, the state universities, and the government bureaucracies, and would even mean banning Jewish Christians from serving in any ministry or office in the churches. And so the Nazis, sometimes preceded by zealous leaders in these arenas, pushed "Jews" right out of all these roles, in many cases long before the Nuremberg Laws made Jewish *disenfranchisement* official in September 1935. This disenfranchisement was so personally crushing to many Jews that they either left the country or killed themselves.[60] For those who remained, it was among the first of many legislated blows to fall upon them.

Any group pushed out of full political participation in the community in which they live have their human rights violated in that very act, and are also desperately vulnerable to further victimization by the state or by their neighbors. A full commitment to the sacredness of every human life demands careful attention to the political status and participation rights of all groups in the community, with special concern for those, resident aliens and illegal immigrants especially, who have no political standing in the state. The implications of this issue for current national and international debates over immigration, for example, should be obvious. Those committed to honoring life must not find themselves on the side of those pressing for the even more forceful marginalization of undocumented immigrants.

9.7. Expulsion and Statelessness

> Article 7. We demand that the State make it its duty to provide opportunities of employment first of all for its own Citizens. If it is not possible to maintain the entire population of the State, then foreign nationals (non-Citizens) are to be expelled from the Reich.

> Article 8. Any further immigration of non-Germans is to be prevented. We demand that all non-Germans who entered Germany after August 2, 1914, be forced to leave the Reich without delay.

Now we see the (inevitable) turn to an economic argument for the expulsion of those just defined as foreign nationals. Built on an assumption of scarcity and written during a time of great economic distress, the platform anticipates that noncitizens will be and should be expelled. The noncitizen population already explicitly included Jews; with Article 8 all post-1914 immigrants were added. (The date was the beginning of World War I.)

Think about it for a minute: President Hindenburg appointed a chan-

---

60. See Christian Goeschel, *Suicide in Nazi Germany* (New York and Oxford: Oxford University Press, 2009), chapter 3. Goeschel opens his chapter this way: "In the Third Reich, suicide became a routine phenomenon among German Jews." Suicides spiked with the Nuremberg Laws, after *Kristallnacht,* and with those scheduled for deportation.

cellor representing a party that for the entirety of its existence called first for the disenfranchisement and then for the expulsion of Jews and other "aliens" from Germany. If concerns about such policy promises had really mattered to Hindenburg, or to the 37 percent of Germans who voted freely for the Nazi Party in July 1932, Hitler would never have come to power. But he did come to power, and he was true to his party's published agenda.

The implications of statelessness in a world built around nation-states are dire indeed. This is an often overlooked dimension of the story we are telling. Anyone who travels internationally knows that no document is quite as important or as powerful as a passport. My passport promises me the assistance of the United States government if I run into trouble abroad.

The National Socialist government of Germany simply removed all such protections from Jews and others whom it disenfranchised. After September 1935 these citizens became unwanted guests, foreign "aliens." After *Kristallnacht* in November 1938, these aliens were placed under extreme pressure to leave the German Reich as quickly as possible. But in a nation-state-centered world, no other country had any legal obligation to help them. During the window when emigration was possible, Jewish resettlement depended on the kindness of nation-states, which are rarely kind. No one had a legal obligation to help, and few felt a moral obligation. All praise goes to the rare lands that showed hospitality, and the diplomats who offered visas when they were told not to do so, from places like Sweden, Switzerland, Japan, China, Albania, and Turkey.[61] All scorn goes to the hard-hearted nations, including our own, that mainly closed their doors. Most Jews were trapped in Germany or somewhere else that the Germans had reached. They were doomed, unless someone saved them.[62]

As a moral conviction, the sacredness of life means that people have human rights before God and neighbor even where legal rights are questionable or do not exist. As a practical matter, stateless people are the most vulnerable in the world, and the easiest to kill.[63] Anyone who cares about the sacredness of life must care about all issues related to refugees, immigration, statelessness, and the expansion and enforcement of global norms requiring the protecting of the rights of the stateless ones among us.

---

61. http://www.globalatlanta.com/article/23926/, accessed April 30, 2011.

62. This is the story I tell in my first book, *Righteous Gentiles of the Holocaust: Genocide and Moral Obligation,* 2nd ed. (Minneapolis: Paragon House, 2003).

63. Rubenstein and Roth, *Approaches to Auschwitz,* p. 373.

9.8. Statist, Racist, Homogeneous Communitarianism

Article 9. All German Citizens must have equal rights and duties.

Article 10. It must be the first duty of every Citizen to carry out intellectual or physical work. Individual activity must not be harmful to the public interest and must be pursued within the framework of the community and for the general good.

Internally, the "Socialism" of National Socialism was the most disputed concept in Nazi circles, at least until the murder of SA chief Ernst Röhm in 1934. Retrospectively, it is now clear that one can distinguish Nazism's stillborn economic "socialism" from the sick nationalistic "socialism" that characterized the regime until its end.

This first Nazi platform strikes a number of notes that sound very much like economic socialism. Article 11 rejects making money through interest ("usury," e.g., commercial loans and banking). Articles 12-17 demand confiscation of money made in war profiteering, nationalization of corporations, profit sharing in big business, "old-age pension schemes," the communalization of large department stores, and land expropriation and reform.[64] Eventually this kind of economic socialism was sacrificed by

---

64. Here is how these articles read, in full:

"We therefore demand:
11. The abolition of all income obtained without labor or effort.

Breaking the Servitude of Interest
12. In view of the tremendous sacrifices in property and blood demanded of the Nation by every war, personal gain from the war must be termed a crime against the Nation. We therefore demand the total confiscation of all war profits.
13. We demand the nationalization of all enterprises (already) converted into corporations (trusts).
14. We demand profit-sharing in large enterprises.
15. We demand the large-scale development of old-age pension schemes.
16. We demand the creation and maintenance of a sound middle class; the immediate communalization of the large department stores, which are to be leased at low rates to small tradesmen. We demand the most careful consideration for the owners of small businesses in orders placed by national, state, or community authorities.
17. We demand land reform in accordance with our national needs and a law for expropriation without compensation of land for public purposes. Abolition of ground rent and prevention of all speculation in land."

Hitler as party leader as he sought to gain the confidence of Germany's business elite during and after his ascent to power. This move also served to sharpen the policy distinctions between German Nazism and Soviet Communism.

It was the nationalistic socialism that survived, and this has very important implications for our study. The Nazis explicitly rejected the centrality and the rights of the individual, privileging instead "the public interest" and "the general good" of the nation, as they defined it. (Notice the relevance to puzzle #2.) That was the project the Nazis began to pursue. It is worth looking at closely.

Not long before he was killed, SA leader Ernst Röhm argued in an April 1934 speech that "the Nazi revolution meant the rupture with the current of thought that had come from the French Revolution and that had elevated to sanctity the basic rights of the person, of the individual."[65] Notice that this formulation, which was common among the Nazis, linked individual rights to the French Revolution, rejecting both, in part because of the very association with France, historic enemy of the Germans. We saw earlier that the turn toward individual rights long predated the French Revolution and was visible not only in John Locke but also in at least one strand of medieval natural rights theory and in the early Baptists (chapter 7). The Nazis had no interest in these approaches either.

Instead they developed an extreme communitarianism in which the individual was sacrificed on the altar of the community, here understood of course as the Nazi state. This helps explain that dimension of Nazi violations of life's sanctity involving the move toward political tyranny even in Germany, the rejection of individual rights to freedom of expression or freedom of conscience, and the collapse of a judicial system that would attend impartially to the case of particular individuals over against the state. One problem, of course, was that the Nazis identified the interests of the community, or the common good, or the public interest, with whatever the desires of the Nazi state or its leaders happened to be at any given time. The will of the Führer simply was the law, which was the public interest, which was the common good. In a reasonably healthy political system, the common good does not equate to the state's policies, but overweening states and their leaders are always tempted to make such equations. If human rights are defended along with and as part of the common good, then individual liberties and the public interest can both be affirmed and protected.

---

65. Mineau, *Operation Barbarossa*, p. 168, paraphrasing Röhm.

The Nazi version of communitarianism was not just statist but also racist. The Nazis sought a social unity that could overcome all prior class distinctions, and they did so by inviting all (approved and racially acceptable) Germans to view themselves as part of a renewed German national community. It was to be all for one and one for all, with the exception of those of bad blood.[66] Hitler and the Nazis, then, sought to coerce and sometimes to inspire Germans to transcend both individualism and social class to become a single "community of the people" *(Volksgemeinschaft),* excluding, of course, those who were defined out of the community.

To this *statist and racist communitarianism* we must add one more element — *reactionary conservatism.* They joined with many others in their era, and in ours, in reacting negatively to social changes brought about by modernization, urbanization, and population movements. These social changes included the emergence of large and diverse urban communities; the surfacing of previously suppressed lifestyles (such as the emergence of gay and lesbian communities); increased openness about sex; the appearance of peoples of diverse race and language on streets in German and Austrian cities; the transiting across national borders of foreign music, books, and other cultural forms (the Nazis sought to suppress, of all things, jazz music); interracial and intercultural dating and marriage; and the perhaps inevitable growth in religious and moral toleration, if not relativism, as various groups intermingled and learned to accept each other.[67] Modern Western cultures are pluralistic, diverse, and multichromatic, and the Nazis desired homogeneity, uniformity, and monochromatic community. This extremely negative reaction to diversity helps explain the later policies of the Nazi state related to suppressing and in many cases killing social outsiders — including but extending far beyond the Jewish people.

Political and moral philosophers are still arguing about some of these themes. There is still, for example, a robust debate between those leaning in a communitarian direction and those who believe that the pursuit of individual dreams and aspirations best reflects the good life and the good society. Debates linger as well over whether the state and its leaders should

66. Michael Burleigh and Wolfgang Wippermann, *The Racial State: Germany, 1933-1945* (Cambridge: Cambridge University Press, 1992), argue that the Nazis tried to restructure a heavily class-conscious society along racial lines, which if successful would defang the appeal of Communism and also create, in their warped view, a sturdier basis for national unity and community.

67. In *Mein Kampf,* Hitler strikes many of these notes, including a surprisingly conservative-sounding prudishness about sexuality. See chapter 10.

have any role whatsoever in promoting a shared communal identity and vision, or whether a democratic state's only role is to provide civic space for individuals to pursue their own versions of happiness and the good life.[68] Suffice it to say here that one lesson of the Nazi desecrations is that extreme forms of communitarianism, especially *homogeneous or racist or otherwise socially intolerant forms of communitarianism,* and most especially if enforced by the state, pose profound threats to the sacredness of human life. And it is not all that bold to observe that some among us who proclaim their commitment to life's sacredness most loudly on selected issues are among those who are most attracted to retrograde projects of homogeneous communitarianism.

9.9. Ruthless Avenging Violence

> Article 18. We demand ruthless battle against those who harm the common good by their activities. Persons committing base crimes against the People, usurers, profiteers, etc., are to be punished by death without regard of religion or race.

Here is the ultimate law-and-order platform statement. Read it carefully, and you can see its murderous implications, especially in light of the history we reviewed in the first part of this chapter.

The goal of these strenuous efforts is, once again, the common good. Those subject to these efforts include "those who harm the common good by their activities [and] persons committing base crimes against the People." In the 1920 context two groups are specifically named: usurers and profiteers. But then there is that notorious "etc." One might say that the Nazis killed an awful lot of people under that "etc." They did indeed deliver what they demanded: "ruthless battle" and "punish[ment] by death." And they killed all kinds of people of all kinds of religions and races.

Both Christian and Enlightenment versions of a sanctity-of-life ethic attempted to impose restraints on violence. We have seen this throughout the book, as well as some of the failures of those attempted restraints. The Lockean Enlightenment version of this political-social ethic had learned from centuries of state abuse of violence to focus considerable attention

---

68. I am grateful to Mercer University student Aaron Kosel for surfacing these themes quite brilliantly in a spring 2011 term paper that has been helpful in this section.

on limiting the state's power, but even Locke granted the state the power to kill, viewing that threat and power as one of the prime reasons people desire to associate in political communities at all.

The paradox of state violence never leaves us: fear of Hobbesian wars of all against all leads us to associate together in community and then to form states, to which, theoretically, we grant very carefully constrained use of the power to coerce and to kill. States then regularly break through their bounds and kill unjustly and without restraint, even in the best of political systems. The twentieth century saw this phenomenon again and again. This first 1920 Nazi Party Platform hardly rings with moral restraint when it comes to violence, and it got worse — the extolling of the virtue and necessity of violence characterized the speeches and then the policies of Hitler and the Nazi regime throughout those dark years, even intensifying as the death toll climbed.

Christian tradition, and then many forms of Enlightenment translation of that tradition, mainly treated violence as a necessary evil rather than a positive good. But neither Hitler nor the Nazis ever treated violence as an evil, not even as a necessary evil. They deployed SA street violence from the beginning, attempted a violent coup in 1923, and used violence at every stage, both domestically in the beginning and internationally until the end — after which the top leaders all killed themselves.

One would think that a man like Hitler, who had witnessed and lived through some of the worst violence in world history as a soldier in the Great War, would have moved in a different direction. After all, that war cost 20 million lives, obliterating a generation of victims and leaving thousands of physically and emotionally ruined survivors. To most of us the natural reaction to surviving a war like that would be to grieve its losses and determine to never again go down such a path. Consider shattering World War I novels like *All Quiet on the Western Front* by German survivor Erich Maria Remarque, or the policies of France and Britain in the interwar period, or even America's growing pacifism during that era.[69]

69. This helps us understand the policies of British leaders like Neville Chamberlain in the late 1930s. Consider this line from historian J. A. S. Grenville: "Chamberlain's attitude stands in stark contrast to Hitler's. He belonged to the generation of the Great War. Humanitarian feelings were the positive motivations of his life. . . . War, to him, was the ultimate waste and negation of human values. He believed in the sanctity of individual human life and rejected the crude notions of a people's destiny, purification through violence and struggle, and the attainment of ends by brute force. He had faith in the triumph of reason and, believing himself to be fighting the good fight for peace, he was prepared to be patient,

But war can have a different impact than this, and people can be emotionally ruined in different ways. In Germany, some men like Adolf Hitler who survived the war actually came back inured to violence and more deeply attracted to its power and its glory. The war had been the high point of Hitler's life. He had been honored for his service. He had found community among his fellow soldiers.[70] And afterward, amidst the bitterness of Germany's defeat, he had found what he believed to be his calling, and his destiny.

Doris Bergen is among those who have claimed that World War I "cheapened human life."[71] Remarque provides a clue about this in his World War I narrative when he has his narrator say: "When a man has seen so many dead he cannot understand any longer why there should be so much anguish over a single individual."[72] Hitler and many around him exhibited no restraints when it came to killing, and this seems inconceivable apart from the intervening event of a war in which tens of thousands died on each given day. Hitler was in the middle of that war, a runner in some of its most infamous battles. He personally witnessed untold deaths on those battlefields.

But for Hitler and the Nazis it was not exactly a cheapening of life. Hitler and other rightist war survivors *so highly valued* the lives of the Germans who had died during the war that they sought to redeem their deaths from meaninglessness. This was *redemptive and avenging violence.* Something very primal was going on here, as was evidenced in countless Nazi songs and ceremonies in which the dead of the war were placed at the very center of Nazi ritual, as if to say: *everything we do is to redeem your deaths.* We defeat Germany's enemies so you will not have died in vain. Indeed: we avenge your deaths through the deaths of your enemies. Especially given the belief of Hitler and others that those enemies who had cost Germany the first war included Jews, every killing of a Jew was an avenging of a German casualty from World War I. The entire war was a sick effort at collective national payback, atonement, and redemption. It was blood for blood. Heinrich Himmler said as much when speaking frankly to his top SS leaders at Posen in 1943 after millions of Jews had already been killed:

---

tenacious and stubborn, drawing on inner resources to maintain a personal optimism even when conditions all around pointed the other way. To the very end he hoped for some miracle that would ensure a peaceful outcome." *A History of the World from the 20th to the 21st Century* (London: Routledge, 2005), p. 221.

70. Bergen, *War and Genocide,* p. 28, though here she did not speak of Hitler personally.

71. Bergen, *War and Genocide,* pp. 26ff.

72. Erich Maria Remarque, *All Quiet on the Western Front* (New York: Barnes and Noble, [1928] 2002), p. 140.

We shall now discuss it absolutely openly among ourselves, nevertheless we shall never speak of it in public. I mean the evacuation of the Jews, the extermination of the Jewish race. . . . For we know how difficult we should have made it for ourselves, if — with the bombing raids, the burdens and the depravations of war — we still had Jews today in every town as secret saboteurs, agitators and trouble-mongers. We would now probably have reached the 1916-17 stage when Jews were still in the national body. . . . We have the moral right, we had the duty to our people to do it — to kill this people who wanted to kill us.[73]

The exaltation of the lives of German war victims (of both wars, actually), and the blaming of the Jews for those deaths, is here explicitly linked to the "evacuation" of the Jews.

Hitler provided a veneer of theorizing on top of this primal motivation when in *Mein Kampf* he explicitly embraced a crude *social Darwinism* positing a perennial war between races and their civilizations.[74] Just as the fittest species survive and others perish, so do nations — that is, for Hitler, ethnic-national people groups. So Hitler explicitly affirmed belief that Germany was in a Darwinian fight to the finish with its enemies — its state enemies, such as the Soviet Union, and its racial enemies, such as the Jews. And it was a matter of either/or — either Germany or the Soviet Union would survive, either Aryans or Jews. This belief undergirded much that he did, including his assault on the Jews and his invasions and colonizations in the east.[75] Only violence could resolve these existential fights to the finish, especially an unwavering "spiritual" violence anchored in a fanatically held worldview.[76] We have seen that Hitler unwaveringly and fanatically initiated just such existential conflict on both fronts when he had the chance.

Let us discuss that horrible word we translate "ruthless." The term was a constant in Nazi propaganda, speeches, literature, and instructions to underlings. "Ruthless" means without pity or compassion, unrelenting, cruel, merciless, hard-hearted. The Nazi ethic — and there was a Nazi ethic, as every community has an ethic — extolled ruthlessness as a high virtue.[77] SS

---

73. http://www.historyplace.com/worldwar2/holocaust/h-posen.htm, accessed April 30, 2011. Both manuscript and audio of this speech survive and can be found on this site.

74. Cf. especially Hitler, *Mein Kampf,* chapter 11.

75. Bergen, *War and Genocide,* p. 36.

76. Hitler, *Mein Kampf,* chapter 5.

77. Claudia Koonz, *The Nazi Conscience* (Cambridge: Harvard University Press, Belknap Press, 2003).

troops were sent out into the killing fields with reminders to be hard, cruel, and pitiless to non-Aryans while loyal to their own kind. Here's Himmler in that same October 1943 speech to his murderous SS leaders:

> We must be honest, decent, loyal, and comradely to members of our own blood and to nobody else. What happens to a Russian or a Czech does not interest me in the slightest. . . . Whether 10,000 Russian females fall down with exhaustion while digging an anti-tank ditch interests me only in so far as the anti-tank ditch for Germany is finished. . . . Most of you know what it means to see a hundred corpses lying together, five hundred, or a thousand. To have gone through this and yet — apart from a few exceptions, examples of human weakness — to have remained decent fellows, this is what has made us hard. This is a glorious page in our history that has never been written and shall never be written.[78]

In this spirit, every effort was made by the SS and others to stamp out any remaining vestiges of Christian or human compassion both among the troops and in the German population. Peter Fritzsche has written that "The SS set for itself the task of breaking down religious affiliations . . . and expunging principles of Christian love and mercy."[79] There could be no pity, no tender compassion, no "weakness." Said Himmler at Posen: "It is absolutely wrong to project our own harmless soul with its deep feelings, our kindheartedness, our idealism, upon alien peoples . . . it is a crime against our own blood to worry about [other peoples] and to bring them ideals."[80]

It was ruthless murder, death everywhere — death to racial subhumans; death to Communists; death to Poles; death to political adversaries or dissenters; death to traitors and turncoats. Death by capital punishment in the homeland, death by shots in the night, death by war, death by starvation, death by beatings, death by torture, death by gas. Redemptive violence brought nothing but death and no redemption. Any who would value the sacredness of human life must look very closely at the blood of all these dead, slain so ruthlessly in the name of vengeance and honor, when reflecting on what it means to protect life's sacredness today.

78. http://www.historyplace.com/worldwar2/holocaust/h-posen.htm.
79. Fritzsche, *Life and Death,* p. 105.
80. http://www.historyplace.com/worldwar2/holocaust/h-posen.htm.

9.10. National Health and Racial Hygiene

> Article 21. The State must raise the level of national health by means
> of mother-and-child care, the banning of juvenile labor, achieve-
> ment of physical fitness through legislation for compulsory gym-
> nastics and sports, and maximum support for all organizations
> providing physical training for young people.

The means envisioned here for this rush toward national health appear
quaint to us in retrospect. Physical fitness and training are one thing. And
who can be against banning child labor? But compulsory sterilization, forced
abortion, involuntary euthanasia, and physician-assisted genocide are something altogether different. The means shifted, radicalizing over time. But the
underlying vision really did not: it was always *national health.* Sometimes it
was described as "racial hygiene." I want to focus here on this manic desire to
get clean, to get healthy, to become pure, not just as individuals but as a people. This group of Germans felt dirty, tainted, ill, and impure. They wanted
to feel clean and pure. Eventually they thought they could kill their way to
cleanliness (in filthy, disease-infested death camps). What lies behind this?

After World War I, a group within Germany interpreted the nation's failures and sufferings as a kind of national illness. Such an illness required a diagnosis. The Nazi diagnosis was that the Aryan race, that is, the true Germans, were suffering from racial illness. Their race had become sick. How
had this happened? The Aryan race had contracted "racial tuberculosis"
from the Jews. The Jews, it seemed, were agents of disease (or parasites, vermin, maggots, germs, etc. — all these horrible terms were used). Germany
had lacked the vigilance to keep these agents of disease out of Germany and
out of Aryan beds. The only possible solution to this medical problem was
likewise medical. Germany must collectively cut out this "canker of decay"
through a program of national surgery. This vision was so widely shared in
the Nazi world that it showed up in official documents, such as when Hans
Frank, head of the General Government, described the Jews he was in the
process of murdering as "a lower species of life, a kind of vermin, which
upon contact infected the German people with deadly diseases." Lifton reports that Frank celebrated the destruction of the Jews of his area with these
words: "Now a sick Europe would become healthy again."[81] The same vision
motivated the less radical earlier steps such as forced sterilization.

---

81. Quoted in Lifton, *The Nazi Doctors,* p. 16.

This medicalized diagnosis and cure depended on the broader blood-racism we discussed above. Hitler and the Nazis fixated on human blood-lines and classified them as superior or inferior, and pure or impure. The theme works its way through *Mein Kampf* and all subsequent Nazi propaganda about human nature. A healthy nation of any type has pure blood. A superior nation has both superior blood and pure blood. That was the goal for Aryan Nazi Germany. Ruthless measures would be required to clean up Aryan blood and restore it to its natural/God-given superiority.

Here is just one example from Hitler's own writings. For those who have never read such odious ideas, one quote really must be offered:

> Historical experience offers countless proofs. . . . It shows with terrifying clarity that in every mingling of Aryan blood with that of lower peoples the result was the end of the cultured people. . . . The result of all racial crossing is therefore in brief always the following:
> (a) Lowering of the level of the higher race;
> (b) Physical and intellectual regression and hence the beginning of a slowly but surely progressing sickness.
> To bring about such a development is, then, nothing else but to sin against the will of the eternal creator.[82]

Therefore, once in power, Hitler led Germany on a delusional program of blood purification, the disastrous results of which were described above. His success was marked in part by his ability to get ordinary Germans to look at themselves and one another in blood-race/purity-impurity terms when many had never done so prior to his regime. This demonstrates the amazing malleability of the human mind — our ability, and curse, to be able to see the world in fundamentally new ways depending on how we are formed/trained/propagandized. What else can explain a physician who had signed the Hippocratic oath saying the following words? These words were actually spoken while looking at Auschwitz's chimneys: "Of course I am a doctor and I want to preserve life. And out of respect for human life, I would remove a gangrenous appendix from a diseased body. The Jew is the gangrenous appendix in the body of mankind."[83]

The rising influence of science played a role in these developments. Early understandings of genetics (a nineteenth-century science) became com-

82. Hitler, *Mein Kampf*, p. 286.
83. Quoted in Lifton, *The Nazi Doctors*, p. 16.

bined with belief in the capacity and responsibility of scientists to engineer a stronger, healthier, fitter population. The population could be manipulated and managed to bring into the world more of the right kind of "stock" and fewer of the bad. What was defined as good or bad could of course vary, focusing on race, or handicap, or whatever variable might be valued or disvalued. And in a context devaluing the individual (or couple, or family) vis-à-vis the community, it was not a stretch to place coercive power over reproduction in the hands of the state, especially its medical professionals.

So the dream of national healing from racial illness, together with the aim of national victory over other nations and peoples, underwrote criminal and murderous intervention with human families, reproduction, and life itself. It wasn't just Nazis who were interested in such projects, at least the milder forms of them. The early-twentieth-century advent of serious advances in birth control, for example, as well as in sterilization techniques, tempted many do-gooders around the world to seek to suppress the birth rates of the "bad" in favor of the good. If American readers of this book are feeling pretty good about our country right now, this might be a good time to say that the United States was the very first nation to undertake compulsory sterilization for eugenic purposes.

Building a better society, a better "race," or a better humanity through medical-technical intervention remains an abiding temptation. Those concerned with the sacredness of each and every human life learn vigilance against state or expert projects to improve or even to clean up humanity along the lines envisioned by one or another regime or ideology. This is especially clear when such efforts are undertaken by government coercion. The more subtle challenge today emerges when individuals, couples, and families seek technical help in such improvement projects themselves.

9.11. Authoritarianism, Propaganda, and Suppression of Civil Liberties

Article 20. . . . The courses of study at all educational institutions are to be adjusted to meet the requirements of practical life. Understanding of the concept of the State must be achieved through the schools (teaching of civics) at the earliest age at which it can be grasped. We demand the education at the public expense of specially gifted children of poor parents, without regard to the latter's position or occupation.

Article 23. We demand laws to fight against *deliberate* political lies and their dissemination by the press.[84]

Article 25. To carry out all the above we demand: the creation of a strong central authority in the Reich. Unquestioned authority by the political central Parliament over the entire Reich and over its organizations in general. The establishment of trade and professional organizations to enforce the Reich basic laws in the individual states.

Article 20 demands a restructuring of the educational system, which the Nazis implemented once in power. They democratized access to the schools while making life miserable for "non-Aryan" children and finally forcing them out. Both in school and in the compulsory Hitler Youth program, children of every social class had the opportunity to turn their attention to "understanding of the concept of the State." Children were given official textbooks like *The Nazi Primer,* teaching them such important truths as "the unlikeness of men," "protection of our racial being," "fate of peoples determined by blood," and the "increasing need for territory" in the east.[85] Twelve years of such propaganda on impressionable minds worked its magic in many cases.

Nazi "coordination" of society did indeed extend to taking control of the press, as in Article 23. Once in power they quickly suppressed the freedom of the press and seized almost every avenue by which opinions were formed and expressed. Therefore they were free to disseminate their own "political lies" for twelve long years without any permitted forms of public dissent or publication of alternative views.

The centralization of power that this required, which is expressed in

84. The statement continues with the following specifics: "a) all editors and editorial employees of newspapers appearing in the German language must be German by race; b) non-German newspapers require express permission from the State for their publication. They may not be printed in the German language; c) any financial participation in a German newspaper or influence on such a paper is to be forbidden by law to non-Germans and the penalty for any breach of this law will be the closing of the newspaper in question, as well as the immediate expulsion from the Reich of the non-Germans involved. Newspapers which violate the public interest are to be banned. We demand laws against trends in art and literature which have a destructive effect on our national life, and the suppression of performances that offend against the above requirements."

85. From *The Nazi Primer: Official Handbook for Schooling the Hitler Youth,* trans. Harwood Childs (New York: Harper and Brothers, 1938).

Article 25, amounted to the creation of one of the worst political tyrannies in history. Here the hope expressed is merely for a strong central parliament in a nation still profoundly decentralized at the time. In almost every venue the Nazis succeeded in moving power to the center from the margins and then taking over the center. Trade and professional organizations were centralized and Nazified quickly, after independent trade unions were smashed.

Centralization, authoritarianism, propaganda, an unfree press, suppression of freedom of expression and conscience emerge as central problems in themselves and as the facilitators of wholesale violations of the sacredness of life, then and now. Such matters must remain a matter of attention for those who care about human dignity.

9.12. The Religious Politics of National Salvation

> Article 24: We demand freedom for all religious denominations, provided that they do not endanger the existence of the State or offend the concepts of decency and morality of the Germanic race. The Party as such stands for positive Christianity, without associating itself with any particular denomination. It fights against the Jewish-materialistic spirit *within* and *around* us, and is convinced that a permanent revival of our Nation can be achieved only from *within*, on the basis of: Public Interest before Private Interest.

This is an extraordinarily fascinating and important statement. What it appears to give to Christianity with one hand it takes away with the other. It seems wholly apt to close this chapter with consideration of the connection between the murderous Nazis and the Christian history we have been reviewing in much of this book. We will do so through the lens of this article in the Nazi Party Platform, and through Hitler's own words in *Mein Kampf.*

The Nazi state did indeed provide freedom for every Christian community that did not "endanger the existence of the State or offend the concepts of decency and morality of the Germanic race." Which is to say, the Nazis provided exactly no space for a morally independent Christianity at all. There was freedom to conform and collaborate and bless. Besides that there was no freedom at all, except the freedom to be imprisoned or to die for standing up for justice, human rights, and the sacredness of life.

It is certainly true that the Nazis pitched themselves as a bulwark of conservative order against the forces of cultural decadence. One way to cement such a self-presentation was to nod in the direction of Christianity in order to appeal to the historically large and temperamentally conservative established Protestant and Catholic churches in Germany. Many of both the leaders and the rank and file of these churches shared concerns about the direction of German culture after World War I, and certainly almost everyone shared at least some sense of aggrievement at the nature of the postwar order. The Nazis served them up an offering of "positive Christianity," Germanic and nationalist, nonsectarian but vaguely Christian and not so vaguely anti-Jewish.

Scholarly literature about the ideological and institutional intersections and divergences between Nazism and Christianity in the Third Reich is vast. At the institutional level, the account is a bit more settled. The Nazis signed a deal with the Vatican in 1933 that promised Catholic religious independence and Nazi nonharassment in exchange for German Catholic abstention from political activity. This killed the once vibrant Catholic Centre Party and suppressed the best moral voices of German Catholicism for most of the Nazi years, while in turn the Nazis freely violated their part of the bargain. On the Protestant side, the Nazis at first tried with bumbling inside help to coordinate the German Evangelical (Protestant) Church right into the Third Reich but, facing considerable resistance from an articulate minority of Protestant pastors led by people like Karl Barth, Martin Niemoller, and Dietrich Bonhoeffer, the Nazis settled for partial coordination and fierce suppression of any who became too visibly resistant.[86] Meanwhile Nazi ideology proved so attractive to some Protestant theologians and church folk that they morphed Christianity into a Nazianity that thoroughly Aryanized the Christian faith, including abandoning the Old Testament and dropping any Jewish-sounding hymns — not to mention the obvious project of excluding Christians of Jewish descent.[87]

86. Victoria Barnett has one of the best accounts of this "German Church Struggle" in her *For the Soul of the People: Protestant Protest against Hitler* (Oxford and New York: Oxford University Press, 1998).

87. Susannah Heschel, *The Aryan Jesus: Christian Theologians and the Bible in Nazi Germany* (Princeton: Princeton University Press, 2008). The worst of these Protestant theologians bought Hitler's claims in *Mein Kampf* that Jesus was not Jewish but Aryan, and not only Aryan but also the sworn enemy of the Jews. Their theological project was to de-Judaize Christianity, and their political project was to swing Protestants into full support for Hitler and his anti-Semitism.

So we know that there were at least some German Christians who succumbed to a religion still called "Christianity" that was in fact a syncretistic Nazi-Christian blend. But was Hitler interested in any of that? Did he think he was doing God's work? Did he care about the churches? Was he in fact a Christian, in his own mind at least? The once-settled consensus was that Nazism was an anti-Christian movement that made tactical feints in the direction of Christianity to seduce or silence the large Christian churches of Germany, but that it was at its core an anti-Christian movement and privately knew itself to be such. Certainly this was the story the German churches told themselves after the war, and many Christian historians still believe it. It is a comforting story.

But I think it is not so simple. Adolf Hitler was a man of Christian background like just about everyone in German society at that time. He was baptized as a Catholic and went to church. He discusses some of those childhood experiences in his memoir. It is impossible to miss the imprint on him of Christian Scripture, history, and imagery. By now he has the settled reputation of a demonic anti-Christian. But I think it is more accurate to describe him as a Christian heretic. He was familiar enough with Christianity to do a great deal of damage while deploying its concepts, images, and vocabulary. I recognize this as a possibility for Hitler because I have seen similar patterns among those carrying the name of Christ during my own career — from a Florida pastor burning the Qur'an in the name of Jesus to a Kansas Baptist church celebrating the deaths of gay men and counting their days of residence in eternal fire. For that matter, some of the behavior of "Christians" that we have reviewed earlier in this volume is not all that different, like roasting natives alive in the Americas or hurling Muslim heads into Damietta. Certainly we cannot rule out the possibility of people desecrating life precisely in the name of God. We have seen it repeatedly. What may be new here is the suggestion that Hitler was one of them.

I have been quoting the Nazi Party Platform and *Mein Kampf* extensively in this chapter. I have shown numerous times that Hitler and his party said exactly what they meant during this period. Yes, it is clear that he lied all the time once it was to his tactical advantage as leader of Germany. But I do not believe there is compelling evidence that he was lying, that is, saying something he did not believe, all the numerous times he spoke of God, the Lord, the Creator, and the Founder of Christianity in *Mein Kampf.* (He never once uses the name "Jesus" in *Mein Kampf.* Watch out for any person of Christian background claiming to speak for

God without concrete reference to the teachings and example of Jesus. And notice how those most likely to resist evil in the name of Christianity — people like Bonhoeffer — do draw explicitly on the teachings and example of Jesus.)[88] And what Hitler says there is completely consistent with the much more concise statement in the platform. Let me summarize the themes and quote him at some length as our last task in this chapter.

1. Hitler says that his struggle against the Jews is undertaken on behalf of "the Lord" and in an effort to ensure the very survival of the human race (puzzle #2 again):

> Should the Jew, with the aid of his Marxist creed, triumph over the people of this world, his Crown will be the funeral wreath of mankind, and this planet will once again follow its orbit through ether, without any human life on its surface, as it did millions of years ago. And so I believe today that my conduct is in accordance with the will of the Almighty Creator. In standing guard against the Jew I am defending the handiwork of the Lord. (p. 59)[89]

2. Hitler says that the German/Aryan people have a divinely assigned mission in the world that justifies the full range of Nazi domestic and foreign policy measures he envisions:

> What we have to fight for is the necessary security for the existence and increase of our race and people, the subsistence of its children and the maintenance of our racial stock unmixed, the freedom and independence of the Fatherland; so that our people may be enabled to fulfill the mission assigned to it by the Creator. (p. 182)

3. He says that his coming racial-surgical efforts against the Jews are intended to protect the image of God (!) in creation and therefore to honor God the Creator:

> The [Jews'] very existence is an incarnate denial of the beauty of God's image in His creation. (p. 154)

---

88. My friend and coauthor Glen Stassen calls this the issue of *incarnational discipleship*.

89. All page numbers in this section are to *Mein Kampf* from the following text: http://www.greatwar.nl/books/meinkampf/meinkampf.pdf, accessed April 30, 2011.

Disease of the body in this case is merely the result of a diseased condition of the moral, social, and racial instincts. But if for reasons of indolence or cowardice this fight is not fought to a finish we may imagine what conditions will be like 500 years hence. Little of God's image will be left in human nature, except to mock the Creator. (p. 214)

On this planet of ours human culture and civilization are indissolubly bound up with the presence of the Aryan. If he should be exterminated or subjugated, then the dark shroud of a new barbarian era would enfold the earth. To undermine the existence of human culture by exterminating its founders and custodians would be an execrable crime in the eyes of those who believe that the folk-idea lies at the basis of human existence. Whoever would dare to raise a profane hand against that highest image of God among His creatures would sin against the bountiful Creator of this marvel and would collaborate in the expulsion from Paradise. (p. 317)

4. He says that "the Founder of Christianity" was the enemy of the Jews and was crucified by the Jews for commercial reasons:

And the Founder of Christianity made no secret indeed of His estimation of the Jewish people. When He found it necessary He drove those enemies of the human race out of the Temple of God; because then, as always, they used religion as a means of advancing their commercial interests. But at that time Christ was nailed to the Cross for his attitude towards the Jews. (p. 254)

5. He says that Germany is a Christian nation:

[O]ur modern Christians enter into party politics and when elections are being held they debase themselves to beg for Jewish votes. They even enter into political intrigues with the atheistic Jewish parties against the interests of their own Christian nation. (p. 254)

6. He says that the failure to intervene to suppress racially undesirable births and to encourage racially desirable ones is a sin against God:

How devoid of ideals and how ignoble is the whole contemporary system! The fact that the churches join in committing this sin against the image of God, even though they continue to emphasize the dignity of that image, is quite in keeping with their present activities. They talk about the Spirit, but they allow man, as the embodiment of the Spirit, to degenerate to the proletarian level. Then they look on with amazement when they realize how small is the influence of the Christian Faith in their own country and how depraved and ungodly is this riff-raff which is physically degenerate and therefore morally degenerate also. (p. 333)

7. He says that God's will is that both of the major Christian denominations must turn their attention to advancing Aryan humanity and stop worrying about sectarian differences:

The two Christian denominations look on with indifference at the profanation and destruction of a noble and unique creature who was given to the world as a gift of God's grace. For the future of the world, however, it does not matter which of the two triumphs over the other, the Catholic or the Protestant. But it does matter whether Aryan humanity survives or perishes. And yet the two Christian denominations are not contending against the destroyer of Aryan humanity but are trying to destroy one another. Everybody who has the right kind of feeling for his country is solemnly bound, each within his own denomination, to see to it that he is not constantly talking about the Will of God merely from the lips but that in actual fact he fulfills the Will of God and does not allow God's handiwork to be debased. For it was by the Will of God that men were made of a certain bodily shape, were given their natures and their faculties. Whoever destroys His work wages war against God's Creation and God's Will. (p. 458)

8. He says that the true believer should pray not for peace but for God's aid in bringing victory to Germany in the next war:

Then, from the child's story-book to the last newspaper in the country, and every theatre and cinema, every pillar where placards are posted and every free space on the hoardings should be utilized in the service of this one great mission, until the faint-hearted cry, "Lord, deliver us," which our patriotic associations send up to Heaven to-day would be transformed into an ardent prayer: "Almighty God, bless our arms when the hour comes. Be just, as Thou hast always been just. Judge now if we deserve our freedom. Lord, bless our struggle." (p. 514)

Saul Friedländer has written of Hitler's "redemptive antisemitism."[90] This was a brilliant intellectual breakthrough on Friedländer's part. But I would argue that Hitler's *entire program and persona* were religiously inflamed, indeed "redemptive." Hitler didn't see himself as just a politician solving a set of problems; nor was he redemptive in his orientation in relation to "the Jewish problem" alone. His whole program was redemptive. His whole identity likewise became self-referentially redemptive. This was a political religion and he was its messiah. God had sent him to save the world. The same was true of the Nazi Party. Have you seen this line from Nazi propaganda chief Joseph Goebbels? "The Nazi party is a political church, where for hundreds of thousands of years German people will be trained to be true National Socialists. We are the political pastors of our people."[91] Goebbels joined Hitler in the belief that the Führer was called and destined to save Aryans, Germany, and the world. This must have been the interpretation Hitler put on his survival for over four long years in the middle of the worst fighting of World War I, when so many around him were mown down. He was spared . . . for a purpose! Hitler certainly put that construction on other near misses during his life, as when he barely survived a 1944 assassination attempt. He was spared — because his work was not yet done! Doris Bergen is most of the way there when she says that "Hitler, and the hard-core Nazis who accepted his views, had a religious fervor, a fanatical conviction that attacks on Jews were necessary to save the world for Aryan Germany."[92]

Christians, can you spot the creation-fall-redemption pattern here? Hitler wrote with a passionate urgency about a fallen world, most viscerally about a fallen Germany. Something had gone terribly wrong. "Paradise" had been lost. But if there was a Fall, there must be a serpent, and the Jews were that serpent. They were not quite human. In a public speech in 1923 Hitler said: "The Jews are undoubtedly a race but not human. They cannot be human in the sense of being an image of God, the Eternal. The Jews are the image of the devil."[93]

Germany was in urgent, dire need of deliverance from this spawn of

---

90. Saul Friedländer, *Nazi Germany and the Jews: The Years of Persecution, 1933-1939* (New York: HarperCollins, 1997), chapter 3.

91. Quoted in William E. Dodd, "The Bible of a Political Church," in *The Nazi Primer*, p. 256.

92. Quoted in Bergen, *War and Genocide*, p. 38.

93. Quoted in Stephen E. Atkins, *Holocaust Denial as an International Movement* (Westport, Conn.: Praeger, 2009), p. 32.

the devil. But who would bring that deliverance? A leader of great vision willing to do everything necessary to redeem the race and the nation before it was too late. Hitler would be that national savior, who would with ruthless fanaticism crush Germany's enemies before they could crush Germany one last time.

And what would be the outcome? A thousand-year Reich! A millennial reign of peace and justice in an ever-more-perfect world: a Nazi World Order with Germans spread all across Europe as colonizers of a vast new empire, her enemies dead or enslaved; a nation with ever greater racial purity and national strength reigning over a kingdom that would have no end.

This was a political religion, or a religious politics. It was a bastardized version of Christianity. It was apocalyptic, eschatological, and messianic. It was everything tame mainstream Christianity was not (and still is not). It was full of drama and meaning. It told a compelling story of great danger, the clock ticking toward midnight, imminent apocalypse, the "funeral wreath of humanity," with a savior riding to the rescue with sword (and machine gun, and poison gas) flashing, bringing in, as out of nowhere, salvation and a new world.

Hitler and the Nazis retained and transfigured Christian Scripture and many of its most problematic elements and scenes. Biblically, one does not have to go far into the book of Joshua to find holy wars of annihilation and conquest. If one wants a fixation on cleanness and purity and being distinct from other peoples, Leviticus provides great material, though it is not race-based. If one wants an apocalyptic triumph over God's enemies, a certain reading of the book of Revelation has some resources. Hitler was Christianity's worst nightmare, claiming all the most dangerous elements of Scripture without any of its truly redemptive themes, texts, or hermeneutical traditions, without any of its calls for repentance from idolatry.

And he had history with him — at least, large parts of history. If one wants a regime demanding conformity of religious belief and worldview, one has Theodosian Europe. If one is interested in bloody military crusades against religious enemies, much material is available over in Damietta. If one wants colonialism in the name of God and the state, and the suppression or annihilation of the local subhumans, one has the Spaniards in the New World. And if one wants resources for hatred of Jews, plenty of that is available as well, in much of the long history of Christian anti-Semitism. The Enlightenment thinkers saw all these problems in the long tradition and history stretching behind them and crafted versions of what they saw as the best of Christian ethics, stripped gradually of Christian theology. Nietzsche gave us his rejection of Christian theology and Christian ethics and the Enlightenment, along with some elements of a new transvalued ethic and an odd new theology.

If *Mein Kampf* is to be believed, Hitler was not really a disciple of Nietzsche, at least not theologically. Hitler gave us a bastardized reading of biblical theology as the driving narrative. Nietzsche utterly rejected any version of the Christian narrative. Ethically, there are more resemblances. But Nietzsche was a better reader of Christian ethics than was Hitler. Nietzsche knew that Christian ethics was about mercy, compassion, and the sacredness of life. He rejected it for that reason, along with its theology. Hitler seems to have believed that mass murder and all the other crimes outlined here conformed to the will of God. The legacy of his moral heresy was 55 million dead bodies and a morally eviscerated world.

9.13. "Contempt for the Sanctity of Human Life"

Looking back on Europe at midcentury, historian J. A. S. Grenville writes the following:

> In chaos a few ruthless men were able to determine the fate of nations, ushering in a European dark age in mid-century. Lenin, Trotsky and Stalin were able to create a more efficient and crueler autocracy than that of the Romanovs. . . . In Italy disillusionment with parliamentary government led to fascism. In Germany, democracy survived by a narrow margin but was demolished when its people despaired once more in the depression of the early 1930s. Hitler's doctrine of race then found a ready response, and his successes at home and abroad confirmed him in power. Different though their roots were, *what these dictators had in common was the rejection of ethics, a contempt for the sanctity of human life, for justice and for equality before the law. They accepted the destruction of millions of people in the belief that it served desirable ends.* They were responsible for a revolution in thought and action that undid centuries of progress.[94]

The question that lies before us is, which path will humanity take in the future — further and perhaps fatal desecrations, or a renewed commitment to consecrating life? To that question we now turn.

94. Grenville, *History of the World*, p. 7.

10. *Honoring Human Life: Twenty-first-Century Challenges*

> An authentic Christian spirituality is utterly subversive to any system that would treat a man or woman as anything less than a child of God. It has nothing to do with ideology or politics. Every praying Christian . . . must have a passionate concern for his or her brother or sister.
>
> Desmond Tutu, *The Words of Desmond Tutu*

10.1. Rebuilding the Moral Order after World War II

The world somehow survived the desecrations and carnage of the period from 1914 to 1945. The apocalyptic catastrophes that fell upon humanity in that period finally ended. The sun rose and set each day, as it always had, by God's forbearing grace. Humanity's survivors attempted to rebuild their lives, their nations, and the fabric of the world. Leaders in multiple sectors of human life sought to do their part: politicians sought to rebuild political order, while religious and secular intellectuals sought to rebuild a decent moral order that would respect human life and dignity.

As I showed in chapter 1, there began a strong recovery of the language of life's sacredness after World War II. It showed up in scholarly and popular sources, Supreme Court decisions and newspaper articles and ethics dictionary entries. The concept was loathed by enemies and loved by advocates, but both sides treated it as a widely understood idea — or even as a settled dimension of Christian moral theology. This historic legacy of biblical faith via Christian civilization, which had largely been secularized or rejected during the eighteenth and nineteenth centuries, resurfaced after the horrors of the 1930s and 1940s. Certainly much of the resurgence of that particular phrase — "the sacredness of life" — had to do with the fight over abortion beginning in the 1970s. But to think that this is the whole story is to badly misread the global mood after World War II. I would instead suggest that much of the ferment on the political, intellectual, and religious landscape after 1945 can be linked to one or another kind of struggle to resacralize human life. Humanity was regrouping, overcoming past blind spots, and trying to find a way forward after thirty years of desecrations.

The horrible legacy of two wars was met by determined efforts to create structures of politics, international peacemaking, and morality that would prevent any recurrence of such global conflagrations. The emergence of a long, frightening Cold War and the proliferation of nuclear weapons made the avoidance of war increasingly a matter not only of human well-being but also of human and even planetary *survival*. Beginning with the formation of the United Nations and the adoption of the Universal Declaration of Human Rights, domestic and international legal structures and moral norms were strengthened to limit tyrannical power, uphold the rule of law, protect human rights, prevent genocide and other war crimes, and hold wrongdoers accountable. A number of countries began to limit the power of their governments to kill their own people for political or other crimes. Especially beginning in the 1950s, racist, nationalist, and imperialist subjugation of dominated peoples was morally delegitimized and politically resisted all around the world, from the anticolonialist struggles of the global south to the civil rights movement of the United States to the antiapartheid movement in South Africa. A global movement for women's rights entered a new stage in the 1960s and 1970s that improved women's lives in large parts of the world while leaving much undone. An international movement on behalf of gay and lesbian rights was born, with effects still being felt. Efforts to tackle global poverty and human health intensified during this same period, accompanied by a growing intolerance of the largely preventable suffering of the world's poor majority. The 1960s also saw the birth of a global environmental movement with many particular concerns ranging from ecosystem damage to species loss to animal rights to long-term human survival.

One can spot a shift and finally a rupture in moral engagement on behalf of life's sacredness after the polarizing legalization of abortion on demand in the United States in 1973. During the same period as this abortion decision, other medical-technological developments began to raise a host of new moral issues, such as how far end-of-life health care efforts should extend, whether contraception should be routinely available to both the married and the unmarried, whether technology is appropriately employed to create pregnancies outside the womb, how to understand the moral status of (frozen and other) embryos, and whether scientists should be free to intervene in the human genome.

Such issues as peacemaking, death penalty abolition, human rights, anticolonialism, environmentalism, and efforts to address global poverty have often been considered "liberal" or "liberationist" causes during the years since World War II. Especially in the United States, in our politics and our religion, such moral concerns have been viewed as an entirely separate matter from the later-developing "sacredness of life" agenda, with its focus on abortion and other bioethical issues. In essence, after the (Christian and other) liberals claimed their issues and called their agenda "social justice," the (Christian and other) conservatives took bioethics and made these concerns their "sanctity of life" battleground. Then for four decades they shot at each other across the political-religious barricades, often entirely convinced of the triviality of each other's concerns — and of the cynicism of the language each side used to talk about them. Examine what is variously taught under the label "Christian ethics" at conservative versus liberal Christian schools, and you will immediately see what I am talking about.

Surely our long journey through the origins, history, and deepest meaning of the conviction that human life is sacred has shown that any reduction of such concerns to either "social justice" issues or bioethical = "sanctity of life" issues is historically groundless. If each and every human life is of sacred worth, unique and incalculably precious, that would apply to *each and every* human life. *Any* issue having to do with the survival, security, and flourishing of large numbers of human beings is a sacredness-of-life issue. It is also a social justice issue, if we understand social justice as a commitment to right relations between people, leading to actions that deliver people from oppression and restore them to right relations in community, with us caring about any of this because each human life is sacred. It is time for the opposing sides to lay down their weapons. All of that oppositional energy could be far better spent.

In this chapter, I will briefly take up six issues facing us today in which life's protection and flourishing are at stake. These discussions should help us work toward finding clarity on several of the original puzzles that we set out to address in chapter 1. I cannot be comprehensive, however much I might wish to be.[1] Moving alphabetically, I will choose some issues from the "social justice" list and some from the "sacredness of life" list and attempt to overcome the distinction once and for all. I will attempt to treat each issue in historical and social context and not in conceptual abstraction, focusing especially on what Christians should be and do, though all readers are invited to consider their opportunities and obligations to honor and protect life. I will try to say something fresh rather than predictable, and point in each case to what I believe to be an important and potentially fruitful way forward at this moment.

10.2. Abortion

Since 1973, a great many Christians have come to believe that the legalization and wide practice of abortion in the United States and large parts of the world represent a massive violation of the sacredness of human life.[2] Opposition to abortion has come to dominate much Christian public ethics while also being quite visible in the life of many local congregations. A desire to remain untainted by any association with abortion has affected Christian stances on a range of other public issues, such as health care reform and women's rights. A small but committed minority of Christians say that they now cast their votes in major elections *entirely* on the basis of their beliefs about abortion.[3] In actuality, this statement could be made of some on the "pro-choice" side as well. The issue has assumed enormous weight for committed activists on both sides.

The conservative Christian posture on abortion has been a reflexive and in some cases extreme reaction to the sudden and equally extreme overturning of legal (and often moral) proscriptions against abortion. In the United States, it also has much to do with the way in which that occurred — through two Supreme Court decisions on January 22, 1973, that

---

1. Readers wanting more treatment of more issues should turn to Glen H. Stassen and David P. Gushee, *Kingdom Ethics: Following Jesus in Contemporary Context* (Downers Grove, Ill.: InterVarsity, 2003).

2. See http://pewforum.org/Abortion/Abortion-Views-by-Religious-Affiliation.aspx.

3. In fall 2010, a Pew poll showed that for 53 percent of white evangelicals, religion was the biggest influence on their opinion about abortion. Sixty-three percent of them believed that abortion should be illegal in all/most cases. The Catholic News Service reported that a U.S. Vatican official said that "voting for a political candidate who favors legal abortion can never be morally justified." http://www.catholicnews.com/data/stories/cns/1004453.htm.

overrode all contrary state laws, leaving many millions of Americans feeling deeply disenfranchised, trampled by judicial fiat. *Roe v. Wade* discovered a federally guaranteed right to an abortion within the right to privacy, and then set up a dubious trimester model (later abandoned in *Planned Parenthood v. Casey,* 1989) for ascribing escalating legal value to fetal life during three artificially designated stages of pregnancy. Only during the third "trimester" (after twenty-six weeks, roughly associated with viability at that time) did fetal life have any meaningful legal status or protection.

But then, in the far less well-known *Doe v. Bolton* case decided the same day in 1973, the justices essentially took away whatever fetal legal protection they had just offered. They did this by permitting third-trimester abortions to protect the mother's life or health, then defined health to include "all factors — physical, emotional, psychological, familial, and the woman's age — relevant to the wellbeing of the patient"[4] as she and her doctor perceived it. While only a tiny percentage of abortions have ever occurred during this third trimester,[5] the fact that a fully viable fetus could be aborted at eight months because the mother was depressed or her marriage was unhappy has outraged the consciences of many thoughtful people. It is hard to overstate the significance of late abortion and the elasticity of the health exception in launching a culture war over abortion in the United States.

There is strong evidence that U.S. Christian opinion about abortion before the 1973 *Roe* and *Doe* decisions was more nuanced than current opinion tends to be. The complexity of the issue, especially in the "hard cases" like rape and incest, was more readily acknowledged. When exactly to attribute full personhood to the fetus was not a matter of unanimity, as it is not discussed directly in Scripture. The gradual evolution of a totally rigid, exceptionless, and highly politicized opposition to current abortion law can be charitably interpreted as conscientious religious dissent to Supreme Court overreach, exacerbated by forty years of conflict that has entrenched the extremes of both the "pro-life" and "pro-choice" sides. Some read it more cynically, at least in its origins, as a political ploy to mobilize conservative Christian voters for the Republican Party.[6] It is certainly a fact

4. J. Blackmun, Opinion of the Court, *Doe v. Bolton,* 410 US 179 (1973).

5. 0.02 percent. From: Stanley K. Henshaw and Kathryn Kost, *Trends in the Characteristics of Women Obtaining Abortions, 1974-2004* (New York: Guttmacher Institute, August 2008).

6. Randall Balmer, *Thy Kingdom Come: How the Religious Right Distorts the Faith and Threatens America — an Evangelical's Lament* (New York: Basic Books, 2006).

that overturning *Roe* is understood as the most important sacredness-of-life concern by many millions of my fellow Christian believers, sometimes with little thought given to what might come afterward if such a goal were fulfilled.

There is certainly support in Christian tradition for profound moral discomfort with abortion. We noted in chapter 3 that the early church clearly and openly rejected both abortion and infanticide. As we saw, these arguments were made on the basis of the incarnation, Jesus' opposition to violence, and the well-being of *both children and women*. This last point provides a critically important clue for addressing abortion today — no treatment of abortion is satisfactory that does not fix its gaze on the sacred lives of both woman and child and does not ask what it might mean for both to live and both to flourish.

The biblical basis for opposition to abortion is disputed, because there is no explicit condemnation of abortion in the canon. However, as we saw earlier, the Bible does contain affirmations that God is the Creator of humanity and of each human life, made in the image of God (Gen. 1:26-27); that fruitfulness in procreation for humanity was part of God's original intent and command (Gen. 1:28); that children are a gift from God (Ps. 127:3); that even in the development process God is depicted as present in providential and superintending ways (cf. Ps. 139:13-16); and that the unjust killing of a human being is a profound violation of God's will, subject to the sternest divine judgment (cf. Gen. 9:5-6; Exod. 20:13). Also, sad human experience leads to the worry that humans have far more often erred on drawing their circle of moral concern too small rather than too large. Still, one might say that the biblical case against abortion is principled and inferential rather than explicit. Not everyone finds the biblical evidence open-and-shut, including Jewish scholars interpreting their own sacred texts. This certainly matters both for public policy debates and in our own internal Christian conversation.

The question of whether a zygote, then an embryo, then a fetus, then a newborn, then a child, then an adult should, at every stage, be viewed as holding exactly the same moral status, is at one level the most pivotal moral question vis-à-vis abortion. If the answer is yes, the biblical ban on murder is ipso facto a ban on abortion. Many Christians have coalesced around the position that a human person with the same moral status as anyone reading this sentence begins at conception — presumably meaning that moment when the egg nucleus and the sperm nucleus fuse to begin the development of a human life. (This actually occurs some twelve hours after an act of sexual intercourse.)[7]

It is perhaps relevant (and not often considered by pro-lifers) that fewer than half of all successfully fertilized eggs last longer than two weeks in *utero*, with a major milestone being the indispensable attachment of the zygote to the mother's uterine wall around the ten-day mark. After that the tiny, fragile embryo-then-fetus depends on maternal nourishment through the placenta, along with maternal (self-)care and much else, even while it begins the amazing, gradual unfolding of its potential for development from day to day during the next thirty-seven hidden weeks.

The flaw of any trimester scheme, really any naming scheme (conception = zygote//two weeks = embryo//nine weeks = fetus//live exit from birth canal = newborn), is its incapacity to fully account for the unbroken daily continuity of the developmental process. Each step builds on the one before, as each milestone precedes the next one. This is true after birth, and just as true before birth, and our science and even photography of prenatal development now allow us to see that continuity in the womb as never before. It should be hard to avoid the commonsense conclusion that the prenatal human being is indeed human from the beginning of her precarious journey, and this fragile humanity simply continues to blossom over the entire course of her life span, with birth one very significant milestone in the journey.

The moral debate over abortion often involves arguments over whether there is a meaningful distinction between human being and human personhood (puzzles #3 and #8). I have already rejected any meaningful distinction between the two. In an instructive contrast, Jewish scholars such as Laurie Zoloth believe it to be more appropriate to speak of fetal life as having full humanity but only *potential* personhood, with that potentiality actualized at live birth.[8] This potentiality approach can be accompanied by high claims (including calls for bans on abortion) related to the appropriate legal status for such human beings who are potentially but not yet persons,

---

7. David G. Myers, *Psychology,* 9th ed. (New York: Worth Publishers, 2009), p. 140. This might open moral space for Christians to support morning-after prescriptions that prevent sperm and egg from meeting.

8. See Laurie Zoloth, "The Duty to Heal an Unfinished World: Jewish Tradition and Genetic Research," *Dialogue* 40, no. 4 (Winter 2001): 299-300, and Laurie Zoloth, "The Ethics of the Eighth Day: Jewish Bioethics and Research on Human Embryonic Stem Cells," in *The Human Embryonic Stem Cell Debate: Science, Ethics, and Public Policy,* ed. Suzanne Holland, Karen Lebacqz, and Laurie Zoloth (Cambridge: MIT Press, 2001).

or it can lead to somewhat more modest legal claims, often involving some kind of incrementalist posture — as fetal life develops, moral status and legal status rightly develop with it. It may be that a permanent split is developing in the United States between moral communities in which abortion cannot be countenanced and others in which it must be permitted. Christians and others who attribute full moral status to the developing unborn child will go far beyond what U.S. law understands are our moral obligations to fetal life, and will often struggle to accommodate the current state of the law.

All who care about life's sacredness must understand the factors that will motivate thousands of women to seek an abortion today, and these must be addressed systematically. Here those whose focus has been on protecting the unborn can and must find common ground with those who have focused on advocating for women, and must swing into common action alongside them.

It is very striking that a disproportionate number of poor women and women of color choose abortions.[9] Abortion rates go up and birthrates go down during times of economic and civil crisis. A surprisingly high percentage of abortions are chosen by married women, often because they fear that a pregnancy or (another) child would snap the fragile bonds that keep their marriage and family together or would tax them financially beyond what they can bear. Abortion is quite often a desperate measure for a crisis moment in a woman's life, so that abortion is not an expression of her agency or freedom but of her tragic desperation. A legal regime that banned or sharply restricted abortion would, on its own, do *exactly nothing* to deal with these problems, and Christians who oppose abortion need service and advocacy strategies that reflect this reality. In the United States, as long as our cultural sexual ethic is so libertine, as long as our social safety net is so fragile, as long as the relationships between men and women are so tenuous, and as long as poverty and hopelessness continue to enfold at least one-fifth of our population, demand for abortion will be high, especially among those whose bodies and spirits bear the costs of most of our other social dysfunctions. It is not too much to say that a society culturally constructed in the way ours now is actually *depends* on abortion to sustain its

---

9. Non-Hispanic black women account for 30 percent of abortions, Hispanic women 25 percent, and women of other nonwhite races 9 percent. Of women obtaining abortions, 42 percent have incomes below 100 percent of the federal poverty level — $10,830 for a single woman with no children. http://www.guttmacher.org/pubs/fb_induced_abortion.html.

way of life. And women — especially poor women — are the ones who must endure the abortions that underwrite our social dysfunctionality.

Christians need to remember that our traditional sexual ethic offers us something better than a regular routine of out-of-wedlock pregnancy and abortion. We need to begin within our own communities in calling one another back to the norm of sexual abstinence outside marriage and fidelity within marriage, regardless of how very difficult it seems to practice this norm today. As we nurture congregations that do not depend on abortion, we will have credibility to offer both moral vision and morally motivated care beyond our families and congregations.

Christian public witness on abortion needs to call boldly for reconsideration of our culture's sexual ethic. We need to support public policies ensuring affordable, quality health care to all Americans, especially pregnant women (married or unmarried) and their young children. Our nation needs a sturdy social safety net that can make having a child a thinkable option for more women, as well as quality education, decent wages, and economic opportunities for everyone so that raising a child is not viewed as a path to financial disaster in hopeless times. Our laws need to improve adoption procedures, and our culture needs to value adoption and the heroic choice to give a child up for adoption. Even Christians who are morally uneasy with contraception need to consider supporting policies that provide access to contraception for those who will not abstain from sex that might produce a child they do not want. We need more loving relationships and fewer abusive and disastrous ones, and men need to take responsibility for the children they conceive. We need to stigmatize casual abortion and men and women whose sexual and contraceptive practices make repeat abortion a way of life. We need stronger and sturdier marriages. The more humane our society, the more covenantal our sexual relationships, the fewer will be our abortions. This project begins in every marriage, family, and congregation. The church can lead the way, as it once did.

10.3. Biotechnological Innovations

The promise and danger of biotechnological innovations have exercised the attention of a sophisticated community of scholars in recent decades. The specific issues range from the new reproductive technologies, which enable the infertile and others to bring new life into the world, usually with considerable medical-technological assistance, to the cloning and genetic engineering of animals (and perhaps human beings one day), to research on embryonic stem cells, to efforts to extend the human life span, to the cracking of the human genome and the possibilities that this opens up for genetic therapy and engineering, and more. In recent years a pattern has emerged in which theologically and sometimes politically conservative bioethicists have offered considerable resistance to most of these developments or their implications — sometimes expressing great alarm about innovations that exist only on the drawing board — while theologically and sometimes politically liberal bioethicists, along with the biotechnology research community, have advocated just as strongly for innovations that also may be decades away. Meanwhile, the research continues apace, in labs that 99.9 percent of us will neither visit nor even know the location of.

Though I will use genetic intervention as something of a case study, I will not attempt to evaluate specific biotechnological innovations here. I confine myself to identifying two broad patterns of response to biotechnology, and trying to relate them to the themes of this volume. The two patterns of response are "more afraid than hopeful" and "more hopeful than afraid." Let's take them in order.

The "more afraid than hopeful" approach begins with a posture of caution toward any biotechnology innovation. This side is not unaware of the possible or promised benefits that could be gained by, for example, genetic therapies, but it is more impressed by what could go wrong with these innovations, or what their moral, legal, medical, or cultural implications could be. A leader on this side is philosopher Leon Kass, who chaired President George W. Bush's bioethics council and helped lead that group toward a generally "more afraid than hopeful" posture. The following statement by Kass aptly summarizes the spirit of this approach: "I surely have no way of knowing whether my worst fears will be realized, but you surely have no way of knowing that they will not."[10] By implication, when one is in doubt about such hugely significant matters, one is wise to move very, very slowly, if at all.

Consider what Kass says about germ-line genetic therapy, which if perfected would aim to cure damaged genes that can be transmitted from one generation to the next during the reproductive process. Advocates of such

___

10. Leon Kass, "The Moral Meaning of Genetic Technology," *Commentary*, September 1999, online version, p. 9. All references to Kass are from this article.

therapies obviously point to all the potential benefits that might come from them. They also seek to deflect the concerns of people like Kass. For example, to the fear that if we start with genetic repairs we will soon be making (putative) genetic enhancements, advocates are confident that the human community will be able to delineate clearly between therapy and enhancement, permitting the one and banning the other. Kass, though, is more afraid than hopeful about this. He is afraid that the line between germ-line therapy and enhancement will erode rapidly once we start doing genetic interventions.

Similarly, where advocates argue that all therapeutic decisions can and will properly be in the hands of patients, Kass fears that geneticists and government authorities will gain a destructive amount of power over patients, and really, over all of us, once we start routinely altering human genes. Advocates think that human freedom will be enhanced as germ-line therapies are added to the menu of medical options in extreme cases; but Kass fears that human freedom will be eroded and the average person will be manipulated by these new genetic powers-that-be in their white coats. Kass fears that economic pressures, such as health insurance decisions, will constrain human freedom very deeply. What if, for example, such companies refuse to pay for health care services for those children whose genes "should have been" repaired in advance, such as, perhaps, those with Down syndrome? Kass fears that genuine reproductive freedom will be eroded as a eugenicist vision prevails in society. In short: far from enhancing life's value, Kass is afraid that if we go down the path of this and other biotechnologies, human dignity will be undermined, human reproduction reduced to manufacture, and human nature diminished or altered beyond recognition.

A theological motif running through Kass's argument on germ-line intervention, and applicable far more broadly, is *a profound fear of human sin in the form of hubris or overreaching*. In this he is not alone. It also seems to be the central motif in negative Christian responses to many biotechnological developments. Genesis 3 and 11 seem to be the primary biblical texts in view. God creates humanity with great potential but also very clear limits and boundaries. Humanity's original sin lies in the attempt to transgress these boundaries, whether in eating the forbidden fruit (Gen. 3) or building a tower to the heavens (Gen. 11). The only thing that God forbids Adam and Eve to do is to attempt to become godlike in their knowledge, so (perversely) this is what they do. They bring ruin on themselves through prideful overreaching.

It is thus the dark shadow cast by the cosmic sin in the Garden, and by the prideful Tower of Babel, that dominates the theological horizon of at least some of those who are more afraid than hopeful. Those of a classical bent, such as Kass himself, often supplement these biblical narratives with a turn to ancient myths that teach the same lesson — like the story of Prometheus, who attempted to steal fire from the gods, or Icarus, who flew too close to the sun with his wings made of wax. Thunderous warnings of possible disaster for transgressing such boundaries can be found in most of the leading (conservative, evangelical, or orthodox) Jewish or Christian voices that have tackled these issues, from C. S. Lewis to Paul Ramsey to Carl F. H. Henry and more contemporary voices like Leon Kass, Gilbert Meilaender, and Edwin Hui. In part due to their influence, "more afraid than hopeful" has become the reigning orthodoxy in the evangelical bioethics and biotechnology conversation, threatening to squeeze out other perspectives entirely.

Jim Peterson is a different kind of evangelical Christian bioethicist, a rare example of the "more hopeful than afraid" posture.[11] Peterson focuses on genetic interventions, but his basic posture could just as easily apply to a wide range of other issues.

Just as Kass recognizes reasons for hope despite his overall posture of being more afraid than hopeful, Peterson offers sober consideration of reasons for fearing genetic research, testing, drugs, and surgery. Yet his overall stance clearly is more hopeful than afraid. He is unwilling to say a clear no to germ-line genetic intervention because he is more hopeful of the goods it can bring about than afraid of its possible dangers. He focuses on the exciting possibility of wiping out such genetic conditions as Tay-Sachs, Huntington's, and Alzheimer's, just as earlier diseases, such as polio, have been reduced or even eliminated. He emphasizes the possibilities that more healthy and capable bodies will make available for human beings if they make use of these bodies wisely through good choices. Therefore, rather than ruling out germ-line intervention, he proposes a moral test for any kind of genetic intervention: it must be safe, it must be a genuine improvement for the recipient, it must increase the recipient's capacity for a more open future, and it must be the best available use of limited resources.[12]

---

11. James C. Peterson, *Genetic Turning Points: The Ethics of Human Genetic Intervention* (Grand Rapids: Eerdmans, 2001). See also his *Changing Human Nature: Ecology, Ethics, Genes, and God* (Grand Rapids: Eerdmans, 2010).

12. Peterson, *Genetic Turning Points*, p. 253.

Peterson clearly envisions the possibility that germ-line genetic intervention could someday meet this test.

This moral stance toward germ-line intervention does not stand alone. It is rooted in a number of principles that Peterson articulates throughout his book. These in part have to do with the basic principles of medical ethics. Some conditions could be treated only through germ-line intervention; others could be treated more efficiently; others could be preempted altogether. If it is possible to provide cures and reduce suffering, as medicine is charged with doing, it is a violation of medical ethics not to proceed to do so. Beyond this, Peterson proposes an ethic of intergenerational responsibility rooted in love for one's own children as well as the value of all human life.[13]

Peterson deflects Kass-type concerns about autonomy by emphasizing that every generation makes choices that affect the next one. To the concern that human beings do not really have the knowledge to discern what is best for future generations, he says they at least have a good idea what will harm them, and are responsible for preventing such harms — as well as presenting to the next generation the good of a well-functioning body if they can. He appears to see no violation of human dignity in such efforts but instead sees a confirmation of that principle.

Underneath Peterson's own principles is a broader theological vision, which he articulates consistently in his book. His reading of the Genesis story, and of the Bible as a whole, finds a mandate to "sustain, restore, and improve" ourselves and the rest of the physical world.[14] The point of human life, says Peterson, is to love God and neighbor. The context in which we offer such love is a created order in which we are called by God to choose the good and to care about God, others, and the world itself. The brokenness of this good world means that much of what we must do is to reconcile the alienated and heal what has been damaged. Even as we do this remedial work, we are called to the bigger and more hopeful vision of transforming the world and improving ourselves.

For Peterson, technology, including genetic technology, should be viewed in Christian perspective as one aspect of our human response to the divine mandate to love God and neighbor in a good-yet-fallen world. We dare not shrink back from new possibilities to fulfill this mandate, however unfamiliar these new possibilities may be when we first encounter

---

13. Peterson, *Genetic Turning Points*, pp. 314-15.
14. Peterson, *Genetic Turning Points*, chapter 3.

them. A good slogan for the "more hopeful than afraid" school could be drawn from this quote from his *Genetic Turning Points:* "Those who argue that genetic intervention is part of the God-given mandate for human beings to share in creation, redemption, and transformation of creation, would see the greater danger not in an attitude of pride, but of sloth."[15] It is this sloth that Peterson most fears.

I struggle to account for the ultimate origins of the split between these two perspectives. Is the issue ultimately about theological *anthropology?* Is it the difference between pessimism about human nature and what humans can accomplish for good on this planet, and a transformationist stance more hopeful about human possibilities? Perhaps the issue is *eschatological:* What does the human future hold anyway? Should we look forward to Christ's return, and only then see significant positive transformation for human life? Or should we expect to catch glimpses of God's reign now, with us having a part in bringing about some of the kingdom's victories? Is the role of morally responsible Christian people to try to prevent things from getting worse and worse, or to hope that things get better and better, and work for that result? Perhaps the split between these two approaches is ultimately *precognitive,* a matter of psychological orientation that divides two types that are familiar to us — those who are generally more hopeful than afraid, and others who are generally more afraid than hopeful. Surely we all know people of both types.

I make no grandiose claims about the ability of the kind of life-honoring vision articulated in this book to resolve these disputes about biotechnology. Surely my posture demands an orientation toward human flourishing (puzzle #12), including human health and well-being, based on the great worth of the human being. Preventable human suffering has always been and must always be an object of strenuous effort for those committed to the flourishing of sacred human lives. The activist posture articulated here also ought to incline us toward openness, indeed enthusiasm, to breakthroughs that bring great gains for human physical wholeness and thus human flourishing. Further, if we recognize that the (re)consecrating of human life is an unfinished, eschatological project in which we have the opportunity to participate, and that as we do so we join a compassionate, just, and activist God in healing a hurting world, our default posture surely will not be to draw back from innovative treatments and technologies that promise gains in human health.

---

15. Peterson, *Genetic Turning Points,* p. 286.

But there are good reasons for caution. First of all, we should be extremely vigilant about guarding the *humanness* of the human being. A presupposition of the entire Christian sacredness-of-human-life tradition is that there is such a thing as a human being, that there is such a thing as human nature, and it is this being, with this nature, whom God has declared to be of sacred worth. There is an intrinsic commitment to keeping human life human in the tradition with which we are wrestling here. God wants humans to flourish, but not at the expense of losing their humanity. Health care should reasonably aim to help human beings flourish within the range of what a normal human existence looks like, not without limits, and always in view of the unfinished nature of all redemptive and life-honoring projects among human beings. Perhaps one thing we can learn from both the Nazi and Communist nightmares is that until Christ returns human beings do better with modest rather than grandiose dreams of salvation.

This discussion perhaps makes necessary a revisiting of the natural law tradition we considered in chapter 7. The category of the "natural" is extremely complex in a faith tradition that sees the world, and human nature, as good-yet-fallen. Any orthodox Christian theological anthropology has to try to account for the "natural" both in terms of what God intended and in terms of what human beings have become in their sin and brokenness. The "more afraid" camp seems inclined toward a posture in which our efforts in health care and biotechnology ought to aim to mitigate some of the worst consequences of human brokenness and sin while accepting that the human condition will not (and should not?) undergo fundamental transformation prior to the end of all things. One might say that precisely in our created goodness and our damaged fallenness we are sacred in God's sight; it is this human being, beautiful yet damaged, to whom God attributes sacred worth. Therefore human beings had better beware of much tinkering with the human, good-yet-fallen as they are. The "more hopeful" posture seems less willing to accept the givenness of humanity in its broken state. It is this very brokenness that we are called to try to repair. This side is far less worried about messing with the fallen part of the human condition and far more concerned about not doing enough to make human life better.

One more point: our exploration of the sacredness of human life has discovered an important theme in *common humanity,* or the fundamental unity of the human family. Realism about starkly differentiated access to health care both within the wealthy nations and around the world motivates many in the "more afraid than hopeful" camp to fear that genetic therapies will become genetic enhancements for those with the money to buy them, leaving leftovers for everyone else. After all, that is already how the U.S. health care system works — some can buy liposuction and cosmetic dentistry while others cannot afford to go to the doctor for an immunization or to treat the flu. One nightmare sci-fi scenario is a species-split between the genetically enhanced and the genetically "natural," based on the ability to afford enhancements. At a much less profound level, sports fans already have witnessed the effects of an uneven human playing field, as, for example, when aging baseball players take performance-enhancing drugs and suddenly develop the strength to hit seventy-five home runs in a season.

A sacredness-of-life perspective will always pay very close attention to the unanticipated (but inevitable) consequences and implications of innovations. Is it really fair in a world of such profound unmet human needs for some to be able to spend tens or hundreds of thousands on exotic biotechnologies? How will the health care system be even further distorted? What will happen to the children who were expected to meet a certain design specification if, somehow, their therapy doesn't quite work for them? What happens to Down syndrome individuals already with us or still to be born if a genetic therapy aimed at snuffing out this condition were to become available? Careful attention to the extraordinary political and social power of the biotechnology industry also leads some of us to be quite fearful of a loss of democratic, participatory decision making on these issues — indeed, on any issue where powerful industries and lobbyists can easily buy access to legislators — which is, well, any issue where big money is involved. Finally, those who still take seriously the abuses of Nazi biomedical programs to protect the "race" from weakness, corruption, and impurity do not easily embrace what might become a new and more powerful version of a similar project. Overall, I find myself more afraid than hopeful. In theory this is a very close call. In the gritty reality of global capitalism and politicians-for-hire and an unjust health care system and an economically stratified world, the smoke clears a bit.

10.4. The Death Penalty

A human family that had adequately absorbed the lessons of the years from 1914 to 1945 probably would have abolished the power of any nation-state to kill its own citizens. So many millions, killed by statute, killed by the state for political crimes or for no particular reason at all other than the offense of their very existence! Actually, all western European countries, on whose soil much of the killing of that period took place, did eventually abolish the death penalty. Europe had lost its taste for blood. The newborn state of Israel, which had plenty of reason to find and kill those war criminals who had tortured and murdered the Jewish people, also chose to do without the death penalty, from the very beginning.[16]

But the United States did not, and still has not, abolished the death penalty. Citizens in thirty-three states (and all of us, with the federal death penalty) still trust government to kill its own people. This makes our country anomalous among our peer nations, and in some eyes places us among the world's routine violators of human rights.

The authority to kill its own citizens is the ultimate expression of government power. The tyrannies we considered in the last chapter eventually developed state killing by fiat. Our country's form of state killing is more "civilized." It is by now an expensive and time-consuming process that involves state actors at every step of the journey — in legislation, law enforcement, the judicial system, the prison system, and the execution system. Citizens who look on with complacency or favor at the use of the death penalty by our states, or by the federal government, reflect a trust in government that they now rarely show in other areas of national life. They assume that the government can be trusted to write laws related to capital crimes fairly, enforce them fairly, and execute fairly. We don't assume that this is the case in consumer law, environmental law, business law, or electoral law. Why should we assume it to be true in criminal law? It is not coincidental that opposition to the death penalty rises among groups whose experiences with the state, and in particular with the criminal justice system, are fraught with injustice — such as African Americans.

The Supreme Court rightly ruled in 1972 in *Furman v. GA* that the use of the death penalty by the states was at that time essentially random and arbitrary and therefore unjustifiable. It looked for a time as if this would be the end of the death penalty in this country, but the response of the majority of the states was to throw together bigger and supposedly better death penalty statutes; so in deference to public opinion, four years later the Court allowed capital punishment to continue (*Gregg v. GA,* 1976). The

---

16. There was one exception to this rule — Adolf Eichmann, who was captured, tried, and executed in 1962 for his pivotal role in organizing the death trains to the east.

Court acknowledged in *McCleskey v. Kemp* (1987; another case from Georgia) that racial bias in death sentencing was statistically indisputable. This meant that death sentencing was worse than arbitrary — it was biased against African Americans. Still the majority decided that a death sentence for a black man in that particular case must be upheld, and they have not overturned the death penalty despite persistent evidence of racial bias in the entire system that churns out these sentences. This tragically myopic decision is a great and terrible example of the continuing impact of structural racism in American life.

There is no logical correlation between committing a murder or a certain type of murder and being executed in the United States. There were 15,241 murders/nonnegligent manslaughters in the United States in 2009, 118 death sentences, and 52 executions.[17] How is that anything other than random? The only predictable patterns are that one is more likely to die if black, if convicted of killing a white person, if poor, if convicted in the South (especially Texas and Virginia), and if convicted under the jurisdiction of district attorneys who are especially fond of the death penalty. And we now know through DNA evidence that the errors inevitable in a class- and race-biased system — and simply put, a human system, run by flawed and self-interested and error-prone human beings — lead to the executions of innocent people. Since 1973, over 130 people have been released from death row with evidence of their innocence. Such flaws have led a few states, most recently Illinois, to abolish the death penalty once and for all.

It would seem that a commitment to tightly limited government and a recognition of the continuing arbitrariness, racism, costliness, and fallibility of our governments' use of the death penalty would be sufficient to ground its suspension if not abolition from a strictly secular and even conservative perspective. There are efforts toward a moratorium along these lines in initiatives led by the Constitution Project and other individuals and groups.

But especially in the South, it seems apparent that a certain reading of the Bible continues to lead to support for capital punishment. People here (I live in Atlanta) still seem to believe that death is the only proper sentence for certain kinds of crimes, and that this is God's will. Citations of the Bible come up in capital cases all over the South. This means that even the purest secularist who cares about the death penalty has to take the biblical issues seriously — which illustrates that in the United States the insti-

---

17. All statistics in this paragraph are derived from http://www.deathpenaltyinfo.org/documents/FactSheet.pdf; accessed July 30, 2012.

tutional separation of church and state definitely does not mean the separation of religion and culture.

The structure of biblical teaching as it relates to the death penalty sets up the following trajectory, much of which we have already seen in this book:

1. Human life is made in the image of God and sacred in God's sight.
2. The sacredness of life is respected by acknowledging a basic human right to life and by establishing a legal framework and moral culture that uphold that right.
3. Human beings must be trained to honor the sacredness of human life and to refrain from attacking and killing each other. (Note: Opposition to the death penalty must never be understood as softness or laxness in relation to the sacredness of human life or the great evil of murder.)
4. When this training fails and we kill each other, the guilty must be apprehended, punished, and prevented from killing again. (Note: Opposition to the death penalty must never be understood as softness or laxness in relation to the need to apprehend, punish, and prevent murderers from killing again.)
5. The Old Testament in its legal sections mandates the death penalty repeatedly, for murder and for a large number of other offenses against God and the community.
6. And yet the Old Testament also sets an extraordinarily high burden of proof for the use of the death penalty (two eyewitnesses — Num. 35), far higher than in our own legal system. This makes comparisons between our justice system and that of the Old Testament problematic. A great number of capital cases in our system would not meet this burden of proof.
7. The Bible also offers numerous stories of God's merciful decision to spare killers from the death penalty (Cain, Moses, David). Whatever the significance of the myriad Old Testament laws instituting the death penalty, God spared several notable murderers.
8. As the rabbinic tradition developed, the rabbis ended up interpreting the texts of Scripture in such a way as to narrow the grounds for use of the death penalty so far that it became essentially unusable. Their ingenious solution to the problem we are considering here was to retain the death penalty as a statement of the seriousness of murder but to sharply limit, and indeed effectively eliminate, its actual use.
9. Jesus never blessed killing. He died for God's kingdom but did not kill for it. His disciples understood the centrality of his radical nonviolence

and became a nonviolent movement in a violent context of imperial oppression and domination. They rejected and recoiled from every form of killing, from abortion to infanticide to the gladiator games to war to the death penalty. They could not bear to see anyone killed, "though justly" (chapter 4).

One sees a kind of theological and ethical evolution here that in the end is a kind of revolution. A religious tradition that begins by saying the sacredness of life requires blood-for-blood punishments ends up concluding that the sacredness of life requires refraining from such punishments. The death penalty teachings stand in the canon as a stern and permanent warning, while the two primary religious and political communities shaped by those teachings came to understand that they must find alternatives to this form of punishment. The value of life had not changed, but beliefs about how best to uphold that value had changed.

Undoubtedly, Jewish and Christian resistance to the death penalty during the formative first and second century C.E. period was deeply affected by being regularly on the receiving end of state killing. These early forebears in faith had no illusions about the justice of how states applied this penalty. It is this Jewish-Christian trajectory, plus a proper nausea at the mass state killings of the twentieth century (and the numberless state killings in every century), plus sober appreciation of the deeply flawed nature of our own criminal justice system, that make any support for the U.S. death penalty unthinkable, in my view.

But it is not because I cannot imagine how someone could support the penalty of death for murder. And it is not because the death penalty is per se a violation of human rights. I do understand how it could seem that the only appropriate punishment for taking a life of sacred worth is to have one's life taken. That is the spirit that lies behind a text like Genesis 9:5-6 if interpreted as a command, and such a text is to be respected at least for its aim of putting a sacred protective boundary around the life of the human being. My thinking here has been reinforced by studying the killings of the twentieth century both in broad outline and in incident-by-incident detail. At one level it is possible to view people like Adolf Hitler — or even those garden-variety camp guards sadistically torturing to death their daily victims — as having lost their legitimate place in the human community because of the desecrations they have inflicted on human life. Can it be that mass murderers constitute a population whose lives we are *not* obligated to seek to preserve, or allow to flourish (puzzle #6)?

We must pause precisely at this precipice. One problem is that no political community appears capable of creating a system that can adjudicate murder cases with consistency and impartial justice. Entrusting states with the routine power to kill their own people repeatedly has proven disastrous, spilling far beyond our own 140 errors in thirty-five years to systemic regimes of state killing. And as Christians at least we must hesitate before the implications of any conclusion that allows us to accept the creation of a category of human beings who are no longer to be viewed as having sacred worth and whose lives we are obligated to end. Perhaps only a very small minority of people, from among the Christian and other communities, will be able to view the Osama bin Ladens and Joseph Stalins and Jeffrey Dahmers of this world as remaining sacred in God's sight even after their crimes. Perhaps we learn that there is a category of cold-blooded killers for which a considerable moral restraint, even moral grandeur, is required for any community to consent to their continued existence and their decent treatment in lifetime imprisonment rather than execution. But this resolution is indeed the one most in keeping with Christian respect for the sacredness of human life. And so, when it comes to state punishment even of the most heinous murderers, Christians should continue to advocate for the state being allowed to take away their *freedom* rather than their *lives,* and to leave the matter of eternal judgment in the hands of God.

10.5. Human Rights

We have already discussed the gradual emergence of a concept of human rights in Western culture, and have puzzled over its relation to a sacredness-of-life ethic (puzzle #11). Besides the biblical roots of the idea (chapter 2), the issue has surfaced throughout much of this book. We saw Las Casas championing the human rights of aboriginal Americans, early Baptists calling for human rights for Jews and other religious dissenters, human rights claims in one strand of the medieval natural rights tradition, and the way human rights figured into the moral and political theories articulated by John Locke and Immanuel Kant. We have also seen the explicit rejection of the idea of human rights in Nietzsche and the absolute crushing of human rights under the murderous Nazi regime.

After World War II, it seemed very important to large parts of the surviving world to develop a robust moral and legal human rights framework, and to do so in such a way that it could be universally embraced. It is not too much to say that human rights became the primary public language in which to discuss all significant ethical issues, and indeed, in which to contest most major domestic and international policy issues. I see in this decision an almost desperate quest to lay some kind of foundation upon which a new world order could be built out of the rubble of two world wars — from Verdun to Rotterdam to Babi Yar to Auschwitz to Hiroshima.

By now, sixty-seven years after the end of World War II, an entire apparatus of human rights declarations, conventions, and treaties has been elaborated. For the first time in human history, individual human rights are now guaranteed by international law; presidents and kings can be indicted by international criminal tribunals for their offenses against individuals.[18] The international community now is charged with a "responsibility to protect" endangered minorities and other groups in any country in the world. These have been extraordinary developments, worthy of celebration despite the tragic and damnable failures of enforcement (as in the Rwandan genocide) that in some cases have evoked the strengthening of these norms. A vast international scholarly literature has also emerged around human rights.[19]

All these treaties, covenants, and books are important, but for our purposes it is the first of the major declarations in the new postwar era that is the most illuminating. That document was the 1948 Universal Declaration of Human Rights, which together with the 1945 founding of the United Nations marked the very first stage of the effort to rebuild a desecrated moral world. I want us to spend a few pages considering the declaration that in many ways set the agenda of a bleeding postwar world.

In the preamble, the Declaration offers four essential reasons to offer a "universal declaration of human rights":

1. Recognition of such rights "is the foundation of freedom, justice, and peace in the world."
2. Disregard for human rights has resulted in outrageous, barbarous acts (the systematic atrocities of World War II hang over this document like a dark cloud).

18. A very helpful, nonspecialist source on these issues is Thomas Buergenthal et al., *International Human Rights in a Nutshell*, 4th ed. (St. Paul: West Publishers, 2009).

19. Two important recent overviews are Lynn Hunt, *Inventing Human Rights* (New York: Norton, 2007) and Ethna Regan, *Theology and the Boundary Discourse of Human Rights* (Washington, D.C.: Georgetown University Press, 2010).

3. The kind of world that would be created by respect for such rights fits with the highest of human aspirations.
4. Member states have already pledged commitment to such standards when they formed the United Nations.[20]

Then the Declaration enumerates an exceedingly wide range of rights "as a common standard of achievement for all peoples and all nations." The thirty articles that follow begin by articulating the universality of human rights — they apply to everyone, without exception. The Declaration then enumerates rights under the broad categories of life, liberty, and security of person. Most rights are articulated negatively (what must *not* be done *to* people — like murder and torture), while others are framed positively (what must be done *for* people — like provisions for social security and rest from labor). The rights articulated are comprehensive; they are civil and political for the most part, but also include social, cultural, and economic rights, an important distinction in human rights theory and law. Just one article emphasizes the *duties* of individuals, a lacuna that has often been noted and will be considered again in a moment. Another article emphasizes the quality of the "social and international order" required for the full realization of these rights. Most focus on the specific rights (in chapter 7, we learned to call these "subjective natural rights") held by human beings just because they are human.

As noted in chapter 7, a number of theological and philosophical critics in the United States, such as Alasdair MacIntyre, have offered influential and damaging attacks on the concept of human rights as a unicorn-like fiction, and the fight for various human rights causes as a distraction from Christianity's real mission, or simply as socially destructive. A fresh reading of the Universal Declaration in light of the inquiry we have been undertaking instead ought to lead to the conclusion that the Declaration is congruent with the commitments generated by a Christian sacredness-of-life ethic while, perhaps inevitably, lacking what is for us the indispensable theological foundation. Rather than rejecting human rights talk and its correlated activism, we should do our own theologically and ethically richer version, in dialogue with other groups doing the same from the perspectives of their own traditions.

There is indeed a profound and visible congruence between this declaration and the vision we have been working on in this book at the level of

20. The Declaration can be accessed online at http://www.un.org/en/documents/udhr/.

moral principle. The Declaration articulates broad moral norms — human freedom, human dignity, human equality, human participation in community, and the immeasurable value of human life — that we have found to be constitutive of a life-revering vision. The Declaration also claims that human beings have an "inherent dignity" (and "equal and inalienable rights"). But no reason is really given for these claims other than the *positive consequences* of their embrace and the *negative past and future consequences* of their abandonment. That's pure consequentialism and not particularly compelling. Language of "inherent" or "intrinsic" dignity is a de-theologized version of the far richer theological claims that are its ultimate origin (puzzle #7). It is not that humans *qua* humans have some kind of intrinsic dignity, inherent mysteriously in our humanity or in some aspect of our nature (e.g., rationality, creativity; puzzle #5). Such claims are easily punctured by those who can point to the thoroughly undignified dimensions of human experience or the particular cases in which one or another supposedly intrinsic-dignity-conferring feature is absent in some of us or present in sharks or apes. It is not because of what we are intrinsically or inherently that human life has dignity and sacred worth; human worth is *conferred worth* based on the character, activity, and declaration of God, as revealed in Scripture and elaborated in Christian tradition. But of course, a "universal" declaration, precisely because of the universality of its audience, cannot make such a claim. Therefore, at least in 1948, it settled for a determined but vulnerable adhesion to the moral norms of the sacredness tradition without an articulated theological foundation.

There is another surprising and little-noted way in which the Universal Declaration of Human Rights fits with the sacredness-of-life theme developed in this book. This congruence is found in its *implicit eschatology*. Hear this line from the Declaration: "The advent of a world in which human beings shall enjoy freedom of speech and belief and freedom from fear and want has been proclaimed as the highest aspiration of the common people." And this one: "Recognition of the inherent dignity and of the equal and inalienable rights of all members of the human family is the foundation of freedom, justice, and peace in the world." That word "advent" cannot help but be striking to a Christian. Advent means "coming." Christians celebrate the weeks before the traditional date of the birth of Jesus as "Advent." Salvation comes into the world; humanity's deepest hopes will soon find realization; light is coming into darkness, at last.

The Universal Declaration of Human Rights is an eschatological document, penned in the ashes of catastrophic utopian schemes built on the

murder of millions. It dreams of the "advent of a world" of justice, freedom, and peace. Another way to say it is that the document dreams of a
world in which life is treated as sacred rather than desecrated in war, torture, and gas chambers. It aspires to such a world, and through its public
articulation of this hope in global community seeks to create the world to
which it aspires. What the Declaration can't say, but believers can, is that
this is also the kind of world God our Creator envisioned when God created; it's the world every biblical moral law is intended to advance; it's the
world the prophets pointed to when they cried out for an end to all the
hurt and killing; and it's the world that Christians believe Jesus came to
initiate. It's *tikkun olam* — the healing of the world, when every tear shall
be wiped away at last, and all flesh shall dwell in peace, freedom, and justice; when human life is (re)sanctified at last.

The Declaration does not and cannot offer a theological account of
how God and/or the church and/or human beings will move the world
from its current burnt-over state to this envisioned state of freedom, justice, and peace. It "proclaims this Universal Declaration of Human Rights
as a common standard of achievement for all peoples and all nations," and
hopes that "every individual and every organ of society . . . shall strive by
teaching and education to promote respect for these rights." Thus human
rights will be advanced by moral suasion; but also "by progressive measures, national and international, to secure their universal and effective
recognition and observance." In sum, the Declaration hopes to reach the
glorious day when human rights are honored through education and various kinds of laws, both domestic and international. A robust Christian
theology will want to say more about how any success in any life-
sacralizing project comes simultaneously as human achievement and as a
gift from God, and flows toward the eschatological future that God has in
store for humanity. But at the same time, we must say a whole lot more
than we now do about the absolute centrality of the rule of the law, both
domestic and international, for advancing life's sacredness in our fallen,
broken kind of world. We must celebrate and therefore advance the recent
strengthening of international human rights law, which in its elevation of
the rights of the "smallest" individual against the "greatest" ruler, and in its
relativizing of national sovereignty and absolutizing of human rights,
stands in profound continuity with the radical egalitarianism and concern
for the human being found in the Christian sacredness-of-life vision.

Finally, let's try to put to rest what is probably the most important
theological source of Christian opposition to rights-talk. Classic Christian

theology finds its center in the cross event. Here, we believe, the innocent, perfect Son of God laid down his life for sinful humanity. It is hard to overstate the centrality of the image of a dying Savior in the Christian moral imagination, and we considered it carefully in chapter 3. The cross functions in the New Testament not just as the central theological image but also as the central *moral paradigm*. Believers are instructed to be like Jesus, who voluntarily set aside all his rights and privileges and condescended to the humility of human nature and the humiliation of crucifixion (Phil. 2:5-11). The imitation of Christ therefore must take the form of a similar self-abnegation, taking up one's own cross and laying down one's privileges and rights in order to love the neighbor above the self. A number of Christian theologians and ethicists find this moral paradigm to be incompatible with an ethic of human rights, because the true Christian may claim no rights for himself, as Jesus claimed no rights. The worry is that rights-talk is selfish talk, always about me claiming my rights. This concern is also sometimes articulated alongside a suspicion that all this rights-talk invites a cultural ethos encouraging the endless elaboration of increasingly dubious rights-claims, including, for example, a purported right to abortion. Wants become rights; freedom becomes license. This is the fear, and there are good reasons for it.

Is there a way beyond this impasse? We saw the earliest version of such an effort in chapter 7. Let me offer another way into it here, starting with duties rather than rights, and with the deep physical/emotional neediness and vulnerability of the human being. The biblical command to love one's neighbor, to treat her as the "sacred animal" (Lactantius) that she is, creates binding duties for the Christian. Examination of the human condition reveals that our neighbors are needy creatures who are vulnerable to harm and even desecration from every side. They have bodies that are exquisitely responsive to pain (this can be exploited to terrorize or torture them); they have relationships that matter deeply to them (this also can be exploited to terrorize or torture them); they need food and shelter (this can be denied them long enough to immiserate or kill them). The obligation to love our neighbors in a manner commensurate with their sacred worth and responsive to their vulnerability and neediness creates a Christian duty to intervene on their behalf when their worth is being violated, their core needs are going unmet, or their vulnerability is being exploited. Contemporary human rights language is a way to systematize and in some cases legalize claims of persons in community upon others, claims corresponding with core human needs and vulnerabilities, and ultimately rooted in divinely conferred sacred worth. So others have rights, which we must act to protect, and we have rights, which they must act to protect, because all of us are humans who stand before God the Creator of all humanity. Rights-talk is a way of making concrete the obligations of neighbor-love when the neighbor has been declared to be sacred in God's sight.

Certainly human rights are a far less coherent notion apart from a biblical theological foundation, but in pluralistic discourse we all do the best we can, and in the Christian community we are entirely free to reanchor human rights language in the best resources of our own theological tradition. I would say more than this: once we Christians have dispensed with our theological reservations about the language and implications of rights claims, we ought to be some of the world's most vigorous champions for the legitimate human rights of our neighbors near and far. Such advocacy and service are an apt expression of our sacredness-of-life ethic, a point of fellow service with people of other faiths and no faith, and a redemptive form of Christian witness in a world fully aware of historic Christian failures and fully weary of meaningless Christian rhetoric.

10.6. Nuclear Weapons

When we try to think about the mass-killing machines humans have invented that we call nuclear weapons, we do well to step back and remember a few things about who we are, and where we are.

According to the Bible, we are the sole species to whom responsibility for the fate of the earth and its inhabitants has been entrusted. There are between 5 million and 100 million species on the planet; 1.7 million have been identified and named. There is just one species that is responsible not just for its own well-being but also for the well-being of all others. That is *homo sapiens.* Us.

The Bible does not treat the disproportionate role and power of humanity on planet earth as an accident. Instead that role is described as a divine decision: first to *create* a certain type of creature in the divine image, and then to *entrust* that creature with dominion over the planet as a whole: "Then God said, 'Let us make humankind in our image, according to our likeness; and let them have dominion over the fish of the sea, and over the birds of the air, and over the cattle, and over all the wild animals of the earth, and over every creeping thing that creeps upon the earth'" (Gen. 1:26).

There is a theological complexity here that has often tested the capacities of people in the biblical tradition. That has to do with how to make sense of *both* the affirmation that "The earth is the LORD's and all that is in it" (Ps. 24:1) *and* the affirmation that "The earth he has given to human beings" (Ps. 115:16). What ought to be an obvious solution often seems to elude people of faith; that is, that *the second affirmation is dependent on the first.* Human responsibility over the earth and its creatures is delegated responsibility, for which we are answerable to the One who delegated it. It is trusteeship, like when a state elects a senator and entrusts her to represent it, or when a board of trustees elects a university president and entrusts him to manage the affairs of the school. These elected officers hold real responsibility. Their decisions really matter. They are not *seemingly* making important decisions with real consequences. They *are* making important decisions with real consequences. But they hold their power in trust on behalf of others.

That is how it is with us in relation to the earth and its creatures. This is God's world, over which we humans have been entrusted with enormous responsibility. In that light, the human invention, deployment, use, and threat of use of nuclear weapons, and our stubborn slowness in stepping away from these weapons even twenty years after the end of the Cold War, despite their manifest danger to the entire planet, are best viewed as a grotesque violation of our delegated trusteeship over the earth that God made. But it is not too late to get this right — even as Ron Rosenbaum in his recent book *How the End Begins* argues that we have come very near nuclear Armageddon numerous times and we remain right on the brink of unleashing nuclear war on one another.[21]

We cannot give in to despair. But we need to remember that what we are talking about are weapons capable of inflicting the greatest mass slaughter in the history of the world. We are talking about mass murder, the ultimate form of state-inflicted killing. We are talking about creatures made in the image of God, using their special, God-given powers of rationality and creativity to dream up weapons that can obliterate millions in a single flash in order to create, not a bloodbath, but something more like an *evaporation* of infinitely precious human beings whom God *loves,* together with the long-term poisoning of the planet itself. It says something profoundly distressing about the limits of human nature that most have become complacent to the continued existence of thousands of these life-desecrating weapons, in the hands of multiple nations.

---

21. Ron Rosenbaum, *How the End Begins* (New York: Simon and Schuster, 2011).

All who care about life's sacredness need to participate in helping our fellow human beings, including the leaders of our own nations, to slowly back away from the brink of mass murder. That is what the use of nuclear weapons is, or what it would be, however we dress it up in the morally exculpatory languages we have created. This is a word of warning to all of us, especially those of us operating in the just-war tradition. In these traditions killing is not necessarily murder if done in self-defense, and the acquisition and threat of weapons are not necessarily evil if these acts deter those who would harm the innocent. This perfectly natural, perfectly logical, moral-legal system, which we considered especially in chapter 6, bumps up against its outer limits here. Mass murder is mass murder, however it is labeled or justified. It will be cold comfort to the dead in a nuclear exchange if we label them as collateral damage in a morally justified act of self-defense. They will be just as dead, along with human civilization.

Jesus says, "If you . . . had only *recognized* on this day the things that make for peace" (Luke 19:42).

This may mean, this must mean, that there are things that we can do to *make peace.*[22] And it may mean, indeed it must mean, that we have *the capacity to discover what these are.* Revering life means moving from sterile arguments about just war to a nuclear peacemaking crusade, like Francis's crusade for peace during his own bloody era. Those who are already engaged in that crusade know the following:

1. As long as possessing nuclear weapons is seen as the best way to secure one's regime or keep one's nation from destruction, leaders of nations like North Korea and Iran will seek them. If any nation feels insecure, all will in fact be insecure. So we need to find ways to meet the legitimate security needs of every nation for the sake of all nations.

2. Relationships between nations can easily default to a Hobbesian state of nature, unless a fabric of international covenants and treaties observed by all nations weaves the peoples together under the rule of law. We need to find ways to strengthen that fabric.

3. Weapons of this level of destructiveness have to be quarantined from other kinds of weapons so that their use is delegitimized. So we need to

---

22. Glen Stassen is right in his career-shaping insight that the heart of the New Testament teaching about war is neither pacifism nor just war but the practices of just peacemaking. See Stassen, ed., *Just Peacemaking: The New Paradigm for the Ethics of Peace and War* (Cleveland: Pilgrim Press, 2008), and *Just Peacemaking: Transforming Initiatives for Justice and Peace* (Louisville: Westminster John Knox, 1992).

find ways to continue to quarantine nuclear weapons from other types of weapons, and delegitimize any possible use of these weapons.

4. It is not just weapons themselves that matter but also the quality of the relationships between the nations that develop and deploy them. So we need to find ways to reduce fear, generate trust, and build friendships between nations. Some of our best and brightest need to enter the diplomatic corps, and the skills of the world's diplomats need strengthening.

5. The human heart, even the collective human heart as found in nations, alternates between fear and hope. So we need to find ways to reduce fear and build hope, such as employing unilateral confidence-building measures as independent peacemaking initiatives.

6. We need to create constant and open channels of communication between nations, even those that view each other as enemies, rather than ever shutting down communication. Too much is at stake to stop talking with other nations.

7. Fear and anger tend to produce a hostile rhetoric of blame that produces more fear and anger, and so forth in a vicious cycle. So we need to train ourselves and require of our leaders a posture of rhetorical restraint, articulated respect for other peoples and nations, and a willingness to confess wrongs that have damaged relations in the past.

The Damocles Sword of nuclear annihilation has hung over our heads since 1945. By God's grace working through responsible human action and restraint, that sword has not fallen. It is one of the twenty-first century's greatest moral challenges to remove that sword from over all of us at last. Thousands of nuclear weapons were left on the international table when the Cold War ended, as if somehow they would dismantle themselves when everyone's attention turned to other issues. They did not dismantle themselves. We human beings must do that. We created them; we must uncreate them. The most heavily armed nation in the world, the United States, must take the lead. We must continue to reduce our nuclear weapons toward zero, preferably by stages under the provisions of multilateral treaties — as we work against nuclear proliferation and nuclear terrorism. The goal is clear; what is lacking is the will. The leading religious community in the United States, Christians, must help build the moral consensus required to move toward this goal. To do so, America's Christians must learn to see nuclear weapons as a leading sacredness-of-life issue, and respond accordingly. We must be the first community in our nation to declare our readiness to live entirely without nuclear weapons.

10.7. Women's Rights

To end this chapter I want to address a set of issues together that are often treated separately — human trafficking, global health, and poverty. I want to tie these issues to the broader question of women's well-being and women's rights, and in this case I want to take a global rather than a national perspective.

In 2009, the husband-and-wife team of Nicholas D. Kristof and Sheryl WuDunn published *Half the Sky*, a global survey of the oppression of women and of individuals and groups making a difference in combating it.[23] Every reader of this book should immediately go find that one and not come back to my next sentence until she has done so. The book has entirely revolutionized my thinking about the world, and in particular, what it means to speak of the sacred worth of women's lives in light of the desecrations inflicted on women all around the world.

I am now embarrassed that until these pages I have rarely written about women's rights issues other than treating the fight among conservative American Christians over the role of women in home, church, and society.[24] That fight for decades has been framed as a battle between "complementarians" and "egalitarians" over whether God's plan for women is to complement and "graciously submit" to male leaders in home and church (and maybe society) or whether the Bible is best understood as teaching full equality and shared leadership for women and men. Since the beginning of my career I have taken the egalitarian position. I still believe that one aspect of honoring women's lives is for Christian churches and families to abandon their objections to a fully egalitarian understanding of the roles of males and females in every sector of life. A large part of conservative Protestant Christianity remains committed to retaining some version of an older patriarchalism. I have personally known many women who have been harmed by it.

These issues are related, but pale in comparison, to the concerns raised by Kristof and WuDunn in their transformative book. We could start with this claim: "It appears that more girls have been killed in the last fifty years, precisely because they were girls, than men were killed in all the battles of the twentieth century."[25] Labeling this a "gendercide," the authors quote

---

23. Nicholas D. Kristof and Sheryl WuDunn, *Half the Sky: Turning Oppression into Opportunity for Woman Worldwide* (New York: Vintage Books, 2009).

24. See Stassen and Gushee, *Kingdom Ethics*, chapter 14, and scattered articles.

25. Kristof and WuDunn, *Half the Sky*, p. xvii.

the great scholar-activist Amartya Sen in claiming that 100 million women are missing from the world who would have been here had it not been for sex-selective abortions targeting girls, honor killings, bride burnings, widespread fatal neglect and infanticide of girl babies and children, lack of the most basic health care for women, easily preventable maternal mortality, and other facets of global discrimination against women. This is "death by discrimination," and it is a global epidemic. Most Americans, including American Christians, have no idea any of this is going on.

Kristof and WuDunn break their study down into three primary areas of women's oppression: sex trafficking/forced prostitution, gender-based violence against women, and maternal mortality.

The major types of human trafficking, according to the U.S. Department of State, are forced labor, sex trafficking, bonded labor, involuntary domestic servitude, forced child labor, child soldiers, and child sex trafficking.[26] The authors of *Half the Sky* focus on sex trafficking, and what they clearly show is a modern-day form of sex slavery inflicted on girls and women (and a small number of boys) in dozens of countries around the world, including the United States. Kristof and WuDunn estimate that 3 million people are currently sex slaves, though it may be many more than this.[27] Those trafficked for sex are part of an overall trafficked population both within and across national borders that has been estimated to be between 10 million and 30 million people, earning for their captors $32 billion (U.S.) per year. According to the United Nations, human trafficking is "the fastest growing criminal enterprise in the world."[28] *Foreign Affairs* magazine has called human trafficking "larger in absolute terms than the Atlantic slave trade," involving 600,000–800,000 victims crossing international borders each year.[29] There are good reasons why human trafficking is simply called "modern-day slavery."

The path into sex slavery begins with being tricked, coerced, or kidnapped and then sold into the hands of sex traffickers, often, though not always, in a form of modern-day debt slavery. Any resistance of children or women to their all-day everyday duty as sex slaves is broken by a brutal regimen of humiliation, manipulation, threats, rapes, beatings, torture,

26. United States Department of State, "What Is Human Trafficking?" www.state.gov/g/tip; accessed April 10, 2011.

27. Kristof and WuDunn, *Half the Sky,* p. 9.

28. Data from http://thecnnfreedomproject.blogs.cnn.com/2011/03/04/modern-day-slavery-a-problem-that-cant-be-ignored/.

29. Quoted in Kristof and WuDunn, *Half the Sky,* pp. 10-11.

and the occasional witnessed murder of a fellow slave. Dominated into submission, these girls and women become enslaved sex workers, servicing a clientele of local and traveling men that often includes "respectable" police officers who should be enforcing laws against trafficking and prostitution. Sometimes sex slavery is intergenerational, as dominated women give birth to children who are raised to serve as the next generation of slaves.

Sex trafficking has taken off in our era of global flows of capital, information, and people. Easy movement across borders is good for trade but also good for trade that is evil, such as the trade in human beings. Thus, for example, the integration of the European economy and ease of transit across European borders have opened up vast new opportunities for trafficking sex slaves from eastern Europe and elsewhere. And certain parts of the world, such as Thailand, are the destination of choice for what are now called sex tourists. The vicious logic of a morality-free global capitalism willing to commodify anything that someone wants to buy is deeply implicated in all forms of trafficking, including sex trafficking. Sometimes it seems that the most indisputable law on the planet is the law of supply and demand, with all moral considerations subservient to that law. The relentless appetite of men for sex, including sex with children or brutalized adult female sex slaves, is for me, as a male, one of the most disgusting aspects of this entire sordid story.

Kristof and WuDunn contrast the "legalize and regulate" approach to the overall problem of prostitution and sex slavery with the "big stick" approach of attempting to crack down on sex trafficking, break up brothels, and rescue women and children from slavery. Both approaches have problems, though I concur with Kristof and WuDunn that on balance it appears that a zero-tolerance "big stick" approach is the better one. Close examination of this issue reveals once again the indispensable role of the rule of law. Both domestic and international laws are routinely flouted in the sex trade, and corruption of local police forces is endemic. If we want a more just world in which life is treated as sacred, power needs to be exerted by the world community, the United States, and Christian advocacy to demand that basic laws respecting human rights are enforced all over the world. Meanwhile, morally thoughtful Christians and others need to become aware of the phenomenon of human trafficking and sex slavery and participate in organizations and efforts that work to end it.[30]

30. See "20 Ways You Can Help Fight Human Trafficking," U.S. Department of State, http://www.state.gov/g/tip/id/help/index.htm.

Kristof and WuDunn claim that "women aged 15 through 44 are more likely to be maimed or die from male violence than from cancer, malaria, traffic accidents, and war combined."[31] Their chapters on the various ways in which women are routinely raped, assaulted, and murdered, often in the name of "honor," are among the most nauseating texts I have ever read. They write of "widespread, cruel, lethal" violence against women around the world.[32] One-third of women face beatings in the home, some of these as part of social customs in which many members of a family feel perfectly authorized to "discipline" women for purported offenses against a family or cultural code. Both men and women perpetuate such violence. One example of the latter is the permission granted to mothers-in-law to beat their daughters-in-law related to disputes in the home. Mothers often adhere to custom in performing infanticide on their own daughters where this is widely practiced.[33] (Kristof and WuDunn try to walk a fine line between naming the elements of external oppression on women and calling on women not to participate in internalizing and practicing the structures and norms that underwrite their own victimization.) Women's noses are chopped off; they are attacked with acid; they are raped by gangs and sometimes murdered, often as punishment handed down by one family on another family in incidents having nothing to do with the victimized women at all.

Men's fixation on and discomfort with women's sexuality are deeply implicated in a wide range of crimes against women, such as honor killings of women believed to have lost their virginity or rapes of virgins in order to despoil their sexual honor and thus shame their family or society. Mass rape has become a favored weapon of war, as has recently been documented in the horrible, endless conflict in the Democratic Republic of the Congo. Kristof and WuDunn actually found a sixteen-year-old soldier willing to articulate in print, with his picture taken for the book, that he and his troops have a "right" to rape women: "If we see girls, it's our right . . . we can violate them."[34] These rapists have become ingenious in their cruelty, finding ways not just to rape women but also to leave them permanently damaged, as when their slicing up of the genital and anal area of women leaves these women's excretory and reproductive systems intentionally ruined. Many

31. Kristof and WuDunn, *Half the Sky*, p. 61.
32. Kristof and WuDunn, *Half the Sky*, p. 67.
33. Kristof and WuDunn, *Half the Sky*, p. 68.
34. Kristof and WuDunn, *Half the Sky*, p. 86.

women are left abandoned, to die humiliated and rejected, once this has been done to them. And yet Kristof and WuDunn find doctors and other specialists who have developed skills to try to heal this particular form of human suffering and restore women to health and community.

Death in childbirth takes one woman's life per minute per year; 99 percent of these deaths occur in poor countries. Many more women survive but have their health permanently ruined by childbearing.[35] Women die in childbirth primarily because of the lack of adequate health care services for them, especially in poor rural areas. But Kristof and WuDunn give numerous examples of poor and even war-torn lands, like Sri Lanka, that have made great strides against maternal mortality simply by choosing to apply their resources to solving the problem. It is simply a matter of valuing women's lives.

Maternal mortality is also intimately related to the issue of contraception, and the politics around contraception and abortion. Almost 125 million women want contraception and cannot get access to it around the world. This is also related to the AIDS problem, especially in Africa, where it is most prevalent, and where women are often infected by husbands who are unwilling to use a condom during sex or cannot get access to them. U.S. abortion politics contributes to this when it defunds family planning agencies because they also, at times, perform abortions, even though they do not use federal money to perform abortions.[36] The flourishing, and sometimes even the survival, of women requires that they be able to gain access to contraception when they need it.

Much of the Kristof/WuDunn book has to do with current best practices related to empowering women. They discuss education and economic opportunity, microcredit as a way for poor women to develop trades and move toward economic self-sufficiency and power balance with their husbands, and a large number of women's empowerment efforts that, as they elevate women, benefit children and entire communities economically and in other ways. They make the convincing case that no society can fully flourish if the talents and potential of half of its population are suppressed or lost, and that community economic development is boosted more dramatically through efforts to empower women economically than by anything else one might try to do. I am entirely convinced that *honoring the sacredness of life in the twenty-first century requires full engagement with global women's rights issues.*

35. Kristof and WuDunn, *Half the Sky*, p. 97.
36. Kristof and WuDunn, *Half the Sky*, p. 134.

I am also convinced that the forms of women's marginalization that still can be found in conservative Christian religion here in the United States contribute to our relative indifference to women's rights issues around the world. And, clearly, the association between women's rights and abortion in the minds of conservative Christians has damaged that cause greatly and quite unfairly. Surely Christians can demonstrate the intelligence to separate issues that are intrinsically distinct from one another.

10.8. Other Issues

This chapter could have included a number of other issues. I regret the lack of space to say more about the current shape of race-related issues and issues related to refugees and immigration, modern-day genocides, poverty and economic injustice, and other matters. Every human life is sacred; in our sinful world we violate that sacredness in myriad ways every day. If we were to address every relevant sacredness-of-life issue, "the world itself could not contain the books that would be written" (John 21:25). But we must move on. In the next chapter, I turn to the question of whether God's creation itself should be treated as sacred, and whether speaking of the sacredness of *human* life is in fact a really bad idea.

11. The Sacredness of God's Creation

> If you have men who will exclude any of God's creatures from the
> shelter of compassion and pity, you will have men who will deal
> likewise with their fellow men.
>
> Francis of Assisi

11.1. The Sacredness of Human Life and Ecological Degradation

There are many reasons to embrace a sacredness-of-human-life ethic. As
articulated carefully (though undoubtedly imperfectly) in this book, this
ethic emphasizes as starkly as possible the *universality* of human moral obligations to other human beings. No one can be excluded. From womb to
tomb, from home to far away, from friend to foe, all are covered. All must
be viewed with reverence and treated with respect and care. To each and to
all I (we) owe particular moral obligations, focusing first on the protection
of their lives and finally, in an open-ended way, on their flourishing in every aspect of what it means for them to flourish as human creatures made
in the image of God.

It is not difficult for most Christians to understand why human beings
should be viewed and treated in this way when the scriptural warrants are
presented. Few Christians today would explicitly reject this vision of their
moral obligations, though it is certainly difficult to pry some people away
from a too-narrow understanding of the implications of this conviction.
Still, the overall concept reflects a kind of exalted theocentric humanism
that coheres well with the best of contemporary Christian thinking about
persons and the world. If we can find ways to motivate more Christians

(and others) to live out this kind of ethic in relation to those they are least inclined to value, it will be a hugely significant accomplishment in the real world.

And yet, it is not at all clear that this kind of Christian ethic is sufficient for addressing the particular challenges created by the ecological degradation of the planet that we face today and into the rest of the twenty-first century. In fact, it can be argued that a sacredness-of-human-life ethic is *part of the problem and cannot be part of the solution.* What a paradox it would be if the highest expression of a Christian ethic that values human life turns out to be at the same time a major source of the ongoing devaluation of the rest of God's creation — and thus, tragically enough, contrary to long-term human well-being. Some very thoughtful analysts have concluded that this is in fact the case. My goal in this chapter is to determine if this is true. I want to explore the capacity of a sacredness-of-human-life ethic to deal with the new kinds of problems created in a context of ecological degradation and potential catastrophe. We may be facing here the most important contemporary objection to the moral vision articulated in this book. It was our puzzle #1, and now it moves to the center of our attention.

11.2. Problems of a Sacredness-of-Human-Life Ethic for the Care of Creation

Without pretending to offer a complete list of the possible problems and limits of a sacredness-of-human-life ethic for our era of ecological crisis, I will briefly elucidate the following issues.

First, the sacredness ethic as I have articulated it sharpens our sense of the immense value of the human person, but as usually stated, it offers no account even of the existence, let alone the value, of other beings. Take a look at our Christian definition once again (see p. 33). We are trained to see human beings (each and every human being) as the center of God's concern when it comes to the affairs of this planet. Even the broad sacredness ethic proposed here still focuses the entirety of its attention on human beings. It is different from narrower versions only in the breadth of its concern for the whole human family and the flourishing of each person everywhere at every stage of existence. The drama of salvation history remains the question of the response of the human being to God our Maker and Redeemer; the drama of ethics remains the question of the response of the human being to other human beings.[1]

As for the moral status of other sentient beings, and the creation itself, my account of life's sacredness has so far remained largely silent. This has been intentional. At least in Western Protestant Christianity we have lacked the language to discuss that which goes beyond and yet includes the vertical and the horizontal, the divine-human and human-human dramas, and my presentation has reflected that lacuna. An earlier generation might have spoken of God's relationship with the angels or the heavenly court. That theme has been absent. And no mention is made of fish, squirrels, or dolphins, or of trees, rivers, air, and crabgrass. A sacredness-of-human-life approach does at least push Christians to pay attention to ethics and not just theology, to how people are treated and not just whether they believe right doctrines, but it does nothing to raise the visibility of the millions of other species with whom we share the created order, or the created order itself in which we and these many other creatures live and move and have our being.

As we have seen, even when Christians do move in the direction of a theology of creation and the other creatures, a common theological move is quickly to sharpen the ontological distinctions between human and nonhuman creatures. The first step in this direction in many theologies is to define the content of the *imago Dei* through some delineation of the ways in which human beings, and only human beings, are made in God's image. Often this is done through the specification of certain capacities of the human that are set against the lack of capacity of other creatures (puzzle #5). Only humans, we say, can reason, or plan, or create, or love, or invent and speak languages. Only humans have a soul that can relate to and love God. This is sometimes called "human exceptionalism," or criticized as human egocentrism, or speciesism, and it goes deep in Western and Christian thought and in its secularized successors.[2] Imagine how different our view of the world would be if our teachings about creation emphasized all that we shared in common with other creatures instead of all that makes us different. Instead, our tradition tends to emphasize human difference, uniqueness, and superiority in fateful ways.

A capacity-based construal of the divine image or human worth is also

1. Richard A. Young, *Healing the Earth: A Theocentric Perspective on Environmental Problems and Their Solutions* (Nashville: Broadman and Holman, 1994), p. 48.

2. On the problem of "exceptionalism," see the excellent discussion in Anna L. Peterson, *Being Human: Ethics, Environment, and Our Place in the World* (Berkeley and Los Angeles: University of California Press, 2001), pp. 28-50.

susceptible to empirical attacks from those who propose or can show that the distinctions between the reasoning, creative, emotive, linguistic, or relational capacities of humans and those of the higher mammals, for example, have been overdrawn. We end up risking a core element of our theology of creation (and even salvation) with every new discovery about the surprisingly advanced capacities of other creatures.

This is one very good reason, as we discussed in chapter 2, for us to follow the suggestions of a number of biblical scholars and understand the image of God in terms of our unique *responsibilities,* not our unique *capacities.*[3] We image God as we bear God's delegated authority to care for the earth and its creatures. This emphasizes our unique power and responsibility in the earth, rather than our increasingly tenuous claim to have unique capacities. Again, it might be helpful here to be reminded of the existence in biblical thought of other entities, some even "higher" than us, such as the angels, to repopulate our theological imaginations with a planet and universe full of diverse forms of life, and to some extent to decenter humanity in our vision of the created order.

One consequence of defining the *imago Dei* in this better-than, over-against paradigm is the implicit or explicit degradation of the status and value of nonhuman creatures relative to human beings. Other creatures are *less than* us because they cannot reason, emote, relate, love, create, or speak. It becomes very important in this approach to delineate the many specific ways in which other creatures are inferior to us in their capacities. Not made in the image of God, not destined for eternal life with God, they occupy an ambiguous and certainly less important role in the divine economy. They are not part of the ultimate drama of salvation, nor are they part of the penultimate drama of ethics. They are barely more than "scenery" on the stage of the divine-human drama.[4] Human uniqueness and status are bought at a high price here — the denigration of the status of each and every one of the other creatures on the planet.

This way of defining what it really means to be human, what it really means to be made in the image of God, can have the dramatic unintended consequence of weakening the moral status of those human beings who lose or never have those distinctive capacities that we have identified as

3. E.g., Claus Westermann, *Creation,* trans. John J. Scullion (Philadelphia: SPCK and Fortress, 1974).

4. See Emil Brunner, *Revelation and Reason: The Christian Doctrine of Faith and Knowledge,* trans. Olive Wyon (Philadelphia: Westminster, 1946), pp. 33-34 n. 4.

constituting the image of God. A child in the womb does not qualify as *imago Dei* material as defined by current capacities. The best we can really say is that one day, if all goes well, this developing child will have those capacities. A person in a persistent vegetative state lacks some or all of the capacities we have named. These weaknesses of a capacity-based defining of the image have been exploited energetically by those with reason to do so. How tragic that the effort to buttress the elevation of what it means to be human vis-à-vis other species has sometimes contributed to the degradation of lives that do not quite qualify by the definitions we have created.

Our exalted definition of the sacredness of human life reveals huge implications for how human beings are to be treated by other human beings, but no ethical framework for human responsibility to other creatures and the creation itself. We can see that each and every human being is to be viewed with reverence, and to be treated in a manner that contributes to the protection and flourishing of their lives. But how are we to view and to treat the monkeys, rats, and dogs — or the roses, oceans, and air?

In a world populated by millions of other species and billions of other nonhuman neighbors, it is impossible for human beings not to operate according to some kind of vision and ethic in relation to these creatures. Some of these are actually codified into law, as we were reminded here in Atlanta when our former star quarterback, Michael Vick, went to jail for grossly mistreating and even murdering dogs. So the state does have laws related to how both animals and ecosystems must be treated. But it appears that the resources for such a legal or moral vision are not available, or not central, in the Christian faith itself. Can that really be so?

In the history of Christian thought there has been at least one identifiable and consistently recurring vision for the moral relationship between human beings and the rest of creation — this is captured in the English word "dominion." The concept is rooted quite firmly in the soil of Genesis 1:26-30, as we saw earlier, a text in which human beings are charged with the responsibility to "rule" or "have dominion" over every kind of creature and apparently "over all the earth" itself. Recent attempts to modify either the translation or the moral vision associated with Christian dominion theology have tended to shift the focus to service and stewardship.[5] If we

---

5. See Calvin B. DeWitt, *Caring for Creation: Responsible Stewardship of God's Handiwork,* ed. James W. Skillen and Luis E. Lugo (Grand Rapids: Baker, 1998); Fred Van Dyke et al., *Redeeming Creation: The Biblical Basis for Environmental Stewardship* (Downers Grove, Ill.: IVP Academic, 1996).

"rule," it must be more like how Jesus taught us to rule — through humble service rather than lordly domination.

Somehow that point was lost on many generations of Christians, especially Western Christians influenced by cultural currents unleashed in the modern era, including technical rationality, expansionist capitalism, and imperial colonialism. The creation and its creatures became "natural resources" to be exploited for the good of humanity, especially dominant human groups that engineered amazing feats involving the reworking of the "raw materials" of creation for the pleasure and advancement of humanity. John Locke's writings about creation are redolent with such themes, and they remain with us in crude and sophisticated form every day of our lives in capitalist societies. Every one of us is the beneficiary of these developments, but looked at with a long view, the "thingification" of the creation and the creatures within it has proven to be spiritually damaging, environmentally degrading, and increasingly unsustainable. In the last chapter we saw what happens when "thingification" is applied to human beings — as in slavery and sex trafficking.

Whether it can be fairly traced to Genesis 1 or to the modern Western reading of Genesis 1 can be argued, but the cultural result in the Western world is undisputed — a human understanding of the world that abstracts one part of creation (human beings) from the rest. "Man" sits at the pinnacle of creation, lord of all he surveys, free to use it as he sees fit. There is "humanity" and then there is "the world," or humanity and "the environment," or humanity and "nature," or humanity and "the creation." Even the more biblical language of "creation" is not often employed to join us to that creation, but instead to abstract us from it.

Throughout Christian history scattered saints have modeled a different way of relating to the creation — one thinks of our dear Saint Francis. But for the most part Christians have both elevated humanity and separated humanity from the fish of the sea and the birds of the air and the livestock that move along the ground — and from the sea, the air, and the ground itself.

We have been trained not to see ourselves as creatures, as part of creation, as dependent upon the well-being of other creatures and of the air, land, and water that we all share. Therefore we have been and remain vulnerable to the overexploitation of these fellow creatures and the gradual degradation of the creation we share with them. We acted as if what we did to other creatures would have no negative effects on us, lords of creation, and as if what we did to creation itself would similarly bounce off of us, its masters. It was not until the late twentieth century that a number of developments — including severe environmental problems, the depletion of what had been treated as infinite "natural resources," the early environmental movement, the revival of nature religions, and the photos of our shared "terrestrial ball" from outer space — *prompted us to understand that what we do to creation and to the other creatures we do to ourselves.* There is no escape, no place to hide, no safe space from which we can benignly view a deteriorating creation. We depend on our particular ecosystems, and our shared planet, no less than the fish of the sea and the birds of the air and the livestock that move along the ground.

One final concern before we move on. It is possible to view this human-centered view of reality, this theologically validated human egocentrism, as a theological leftover, a vestige of a prescientific, pre-Darwinian, pre-ecological worldview in which the earth was the center of the universe, human beings were the center of events on the earth, and God guaranteed the continued well-being of this planet made for humans. It is not difficult to recall how deeply threatened church leaders felt at the suggestion that the earth orbits the sun and not the other way around. Then it was discovered that this is but one sun and one solar system among other suns and other solar systems. It became harder and harder to believe that the only thing God cared about in the whole universe was what was happening on this "third rock from the sun."

This same prescientific worldview suggested that not only was the earth the center of the universe, but also human beings were the center of (what matters on) the earth. Darwin is the name most associated not only with the idea that human beings are but one species among many on this earth (which we knew) but also with the more radical notion that human beings are but one late-evolving species on this earth and share an ancestry with other creatures and even the humblest life-forms that exist here.

This latter move has been too much to swallow even today for large sections of the human family, especially religious believers, and not only Christians. It challenges nearly every element of the historic Christian approach we have been discussing in this section, from the elevation of humanity, to the distinctions between human and nonhuman creatures, to the abstraction of human beings from the ecosystems and the earth they share with other creatures.

This is not a chapter about Darwin or evolution, and I do not believe that Christians are dependent on a particular approach to evolution for a response to the ecological crisis. But I do think that what are often thought of as two separate "faith and science" issues — evolution and the environment — actually are best considered in conversation with one another. And I think that the discovery, through modern genetic research, of our considerable shared DNA with all living creatures on this planet confirms a central thesis I am pursuing here — that whatever else we may say about the special moral status of human beings before God, we must also say that we creatures of God and earth, of spirit and humus, are somehow fellows, somehow kin, somehow morally related to and responsible to the other creatures of the earth with whom we share so much — including being beneficiaries of God's creative and redeeming love.[6]

11.3. The Development of Alternative Theological Paradigms

In a famous 1967 article called "The Historical Roots of Our Ecologic Crisis," scientist Lynn White Jr. charged that "Christianity bears a huge burden of guilt" for the environmental problems afflicting Western society and now the whole world.[7] Probing many of the issues discussed in the last section, White argued that the Bible desacralized nature, licensed human beings to dominate and overpopulate the earth, and created an anthropocentric view of creation.[8] The Bible has also been charged with encouraging a dualistic view of reality that creates a contempt for this world and all things physical, and with nurturing an eschatological framework in which Christ's second coming distracts Christians from an ultimate commitment to the well-being of the one earth on which we actually live.[9] While more recent scholarship has clearly demonstrated that ecological catastrophe is not a uniquely Western or Christian problem, the effects of White's thesis and the significance of his concerns linger still.[10]

Many have found such contentions attractive, leading or contributing both to the explicit rejection of the Bible and/or Jewish and Christian faith and to the embrace of starkly different religious and philosophical

---

6. Larry L. Rasmussen, *Earth Community, Earth Ethics* (Maryknoll, N.Y.: Orbis, 1996).

7. Lynn White Jr., "The Historical Roots of Our Ecologic Crisis," *Science* 155 (March 1967): 1203, 1206.

8. White, "The Historical Roots," pp. 1203-7.

9. See Young, *Healing the Earth*, for a careful analysis and response.

10. See generally Jared Diamond, *Collapse: How Societies Choose to Fail or Succeed* (New York: Penguin, 2005), an immensely important book, which tells the story of numerous societies that collapsed ecologically for a variety of reasons.

visions seen as more nature-friendly. This association of environmental concern with a rejection of orthodox Christianity has had the disastrous effect of discrediting the environmental movement in the eyes of millions of traditional-minded Christian believers. Only recently have many serious Christians been willing to consider environmentalism, or "creation care," in any significant way, and they often find their efforts resisted fiercely by other Christians on the basis of fears that ecological concern is the path to heresy.

Meanwhile, various Christian thinkers have attempted to offer more ecologically sensitive versions of Christian faith — sometimes with elements drawn from other religions or sometimes from a rethinking of biblical or theological resources. Some of these revised theologies stray quite profoundly from recognizable Christian faith, helping to confirm the fears of Christians worried about ecological concern infiltrating Christianity. Other times the reforms stay more carefully within Christian theological boundaries.

A variety of theological moves have been made to create or retrieve a more environmentally friendly stance. I will name just a few of these here.

For those who believe that biblical faith's primary sin is in desacralizing nature, robbing it of the felt sense of the divine presence as it locates all divinity in one transcendent God, one option is to retrieve or create nature religions that redivinize nature in its individual parts or as a whole. Just as once the ancients experienced and worshiped the divine in the air, land, and sea, in the various creatures, and in the mysterious processes of nature on which all life depends, today some have returned to various forms of such beliefs.

Another possibility, especially appealing to some in view of the growing appreciation of the creation as a single, intricate entity, a vast ecosystem that sustains all life (the "Gaia hypothesis"), has been a retrieval of a kind of pantheism in which God is all and all is God, or a panentheism in which God is to be identified with or experienced directly in everything that exists.[11]

A third move is toward a kind of feminist nature religion. Here the critique of biblical thought categories is further specified as a critique of the patriarchy or androcentrism that has distorted all these thought categories, such as the dualism that diminishes the female in favor of the male,

---

11. The concept began as a scientific hypothesis and developed in a metaphysical/religious direction. See J. E. Lovelock, *Gaia: A New Look at Life on Earth* (Oxford: Oxford University Press, 1979).

the natural in favor of the spiritual, the body in favor of the soul, and this life in favor of the next one.[12] In one version of this approach, the earth is personified as our divine Mother, who must be loved as a whole and in her constituent elements — every tree, river, and frog. Some who are attracted to this approach seek to retrieve ancient matriarchal religions that, they argue, contained elements of this kind of mysticism and spirituality and were displaced centuries ago in most of the world by the violent patriarchal religions of Judaism, Christianity, and Islam.[13]

The evolutionary approaches to life on the earth have been fully embraced by some who then weave an eco-spirituality around evolution. One approach is to find a kind of life-force spirituality at work in the multi-billion-year process by which life has unfolded on this planet and presumably elsewhere. All life is related to all other life, all life seeks to extend itself, and in the development and infinite elaboration of life-forms on this planet one has many reasons for religious awe and wonder, as well as the basis of an ethic of reverence and respect and even "sacredness of life" in all its forms.[14]

One influential philosophical (rather than theological) move has been the embrace of a kind of eco-utilitarianism by the philosopher Peter Singer. Singer offers a new kind of moral universalism in which at least some non-human creatures are valued equally to human beings and thus become the bearers of moral claims that must be respected by human beings. Unfortunately, Singer grounds his elevation of the moral status of the higher mammals in a consciousness-based or capacity-based evaluation of that status. This simultaneously elevates the moral status of the higher mammals that have been shown to be near or equal to human beings in their capacities and consciousness, but at the same time demotes human beings who lack such capacities and consciousness. This move lies at the root of Singer's terrible suggestion that infanticide and euthanasia should be permitted. For Singer, the capacities of an infant or an Alzheimer's patient fall below those of a fully functioning gorilla, and their respective rights should be treated correspondingly.[15]

---

12. Peterson, *Being Human*, pp. 28-50.

13. See, e.g., Riane Eisler, *The Chalice and the Blade: Our History, Our Future* (San Francisco: Harper and Row, 1987).

14. Thomas Berry, *The Dream of the Earth* (San Francisco: Sierra Club Books, 1988), pp. 123-37.

15. Peter Singer, *Practical Ethics*, 2nd ed. (Cambridge: Cambridge University Press, 1993), pp. 175-217.

Another move suggested in recent literature has been more explicitly po-litical. It involves a rethinking of political community to include all crea-tures. If one thinks of modern history as involving a gradual recognition of the moral and thus political status of all human beings, and not just some categories of human beings (men, landowners, white people), then the ex-tension of this status to nonhuman creatures can be seen as the next logical step. Animals join humans in the kingdom of ends, to reframe our friend Immanuel Kant. In an extension of the categorical imperative, animals must be counted among those viewed as ends also and not merely as means to someone else's ends. This ultimately leads to a reframing of the concept of citizenship, with animals included in a kind of global-earth community with rights that must be respected even if they cannot speak for themselves.[16]

I have already suggested that a number of Christian theologians have attempted to reframe Christian theology in radical ways that, in my view, essentially introduce elements of nature religions into Christian faith. While this is not the place to offer an introduction to all these approaches, what they have in common is generally the explicit abandonment of core doctrinal elements of Christian faith and often the introduction of theo-logical concepts and images that have little precedent in biblical or histori-cal theology. Two examples of this are the mystical pantheism of Matthew Fox's creation spirituality[17] and the feminist embrace of a kind of Mother Earth theology, such as Sallie McFague's suggestion that the earth should be viewed as God's body.[18]

Perhaps it is easy for some Christians to dismiss all the foregoing moves as dangerous overreactions. They should instead be viewed as rele-vant evidence of the earth's distress and of culture's responses to that dis-tress — and some of our Christian brothers' and sisters' responses. Some represent the retrieval of centuries of wisdom about sustainable human living on this planet. Even those that go too far should speak to us about our own need as Christians to respond far better than we have done.

16. For an example of how this can be framed philosophically as an expansion of Kant, see Paul W. Taylor, *Respect for Nature* (Princeton: Princeton University Press, 1986) (or as an expansion of Mill, see Peter Singer, *Unsanctifying Human Life*, ed. Helga Kuhse [Oxford: Blackwell, 2002]). For an example of how it can be framed theologically, see Rasmussen, *Earth Community, Earth Ethics.*

17. Matthew Fox, *Original Blessing: A Primer in Creation Spirituality Presented in Four Paths, Twenty-six Themes, and Two Questions* (Santa Fe, N.Mex.: Bear and Co., 1983).

18. Sallie McFague, *Models of God: Theology for an Ecological, Nuclear Age* (Philadelphia: Fortress, 1987).

A number of Christian theologians and ethicists have attempted to offer a more modest reframing of Christian ethics to shift and improve our moral paradigms, and thus improve Christian approaches to the environment. One move is to tackle the "dominion mandate" and to redefine it with language such as "stewardship," "earth keeping," or "creation care." The focus remains Genesis 1–2, and the goal is to pull Christians away from a reading of dominion as domination and toward dominion as a more humble stewardship, care, or earth keeping. This move also nudges Christians to pay more attention to nonhuman creatures and the creation itself, as an aspect of proper obedience to the "dominion mandate." Cal DeWitt, working in the Reformed tradition, long has been a pioneer in these efforts.[19]

I think it has become clear recently that the theology and ethic of creation of many Christians are too weak to bear this added pressure. In other words, they would have to really care about *creation as a theological category* for this revision of a theology of creation to get their attention. But, focused as they have been on soteriology, on God's saving relationship to the human, and the human response to the divine, it would require a deep revolution in their working theology to move them toward any kind of deep concern with a theology or ethic related to creation or its renewal. This helps explain why some recent theological work has moved closer to the core of classic Protestant theology, trying to take account of ecological concerns when thinking about the meaning of Jesus Christ, sin, salvation, and eschatology. A full-blown ecological theology will involve serious work in these areas. Some of the needed elements will be suggested in the next section.

11.4. Toward a Broadened Christian Sacredness-of-Life Ethic

Perhaps if properly modified, the sacredness of life still can be the organizing framework or paradigm that we need for an era of ecological crisis. If this effort is successful, concern for God's creation can be, at least in part, anchored in a moral commitment that is already widely shared in the church, which is a considerable advantage for those trying to affect the beliefs and behaviors of the average Christian today. And it can tie care for creation right into the heart of the vision we have been pursuing in this book.

19. E.g., DeWitt, *Caring for Creation*.

I have argued that in biblical thought the character of God, together with the free decision of God to decide and declare the unique, incalculable value of human life, entirely grounds any ascription of sacredness to human life. Therefore, it is wrong to say that human beings and their lives are somehow intrinsically sacred (puzzle #7), if we are not at the same time saying that what makes human lives sacred is God's action and declaration toward them. The more precise way to say it is that in theocentric perspective all value is *conferred value,* in that the Creator is the one who authoritatively declares the value of all things that God has made.

In the critically important Psalm 8, for example, it is God's name that is "majestic . . . in all the earth!" (Ps. 8:1). It is God's decision to choose to be "mindful" of humanity amidst all of God's other majestic creations (8:4). It is God who made us "a little lower than the divine beings" (8:5), and "crowned [us] with glory and honor" (8:5). It is God who chose to make us ruler "over the works of [his] hands" (8:6). Human life can be described as sacred insofar as the majesty, holiness, presence, love, and care of God touch it, are related to it, and are directed toward it. To honor human life and treat it with reverence is an appropriate theological, spiritual, and ethical response to God's character and actions.

Insofar as ecological degradation and catastrophe hurt human beings, those creatures toward whom God's actions and declarations reveal such exalted value, then Christians are duty-bound to respond with steps to ease the suffering of their human neighbors. Therefore one of the best things that concerned Christian environmentalists can do to advance their commitments is to (a) remind their brothers and sisters of their obligations toward their human neighbors, whom God loves so dearly, and (b) show concretely how ecological degradation is already sickening and killing those neighbors. This is not hard to do. Far from setting up environmental concern as a conflict of interest between babies and polar bears, we must instead show the ways in which the same problems, such as climate change, hurt both babies and polar bears. This would be a huge step forward.

But then we must also find ways to demonstrate theologically that these polar bears themselves, as well as the other creatures, and the creation as a whole, are also sacred. They may not be sacred to the same degree or in the same way that human beings are, especially if we tie sacredness in any strong way to the *imago Dei,* and if we preserve some species-uniqueness as part of that divine image. But they are indeed sacred — if we understand sacred, again, to mean ascribed worth as a result of God's action and declaration toward them and relationship with them. When we then reopen the text of the Bible and look especially for God's relationship to other creatures and the creation, we find a God who creates other creatures (and the creation) (Gen. 1–2), who declares them good (Gen. 1:31), who feeds and sustains them (Ps. 104; Matt. 6:26), who takes delight in them,[20] who makes covenants with them (Gen. 9), who protects them in his laws (Lev. 25; Deut. 6:14), who hears their groaning (Rom. 8:22), and who promises their ultimate liberation from bondage to decay (Rom. 8:20-21) and the renewal of all things (Matt. 19:28). We have ample biblical grounds for looking upon them with reverence and treating them with respect and care.

It is not too much to say that, to the extent that we Christians have failed to acknowledge God's relationship to other creatures and the creation, and their ascribed worth in God's eyes, we have sinned against God, against other creatures, and against the creation we share with them. Our failures call for repentance, which includes both grief over sin and a new commitment to a different way of relating. We must learn to perceive our moral obligations as people to those other creatures also loved and valued by God. This is the starting point for a fresh look at the particular resources found in the Scriptures that are relevant to ecological concern.

Once we open ourselves to seeing and sensing God's immense valuing of the creation and its creatures, a whole new range of biblical resources becomes available to us. Significant work has already been done, and more is needed to mine these extensive biblical resources that teach us in various ways a high valuing of the creation, its ecosystems, and its creatures. These can be of especially great value in church settings precisely because they do not rely on esoteric theological moves but can simply be read in the biblical texts. Let me suggest at least a few places to look.

11.5. Rediscovering Scripture

We should pay more attention to Genesis 1–2, and to developing a more robust theology of creation (and fall, in Genesis 3). We should work harder at "seeing" nonhuman life and the creation itself as they appear in Genesis, populating our Christian moral imagination with creatures that matter to God who are not human beings. We must learn to read, and to tell, the primal biblical story differently.

20. Implicit in the declarations of the goodness of creation in Gen. 1; cf. Prov. 8:29-31.

We should spend much more time in Genesis 6–9, paying attention to the terrible suffering that befell the creation due to human sin — a paradigmatic pattern that continues today. The ark itself has become something of a symbol of human-animal community — there creaturely life survived together. In one sense the entire earth is an ark — either we survive together or maybe none of us will survive at all. (An image picked up explicitly in the apocalyptic thriller *2012*.) The Noahide covenant is rich with theological significance, for nowhere is divine-human-animal-creation community more clearly suggested. Most breathtakingly, God makes a covenant through Noah and "every living creature that [was] with you" to and with all human beings and "every living creature . . . for all future generations" (Gen. 9:8-12). This means that yesterday, today, and tomorrow God chooses to stand in an ongoing covenant relationship with every creature. This suggests a creaturely status before God that is not contingent on the creature's status before or with humans. It also reminds us that when we mistreat any creature, we mistreat one who stands in covenant relation to God. And when our actions contribute to the destruction of all members of a species and therefore its total extinction, one might fairly say that we are reversing the obedient work of Noah and destroying a species-family with which God our Creator intended to remain in a covenant relationship in perpetuity.

Strangely and suggestively, even animals are treated as moral agents when the text says in Genesis 9:5-6 that both people and animals will be held accountable for the shedding of blood on the earth. Can it be that before God even the animals have a kind of moral responsibility? Certainly it is clear in Old Testament law that human beings bear responsibility for the negligent care of their animals and any harm that comes to others as a result of such negligence (Exod. 21:29-32). But in this same case, the animal is put to death for its killing of a human even if its owner is not found negligent. Surely this provision aims at the protection of human life, but it also raises the interesting possibility of a kind of limited moral accountability for animals (see, e.g., Gen. 9). This is important because it is precisely moral agency that is often specified as a key demarcation point between human beings and other species.

Old Testament law contains several provisions protecting both land and animals. This is especially clear in Deuteronomy's version of Sabbath law. Here rest is entirely democratized and universalized, extending not just to every human member of the household (including servants and aliens, in an important egalitarian move) but also to the household's oxen, donkeys, and other animals (Deut. 5:12-14). If all these are resting, the land must rest as well, a point made explicit in the instructions for Sabbath years and the Jubilee Year (Lev. 25); in both cases, "the land is to have a sabbath of rest, a sabbath to the LORD. . . . The land is to have a year of rest" (Lev. 25:2-5 NIV). Even the holy war regulations contain surprising provisions sparing fruit-bearing trees from being cut down during city sieges (Deut. 20:19). Note that there are good human reasons for these laws, and in the end they protect the long-term sustainability of the land and therefore human well-being. But the texts are explicit in protecting animals and the land, apparently for their own sake as well.

The psalms are notable for their celebration of God-as-Creator and for their sometimes quite detailed descriptive celebrations of God's care for creation. A particular favorite of Christian environmentalists is Psalm 104, which, like Psalm 8, begins with a celebration of God's majesty, splendor, and greatness (Ps. 104:1). This is particularized through careful descriptions of the phenomena of the heavens and the earth, the waters and the air (104:2-9). This psalm notes and celebrates the dependence of the creatures on God's continual provisions for them in creation, including the springs from which the beasts drink; the grass eaten by the cattle; the plants, bread, and wine that God provides and people eat and drink; the carefully described niches in which the various particular named creatures dwell; the cycles of day and night, and the seasons (104:10-23). Our commonality with other creatures is marked as Psalm 104 ends, for "all look to you / to give them their food at the proper time," and for all creatures,

> when you take away their breath,
>   they die and return to the dust. (104:27-29 NIV)

"May the LORD rejoice in his works," says the psalmist, and those works are all of us, all creatures, entirely dependent on God's creation, provision, and care, in a fundamental sense a democracy of creaturely gratitude and need, a fact so often forgotten by proud human image-bearers (104:31). A similarly detailed and awe-inspiring text of this sort is Job 38–41, in which God takes the questioning Job on a detailed tour of creation. These are profound, passionate, loving depictions of the details of creaturely existence and the created world. They reflect a profound sense of creation's sacredness and human embeddedness in creation.

Constructive resources for an ecologically friendly ethic extend to the wisdom sayings of both the Old Testament and the New. These regularly refer to the created order, its regularities and moral structure established from the beginning of creation (Prov. 8), and the behaviors of other creatures that in various ways teach human beings lessons for living their lives (Prov. 17:12; 25:13-14, 25-26; 26:1-3, 11, 17; 27:8; 28:3, 15; 30:17-19, 24-31). One text even describes a righteous person as one who "cares for the needs of his animal" (12:10 NIV), reminiscent of a similar saying by Saint Francis: "If you have men who will exclude any of God's creatures from the shelter of compassion and pity, you will have men who will deal likewise with their fellow men."[21] These observations and exhortations can broaden our sense of the way God stands in relationship to the entirety of the creation, as well as our awareness of sharing a kind of moral community with other creatures whose lives are also governed by the loving and just God of the universe.

The sorrowful brokenness of the creation, despite God's ongoing care, becomes a theme in the prophetic writings — along with promises of the renewal of the whole creation (as we saw in chapter 2), and the healing of the conflicts and fears that separate not just humans from each other but animals from humans as well. So indeed, at the end, in that blessed Day of the Lord, predators will no longer kill, animals will live in community with each other, and neither children nor their parents will have to fear animals —

they will neither harm nor destroy
    on all my holy mountain. (Isa. 11:9 NIV)

When "the Spirit is poured upon us from on high" (Isa. 32:15 NIV), the creation will be renewed. Deserts will become fertile ground, peace will prevail in human community, the land will be fruitful, and both people and animals will dwell in safety (Isa. 32:16-20). The later prophetic writings mix warnings of a fierce coming judgment on God's enemies with promises of the glorious transformation that will then come upon both Israel and the world. First there will be a purgative judgment, then a holistic planetary renewal leading to secure, joyful existence for all creatures (Isa. 65:1-25). How often does our treatment of biblical eschatology address these themes? Do our love and hope extend this far?

Jesus reflects this thoroughly Jewish and prophetic eschatology when he speaks of the restoration (Matt. 17:11) and "the renewal of all things"

---

21. See http://www.all-creatures.org/quotes/francis_saint.html; accessed March 18, 2009.

(Matt. 19:28), and there are certainly far worse summaries of his ministry. I have discussed the centrality of the kingdom or reign of God in the ministry of Jesus (chapter 3), and here would only emphasize that part of that reign was and is the renewal and healing of the broken creation and broken creatures.[22] Not only did Jesus heal the sick and raise the dead, he also calmed the threatening storm and pointed to the future renewal of all things — a renewal gloriously depicted in Revelation in the same words used by Isaiah. One day there shall be no more hurting or destroying, no more suffering or crying or mourning or pain (Rev. 21:1-5; see Isa. 65:17-25). Is it too much to wonder whether this end of suffering, crying, and pain extends to our nonhuman neighbors who also suffer and die? Can that be what Paul refers to when he speaks of the liberation of creation from its bondage to decay (Rom. 8:21)?

These themes take us right into the heart of a Christian theology of salvation, which is logically interconnected with our theology of creation, sin, covenant, and eschatology. Here we are well beyond tweaking an ethic of dominion.

A thoroughgoing concern for God's creation is today contributing to a discovery or rediscovery of a planetary or cosmic rather than human-centered biblical narrative. The whole biblical story is being reframed, moving away from a sole focus on the divine-human drama of creation, fall, and redemption toward a planetary drama involving all God's creatures. Admittedly, staying close to the biblical text entails a special place for humanity — in creation, in sin (and in evoking a divine judgment that sweeps up all creatures into its effects), in redemption, and in the final eschatological drama. But the rest of the created order has begun to reappear in Christian theological treatments of soteriology and eschatology.[23]

In this more cosmic vision, as we have already seen, from the beginning a theology of creation is much more attentive to the full range of God's creatures. While sin is (apparently) a possibility only for human beings (and higher beings, such as the angels), all creation and its creatures are affected. God's long march of redemption begins with Noah and a covenant made with all creatures.

As for the decisive covenant that centers in Jesus Christ, more and

22. Glen H. Stassen and David P. Gushee, *Kingdom Ethics: Following Jesus in Contemporary Context* (Downers Grove, Ill.: InterVarsity, 2003); cf. Isa. 35; Luke 4:16-20.

23. For a recent treatment, see N. T. Wright, *Surprised by Hope: Rethinking Heaven, the Resurrection, and the Mission of the Church* (New York: HarperOne, 2008).

more attention is being paid to grand texts like John 1 and Colossians 1. Together, these texts:

- position the Word as the One through whom all things were made and as the source of "life," apparently both physical and spiritual life, if the distinction is relevant (John 1:3; Col. 1:16);
- describe the Word as "bec[oming] flesh" (John 1:14) in Jesus Christ, forever elevating the value of all fleshly life through the reality of the incarnation (cf. chapter 3);
- describe Christ as the "image of the invisible God" (Col. 1:15), and thus present him as the source and beginning of a renewal of human nature (Col. 1:15-20);
- list a mysterious and extensive array of entities and creatures created by Christ;[24]
- assert that all these were not only created by him but also for him — he is their source, their purpose, and their destiny (Col. 1:16);
- state that "in him all things hold together" (Col. 1:17), which suggests that Christ is somehow the sustaining and centering power of the universe in an ongoing way;
- assert that by being "before all things" and "the firstborn from the dead" (Col. 1:17-18), Christ has supremacy in everything — he is Lord of all who exist, all that exists; and
- assert that God's purpose through Christ is to reconcile to himself "all things, whether on earth or in heaven" (Col. 1:20).

These are exalted themes, high points of biblical revelation. They offer a much bigger story than the relationship between God and humanity. Jesus Christ becomes the hinge and pivot of the entire planetary drama from beginning to end; no creature comes into existence or stays in existence apart from him; and no creature is unaffected by the gospel, the good news that God was in Christ, reconciling the world to himself (2 Cor. 5:19; cf. Mark 16:15).

Paul's treatment of these themes in Romans 8 seems to suggest a relationship between the salvation of humans and the rest of creation in which just as human sin brought creation's groaning, so the salvation of human beings in Christ brings creation's reclamation. That is why a (personified)

---

24. John 1:3; Col. 1:16. "All things in heaven and on earth were created, things visible and invisible, whether thrones or dominions or rulers or powers."

creation can be depicted as "wait[ing] in eager longing for the revealing of the children of God" (Rom. 8:19). In Adam, humans sinned and creation suffered; in Christ, redemption begins and creation rejoices. We are the God-designated servant-leaders of the rest of creation (Gen. 1:26-28), but we are forever connected to that creation as well. When God sent Christ into the world, Paul seems to be saying, his central purpose was to reclaim humanity, but in so doing he acted to reclaim the entirety of the created order, which of course only needed to be reclaimed because human sin brought it low. When we see this, when we see that God was in Christ, reconciling the world to himself, every creature included, we see the ultimate evidence of God's immense valuing of a universe made sacred by divine design, decision, and declaration.

This, finally, is the theological reason why God's ultimate intention for this planet cannot be its destruction by fire. It is hard to overstate how much damage has been done by this particular interpretation of the events of the end, and especially of 2 Peter 3. It seems clear that 2 Peter 3 is much better interpreted as a purgative judgment preliminary to the final renewal of all things. That coheres better with the rest of the Scriptures, in which warnings of ultimate judgment at the Day of the Lord are coupled with promises of the final "renewal of all things." The "new heaven and the new earth" of 2 Peter 3 and Revelation 21 are actually a renewed heaven and renewed earth, where God's intention for this planet at the creation is at last fulfilled. It is hard to see how a God who cares so profoundly for the creatures and all creation could end the planetary drama with raw destruction rather than renewal.

11.6. Some Moral Implications

This theological reframing and rediscovery of the creation dimension of the Bible have certain important moral implications. These I present briefly and will not attempt to develop in detail.

1. We must always treat human beings as part of creation; they are affected by all that is done to creation. We are part of the community of earth creatures, as Larry Rasmussen has put it, and our ethical obligation extends to the whole earth.
2. We must learn to pay attention to evidences of the spillover effects of human actions on the creation, and of creational ills on human well-

being. Consider the rise in various forms of cancer, in infertility and asthma and so much more. What we do to creation we do to ourselves. There is no "nonsmoking" section on the planet.

3. We must learn from other traditions and our own tradition to (re)gain reverence for all creation and creatures and to live more gently on the earth. Francis of Assisi is a great place to start.

4. Even while retaining the concept of the unique *imago Dei,* we must stop treating "humanness" as the standard of valuation of all that counts or matters in creation. This is indeed a kind of human egocentrism, and it has been damaging.

5. We must extend the presumption against (unnecessary) killing and harm-doing to the nonhuman creation; even without embracing full-fledged vegetarianism, this has profound implications for our agricultural, food production, and eating practices.

6. We must look for win-win solutions related to ecological and economic challenges and take a long-term perspective. We must seek what benefits humans, other creatures, and the creation itself in the long term; conversely, what harms one of these three ultimately harms all three.

7. We must understand that ecological ethics is not one discrete area of inquiry but instead is relevant to all areas. What we might call "eco-sacredness" reframes all human enterprises because all depend on the ecological systems that sustain life.

11.7. Embracing a Sacredness-of-Created-Life Ethic

Our question in this chapter has been whether the sacredness-of-life ethic is adequate for an age of ecological degradation and threatened catastrophe. Our happy discovery is that the Scriptures very clearly reveal "a wideness in God's mercy," and that the Bible is full of evidence that God has revealed profound care for nonhuman creatures and the creation in ways that, to our shame, we Christians often miss. It is fair to say from Scripture that a *sacredness-of-created-life* ethic can be found that includes but is not limited to human life. Human beings occupy a special servant-leadership role in creation, but as Scripture consistently teaches, leadership roles entail disproportionate responsibility and not unique status or special privileges. Human failures before God, neighbor, and fellow creatures have damaged relationships at every level. The good news is that Christ's redeeming love is big enough to include the entire created order, which was, after all, made by him, through him, and for him.

A sacredness-of-human-life ethic can be (must be) expanded to include other creaturely neighbors. As Helen Fein wrote in relation to the sad history of indifference to the plight of the Jews during the Holocaust, what is needed is an *expansion* (not abandonment) of a sacred universe of moral obligation.[25] Christians who turned away from Jews when the Nazis were trying to kill them believed that certain lives were sacred, but just not these (Jewish) lives. They would lay down their lives for their own family members, but not for Jewish strangers. This may be understandable at a human level, but it did not reflect the teaching of Jesus. He taught that the stranger and even the enemy must be treated as falling within that sacred universe of moral obligation, and he proved it by living and dying for them — for us.

I do not believe that we must abandon a biblically based sacredness-of-human-life ethic in order to care adequately for God's creation. To the contrary, having recovered the majestic worth of the human person, we can expand our vision to discover the extraordinary value of God's other creatures — and the foundation of both in the majesty and love of God. Indeed, we can make the argument more strongly to say that to recover the true roots of the sacredness of human life in God is also to recover the true roots of the sacredness of all created life. This is at least as much a spiritual experience as it is a theological move. Those who tremble in loving awe before the God of all creation will in turn love and honor all God's creatures. Worship of God is the ultimate origin of a true appreciation for life's sacredness in any of its forms.

As we fall on our knees before God, may we also (re)discover the God-given connectedness of all created life. The evidence is clear all around us that as we care for God's creation well, we care for each other well, and, sadly, the reverse is also true. Human beings are permanently and inextricably connected to other creatures and the rest of the creation. We may be the planetary servant-leaders, but our story is the story of those we lead, our destiny intertwined with theirs, from creation to the end of time. We are as dependent on the rest of creation as it is on us, with the whole dependent on God-in-Christ. The astonishing discovery from Scripture is that God revealed this long ago, through the Word written and the Word

25. Helen Fein, *Accounting for Genocide: National Responses and Jewish Victimization during the Holocaust* (Chicago: University of Chicago Press, 1984), p. 33.

made flesh. Christians lost track of it for a long while. May we recover, internalize, and be transformed by these truths without further delay, taking our appropriate role in the global effort to restore and honor God's sacred yet damaged creation.

12. Final Words: For the Church and Its Neighbors

I call heaven and earth to witness against you today that I have set before you life and death, blessings and curses. Choose life so that you and your descendants may live, loving the LORD your God, obeying him, and holding fast to him; for that means life to you and length of days.

Deuteronomy 30:19-20a

12.1. Where We Started: What It Means to Say That Human Life Is Sacred

This is where we started, with our Christian definition of the sacredness of human life:

Human life is sacred: this means that God has consecrated each and every human being — without exception and in all circumstances — as a unique, incalculably precious being of elevated status and dignity. Through God's revelation in Scripture and incarnation in Jesus Christ, God has declared and demonstrated the sacred worth of human beings and will hold us accountable for responding appropriately. Such a response begins by adopting a posture of reverence and by accepting responsibility for the sacred gift that is a human life. It includes offering due respect and care to each human being that we encounter. It extends to an obligation to protect human life from wanton destruction, desecration, or the violation of human rights. A full embrace of the sacredness of human life leads to a full-hearted commitment to foster human flourishing.

12.2. Summary of Major Discoveries

In exploring the origins and implications, as well as the affirmations and negations, of this Christian ethical vision, we have made a number of discoveries and observations along the way. Here are some of the most important ones, taken roughly in the order in which we encountered them.

We have learned (chapter 1) that to ascribe sacredness to something is to consecrate, hallow, or venerate it, often because of its connection with the divine and always because of its profound importance and differentiation from the ordinary. We Christians ascribe sacredness to human life (or created life more broadly) because we believe we have received divine revelation that God has ascribed such sacred worth to life. Life is sacred, then, not because of anything about it, or intrinsic to it, but because of its connection with the God who created it and who has communicated the breathtaking divine choice to value it as sacred (our final answer to puzzle #7). This comes to us as sheer gift from God, before whom we can only bow in gratitude and awe.

The moral conviction that each individual human life is sacred is a legacy of biblical faith, a product of Jewish and Christian ethics as it emerged from these faith communities, was articulated and practiced in synagogue and church, and shaped the cultures they affected. Indisputably, this is its ultimate origin. The most perceptive secular critics of this conviction agree; Nietzsche, Freud, and Peter Singer are among the most perceptive critics of the religious underpinnings of belief in the sacredness of human life, albeit rejecting that belief. Efforts to retain the substance of the conviction apart from the theological foundations are still attempted and have considerable practical value in offering protections to human rights and dignity, but they have proven deeply vulnerable to incoherence or collapse (our final answer to puzzle #15).

Within the thought-world of historic Christian belief, the conviction that human life is sacred is understood to be a response to divine revelation in God's acts and declarations as recorded in Scripture and culminated in Jesus Christ. Christians have never believed they "invented" this concept, but instead have heard it as God's command and have sought to respond in faithful obedience.

Particularly through our explorations in Nietzsche and in the Nazi era, but also in our glimpse of the treatment of Muslims during the Crusades and the natives during the conquests of the New World, it has become clear that even for Christians (who had Scripture and tradition available!), but really for everyone, fallen human beings all, viewing other humans as persons of sacred worth and inviolable dignity is *not at all* "natural." The opposite seems truer. We humans naturally notice differences and naturally rank people according to those differences, especially when it is in our interests to do so. We have to be *taught* to see each person as equal, valuable, and sacred. We have to *believe* that this teaching carries binding divine command. We have to *choose* (again and again) to retrain our instincts accordingly. We can go wrong at any of these steps. (How often we have indeed gone terribly wrong!) It was not nature that taught us to see people of different abilities, races, and religions as equally and immeasurably valuable. It was divine revelation and the Scriptures and traditions that grew out of it.

This leads to the conclusion, in passing, that probably the natural law tradition should be understood mainly as an ingenious presentation of insights about human nature and vocation that were originally derived from biblical revelation but had become so embedded in Christian culture as to seem to be derivable apart from that revelation. Studying human desecrations of other humans in thought and deed has made me a more convinced skeptic of most claims to nature or natural law, and a more convinced adherent of those who root their theological and moral claims in divine revelation, God's Word to humanity.

We discovered (also in chapter 1) that the term "human dignity" functions today as a modest secularization of "sacredness" useful for discourse in our era. It is a term that post-Christian culture seems to find more congenial as it is somewhat less redolent of incense and church bells and more accessible in multifaith communication. But I sought to show that the roots of that particular term are more classical than biblical, emerging from stratified Greco-Roman cultures in which the original obligation was to treat those of high or noble worth/birth with due reverence and respect, with a different standard of treatment for those of low or humble worth/birth. Judaism and Christianity, when true to their own beliefs, emphasized *the dignity of all persons in community,* but did so with the stronger and theologically richer concept of sacredness. Today many Christians have decided to use the term "dignity" when what they mean is "sacredness," usually importing the theological content of "sacredness" into the vocabulary of "dignity." "Dignity" is certainly not a bad term, and I can readily endorse it when that is the language Christians choose to deploy. Yet I do not believe it is the very best one to reflect the original theological conviction.

413

A key purpose of this book was to offer a more robust account of the biblical materials that helped shape the sacredness-of-life ethic than is usually presented (puzzle #17). As we saw in chapter 2, the Hebrew Bible teaches the sacredness of human life across its genres, and not just through the concept of the image of God. I focused on creation theology, exodus-deliverance themes, covenant-legal materials, and prophetic exhortations, warnings, and visions of shalom. I acknowledged that there are gaps and problems in the Old Testament record in terms of the full application of sacred and equal status to women, slaves, and enemies in war, and that we must frankly admit that faith communities have always sifted through the biblical materials in search of God's Word as it pertains to human worth.

The Old Testament does introduce many of the most important and distinctive features of the sacredness-of-human-life tradition that carry forward into the New Testament and then into the bloodstream of every culture affected by the Bible:

a. It is rooted in claims about God's character, will, and relation to the world.
b. It applies to all human beings and thus has egalitarian implications.
c. It focuses especially on preventing violent killing through its stern bans of murder and threatened punishments.
d. It attends especially to abuses of the weak and powerless and how to prevent them.
e. It inculcates mercy, compassion, and pity toward those in need and in trouble.
f. It sets a transcendent standard of divine justice to which all are accountable.
g. It begins the development of a concept of human rights, focusing especially on the obligation to come to the aid of those who are unable to defend themselves, such as widows, orphans, aliens, and strangers.
h. It constrains human power, especially through divine law and human legal institutions, and thus is one basis of Western traditions of limited government and the rule of law.
i. It establishes a future horizon of "shalom" in which life is lived as God intended it to be.
j. It pictures an activist God who works for this kind of Israel, and this kind of world, and also inculcates a human activism toward these ends. There is no world-weary or complacent acceptance of the world as it is (with the exception of Ecclesiastes).

k. It includes creatures and the creation, though this strand has far too often been overlooked.

This is a considerable heritage! The New Testament (chapter 3) builds on it, as it proclaims that the shalom promised by the Old Testament prophets has dawned in Jesus Christ. The disparate Old Testament strands that had contributed to the sacredness ethic are drawn together, exemplified, and *personalized* in the ministry of Jesus Christ. Jesus incarnates the message of human life's sacred worth, and intensifies it through his teaching that one's (de)sacralizing of the life of the lowliest human being is one's (de)sacralizing of God (Matt. 25:31-46).

New Testament reflection on Jesus Christ himself — his birth, ministry, death, resurrection, and exaltation/ascension — deepens the theological basis of life's sacredness in Christianity by tying the entirety of human existence to the sacred journey of the God-man, Jesus Christ. This also spills over into new thinking about human nature and the reclamation of the originally intended personal and social sacredness of human existence. We saw that the concept of the image of God takes on profound new possibilities as it is reframed as the image of Christ.

The early church (chapter 4) taught and largely lived a life-revering ethic that stands in fundamental continuity with the Old Testament and New Testament themes just outlined. The early church, because of its marginality and political powerlessness, could not hope to affect the major directions of imperial state policy. The church concentrated on living out its distinctive way of life in congregational community and local ministry. The early Christians developed a marked egalitarianism, inclusiveness, holistic rejection of violence, and explicit affirmation of the God-given sacredness of human life over against the divinizing of the emperor, or various demigods, or the creation. We can learn important lessons from how Christianity retained its distinctive moral vision in that context that can be applied to any context.

The emergence of Christendom in the fourth century (chapters 5–6) brought a division in the soul of Christianity, along with paradoxical moral consequences. Despite gains achieved through alliance with the state, the church's prior nonviolence gave way to a support for state-sanctioned violence not only to defend the state but also to defend orthodox Christianity. (The church has wrestled with the issue of violence ever since this time, and I have wrestled with it frequently here, not quite embracing the early church's total rejection of violence but coming to a focus on holy peacemaking, as in Francis of Assisi and nuclear abolition. This is my final word on puzzle #10.) And yet exemplars like Francis and Las Casas and the movements they represent show that the life-revering resources of Scripture and tradition could be submerged and even at times desecrated but never destroyed or extirpated. The sacred worth of each as God's image, human equality, preventing unjust and violent killing, concern for the weak and powerless, deep compassion and pity, affirmation of a transcendent standard of justice, human rights, and constraints on absolute power under the rule of law all surfaced during the Christendom era — and not only with occasional saints, but also within more mainstream traditions such as just-war theory and some aspects of natural law (chapter 7).

The story of theological and state anti-Semitism (chapter 6) reveals a pre-Christendom flaw rooted in unique features of the birth of Christianity from the womb of Judaism in the first century. The inability to tolerate religious cognitive dissonance began here and worked its way disastrously through the Christian tradition until Christian dissenters such as Richard Overton began the resistance that eventually led to bans on that kind of state power for the church. Finally it was recognized that freedom, especially religious liberty, is fundamental to the sacredness of human life before God and in human community. A theme — freedom — that is arguably a minority strand within the biblical tradition became more and more important politically and theologically in the early modern period and then forward from there (chapter 7). This was the beginning of the modern expansion of human rights, claims to universal human equality, incipient democracy, the rule of law, and limited government. In its earliest stage these themes were not rejections of the Christian moral tradition but instead efforts to protect its insights while preventing the church from politically enforcing its orthodoxy/ies. Locke and Kant were profiled to help illustrate this part of the story. I venture the provocation that Christianity's original sin was anti-Semitism, that the fruit of that sin was 1,500 years of state-religious persecution of those who did not adhere to the reigning Christian orthodoxy, and that the punishment the church received for that sin was political disestablishment (which was good) and intellectual rejection of Christianity itself (which in many ways proved disastrous). In any event, the foregoing paragraphs offer my final answer to puzzle #16, my assessment of how at least some very notable Christians have discharged their responsibilities to treat human life as sacred.

Nietzsche (chapter 8) was profiled because he is the best exemplar of the intellectual rejection of Christianity, of the collapse of both the theological foundations and moral convictions that had shaped Christian culture. He first *described* their weakening and then *evangelized* for their demise. Eventually he explicitly rejected every aspect of the sacredness tradition in the name of the flourishing of the "best" of the species, which marked a dangerous kind of aristocratic naturalism pitting the flourishing of some against the basic well-being and dignity of all (puzzles #2, #12). Nietzsche's epistemological skepticism (not to mention Kant's skepticism) shakes the revelational foundations of the sacredness claim. We do live on the other side of the epistemological crisis of modernity. But still, even if we were to grant that skepticism, I would happily lay the fruits of the biblical sacredness-of-life tradition against the fruits of Nietzsche's theology and ethics and those who have claimed him, which may be the best we can do in these postmodern times in publicly assessing competing truth claims.

Among those movements redolent with Nietzschean themes was Nazism (chapter 9). We amply explored the moral sickness of that ideology and the moral disaster it produced. Perhaps our greatest surprise was the way in which Hitler and the Nazis scooped up and radicalized almost all the most problematic strands of Western/Christian history and thought, implementing them with fanatical ruthlessness, aided and abetted by modern state bureaucracy and then-modern technology — such as gas chambers and crematoria.

Many have pointed out that the ancient human capacity for hatred combined with new human technological capacities means that humanity's ability to desecrate one another and the creation is greater than ever. We can abort children at will, now through a prescription. We can tinker with the very genetic code. We can kill criminals at the press of a button. We can enslave and mutilate women on a vast scale. We can push the nuclear button and end it all more or less instantaneously, or slowly poison the ecosystems, other creatures, and ourselves (chapters 10–11). We must, quite literally, "choose life so that [we] and [our] descendants may live" (Deut. 30:19).

I think this study has contributed insights that can thicken the original Christian definition of the sacredness of life as well as help us understand how to resolve the most important remaining puzzles associated with it.

We have learned, in considering puzzle #2, that revering human life requires attending simultaneously to each individual, holistically understood, unique and irreplaceable; but it also demands attention to the multifaceted structures of human community in which human dignity is protected and human flourishing advanced, and the well-being of the species and planet as a whole. Nietzsche and the Nazis have taught us to be especially vigilant about the dangers of emphasizing group and species interests over the rights and needs of each and every individual, but our contemporary ecological challenges have forced us to a more connectional understanding of the way in which human beings, communities, and ecosystems are inextricably related to one another. We must protect individual human rights, for sure, but we also must create cultures and economic practices that are sustainable in the interests of long-term human well-being.

We have found ourselves returning constantly to a reaffirmation of human rights (puzzle #11), even in the face of critics. To affirm the sacredness of life requires the prevention of victimization of all people, without exception, through war, torture, crime, abuse, rape, neglect, and, yes, abortion and involuntary euthanasia (puzzle #3), as well as other attacks on the security of body, person, and community. It leads us into active, compassionate mercy on behalf of the poor, the weak, the powerless, the sick, the suffering, and any others who cannot fully protect their own interests, which is all of us some of the time and some of us all of the time. It makes us especially vigilant about our human temptation to exempt certain groups from fully human or fully personal status (puzzle #8) so that we might more readily work our will against them, as well as any tendency to put a price on the value of a human life, which Kant helped us to see is the antithesis of human dignity (our final answer to puzzle #4). It leads us to a commitment toward empowerment of communities so that powerless people can gain power and full and equal moral/legal status, and not have to depend on the vagaries of human compassion.

Protecting human rights — as an aspect of honoring the sacredness of human life — is everyone's responsibility (puzzle #14). It demands the establishment not just of churches committed to human rights but also of civic and political structures advancing justice, including limited, participatory government under the rule of law, the protection of liberty of religion and conscience, and other God-given human rights and freedoms. It depends on the creation of cultures that elevate the dignity of human life rather than allow the routine desecration of life, whether in entertainment, family life, religion, sports, or any other social practice. It requires vigilant resistance to all ideologies, hatreds, and passions tending toward the dehumanization and degradation of the "other."

Our wrestling with what exactly makes human life sacred began with our discussion of the meaning of the image of God. There we learned to be suspicious of historic and contemporary, Christian and secular, treatments of human (or animal) worth based on some rendering of person- or worth-making capacities or qualities, perhaps capacities that define a life as carrying intrinsic dignity (we rejected all "intrinsic" or "inherent" language — puzzle #7). By moving worth-making or sacredness-ascribing entirely into God's hands, we sought to avoid the dangers that emerge with capacities-based understandings and behavior-based ascriptions. Such dangers include the loss of full sacredness/dignity/worth through loss of capacities, or the forfeiting of sacred worth through some (purported) act or shortcoming such as murder or terrorism. Our final answer to puzzles #5 and #6 is that no capacity a human can lose, and no act a human can perform, can cause a human being to lose or forfeit his ascribed status as sacred in God's sight. Our final answer to puzzle #1 is that this theocentric understanding of where sacred worth comes from is applicable to other creatures in their own distinctive ways and is a theme visible in the Scriptures when they are revisited with fresh eyes. It is not necessary to buy human value at the expense of denigrating other species if the focus is on God rather than on capacities.

A full-hearted Christian vision of life's sacred worth moves beyond respect for each and every human life toward an expansive vision of human flourishing, the creation of social conditions in which all human beings can reach their God-given potential (puzzle #12). Our discussion of the Ten Commandments helped clarify that different relationships do create different responsibilities, with the more intimate ties of marriage and family life, for example, leading to more profound and direct responsibilities to contribute to the flourishing of particular human beings. We acknowledged that there might indeed be a plausible set of distinctions drawn between minimal and maximal obligations to human beings depending on our particular relationships with them (puzzle #9).

And yet this was affirmed without abandonment of the broader claim that if each and every human life is sacred in God's sight, then each and every life must be perceived as sacred by everyone who believes in and seeks to honor God. One might say that communities of religious believers — churches — are called to accept an obligation to adopt a posture of reverence and to work for the flourishing of every human life even if and when our societies fail to perceive such an obligation. This claim is itself a reminder that belief that human life is sacred emerged from the particular experiences of the Jewish and Christian communities with the God who spoke to them, and that with this privilege of hearing God's Word come responsibility to live in obedience, and a coming accountability before God, that may be different from the responsibilities and accountabilities of others (our final answer to puzzle #13).

Honoring life is a holistic, comprehensive, and unfinished project, extending across the human life span and the span of human and planetary history. It is a project encompassing creational, social, interpersonal, and individual life, addressing the human being in her wholeness as a spiritual and physical being, a creature of God and earth. The very idea that respecting life's sacred worth is *the* central human project is itself biblically rooted and flows from the depiction of God's activities in the biblical canon. The biblical picture is that we join a compassionate, just, and loving God in an activist, responsible, eschatological project of (re)sacralizing life, even as we await God's gracious consummation of this project at the end of time. Amidst heartbreaking failures and occasional breakthroughs, we work and we wait for a world in which human life is treated as it should be and the creation flourishes under humanity's tender care.

12.3. The Thirty-six Righteous

Throughout this book the contrast between the beautiful vision of life's immeasurable sacredness and the desecrations inflicted upon the world by human beings has been at times overwhelming and unbearable. At least it has been for me. If I have done my work well, it will have been for you as well.

Often I have been reminded of Nietzsche's claim that if any human being were actually able to shift his focus from his own affairs and enter into the lives of others, "[he] would have to despair about the value of life; if he were able to grasp and feel mankind's overall consciousness in himself, he would collapse with a curse against existence." Of course, for Nietzsche the thing about human existence that would evoke such despair would be "the ultimate aimlessness of men." For me, the temptation to despair is found in the sheer volume and creativity of human desecrations in this good world made by a good God. We don't just squander our lives in aimlessness — we desecrate them, along with the entire creation. And we do so using a cunning and ingenuity that only creatures of high gifts and talents could reach.

Have you wondered while reading this book, as I have while writing it, why God puts up with us? Have you wondered why a holy God who made us for sacredness permits the species to live another day amidst our desecrations of life? Or perhaps, have you wondered about whether God is good, or whether God is there at all? The contrast between the sacredness toward which we aspire and the desecrations we so often inflict and endure must raise the question of theodicy. Where is God in a world like this?

I am reminded of a story from Jewish tradition that I discovered while writing my first book, *The Righteous Gentiles of the Holocaust.* One strand of the Jewish tradition built upon the story of Abraham's negotiations with God over the fate of Sodom (Gen. 18) to propose that God bears with the world for the sake of thirty-six righteous persons whose goodness holds back his wrath. These are the *lamed vav zaddikim* — the thirty-six righteous. They are scattered throughout the world, according to this lovely legend. They are not confined to the Jewish people. And God makes sure that in every generation there are at least thirty-six.

These *lamedvovniks* (the thirty-six righteous, in Yiddish!) are the kinds of people Nick Kristof and Sheryl WuDunn write about in their book *Half the Sky* (and the kind of people they *seem to be*, actually). These are the people who go to the poorest, harshest, and most dangerous places on earth to do things like stitch up raped women's bowels and break up sex trafficking rings. They are the people who visit death row prisoners and treat them with dignity while also grieving with crime victims. They are the human rights protesters who stare down tyrants in the name of human worth. They are ecologists who share a sacred bond with earth's disappearing species and seek to save them. They are the fighters against racism, against misogyny, against starvation, against xenophobia, against nuclear proliferation, against hatred of gays. They are the families that take in abandoned children and walk through a pregnancy with a woman in crisis. They are the diplomats who broker peace agreements and the activists who lay down in front of the world's parliaments to end modern-day slavery. They are the thirty-six. They hold back God's wrath and perhaps bring a smile now and again to God's weeping countenance.

At a theological level, I find some comfort if not clear answers in the idea that when Jesus was on the cross he indeed took upon himself the sin and suffering of every human being who ever lived. He lived what Nietzsche speculated. And in that moment he did cry out, "My God, my God, why have you forsaken me?" It was not a curse against existence; but it was a howl of pain. I find sad, strange comfort in the idea that the way a good God redeems a world like this is to come in human flesh and take every drop of blood and pain into the Godhead, to die under the weight of human suffering and so somehow to transfigure and redeem that suffering.

At a moral level, I am quite convinced that the meaning of human existence in this desecrated world is found precisely where we participate in its healing, its resacralization. Every time we treat human beings with tender reverence, take responsibility for the sacred gift of human life, protect people from wanton destruction and desecration, and commit our best efforts to human flourishing, we are doing what we were made to do. Could it be that as long as God finds the "thirty-six" out there doing such work, God will bear with us? Could it be that the only proper response to this book is to try to be one of those thirty-six? Not words about life's sacredness, but deeds that make life truly sacred — that is what most matters . . .

12.4. Honoring Life Together

I want to say a final word to my Christian brothers and sisters. We are the trustees of a great tradition, and an even greater revelation. To us and our Jewish elder brothers we were given the divine revelation that before God each and every human life is sacred, and that it is our task to nurture a world that recognizes that sacredness. Even today, in a very special and unique way, together with our Jewish friends, we bear that tradition forward into the world.

Sometimes Christian spokespeople speak and write as if they are oh-so-proud of Christian moral superiority and Christian responsibility for creating and delivering this great tradition to the world. But as Scripture itself says, "It is not because of your righteousness or the uprightness of your heart" that God chose you (Deut. 9:5a). God calls whom God wills; God speaks to whom God wills. That God chose to deliver a word to the world to and through the Jewish and Christian peoples is no cause for pride. Certainly we Christians in particular have plenty of reason for humility when we consider the very, very many ways in which we botched our responsibilities, including when we turned against our own covenant sibling. And when we got our hands on political power, we used that power to advance our own interests rather than life's sacredness, and often at the cost of life's sacredness. The earth became drenched with the blood that we spilled! Much of our history is utterly revolting!

So "the kingdom [was] taken away from [us]" (Matt. 21:43). During and after the Enlightenment a culture that had once *desired* the marriage of church and state *rejected* such arrangements. We lost the power to rule and eventually lost the power to exercise intellectual hegemony over a culture we had once dominated. Even today, many of our most thoughtful (and some of our least thoughtful) leaders seethe with resentment over our lost kingdom.

But our loss of power may have been a gain for our moral witness. In fewer and fewer places do we have the power to impose our will or to order violence for our various causes. Many of us have been led back to our core vision and to the noncoercive way, the only way available to us, to advance it. And even in "Christian" America, if we want to advance the sacredness-of-life vision (or any other one), we Christians must do so in humble partnership with people who do not share our religious beliefs.

The project of respecting the equal, immeasurable, and sacred worth of each and every human being and God's awesome creation now belongs to all humanity. Because of our enhanced power to destroy each other and creation, we *together* must choose to continue life on earth. And we have a precious resource to help us do that: the sacredness-of-life tradition. An ancient biblical vision has become key to the world's future. We will honor creation and human life together, across religions, nations, and cultures, or we will perish together. Treat life as sacred! This is God's command — to all humanity. The response is up to all of us.

Bibliography

Aldunate, José. "La Acción que Habla a las Conciencias." In *La No Violencia Activa: presencia y desafíos,* edited by José Aldunate, S.J., et al. Santiago: ILADES, 1988.

Allman, Mark J. *Who Would Jesus Kill? War, Peace, and the Christian Tradition.* Winona, Minn.: St. Mary's Press, 2003.

Ameriks, Karl. "Immanuel Kant." In *The Columbia History of Western Philosophy,* edited by Richard Popkin, pp. 494-502. New York: Columbia University Press, 1999.

Armstrong, Karen. *Holy War.* New York: Anchor Books, 1992.

Atkins, Stephen E. *Holocaust Denial as an International Movement.* Westport, Conn.: Praeger, 2009.

Atkinson, David J., et al., eds. *IVP New Dictionary of Christian Ethics and Pastoral Theology.* Downers Grove, Ill.: InterVarsity, 1995.

Bainton, Roland. *Christian Attitudes toward War and Peace.* Nashville: Abingdon, 1960.

Barnett, Victoria. *For the Soul of the People: Protestant Protest against Hitler.* Oxford and New York: Oxford University Press, 1998.

Barth, Karl. *Dogmatics in Outline.* New York: Harper and Row, 1959.

———. *Church Dogmatics III/2: The Doctrine of Creation.* Translated by H. Knight et al. Edinburgh: T. & T. Clark, 1960.

Barton, John. *Understanding Old Testament Ethics: Approaches and Explorations.* Louisville: Westminster John Knox, 2003.

Barton, Stephen C., ed. *Holiness: Past and Present.* London and New York: T. & T. Clark, 2003.

Bauckham, Richard. *The Climax of Prophecy.* Edinburgh: T. & T. Clark, 1993.

———. *Gospel Women: Studies of the Named Women in the Gospels.* Grand Rapids: Eerdmans, 2002.

Bauer, Susan Wise. *The History of the Medieval World.* New York: Norton, 2010.

Beasley, David. "Exhibit Honors Diplomats Who Saved Jews from Holocaust." *Global Atlanta.* http://www.globalatlanta.com/article/23926/. Accessed April 30, 2011.

Beker, J. Christiaan. *Paul the Apostle: The Triumph of God in Life and Thought.* Philadelphia: Fortress, 1980.

Bellamy, Chris. *Absolute War: Soviet Russia in the Second World War.* New York: Vintage Books, 2007.

Benhabib, Selya. *Situating the Self: Gender, Community, and Postmodernism in Contemporary Ethics.* New York: Routledge, 1992.

———. *The Rights of Others: Aliens, Residents, and Citizens.* Cambridge: Cambridge University Press, 2004.

Bergen, Doris L. *War and Genocide: A Concise History of the Holocaust.* Lanham, Md.: Rowman and Littlefield, 2002.

Bernardin, Joseph Cardinal. *Consistent Ethic of Life.* Kansas City, Mo.: Sheed and Ward, 1988.

Berry, Thomas. *The Dream of the Earth.* San Francisco: Sierra Club Books, 1988.

Birch, Bruce C. *Let Justice Roll Down: The Old Testament, Ethics, and Christian Life.* Louisville: Westminster John Knox, 1991.

Bonhoeffer, Dietrich. *Discipleship.* Vol. 6 of *Dietrich Bonhoeffer Works.* Minneapolis: Fortress, 2003.

———. *Ethics.* Vol. 4 of *Dietrich Bonhoeffer Works.* Minneapolis: Fortress, 2005.

Borg, Marcus J. *Conflict, Holiness, and Politics in the Teachings of Jesus.* Harrisburg, Pa.: Trinity, 1984.

———. *Jesus: A New Vision; Spirit, Culture, and the Life of Discipleship.* San Francisco: Harper and Row, 1987.

Boyd, Gregory A. *The Myth of a Christian Nation: How the Quest for Political Power Is Destroying the Church.* Grand Rapids: Zondervan, 2005.

Brague, Rémi. *The Law of God: The Philosophical History of an Idea.* Translated by Lydia G. Cochrane. Chicago: University of Chicago Press, 2007.

Brands, H. W. *American Colossus: The Triumph of Capitalism, 1865-1900.* New York: Doubleday, 2010.

Brown, William P. *The Ethos of the Cosmos.* Grand Rapids: Eerdmans, 1999.

———, ed. *The Ten Commandments: The Reciprocity of Faithfulness.* Louisville: Westminster John Knox, 2004.

Browning, Christopher R. *Ordinary Men: Reserve Policy Battalion 101 and the Final Solution in Poland.* New York: HarperCollins, 1992.

Brueggemann, Walter. *Living toward a Vision: Biblical Reflections on Shalom.* 2nd ed. New York: United Church Press, 1982.

———. *A Social Reading of the Old Testament: Prophetic Approaches to Israel's Communal Life.* Minneapolis: Fortress, 1994.

Brunner, Emil. *Revelation and Reason: The Christian Doctrine of Faith and Knowledge.* Translated by Olive Wyon, chapter 11. Philadelphia: Westminster, 1946.

Buber, Martin. *I and Thou.* New York: Simon and Schuster, 1970.

Budzeszewski, J. *Written on the Heart: The Case for Natural Law.* Downers Grove, Ill.: InterVarsity, 1997.

————. *What We Can't Not Know: A Guide.* Dallas: Spence Publishing, 2003.

Burleigh, Michael, and Wolfgang Wippermann. *The Racial State: Germany, 1933-1945.* Cambridge: Cambridge University Press, 1992.

Burridge, Richard A. *Imitating Jesus: An Inclusive Approach to New Testament Ethics.* Grand Rapids: Eerdmans, 2007.

Cahill, Lisa Sowle. *Love Your Enemies: Discipleship, Pacifism, and Just War Theory.* Minneapolis: Augsburg Fortress, 1994.

Callahan, Daniel. "Defending the Sanctity of Life." *Society* (July/August 2001): 16-19.

Carroll, James. *Constantine's Sword.* New York: Houghton Mifflin, 2001.

Castro, Daniel. *Another Face of Empire: Bartolomé de Las Casas, Indigenous Rights, and Ecclesiastical Imperialism.* Durham, N.C., and London: Duke University Press, 2007.

Catechism of the Catholic Church. 1934. New York: Doubleday, 1995; 2nd ed. 1997.

Charles, J. Daryl. *Between Pacifism and Jihad: Just War and Christian Tradition.* Downers Grove, Ill.: InterVarsity, 2005.

Chesterton, G. K. *Saint Francis of Assisi.* New York: Image Books, [1924] 1957.

————. *Orthodoxy: The Romance of Faith.* New York: Doubleday, [1908] 1990.

Childress, James F., and John Macquarrie, eds. *The Westminster Dictionary of Christian Ethics.* Philadelphia: Westminster, 1986.

Childs, Brevard. *Old Testament Theology in a Canonical Context.* Philadelphia: Fortress, 1985.

Chilton, Bruce, and J. I. H. McDonald. *Jesus and the Ethics of the Kingdom.* Grand Rapids: Eerdmans, 1979.

Chrysostom, John. "Antioch Sermons." In *The Fathers of the Church,* translated by Paul W. Harkins. Washington, D.C.: CUA Press, 1979.

Claiborne, Shane, and Chris Haw. *Jesus for President.* Grand Rapids: Zondervan, 2008.

Clough, David L., and Brian Stiltner. *Faith and Force: A Christian Debate about War.* Washington, D.C.: Georgetown University Press, 2007.

Colson, Charles, with Ellen Santilli Vaughn. *God and Government.* Grand Rapids: Zondervan, 2005.

Cone, James H. *God of the Oppressed.* New York: HarperCollins, 1975.

Constantine, Augustus, and Licinius Augustus. "The Edict of Milan." Translated by the University of Pennsylvania Department of History. http://gbgm-umc.org/UMW/Bible/milan.stm. Accessed March 26, 2010.

Conyers, A. J. *The Long Truce: How Toleration Made the World Safe for Power and Profit.* Dallas: Spence Publishing, 2001.

Coons, John E., and Patrick M. Brennan. *By Nature Equal: The Anatomy of a Western Insight.* Princeton: Princeton University Press, 1999.

Couenhoven, Jessie. "Christianity, the Enlightenment, and Political Life: A Transformed Landscape?" Presented at a meeting of the Society of Christian Ethics, New Orleans, January 2011.

Crossan, John Dominic. *The Historical Jesus: The Life of a Mediterranean Jewish Peasant.* New York: HarperSanFrancisco, 1991.

———. *God and Empire: Jesus against Rome, Then and Now.* New York: HarperCollins, 2007.

Culpepper, R. Alan. "The Gospel of John and the Jews." *Review and Expositor* 84 (1987): 273-88.

Daly, Mary. *Beyond God the Father: Toward a Philosophy of Women's Liberation.* Boston: Beacon Press, 1993.

Davies, Stevan L. *Jesus the Healer.* London: SCM, 1995.

Davis, James Calvin. *The Moral Theology of Roger Williams: Christian Conviction and Public Ethics.* Louisville: Westminster John Knox, 2004.

Dawson, Christopher. *The Formation of Christendom.* San Francisco: Ignatius, [1965] 2008.

Deloria, Vine, et al. *God Is Red: A Native View of Religion.* 30th anniversary ed. Golden, Colo.: Fulcrum Publishing, 2003.

DeWitt, Calvin B. *Caring for Creation: Responsible Stewardship of God's Handiwork.* Edited by James W. Skillen and Luis E. Lugo. Grand Rapids: Baker, 1998.

Diamond, Jared. *Collapse: How Societies Choose to Fail or Succeed.* New York: Penguin, 2005.

Dodd, William E. "The Bible of a Political Church." In *The Nazi Primer,* translated by Harwood L. Childs, pp. 256-80. New York: Harper and Brothers, 1938.

Dyck, Arthur J. *Rethinking Rights and Responsibilities: The Moral Bonds of Community.* Rev. ed. Washington, D.C.: Georgetown University Press, 2005.

Eisler, Riane. *The Chalice and the Blade: Our History, Our Future.* San Francisco: Harper and Row, 1987.

Elliott, Neil. *The Arrogance of Nations: Reading Romans in the Shadow of Empire.* Minneapolis: Fortress, 2008.

Elshtain, Jean Bethke. *Who Are We? Critical Reflections and Hopeful Possibilities.* Grand Rapids: Eerdmans, 2000.

Eusebius. *The History of the Church.* Translated by G. A. Williamson. London: Penguin, 1965.

Fein, Helen. *Accounting for Genocide: National Responses and Jewish Victimization during the Holocaust.* Chicago: University of Chicago Press, 1984.

Ferguson, Niall. *Empire: How Britain Made the Modern World.* London: Penguin Books, 2003.

Finnis, John. *Natural Law and Natural Rights.* Oxford: Clarendon, 1980.

Flannery, Fr. Edward. *The Anguish of the Jews.* New York: Macmillan, 1965.

Ford, J. Massyngbaerde. *My Enemy Is My Guest: Jesus and Violence in Luke.* Maryknoll, N.Y.: Orbis, 1984.

Forrester, Duncan. *On Human Worth.* London: SCM, 2001.

Fox, Matthew. *Original Blessing: A Primer in Creation Spirituality Presented in Four*

Paths, Twenty-six Themes, and Two Questions. Santa Fe, N.Mex.: Bear and Co., 1983.

Fox, Robin Lane. *Pagans and Christians.* San Francisco: Harper and Row, 1986.

Francis, Saint. In "Quotations Archive." *All-creatures.org.* http://www.all-creatures .org/quotes/francis_saint.html. Accessed March 18, 2009.

Fredriksen, Paula. *Augustine and the Jews: A Christian Defense of Jews and Judaism.* New York: Doubleday, 2008.

Freeman, Michael. "National Self-Determination, Peace, and Human Rights." *Peace Review* 10, no. 2 (Summer 1998): 157-63.

Frend, W. H. C. *The Early Church.* Philadelphia: Fortress, 1982.

Freud, Sigmund. *The Future of an Illusion.* Translated by James Strachey. New York: Norton, 1961.

Friedländer, Saul. *Nazi Germany and the Jews: The Years of Persecution, 1933-1939.* New York: HarperCollins, 1997.

———. *The Origins of Nazi Genocide: From Euthanasia to the Final Solution.* Chapel Hill: University of North Carolina Press, 1997.

Fritzsche, Peter. *Life and Death in the Third Reich.* Cambridge: Harvard University Press, Belknap Press, 2008.

Furfey, Paul Hanly. "Social Action in the Early Church, 30-180 A.D." *Theological Studies* 2, no. 2 (1941): 89-108.

Furtak, Rick Anthony. Introduction to *The Birth of Tragedy,* by Friedrich Nietzche, translated by William A. Hausmann, pp. vii-xiii. New York: Barnes and Noble, 2006.

Galston, William A. *Public Matters: Politics, Policy, and Religion in the 21st Century.* New York: Rowman and Littlefield, 2005.

Gamwell, Franklin I. *The Divine Good: Modern Moral Theory and the Necessity of God.* New York: HarperCollins, 1990.

Geisler, Norman L. *Christian Ethics: Options and Issues.* Grand Rapids: Baker, 1989.

Gellately, Robert. *Backing Hitler: Consent and Coercion in Nazi Germany.* Oxford and New York: Oxford University Press, 2001.

Getty-Sullivan, Mary Ann. *Women in the New Testament.* Collegeville, Minn.: Liturgical Press, 2001.

Gillespie, Michael Allen. *The Theological Origins of Modernity.* Chicago and London: University of Chicago Press, 2009.

Goeschel, Christian. *Suicide in Nazi Germany.* New York and Oxford: Oxford University Press, 2009.

Goldhagen, Daniel Jonah. *Hitler's Willing Executioners: Ordinary Germans and the Holocaust.* New York: Knopf, 1996.

González, Justo L. *The Story of Christianity.* Vol. 1. New York: HarperCollins, 1984.

Gorman, Michael J. *Abortion and the Early Church: Christian, Jewish, and Pagan Attitudes in the Greco-Roman World.* Eugene, Oreg.: Wipf and Stock, 1998.

Grassi, Joseph A. *Jesus Is Shalom: A Vision of Peace from the Gospels.* New York: Paulist, 2006.

Gray, John. *The Biblical Doctrine of the Reign of God.* Edinburgh: T. & T. Clark, 1979.

Greenberg, Irving. *For the Sake of Heaven and Earth: The New Encounter between Judaism and Christianity.* Philadelphia: Jewish Publication Society, 2004.

Grenville, J. A. S. *A History of the World from the 20th to the 21st Century.* London: Routledge, 2005.

Grenz, Stanley J., and Jay T. Smith. *Pocket Dictionary of Ethics.* Downers Grove, Ill.: InterVarsity, 2003.

Gundry-Volf, Judith M. "The Least and the Greatest: Children in the New Testament." In *The Child in Christian Thought,* edited by Marcia J. Bunge, pp. 29-60. Grand Rapids: Eerdmans, 2001.

Gushee, David P. *Righteous Gentiles of the Holocaust: Genocide and Moral Obligation.* 2nd ed. Minneapolis: Paragon House, 2003.

————. *Getting Marriage Right.* Grand Rapids: Baker, 2004.

————. "Five Reasons Torture Is Always Wrong." *Christianity Today,* February 2006, pp. 33-37.

————. *The Future of Faith in American Politics: The Public Witness of the Evangelical Center.* Waco, Tex.: Baylor University Press, 2008.

Gushee, David P., and Sheri B. Lovett. "The *Porraimos:* Toward the Reclamation of the Gypsy Experience of the Holocaust." Paper presented at 1999 Scholars' Conference on the Holocaust.

Gutiérrez, Gustavo. *A Theology of Liberation.* Maryknoll, N.Y.: Orbis, 1973.

————. *Las Casas: In Search of the Poor of Jesus Christ.* Maryknoll, N.Y.: Orbis, 1993.

Hanke, Lewis. *All Mankind Is One: A Study of the Disputation between Bartolomé de Las Casas and Juan Ginés de Sepúlveda on the Religious and Intellectual Capacity of the American Indians.* De Kalb: Northern Illinois University Press, 1974.

Harrelson, Walter. *The Ten Commandments and Human Rights.* Philadelphia: Fortress, 1980.

Hartman, Donniel. "'I Am the Lord Your God': God as Advocate — God as Foe of the Ethical." Unpublished paper, February 8, 2011.

Hauerwas, Stanley. *After Christendom?* Nashville: Abingdon, 1991.

Haynes, Stephen. *Noah's Curse: The Biblical Justification for American Slavery.* New York: Oxford University Press, 2002.

Hays, Richard B. *The Moral Vision of the New Testament: Community, Cross, New Creation.* New York: HarperOne, 1996.

Headley, John. *The Europeanization of the World: On the Origins of Human Rights and Democracy.* Princeton: Princeton University Press, 2008.

Hendricks, Obery, Jr. *The Politics of Jesus.* New York: Doubleday, 2006.

Henkin, Louis, et al. *International Law: Cases and Materials.* 2nd ed. St. Paul: West Publishing Co., 1987.

Heschel, Susannah. *The Aryan Jesus: Christian Theologians and the Bible in Nazi Germany.* Princeton: Princeton University Press, 2008.

Hiers, Richard H. *Justice and Compassion in Biblical Law.* New York and London: Continuum, 2010.

Hilberg, Raul. *The Destruction of the European Jews.* Rev. ed. New York: Holmes and Meier, 1985.

Hill, Jonathan. *What Has Christianity Ever Done for Us?* Downers Grove, Ill.: InterVarsity, 2005.

Himmelfarb, Gertrude. *The Roads to Modernity: The British, French, and American Enlightenments.* New York: Knopf, 2004.

Himmler, Heinrich. "Audio Excerpts from the Speech Given by Heinrich Himmler to SS Group Leaders in Posen, Occupied Poland." *The History Place.* http:// www.historyplace.com/worldwar2/holocaust/h-posen.htm. Accessed April 30, 2011.

Hitler, Adolf. *Mein Kampf.* Boston: Houghton Mifflin, [1925] 1971.

Hoekema, Anthony A. *Created in God's Image.* Grand Rapids: Eerdmans, 1986.

Horsley, Richard A., ed. *In the Shadow of Empire: Reclaiming the Bible as a History of Faithful Resistance.* Louisville and London: Westminster John Knox, 2008.

Horsley, Richard A., and Neil Asher Silberman. *The Message and the Kingdom: How Jesus and Paul Ignited a Revolution and Transformed the Ancient World.* Minneapolis: Fortress, 1997.

House, Adrian. *Francis of Assisi: A Revolutionary Life.* Mahwah, N.J.: HiddenSpring, 2000.

Hunt, Lynn. *Inventing Human Rights: A History.* New York: Norton, 2008.

Huntington, Samuel P. *The Clash of Civilizations and the Remaking of World Order.* New York: Simon and Schuster, 1996.

Isaac, Jules. *Jesus and Israel.* Translated by Sally Gran. New York: Holt, Rinehart and Winston, [1959] 1971.

Jacob, Edmond. *Theology of the Old Testament.* New York: Harper and Brothers, 1958.

Janzen, Waldemar. *Old Testament Ethics.* Louisville: Westminster John Knox, 1994.

Jarausch, Konrad H. "The Conundrum of Complicity: German Professionals and the Final Solution." United States Holocaust Memorial Museum, 2002.

Jennings, Willie James. *The Christian Imagination: Theology and the Origins of Race.* New Haven and London: Yale University Press, 2010.

John Paul II. *The Gospel of Life.* New York: Random House, 1995.

Johnson, Luke Timothy. *Among the Gentiles: Greco-Roman Religion and Christianity.* New Haven and London: Yale University Press, 2009.

Jolley, Nicholas. "Locke on Faith and Reason." In *The Cambridge Companion to Locke's "Essay concerning Human Understanding,"* edited by Lex Newman, pp. 436-55. Cambridge: Cambridge University Press, 2007.

Jones, L. Gregory. *Embodying Forgiveness: A Theological Analysis.* Grand Rapids: Eerdmans, 1995.

"Judaism: Euthanasia and Suicide." *BBC online.* July 21, 2009. http://www.bbc.co.uk/religion/religions/judaism/jewishethics/euthanasia.shtml.

Kaiser, Walter J., Jr. *Toward Old Testament Ethics.* Grand Rapids: Zondervan, 1983.

Kant, Immanuel. *Groundwork of the Metaphysic of Morals.* Translated and analyzed by H. J. Paton. New York: Harper and Row, 1948.

———. "The Critique of Pure Reason." In *Great Books of the Western World,* edited by Robert Maynard Hutchins, 42:1-252. New York: Encyclopaedia Britannica, 1952.

Kass, Leon R. *Life, Liberty, and the Defense of Dignity.* San Francisco: Encounter Books, 2002.

Kaufmann, Walter. Translator's preface to *Thus Spoke Zarathustra,* by Friedrich Nietzsche, edited and translated by Walter Kaufmann, pp. xiii-xxii. New York: Penguin, 1966.

———. *Nietzsche: Philosopher, Psychologist, Antichrist.* 3rd ed. Princeton: Princeton University Press, 1968.

———, ed. and trans. *The Portable Nietzsche.* New York: Penguin, 1954.

Kee, Howard Clark, et al., eds. *Christianity: A Social and Cultural History.* Upper Saddle River, N.J.: Prentice-Hall, 1998.

Keener, Craig S. *Paul, Women, and Wives.* Peabody, Mass.: Hendrickson, 1992.

Keller, Catherine, Michael Nausner, and Rivera Mayra. *Postcolonial Theologies: Divinity and Empire.* St. Louis: Chalice, 2004.

Kelly-Gangi, Carol. *Saint Francis of Assisi: His Essential Wisdom.* New York: Fall River Press, 2010.

Kierkegaard, Søren. *Fear and Trembling.* Translated by Howard V. Hong and Edna H. Hong. Princeton: Princeton University Press, 1983.

King, Martin Luther, Jr. "Letter from Birmingham City Jail." In *A Testament of Hope,* edited by James Melvin Washington, pp. 289-302. San Francisco: Harper and Row, 1986.

Koonz, Claudia. *The Nazi Conscience.* Cambridge: Harvard University Press, Belknap Press, 2003.

Kreider, Alan. "Rediscovering Our Heritage: The Pacifism of the Early Church." In *Waging Peace,* edited by Jim Wallis. San Francisco: Harper and Row, 1982.

Ladd, George Eldon. *The Gospel of the Kingdom: Scriptural Studies in the Kingdom of God.* Grand Rapids: Eerdmans, 1959.

Ladd, John. Translator's introduction to *Metaphysical Elements of Justice,* by Immanuel Kant, translated by John Ladd, pp. xv-liv. 2nd ed. Indianapolis: Hackett, 1999.

Las Casas, Bartolomé de. *In Defense of the Indians.* Translated by Stafford Poole. De Kalb: Northern Illinois University Press, 1992.

———. *A Short Account of the Destruction of the Indies.* Translated by Nigel Griffin. London: Penguin Books, 1992.

Laslett, Peter. Introduction to *Two Treatises of Government,* by John Locke, pp. 15-135. New York: New American Library, 1963.

Bibliography

Latourette, Kenneth Scott. *A History of Christianity.* Vol. 1. New York: Harper and Row, 1975.

Lazar, Moshe. "The Lamb and the Scapegoat: The Dehumanization of the Jews in Medieval Propaganda Imagery." In *Anti-Semitism in Times of Crisis,* edited by Sander L. Gilman and Steven T. Katz, pp. 38-80. New York: New York University Press, 1991.

Lebacqz, Karen. *Six Theories of Justice: Perspectives from Philosophical and Theological Ethics.* Minneapolis: Augsburg Fortress, 1987.

Leithart, Peter J. *Defending Constantine.* Downers Grove, Ill.: InterVarsity, 2010.

Levi, Primo. *Survival in Auschwitz.* New York: Collier, 1961.

Levine, Amy-Jill. *The Misunderstood Jew: The Church and the Scandal of the Jewish Jesus.* New York: HarperOne, 2006.

Lifton, Robert Jay. *The Nazi Doctors: Medical Killing and the Psychology of Genocide.* New York: Basic Books, 1986.

Lilla, Mark. *The Stillborn God.* New York: Knopf, 2007.

Littell, Franklin. *The Crucifixion of the Jews: The Failure of Christians to Understand the Jewish Experience.* Macon, Ga.: Mercer University Press, [1975] 1986.

Locke, John. *An Essay concerning Human Understanding.* In *Great Books of the Western World,* vol. 35, edited by Robert Maynard Hutchins, pp. 85-395. New York: Encyclopaedia Britannica, 1952.

————. *A Letter concerning Toleration.* In *Great Books of the Western World,* vol. 35, edited by Robert Maynard Hutchins, pp. 1-22. New York: Encyclopaedia Britannica, 1952.

————. *Two Treatises of Government.* New York: New American Library, 1963.

Longman, Tremper III, and Daniel G. Reid. *God Is a Warrior.* Grand Rapids: Zondervan, 1995.

Lossky, Vladimir. *Orthodox Theology: An Introduction.* Crestwood, N.Y.: St. Vladimir's Seminary Press, 1978.

Lovelace, Richard F. *Dynamics of Spiritual Life.* Downers Grove, Ill.: InterVarsity, 1979.

Lovelock, J. E. *Gaia: A New Look at Life on Earth.* Oxford: Oxford University Press, 1979.

Luther, Martin. *Luther's Works.* Vol. 1. Edited by Jaroslav Pelikan. Translated by George V. Schink. St. Louis: Concordia, 1958.

————. "On the Jews and Their Lies." In *Luther's Works,* vol. 47, edited by Franklin Sherman, pp. 121-306. Philadelphia: Fortress, 1971.

Maass, Peter. *Love Thy Neighbor: A Story of War.* New York: Knopf, 1996.

MacGregor, Kirk R. "Nonviolence in the Ancient Church and Christian Obedience." *Themelios* 33, no. 1 (2008): 16-28.

MacIntyre, Alasdair. *After Virtue.* 2nd ed. Notre Dame, Ind.: University of Notre Dame Press, 1984.

Mackie, J. L. *Ethics: Inventing Right and Wrong.* New York: Penguin, 1977.

Majer, Diemut. *"Non-Germans" under the Third Reich: The Nazi Judicial and Administrative System in Germany and Occupied Eastern Europe, with Special Regard to Occupied Poland, 1939-1945.* Baltimore: Johns Hopkins University Press, 2003.

Malina, Bruce. *The Social Gospel of Jesus: The Kingdom of God in Mediterranean Perspective.* Minneapolis: Fortress, 2001.

Manent, Pierre. *Tocqueville and the Nature of Democracy.* New York: Rowman and Littlefield, 1995.

Marshall, Christopher. *Crowned with Glory and Honor.* Telford, Pa.: Pandora Press, 2001.

Massaquoi, Hans J. *Destined to Witness: Growing Up Black in Nazi Germany.* New York: Morrow, 1999.

Mauser, Ulrich. *The Gospel of Peace: A Scriptural Message for Today's World.* Louisville: Westminster John Knox, 1992.

McFague, Sallie. *Models of God: Theology for an Ecological, Nuclear Age.* Philadelphia: Fortress, 1987.

Meagher, John C. "As the Twig Was Bent: Antisemitism in Greco-Roman and Earliest Christian Times." In *AntiSemitism and the Foundations of Christianity,* edited by Alan T. Davies, pp. 1-26. New York: Paulist, 1979.

Meeks, Wayne A. *The Moral World of the First Christians.* Philadelphia: Westminster, 1986.

Meier, John P. *A Marginal Jew: Rethinking the Historical Jesus.* Vol. 2, *Mentor, Message, and Miracles.* New York: Doubleday, 1994.

Milbank, John. *Theology and Social Theory: Beyond Secular Reason.* Oxford: Blackwell, 1990.

Miller, Patrick. "Divine Command and Beyond: The Ethics of the Commandments." In *The Ten Commandments: The Reciprocity of Faithfulness,* edited by William P. Brown. Louisville: Westminster John Knox, 2004.

Miller, William Lee. *The First Liberty: America's Foundation in Religious Freedom.* Washington, D.C.: Georgetown University Press, 2003.

Mills, Watson E., and Richard F. Wilson, eds. *Mercer Commentary on the Old Testament.* Macon, Ga.: Mercer University Press, 2003.

Mineau, André. *Operation Barbarossa: Ideology and Ethics against Human Dignity.* Amsterdam: Rodopi, 2004.

Moses, Paul. *The Saint and the Sultan.* New York: Doubleday, 2009.

Mouw, Richard J. *The God Who Commands.* South Bend, Ind.: University of Notre Dame Press, 1991.

Muilenberg, James. *The Way of Israel: Biblical Faith and Ethics.* New York: Harper and Row, 1961.

Muller, Richard A. *Dictionary of Latin and Greek Theological Terms.* Grand Rapids: Baker, 1985.

Mullin, Robert Bruce. *A Short World History of Christianity.* Louisville: Westminster John Knox, 2008.

Murphy, Nancey. *Beyond Liberalism and Fundamentalism*. Valley Forge, Pa.: Trinity, 1996.

"Nazi Conspiracy and Aggression, Volume 1, Chapter XIII — Germanization and Spoliation." *The Avalon Project: Documents in Law, History, and Diplomacy.* Yale Law School Lillian Goldman Law Library. http://avalon.law.yale.edu/imt/chap_13.asp. Accessed April 30, 2011.

Nazi Primer, The: Official Handbook for Schooling the Hitler Youth. Translated by Harwood Childs. New York: Harper and Brothers, 1938.

Neuhaus, Richard John. *The Naked Public Square*. Grand Rapids: Eerdmans, 1984.

Niebuhr, Reinhold. *Moral Man and Immoral Society*. New York: Scribner's, 1933.

Nietzsche, Friedrich. *Beyond Good and Evil: Prelude to a Philosophy of the Future.* Translated and edited by Walter Kaufmann. New York: Vintage Books, 1966.

―――. *On the Genealogy of Morals*. Translated by Walter Kaufmann and R. J. Hollingdale. New York: Vintage Books, 1967.

―――. *The Anti-Christ*. Translated and edited by R. J. Hollingdale. New York: Penguin, 1968.

―――. *Twilight of the Idols*. Edited and translated by R. J. Hollingdale. New York: Penguin Books, 1968.

―――. *The Will to Power*. Translated by Walter Kaufmann and R. J. Hollingdale. Edited by Walter Kaufmann. New York: Vintage Books, 1968.

―――. *The Gay Science*. Edited and translated by Walter Kaufmann. New York: Vintage Books, 1974.

―――. *Human, All Too Human: A Book of Free Spirits*. Translated by Marion Faber, with Stephen Lehmann. Lincoln: University of Nebraska Press, 1984.

―――. *Daybreak: Thoughts on the Prejudices of Morality*. Edited by Maudemarie Clark and Brian Leiter. Translated by R. J. Hollingdale. Cambridge: Cambridge University Press, 1997.

―――. *The Birth of Tragedy*. Translated by William A. Hausmann. New York: Barnes and Noble, 2006.

―――. *On Truth and Untruth*. Translated and edited by Taylor Carman. New York: HarperPerennial, 2010.

Noakes, J., and G. Pridham, eds. *Nazism: A History in Documents and Eyewitness Accounts*. Vol 1. New York: Schocken, 1983.

Noonan, John T., Jr. *A Church That Can and Cannot Change*. Notre Dame, Ind.: University of Notre Dame Press, 2005.

Norman, Richard. *The Moral Philosophers: An Introduction to Ethics*. Oxford: Oxford University Press, 1998.

Novak, David. *The Sanctity of Human Life*. Washington, D.C.: Georgetown University Press, 2009.

Nussbaum, Martha. *Frontiers of Justice: Disability, Nationality, Species Membership*. Cambridge: Harvard University Press, Belknap Press, 2007.

O'Connell, Mary Ellen. *The Power and Purpose of International Law.* New York: Oxford University Press, 2008.

Oden, Thomas C., and Christopher A. Hall, eds. *Ancient Christian Commentary on Scripture: Mark.* Downers Grove, Ill.: InterVarsity, 1995.

O'Donovan, Oliver. *The Desire of the Nations: Rediscovering the Roots of Political Theology.* Cambridge: Cambridge University Press, 1996.

O'Donovan, Oliver, and Joan Lockwood O'Donovan, eds. *From Irenaeus to Grotius: A Sourcebook in Christian Political Thought.* Grand Rapids: Eerdmans, 1999.

Oh, Irene. *The Rights of God: Islam, Human Rights, and Comparative Ethics.* Washington, D.C.: Georgetown University Press, 2007.

"O Sacred Head, Now Wounded." Words by Paul Gerhardt. 1656. Hymn 105. *Baptist Hymnal.* Nashville: Convention Press, 1975.

Outka, Gene. *Agape: An Ethical Analysis.* New Haven: Yale University Press, 1972.

Oxford Classical Dictionary, The. Edited by Simon Hornblower and Antony Spawforth. 3rd ed. Oxford and New York: Oxford University Press, 1996.

Padgen, Anthony. Introduction to *A Short Account of the Destruction of the Indies,* by Bartolomé de Las Casas. Translated by Nigel Griffin. London: Penguin Books, 1992.

Pagels, Elaine. *The Origin of Satan: How Christians Demonized Jews, Pagans, and Heretics.* New York: Vintage Books, 1995.

Patterson, Orlando. *Freedom in the Making of Western Culture.* New York: Basic Books, 1992.

Pelikan, Jaroslav. *The Christian Tradition: A History of the Development of Doctrine.* Vol. 1. Chicago: University of Chicago Press, 1971.

Peterson, Anna L. *Being Human: Ethics, Environment, and Our Place in the World.* Berkeley and Los Angeles: University of California Press, 2001.

Phillips, Jonathan. *Holy Warriors: A Modern History of the Crusades.* New York: Random House, 2009.

Pleins, J. David. *The Social Visions of the Hebrew Bible.* Louisville: Westminster John Knox, 2001.

Pontifical Council for Justice and Peace. *Compendium of the Social Doctrine of the Church.* Washington, D.C.: United States Council of Catholic Bishops, 2004.

Pope, Stephen J. "'Equal Regard' vs. 'Special Relations': Reaffirming the Inclusiveness of Agape." *Journal of Religion* 77, no. 3 (July 1979): 353-79.

Rad, Gerhard von. *Old Testament Theology.* Translated by D. M. G. Stalker. Vol. 1. Louisville: Westminster John Knox, [1957] 2001.

Ramsey, Paul. *Basic Christian Ethics.* Louisville: Westminster John Knox, 1950.

Rasmussen, Larry L. *Earth Community, Earth Ethics.* Maryknoll, N.Y.: Orbis, 1996.

Rawls, John. *A Theory of Justice.* Cambridge: Harvard University Press, Belknap Press, 1971.

Reed, Esther D. *The Ethics of Human Rights: Contested Doctrinal and Moral Issues.* Waco, Tex.: Baylor University Press, 2007.

Richardson, Kurt Anders. "Imago Dei: Anthropological and Christological Modes of Divine Self-Imagining." *Journal of Scriptural Reasoning* 4, no. 2 (October 2004).

Rivera, Luis N. *A Violent Evangelism: The Political and Religious Conquest of the Americas.* Louisville: Westminster John Knox, 1992.

Roberts, Alexander, and James Donaldson, eds. *Ante-Nicene Fathers.* Buffalo: Christian Literature Publishing Co., 1885.

Roberts, Christopher Chenault. *Creation and Covenant: The Significance of Sexual Difference in the Moral Theology of Marriage.* London: T. & T. Clark, 2007.

Robinson, Michael. "Divine Image, Human Dignity and Human Potentiality." Unpublished paper.

Royal, Robert. *The God That Did Not Fail: How Religion Built and Sustains the West.* New York: Encounter Books, 2006.

Rubenstein, Richard L., and John K. Roth. *Approaches to Auschwitz: The Holocaust and Its Legacy.* Rev. ed. Louisville: Westminster John Knox, 2003.

Ruether, Rosemary Radford. *Faith and Fratricide.* New York: Seabury Press, 1974.

————. *America, Amerikkka: Elect Nation and Imperial Violence.* London: Equinox Publishing, 2007.

Rufinus. "Summa Decretorum." In *From Irenaeus to Grotius: A Sourcebook in Christian Political Thought,* edited by Oliver O'Donovan and Joan Lockwood O'Donovan, pp. 297-305. Grand Rapids: Eerdmans, 1999.

Russell, Jeffrey Burton. *A History of Medieval Christianity.* Arlington Heights, Ill.: Harlan Davidson, 1968.

Ruston, Roger. *Human Rights and the Image of God.* London: SCM, 2004.

Samra, James George. *Being Conformed to Christ in Community: A Study of Maturity, Maturation, and the Local Church in the Undisputed Pauline Epistles.* London: T. & T. Clark, 2006.

"Sanctitas." *Langenscheidt's Pocket Latin Dictionary.* Berlin: Langenscheidt, 1955.

"Sanctity." *The Oxford English Dictionary.* 2nd ed. Oxford: Clarendon, 1989.

"Sanctity." *Webster's New Universal Unabridged Dictionary.* New York: Barnes and Noble, 1989.

Sanders, E. P. "Reflections on Anti-Judaism in the New Testament and in Christianity." In *Anti-Judaism and the Gospels,* edited by William R. Farmer, pp. 265-86. Harrisburg, Pa.: Trinity, 1999.

Scaruffi, Piero. "1900-2000: A Century of Genocides." http://www.scaruffi.com/politics/dictat.html. Accessed April 30, 2011.

Schmitz, Elisabeth. "On the Predicament of the Non-Aryans." Translated by Steven Martin. Unpublished document, 1935.

————. "Letter to Gollwitzer." Unpublished letter, November 15, 1938.

Schockenhoff, Eberhard. *Natural Law and Human Dignity: Universal Ethics in an Historical World.* Translated by Brian McNeil. Washington, D.C.: Catholic University of America Press, 2003.

Schüssler Fiorenza, Elisabeth. *In Memory of Her.* New York: Crossroad, 1987.

Second Vatican Ecumenical Council, Pastoral Constitution. *Gaudium et Spes.* In *Vatican Council II,* edited by Austin Flannery, pp. 903-11. Rev. ed. Collegeville, Minn.: Liturgical Press, [1966] 1999.

Siker, Jeffrey. *Disinheriting the Jews: Abraham in Early Christian Controversy.* Louisville: Westminster John Knox, 1991.

Singer, Peter. *Practical Ethics.* 2nd ed. Cambridge: Cambridge University Press, 1993.

———. *Unsanctifying Human Life.* Edited by Helga Kuhse. Oxford: Blackwell, 2002.

Smith-Christopher, Daniel L. *Jonah, Jesus, and Other Good Coyotes: Speaking Peace to Power in the Bible.* Nashville: Abingdon, 2007.

Soulen, R. Kendall, and Linda Woodhead, eds. *God and Human Dignity.* Grand Rapids: Eerdmans, 2006.

Staniforth, Maxwell, and Andrew Louth, trans. and eds. *Early Christian Writings: The Apostolic Fathers.* London: Penguin Books, 1987.

Stark, Rodney. *The Rise of Christianity.* New York: HarperCollins, 1996.

———. *The Victory of Reason: How Christianity Led to Freedom, Capitalism, and Western Success.* New York: Random House, 2005.

———. *God's Battalions: The Case for the Crusades.* New York: HarperOne, 2009.

Stassen, Glen H. *Just Peacemaking: Transforming Initiatives for Justice and Peace.* Louisville: Westminster John Knox, 1992.

———, ed. *Just Peacemaking: The New Paradigm for the Ethics of Peace and War.* Cleveland: Pilgrim Press, 2008.

Stassen, Glen H., and David P. Gushee. *Kingdom Ethics: Following Jesus in Contemporary Context.* Downers Grove, Ill.: InterVarsity, 2003.

Stern, Fritz. *The Politics of Cultural Despair: A Study in the Rise of the Germanic Ideology.* Berkeley and Los Angeles: University of California Press, 1961.

Stewart, Angus. "The Image of God in Man: A Reformed Reassessment." http://www.cprf.co.uk/articles/imageofgod.htm. Accessed July 8, 2009.

Stewart, Herbert L. "Euthanasia." *International Journal of Ethics* 29, no. 1 (October 1918): 48-62.

Stout, Jeffrey. *Ethics after Babel: The Languages of Morals and Their Discontents.* Princeton: Princeton University Press, 2001.

———. *Democracy and Tradition.* Princeton: Princeton University Press, 2004.

Swartley, Willard M. *Slavery, Sabbath, War, and Women.* Scottdale, Pa.: Herald, 1982.

———. *Covenant of Peace: The Missing Piece in New Testament Theology and Ethics.* Grand Rapids: Eerdmans, 2006.

———, ed. *The Love of Enemy and Nonretaliation in the New Testament.* Louisville: Westminster John Knox, 1992.

Tacitus. *Annals,* 15.44. In Justo Gonzalez, *The Story of Christianity.* Vol. 1. New York: HarperCollins, 1984.

Tarnas, Richard. *The Passion of the Western Mind.* New York: Ballantine Books, 1991.

Taylor, Charles. *Sources of the Self: The Making of Modern Identity.* Cambridge: Harvard University Press, 1989.

————. *A Secular Age*. Cambridge: Harvard University Press, Belknap Press, 2007.

Taylor, Paul W. *Respect for Nature*. Princeton: Princeton University Press, 1986.

Ten Boom, Corrie. *The Hiding Place*. New York: Bantam Books, 1971.

Teresa (Mother), and Jose Luis Gonzalez-Balado. *Mother Teresa: In My Own Words*. New York: Gramercy Books, 1996.

Thiselton, Anthony C. *The First Epistle to the Corinthians*. Grand Rapids: Eerdmans, 2000.

Thurman, Howard. *Jesus and the Disinherited*. Richmond, Ind.: Friends United Press, [1949] 1981.

Tierney, Brian. *The Idea of Natural Rights*. Grand Rapids: Eerdmans, 1997.

————. "Natural Law and Natural Rights." In *Christianity and Law: An Introduction*, edited by John Witte Jr. and Frank S. Alexander, pp. 89-103. Cambridge: Cambridge University Press, 2008.

Tietz, Christiane. "Particular Justifications for Universal Claims — Exemplified through the Protestant Concept of Imago Dei as Foundation for Human Rights." Unpublished paper for Center for Theological Inquiry Consultation, September 2009.

Tinder, Glenn. *Liberty: Rethinking an Imperiled Ideal*. Grand Rapids: Eerdmans, 2007.

Tinker, George. *Missionary Conquest: The Gospel and Native American Cultural Genocide*. Minneapolis: Fortress, 1993.

Tocqueville, Alexis de. *Democracy in America*. 1835. Washington, D.C.: Library of America, 2004.

Townsend, John T. "The Gospel of John and the Jews." In *AntiSemitism and the Foundations of Christianity*, edited by Alan T. Davies, pp. 72-97. New York: Paulist, 1979.

Trible, Phyllis. *Texts of Terror: Literary-Feminist Readings of Biblical Narratives*. Philadelphia: Fortress, 1984.

Trinkaus, Charles. *In Our Image and Likeness*. Notre Dame, Ind.: University of Notre Dame Press, 1995.

Tuck, Richard. *Natural Rights Theories: Their Origin and Development*. Cambridge: Cambridge University Press, 1979.

Twomey, Fr. Vincent, S.V.D. "Pope Benedict XVI on Conscience." http://www.catholicculture.org/culture/library/view.cfm?recnum=8598. Accessed February 17, 2010.

Van Dyke, Fred, et al. *Redeeming Creation: The Biblical Basis for Environmental Stewardship*. Downers Grove, Ill.: IVP Academic, 1996.

Veatch, Robert M. *The Foundations of Justice: Why the Retarded and the Rest of Us Have Claims to Equality*. New York and Oxford: Oxford University Press, 1986.

Waldemar, Janzen. *Old Testament Ethics*. Louisville: Westminster John Knox, 1994.

Waldron, Jeremy. *God, Locke, and Equality: Christian Foundations in Locke's Political Thought*. Cambridge: Cambridge University Press, 2002.

―――. "Dignity and Rank." *Archives Européenes de Sociologie* 48 (2007): 201-37.

―――. "Dignity, Rank, and Rights." Tanner Lectures, University of California at Berkeley. April 2009. http://www.law.nyu.edu/ecm_dlv3/groups/public/@nyu _law_website__news/documents/documents/ecm_pro_061884.pdf. Accessed September 30, 2009.

―――. "The Image of God: Rights, Reason, and Order." Paper presented at Center for Theological Inquiry, Princeton, September 2009.

Walsh, Michael. *Warriors of the Lord: The Military Orders of Christendom.* Grand Rapids: Eerdmans, 2003.

Walzer, Michael. *Exodus and Revolution.* New York: Basic Books, 1985.

"Wannsee Conference, The." *The History Place.* http://www.historyplace.com/ worldwar2/holocaust/h-wannsee.htm. Accessed April 28, 2011.

Ware, Timothy. *The Orthodox Church.* London: Penguin, 1993.

Washington, James Melvin, ed. *A Testament of Hope.* San Francisco: Harper and Row, 1986.

Webb, William J. *Slaves, Women, and Homosexuals.* Downers Grove, Ill.: InterVarsity, 2001.

Wennberg, Robert N. *God, Humans, and Animals: An Invitation to Enlarge Our Moral Universe.* Grand Rapids: Eerdmans, 2003.

West, Cornel. *Democracy Matters.* New York: Penguin, 2004.

Westermann, Claus. *Creation.* Translated by John J. Scullion. Philadelphia: SPCK and Fortress, 1974.

White, Lynn, Jr. "The Historical Roots of Our Ecologic Crisis." *Science* 155 (March 1967): 1203-7.

Wickham, Chris. *The Inheritance of Rome.* New York: Viking Penguin, 2009.

Wiesel, Elie. *Night.* Rev. ed. New York: Hill and Wang, 2006.

Wilken, Robert L. *The Christians as the Romans Saw Them.* New Haven and London: Yale University Press, 1984.

Williams, Rowan. *Grace and Necessity: Reflections on Art and Love.* Harrisburg, Pa.: Morehouse Publishing, 2005.

Willis, Wendell, ed. *The Kingdom of God in 20th Century Interpretation.* Peabody, Mass.: Hendrickson, 1987.

Winnington-Ingram, Bishop A. F. *The Potter and the Clay.* London, 1917.

Wistrich, Robert. *Antisemitism: The Longest Hatred.* New York: Pantheon Books, 1991.

Witherington, Ben. *Women in the Ministry of Jesus: A Study of Jesus' Attitude toward Women and Their Roles as Reflected in His Earthly Life.* Cambridge: Cambridge University Press, 1987.

Witte, John. *God's Joust, God's Justice: Law and Religion in the Western Tradition.* Grand Rapids: Eerdmans, 2006.

Wogaman, J. Philip. *Christian Ethics: A Historical Introduction.* Louisville: Westminster John Knox, 1993.

Bibliography

Wolfe, Alan. *Moral Freedom: The Search for Virtue in a World of Choice*. New York: Norton, 2002.

————. *The Future of Liberalism*. New York: Vintage Books, 2010.

Wolterstorff, Nicholas. *Justice: Rights and Wrongs*. Princeton and Oxford: Princeton University Press, 2008.

Wood, Allen W. *Kant*. Malden, Mass.: Blackwell, 2005.

Woodruff, Paul. *Reverence: Renewing a Forgotten Virtue*. New York and Oxford: Oxford University Press, 2001.

Woods, Thomas E., Jr. *How the Catholic Church Built Western Civilization*. Washington, D.C.: Regnery, 2005.

Wright, Christopher J. H. *Old Testament Ethics for the People of God*. Downers Grove, Ill.: InterVarsity, 2004.

Wright, N. T. *Jesus and the Victory of God*. Minneapolis: Fortress, 1996.

————. *Surprised by Hope: Rethinking Heaven, the Resurrection, and the Mission of the Church*. New York: HarperOne, 2008.

Yahil, Leni. *The Holocaust*. New York: Oxford University Press, 1990.

Yoder, John Howard. *The Politics of Jesus*. Grand Rapids: Eerdmans, [1972] 1994.

————. *The Jewish-Christian Schism Revisited*. Edited by Michael G. Cartwright and Peter Ochs. Grand Rapids: Eerdmans, 2003.

————. *The War of the Lamb*. Edited by Glen Stassen et al. Grand Rapids: Brazos, 2009.

Yoder, Perry B., and Willard M. Swartley, eds. *The Meaning of Peace: Biblical Studies*. Louisville: Westminster John Knox, 1992.

Young, Frances M. "The Early Church: Military Service, War and Peace." *Theology* 92, no. 750 (November 1, 1989): 491-503.

Young, Richard A. *Healing the Earth: A Theocentric Perspective on Environmental Problems and Their Solutions*. Nashville: Broadman and Holman, 1994.

Index of Subjects and Names

Early Christianity and the sacredness
of life; Roman Empire
Greek culture, pre-Socratic, 266-74
Greenberg, Irving, 12n, 13-14, 79, 203n
Gregg v. GA (1976), 368-69
Gregory of Nyssa, 205n
Gregory the Great, Pope, 156n
Grenville, J. A. S., 335n, 351
Grenz, Stanley J., 29-30, 32
Gundry-Volf, Judith M., 90n
Gushee, David P., 2n, 15n, 112n, 189n,
190n, 320n, 355n, 382n, 405n
Gutiérrez, Gustavo, 58, 117, 197n
Gypsies (Sinti and Roma), 308, 310n, 311,
320, 327

Half the Sky (Kristof and WuDunn), 382-
87, 421
Hall, Christopher A., 104n
Hanke, Lewis, 192n, 194n, 195n, 196
Harnack, Adolf von, 69n
Harrelson, Walter, 41n, 42n, 68n
Hartman, Donniel, 73-74
Hauerwas, Stanley, 114, 116, 117n
Haw, Chris, 92n, 117n
Haynes, Stephen, 76n
Hays, Richard B., 103n, 114-15; *Moral Vi-
sion of the New Testament*, 114
Headley, John, 224n, 240, 241n
Hebrew Bible. *See* Old Testament and
the sacredness of life
Helyws, Thomas, 209n, 210
Hendricks, Obery, Jr., 92n
Henkin, Louis, 65n
Henry, Carl F. H., 363
Henshaw, Stanley K., 356n
Heraclitus, 275
Heschel, Susannah, 344n
Heydrich, Reinhard, 319
Hiers, Richard H., 52n
Hilberg, Raul, 186, 207-8
Hill, Jonathan, *What Has Christianity
Ever Done for Us?*, 118
Himmelfarb, Gertrude, 240n, 241n
Himmler, Heinrich, x-xi, 319, 336-37, 338
Hindenburg, Paul von, 306-7, 329-30

Hippolytus, 123
Hitler, Adolf, 304, 306-21; and anti-
Semitism, 40-41, 304; ascension to
power, 307-8; Catholicism of, 345;
First World War military service,
306, 335-36; *Mein Kampf*, 306, 325,
333n, 337, 340, 343-48; and social
Darwinism, 337. *See also* Nazi Ger-
many
Hobbes, Thomas, 235-36, 246n; *Levia-
than*, 235-36
Hoche, Alfred, 315
Hoekema, Anthony A., 42n
Holland, Suzanne, 358n
Hollingdale, R. J., 261n, 277n, 282n,
283n, 286n
Hornblower, Simon, 125n
Horsley, Richard A., 116, 117n
House, Adrian, 167n, 172n
Hui, Edwin, 363
"Human dignity": and contemporary
human rights concepts, 19-20, 27,
374-75, 413; Greco-Roman, 19, 413;
Kant and, 252-53, 254-55, 255n; lan-
guage of "inherent" or "intrinsic"
dignity, 374-75; Locke and, 229-30;
Nietzsche and, 273; post–World
War II human rights framework, 27,
374-75
Human rights, 27, 353, 372-78, 418; and
Christian reservations about rights-
talk, 376-78; and concept of "natu-
ral rights," 216n; and duties of indi-
viduals, 374, 377; and "human dig-
nity," 19-20, 27, 374-75, 413; Old
Testament concept, 52-54; post–
World War II framework, 27, 353,
372-78
Human trafficking, 383-84
Hunsinger, George, 101
Huntington, Samuel P., 118n, 175n
Hutchins, Robert Maynard, 228n,
232n, 242n

Ignatius of Antioch, 141, 207
Imago Dei: capacities-based construals

Index of Scripture References

Puzzle #1: Does the elevation of "each and every human being" to special dignity and rank require or imply a denigration of other species, even if the definition as stated on page 33 says nothing about other species? How does this old-new Christian tradition of human life's sacredness relate to the value of other forms of life? Can it be sustained alongside proper valuing of God's creation and its other species?

Puzzle #2: Is the focus of "the sacredness of human life" on the human individual, the human community, or the human species? Or is it perhaps even some *aspect* of the individual, such as the human body, the human spirit, or even the human "personality" or human "potential"? Might there ever be conflicts of interest and vision between those seeking to defend human worth and well-being at these various levels?

Puzzle #3: What does it mean to say that the sacredness of human life applies "without exception and in all circumstances"? Is it clear from divine revelation that this includes the developing human being in the womb, for example? Or the embryo in the lab? Or the human being lingering in a persistent vegetative state?

Puzzle #4: What does it mean to say that human beings are "incalculably" precious? Does that mean the same thing as "infinite" or "immeasurable"? Can any kind of "price" be put on a human life? Are some human lives ever "worth" more than others?

Puzzle #5: What exactly makes human life so precious and sacred? Is it some quality, capacity, or particular set of characteristics that (most) humans have? Is it possible for a human being to lose whatever characteristics or qualities make him or her worthy of the designation "sacred"?

Puzzle #6: Does human behavior matter at all to this ascription of sacredness? Can a human being behave in such a way as to forfeit his or her sacredness — or at least forfeit the respect and protection that goes with that status, as defined here? Does the mass murderer or perpetrator of genocide still hold sacred worth?

Puzzle #7: The definition never uses the words "intrinsic" or "inherent," as in "intrinsic worth" or "inherent dignity." Why not? If human worth is not intrinsic, does this mean it can be forfeited?

Puzzle #8: The definition also never uses the word "person." Can there ever be a difference between a "human being" and a "person"? What about the distinction that is sometimes drawn between "potential" and "actual" human beings and/or persons?

Puzzle #9: Is it possible to specify minimum and maximum obligations to human beings? "Respect" sounds minimal in comparison with "reverence." Are

some human beings worthy of respect and others of reverence? Could different obligations be related to different relationships, such as the differences between a parent-child relationship and that of two strangers on a subway?

Puzzle #10: The definition speaks of protecting human life from "wanton destruction" but does not say "killing" or "destruction of an innocent human being." Does belief in the sacredness of human life require rejection of any and
all violence and killing? Is this book embracing a "consistent ethic of life" that
rejects all violence?

Puzzle #11: What is meant by "human rights" here? How would one know
what these rights are? Does belief in the sacredness of human life require belief
in (a particular set of) human rights?

Puzzle #12: That's a pretty large statement at the end about a "commitment to
foster human flourishing." What exactly does that entail? And whose responsibility is it to foster human flourishing in particular? Is there no limit to this obligation?

Puzzle #13: Who exactly is the recipient of this purported divinely established
set of obligations? To whom did/does God communicate these obligations?
Are these obligations for believers only, or for all people? Is this a religious/
Christian ethic or a universal human ethic? Who exactly will be held accountable, and by whom?

Puzzle #14: If one grants the obligations imposed on humanity by these claims
to life's sacredness, what are the best ways to move toward their fulfillment? In
particular, what are the respective roles of the individual, the faith community,
and the state?

Puzzle #15: These claims are grounded in divine revelation, Scripture, and
Christ. But what weight can they carry for those who do not accept such authorities? Could the ethic survive if it were retrofitted back to the analytical
definition and stripped of all the religious language and authority? Could secular people embrace at least the spirit of this ethic? As a matter of historical
fact, have they done so? Does secularization of this ethic change it in any fundamental way?

Puzzle #16: Christians have purportedly received this moral obligation
through ancient divine revelation. How have they done with it? Have they always recognized and lived by it? What has gone right, and what has gone
wrong, in their effort to advance life's sacredness? What can history tell us?

Puzzle #17: The definition is pretty vague about what exactly elements of the
Bible teach this moral obligation to honor human life as sacred. What does the
Bible really say that can fill out the details left unexplored here?